CORE

Visual Basic 5

PRENTICE HALL PTR
CORE SERIES

CORE
Visual Basic 5

GARY CORNELL • DAVE JEZAK

Prentice Hall PTR, *Upper Saddle River, NJ 07458*
http://www.phptr.com

Editorial/Production Supervision: Joe Czerwinski
Acquisitions Editor: Greg Doench
Editorial Assistant: Mary Treacy
Marketing Manager: Stephen Solomon
Manufacturing Manager: Alexis Heydt
Cover Design: Design Source
Cover Design Direction: Jerry Votta
Art Director: Gail Cocker-Bogusz

© 1998 Prentice Hall PTR
Prentice-Hall, Inc.
A Simon & Schuster Company
Upper Saddle River, NJ 07458

Prentice Hall books are widely used by corporations and government
agencies for training, marketing, and resale.

The publisher offers discounts on this book when ordered in bulk quantities.
For more information, contact

Corporate Sales Department,
Prentice Hall PTR
One Lake Street
Upper Saddle River, NJ 07458
Phone: 800-382-3419; FAX: 201-236-714
E-mail: corpsales@prenhall.com

Printed in the United States of America

10 9 8 7 6 5 4 3 2 1

ISBN 0-13-748328-7

Prentice-Hall International (UK) Limited, London
Prentice-Hall of Australia Pty. Limited, Sydney
Prentice-Hall Canada Inc., Toronto
Prentice-Hall Hispanoamericana, S.A., Mexico
Prentice-Hall of India Private Limited, New Delhi
Prentice-Hall of Japan, Inc., Tokyo
Simon & Schuster Asia Pte. Ltd., Singapore
Editora Prentice-Hall do Brasil, Ltda., Rio de Janeiro

For Bruce, Caroline, and Kurt—with more than simple friendship

Gary Cornell

To Hannah and Michael with eternal love. Let them always see Him in me

Dave Jezak

Contents

5   MORE ON VISUAL BASIC'S PROGRAMMING
        LANGUAGE 176

FIGURES

Preface

With more than 3 million users, Visual Basic is the most popular tool for programming in the world today. However, there have always been a few things that Visual Basic couldn't do:

- It couldn't create native code executables.
- It couldn't create reusable servers that other programs could use.
- It couldn't even make the controls that were the foundation of its success.

(Control is the term used in Visual Basic for things like the text boxes and command buttons that are the building blocks for graphical user interfaces.) These features were traditionally the domain of C++; one result was that even with the powerful Wizards available, the construction job was never pleasant.

In March 1997, Microsoft released the long awaited Visual Basic Version 5.0. This extraordinarily powerful upgrade had the power to take existing controls and make them better—or even to make new controls from scratch. It could build DLLs and EXE servers for use by other programs. It had powerful features for working with the Internet. It was almost completely customizable through its new extensibility model. In short, it could do most everything VB programmers had long wanted and hoped for. If all this wasn't enough, it was also faster, more object oriented, and offered a native-code compiler for the first time. There's even a version that will run on the first non-Windows machines. (Certain RISC machines, like a DEC Alpha running Windows NT.)

Since these new features are used pretty much by following the previous Visual Basic model, millions of Visual Basic programmers can now (finally!) liberate themselves from the burden of C++ programming. Moreover, Visual Basic 5.0 follows the Visual Basic rule of being powerful, easy to use, and fun!

About This Book

This book is a complete guide to the Visual Basic 5.0 for experienced programmers, no matter what language you are coming from. We do not assume you have ever programmed in Visual Basic before—the beginning of this book gives a concise yet complete treatment of the underlying programming language in Visual Basic 5. (Obviously users of previous versions Visual Basic can skip the concise introduction to VB found in Chapters 3-6). As with all Core Books, it is filled with real examples that we hope will provide a basis for your own code.

For example, even simple concepts like file handling are illustrated with a recursive file handler and a file encrypter program. The (new) key object-oriented features of Visual Basic are not illustrated with toy classes of animals biting each other but rather with the start of a personnel management system and a generic sorting class. We have provided a set of templates that make it easier to build more powerful controls. Perhaps the biggest time saver we provide is a set of full featured Add-Ins that you can use to make your VB environment more productive, such as an Add-In that makes it easy to clone a VB project. (Of course, all our Add-Ins come with full source code, most of which is explained in some detail in the text.)

How This Book Is Organized

Programmers familiar with Visual Basic might want to skim the early chapters and spend more time on the later chapters where we cover the new features of VB5. (But we hope you will find some of the example code in the earlier chapters interesting. Also note that Chapter 6 has a discussion of a new feature of VB called OLE Drag and Drop.) Anyone familiar with COBOL, Pascal, or C but not an event-driven language like Visual Basic might want to spend more time on the early chapters. In any case, no matter what your language background, we suggest at least skimming these early chapters.

Here are brief descriptions of the chapters:

- Chapter 1 gives an introduction to Visual Basic 5 and shows how to build a simple image viewer and an equally simple, but still useful, extension of the ordinary text box.

- Chapter 2 is really for reference; it's a complete discussion of the Visual Basic 5 environment.

- Chapter 3 starts with the notion of a customizable window (called a form) that is the heart of every control. You'll see how to add and manipulate the fundamental Visual Basic objects, such as command buttons, places to enter text, labels, and timers.

- Chapters 4 and 5 survey the underlying programming language in Visual Basic 5.

- Chapter 6 goes further into the user interface, including a brief but complete treatment of graphics and the mouse, including a feature new to VB: OLE Drag and Drop.

- Chapter 7 starts you on the road to mastering Visual Basic 5's take on object-oriented programming. Object-oriented programming in Visual Basic 5 is far more sophisticated than in earlier versions of Visual Basic.

- Chapter 8 covers more advanced features of object-oriented programming in VB5, including the subtle but important new notion of *implementing* an interface. We also give a brief introduction to COM (common object model), the technology that underlies VB5's approach to object-oriented programming.

- Chapter 9 shows you how to use VB's debugging features.

- Chapter 10 explains the basic techniques for optimizing your VB programs, but also includes an introduction to one of the less well known features of VB—a full code profiler.

- Chapter 11 is an introduction to data structures. In particular, we show you how VB implements the *pointers* that are necessary for sophisticated data structures and that people have thought VB lacked!

- Chapter 12 is an introduction to the Windows API and the Registry that tries to cover what a working VB programmer needs to know. It also includes an Add-In that goes beyond what the API viewer supplied with VB can do.

- Chapter 13 is a complete introduction to the techniques needed to build controls, including adding custom properties and methods to your controls, the Control Interface Wizard and property pages.

- Chapter 14 is an introduction to ActiveX servers, multiprocessing and multithreading. You'll see how to use VB to make object factories that other programs—not just VB—can use.

- Chapter 15 is one of our favorites. It shows you how to use VB5's new *extensibility model* to add new features to the VB5 environment. For example, we show you an Add-In that lets you clone a VB project and one that lets you add line numbers to a procedure for those desperate days when no other debugging technique seems to work!

- Chapter 16 shows you how to build your own Wizards, step-by-step applications that are so common today.

- Chapter 17 shows you how to use templates, are a new feature in VB5 designed to make reusing code easier.

- Chapter 18 shows you how VB5 can work with the Internet. There's an introduction to the ActiveX document technology that allows you to embed a VB application in Internet Explorer and an introduction to the powerful Internet-enabled controls supplied with VB. We even show you how to build a simple browser that has the ability to exclude sites by name or pages that contain forbidden words.

- Chapter 19 is an introduction to another hidden treasure in VB5—the Visual Component Manager. It lets you easily store, manipulate, and search all the objects that go into a VB5 application.

- Chapter 20 explains the techniques needed to deploy an application or a control.

- The Appendix is an overview of the \Tools directory on your VB CD, since Microsoft neglected to provide one.

Conventions

Keys are set in small capital letters in the text. For example, keys such as CTRL and ALT appear as shown here. Arrow and other direction keys are spelled out and also appear in small capital letters. For example, if you need to press the right arrow key, you'll see, "Press RIGHT ARROW." Code that is in line appears in courier typeface.

When you need to use a combination of keys to activate a menu item, the keys will be separated by addition signs and the entire key combination will appear in small capital letters. For example, "Press CTRL+ALT+DEL" is how we would indicate the "three-fingered salute" that (thankfully) is a lot less common in Windows 95. On the other hand, ALT F, P means press the ALT and F keys, and then the P key—you don't have to hold down the ALT key. Menu choices are indicated with a bar between them, e.g., "Choose Run|Run."

Programs are set in a monospace font, as shown here:

```
Private Sub Form_Click( )
   MsgBox "Hello world!"
End Sub
```

Tip, Note, Caution

Tips, Notes, and Cautions are indicated by the globe icon:

Be sure to check out Microsoft's Web site (www.microsoft.com) for updates to VB5.

People have asked us about the licensing rules for our code. You may freely use any of our code as the basis for a noncommercial product. You may not post our source code on your Web site without our permission. If you use our code as the basis for code of your own, then either everyone on the development team for the product that is using our code must own a copy of this book or you must contact us for a site license. And, obviously, you may not simply repackage our code and sell it!

Finally, in a book as long as this errors inevitable creep in. We have a web page available at www.corebooks.com where we will maintain an errata list and add other material as needed. We hope you will write us with errata as well as suggestions and improvements for the next edition! Our e-mail addresses are:

gcornell@ix.netcom.com
daveje@microsoft.com

Acknowledgments

One of the best parts of writing a book is when the authors gets to thank the people who helped them, for rarely (and certainly not in this case) is a book produced by the authors alone. First and foremost, we have to thank the team at Prentice Hall whose patience and good cheer as this book dragged on was endless. In particular, we need to thank Joe Czerwinski who did a masterful job at producing a book under intense pressure. Both he and our long-suffering editor Greg Doench went way beyond the call of duty. Thanks also to Mary Treacy, who was always there when we needed her. Next, we want to thank our two technical editors: Brad Hoffman and Brian Engler, who went way beyond what one could have hoped for—or expected in—tech reviewers. Finally, we need to thank the whole Visual Basic team at Microsoft who created Visual Basic 5: It's far more than a simple upgrade, it's most of what VB programmers have long been waiting for.

Next, Gary wants to first and foremost thank Dave's family. They put up with seemingly endless phone calls as this project lasted so long and took far too much of Dave's time. He also needs to thank his nieces: Shara, Rebecca, Alyssa, Debbie, Emma, and Julia. Their love provided him an anchor in all too hectic times. Finally, he needs to thank all his friends who put up with his strange ways and his occasionally short temper: no visits and a short temper was all they got for so many, many months.

Dave must first thank his wife Cheryl for her love and support, and for constantly reminding him that his talent was not his but rather a gift from God. Next he would like to thank his kids Hannah and Michael for just being themselves because no dad could ever ask for a better pair of children than them. He would also like to thank the members of the Visual Basic team that he works with every day, who helped create such a great product and one that is fun to write about. Finally, his true friend Brad Hoffman, who was always there when he needed him.

CORE
Visual Basic 5

INTRODUCTION

Topics in this Chapter

- Introduction
- ActiveX Controls
- Building Simple Applications in VB
- Building a Simple ActiveX Control
- Adding an Event

Chapter 1

This chapter introduces you to Visual Basic 5; we include a brief tour of ActiveX technologies in general, and ActiveX controls specifically. So as not to get bogged down in generalities, after a short introduction we'll move on to showing you a sample of how fast the development process in Visual Basic can be. We'll show you how to build:

- An image viewer with three lines of code.
- A reusable (if not perfect) ActiveX control for accepting non-negative integers with hardly any more code.

(Control is the term used in Visual Basic for things like the text boxes and command buttons that are the building blocks for graphical user interfaces. Other languages may call them something else, for example, *widgets* in X programming.)

Note, however, that since we are assuming you are not a naive user, this chapter (and book) will not show you how to install Visual Basic, start it, manipulate windows within the Windows environment, and so on. However, we are *not* assuming any expertise in Visual Basic or Windows programming—just a general level of programming sophistication (Of course, as a result, experienced VB programmers can skim or even skip this chapter—although the section on building an ActiveX control might be fun to look at if you have never worked with VB5 before.)

Introduction

A few years ago in *The New York Times*, Charles Petzold, who wrote two of
the standard books on Windows programming, said this about the first version of Visual Basic: "For those of us who make our living explaining the complexities of Windows programming to programmers, Visual Basic poses a real
threat to our livelihood." To a large extent, that has become true. Visual Basic
is currently, by most accounts, the world's most popular programming language and the main reason for its success is that Visual Basic shields us from
most of the complexities of Windows programming. No cryptic hWnd's or
event processing loops to worry about. However, there have always been two
things Visual Basic couldn't do. First off, earlier versions of VB:

- Couldn't compile code into a native Windows EXE or
  Windows's DLL (dynamic link libraries).

(EXEs are stand-alone programs, DLLs are executable code that can be
shared by many applications at the same time. You can think of Windows
itself as being a group of shared DLLs.) The inability to make native code
meant that Visual Basic code often ran too slowly for certain situations. The
inability to build DLLs meant Visual Basic code couldn't easily be used by
other Windows applications.

Next, earlier versions of VB:

- Couldn't make the external *controls* (VBXs prior to VB 4.0 and
  OCXs since 4.0, now they are called ActiveX controls) that
  were the foundation of its success.

Visual Basic controls always needed to be built-in languages like C, C++
or, more recently, Delphi. Visual Basic 5 fills this gap. All versions of Visual
Basic now come with the ability to build controls. (In fact, the Visual Basic 5.0
Control Creation Edition is designed solely to build controls and, hard as it
might be to believe, this version of Visual Basic 5 is *free* for downloading. It
also comes free with the Learning Edition of VB since this "study" version of
VB does not come with the ability to make controls.)

Moreover, the controls you build with Visual Basic can be used without any
royalties in any program that can accept ActiveX controls. This includes ordinary Visual Basic programs, Internet Explorer (activated via VBScripting),

and VBA hosts such as MSWord, Excel, or Access. Microsoft has also made the engine for ActiveX scripting freely available: Expect to see lots more hosts for Visual Basic in the near future.

Note

ActiveX has become the "magic word" for Microsoft. In October of 1996, Microsoft announced its support for what they called the "Active Platform." ("The Active Platform is an open platform that enables developers to take full advantage of Microsoft's leading, standard-based implementations of HTML, open scripting, component architecture and underlying operating system services.") Even though this is written in typical Microsoft-speak, it is noteworthy. Why? Well, as Bob Muglia, a Microsoft VP, said, "Keep in mind when we don't use the word platform lightly. Windows 95 is a platform, as is Windows NT. Applications like Office are not platforms." An essential part of the Active Platform is ActiveX technology.

So, what is ActiveX? In a nutshell, ActiveX is Microsoft's attempt to come up with a cross platform, language-independent technology to use in networked environments—specifically, the Internet and corporate "intranets." Microsoft has, in fact, made the nearly unprecedented step of releasing control of the standards for ActiveX technology to a third party (the Open Group). ActiveX is built on a specification for objects called COM, or the Common Object Model. (See Chapters 7 and 8 for a short course in Object-Oriented Programming (OOP); see Chapter 8 for a brief introduction to COM.)

ActiveX Controls

ActiveX controls are the most common manifestation of ActiveX technology. In particular, Microsoft clearly wants to see ActiveX controls everywhere: the desktop, the Internet and the Intranet. ActiveX controls give the developer small footprints, reusable software components. These components can easily be activated through development tools, browsers and applications. In turn, these components can give the user a richer and more rewarding experience than could be hand-coded in a reasonable amount of time by most developers.

Note

For those who have worked with OCX controls before: roughly speaking, an ActiveX control is a lightweight OCX. The main difference is that instead of needing to support multiple interfaces, an ActiveX control need only support IUnknown and be self-registering. This makes it much smaller, hence, much easier to deliver via slow network connections. See Chapter 8 for more on what these words mean.

Here is the typical situation where a control makes you much more productive: you want your user to be able to enter a date. Wouldn't it be nice to click on an icon that pops up to a calendar? Then it would be easy to choose the date. And wouldn't it be even nicer if the calendar would show weekends and holidays in gray? You wouldn't want to write this from scratch; the rules for leap years are a pain, the GUI needed would be no fun to maintain. The point is you can drop an ActiveX calendar control into a Web page with a few keystrokes using a tool like the ActiveX Control Pad. The result is a Web page that is more useful to the browsing public. Using an ActiveX control, you could accomplish this with far less effort than by programming a calendar control in Java, C, or C++.

For a more sophisticated example, consider something you would probably never want to program by hand: suppose you want to allow a user to access information from a database on a Web page. Using the appropriate ActiveX control, here's all you have to do:

1. Put a data control and some bound (data-aware) controls on your page;
2. Tell the data control the name of the database via a property setting at design time or via VB Script code that sets a property at run time; and
3. Tell the data bound control the name of the table or the query you want it to display, also via a property setting at design time or run time.

The control will then:

1. Fetch the data;
2. Resize itself automatically, based on the data it receives (adding scroll bars if necessary); and
3. Display the data.

All this can be done at design time or run time and takes, at most, five lines of code for the run-time version.

Note

The VB Control Creation Edition does not come with the data control needed to bind data-aware controls. All other versions of Visual Basic do have this control.

Finally, keep in mind that the controls you build using VB 5 most often will be based on existing controls. You rarely will be building a control totally from scratch. Since there are more than 3,000 ActiveX controls already commercially available (and too many free or shareware controls to count), you have lots of controls to extend.

Tip

The most complete list of commercial ActiveX controls that we know of can be found at: http://204.203.124.10/activexisv/direct.htm

Working with Visual Basic

The Visual Basic compiler is very fast and even lets you do background compilation or compile only the code that is needed to start the application. This means that any changes needed to correct the routine programming and typographical errors that are so common when you begin building an application are a snap. Of course, Visual Basic also provides sophisticated error handling for the all-too-common task of preventing end users from bombing an application. It has an extensive online help system for quick reference while you're developing an application.

But as impressive as all this is, it isn't why Visual Basic is so popular. To understand this step back and think how older programming languages work:

- Execution starts from the first line and moves with the flow of the program to different parts as needed.

A Visual Basic program usually works completely differently. The core of a Visual Basic program is a set of independent pieces of code that are *activated* by, and so *respond* to, only the events they have been told to recognize. This is a fundamental shift. Now, instead of a programmer designing a program to do what the programmer thinks should happen, the user is in control.

Building a Visual Basic Application

The first step in developing a Visual Basic application is to plan what the user will see. What menus do you want? How large a window should the application use? How many windows should there be? Should the user be able to resize the windows? Where will you place the *command buttons* that the user will click on to activate the applications? Will the applications have places (*text boxes*) in which to enter text? With Visual Basic building the interface is easy: you draw the user interface, almost as if you were using a paint program. In addition, when you're done drawing the interface, the containing windows, command buttons and other controls that you have used will automatically recognize user actions, such as mouse movements and button clicks. Only after you design the interface does anything like traditional programming occur.

After you design the interface the next step is to make the interface behave the way you want. The way this works is that Visual Basic objects generally have:

- Properties that you can set;
- Methods to perform actions;
- Events that they can respond to.

The properties of a VB object (such as a control) can describe how wide or high it is, what color it is, what font it uses to display information, and so on. You can set the properties of a Visual Basic object at design time, run time, or both. Methods are called at run time via code. You might call a method to add or to remove a row or column in a grid control, or add to the list of items in a list box. An event, on the other hand, is something to which a VB object can respond. For example, a button might respond only to a single click but another kind of control would respond (differently) to single and double clicks. Most objects you use in Visual Basic will automatically recognize certain events, for example command buttons will be able to respond to mouse clicks. How the objects respond to the event depends on the code you write. In particular, you will almost always need to write code in order to get useful responses to events. This makes Visual Basic programming fundamentally different from the kind of conventional procedural-oriented programming found in early versions of Basic, Pascal, or C because the program must be reactive rather than proactive.

The code that determines how a control responds to events is contained in what VB calls an *event procedure*. For example, the code to respond to a button click might look like this:

```
Sub Command1_Click()
    MsgBox You "clicked me!"
End Sub
```

Of course, the event procedures can and will use functionality supplied by other parts of your application. In VB5 the functionality can be supplied by objects created in VB5 using modern oriented techniques, functions exported by external libraries (such as the Windows API) or libraries created in other languages, such as C or C++.

Here is what happens when the application is running:

1. Visual Basic monitors the windows and the controls in each window for *all* the events that each control can recognize (mouse movements, clicks, keystrokes, and so on).

2. When Visual Basic detects an event, if there isn't an internal built-in response to the event, Visual Basic examines the application to see if you've written an event procedure for that event.

3. If you have written an event procedure, Visual Basic executes the code that makes up that event procedure and goes back to step 1.

4. If you have not written an event procedure, Visual Basic waits for the next event and goes back to step 1.

These steps cycle continuously until the application ends.

Building Simple Applications in VB

In the rest of this chapter we want to lead you through some sample sessions with VB so we will be assuming you have successfully installed some version of VB. First off, when you first start VB you first see a copyright splash screen. After that, the New Project dialog box shows up. This is a screen like Figure 1-1 although the number of items you will see depends on the version of VB you have. (Figure 1-1 was taken with the Enterprise Edition of VB).

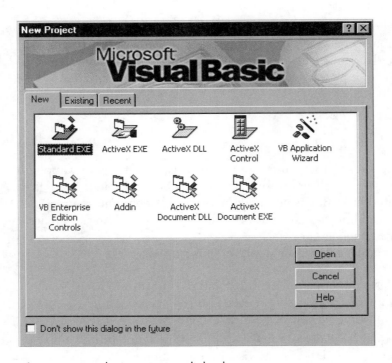

Figure 1-1   The New Project dialog box

Note

If you choose the VB Application Wizard in the dialog box shown in Figure 1-1 you will be led through a step-by-step process for building certain common applications. The idea, like all Wizards, is that you fill in screens that describe what you want done. The Wizard then takes this information and generates the framework code for the application. Since we are assuming that you are an experienced programmer, we will let you experiment with the Application Wizard rather than work through an example of the step-by-step process that the Wizard uses. (It really is very easy to use.) But, we do encourage you to play with the Application Wizard, as you will see in later chapters the code that the Application Wizard generates can save you a lot of work. For example, we will use the Wizard to generate the starting point for a couple of our samples, such as the MDI notepad example in Chapter 6 and our special purpose Internet browser in Chapter 18.

For our first sample program we want to build a simple image viewer. To start the process choose the Standard EXE type from the New Project Window shown in Figure 1-1. You'll see a screen like Figure 1-2. Note the blank window in the center of the screen, which has a grid of dots inside a larger window. This is the *form* that you will customize (form being the term used in VB for a customizable window). You use the grid to align controls such as command buttons and list boxes on the screen (you'll learn more about the grid in Chapter 3). When you run your project (or compile it so that it can be run independently of the Visual Basic development environment), forms become the windows that users see. Next, notice at the top of the blank form is the title bar with its *caption*. (Caption is the Visual Basic term for what appears in the title bar of the form.) Currently, this form is titled Form1, which is the default caption that Visual Basic gives to a form when you start working on a new project.

Figure 1-2　　The initial VB environment

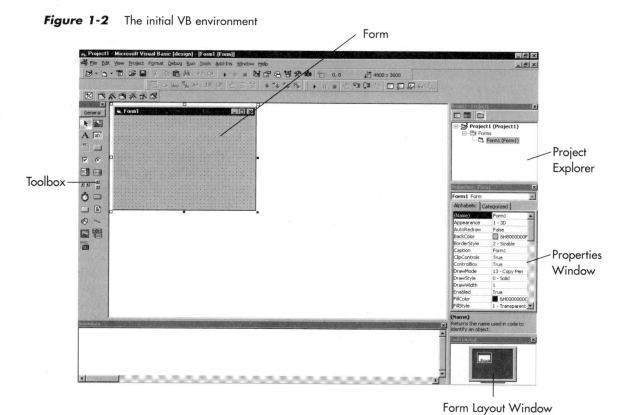

To the left of the Form1 window is the Toolbox. (If you do not see it, press ALTV, X to reveal it.) The Toolbox is where you find the controls you will place on the form. To the right is the Project Explorer, which gives you information about the files in your project (VB-speak for the totality of code you are developing at a given time). The Properties window is where you go to customize the form and the various controls you'll place on a form at design time. (The Form Layout window below the Properties window gives you one way to control the initial location of your screen at run time—see Chapter 3 for more on this window.)

For now, concentrate on Form1. You should be completely comfortable with the methods for changing the size and location of this form before you move on. In many Visual Basic applications, the size and location of the form at design time is the size and shape that the user sees at *run time*. This is not to say that Visual Basic doesn't let you change the size and location of forms as a project runs (see Chapter 4); in fact, an essential property of Visual Basic is its ability to make dynamic changes in response to user events.

One way to resize a form that is common to all Microsoft Windows applications is to first click inside the form so that is active. (You can always tell when a window is active because the title bar is highlighted.) Then move the mouse to any part of the border of the form. The mouse pointer changes to a double-headed arrow when you're at a hot spot. At this point, you can drag the form to change its size or shape. Similarly, to move the form, you can click anywhere in the title bar and then drag the form to a new location. The size and location of a form are examples of properties of the form. (You may need to enlarge the Window that contains the form to do this successfully.)

Our aim is to show you the first steps you would take to build a graphics file viewer. Using two controls and a few lines of code, you can have a Windows application that will display any bitmap. Of course, you don't yet know how to save the project, bulletproof it, or make it truly user friendly—but it's only the first chapter after all! So, first off make sure you are working with a new project by choosing Standard EXE in the New Project Dialog box shown in Figure 1-1 (choose File|New Project if you happen to be in VB already).

We want to add two controls to the blank form: an *Image* control for displaying graphics and a *Common Dialog* control for displaying the file/directory structure. To get an Image control onto the form, double-click on the Image control icon (it looks like a landscape with a sun over a mountain) that the cursor is pointing to here.

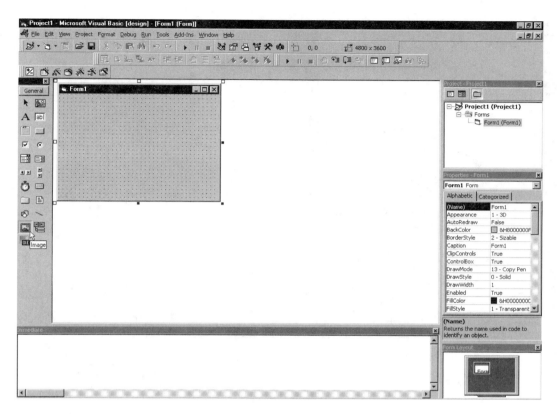

Figure 1-3 The Image control

Next, we need to add the Common Dialog control to the form. The icon for this control looks like that shown in Figure 1-4.

This tool may not be in your toolbox. If not, you will have to add it. For this:

1. Choose Project|Components.
2. In the dialog box (shown in Figure 1-5 on page 15) that pops up, scroll down until you see the item marked Microsoft Common Dialog Control 5.0 and make sure it is checked.
3. Click on OK.

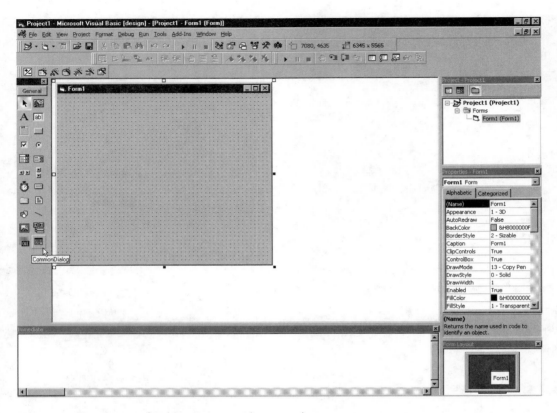

Figure 1-4   The icon for the Common Dialog control

Once you have the Common Dialog control in your toolbox, add it to the form by double-clicking on the icon.

Your screen will look like Figure 1-6.

The Inner box is the design time representation of the Common Dialog control and the outer box is the design time representation of the Image control. (You could move them by dragging them around—see Chapter 3—but for now we will leave everything in their default positions.)

We now need to set the *Filter* properties of the Common Dialog control so that only files that the Image control can handle will show up. These are bitmaps (.BMP), icons (.ICO), GIFs (.GIF), Windows metafiles (.WMF) and JPEGs (.jpg). To set the Filter property make sure the Properties window shows that you are working with the CommonDialog1 control as shown in Figure 1-7 on page 16.

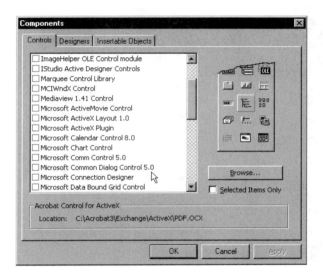

Figure 1-5   The Components dialog box

Figure 1-6   Initial screen for image viewer

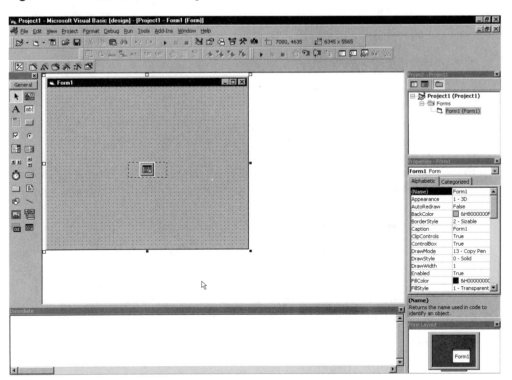

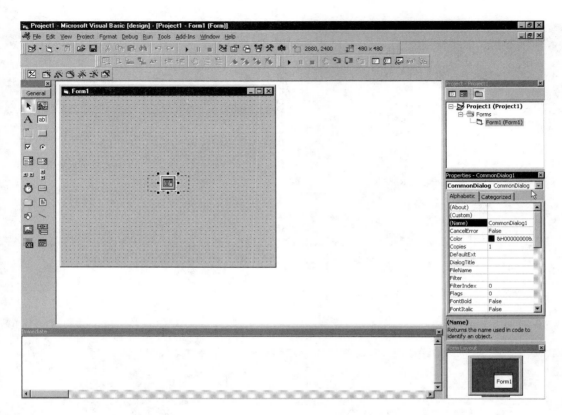

Figure 1-7   The Properties window for the Image control

If it doesn't look like this, click inside the CommonDialog icon on the form, as shown in Figure 1-6, and then hit F4 again. Move through the Properties window until you get to the Filter property of this control. Click in the right column and type the following exactly as we have indicated:

```
Pictures (*.bmp; *.ico;*.gif; *.wmf; *.jpg)|*.bmp;
*.ico;*.gif; *.wmf; *.jpg
```

(The | symbol is usually found above the backslash on your keyboard.) This tells the CommonDialog box to display only files that end in these extensions.

Next, enter the text Choose Image in the right column of the DialogTitle property. Figure 1-8 is an enlarged view of what your Properties window for the common dialog box will look like at this point.

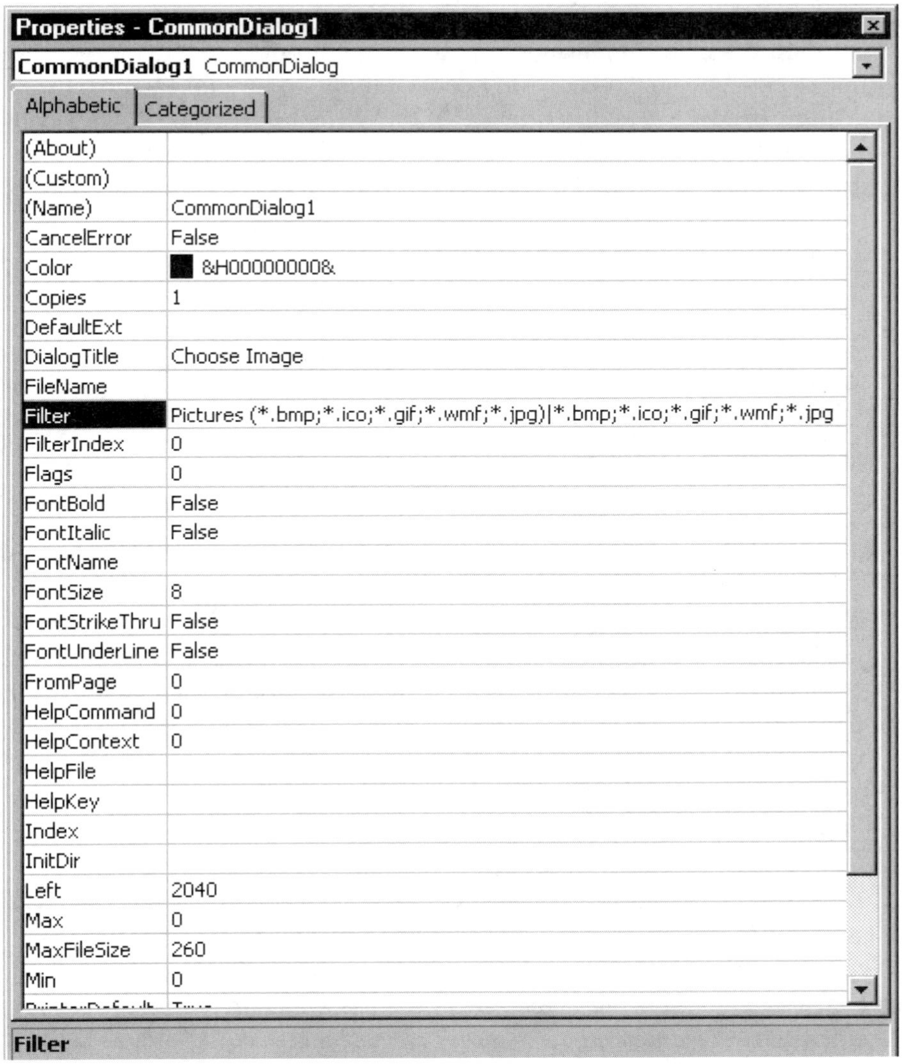

Properties - CommonDialog1	☒

CommonDialog1 CommonDialog	▾

Alphabetic	Categorized

(About)		▲
(Custom)		
(Name)	CommonDialog1	
CancelError	False	
Color	■ &H00000000&	
Copies	1	
DefaultExt		
DialogTitle	Choose Image	
FileName		
Filter	Pictures (*.bmp;*.ico;*.gif;*.wmf;*.jpg)|*.bmp;*.ico;*.gif;*.wmf;*.jpg	
FilterIndex	0	
Flags	0	
FontBold	False	
FontItalic	False	
FontName		
FontSize	8	
FontStrikeThru	False	
FontUnderLine	False	
FromPage	0	
HelpCommand	0	
HelpContext	0	
HelpFile		
HelpKey		
Index		
InitDir		
Left	2040	
Max	0	
MaxFileSize	260	
Min	0	

Filter

Figure 1-8   The Properties window for the Common Dialog Box control

By the way, if you try to run the project now, nothing will happen. The CommonDialog box needs to be activated in order to be displayed. To activate the CommonDialog box, you need to use a *method*. (Roughly speaking, in Visual Basic, properties determine what controls *are*, methods determine what they *do* and events are normally user-triggered actions.) The method we need is called the ShowOpen method, and we will put it together with the other line of code we need inside the Load event procedure for the form. The Load event procedure is a little unusual in that Visual Basic calls it whenever a form is loaded for the first time—which happens in this case when the project starts running. To get to the event procedure template for Form_Load:

* Double-click on any blank area in the form.

This will open up the event procedure template for the Load event. Now enter the following two lines of code so that your event procedure template looks like this:

```
Private Sub Form_Load()
  On Error Resume Next

  CommonDialog1.ShowOpen
  Image1.Picture = LoadPicture(CommonDialog1.FileName)
End Sub
```

That's it. If you run this project, you'll be presented with an ordinary Windows dialog box (with the caption "Choose Image") that will be restricted to displaying only files with the extensions we specified. You can navigate among the directories on your drives by clicking and double-clicking as is usual with a CommonDialog box in Windows. Find an image, click on OK, and Visual Basic will display the image on the form (and will try to resize the image box to the correct size as well).

Note

The On Error Resume Next that we used is a pretty crude way of preventing the program from crashing if the user tries to enter a file name that the Image control can't handle or if he or she hits the Cancel button. There are much better ways to do this but they all need more code than we wanted to use here.

Building a Simple ActiveX Control

Our simple control will be a text box that accepts only numerals (0–9), i.e., only non-negative integers. Once we build it, we will add an event called

BadEntry that is triggered (*raised* is the technical term) whenever the user tries to enter a non-numeral or pastes a non-integer into the box. To get started, (assuming you are in the VB Environment):

- Choose File|New Project and then choose ActiveX Control

After you click on Open you are taken into a slightly different version of the initial screen for Visual Basic. For example, the Initial Form says User Control1 rather than Form1. Since UserControl1 is not a very good name for a non-negative integer-only text box, change it to better reflect the object's functionality. For this go to the Properties window in the right-hand side of the window. If the Name property isn't highlighted in the Properties window, click in the left-hand column to highlight it. Change the name to NonNegativeIntegerTextBox. For this:

1. Double-click in the right-hand column of the Name property.
2. Enter the term NonNegativeIntegerTextBox.
3. Press ENTER.

Notice the title bar has changed to reflect the new name. We now want to add the text box that we will customize to the User Control object. For this:

- Double-click on the text box icon in the toolbox. (It is on the second line and says "ab" in it.)

This gives you a text box in the default size and location, as shown in Figure 1-9 on the next page.
Make sure the text box is blank. For this:

1. If the Properties window doesn't say Text1 TextBox on the top, click inside the text box.
2. Use the scroll bars to move through the Properties window until you get to the Text property in the left column. (It should say Text1 in the right-hand column.)
3. Erase the value in the right-hand column by double-clicking and then pressing Delete.

Notice that the text box in the User Control object is now blank. We need to add the code to the text box to reject any non-numerals that are typed. For this:

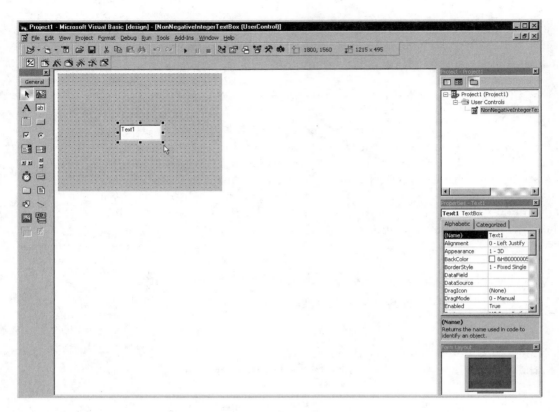

Figure 1-9   A text box in the User Control object

- Double-click inside the text box. This brings up the Code window, as shown in Figure 1-10.

The Code window shows you an event template for the Change event of the text box. We want to write the code that will make sure the user pastes in only non-negative integers. For this:

1. Move the cursor in the blank line between the two lines of the template.

2. Type the following lines before you get to the End Sub. (Don't worry about all the "statement completion boxes" that appear when you press the space bar or a period. These will make your life easier as soon as you become more comfortable with the Visual Basic environment.)

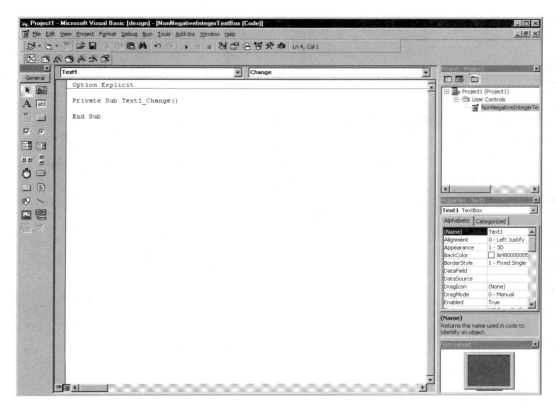

Figure 1-10   The Code window for the NonNegativeIntegerTextBox

```
If Text1.Text = "" Then Exit Sub
If Not (IsNumeric(Text1.Text)) Or Val(Text1.Text) < 0 _
Or (Int(Val(Text1.Text)) <> Val(Text1.Text)) Then
    Text1.Text = ""
End If
```

Now we want to make sure the user can only type numerals (0–9). For this, we need to write some code in the KeyPress event procedure that is triggered whenever the user types something in the box. To do this:

1. Click on the DOWN ARROW near the box that currently says Change.

2. Move through the drop-down list box until you get to the KeyPress event. (Pressing "K" twice does this.)

3. Type the following code inside the KeyPress event template.

```
If KeyAscii < Asc("0") Or KeyAscii > Asc("9") Then
    KeyAscii = 0
End If
```

That's it, the control is ready for use. Figure 1-11 shows what your code looks like.

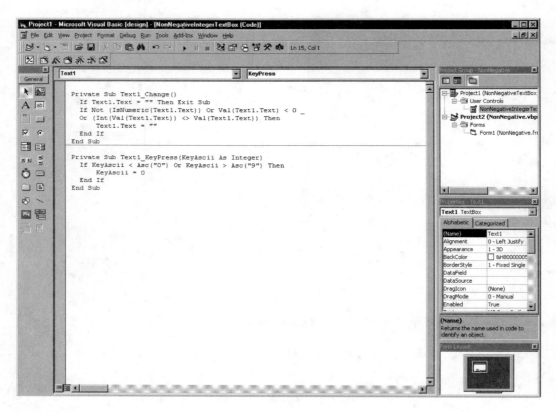

Figure 1-11   First steps in code

The next section describes the usual way to test a custom control and the last section shows how to add an event to this control. (We will leave adding custom properties to this control for Chapter 13.)

Testing the Control

The usual way to test a control you have built is to start another project within the Visual Basic environment. (You could compile it and start another environment to test it, but our way is much easier.) Think of this new project as a stand-alone VB program that would use your control. For this:

1. Choose File|Add Project.
2. When you see the Project dialog box, choose Standard EXE and click on Open.

   At this point, your Project Explorer window in the top right corner should contain two projects. Figure 1-12 shows an enlarged view of the Project Explorer in this state.

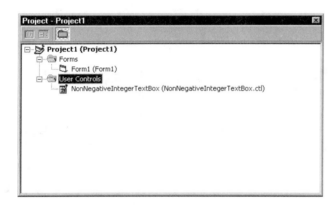

Figure 1-12 Project Explorer with two projects

3. Double-click on Form1 in the Forms folder to bring up the form in this project.

Look where the arrow is pointing in Figure 1-13 (the right corner of the toolbox). You can see a grayed outline of the default icon for a custom control along with a tooltip that describes it. The tooltip is added automatically by Visual Basic. (You will see how to add meaningful icons for your custom controls in Chapter 13.)

Our custom control is currently inactive. This is because the User Control designer is still active and, so to speak, it has control of the control. To activate the control:

1. Double-click on the NonNegativeIntegerTextBox line in the Project Explorer to make the NonNegativeIntegerTextBox designer window active.

2. Close the designer by clicking on the X button in the menu bar (not on the X button in the title bar).

Figure 1-13   Toolbox with grayed custom icon

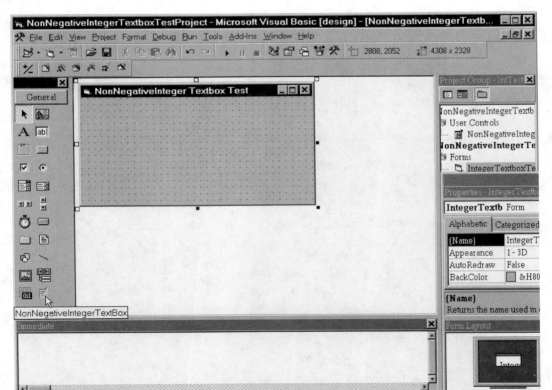

That's it, the non-negative integer text box is now an active control on the toolbox for Form1. To test it:

1. Double-click on its icon in the bottom right corner of the toolbox—this will place the control on Form1.
2. Press F5 to run Project2.

Try typing in this box. Notice that you can only type non-negative integers in it. If you want to test if you can only cut and paste non-negative integers in it, try cutting and pasting something that isn't one from another Windows application; the box will immediately go blank.

Adding an Event

For our final demonstration of the power you now have at your hands, we want to add a BadEntry event that we can program within the Form window of our Standard EXE. For this:

1. End the program if it is still running.
2. Move to the Code window for the NonNegativeIntegerTextBox by highlighting the line with NonNegativeIntegerTextBox in the Project Explorer and choosing View|Code.
3. Add the following line above the Text1_Change event.

   ```
   Public Event BadEntry()
   ```

4. Add the code indicated in boldface below to your previous code so that your code reads like Listing 1-1:

Listing 1-1: Adding a BadEntry Event

```
Private Sub Text1_Change()
    If Text1.Text = "" Then Exit Sub
    If Not (IsNumeric(Text1.Text)) Or (Int(Val(Text1.Text)) _
    <> Val(Text1.Text)) Or Val(Text1.Text) < 0 Then
        RaiseEvent BadEntry
        Text1.Text = ""
    End If
End Sub
```

```
Private Sub Text1_KeyPress(KeyAscii As Integer)
    If KeyAscii < Asc("0") Or KeyAscii > Asc("9") Then
        KeyAscii = 0
        RaiseEvent BadEntry
    End If
End Sub
```

That's it. We have added the code to raise an event whenever the user enters a non-integer. To test it, we need to go back to Form1:

1. Double-click in the Form1 line of the Project Explorer.
2. Double-click on the NonNegativeIntegerTextBox. Notice that this brings up an event procedure for the BadEntry event, as shown in Figure 1-14.

Figure 1-14   The BadEntry event procedure

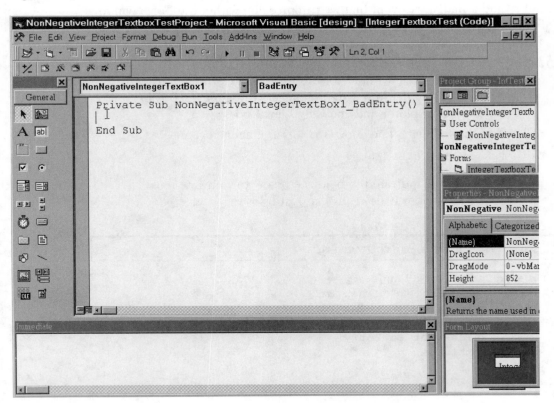

3. Type the following line of code inside the template.

    ```
    MsgBox "Please enter only non-negative integers!"
    ```

That's it! If you run the program, you'll see that it accepts only non-negative integers and any attempt to enter anything except a non-negative integer shows the message box (proving that our control does, indeed, respond to a custom event!).

Note

Obviously, there is a lot more that can be done to this control. In particular, the area for this customized text box is surrounded by a lot of "white space." You will see in Chapter 13 how to make your controls resize themselves automatically so there is no unintended white space, for example.

VISUAL BASIC 5'S ENVIRONMENT

Topics in this Chapter

- Visual Basic 5 Environment Overview
- An Overview of the Main Window
- The Different Child Windows
- Context Menus
- Miscellaneous Dialog Boxes

Chapter

The purpose of this chapter is to show you the Integrated Development Environment (IDE) of Visual Basic 5, and provide a handy reference that you can return to as needed. Most of the menus and toolbar buttons are fairly self-explanatory, so we suggest skimming the information and returning to this chapter after you get a little further into VB.

Visual Basic 5 Environment Overview

If you are already familiar with Visual Basic 4.0, then much of the environment will seem familiar. The big difference is that in earlier versions of Visual Basic, the IDE consisted of a main window made up of a menu and toolbar. All other windows were free-floating on the screen. (This is called single document interface or SDI.) However, Visual Basic 5 gets a new multiple document interface (or MDI) as its default, although the older SDI mode is still available as an option (see below). In MDI, all the windows are child windows of a parent window. With the introduction of the new MDI mode also comes *dockable windows*. Dockable windows enable you to connect child windows into groups of docked windows that can be moved and sized together.

Also new to the IDE is the ability to load multiple projects at the same time, known as *project groups,* which you saw in Chapter 1. This feature allows you to load another project with which to test your control while developing it, which is necessary for the testing of user controls.

The MDI IDE consists of a main window that has a menu and toolbar on top with all other child windows residing somewhere within the MDI space (see Figure 2-1). In SDI mode, the difference is that the child windows float freely and you can see your desktop in between them. See Figure 2-2 for what the default SDI desktop looks like—you will need to make other windows visible via the View menu to get something similar to Figure 2-1.

The default mode for Visual Basic 5 is the new MDI mode, but you can change it to SDI using the Tools|Options Advanced tab. The change will take effect the next time you start VB5. If you are an experienced Visual Basic user with a big screen, try the MDI mode; it is a little uncomfortable at first, but it grows on you.

Figure 2-1 MDI mode

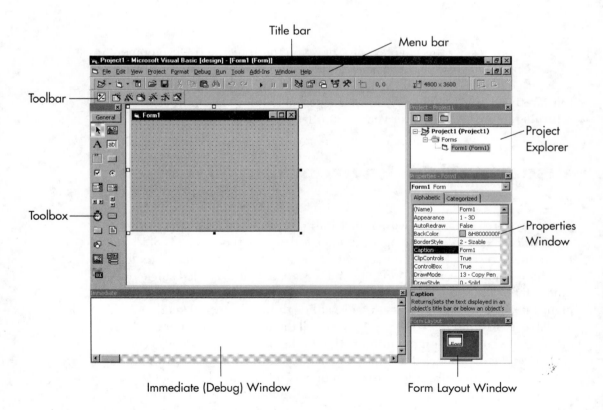

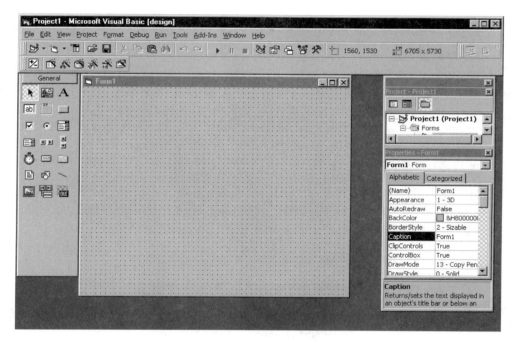

Figure 2-2 SDI mode

Tip

If you are using anything less than 800 × 600 resolution, you will probably want to use SDI mode for coding. The code window in a low resolution MDI is ridiculously small.

Another new feature is customizable dockable toolbars. The Standard toolbar is visible by default but the other ones (Debug, Edit and Form Editor) are available by choosing View|Toolbars menu and selecting them. (See the Toolbar(s) section later in this chapter.)

If all this were not enough, in addition to the main window, main menu and toolbars, the IDE contains nine other windows that may be made visible or invisible from the View menu. Finally, there are numerous dialog boxes that pop up when you invoke various commands and operations.

An Overview of the Main Window

When you start up Visual Basic 5, you see a copyright screen indicating to whom the copy of the program is licensed. After a short delay, a tabbed dialog box appears as shown in Figure 2-3 for the Enterprise Edition of VB (other versions of VB will have fewer options). The first tab, as you can see in Figure 2-3, gives you a wide choice of options. You have three of them already: Standard EXE, ActiveX Control, and the VB Application Wizard. The other options will be covered later on in this book. Choosing the Existing tab gives you a standard File Open dialog box, as shown in Figure 2-4. Choosing the Recent tab shows a list of your most recent projects. An example of what you will see in this case may be found in Figure 2-5.

Figure 2-3   The New Project dialog box

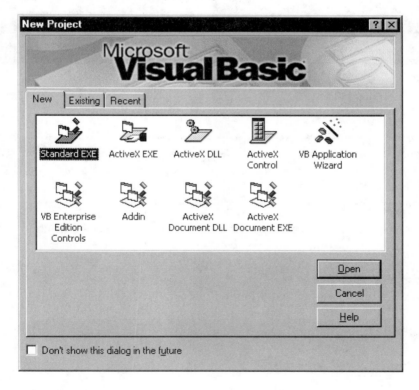

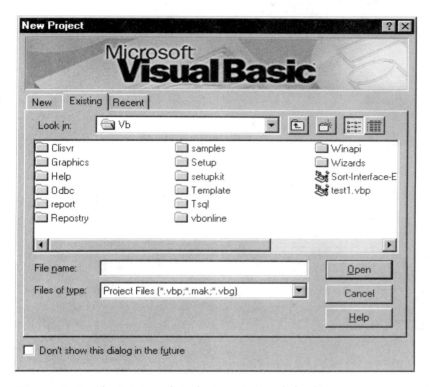

Figure 2-4   The Existing tab in the New Project dialog box

Note

Although Visual Basic 5 gives you the option of not using this dialog box as your gateway into it, (click off the check box shown in the left corner of Figure 2-3), we don't recommend it. If you want to get it back, select Prompt for Project in the Tools|Options|Environment dialog.

After you choose one of the options, you'll be taken to the main window. As mentioned earlier, this will either be the MDI interface shown in Figure 2-1 or the SDI interface of Figure 2-2.

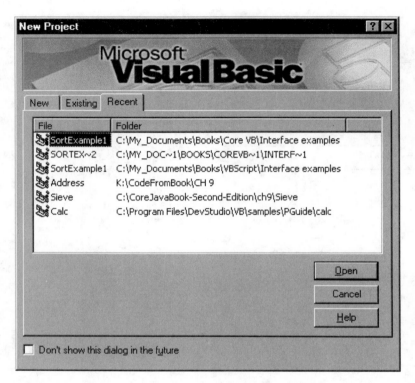

Figure 2-5   The Recent tab in the New Project dialog box

Note

Visual Basic 5 remembers your last screen arrangement and reuses it. For this reason, your screen may look different from Figure 2-1 or 2-2. (This information is kept in the Windows Registry.) Visual Basic 5 also remembers the state of a project and restores the environment as you left it. This information is kept in a file with the same name as your project but with the extension .vbw, which stands for Visual Basic Workspace.

Title Bar

The title bar is the horizontal bar located at the top of the screen; it gives the name of the application and is common to all Microsoft Windows applications. Interactions between the user and the title bar are handled by Windows, not by the application. Everything below the title and menu bar in a Windows application is called the *client area*. Your application is completely responsible for the look, feel, and response of the objects you place in this area.

For example, if you are working with a new Standard EXE in Visual Basic 5, the title bar starts out by displaying:

Project1 - Microsoft Visual Basic [design]

This is typical of Microsoft Windows applications: in sophisticated programs (like Visual Basic 5) that have multiple states, the title bar changes to indicate the different states. For example, when you are testing a Standard EXE, the title bar switches to something like:

Project1 - Microsoft Visual Basic [run]

and when you are debugging and have temporarily stopped the program, the title bar switches to something like:

Project1 - Microsoft Visual Basic [break]

The Menu Bar

In Visual Basic 5, the menu bar gives you the tools needed to develop, test, and save your application. Most of the options have toolbar equivalents and keystroke shortcuts. For example, the File menu contains the commands for working with the files and projects that go into designing and testing a user control. The Edit menu contains editing tools that will help you write the code to activate the interface you design for your application, including the search-and-replace editing tools. (Only a few are available on the Edit toolbar.) The View menu gives you fast access to the different parts of your program and the Visual Basic 5 environment. The Project menu gives you access for inserting new objects and setting project properties. The Format menu provides tools to arrange the controls on a form. The Debug menu gives you the command you need to operate in a debugging session. The Run menu lets you test your application while developing it. The Tools menu gives you commands to add/modify items in a code module, add/modify menus, and set the options for the IDE. The Add-Ins menu gives you access to tools and Wizards that are added into the Visual Basic environment. The Window menu helps organize your windows. Finally, you use the Help menu to gain access to the help system provided with VB5. This menu also has the very useful Microsoft on the Web option that, if your machine is equipped for it, lets you connect to the World Wide Web for up-to-the-minute information from Microsoft.

In Windows applications, all the menus have access keys. Pressing ALT and the underlined letter opens that menu. Use the arrow keys to move around the menu bar. Once a menu is open, all you need is a single *accelerator key* (also called an *access* or *hot key*) to select a menu option. Accelerator keys are not case-sensitive. Some menu items have shortcut keys. For example, as is common in Windows applications, pressing ALT+F4 lets you exit Visual Basic 5 without going through the File menu.

The Toolbar(s)

Visual Basic 5 contains four toolbars also referred to as command bars since they are based on Office 97 technology. This section describes the toolbars: Standard, Debug, Edit and Form Editor. There is a fifth toolbar that is used with Add-ins (see Chapter 15).

Tip

Since the toolbars are dockable in the IDE by simply dragging them around, you might want to experiment with their arrangement to have all the toolbars available at one time. The most compact arrangement we have found is to have the Standard and Form toolbars on one line and the Edit and Debug toolbars on the other.

Note

The toolbars can be customized. See the section on the Context-Sensitive Menus later in this chapter.

Standard Toolbar

Reading from left to right, here is what the tools on this toolbar do:

Table 2-1:	**The Standard Toolbar Icons**	

Icon	*Name*	*Purpose*
	Add Project	Lets you add a new project of the various types to the IDE. This is the same as File|Add Project. The little down arrow to the right of the button selects a different project type than the one currently shown. The ActiveX EXE and DLL options are not available in the Control Creation Edition version of Visual Basic.
	Add Form	Lets you add a component to the current project. A component can be a Form, MDI form, Module, Class Module, User Control, Property Page, User Document, ActiveX Designer or a file of your choice. The User Document and ActiveX Designer options are not available in the Control Creation Edition version. Clicking the little down arrow to the right of the button opens a dialog that lets you choose a new component template or an existing file of that type. These functions may also be found on the Project menu.
	Menu Editor	This opens the Menu Editor, which is only available when a form or User Control is currently open in design mode.
	Open Project	Lets you open a new project. This will close the current project or project group in order to load the new one you select. This is the same as File|Open Project.
	Save Project or Project Group	This allows you to save the current Project or, if more than one project is loaded, the entire Project Group will be saved. This is the one-click way of saving every item that is currently *dirty* (modified since the last save).
	Cut, Copy, Paste	These are the standard editing commands that work with text and objects in the IDE. These are available on the Edit menu and with the shortcut keys CTRL+X, CTRL+C, and CTRL+V, respectively.
	Find	Opens the Find dialog box when a code window is visible. From this dialog box you can also perform find and replace operations. This is the same as Edit|Find and CTRL+F.

Table 2-1:	The Standard Toolbar Icons (continued)	
Icon	*Name*	*Purpose*
	Undo	Undoes the last operation, if possible. For example, if you inadvertently delete a control from a form, clicking this button will put it back. This is the same as Edit|Undo and CTRL+Z. Visual Basic 5 has multiple levels of undo. Each click on this button undoes another action.
	Redo	Redoes the last Undo operation, if possible. For example, if you inadvertently undo too many changes in a code module, clicking this button will reverse the undo operations, one at a time. This is the same as Edit|Redo.
	Start	Runs the current project. Same as Run|Start or F5.
	Break	Puts the current project into break mode. Same as Run|Break or CTRL+BREAK.
	End	Stops the current project. Same as Run|End.
	Project Window	Makes the Project Explorer window visible and sets focus to it. This window is explained in detail later in this chapter.
	Properties Window	Makes the Properties window visible and sets focus to it. This window is explained in detail later in this chapter.
	Form Layout Window	Makes the Form Layout window visible and sets focus to it. This window is explained in detail later in this chapter.
	Object Browser	Makes the Object Browser window visible and sets focus to it. This window is briefly explained in this chapter and in some detail in Chapter 7.
	Toolbox	Makes the Toolbox window visible and gives it the focus. This window is explained in detail later.
1080, 1320	Current X, Y	Shows the current X and Y position of the current object, whether it is a form or a control on a form.
1215 × 495	Current Width, Height	Shows the current width and height of the current object, whether it is a form or a control on a form.

Debug Toolbar

Reading from left to right, here is what the tools on this toolbar do:

Table 2-2:	The Debug Toolbar	
Icon	*Name*	*Purpose*
▶	Start	Runs the current project. Same as Run|Start or F5.
‖	Break	Puts the current project into break mode. Same as Run|Break or CTRL+BREAK.
■	End	Stops the current project. Same as Run|End.
✋	Toggle Breakpoint	Turns the breakpoint on the current line on or off depending upon its current state. Same as Debug|Toggle Breakpoint and F9.
	Step Into	Executes the next line of code while in break mode, and steps into a sub program if one is called. Same as Debug|Step Into or F8.
	Step Over	Executes the next line of code while in break mode, and steps over a sub program if one is called. Same as Debug|Step Over or SHIFT+F8.
	Step Out	Steps out of a sub program that you entered with Step Into. Same as Debug|Step Out or CTRL+SHIFT+F8.
	Locals Window	Displays the Local variables window and sets focus to it. Same as View|Locals Window. This window is explained later in the chapter.
	Immediate Window	Displays the Immediate window and sets focus to it. Same as View|Immediate Window or CTRL+G. This window is explained in Chapter 9.
	Watch Window	Displays the Local variables window and sets focus to it. Same as View|Watch Window. This window is explained later in the chapter.
👓	Quick Watch	Displays the value of the currently highlighted text in a code window. Same as Debug|Quick Watch or SHIFT+F9.
	Call Stack	Displays the value of the current call stack (all of the procedure calls executed in the current operation). Same as View|Call Stack or CTRL+L.

Note

The functions on the Debug toolbar are discussed in detail in Chapter 9.

Edit Toolbar

Table 2-3:	The Edit Toolbar	

Icon	Name	Purpose
	List Properties/ Methods	Displays a pop-up list of the properties and methods for the object preceding the period. CTRL+J is the keyboard equivalent.
	List Constants	Displays a pop-up list of the valid constants after you type an = sign. CTRL+SHIFT+J is the keyboard equivalent.
	Quick Info	Gives the syntax for the procedure or method. CTRL+I is the keyboard equivalent.
	Parameter Info	Provides the parameter list for the current function call. CTRL+SHIFT+I is the keyboard equivalent.
	Complete Word	Completes the keyword or object when enough information is there. CTRL+SPACE is the keyboard equivalent.
	Indent	Indents the selected text one tab stop. TAB is the keyboard equivalent.
	Outdent	Moves the selected text back one tab stop. SHIFT+TAB is the keyboard equivalent.
	Toggle Breakpoint	Used for debugging (see Chapter 9). F9 is the keyboard shortcut.
	Comment Block	There is no default keyboard equivalent for this. (See Chapter 4 for more information on comments.)
	Uncomment Block	There is no default keyboard equivalent for this tool.
	Toggle Bookmark	Bookmarks allows easier navigation between parts of your code.

Icon	Name	Purpose
	Next Bookmark	Jumps to the next saved bookmark.
	Previous Bookmark	Jumps to the previously saved bookmark.
	Clear All Bookmarks	Clears all bookmarks currently saved. Bookmarks do not persist when you exit the IDE so they will be cleared then, as well.

Note

This toolbar is explained in more detail in Chapter 4.

Form Editor Toolbar

Reading from left to right, here is what the tools on this toolbar do:

Table 2-4:   The Form Editor Toolbar

Icon	Name	Purpose
	Bring to Front	Sets the ZOrder of the currently selected control to 0, causing it to display on top of the other controls. (See Chapter 6 for more on ZOrder.) Same as Format|Order|Bring to Front or CTRL+J.
	Send to Back	Sets the ZOrder of the currently selected control to 1, causing it to go behind any controls that reside in the same area. Same as Format|Order|Send to Back or CTRL+K.
	Align	Allows you to align multiselected controls to the Left, Center, Right, Top, Middle, Bottom or to the Grid. Same as Format|Align. (See Chapter 3 for more on this.)
	Center	Allows you to center the selected controls horizontally or vertically. Same as Format|Center.

Table 2-4:	The Form Editor Toolbar (continued)	
Icon	*Name*	*Purpose*
	Make Same	Allows you to make the selected controls the same Height, Width or both. Same as Format|Make Same Size.
	Lock Controls Toggle	Locks or unlocks the controls on a form so they can be sized or moved with the mouse (unlocked) or prevented from being sized or moved by the mouse (locked). A locked control or set of controls can still be sized or moved with the keyboard using the SHIFT+ARROW and CTRL+ARROW keys, respectively.

The Different Child Windows

This section briefly discusses the nine possible windows in VB5.

Form Designer

The initial Form Designer window, as shown in Figure 2-6, takes up part of the center window in the MDI. (In Visual Basic programming, the convention is to use the term *form* for a customizable window.) It is simply a window with a grid of dots. (See Chapter 3 for more details on the Form Designer window.)

Note

Form designers are used for user control design, testing form design and Property Page design (Chapter 13). They all use the same designer and, while there are a few subtle differences that we cover later on, they work basically in the same way.

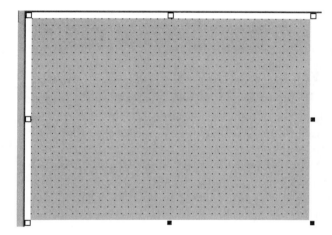

Figure 2-6 Form Designer window

Code Window

Visual Basic comes with a full-screen programming editor. Since it is a programming editor, it lacks features like word wrap and print formatting that even a primitive word processor like WordPad has. On the other hand, it does add features like syntax checking that can spot certain common programming typos, as well as many new features not found in previous versions of Visual Basic, such as Quick Info. The Visual Basic program editor also color-codes the various parts of your code. For example, Visual Basic commands can be in one color, comments in another. The colors used are customizable via the Editor page from the Tools menu's Options dialog box. The Visual Basic program editor is activated whenever you are writing or viewing code. The font used in the editor can be changed to suit your needs.

Note

This window is explained in detail in Chapter 4.

Object Browser

The Object Browser, shown in the center of Figure 2-7, lets you view properties, methods, events and constants from the object libraries currently loaded in the IDE. By default, the browser loads a few standard libraries, such as the one for standard parts of Visual Basic 5. Visual Basic 5 also loads all the parts of the currently loaded project(s). Whenever you use the Project menu to add a reference to another library or a custom control, that library will appear in the browser as well.

Although we will cover the browser in more detail in Chapter 7, we want to give you a hint of its powers here. It is a great source of information on the available programming resources in the IDE. For example, to see all of the available properties and methods for the App object, load the browser using the F2

Figure 2-7   The Object Browser at work

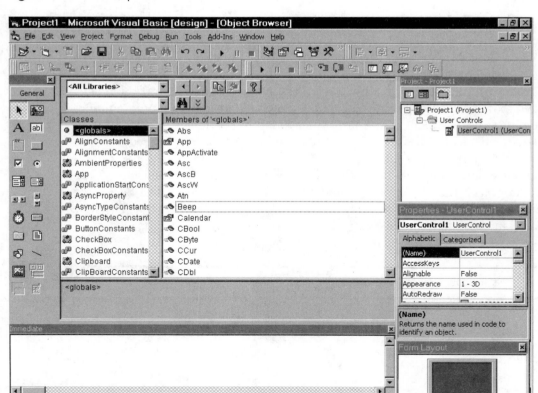

key and choose VB in the top drop-down list. Then click on App in the Classes list. As you can see in Figure 2-8, the browser gives you a short description of the object. (For the App object, this is "Contains general information about an application.") A complete list of the Members of App is shown in the right-hand pane. (*Members* is the standard term in object-oriented programming for everything in that particular object. This includes its properties and methods— see Chapters 7 and 8 if you are not familiar with these terms.)

Playing with the Object Browser is a great way to discover powerful features that would otherwise go unnoticed. As you can see in Figure 2-8, each item will display a short description in the bottom of the window when it is selected.

It is possible to search for a word in a single library or in all the available libraries. Just type in the word in the lower drop-down combo box and click

Figure 2-8   The Object Browser for the App object

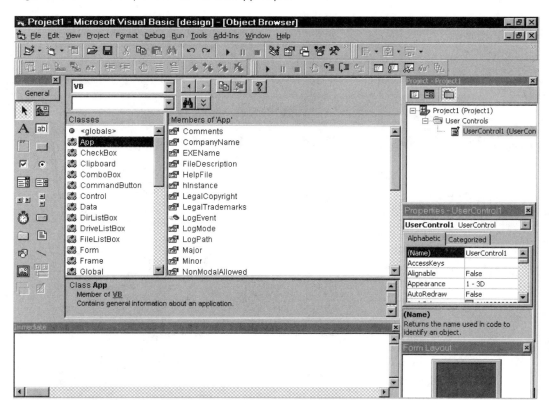

the little binoculars button. For example, let's assume you still have "VB" listed as the object to browser:

1. Type the word "click" in the box.
2. Click the binoculars button.

A new pane will open every occurrence of the word "click" in the VB object, as shown in Figure 2-9. (What you are seeing is the list of all controls built into Visual Basic that have a Click or DblClick event.)

Note

For more on the Object Browser, please see Chapter 7.

Figure 2-9   Object Browser example screen

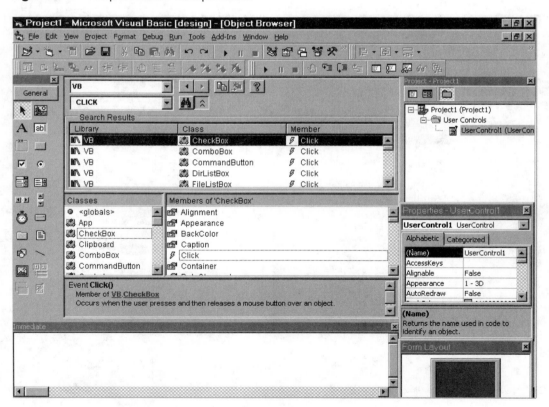

Immediate Window (Debug Window)

The Immediate window (or Debug window, as it is commonly called) was a useful tool in earlier versions of VB. It has been made much more powerful in Visual Basic 5, allowing you to test functions, load forms, evaluate expressions and view the values of objects, variables and properties. It is usually located at the bottom of the screen (see Figure 2-1) and is explained in detail in Chapter 9.

Locals Window

Newly added to Visual Basic is the Locals window. This window is usually hidden; choose View|Locals Window to bring it up. The Locals window displays the names and values of every local variable in the current procedure. It shares similar functionality with the Watch window (explained below). The benefit of the Locals window is that it follows the flow of your program, giving all the values in the current scope. The disadvantage is that you cannot see any values outside of that scope. Of course, that is what the Watch window is for. You can also change the value of any assignable variable. Objects (such as forms and controls) cannot be set, but they may be expanded and their properties can be changed.

Watch Window

This window is used to display the value of variables and expressions for any scope from the current procedure to the entire application. In addition to all of the features available for the Locals window, the Watch window allows you to Add, Edit and Delete items. Edit is the most powerful as it allows you to set the scope of the item and what type of watch statement you want to use for it. This window is also discussed in more detail in Chapter 9 in the section on Testing and Debugging. The Watch window allows the same value modification as described above for the Locals window.

Project Explorer

The Project Explorer (or Project Window) lists all projects and their components (forms, modules, user controls property pages) that are currently loaded in the IDE. Figure 2-10 shows one of the samples supplied with VB5. (If the Project Explorer is not visible, choose View|Project or CTRL+R.)

Figure 2-10   Project Explorer in Folder view

There are actually two ways to see the Project Explorer. Figure 2-10 gives the default Folder view where all similar components for each project are kept in a folder and are not visible until you open that folder. This is useful when you have a large number of components of various types and you want to see only certain types at a time.

The other view is a simple hierarchy of projects and components with all components listed alphabetically for each project. An example is shown in Figure 2-11. (Use the last button, Toggle Folders, on the Project Explorer

Figure 2-11   Project Explorer in Hierarchical
view

toolbar to change to this view.) This view is better when you want to access
any component quickly—you won't have to open a folder. The disadvantage
is that it takes more room to display the entire list. Each component type has
a specific icon, such as the pencil used for a user control (`ctl` file), so it is
easy to distinguish the different types of components.

Figure 2-12 shows what the initial Project window looks like for a Standard
EXE project.

Notice in Figure 2-12 that one item is already listed in the Project window.
This is the initial form (or user control) on which you will build the application. Click on the first tool (View Code) in the Project Explorer to quickly see
the code, and use the second tool (View Object) to send that part of the highlighted component to the forefront or use the Context menu.

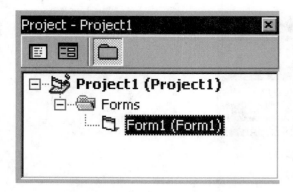

Figure 2-12   Initial Project Explorer for a
Standard EXE

Although Visual Basic separately stores all the files that go into making up
the project, it keeps track of where they are. It creates a file, called the
Project file, that tells it (and you, if you look at the file with an editor) where
the individual files are located. Visual Basic creates the Project file whenever
you choose Save Project from the File menu, or the Save Project tool from
the toolbar. It creates a different Project file whenever you choose Save
Project As. Project files have the extension .vbp in their filename.

If you have more than one project loaded in the IDE, you have, by default,
created a *project group*. Visual Basic saves the information about the group
(such as what projects were in it) in a .vbg file. The new project group feature
of VB5 makes it easy to create a test project group with designed controls and
a Standard EXE project that allows you to test the controls.

Properties Window

The Properties window, an example of which is shown in Figure 2-13, is
where you set and view the properties of the currently selected item in the
Project Explorer or the currently selected control on a form or user control.
The default view of the Properties window is an alphabetical list of all properties that are available at design time.

Note

*For more on the Properties window, see Chapter 3. You can also use the
Object Browser discussed previously to see all of the properties of an object.*

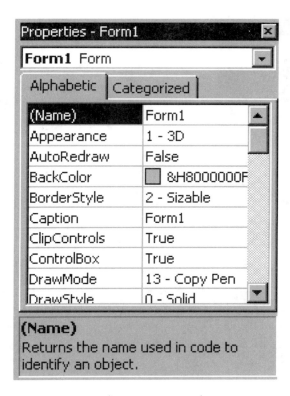

Figure 2-13   The Properties window

The Properties window can also use a Categorized view. In this view, all properties of a control or component fall into categories such as Appearance, Behavior, DDE, Font, Misc, Position, Scale and Text, as shown in Figure 2-14 on the next page. When you create your own controls, you can place the properties in a category using the Tools|Procedure Attributes dialog box discussed in Chapters 7,8, and 13.

Form Layout

The Form Layout window shows you the position and size of your form, relative to the entire screen. This is very helpful for designing forms and user controls that must work well in many resolutions. The Form Layout window optionally shows resolution guides to show how your form fits in various resolutions. (Right-click in the Form Layout window to see this feature at work.)

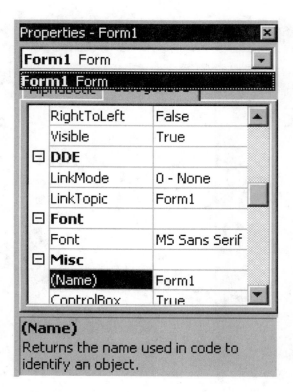

Figure 2-14   The Properties window in
Categorized view

The Form Layout window default is to be visible directly under the Properties window. It is also available from the View|Form Layout command.

The Toolbox

The toolbox is located at the left of the screen by default, just below the toolbar. It contains the available controls used to develop the UI (user interface) of your forms and user controls. How many tools are available depends on your custom controls. Use the toolbox to place command buttons, text buttons, and the other controls in your application. See Chapter 3 for more on the toolbox.

Color Palette

The color palette is a handy window that allows you to set the ForeColor and BackColor of any object that exhibits these properties. The window eliminates the need to go to the Properties window to set these color properties. It is not loaded by default, but is available from the View|Color Palette command. See Chapter 3 for more on the Color Palette.

Context Menus

Virtually every window in the IDE has a context menu that pops up when you click the right mouse button, displaying commands that pertain to the object you clicked. (Most are available on the usual menus or via the toolbar.) Once you get comfortable with context menus, they can be one of the most useful features in the IDE. We describe the main features of the most interesting context menus for the different windows in the sections that follow.

Context Menu for the Toolbox

Figure 2-15 on the next page shows you the Context menu for the Toolbox.

The Components item leads to a dialog box for adding custom controls. The Add Tab item lets you add a new tab to the toolbox when you have too many controls to easily fit. For example, Figure 2-16 on page 55 shows what you get if you add a Common Controls tab with the usual Windows Common controls.

Context Menu for Toolbars

If you right-click in the toolbar, you'll see a list of all the toolbars (checked ones are visible). Click on any toolbar in the context menu to display or hide it. The last item is, potentially, the most useful. Click on the Customize option and you see a screen like Figure 2-17 on page 55. Use this dialog box to add your own toolbars or to customize an existing toolbar.

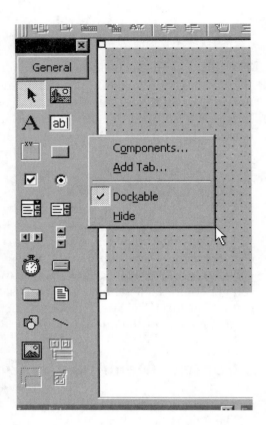

Figure 2-15   The Context-Sensitive menu for the Toolbox

Adding a Custom Toolbar

Custom toolbars can contain items from any of the VB5 menus. To build one:

1. Choose View|Toolbars|Customize.
2. Choose New.
3. Give your new toolbar a name in the dialog box that pops up and click on OK.

Your screen will now look like Figure 2-18 on page 56. Notice the toolbar in the center of the Customize dialog box. All you have to do is drag items from the Commands pane (in the Command tab) to the toolbar.

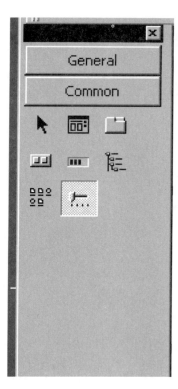

Figure 2-16   Toolbox with an additional tab

Figure 2-17   Customizing a Toolbar dialog box

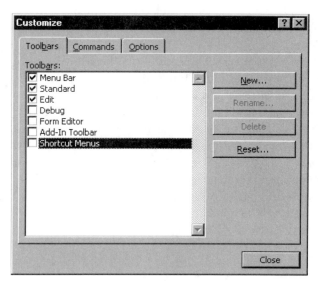

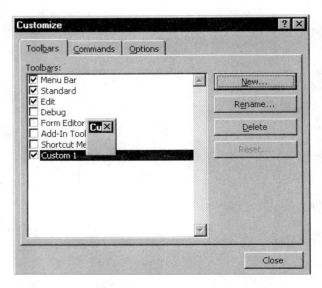

Figure 2-18   Creating a Custom toolbar

Customizing an Existing Tool Button

While you have the Customize dialog box open, Visual Basic 5 gives you the ability to further customize any of its buttons. For this,

1. Right-click on a command bar and choose Customize.
2. While the Customize Dialog is up, right-click on the button you want to customize. This shows a pop-up menu.

For example, Figure 2-19 is what your screen will look like while you are trying to further customize the comment block tool button.

Since we use this tool a lot, we will give it a keystroke shortcut. For this, go to the pop-up menu and change the name to something like Comment & Block. This will assign the keystroke combination of ALT +B to the Comment Block tool. (Note that the Edit toolbar must be active and the text in the caption must be visible for this shortcut to work.) This pop-up menu also gives the option of using the most innovative invention in toolbars since they were first invented—Text. If you are like some people and prefer buttons with textual descriptions to confusing pictures, the Text option shown in Figure 2-19 is ideal.

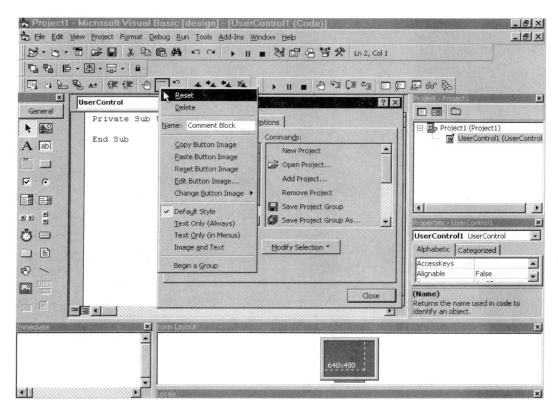

Figure 2-19   Customizing a button

Context Menu for the Form Designer

Figure 2-20 on the next page shows the Context menu for the Form Designer. The options on this menu are discussed in Chapter 3.

Context Menu for the Code Window

Figure 2-21 on page 59 shows the Context menu for the Code window. The options on this menu are discussed in Chapter 4.

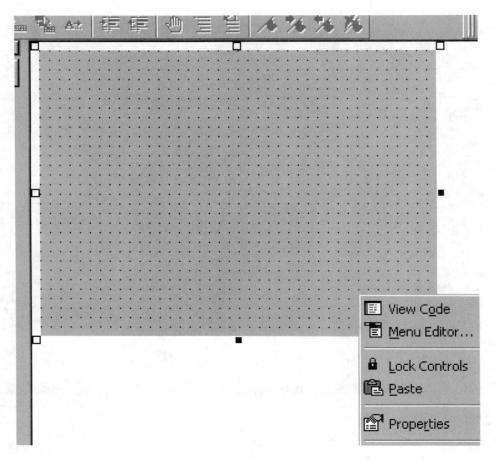

Figure 2-20   Context menu for the Form Designer

Context Menu for the Project Explorer

There are actually two Context menus available for this window, depending on whether you right-click on a project or one of the objects like a form or control in a project. The functionality of both Context menus is similar. Figure 2-22 on page 60 shows the Context menu when you right click on a form.

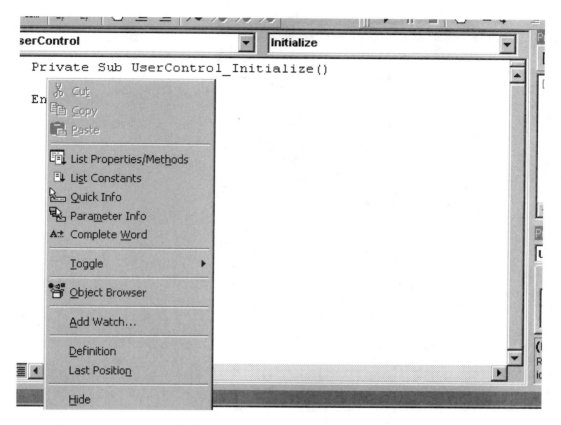

Figure 2-21   Context menu for the Code window

Miscellaneous Dialog Boxes

Numerous dialog boxes throughout the IDE may not be easily discoverable or intuitive in use. We will explain a few of them here.

Figure 2-22   Context menu for a form in the
Project Explorer

REGISTRY NOTES

All of the values set here are currently stored in the system registry under the following key:

HKEY_CURRENT_USER\Software\VBA\Microsoft Visual Basic

If you run REGEDIT and look at this key, you will find numerous settings and values, some of which make sense and some that look cryptic. We do not recommend that you change the settings directly in the registry unless absolutely necessary. If you do change a registry entry, the IDE may have problems functioning and issue an error. On the other hand, some entries given here may need to be changed if your IDE gets really confused and you want to bring it back to its defaults.

Options

The Options dialog box available off the Tools menu is the place to go to change a setting in the IDE. Brief explanations of the six tabs found on this dialog box follow.

Editor Tab

As its name suggests, the Editor tab (shown in Figure 2-23) affects the way the code editor works. Following are explanations of its options.

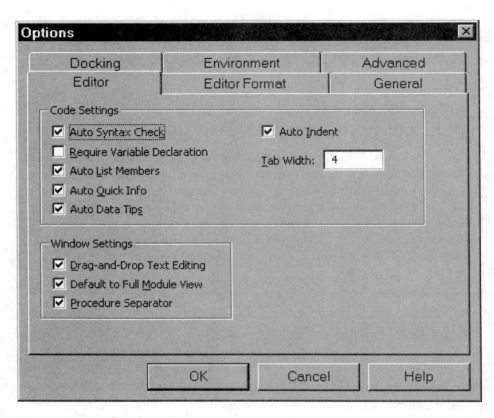

Figure 2-23   The Editor tab

Table 2-5: The Editor Tab	
Option	**Purpose**
Auto Syntax Check	When checked, the editor will issue an error if you move off a line that contains invalid code, such as leaving off the "Then" on an If/Then line.
Require Variable Declaration	Checking this option tells the IDE to add the "Option Explicit" line to the top of every new code module created. We recommend this as a means of preventing misspelled variable names.
Auto List Members	Checking this tells the editor to display a drop-down list of available members of an object whenever you type the Object Name followed by a period.

Option	*Purpose*
Auto Quick Info	This option tells the editor to list the parameters of the function with which you are working. This feature works for VBA functions, other library functions, and even your own user-defined functions.
Auto Data Tips	When activated, this feature lets you see the current value of a variable in break mode. Hold the mouse cursor stationary for a second on the variable you want to examine.
Auto Indent	This option, when checked, will automatically indent the next line of your code to the starting position of the previous line when you press ENTER. If unchecked, the cursor will return to the left margin when you press ENTER.
Tab Width	This is the number of spaces that will be added by the editor when you press the TAB key. It also applies when you use the Indent and Outdent buttons or their TAB and SHIFT+TAB equivalents.
Drag-and-Drop Text Editing	This box enables the type of drag-and-drop editing that is used in Microsoft Word. When you highlight some text, drag it by holding down the left mouse, then drop it in the desired position. This makes moving text fast and easy.
Default to Full Module View	When checked, the editor will display procedures in a streaming fashion. When unchecked, only one procedure will be displayed at a time, as it was in earlier versions of Visual Basic.
Procedure Separator	While in full module view, this option tells the editor whether or not to show the separator lines between procedures.

Editor Format Tab

The editor format tab, shown in Figure 2-24, is fairly self-explanatory. It is the place you go to set the colors and font the editor uses for code. Keep in mind the only way to set the editor back to default settings from this dialog box is one at a time.

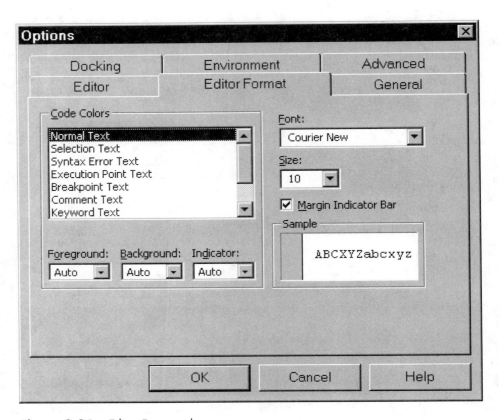

Figure 2-24   Editor Format tab

Note

If you really mess up, you can use REGEDIT and delete the CodeForeColor and CodeBackColor values from the Visual Basic key entry. This will force the IDE to return to its defaults.

General

The General tab, shown in Figure 2-25, is used when designing a form or building a control. It also controls how VB5 handles errors at design time (see Chapters 6 and 9).

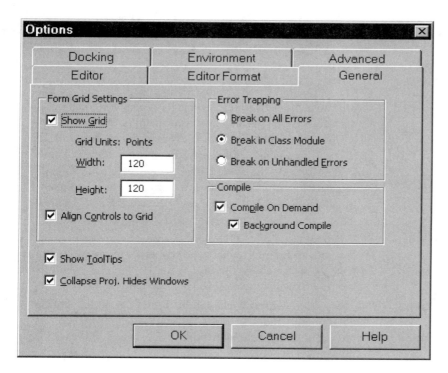

Figure 2-25   General tab

Table 2-6:   The General Tab

Option	Purpose
Form Grid Settings	If the Show Grid option is checked, all form, user control and Property Page designers will display dots in a grid to help you line up controls. The spacing of the dots is determined by the number of points you enter in the Width and Height fields. The Align to Grid option forces controls to jump to the nearest grid line. See Chapter 3 for more on the grid.

Table 2-6:   The General Tab (continued)

Option	*Purpose*
Error Trapping	This option has three possible settings. *Break on All Errors* will cause the IDE to break on any error in any code module, regardless if there is an active error handler (Chapter 6 covers error handlers). *Break in Class Modules* causes the IDE to break on any unhandled error in a class module (Chapter 7). This includes the code behind forms, user controls and Property Pages because they are technically class modules. Finally, *Break on Unhandled Error* causes the IDE to break on any error that occurs with no error handler present.
Show ToolTips	When checked, the IDE will display a brief description of the buttons on the toolbars and the items in the toolbox. Let your mouse sit above the button for a second or so and the tooltip text will appear.
Collapse Proj. Hides Windows	This option, when checked, tells the IDE to hide all of the component windows (forms, code, etc.) when you collapse the project in the Project window. This is helpful when you have more than one project loaded and you need a quick way to show only the current projects' windows.

Docking Tab

This tab simply tells the IDE which child windows can be docked. By default, all windows other than the Object Browser are dockable. This is the same as the Dockable item available on the Context menu in each window.

Environment Tab

This tab, shown in Figure 2-26, controls how the IDE works. It includes the very useful options for autosaving your projects.

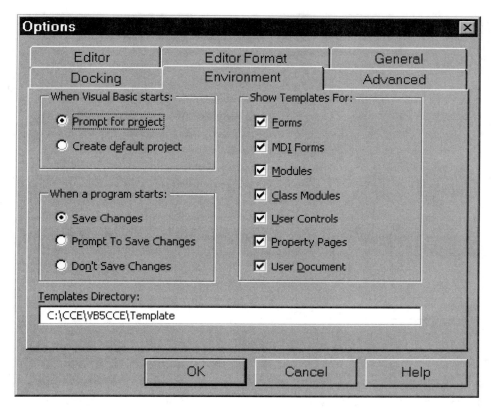

Figure 2-26   Environment tab

Table 2-7:   The Environment Tab

Option Group	Purpose
When Visual Basic starts	*Prompt for Project* tells the IDE to give you a dialog box that asks you to open a project on startup. If you do not like this dialog box to appear, choose Create Default Project and VB5 will simply create a user control project every time you load the IDE.
When a program starts	*Save Changes* causes the IDE to automatically save all *dirty* files to disk when you go to run mode. (Dirty is the jargon for any file that has been changed since the last save.) *Prompt To Save Changes* does the same except that it asks you before saving the changes.

Table 2-7: The Environment Tab (continued)	

Option	Purpose
	Don't Save Changes leaves you to save your changes before you run. We highly recommended that you either get in the habit of saving your changes regularly, or allow VB5 to do it for you prior to running the application.
Show Templates For	This option tells the IDE whether or not to display the new object dialog box when you add a new component to your project. If you uncheck a component type, you will get a blank object when you choose Project|New.
Templates Directory	This tells the IDE where you store your templates. By default, it is in the Template directory directly under VB5's directory. You may, however, point to a network server or any other location that makes sense. See Chapter 17 for more on templates.

Advanced Tab

The Advanced tab has a few options that are especially useful when working larger projects. It is also where you go to switch between the MDI and SDI environments.

Table 2-8: The Advanced Tab	

Option	Purpose
Background Project Load	If checked, VB5 will load your project components in the background allowing you to start working right away after loading a large project.
Notify when changing shared project items	This option tells the IDE to let you know when a change you are making will affect more than the current project. It only works for projects currently loaded in the IDE. For example, it is common to have code libraries that you add to all of your projects. Changing a procedure in such a library can affect the operation of all applications that use that code.

Option	*Purpose*
SDI Development Environment	If you prefer to have the old style Visual Basic environment of floating windows and desktop showing through, this option lets you set it. You can start Visual Basic from the command line with a switch telling it which mode to use, VB/SDI or VB/MDI. The switch from the command will stick until you change it again from this dialog box or the command line.

Project Properties

The project properties dialog box (Project|Project Properties brings it up) is somewhat limited in certain versions of VB5. Therefore, some of the options in this dialog box may be disabled in your version. There are four tabs in this dialog box: General, Make, Compile and Component.

General Tab

The General tab, shown in Figure 2-27, controls global properties of your project. The non-disabled parts of this dialog box are described in the table below.

Table 2-9:   The General Tab

Property	*Purpose*
Project Type	This drop-down list box shows you what the possibilities for projects that your version of VB5 affords. This corresponds to the choice you made in the initial VB screen.
Startup Object	For a Standard **EXE** project, this can be a form or Sub Main. A form name implies that the code project will start by loading the form. Sub Main tells Visual Basic to execute the code in the Main sub procedure. It must be in a standard code module. For a user control ActiveX **EXE** or ActiveX **DLL**, it can be either Sub Main or None. If None is chosen, the control simply goes into run mode without actually executing any basic code.

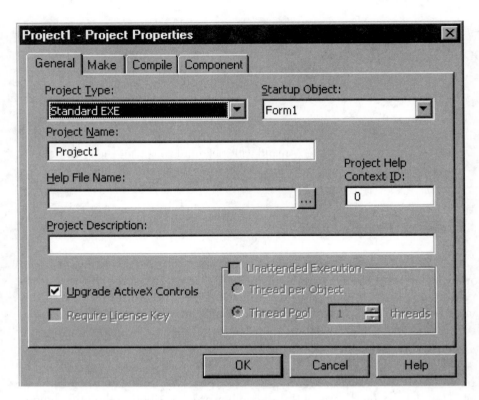

Figure 2-27 General tab in the Properties dialog box

Table 2-9: The General Tab (continued)	
Property	*Purpose*
Project Name	This is the name that will be used to register the user control in the system registry along with the controls class name. It must adhere to the VB5 naming convention of no spaces or punctuation (other than an underscore), and must start with a letter.
Help File Name and Context ID	This is the help file and starting context ID that will be used if a user presses F1 while the application is running.
Project Description	This is the text that will appear in the Object Browser when this project is chosen from the available libraries.

Property	Purpose
Upgrade ActiveX Controls	This enables the host application to upgrade your control if a newer version is available.
Require License Key	This tells VB5 to create a VBL (licensing) file when the project is made executable. The information in the VBL must be registered in order for the control to be usable on another system. The Setup Wizard handles this for you. See Chapter 20 for more on the Setup Wizard.

Make Tab

This dialog box, shown in Figure 2-28, is especially useful for version control since VB5 has none integrated. The following table describes this tab. This

Figure 2-28   The Make tab

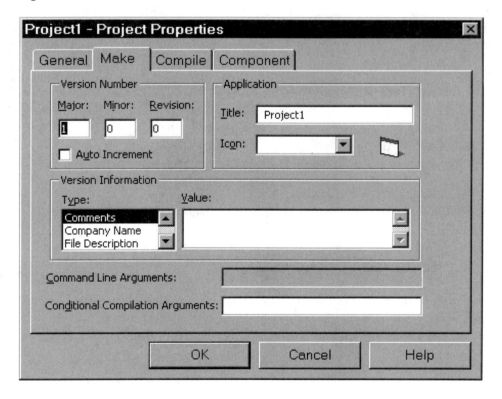

tab is also available when you click the Options button on the Make Project dialog (File|Make Project.ocx).

Table 2-10: The Make Tab	
Property	*Purpose*
Version Number	Sets the version number you want placed in the system registry for this project. Checking Auto Increment tells the IDE to increment the revision value each time the application is built.
Application Title	This is the title that will be displayed whenever a MsgBox function is used and the title parameter is left off. It is also the value of App.Title at run time.
Application Icon	This is the icon that will be stored in the OCX or EXE for use by the OS in creating shortcuts. It is not the Toolbox Bitmap used for your user control, which is set in the User Control Properties window.
Version Information	This is the data that will be displayed when a user selects Properties from the Win95 Explorer utility. It also will be available at run time from the App object. For example, the value of App.CompanyName will reflect what you enter here as the company name.
Command Line Arguments	Only applies to EXE projects.
Conditional Compilation	This is where you enter data, such as Debug=1, to cause the compiler to use lines of code that are encased in #IfDef statements. Conditional compilation is explained in Chapter 9.

Compile Tab

If you have never worked with Visual Basic before, then the options on this tab won't make a whole lot of sense. We suggest returning to this section when you are more familiar with VB. Also, what you can use in the Compile Tab (Figure 2-29) depends on the version of VB5 you have. The options shown in Figure 2-29 are enabled only when you have the Professional or Enterprise editions of VB. However, if you have one of these products, this tab is where you go to unleash one of the most eagerly awaited features of VB5: native code compilation.

First off, P-code is an intermediate step between Visual Basic source code and your machine's native executable format. Visual Basic transforms your Visual Basic source code into the machine language of a hypothetical machine (much as Java does, by the way). The resulting code is interpreted by the Visual Basic Virtual Machine (or run time as it used to be called). The file for the virtual machine is called Msvbvm50.dll. It is about 1.3 megs and can be found in the WINDOWS\SYSTEM directory. Compiling to P-code was your sole option in earlier versions of Visual Basic and is still the only option available in the Control Creation and Learning editions of VB. The advantage of P-code is that the resulting file has the smallest footprint. The disadvantage is that it will run more slowly (sometimes much more slowly) than using the native code option, which is activated by the next option button.

Figure 2-29   The Compile tab

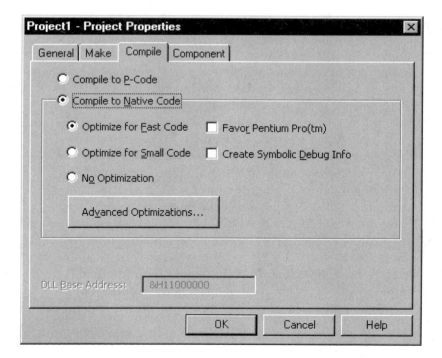

As you might expect, choosing the native code option tells VB to compile your code to a true executable. As we just said, this potential was one of the most requested features that users of previous versions of VB had requested for VB5. But, while it certainly can be useful, it is hardly a cure-all. In particular, how much faster the native code version of your application is than the P-code version depends on what you are trying to do. Some programs speed up 10 times, others barely speed up at all. You might want to try both the P-code and the native option before jumping to conclusions on which version to distribute. Table 2-11 describes the options you have available once you choose native code.

FOR EXPERIENCED WINDOWS USERS

Note that even when you choose the native code option, you still need the VB Virtual Machine (run time) that is used for interpreting the P-code. You may be wondering why; many people think of the run time as simply being the P-code interpreter. It turns out the P-code interpreter is less than 200k, the bulk of the VB run time is the support routines that the VB5 program needs, regardless of which compiler option you chose.

The problem is that the only alternative to a shared run time (a dynamic link library as they are called in Windows speak), is to statically link the necessary support routines into a VB5 executable. If you did this, the resulting executable would be very, very large and *nothing could be shared when you had other VB programs running at the same time.* For example, suppose you had 10 statically linked VB5 applications running at the same time, you would end up with a 13 meg memory requirement just for the overhead for these 10 programs. By using a dynamically linked run time, the same 10 programs could share the 1.3 meg run time and only the added functionality of each program would be added to their memory requirement.

Finally, we want to note that the requirement for a run time is hardly unique to VB—Java always requires a hefty run time containing its virtual machine, as does Windows C++ programming when using MFC.

Table 2-11: Native Code Options	
Option	*Purpose*
Optimize for Fast Code	This gives the fastest executable but may increase compile time. The resulting files may also be larger since you are telling the VB to favor speed over size.
Optimize for Small Code	Minimizes the size of the .exe and .dll files by instructing the compiler to favor size over speed. If this is a problem, you might be better off choosing the P-code option instead!
No Optimization	Compile without optimizations. Why bother?
Favor Pentium Pro	Optimizes the code created to favor the Pentium Pro. Don't use this unless you are sure the program will run almost exclusively on Pentium Pro's. (If you choose this option, the program will definitely run more slowly on an ordinary Pentium.)
Create Symbolic Debug Info	A very useful option if the VB debugger (see Chapter 9) is not sufficient and you need to move on to a product like the one in Visual C++ or the one from NuMega. Obviously, once you debug your program, you will want to recompile it with this option off.
DLL Base Address	This sets a base address for any DLL's (including ActiveX controls) that you may create with VB5. There is actually some argument to be made for changing the default at 0X10000000 to any random location *providing it ends in four zeroes and is less than &H80000000*. Using a random address in the correct range could speed up your program by avoiding conflicts. (This is especially true as lots of VB developers will just accept the default and rely on the OS to manage the conflicts.)

When you click on the Advanced Optimization button you are taken to a screen like Figure 2-30. This controls some more esoteric possible optimizations that are described in Table 2-12. *They should only be used after you have thoroughly debugged your program.*

Table 2-12:   Advanced Optimization Options

Option	*Description*
Assume No Aliasing	This tells the compiler that your program does not use aliasing. Aliasing is the technical term for when a parameter used in pass by reference refers to the same variable as a global variable. It usually isn't worth bothering with this option.
Remove Array Bound Checks	By default, Visual Basic checks that you are never trying to access a l entry in an array that is outside the range defined for the array. This takes time. If you are sure that you are not overstepping the bounds of arrays, this option can speed things up considerably. The risk is very weird bugs if you try to use the 11th entry in an array that holds 10!
Remove Integer Overflow Checks	By default, Visual Basic checks that calculations for bytes, integers, and longs are within the correct ranges. Choosing this option (again for a thoroughly debugged program) speeds up the calculations but again you risk weird bugs if you overflow the range for the type.
Remove Floating Point Error Checks	Works similarly as the previous check only for floating point types, such as Single and Double.
Allow Unrounded Floating Point Operations	This makes floating point calculations faster at the cost of maintaining more digits internally than would otherwise have been needed. This one has no downside providing you never compare floating point types for equality (which you shouldn't do anyway).
Remove Safe Pentium FDIV Checks	Eliminates the code that checks for Intel's (in)famous bug.

Figure 2-30   The Advanced Optimizations Page

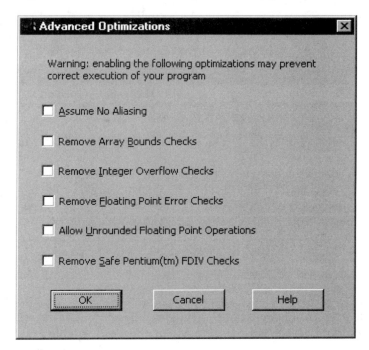

Component Tab

The Component tab is also somewhat specialized and you will rarely, if ever, need to change the defaults. The following table summarizes the various options on this tab.

Table 2-13:   The Component Tab

Property	Purpose
Remote Server	When checked, VB5 creates a VBR file to make it possible to run this user control from a remote server. This allows you to distribute the processing of your components across servers. It is more applicable to ActiveX EXEs, which are discussed in Chapter 14.

Table 2-13: The Component Tab (continued)	
Version Compatibility	*No Compatibility* means that compatibility with previously built and registered versions of your project is not enforced. This can lead to numerous entries in your registry for the same object. *Project Compatibility* tells the IDE to maintain compatibility with the project shown in the location field. If you select *Binary Compatibility*, the IDE will enforce that you do not change the interface of the user control from the file shown in the location field. If you do, a dialog will be presented showing the discrepancies between the two at the time of the build. You will be prompted to accept each change one by one, accept them all, or edit the changes before you continue. This helps insure that you do not inadvertently change your interface without warning.

References

The References dialog box, available from the Project|References command, allows you to view and add object libraries to your application. As shown in Figure 2-31, it consists of a list box of all available libraries. The currently loaded ones have checkmarks next to them. You can check or uncheck libraries, or browse for new libraries not listed because they may not be registered yet.

Note

You may also set the priority order for the checked libraries. Changing the priority is used to resolve conflicts in object models. Say you have the same object name in two loaded libraries. If you do not use the library prefix, VB5 will use the highest library in priority. Therefore, set the library you use the most as the highest priority so you do not have to use the library prefix every time you use members from that object.

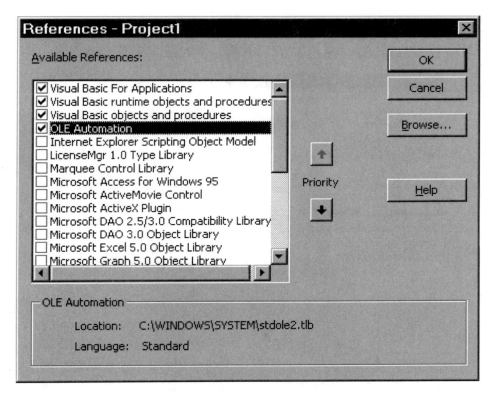

Figure 2-31 The References dialog box

Components

This dialog box, shown in Figure 2-32 on the next page, is available off the Project menu. It displays the Controls and Insertable Objects available to your application. The control list will reflect every OCX that is registered on your system, including the ones you create with Visual Basic 5. This also includes OCXs in Visual Basic 4.0 and any third-party OCXs you have on your system.

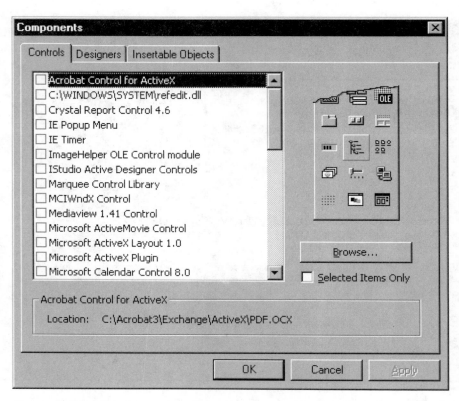

Figure 2-32   The Components dialog box

Note

If you see a duplicate entry, it was caused by the same control being built again without any compatibility enforced. The only way to get rid of these orphaned entries is to remove them from the registry yourself. Since this is not an easy process, we recommend that you use project compatibility to avoid it in the first place. However, if worse comes to worst, Microsoft does make available a program called RegClean that can help. (Search for RegClean at the Microsoft site: www.microsoft.com.)

The Insertable Objects tab list displays objects that are registered as being—you guessed it—insertable. This includes OLE server applications such as MSPAINT, Word and Excel. These cannot be placed on a user control but can be used on a form that is part of a user control project or in any standard EXE. For example, you could create a form that displays a bitmap using the Bitmap Image object that pops up when the user clicks a button found on your user control.

Note

If an item that you know is on your system is not listed, you can use the Browse function to find it and register it, making it available on the list.

Print

The Print dialog box, shown in Figure 2-33, is available off the File menu as well as through the Project window context menu. Visual Basic 5 allows you to print all or part of your project. You may choose whether you want the form image (applies to user control and Property Page as well), the code and/or the entire text of the form (the .frm, .ctl or .pag file).

You can print the *Form Image* (the form as you see it in design mode), the *Code* (only the code portion of the form), and the *Form as Text* (what you would see if you loaded the FRM file into Notepad). The *Print to File* option allows you to send the output to a file of your choice, as opposed to a printer.

Figure 2-33   The Print dialog box

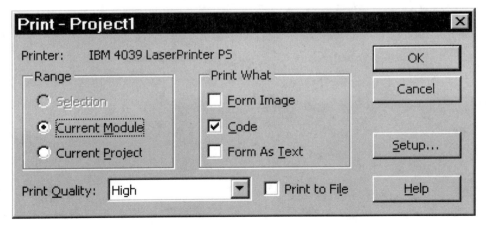

BUILDING THE USER INTERFACE

Topics in this Chapter

- Properties
- Working with the Properties Window
- Forms
- Controls
- Common Control Properties and Events
- Designing Menus
- The Text Representation of a Form or User Control

Chapter 3

M
ost programs or controls that you build will need to present a winning face to the world. Also, you need to be able to design realistic interfaces in order to test the controls that you build. This chapter will show you how to do both. Any visual part of a Visual Basic project, the test bed for a user control, and the control itself are all built on a window that is usually called a *form* in all versions of Visual Basic. Changing the appearance of a form or control can be done via the Properties window at design time or by using code at run time. This chapter concentrates on design time and leaves most of the coding tasks to the next chapter.

Included in this chapter is a short introduction to the controls supplied with Visual Basic 5, how to use the menu designer, as well as an introduction to the event-driven model of programming that is so important for using VB.

Note

Anyone familiar with early versions of Visual Basic will recognize most of this material. However, VB5 has some neat improvements for laying out controls. There are a few subtleties in how layout and event handling work because of the differences between a user control and a traditional VB project. Therefore, you may want to skim this chapter.

Properties

Properties affect the appearance of an object, and can be changed at design time or at run time. When they are changed at run time, the syntax takes the form:

```
object.property = new value
```

(For more on coding techniques, see Chapter 4.)

For now, we want to concentrate on the properties you can set at design time using the Properties window. First, press F4 (or View|Properties Window) to bring the Properties window to the top if it is obscured or hidden. Figure 3-1 is a picture of the Properties window.

(If you prefer to see the properties characterized by function, click on the Categorized tab.)

Notice the bottom of the Properties window gives you a short description of the property. The drop-down list box on top shows the object you are working with. When you click on the arrow for the drop-down dialog at the top of the Properties window, VB5 shows all the controls that are currently on the form. If the control (or the form itself) that you want to work with is not shown here, simply drop the list down and choose it.

Naming Your Objects

The first property listed in the Properties window is the all-important Name property. The Name property lets you give meaningful names to your VB5 objects. Visual Basic 5 sets up a default name like Form1 for the first form, Form2 for the second, UserControl1 for the first user control, TextBox1 for the first text box, and so on.

Note

Naming conventions for objects have inspired quite a lot of flaming. Many people add a lowercase prefix that indicates the object, followed by the meaningful name. Examples of this might be frmAbout or frmInitial. Most people set the name for their user controls using mixed case, for example, StretchLabel. Since these are the conventions Microsoft suggests, we use them in this book.

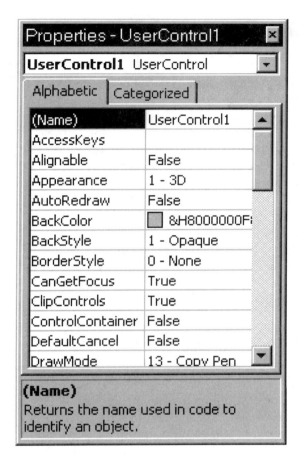

Figure 3-1   The Properties window

The rules for naming an object are:

- Names can be up to 128 characters.
- The first character must be a letter.
- The rest of the name can include any combination of letters, numbers, and underscores, but no spaces, punctuation marks or non-alphanumeric characters.

The case of the letters in the object name is irrelevant.

Working with the Properties Window

There are various ways of setting properties using the Properties window. For instance, the Caption property is an example of the simplest kind of property to set. Just click in the right, or *value*, column and enter the text or the value there. You can use standard Windows editing techniques for cutting and pasting in the value column. Visual Basic 5 actually checks to make sure that what you entered makes sense. If you enter something that isn't valid, VB5 will pop up an "Invalid property value" message box and reset to its original value. For example, VB5 won't let you enter a string if a number is called for.

For properties like BorderStyle, where you have a finite number of choices, VB5 uses a drop-down list box. You have to click in the row for that item in order to see the drop-down arrow. Figure 3-2 shows what you see for the BorderStyle property of a form.

To choose from the drop-down list of properties:

1. Open the list by clicking the down arrow (or with focus on the value box, press ALT+DOWN ARROW). Then select the item you want.

   or

2. If there is a fixed and known set of possible values, repeatedly double-clicking in the value column will cycle through the set. If you know the value you want, you can simply enter it.

When you need to work with a color property like ForeColor, clicking on the arrow brings up a tabbed dialog box. The first tab lists system-supplied colors; the second, a palette. Click on the appropriate-colored box to set the color.

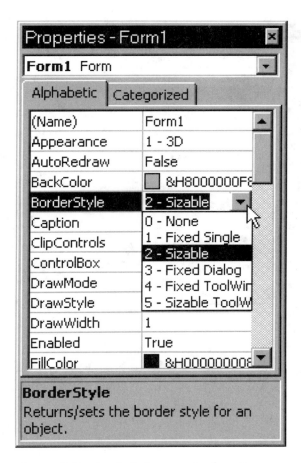

Figure 3-2   BorderStyle properties for a Form

Next, VB5 follows the standard Windows convention where an ellipsis means a dialog box is available. The ellipsis shows up when you click in the value column. Click on the ellipsis to reveal the dialog box, or double-click in the value column. This is usually necessary when the property value type is an object, such as a bitmap, icon or font. The typical example is the Font property dialog box, shown in Figure 3-3.

When you are finished adjusting the settings in the dialog box, click OK and they will go into effect.

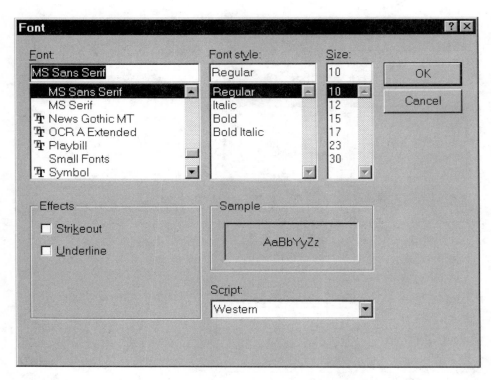

Figure 3-3   The Font dialog box

Forms

The forms for ordinary VB projects and the form used for building a control are similar but there are a few properties that they do not share. In a handful of cases, similarly named properties work differently. For example, the BorderStyle property for a form used for an ActiveX control has only two possible values instead of the six for an ordinary form. Forms for user controls have 42 properties you can set at design time; forms used as test beds for your controls in VB5 or in ordinary VB applications have 49 properties. Both ordinary forms and user control forms can respond to 31 events, although the sets of events are not precisely the same. The next few sections will introduce you to some of the most important properties and events for both kinds of forms. (The forms that are specialized for use in creating controls are covered in depth in Chapter 13.)

Form Properties

What follows is a short discussion of the most important basic properties of a form that you can set at design time. We will not bother describing properties that are completely explained by their names or for which the brief description given in the Properties window is enough. (For example, Caption for an ordinary form is explained here as "resets/sets the text displayed in the object's title bar," which seems sufficient.) More advanced properties, such as OLE Drop Mode, will be covered later.

Appearance

Leave this set at the default value of 1–3D to tell VB5 to display controls on the form with a three-dimensional look.

AutoRedraw

This is an extremely important True/False (Boolean) property. It determines whether information displayed on your form persists when the form is repainted. For example, if AutoRedraw is False (the default), then anything on the form will vanish when the form is covered by another form and then uncovered. Of course, setting AutoRedraw to True means more memory is used to save the bitmap. (See Chapter 6 for more on this property.)

BorderStyle

This property determines how the boundary of the form appears. For ordinary forms there are five possible values, as shown in the following table.

Table 3-1: Border Style Values

Value	Description
0	No border, no system menu, and no min/max or close buttons.
1	*Fixed Single.* The user cannot resize the form with a mouse, but it can still have a control menu box, a title bar, and min/max buttons to minimize or maximize the form.
2	*(Default) Sizable.* The user can resize the form with a mouse.

Table 3-1: Border Style Values (continued)	
Value	*Description*
3	*Fixed Dialog*. Generally used for custom dialog boxes and is not resizable by the user. May have a control box but can't include min/max buttons.
4	*Fixed ToolWindow*. This displays the Close button as well as the title bar text in a smaller font. The form also will not appear in the Windows task bar and will not display an icon.
5	*Sizable ToolWindow*. Does not display min/max buttons but is resizable by the mouse. Gives you a Close button. Displays the title bar text in a smaller font. The form also does not appear in the Windows task bar and will not display an icon.

When you change the setting of the BorderStyle property, you may affect the properties that control the buttons in the title bar. For example, when the BorderStyle property is set to 0 (None), 3 (Fixed Dialog), 4 (Fixed ToolWindow), or 5 (Sizable ToolWindow), the MinButton, MaxButton, and ShowInTaskbar properties are automatically changed to False. The changes you make will not become apparent until the form goes into run mode.

Note

As mentioned earlier, forms for building user controls have only 0 (None) and 1 (Fixed Single) as possible settings for their BorderStyle.

ClipControls

This True/False property determines whether VB5 repaints the whole form or just the newly exposed areas. Obviously, it is faster to paint only the newly exposed areas.

ControlBox

The ControlBox property determines whether VB5 puts a control box in the left-hand corner of an ordinary form. It is obviously not an available property for a user control. If this property is set to False, then the form will no longer respond to the ALT+F4 shortcut combination for closing it, nor will an exit button appear on the title bar. (You would have to provide some other method for closing the form or bring up the Close program dialog box via the CTRL+ALT+DEL combination in order to end the task.)

Enabled, Visible

If the Enabled property is changed from the default value of True, the form will no longer respond to any events. Usually this property is manipulated at run time. The Visible property, on the other hand, controls whether the user can even see the form—it is available for user controls in certain hosts, such as VB itself.

FontTransparent

This True/False property is used with graphics to determine whether graphics show through text. It is quite useful for special effects.

Height, Width

These properties measure (or set) the height and width of the whole form—including the borders and title bar for a non-user control form. Both are measured in *twips*. Theoretically, a twip is $\frac{1}{20}$ of a printer point or $\frac{1}{1440}$ inch ($\frac{1}{567}$ of a cm), but how twips translate on a screen depends on the size of the screen. On one 17-inch monitor that we looked at, 4320 twips actually take up five inches and not three. (On the other hand, Windows printer drivers are set up so that when you design an object using twips, you can be sure it will print out at the correct measurement. For example, if you want a form to be three inches high when printed, you should make its height 3*1440 twips (= 4320) and not worry about how it looks on the screen, then let the Windows printer drivers take over.

HelpContextId

This property is only available for ordinary forms, although the components that make up your user control can have individual HelpContextId's. This should come as no surprise. After all, it is the components in your user control that the user needs help on, not the container. For a form, this property is used when writing a Windows-compatible help system for your application.

Icon

This property determines the icon used for the control on the toolbox or the form when the form is minimized.

KeyPreview

The default for this property is False. If you change it to True, then most key-strokes are processed by the form's Key events first, rather than the control that has the focus. (See Chapter 5 for more on the Key events.) This property is extremely useful for a user control with constituent controls that can accept keystrokes, but you want to determine which control gets what keystroke. It is less often used for standard EXEs.

Left, Top

These properties determine where an ordinary form is, relative to the left top edge of the screen. It is measured in twips. (Determining where a control is relative to the form is, of course, a design-time task, or can be done using code at run time. See Chapter 13 for how to do this for user controls.)

MousePointer, MouseIcon

This property lets you determine the look of the cursor when the mouse is on the form. There are 15 standard shapes, ranging from the usual arrow or hourglass to more exotic shapes. If you set this value to 99 ("Custom"), then you can use the MouseIcon property to assign a custom mouse pointer to your form or control. Regardless of the setting, you can use code to change the mouse pointer.

Picture

This brings up a dialog box that lets you place a picture (bitmap, icon, or Windows metafile) on the form or user control. This is useful for giving your form or user control a nice window to the world.

ScaleHeight, ScaleWidth

The ScaleHeight and ScaleWidth properties let you set up your own scale for the height and width of the form. For example, if you set the value of each of these properties to 100, the form uses a scale that has point 50, 50 as its center. (Resetting these properties has the side effect of setting the value of the ScaleMode property back to 0.)

Note

These properties also represent the height and width of the usable part of the form—the part excluding the borders. For user control forms they are interchangeable with height and width. They are commonly used in code to make sure that the components of your control are correctly sized. (See the discussion of the Resize event in Chapter 6.)

ScaleLeft, ScaleTop

The ScaleLeft and ScaleTop properties describe what value VB5 uses for the left and top corner of the form or control. The original (default) value for each of these properties is 0, 0.

ScaleMode

The ScaleMode property allows you to change the units used in the form's internal coordinate system. Tired of twips? There are seven other possibilities. You can create your own units by setting it to 0, keeping the default twips (this value is 1), or using one of the six remaining choices. A useful setting, especially for graphics, is 3 *pixels* (a picture element—the smallest unit of resolution on your monitor, as determined by Windows) as the scale.

StartUp Position

This new property was added to VB5 to give you a quick way to position your form when it starts up. The choices are explained in the following table.

Table 3-2: StartUp Position Settings	
Setting	*Purpose*
0 Manual	You have to position the form where you want.
1 CenterOwner	Used when your form is embedded in another window (uncommon in VB).
2 StartUpScreen	Center on the whole screen.
3 StartUp Windows Default	Top-left corner.

Tag

This property isn't used by VB5. It exists solely to provide programmers a way to attach information to a control that would otherwise not be available at run time.

WindowState

This property is only available for ordinary forms not user control forms. There are three values for this property. The default, Normal (0), leaves the form neither maximized nor minimized. You normally use code to change this property to one of the other two values: Minimized (1) or Maximized (2).

Form Events

The ability to recognize events is the key to VB5's power, but if you do not write the code in the appropriate event handler, nothing will happen. For EXEs, the event is key to making your programs do what the user wants. The idea for your user controls, of course, is to take the events recognized by the user control-building components and do more with them. For example, in Chapter 1 we modified the ordinary KeyPress event for a TextBox in order to add new functionality by rejecting non-numeric characters.

The first thing you need to do when writing an event handler is to generate the event procedure template. The general method of generating an event procedure template is to:

1. Bring up the code window by pressing F7 or choosing View|Code.

2. The code window has two drop-down list boxes. The right-most
   one, usually called the Procedure box, gives all the events the
   control or form (selected in the leftmost drop-down list) can
   recognize. Click on the name of the event procedure with
   which you want to work.

Figure 3-4 is an example of the Code window with the event procedure list
box dropped down.

Note

*If you double-click on a form, a user control, or an ordinary control, VB5
pops up the default event procedure template for that object. (For forms, it
is the Load event; for user controls, it is the Initialize event.)*

Figure 3-4   The Procedure list box

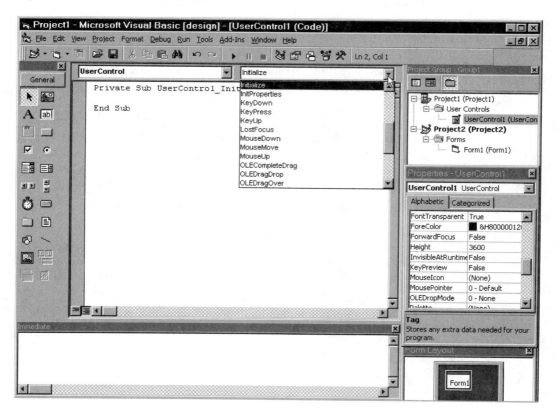

Ordinary Form Life Cycle Events

There are four events that happen when VB5 starts running an ordinary form or a form that you are using for testing: Initialize, Load, Activate, and GotFocus. These events can be confused because they are triggered under similar circumstances. It is important to keep in mind the order in which they are triggered by VB5.

First is the Initialize event. It is triggered first, and only once, when the form is first created. The Initialize event occurs before the Load event. As its name suggests, the Initialize event is where you place code used for setting initial properties of the form.

The Load event is triggered when a form is loaded into memory; it occurs after the Initialize event. Usually this code is triggered only once. (However, using code, it is possible to unload and then reload a form, so you can have this event triggered more than once.) When you start a program with a single form, it will generally be loaded automatically, thus triggering this event.

The Activate event occurs whenever a form becomes the active window. As such, it can be triggered repeatedly, for example, whenever the user clicks in a previously inactive window.

Finally, after the Activate event is triggered, VB5 will trigger the GotFocus event for the form only if all visible controls on it are disabled. (For this reason, programmers rarely use the GotFocus event for a form and it would certainly be strange in a form used as test bed for a user control.)

Three events occur at the death of a form. The QueryUnload event is triggered when the user tries to close the form, for example, by double-clicking on the control box. You can use this event for clean-up code, or even to prevent the form from closing. The Unload event, on the other hand, is triggered after the form closes. The Terminate event is the last event triggered. It occurs when all references to the form are removed from memory.

User Control Life Cycle Events

There are five events that define the life cycle of a user control. In this section, we give a brief overview of them; you'll see a more detailed discussion in Chapter 13. Before we begin, it is important to realize that a user control can come into existence in two ways:

- When you close down the designer of a user control in order to put an instance of the control on a test form ("design time").

- When you run the test bed form or run any code that uses the OCX control you were building ("run time").

The first event for a user control is the Initialize event. This occurs at both run and design time. It is triggered when a control is created. In particular, this event occurs when you switch to your test project and place your user control on the test form, and also when you run the test bed form. Next comes the InitProperties event—you can use this event to give intitial values to your controls. The ReadProperties event occurs next. This lets you read back any properties that were saved about that control, for example, its default property values. This is a design-time event only. Then the Resize event procedure is called, which is both a design-time and run-time event. These four events define the birth of the control.

The death of the control triggers two events. The first is the WriteProperties event. This occurs only when a control is used at design time. It never occurs at run time. This event is triggered when you close the form on which you are testing the control. As you will see in Chapter 13, this gives you a chance to save any properties of the control that were set at design time. The Terminate event, on the other hand, occurs at both design and run time and is the last event triggered by the control's death.

Common Form Events

Now we want to discuss some of the most common events that both user controls and ordinary forms can respond to.

Click, DblClick

This event is triggered when the user clicks (double-clicks) in a blank area of the form. (The Click event will always be triggered first, even when the user double-clicks.)

DragDrop, DragOver, MouseDown, MouseMove, MouseUp

These events are used with code to detect mouse movements (see Chapter 6).

KeyDown, KeyPress, KeyUp

You saw one of these events at work in Chapter 1. These events let you determine what the user is doing with the keyboard. (See Chapter 4 for more on this.)

Resize, Paint

The Resize event is triggered whenever the user resizes a form. You usually place code in the Resize event procedure to reposition controls as needed. The Paint event is triggered whenever part of the form is re-exposed or after the form has been enlarged (after the Resize event).

Note

Both events are triggered when a user control first loads, and the Paint event is fired when a form loads.

Controls

Ironically, existing controls are the nuts and bolts of your user controls. You will rarely build a control totally from scratch using only VB5's graphic capabilities. Just as with a form, controls have properties that you can set at design time via the Properties window, or at run time via code. Many properties, such as Height and Width or Name, work essentially the same way for both forms and controls.

Note

*Visual Basic 5 allows you to add specialized **custom controls** to your project, which you can then (licensing agreements permitting) use as a basis for your projects or user controls. There are custom controls for everything from multimedia to spell-checking to running laboratory equipment. You can use any OCX controls, as they are usually called (named after the extension used for their filenames). If your goal is to use the control in a browser, it is best to get controls that follow the more lightweight ActiveX standard rather than the older OCX standard. (They have the same extension, though, and you will need to check with the vendor to see what standard they follow.)*

To add a custom control, choose Project|Components (CTRL+T). This opens a dialog box like Figure 3-5:

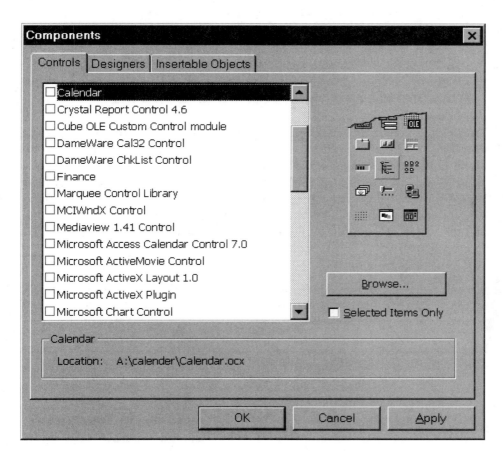

Figure 3-5   The Components dialog box

Now check the control you want to add. (The Windows 95 common controls are quite useful to add.) You can click on the Browse button to search for controls that may exist on your system but aren't registered. Once you add a custom control, Visual Basic 5 places it on the toolbox along with the standard controls. To remove a custom control, bring up the dialog box and remove the checkmark.

Tip

There are many custom controls available on the Net. We give a few samples on the CD. Another good starting point is Microsoft's ActiveX gallery at its Web site.

An Overview of the Standard Controls

There are 20 controls that are always standard in the VB5 Toolbox except in the Control Creation Edition, which lacks the last two in Table 3-3. The Toolbox itself is usually located to the left of the form but you can drag it around to a new location. (To make the Toolbox visible if it is hidden, choose View|Toolbox.) This section gives you an overview of these standard controls. The following table supplies Microsoft's suggested prefix when writing code for the controls' name, for example, cmdButton would be a use suggested by Microsoft.

Note

As always, whether you choose to use Microsoft conventions is up to you.

Table 3-3:   Standard Controls

	Name (and prefix)	Purpose
![pointer]	Pointer	Strictly speaking, this isn't a control. It is used to resize or move a control after you have placed it on the form.
![picturebox]	PictureBox (pic)	Used to display graphics. You can both display existing images and draw on picture boxes. Also used as a container for other controls.
A	Label (lbl)	Used for text that you don't want the user to change.
ab|	TextBox (txt)	Used for user input.

Name (and prefix)	Purpose
Frame (fra)	Used to group controls (both visually and functionally).
CommandButton (cmd)	Used for buttons that the user can click on.
CheckBox (chk)	Used for yes/no choices.
OptionButton (opt)	Used in groups when there is only one possibility from the group.
ComboBox (cbo)	Used when you need a combination of a list box and a place to enter a choice. The idea is that you can either choose from the list or enter your own choice directly.
ListBox (lst)	Used when you want to give the user a fixed list of items from which to choose.
HScrollBar (hsb)	This is a horizontal scroll bar. You can use this to give users an analog tool for moving through a list.
VScrollBar (vsb)	This is a vertical scroll bar.
Timer (tmr)	Used to trigger events periodically.
DriveListBox (drv)	Used to display the disk drives available.
DirListBox (dir)	This is a directory list box.
FileListBox (fil)	Used to display a list of files.
Shape (shp)	Used for rectangles, circles, and other shapes. Quite sparing of Windows resources.
Line (lin)	Used to draw lines on a form—also quite sparing of Windows resources.

Table 3-3:	Standard Controls (continued)	
	Name (and prefix)	*Purpose*
	Image (img)	Like a picture box, can be used to display a graphical image from a bitmap, icon, or metafile on your form. You cannot draw on an Image control, however, and Image controls use fewer Windows resources than picture boxes.
	Data (dta)	This is used with databases. (This control is not covered in this book except for occasional use as an example.)
	OLE (ole)	Used in OLE.

Adding Controls to a Form

Once you decide which control you want to add to a form or a user control, there are a couple of ways to place it there. If you double-click on the control, VB5 adds the control in the default size and shape to the middle of the form. (If there are controls already in the center of the form, the new one is placed on top of the previous one.)

If you want to add a control at a specific location:

1.   Click on the control.

2.   Click and hold down the button at the spot on the form where you want the upper-left corner of the control to appear.

3.   Drag the mouse pointer. As you drag, VB5 gives you an outline that shows the size and position of the control. Release the mouse button when you are happy with the control's size and position.

Adding Multiple Controls to a Form

You may want to add multiple controls of the same type to a form, for example, multiple command buttons or edit boxes.

To add multiple controls of the same type:

1. Hold down the CTRL key.
2. Click on the control in the palette. (Release the CTRL key after you select the control.)
3. Click at the place on the form where you want the upper-left corner of each copy of the control to appear, and drag to make it the correct size and shape.

Note

If you use this method, be sure to click on the pointer icon in order to go back to the usual method of working with controls.

Container Controls

When you use controls like option buttons, keep them in groups. That way, VB5 knows which ones to turn off when one is turned on. Among the standard VB5 controls (besides the form itself), both Frames and PictureBoxes can serve as *container* controls. The idea of a container is that all the controls will behave as one—this is sometimes called a *parent-child relationship*. For example, when you move a container control, the child controls move with it, or when you set the Enabled property of the container to false, all of the child controls are disabled as well.

Note

Properties that measure where a control is, such as Left and Top, are always calculated relative to the boundaries of the container control. See Chapter 13 for how to access these properties for the user controls that you write.

The easiest way to create a container is to add it to the form before you add the child controls. Once you have placed the container on the form, make sure that the container control is selected. Then add controls as you normally would by, for example, clicking inside the container and dragging. (Note that even if the container is in the center of the form, double-clicking on a control will not make it a child of the container control.) You can also set the container property at run time.

Note

You can also add multiple copies of the same control to a container control that is currently active by using the CTRL+CLICK method.

Working with Existing Controls

Before you can work with a control that is already on a form, you need to select it by simply clicking inside the control. If you are working inside the form's designer window, you can also use the TAB key to move the focus among the controls on the form. When a control is selected on a form, small black squares called *sizing handles* appear on the perimeter. Dragging on them lets you resize the control. (See "Resizing and Reshaping Controls" later in the chapter.)

Selecting Multiple Controls

You will often need to work with many controls at once, for example, when you have to align them. The easiest way to select multiple controls is:

1.   Hold down the SHIFT key.
2.   Click on each of the controls.

There is one other method for selecting multiple controls that is occasionally useful.

1.   Imagine a rectangle that includes only those controls you want to select. Move to one corner of this imagined rectangle and click the left mouse button.
2.   Hold the left mouse button down and drag the dotted rectan-

gle until it includes all (and only) the controls you want to select. Then release the mouse button.

Regardless of which way you select a group of controls, when you finish selecting you know you were successful when they all show gray sizing handles. Only controls at the same level will be selected. In the case of a container control, the child controls will not be selected.

Tip

When you have selected multiple controls, the Properties window shows only their common properties. When you change one of the properties listed, all the selected controls are changed accordingly.

For example, one way to align the edges of a group of controls is to select the controls and set the Left property to the same value; to align the tops, use the Top property.

Tip

It is often easier to select the controls and then choose Format|Align or use the equivalent tool on the Form Editor toolbar. You can also use the Format menu to center selected controls on the form, and so on. You can even change the spacing of the controls relative to each other using this menu.

Moving Controls

To move a control to a different location:

1. Select the control.
2. Place the mouse inside the control, and drag the control to its new location. Be careful not to drag the sizing handles or you will resize it instead of moving it.

Notice that, as you manipulate the control, it seems to move in fits and starts, not smoothly. As the old computer joke goes, this is not a bug, it's a feature. The position of controls on a form defaults so that they are located only at grid points. The General page available on the Tools|Options dialog box lets you control this feature, which is called Align Controls to Grid. You can also make the grid more or less fine by changing options in this dialog box.

Note

When you have selected a group of controls, they all move in unison.

Finally, if you want to move a control by only one grid line at a time, select the control and then use CTRL and the appropriate arrow key.

Tip

Choosing the Lock Controls item on the Format menu prevents you from inadvertently moving any control on the form.

Resizing and Reshaping Controls

The sizing handles are the easiest way to change the shape and size of a control. To resize a single control, first select it. You should be able to see the black sizing handles. Now drag the appropriate sizing handle. If you need to resize multiple controls, first select them. Then you can use the Properties window to change the height and width properties or use other nifty features available either on the Format menu or the Form Editor toolbar. In particular, once you have selected multiple controls, the Format menu makes it easy to make them all the same size and shape. And, if you want to increase or decrease the size by only one grid unit at a time, select the control(s) and then use SHIFT and the appropriate arrow key.

Deleting Controls

If you need to delete controls on the form, first select them. Then press the DELETE key, or choose Edit|Delete. If you delete a container component, all its child components are cut as well.

Cutting, Copying, and Pasting Controls

Visual Basic 5 lets you cut, copy, and paste controls between forms, or between a form and a user control form or any form and a container control on it, using standard Windows conventions (CTRL+X for cut, CTRL+C for copy, and so on). You can also use the appropriate options on the Edit menu. (Copying a control leads VB5 to think you want to create a control array. Please see Chapter 7 for more on this feature.)

Common Control Properties and Events

This section discusses some common control properties and events that are important when manipulating the focus for controls. We follow this with a discussion of the standard controls.

While we discuss some of the most important properties and events that occur for controls, we will not repeat discussions of the many properties and events (such as Color, Cursor, Enabled, Left, Name, Top, Visible, Width, Click, DblClick, and so on) that work essentially the same for forms and controls.

Note

Properties like Left and Top are always calculated relative to the container component.

Focus Properties and Events

Only a single control can be active—that is, have the *focus*—at any given time. (The form has the focus only when no control on it can have the focus.) Visual Basic 5 determines which control to give the initial focus to by first looking at the controls whose TabStop property is set to True, then to the one with the lowest TabIndex value. (If the TabStop property is set to False, the user won't be able to tab to that component, however, this does not prohibit the control from getting focus with the mouse.)

When a project loads, VB5 (and Windows, for that matter) moves the focus to the visible and enabled control with the lowest value for the TabIndex. property. Visual Basic 5 sets the TabIndex property numerically according to the order in which you create the controls. You can change the TabIndex property and the order by using the Properties window.

The two focus events are GotFocus and LostFocus, which are triggered when the control gets or loses the focus, respectively.

Note

Only visible and enabled controls can receive the focus. Frames, labels, menus, lines, shapes, images, and timers can never receive the focus.

Caption Properties and Accelerator Keys

Many Windows applications use accelerator keys to quickly move the focus or to click a button. These keys are indicated by an underline in the caption. Users can then press ALT and the underlined letter to click the button or move the focus.

To set up an accelerator key for the VB5 control, add an ampersand (&) right before the accelerator (underlined letter). For example, if you set the Caption property of a command button to &Quit, the user can then use ALT+Q instead of clicking on the button to activate its Click event procedure.

Command Buttons

Placing buttons on a form so that the user can click on them to do something is very common in Windows applications (although many controls can detect the Click event and, therefore, have a Click event procedure associated with them). Most of the properties of command buttons are already familiar to you. However, even experienced VB users need to be aware of the neat new functionality that has been added to ordinary command buttons.

Cancel

Sometimes you want to press the Esc key to trigger an event. For this to happen, set the Cancel property of the command button to be True. Once you have done this, VB5 triggers the Click event handler for this button whenever the user presses the Esc key. Only one command button can have this property set to True on a form, so setting it True will reset previously set controls to False.

Default

The Click event for a default button (one whose Default property is True) is triggered whenever the user presses the ENTER key. To make a button the default button, set the button's Default property to be True.

Note

If the user presses ENTER when a button has the focus, then VB5 triggers the Click event for that button. This happens whether or not you have set up a default command button.

DisabledPicture, DownPicture, Picture, Style

These are new properties for command buttons. As the names suggest, icons can be added to ordinary command buttons. You can have different pictures for when the control is disabled, clicked and not clicked. To place a picture on a command button, set the Style to 1–Graphical.

Text Boxes

Text boxes are the primary method for accepting input and displaying output in the controls you build with VB5. Extending them is, therefore, among the most common ways to build a useful custom control. (Of course, there are already many custom controls available with fancier forms of text input, such as the Microsoft RichTextBox, which allows multiple fonts.)

Text boxes never treat what a user types in as a number; this means that getting numeric information to the VB5 program requires transforming a string of digits into a number by using a built-in function or VB5's built-in automatic conversions (see Chapter 4).

There are more than 40 properties for text boxes, many of which should be familiar to you. As before, the Name property is used only for the code you write; the user never sees it. The Font property gives you a dialog box for setting font properties, and, in this case, they will affect what the user enters or sees. (Unlike RichTextBoxes, which support multiple fonts in the same box, ordinary text boxes allow you only one font for all the text in the box.)

There are three properties you have not seen before and one property that works differently for text boxes than for forms. The three new properties are Text, MultiLine, and ScrollBars. The BorderStyle property works differently for text boxes than for forms.

Text

The Text property is the analog of the Caption property for a command button or a form. The Text property controls the text the user sees. When you create a text box, the default value for this property is set to the default value for the Name property for that control—Text1, Text2, and so on. If you want a text box to be empty when the application starts up, select the Text property and blank out the original setting.

ScrollBars

The ScrollBars property determines if a text box has horizontal or vertical scroll bars. This is useful because VB5 allows you to accept long or multiple lines of data from a single text box; roughly 32,000 characters is the usual limit. There are four possible settings for the ScrollBars property:

Table 3-4:	ScrollBars
Value	*Meaning*
0	This is the default value. The text box lacks both vertical and horizontal scroll bars.
1	The text box has horizontal scroll bars only (limits text to 255 characters).
2	The text box has vertical bars only.
3	The text box has both horizontal and vertical bars.

MultiLine

The MultiLine property determines if a text box can accept more than one line of text. (It is usually combined with resetting the value of the ScrollBars property.) When this property is True, the user can always use the standard methods in Microsoft Windows to move through the text box: the arrow keys, HOME, CTRL+HOME, END, and CTRL+END. Visual Basic 5 automatically word-wraps when a user types more than one line of information into a text box with MultiLine set to be True, unless you've added horizontal scroll bars to the text box.

Note

You can use the ENTER key to separate lines unless you've added a default command button to the form. If you have a default command button, press CTRL+ENTER to break lines.

Finally, we should point out that allowing users to switch between single line and multiline for a custom control is a bit tricky. We provide you with a template to simplify the task (see Chapter 11).

BorderStyle

There are only two possible settings for the BorderStyle property for a text box. The default value is 1, which gives you a fixed single border. If you change the value of this property to 0, the border disappears.

MaxLength

This property determines the maximum number of characters the text box will accept. The default value is 0, which (somewhat counter-intuitively) means there is no maximum other than the roughly 32,000-character limit for multiline text boxes. Any setting other than 0 will limit the data to that number of characters entered into that text box.

PasswordChar

As you might expect from the name, this lets you limit what the text box displays (although all characters are accepted and stored). The convention is to use an asterisk (*) for the password character. Once you set this property, all the user sees is a row of asterisks. This property is often combined with the MaxLength property to add a password feature to your programs.

Locked

If this is set to False, the user cannot edit what is displayed in the text box.

Event Procedures for Text Boxes

Text boxes can recognize 17 events. Events like GotFocus and LostFocus work exactly as before. Three others—KeyDown, KeyUp, and KeyPress—are for monitoring exactly what the user types. You saw the KeyPress event in Chapter 1; the rest are covered in Chapter 5. The Change event lacks the flexibility of the key events you'll see in Chapter 4, but it is occasionally useful. Visual Basic 5 monitors the text box and triggers this event procedure whenever a user makes any changes in the text box. For example, you can warn users that they should not be entering data in a specific text box, since they are blanking out what they typed.

Caution

Be very careful not to put any code in the Change event procedure that changes the contents of the text box. This will cause the system to continually trigger the event until the program crashes. (This is usually called an **event cascade.***)*

Labels

Labels are used for text that identifies the controls they are next to, for example, you will want to label text boxes. They can also be used to display text that users can't edit.

Tip

You can use a label to give an accelerator key for controls that do not have a caption property (like edit boxes). The idea is that when the user uses the accelerator key, the control that follows it in tab order receives the focus.

Alignment

There are three possible ways to align text. For example, if you set the value of this property to 0 (the default), VB5 will left-justify the text. The other possible values are 1 for right-justified and 2 for centered.

AutoSize, WordWrap

If the AutoSize property is set to True, the label automatically resizes horizontally to fit the text. If WordWrap is True, the label will grow vertically to fit the caption.

BorderStyle, BackStyle

The BorderStyle property has two possible values. The default is 0 (no border). Set the value to 1, and the label resembles a text box. This is occasionally useful when your program displays results. The BackStyle property determines whether the label is transparent or opaque.

ListBox and ComboBox Controls

Both the ListBox and ComboBox controls let you display a scrollable list of items from which users can select. The difference is that the user cannot change the entries in a list box. (Combo boxes provide an edit area in which the user can enter information.) You usually use code to enter the items in these controls, but VB5 allows you to enter them directly via the List property in the Properties window at design time. To do this:

1. Choose the List property.
2. Enter the items, pressing CTRL+ENTER after each one. (Not ENTER, which closes the box.)

The most important properties of these controls that you may want to set at design time are discussed next.

Columns and MultiSelect

The Columns property controls the number of columns in a list box. If the value is 0 (the default), you get a normal single-column list box with vertical scrolling. If the value is 1, you get a single-column list box with horizontal scrolling. If the value is greater than 1, you allow (but do not require) multiple columns, which show up only when the items don't fit into the list box. (To force multiple columns, reduce the height of the list box accordingly.) The MultiSelect property controls whether the user can select more than one item from the list. There are three possible values for this property:

Table 3-5:   Multiselect

Type of Selection	Value	How It Works
No multiselection allowed	0	Click the mouse or press the spacebar..
Simple multiselection	1	SHIFT+CLICK extends the selection to include all list items between the current selection.
Extended multiselection	2	CTRL+CLICK selects or deselects a single item.

Sorted

This property applies to both controls. It determines if VB5 keeps the items sorted as you add more items to the list or combo box.

Tip

An invisible list box with the sorted property set to True is a convenient way to sort small lists.

Style

This property lets you determine the style of the combo box. There are three possibilities. The default value, 0 (Dropdown Combo), gives you the usual drop-down list with an edit area. If the value of the Style property of a combo box is 1 (Simple Combo), the user sees the combo box with the list already dropped down.

Notice that in both these cases the user still has a text area to enter information. On the other hand, the final possible choice for the Style property for combo boxes, a value of 2 (Dropdown List), gives you a drop-down list box with no edit area.

CheckBox and Option Button Controls

Use check boxes when you want to provide nonexclusive options to the user. You then use code to determine if the user checks or unchecks a specific check box (using the value of the Value property). On the other hand, use a group of option buttons when you need to present mutually exclusive choices to the user. Whenever a user clicks on one radio button in a group, the other buttons are switched off. In any case, as one would expect, when the user clicks on a box or button, VB5 also triggers the Click event for that control.

Note

Since option buttons work as a group, the only way two option buttons on a form can be checked at the same time is if they are in separate container controls.

Timers

Use a Timer control whenever you want something—or "nothing," such as a pause—to occur periodically. For example, you might want to have a control that "wakes up" at intervals. Timers are not visible to the user; the icon appears only at design time. For this reason, where you place or how you size the timer control at design time is not important.

Enabled

Enabled is a Boolean (True/False) property that determines whether or not the timer should start ticking. If you set this to True at design time, the clock starts ticking when the form loads. (Ticking is meant metaphorically; there's no noise unless you program one.) Also, because timer controls are invisible to the user, he or she may be unaware that a timer has been enabled. For this reason, you may want to notify the user that a timer is working by means of a message box, an image control, or a picture box with a clock icon inside of it.

If you set the Enabled property to False at design time, the timer control starts working only when you switch this property to True in code. Similarly, you can disable a timer inside code by setting its Enabled property to False.

Interval

The Interval property determines how much time VB5 waits before calling the Timer event procedure (see the next section). The interval is measured in milliseconds, and the theoretical limits are between 1 millisecond and 65,535 milliseconds (a little more than one minute and five seconds). The reason these are only theoretical limits is that the underlying hardware reports the passage of only 18 clock ticks per second. Since this is a little less than 56 milliseconds per clock tick, you can't really use an Interval property less than 56, and intervals that don't differ by at least this amount may give the same results. (You can, however, use API functions, described in Chapter 12, for smaller time intervals.)

The smaller you set the Interval property, the more CPU time is spent waking up the Timer event procedure. If you set the Interval property too small, your system performance may slow to a crawl.

Note

An Interval property of 0 disables the timer.

The Timer Event

Visual Basic 5 tries to trigger the Timer event procedure as often as you have set the Interval property. But since the CPU may be doing something else when the time determined by the interval elapses, you cannot be guaranteed that Windows will call the Timer event procedure exactly when you want it. (Windows will know when the interval has elapsed, but it may need to finish what it is doing before activating the Timer event.) If the time has elapsed, Windows will call the Timer event procedure as soon as it is free to do so. You can use code to determine if more time has elapsed than you planned.

For example, suppose you want to develop a "clock control" with a clock that will update itself every second. It takes about two seconds and one line of code.

1. Add a label and a timer to a blank user control form.
2. Set the BorderStyle property of the label to 1. Set the AutoSize property of the label to be True and the font size to be 18. Set the Interval property of the timer control to be 1,000 (1,000 milliseconds = 1 second).

Now write the following code in the Timer event procedure for the Timer1 control:

```
Private Sub Timer1_Timer()
    Label1.Caption = Time
End Sub
```

Visual Basic 5 will call this event procedure and update the clock's time roughly every second because the Interval property was set to 1,000. (See Chapter 4 for more on the date/time functions used in this example.) That's it, you now have a "clock control."

Tip

If you want to have a Timer event procedure do something less frequently than about once a minute (the maximum setting for the Interval property), you need to add a static variable to the Timer event procedure. This variable will let you keep track of the number of intervals that have elapsed. (See Chapter 4 for more on these kinds of variables.)

Designing Menus

Ordinary forms will use menus frequently. Although one rarely thinks of a user control as having menus, add them as pop-ups if the control functionality calls for it.

Think of menu items as specialized controls that you add to your forms. Menu items respond only to a Click event. Designing the right kind of menus will make your applications much more user-friendly. Visual Basic 5 lets you build multilevel menus and add pop-up menus as well.

Menus that contain submenus are usually called *hierarchical* (or *cascading*) menus. Of course, using too many levels of menus can make the application confusing to the user. Four is certainly too many; two or three levels are what you usually see. The user knows that a submenu lurks below a given menu item when he or she sees an arrow following the menu item.

Tip

Instead of using lots of submenus, consider designing a custom dialog box for the options.

To add a menu to your form, use the Menu Design window available from the Tools menu on the VB5 main menu bar. The menu design window looks like the one in Figure 3-6 on the next page. A short description of each of the components of this dialog box follows.

Caption

What you type in the Caption text box is what the user sees. The caption also shows up in the text area inside the dialog box. Unlike other VB5 controls, menu items do not have default captions. As with other controls, use an ampersand (&) in the caption to give the item an access key.

Tip

If you set the Caption property for a non-main menu to a hyphen (-), a separator bar shows up.

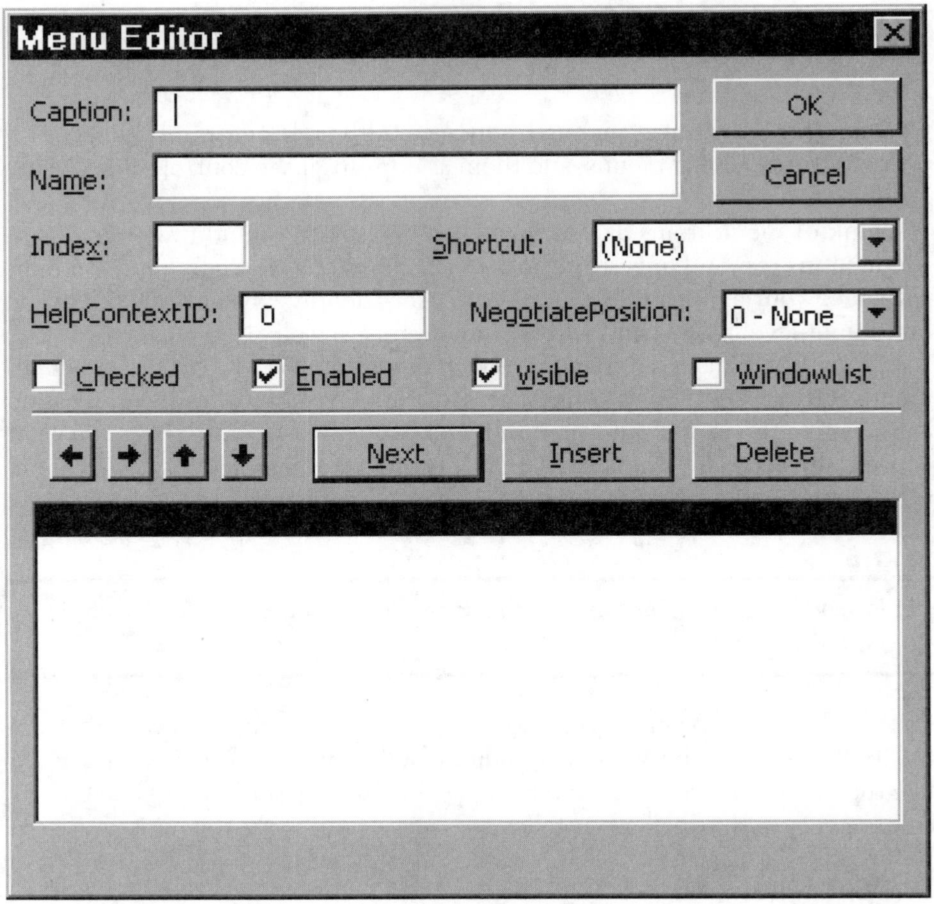

Figure 3-6   The Menu Design window

Name

Each menu item must have a control name. Unless the menu items are part of a control array (see Chapter 7 for more on control arrays), they must have different control names. The Microsoft convention is to use a mnu prefix for menu item control names.

The OK and Cancel Buttons

Click the OK button when you are finished designing the menu. Click the Cancel button if you decide not to build the menu. Even after you've finished designing a menu and clicked on the OK button, you can return to the Menu Design window and make changes.

The Index Box

Use the Index box if you want to make a menu item part of a control array (see Chapter 7).

The Shortcut Box

The Shortcut box gives you a drop-down list box from which you can choose accelerator keys to your menu items. Recall that accelerator keys are either function keys or key combinations that activate a menu item without the user having to open the menu at all. (The shortcut key is automatically added to the caption.)

Tip

The ALT+F4 shortcut to close a window is not an allowable shortcut key. Response to this key combination is built into the form unless you remove the control box at design time. If you have a File menu and a control box on an ordinary form and want to show ALT+F4 as a shortcut for the Exit item, place this shortcut as part of the caption and use the QueryUnload event to call the Click procedure of the Exit item.

Window Lists

Window lists are used when you have MDI windows. (See Chapter 6 for more on MDI forms.)

The Checked Check Box

The Checked check box determines whether a checkmark shows up in front of the menu item. It is much more common to switch the Checked property to True when a user selects the item while the program is running than to set it at design time.

The Enabled Check Box

The Enabled check box determines the value of the Enabled property of the menu item. A menu item that is Enabled will respond to the Click event. An item that has this property changed to False—either at design time by toggling the box off or at run time via code—shows up gray.

The Visible Check Box

The Visible check box determines the value of the Visible property of the menu item. If a menu item is made invisible, all its submenus are also invisible and VB5 moves the menu items to fill in the gap.

The Arrow Buttons

The arrow buttons work with the current menu items. The menu item you're currently working with is highlighted in the large text window below the arrow buttons. Submenus are indicated by the indentation level in this text window. The LEFT and RIGHT ARROW buttons control the indentation level. Clicking on the LEFT ARROW button moves the highlighted item in one level; clicking on the RIGHT ARROW button moves it one indentation level deeper. You cannot indent an item more than one level deeper than the item above it. If you try, VB5 will not let you leave the Menu Design window until you fix it.

Clicking on the UP ARROW button interchanges the highlighted menu item with the item above it; clicking on the DOWN ARROW button interchanges the highlighted item with the item below it. The UP and DOWN ARROWS do not change the indentation pattern of an item.

The Next Button

Clicking the NEXT button moves you to the next menu item or inserts a new item if you are at the end of the menu. The indentation of the new item is the same as the indentation of the previous item.

The Insert Button

Clicking the INSERT button inserts a menu item above the currently high-lighted menu item.

The Delete Button

Clicking the DELETE button removes the currently highlighted item. You cannot use the DEL key to remove menu items.

Pop-up Menus

One of Windows 95's conventions is that a right mouse-click brings up a context-sensitive menu. In order for a pop-up menu to exist, you must first create it as an ordinary menu, complete with captions and names for the item. Visual Basic 5 allows any menu with at least one item to be a pop-up menu.

Tip

If you don't want the user to see it on the main menu bar, set the Visible property of the top level menu item to be False. (For more on pop-up menus, see the section on Mouse events in Chapter 6.)

Finally, in VB5, once you have created a menu with the Main Editor, you can use the Properties window to change its state. (Although we still find it easier to use the Menu Editor to do so!)

The Text Representation of a Form or User Control

The text file that contains an ASCII representation of a form or control is an extremely useful debugging tool, and is often an excellent way to get a sense for how the control was made. Using it, you can easily make sure the properties of the container form and its component controls are exactly what you want and that the code is correct relative to the interface.

Tip

We suggest not modifying the properties of a form or a control using an ordinary text editor on this file, although you may want to do this in unusual circumstances when you are globally changing the names for components.

Here is the .frm file for the Image Viewer from Chapter 1.

Listing 3-1:   .frm File for Image Viewer

```
VERSION 5.00
Object = "{F9043C88-F6F2-101A-A3C9-08002B2F49FB}#1.1#0";  "COMDLG32.OCX"
Begin VB.Form Form1
    Caption         =    "Form1"
    ClientHeight    =    3240
    ClientLeft      =    60
    ClientTop       =    300
    ClientWidth     =    4680
    LinkTopic       =    "Form1"
    ScaleHeight     =    3240
    ScaleWidth      =    4680
    StartUpPosition =    3    'Windows Default
    Begin MSComDlg.CommonDialog CommonDialog1
        Left        =    840
```

```
      Top                =     360
      _ExtentX           =     847
      _ExtentY           =     847
      _Version           =     327680
      DialogTitle        =     "Choose Image Type"
      Filter             =     "Pictures  (*.bmp; *.gif; *.jpg; *.wmf;_
*.ico)|*.bmp;*.gif;*.jpg;*.wmf;*.ico"
   End
   Begin VB.Image Image1
      Height             =     495
      Left               =     1800
      Top                =     1440
      Width              =     1215
   End
End
Attribute VB_Name = "Form1"
Attribute VB_GlobalNameSpace = False
Attribute VB_Creatable = False
Attribute VB_PredeclaredId = True
Attribute VB_Exposed = False
Private Sub Form_Load()
  On Error Resume Next
  CommonDialog1.ShowOpen
  Image1.Picture = LoadPicture(CommonDialog1.filename)
End Sub
```

And here is the .ctl file for the simple NonNegativeIntegerTextBox control we built in Chapter 1. First comes the version of Visual Basic with which you are working. Next are descriptions of the controls we placed on the form, along with any properties not set at their default values. The text about attributes describes certain global properties of the user control, but you don't need to be concerned about them.

Listing 3-2:   .ctl File for NonNegativeIntegerTextBox

```
VERSION 5.00
Begin VB.UserControl NonNegativeIntegerTextBox
    ClientHeight    =    3600
    ClientLeft      =    0
    ClientTop       =    0
    ClientWidth     =    4800
    PropertyPages   =    "NonNegativeIntegerTextBox.ctx":0000
    ScaleHeight     =    3600
    ScaleWidth      =    4800
    Begin VB.TextBox Text1
        Height        =    495
        Left          =    1800
        TabIndex      =    0
        Top           =    1560
        Width         =    1215
    End
End
Attribute VB_Name = "NonNegativeIntegerTextBox"
Attribute VB_GlobalNameSpace = False
Attribute VB_Creatable = True
Attribute VB_PredeclaredId = False
Attribute VB_Exposed = True
Public Event BadEntry()

Private Sub Text1_Change()
    If Text1.Text = "" Then Exit Sub
    If Not (IsNumeric(Text1.Text)) Or (Int(Val(Text1.Text)) _
    <> Val(Text1.Text)) or Val(Text1.Text) < 0
        RaiseEvent BadEntry
        Text1.Text = ""
    End If
End Sub
```

```
Private Sub Text1_KeyPress(KeyAscii As Integer)
   If KeyAscii < Asc("0") Or KeyAscii > Asc("9") Then
     KeyAscii = 0
     RaiseEvent BadEntry
   End If
End Sub
```

PROGRAMMING BASICS

Topics in this Chapter

- Mechanics of Entering Code
- Statements in Visual Basic
- Assignment and Property Setting
- Method Calls
- Variables
- Strings
- Numbers
- Constants
- Repeating Operations—Loops
- Conditionals—Making Decisions
- Select Case
- The GoTo

Chapter 4

This chapter has two purposes:

- To show the mechanics of writing code in VB5.
- To show the fundamentals (variables, data types and control structures) of the programming language built into VB5.

Before we begin, we want to stress that the key to Visual Basic programming is recognizing the importance of event handling. If you think of the code in a Visual Basic program or a control as a set of independent parts that "wake up" only in response to events they have been told to recognize, you won't be wrong, but if you think of the code as having a starting line and an ending line and moving from top to bottom, you will. In fact, unlike some programming languages, executable lines in a Visual Basic program must be inside procedures or functions. (For illustration purposes, we may show you fragments of a program, but they are not meant to, nor can they, work independently.)

Note

Except for the mechanics of entering code, which have gotten even easier, programmers coming from earlier versions of VB4 can skim or even skip most of this chapter; the only new features described here are the decimal type and the IntelliSense features that make code entry easier.

Mechanics of Entering Code

First off, as you have already seen, you always write code in a Code window. The editor built into VB5 automatically color-codes the elements of your program. For example, the default is that keywords are in blue and syntax errors' text is in red. You can change the defaults with the Editor page on the Tools|Options dialog box. The editor is also tied into the compiler. For this reason, you will see an error message box if what you type doesn't make sense to the compiler. (Usually what you see is a message box with "compiler error" after you move off the current line.)

The editor has lots of nifty features to make writing code easier. (Microsoft calls this *IntelliSense*.) For example, when you enter a keyword followed by a space or opening parenthesis, a tip appears that gives the syntax for that element. Figure 4-1 shows an example of this QuickInfo feature at work.

We will explain the syntax for these QuickInfo tips a little later. (You can turn this off by using the Editor page on the Options dialog box. In this case, you can use CTRL+I to access QuickInfo for a specific procedure or method.)

The next nifty feature is called List Properties/Methods. It gives you a list of the properties and methods of an object right after you type the period. For example, if you have a TextBox named Text1 and you type `Text1.`, you will immediately see something like the screen shown in Figure 4-2. (CTRL+J is the keyboard shortcut.) Select the item you want and then press the TAB key to insert the item.

The final nifty feature gives you a list of available constants. For example, if you had a text box named Text1 on your control and entered

```
Text1.Enabled =
```

you would see a pop-up box listing True or False. (Again, select the one you want and press TAB or ENTER to complete it.)

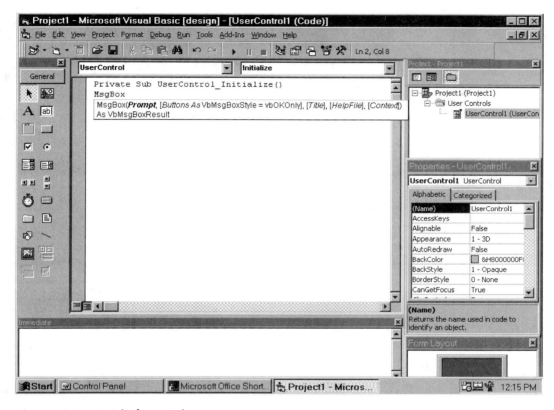

Figure 4-1   QuickInfo at work

In general, the Code window has two list boxes and an area for editing your code. The left list box, usually called the Object list box, lists all the controls on the control or form, plus an object called General that holds common code used by all the procedures attached to the control or form. The right-hand list box is usually called the Procedure list box. As you have seen, this list box shows all the events recognized by the object selected in the Object list box. If you have already written an event procedure, it shows up in boldface in the Procedure list box. User-defined functions and procedures will show up in the right-hand list box as well.

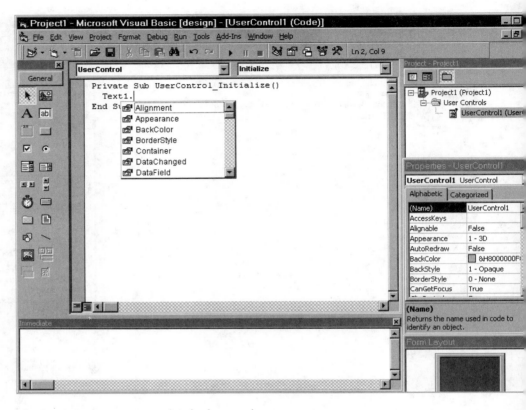

Figure 4-2 List Properties/Methods at work

Advanced Editing Features

The Visual Basic editor follows the standard Windows conventions, such as
CTRL+X for cut and CTRL+V for paste. The Edit menu, as discussed in
Chapter 2, gives you access to most of the editing features, although the Edit
toolbar described in Table 4-2 is also useful. The search/replace feature is
quite powerful and includes the ability to search:

- selected text
- current procedure
- current module
- current project

You can search up or down or in both directions, find whole words, match case, or use pattern matching. (Make sure the Use Pattern Matching box is checked in the Search or Replace dialog box.)

The following table summarizes the wildcard characters you can use for pattern matching.

Table 4-1:	Wildcard Characters in Pattern Matching
Pattern Used	*Matches*
?	Any single character.
*	Zero or more characters.
#	Any single digit (0–9).
[charlist]	Any single character in the charlist.
[!charlist]	Any single character not in the charlist.

For example, with the "Find Whole Words Only" and the "Use Pattern Matching" boxes checked, Count* would match Count, Counts, Counter, but Count? would not match Counter. As another example, you can use [AEIOU] to find vowels.

Note

To match the opening bracket ([ ), question mark (?), pound sign (#), and asterisk (*), enclose them in brackets. The closing bracket ( ]) can't be used inside brackets to match itself, but it can be used outside a group as an individual character.

Finally, in addition to using the braces for a simple list of characters, you can specify a range of characters by using a hyphen (-) to separate the upper and lower bounds of the range. For example, using [A-z] lets you search for any alphabetical character. You can even use multiple ranges inside the brackets: [a-zA-Z0-9] matches any alphanumeric character.

Edit Toolbar

Many useful editing features have button equivalents on the Edit toolbar. However, as we write this, some of them, unfortunately, do not have keyboard equivalents. (See Chapter 2 for a way to add them.) For this reason, you might want to choose View|Toolbars and add the Edit toolbar to your environment. (The Edit Toolbar is also a way to quickly get at the IntelliSense features if you have disabled them from automatically popping up.) The following table summarizes the tools available on this toolbar.

Table 4-2:	The Edit Toolbar		
Tool	*Function*	*Keyboard equivalent, if any*	*Description*
	List Properties/Methods	CTRL +J	Displays a pop-up with a list of the properties and methods for the object preceding the period.
	List Constants	CTRL+SHIFT+J	Displays a pop-up with a list of the valid constants after you type an = sign.
	Quick Info	CTRL+I	Gives the syntax for the procedure or method.
	Parameter Info	CTRL+SHIFT+I	Provides the parameter list for the current function call.
	Complete Word	CTRL+SPACE	Completes the keyword or object when enough information is there. (For example, msg would complete to MsgBox.)
	Indent	TAB	Indents the selected text one tab stop. (Use the Editing page on the Tools|Options dialog box to change the number of spaces.)

Tool	Function	Keyboard equivalent, if any	Description
	Outdent	SHIFT+TAB	Moves the selected text back one tab stop.
	Toggle Breakpoint	F9 (Left-clicking in the left margin next to a line of code also toggles the breakpoint.)	Used for debugging, see Chapter 12.
	Comment Block	None	See the next section for more information on comments.
	Uncomment Block	None	See the next section for more information on comments.
	Toggle Bookmark	None	The editor allows you to put multiple bookmarks at specific places in your code. The four bookmark buttons let you use bookmarks for easier navigation between code segments.
	Next Bookmark	None	
	Previous Bookmark	None	
	Clear All Bookmarks	None	

Statements in Visual Basic

When you enter a statement in the Code window, Visual Basic analyzes it. Many typos are detected by Visual Basic at this stage. The editor can actually correct some common typos like leaving off a closing " on a string.

Caution

Unless they are within quotation marks, Visual Basic is not case sensitive nor is spacing relevant to Visual Basic.

Nonetheless, Visual Basic does try to impose its own conventions. It capitalizes the first letter of command words and often adds extra spaces for readability. For example, no matter how you capitalize the command word Print—`PRint`, `Print`, `print`, and so on—moving off of the line will change it to `Print`.

Statements in Visual Basic rarely use line numbers, and each statement generally occurs on its own line. Lines are limited to 1023 characters but can be extended to the next line by using the underscore character (_) preceded by a space as the end of the line. Thus, unless a line ends with an underscore, pressing the ENTER key indicates a line is done. (There's no semicolon statement separator like in some languages.) You can combine statements on one line by placing a colon (:) between them. If you use a line with more characters than can fit in the window, Visual Basic scrolls the window to the right, as needed.

Note

Sometimes in this book you'll see lines that easily fit this limit but are longer than can fit on one line of a printed page. We will use the underscore as the line continuation character whenever possible. Since the underscore does not work as a line continuation character inside quotes, in this case, look for the closing quote.

```
MsgBox "Please click a button" vbOKCancel _
+ vbExclamation, "Test Button"
Print "This is an example of text inside quotes
that won't fit on a single line of the printed
page."
```

Comments

As with any programming language, commenting your code is up to you. Comment statements are neither executed nor processed by Visual Basic. As a result, they do not take up any room in your compiled code. There are two ways to indicate a comment. The usual way is with a single quote.

```
Sub Command1_Click ()
   'A comment describing the procedure would go here
   '

End Sub
```

(You can also use the older Rem keyword.)

You can add comments to the ends of lines. In this case, it is easier to use the single quotation mark because the Rem form requires a colon before it. For example:

```
Print "Hello world" 'every one uses this
```

or

```
Print "Hello world" :Rem A bit more cumbersome
```

Everything on a line following a Rem statement is ignored, regardless of whether or not it is an executable Visual Basic statement.

Tip

Although VB5 has conditional compilation (see Chapter 9), commenting out executable statements is still a common technique to help debug your programs. This is especially true because the Edit toolbar has the neat Comment/Uncomment Block tools.

The End Statement

When Visual Basic processes an End statement, the program stops. The various Unload events are not triggered, and if you are developing a program, you are dumped back into the development environment. The effect is exactly the same as choosing the End option on the Run menu. While you may have an End statement in a project used for a test bed, you cannot place End statements in any code for a user control and, in any case, even for ordinary projects, we use End rarely since it may prevent VB from cleaning up memory it allocated.

Assignment and Property Setting

Giving values to variables and resetting properties are two of the most common tasks in Visual Basic code. Visual Basic uses an equal sign for both these operations, for example:

```
Count = 1
```

You can also use the optional keyword `Let` that was common in earlier versions of BASIC:

Let *Variable*Name = *value*

If you want to change a property setting for a Visual Basic object, place the object's name followed by a period and then the name of the property on the left side of the equal sign, and put the new value on the right-hand side:

object.*property* = *value*

For example, suppose you have a text button (control name of TextBox1) and want to blank it out in code rather than use the properties bar:

```
Text1.Text = ""
```

Since there is nothing between the quotation marks, the text assigned to this property is blank. Similarly, a line like

```
Text1.Text = "Hello world"
```

in an event procedure changes the setting for the text property to the text in the quotation marks.

Note

Every Visual Basic object has a default property (for example, text boxes have the Text property). When referring to the default property, you don't need to use the property name. For example, you can enter

```
TextBox1 = "This is new text"
```

However, this approach can lead to less readable code and requires you to remember what the default property of the control is. Thus, in spite of the very small gain in speed this approach yields, this book doesn't emphasize this feature of Visual Basic. In addition, the default property may change in future versions of the object, which would cause your program source code to need reworking.

Boolean Properties

Properties that take only the value true or false are usually Boolean properties, after the English logician George Boole. Boolean properties specify whether a command button is visible, enabled, or is the default for cancel or command button. Visual Basic has built-in constants for true and false. For example,

```
Command1.Visible = False   'false works too of course
```

hides the command button. The control stays hidden until Visual Basic processes the statement

```
Command1.Visible = True
```

As another example, to have the TAB key skip over a control while a program is running, change the `TabStop` property to False:

```
Control.TabStop = False
```

Internally, Visual Basic uses the values 0 for False and –1 for True (actually, any non-zero value will work for True). The `Not` operator lets you toggle between Boolean properties. For example,

```
Command1.Visible = Not(Command1.Visible)
```

switches the state of the command button.

Note

For the Not operator to work properly in toggling a Boolean property between on and off, you must use the built-in True constant or a value of -1 for True.

An Example: Setting Fonts

Which fonts and font sizes you can use depends on what kind of hardware is available to the system in which you run the application. Visual Basic lets you find out this information by analyzing the Fonts property of the Screen or Printer objects. In this case, you should think of the Font object as being a "sub-object" of an existing VB object.

For example, to assign a font name in code, use the Name property of the Font object and place the name in quotation marks on the right-hand side of an assignment statement:

```
ObjectName.Font.Name = "Modern"
ObjectName.Font.Name = "Helv" 'Helvetica
```

For example:

```
Printer.Font.Name = "Modern"
```

All objects that display text let you set these properties. These include forms, command buttons, labels, and text boxes. Of these, only forms (rich text boxes and picture boxes) let you combine different fonts. If you change these properties at run time for any other control, all the old text switches to the new font as well. The rule is that if text is specified by a property (like the Caption property for command buttons), changing a font changes the previous text. On the other hand, if you display text by using the Print method, the changes are not retroactive and, therefore, go into effect only for subsequent Print statements.

You can change all the font properties via code. Except for `Font.Size`, they are all Boolean properties. As with `Font.Name`, any control that displays text lets you set these properties of the Font object. For example:

```
Screen.Font.Size = 24              '24 point type
Screen.Font.Bold = False
Screen.Font.Italic = True
Screen.Font.Strikethru = True
Printer.Font.Underline = True
```

As with changing fonts, only forms (and picture boxes) let you mix these font properties.

Forms, picture boxes, and the printer have one other font property you may occasionally find useful: `FontTransparent`. If you set this to True, background graphics and background text will show through the text displayed in the transparent font.

These properties can be combined in almost any way you want. If your hardware and software support it, you can have 24-point bold italic script type in a control.

Method Calls

If you want your Visual Basic objects to actually do something, you will need to work with built-in methods. For example, if you want to set the focus to a specific control at run time, you need to use the SetFocus method:

```
TextBox1.SetFocus
```

In general, of course, the syntax for a method is:

```
Object.NameOfMethod ListOfWhatToUse
```

The ListOfWhatToUse (more correctly called the *argument* or *parameter* list) would contain a list of items separated by commas. For example, the Move method, which can be used to move a control around inside its current container, has the following syntax:

```
Object.Move left, top, width, height
```

```
TextBox1.Move Screen.Width/2, Screen.Height/2, _
25*Screen.Width, .25*Screen.Height
```

would move a text box to roughly halfway inside the usable area and make its width and height ¼ of the usable area.

Variables

Variable names in Visual Basic can be up to 255 characters long and, provided the first character is a letter, can include any combination of letters, numbers, and underscores. All characters in a variable name are significant but, as with most things in Visual Basic, case is irrelevant. `BASE` is the same variable as `base`. On the other hand, `Base` is a different variable from `Base1`, and both are different from `Base_1`.

The Visual Basic editor always changes the form of the names of your variables to reflect the capitalization pattern you last used if you didn't explicitly declare the variable. If the variable was explicitly declared, the VB editor always converts it to the case which was declared. If you use `Yearlyinterest`, `yearlyinterest`, and `YearlyInterest` successively as variable names, when you move off the line, Visual Basic will automatically change all occurrences to `YearlyInterest` because this was the last one you used. However, if you had originally declared it with `Dim Yearlyinterest As Single`, then it would retain that case no matter how you used it in the following code.

This feature is occasionally useful in detecting typos in variable names. If you think a misspelled variable name is causing a problem, change one occurrence to all caps, move off the line, and scan the program to see if all the occurrences of the variable name have been changed. If you find one that wasn't changed, you will know that variable name contains a typo. Correct the error and then change the variable name back to the form you want; all occurrences of the name will change as well.

Note

For a better method of finding misspelled variables, see the section on "Declaring Variables."

You can't use names reserved by Visual Basic for variable names. For example, Print is not acceptable as a variable name. Visual Basic will present an error message if you try to use a reserved word as a variable name, usually immediately after you move off of the line. However, you can embed reserved words within a variable's name. For example, PrintIt is a perfectly acceptable variable name.

The most common convention in Visual Basic for variable names is to use capitals only at the beginning of the words that make up the parts of it (for example, `YearlyInterest`, not `Yearlyinterest`).

Variable Types

Visual Basic handles 12 standard types of variables. It is also possible to define your own variable types, as you will see in the next chapter. Many of these types have special identifiers for variables that will hold information of that type. This was more common in earlier versions of BASIC and most people don't use them very much now. (See the section on "Declaring Variables" later in this chapter for more information on this.)

Boolean

Boolean variables are stored as two-byte numbers, but can only hold the value True or False. Boolean variables have no type-declaration character.

Byte

Byte variables hold (unsigned) integer values between 0 and 255. The Byte data type has no type-declaration character.

Currency

The currency type is designed to avoid certain problems inherent in switching from binary fractions to decimal fractions. (It's impossible to make $\frac{1}{10}$ out of combinations of $\frac{1}{2}$, $\frac{1}{4}$, $\frac{1}{8}$, $\frac{1}{16}$, and so on.) The currency type can have four digits to the right of the decimal place and up to 14 to the left of the decimal point. Arithmetic will be exact within this range. The identifier is an "at" sign (@)—not the dollar sign, which identifies strings. While calculations other than addition and subtraction are about as slow as for double-precision numbers, this is the preferred type for financial calculations of reasonable size. (For those who are interested, this type uses 19-digit integers, which are then scaled by a factor of 10,000. This gives you 15 places to the left of the decimal point and four places to the right.)

Date

Date variables are stored as eight-byte numbers with possible values in the range January 1, 100 to December 31, 9999. Date has no type-declaration character. Dates are indicated by surrounding the date by #'s, for example:

```
Millenium = #1/1/2000#
```

Essentially, VB5 will accept whatever standard formats for dates that your locale uses.

You can do ordinary arithmetic on Date variables and the results are what you might expect:

```
Tomorrow =  Now + 1
```

Generally, adding or subtracting integers affects the day; adding or subtracting fractions will also affect the hour.

Decimal

A type new to VB, this is currently a subtype of the Variant data type described later. Decimal variables are stored as roughly 29-digit (actually 96-bit unsigned) integers. They are then scalable by a variable power of 10 that specifies the number of digits to the right of the decimal point, and ranges from 0 to 28.

Integer

Integer variables hold relatively small integer values, between –32,768 and +32,767. Integer arithmetic is very fast but is restricted to these ranges. The identifier that can be used is the percent sign (%):

```
AnIntegerVariable% = 37
```

Long Integers

This type holds integers between –2,147,483,648 and +2,147,483,647. The identifier used is the ampersand (&). Long integer arithmetic is also fast, and there is very little performance penalty on 486DX, or Pentium class machines for using long integers rather than ordinary integers.

```
ALongIntegerVariable& = 99999789
```

Object

Object variables hold address information that refers to objects. (See Chapter 7 for more on objects.)

Single Precision

For single-precision numbers, the identifier is an exclamation point (!). These variables hold numbers that are approximations. You can be sure of the accuracy of only seven digits. This means that if an answer comes out as 12,345,678.97, the answer could just as likely be 12,345,670.01. The range for these numbers is up to 38 digits. Calculations will always be approximate. Moreover, arithmetic with these numbers is slower than with integer or long integer variables.

Double Precision

Double-precision variables hold numbers with 16 places of accuracy and allow more than 300 digits. The identifier used is a pound sign (#). Calculations are also approximate for these variables. You can rely only on the first 16 digits. Calculations are relatively slow with double-precision numbers. Double-precision variables are mainly used in scientific calculations in Visual Basic because of the Currency and Decimal data types described earlier.

String

String variables hold characters. The older (but still accepted) method to identify string variables is to use a dollar sign ($) at the end of the variable name:

```
AStringVariable$
```

String variables can theoretically hold up to 32k characters, although a specific machine may hold less due to memory constraints, overhead requirements for Windows or the number of strings used in the form. For example, since the information in a text box is stored as a string, you would use a string variable to pick up the text contained in a text box. For example,

```
ContentOfTextBox1$ = TextBox1.Text
```

assigns the string contained in the text box to the variable named on the left-hand side.

The Variant Type

The variant data type is designed to store all the different possible Visual Basic data received in one place. It doesn't matter whether the information is numeric, date/time, string, or an object; the variant type can hold it all. Visual Basic automatically performs any necessary conversions so you don't (usually) have to worry about what type of data is being stored in the variant data type. The built-in VarType function lets you determine whether data stored in the variant type is numeric, date/time, or string. Using variants rather than the specific type is a little slower because of the conversions needed, and some programmers feel relying on automatic type conversions leads to sloppy programming. Variants can also hold two special values "empty," which means nothing is being stored and the special Null value is used. (Using a Null variant in an expression will always give you Null as the value of the expression.)

Declaring Variables

One of the most common bugs in programs is the misspelled variable name. Most versions of BASIC allow you to create variables "on the fly" by merely using the variable name in your program. (And, unfortunately, VB5 kept this "feature.") This is not permitted, for good reason, in strongly typed languages, such as Java or Pascal. Obviously, if you create variables on the fly, you can easily misspell a variable name, and a misspelled variable name will almost certainly yield a default value that causes your program to behave incorrectly. Such an error is among the most difficult to eradicate, because you need to find the misspelled variable name.

One way to avoid this problem is to force all variables to be declared. Then you will be notified if a variable name is spelled incorrectly in a procedure. The designers of Visual Basic give you this option but do not force you to use it. To turn on this option, add the command Option Explicit in the General code section. After Visual Basic processes this command, it will no longer allow you to use a variable unless you declare it first.

Note

You can also use the Editor page of the Options dialog box on the Tools menu to require variable declaration. This inserts the Option Explicit command automatically.

The most common way to declare a variable inside an event procedure is with the Dim keyword. Here are some examples:

```
Sub Command1_Click()
  Dim I As Integer
  Dim InfoInTextBox As String
  Dim Interest As Currency
End Sub
```

You can combine multiple declarations on a single line but you must include the type with each variable.

```
Dim Year As Integer, Rate As Currency, Name As _
String
```

Caution

Do not use:

```
    Dim I, J, K As Integer
```

since this will only make K *an integer variable. The other two are variant variables.*

You can use the type identifier instead of the "As:"

```
Dim I%, MyName$
```

Note

If a variable is declared in a Dim statement, then trying to use variables with the same name but a different type identifier at the end of the variable will cause a "Duplicate definition" error when the program is run.

To give a variable the variant data type, just use the Dim statement without any As clause or identifier:

```
Dim Foo      'makes Foo have the variant data type
```

You can also use:

```
Dim Foo As Variant    'easier to check
```

Note

You can not currently declare a variable as being of the decimal type. Instead, you must store the information in a variant and either rely on Visual Basic to make the conversion or use a conversion function.

Finally, as with naming conventions for objects, naming conventions for variables have also inspired quite a lot of flaming. Many complicated systems of prefixes exist that indicate, at a glance, the type of a variable. In this book, we use prefixes only in a very limited way: we try to indicate the scope of a variable (see later in this chapter and also in the next chapter) by a prefix. Also, when the routine is complicated and it is not obvious what type a variable is, we will usually use a prefix like "s" for string or "n" for integer. (Except, we, like almost everyone else, often use a simple "I" or "J" for integer counters—go figure.)

Default Values

The first time you use a variant variable, VB temporarily assigns it a default value of "empty" and gives it the variant type. The "empty" value disappears the moment you assign a value to the variable. Every other type of variable also has a default value. For string variables, this is the null (empty) string— the one you get by assigning " " to a string variable. For numeric variables, the default value is zero.

Scope of Variables

Visual Basic is not like the BASIC of old; it has true local and global variables so that you can isolate variables within procedures. (See the next chapter for more on procedures.) Unless you specifically arrange it, changing the value of a variable named Total in one procedure will not affect another variable with the same name in another procedure.

Of course, occasionally you will want to share the values of variables across event procedures. For example, if an application is designed to perform a calculation involving one interest rate at a time, that rate should be available to all the procedures in the form for the control or the test form. Variables that allow such sharing among all the code in a form (including the form used for a control) are called, naturally enough, *form-level variables*. (You can also have true global variables when you have a multiform application—see the Global Variables section in the next chapter for more on this.)

Put the Dim statements for form-level variables in the General section of the code. For example, if you open the Code window, select Declarations for the General object, and enter:

```
Dim InterestRate As Currency
```

then the following is true:

- The value of the variable named InterestRate will be visible to all the procedures attached to the form.
- Any changes made to this variable in one event procedure will persist.

Obviously, the last point means you have to be careful when assigning values to form-level variables. Any information passed between event procedures is a breeding ground for programming bugs. Moreover, these errors are often hard to pinpoint.

You can use the same variable name as both a local and a form-level variable. Any Dim statements contained in a procedure take precedence over form-level declarations—they force a variable to be local. Therefore, you lose the ability to use the information contained in the form-level variable. Duplicating the names makes the form-level variable invisible to the procedure. Visual Basic doesn't tell you whether a form-level variable has been defined with the same name as a local variable. This is one more reason to make sure that variables you want to be local really are local by dimensioning them inside the procedure. This forces the variable to be local to that procedure.

Note

As mentioned, we like to prefix form-level variables with the letter "f" (for example, fInterest) and global variables with the letter "g" (for example, gInterest).

Note

Visual Basic also has Private/Public and Friend identifiers that can be used to scope variables or procedures. Private, in fact, works just like Dim for form-level variables. (For more on these keywords, please see the next chapter; for the Friend keyword, see Chapters 7 and 8.)

Static Variables—Having Values Persist

When Visual Basic invokes an event procedure, the old values of local variables are wiped out and they go back to their default values. These kinds of dynamic variables are not enough for all programming situations. For example, suppose you need to keep track of how many times a command button has been clicked. If the counter is always set back to zero, you're in trouble. You could have the values persist by using a form-level variable, but most programmers reserve form-level variables for sharing information among procedures. The solution is to use *static variables*. Static variables are not reinitialized each time Visual Basic invokes a procedure. Besides being ideal for counters, static variables are useful for making controls alternately visible or invisible (or for switching between any Boolean properties, for that matter), and as a debugging tool.

To make a variable static within a procedure, replace the keyword Dim in the declaration with the keyword Static:

```
Static Counter As Integer, IsVisible As Boolean
```

Here is an example of an event procedure for a command button that counts the clicks and displays the number:

```
Sub Command1_Click()
   'This procedure uses a static variable to count
   'clicks
   Static Counter As Integer    ' Counter starts at 0
   Counter = Counter + 1
   MsgBox Counter
End Sub
```

The first time you click, the counter starts out with its default value of 0. Visual Basic then adds 1 to it and prints the result. Notice that by placing the MsgBox statement after the addition, you are not off by 1 in the count.

Occasionally, you want all local variables within a procedure to be static. To do this, add the keyword Static before the word Sub that starts any procedure:

```
Static Sub Command1_Click()
```

Strings

As you have seen, strings are indicated by double quotes. To put two strings together (*concatenate* them), use a plus sign (+) or an ampersand (&). The recommended method is to always use the ampersand. For example, if

```
Language = "Visual Basic"
Version = " 5.0"
```

then

```
LanguageVersion = Language & Version
LanguageVersion = "Visual Basic 5.0"
```

have the same effect.

The & (or the +) joins strings in the order in which you present them. Thus, unlike when you add numbers together, order is important when you use the + sign to join two strings together.

Tip

The ampersand (&), unlike the + sign, lets you combine numbers and strings into a string equivalent. For example, C=A% & B$ concatenates an integer variable and a string variable by changing them both to variants.

ANSI Codes

Windows (hence, Visual Basic) uses the ANSI character set. The control characters and such special keys as TAB and line feed have numbers less than 32. The value of the function Chr (n) is the string consisting of the character of ASCII value n in the current font. For instance, the statement

```
Print Chr(169)
```

prints the copyright symbol (©) on the screen if you are using the Courier font.

Given the special nature of quotes for Visual Basic strings, you can use the ANSI value for the quotation mark, 34, to display a sentence surrounded with quotation marks.

```
Print Chr(34) & "Necessity is the mother of
    invention." & Chr(34)
```

This gives

```
"Necessity is the mother of invention."
```

(You can also use

```
Print """Necessity is the mother of invention."""
```

since Visual Basic treats `"""` as the literal quotation mark inside Print statements.)

Tip

Many common strings have constant equivalents built into Visual Basic. For example, vbCrLf gives you the Chr(13)+Chr(10) carriage return/line feed combination and vbTab gives you the tab character.

Visual Basic has a function called Asc that takes a string expression and returns the ANSI value of the first character. If the string is empty (the null string), using this function generates a run-time error.

Note

ANSI order is what Visual Basic uses, by default, to compare strings when you use relational operators like < or >.

Fixed-Length Strings

A fixed-length string is created with a Dim statement. Here is an example:

```
Dim ZipPlusFour As String * 10
```

This variable will always hold strings of length 10. If you assign a longer string to a fixed-length string, the right part will be cut off. If you assign a shorter string to ShortString, like this:

```
ZipPlusFour="11234"
```

then you still get a string of length 10. Only this time, the variable is padded on the right with spaces.

Example: Strings at Work: Input Boxes

Text boxes are the normal way for a Visual Basic application (and, especially, a control) to accept data. There is one other method that is occasionally useful. The InputBox function displays a modal dialog box on the screen. This is the principal advantage of input boxes; it is sometimes necessary to insist that a user supply some necessary data before letting him or her move on. (We also use them frequently when writing a quick and dirty test bed.) The disadvantages are that the dimensions of the input box are fixed beforehand and you lose the flexibility that text boxes provide. Figure 4-3 shows an example of an input box:

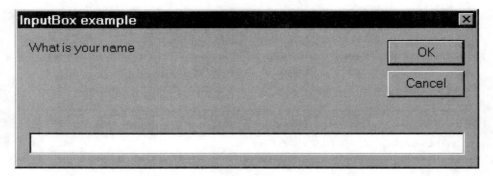

Figure 4-3   An input box

As you can see, input boxes have a title bar and four components, three of which are controls. The first is the prompt, "What is your name." There are always two command buttons labeled OK and Cancel. Finally, there is a text box at the bottom. Visual Basic always places the focus here when it processes a statement containing an InputBox function. The simplest syntax for the InputBox function is

```
StringVariable = InputBox(prompt)
```

where the prompt is a string or string variable. This gives a dialog box that is roughly centered horizontally and one-third of the way down the screen.

Now the user types whatever he or she wants in the text box. Pressing ENTER or clicking the OK button makes whatever is in the text box become the value of the string variable. Pressing ESC or clicking the Cancel box causes Visual Basic to assign the null string to the variable.

A GUIDE TO
QUICKINFO SYNTAX ENTRIES

If you enabled the QuickInfo feature, you can see that the full syntax for the InputBox function is:

`InputBox(`***Prompt*** *[,* ***Title]*** *[,* ***Default]*** *[,* ***Xpos]*** *[,* ***Ypos]][,* *Helpfile,* *Context])*

This is pretty typical of a QuickInfo help item: optional parameters are indicated by enclosing them in square brackets. In this case, only the Prompt parameter is required. If you use an optional parameter, you must separate it with commas. If you skip a parameter, you must still use the extra comma.

In certain cases, including the InputBox function, you can use what are called *named arguments* to avoid dealing with the commas for optional arguments. Named arguments show up in bold italic when using the QuickInfo feature. For example, all parameters in the InputBox function can use named arguments. (See the next chapter for more on named arguments.)

Here is a more detailed description of the parameters for the InputBox function:

Prompt
: This is the string or string variable whose value Visual Basic displays in the dialog box. It is limited to roughly 255 characters. The prompt doesn't wrap, and you have to explicitly add line separators (use vbCrLf).

Title
: The title parameter is optional and gives the caption used in the title bar. There is no default value; if you leave this out, nothing is displayed in the title bar.

Default
: The default parameter is also optional. It lets you display default text in the Edit box, where the user will enter information.

xpos,ypos
: These parameters are also optional. Both xpos and ypos are integral numeric expressions: xpos is the distance in twips between the left edge of the input box and the left edge of the screen, and ypos is the distance in twips between the top of the box and the top of the screen.

Helpfile   The helpfile parameter is also optional. It is a string value to
                    identify the help file to use. If a helpfile parameter is specified,
                    then the context parameter must also be specified.

Context   The context parameter is a numeric expression that is the help
                    context identification number assigned to a help topic. If context
                    is specified, then the helpfile parameter must also be specified.

Numbers

Numbers in Visual Basic cannot use commas to delineate thousands. They
can use a decimal point, unless they are integers. They will be displayed in
scientific notation if they are very large.

If you need to give a numeric value to a variable, place the number or
numeric expression on the right-hand side of the assignment statement. If
you assign a number with a decimal point to an integer variable, it is automatically rounded off. If you assign a number larger than the limits for the
given variable, Visual Basic gives you an error message at run time. To change
a string of digits to a number, use the built-in function Val:

```
Val("3001") is 3001
```

The Val function reads through the string until it encounters a non-numeric
character (or a second period). The number you get from it is determined by
where it stopped searching:

```
Val ("30Something") is 30
```

Similarly, you will want to change a number back to a string of digits when
you display it in a text box. There are many ways to do this, depending on the
form you want the number to take. The function Str is the simplest. It converts a number to a string but doesn't clean it up in any way. It also leaves a
space in front of positive numbers.

To polish the display, the Str function is often replaced by the Format function described in the next section.

Note

Another possibility to store information is the variant data type. If you assign a variable that holds numeric information currently stored in the variant data type to a numeric variable, then Visual Basic will perform the conversion automatically. However (unlike when you use the Val command, for example), you must be careful that the variable of the variant data type holds something with no extraneous characters or extra periods beyond the one allowed, otherwise, you'll get a run-time error.

The Format Function

The Format function gives you complete control over how a string or number will be displayed. The Format function returns a new string in the given format. The basic syntax for the Format function is:

Format(expression[, format[, firstdayofweek[, firstweekofyear]]])

For example,

```
WeeklySalary = Format(1000000/52,"Currency")
```

gives the WeeklySalary variable a value which is the string equivalent of 1,000,000/2 using a standard currency (in the U.S., a $ sign, two decimal points and commas) format. Thus, this line of code is equivalent to:

```
WeeklySalary = "$1,923.08"
```

In general, the expression parameter is what you want to format. The format parameter describes the format to be used. As in the example above, many common formats have names, for example,

```
Print Format(Now, "Long Date")
```

might give

```
Saturday, November 23, 1996
```

The following table identifies the predefined date, time and numeric format names, which, as the examples above indicate, must be enclosed in quotes.

Table 4-3:	Predefined Format Names
Format Name	*Description*
General Date	Displays a date and/or time in m/d/y format using a 24-hour clock.
Long Date	Displays a date according to your system's long date format.
Medium Date	Displays a date using the medium date format (23-Nov-96, for example).
Short Date	Displays a date using your system's short date format (m/d/y).
Long Time	Displays hours, minutes and seconds using your system's long time format (2:40:23 A.M., for example).
Medium Time	Displays time in 12-hour notation using hours and minutes with an A.M./P.M. designator.
Short Time	Displays a time using 24-hour notation, for example, 17:45.
General Number	Displays number with no thousand separator.
Currency	Displays number with thousand separator, if appropriate, and also displays two digits to the right of the decimal point.
Fixed	Displays at least one digit to the left and two digits to the right of the decimal point.
Standard	Displays number with a thousand separator, at least one digit to the left and two digits to the right of the decimal point.
Percent	Converts and displays number to a percent by multiplying by 100; always displays two digits to the right of the decimal point.
Scientific	Uses standard scientific notation.
Yes/No	Displays No if number is 0; otherwise, displays Yes.
True/False	Displays False if number is 0; otherwise, displays True.
On/Off	Displays Off if number is 0; otherwise, displays On.

You can also make your own number formats by using the following special format characters in the form of a format string. For example,

```
Print Format(987.654321,"###.##")
```

yields 987.65. Visual Basic rounds the number off so there are only two digits after the decimal point.

The Format function, unlike the Str function, does not leave room for an implied + sign. This means that in a statement like

```
Print "Your salary is ";Format(Payment,"####.##")
```

the extra space after the word "is" is essential.

In general, a # is the placeholder for a digit, except that leading and trailing zeros are ignored and you don't have to worry about having too few #s before the decimal point in the format string. Visual Basic will always give all the digits to the left of the decimal point.

If you want to have Visual Basic keep leading and trailing zeros, use a zero in place of the # in the format string. For example,

```
Print Format(987.6500,"000.000")
```

yields 987.650.

To display numbers with commas every three digits, place a comma between any two-digit placeholders. For example,

```
Print Format(123456789.991,"#,#.##")
```

gives 123,456,789.99.

Note

If you place the comma immediately to the left of the decimal point (or use two commas), Visual Basic interprets this to mean it should skip the three digits that fall between the comma and the decimal point (or between the two commas). This is occasionally useful in scaling numbers. If your program deals with Japanese yen and you need to display one hundred million yen, you might want to write 100 million yen rather than 100,000,000 yen. To do this, use the following statement:

```
Print Format(100000000,"#00,,");" million yen"
```

Combining the # with the zero in the format string ensures that trailing zeros aren't suppressed.

Finally, if you need to display a –, +, $, (,), or spaces, use them in the format string exactly in the place you want them to occur. For example, if you want to have a dollar sign in front of a value, use this:

```
Print Format(YourSalary,"$#,##.##")
```

Note

You can use Format in any Visual Basic statement that expects a string, not only with the Print method. For example,

```
M$ = "Your balance is " & Format(CurrentBalance, _
"$###.##")
MsgBox M$
```

The following table summarizes the format characters you can use in your format strings.

Table 4-4:   Format Characters

Format character	Use
(0)	Always uses a digit.
(#)	Digit placeholder, but if the digit isn't there displays nothing.
(.)	Decimal placeholder. (In some locales, a comma is used as the decimal separator.)
(%)	Percentage placeholder. The expression is multiplied by 100. The percent character (%) is inserted in the position where it appears in the format string.
(,)	Thousand separator.
(:)	Time separator.
(/)	Date separator.
(E– E+ e– e+)	Scientific format.
– + $ ( )	Displays the indicated character. To display a character other than one of these, precede it with a backslash (\) or use double quotes.
(\)	Displays the next character in the format string.

Arithmetic Operators

The following table gives you the symbols for the five fundamental arithmetic operations.

Table 4-5:   Arithmetic Operators

Operator	Operation
+	Addition.
–	Subtraction (and to denote negative numbers).
/	Division.
*	Multiplication.
^	Exponentiation.

For integers and long integers, there is one symbol and one keyword for the arithmetic operations unique to numbers of these types:

Table 4-6: Unique Arithmetic Operator/Keyword	
Operator/Keyword	*Operation*
\	Integer division (this symbol is a backslash).
Mod	The remainder after integer division.

The ordinary division symbol (/) gives you a value that is a single-precision, double-precision, or currency answer, depending on the objects involved. The backslash (\), on the other hand, throws away the remainder in order to give you an integer. For example, 7\3 = 2. Since a / gives either a single- or double-precision answer, use a \ or the Mod operator if you really want to work with integers or long integers.

The Mod operator is the other half of integer division. This operator gives you the remainder after integer division. For example, 7 Mod 3 = 1. When one integer perfectly divides another, there is no remainder, so the Mod operator gives zero: 8 Mod 4 = 0.

Parentheses and Precedence

To do calculations, you have two ways to indicate the order in which you want operations to occur. The first way is by using parentheses, and you may prefer this method. Parentheses let you easily specify the order in which operations occur. Something like 3 + (4 * 5) gives 23 because Visual Basic does the operation within the parentheses (4 times 5) first and then adds the 3. On the other hand, (3 + 4) * 5 gives 35 because Visual Basic adds the 3 and the 4 first to get 7 and then multiplies by 5.

Visual Basic allows you to avoid parentheses, provided you follow rules that determine the precedence of the mathematical operations. For example, multiplication has higher precedence than addition. This means 3 + 4 * 5 is 23 rather than 35 because the multiplication (4 * 5) is done before the addition.

The following list gives the order (hierarchy) of operations:

1. exponentiation (^)
2. negation (making a number negative)

3. multiplication and division
4. integer division
5. remainder (Mod) function
6. addition and subtraction

For example, $-4 \wedge 2$ gives -16 because Visual Basic first does the exponentiation ($4 \wedge 2 = 4 * 4 = 16$) and only then makes the number negative.

Operations are done in order of precedence and then from left to right when two operators have the same precedence. For example:

    96 / 4 * 2

is 48. On the other hand, $96 / 4 \wedge 2$ is 6. This is because the exponentiation is done first, yielding 16, and only then is the division done.

Number Defaults and Conversions

When you use numbers in your program and do not assign them to a variable of the variant type, Visual Basic assumes the following:

- If a number has no decimal point and is in the range -32768 to 32767, it's an integer.
- If a number has no decimal point and is in the range for a long integer ($-2,147,483,648$ to $2,147,483,647$), it's a long integer.
- If a number has a decimal point and is in the range for a single-precision number, it is assumed to be single precision.
- If a number has a decimal point and is outside the range for a single-precision number, it is assumed to be double precision.

These built-in assumptions occasionally lead to problems. This is because the realm in which an answer lies is determined by where the questions lie. If you start out with two integers, Visual Basic assumes the answer is also an integer. For example, a statement like

```
Print 19999*6789
```

starts with two integers, so the answer is also assumed to be an integer. But the answer is too large for an integer, so you would get an overflow error. The solution is to add the appropriate identifier to at least one of the numbers. Use the statement

```
Print 19999&*6789
```

and Visual Basic treats both 19999 and the answer as long integers.

Caution

VB, in our opinion, carries the automatic conversion process too far. It will even convert strings of digits to numbers if this seems appropriate for the function or method. This "evil type coercion," as it is sometimes called, can lead to very subtle bugs, so be careful.

You can also use a built-in function to force a type conversion.

Table 4-7: Conversion Functions

Conversion Function	*What It Does*
CBool	Makes an expression a Boolean.
CByte	Makes an expression a byte.
CInt	Makes a numeric expression an integer by rounding.
CLng	Makes a numeric expression a long integer by rounding.
CSng	Makes a numeric expression single precision.
CDate	Makes a date expression a date.
CDbl	Makes a numeric expression double precision.
CCur	Makes a numeric expression of the currency type.
CStr	Makes any expression a string.
CVar	Makes any expression a variant.
CDec	Specifies that the value held in a variant is to be treated as being of the decimal type.

Conversions will be performed only if the numbers you're trying to convert are in the range of the new type; otherwise, Visual Basic generates an error message.

If possible, Visual Basic will automatically coerce the contents of a numeric variable from one type to another after an assignment statement (using rounding, if necessary). For example,

```
Dim AnInteger As Integer
Dim ADecimal As Single
ADecimal = 1.3
AnInteger = ADecimal
```

gives `AnInteger` the value 1.

(In fact, using the numeric conversion function has the same effect as assigning the numeric expression to a variable of the type specified.)

Visual Basic will also coerce numbers to strings of numerals if that is appropriate. For example,

```
Dim I As Integer
I = 37
TextBox1.Text = I
I = TextBox1.Text + 1
Print I
```

works just fine, and prints 38. (In theory, the Text property uses strings. We find this disconcerting and tend to use the Str and Val functions in these situations.)

Constants

Visual Basic has built-in predefined global constants to use in your programs. They are usually given a prefix of vb (lowercase). For example, when you use the MsgBox function you can use built-in constants like `vbOKOnly` to get only an OK button. You can use the Object Browser discussed in Chapter 8 to examine all the built-in constants.

Visual Basic also has *named constants* to allow you to use mnemonic names for values that never change. Constants are declared just like variables, and the rules for their names are also the same: 255 characters, first character a letter, and then any combination of letters, underscores, and numerals. Our convention is to use all capitals for constants.

If you have only one form or want the constants visible to the event procedures for only one form (as would be the case in a user control), put them in the Declarations section for the General object. You can also define a constant within a procedure, but this is less common, and only that procedure would have access to the constant. Set up a constant by using the keyword Const, followed by the name of the constant, an equal sign, and then the value:

```
Const PIE = 3.14159
```

You can set up string constants:

```
Const USERNAME = "Bill Smith"
Const LANGUAGE = "Visual Basic Version 5.0"
```

You can even use numeric expressions for constants, or define new constants in terms of previously defined constants:

```
Const PIEOVER2 = PIE/2
```

Visual Basic uses the simplest type it can for a constant, but you can override this by adding a type identifier to a constant. For example,

```
Const THISWILLBEALONGINTEGER& = 37
```

or

```
Const THISWILLBEALONGINTEGER As Long = 37
```

forces Visual Basic to treat the constant 37 as a long integer instead of an ordinary integer. Even if you use a type identifier at the end of the constant when you define it, you don't need to use the identifier in the program. Using the preceding example, all subsequent occurrences of this constant can be

```
THISWILLBEALONGINTEGER
```

As mentioned, our convention is to use all caps for constants, but this is not required. Moreover, references to constants don't depend on the case.

Repeating Operations—Loops

Visual Basic, like most programming languages, has language constructs for loops that repeat operations a fixed number of times, for continuing until a specific predetermined goal is reached, or until certain initial conditions have changed.

Determinate Loops

Use the keywords For and Next to set up a loop to repeat a fixed number of times. For example, the following code

```
Dim I As Integer
For I = 1 To 10
   Print I
Next I
```

prints the numbers 1 to 10 on the current form.

For and Next are keywords that must always be used together. The statements between the For and the Next are usually called the *body* of the loop, and the whole control structure is called, naturally enough, a For-Next loop. The keyword For sets up a counter variable. In the preceding example, the counter is an integer variable I whose initial value is 1. The ending value is set to 10.

In general, Visual Basic first sets the counter variable to the starting value. Then it checks whether the value for the counter is less than the ending value. If the value is greater than the ending value, nothing is done. If the starting value is less than the ending value, Visual Basic processes subsequent statements until it comes to the keyword Next. (The variable name is optional.) At that point, it defaults to adding 1 to the counter variable and starts the process again. This process continues until the counter variable is larger than the ending value. At that point, the loop is finished, and Visual Basic moves past it.

Tip

Although you can use variables of any numeric type for the counters, choose integer or long variables whenever possible. This allows Visual Basic to spend as little time as possible on the arithmetic needed to change the counter and, thus, speed up the loop. Loops with variant counters run very, very slowly.

Finally, you may have noticed that the body of the For-Next loop is indented. As always, the purpose of the spacing in a program is to make the program more readable and, therefore, easier to debug. The designers of Visual Basic made it easy to consistently indent code. The Visual Basic editor remembers the indentation of the previous line, and every time you press ENTER, the cursor returns to the spot directly below where the previous line started. To move the cursor back, you can use the LEFT ARROW key. Or if you get into the habit of using the TAB key to start each level of indentation, you can use the SHIFT+TAB combination to move backward one tab stop. (If you've used the

TAB key, you can undo the indentation pattern for a block that you've used by selecting the block of text and then pressing SHIFT+TAB or the equivalent toolbar tools.)

More on For-Next Loops

You don't always count by ones. Sometimes it's necessary to count by twos, by fractions, or backward. You do this by adding the Step keyword to a For-Next loop. The Step keyword tells Visual Basic to change the counter by the specified amount rather than by 1, which is the default. For example, a space simulation program would not be complete without the inclusion, somewhere in the program, of the fragment

```
Dim I As Integer
For I = 10 To 1 Step -1
   Print "It's t minus "; I; " and counting."
Next I
Print "Blastoff!"
```

When you use a negative step, the body of the For-Next loop is bypassed if the starting value for the counter is smaller than the ending value. This is most useful when performing an operation such as deleting items from a list. If you went from 0 to ListCount, at the midpoint, you would run out of items while going from ListCount to 0 while step –1 removes the highest item to the lowest item correctly.

You can use any numeric type for the Step value. For example,

```
For YearlyInterest = .07 To .09 Step .0125
```

begins a loop that moves from 7 percent to 9 percent by ⅛ percent increments.

Nested For-Next Loops

Visual Basic allows you to nest loops essentially to unlimited depths. A fragment such as

```
For J = 2 To 12
   For I = 2 To 12
      Print I%*J%,
   Next I
   Print
Next J
```

gives an entire multiplication table.

The rule for nesting For-Next loops is simple: the inner loop must be completed before the Next statement of the outer loop is encountered.

An Example: The Screen Object and Available Fonts

You can find out the fonts available to the system using a simple For-Next loop to analyze a property of the Screen object. To analyze available fonts, you need two properties of the Screen object. The first is the FontCount property, which gives you the number of available fonts that the printer or screen has available:

```
NumberOfScreenFonts = Screen.FontCount
NumberOfPrinterFonts = Printer.FontCount
```

The second is the Fonts property. Screen.Fonts(0) is the first font for your display, Screen.Fonts(1) is the second, and so on, up to Screen.Fonts (Screen.FontCount –1), which is the last. To run this program, create a new project with a blank form. Add the Click procedure given here, press F5, and then click anywhere in the form.

```
Sub Form_Click()
   Dim I As Integer

   Print "Here is a list of the fonts for your display."
   For I = 0 To Screen.FontCount - 1
      Font.Name = Screen.Fonts(I)
      Print "This is displayed in " ;Screen.Fonts(I)
   Next I
End Sub
```

To report on the fonts that Windows can pull out of your printer, change the keyword Screen to the keyword Printer.

Indeterminate Loops

Loops often need either to keep on repeating an operation or not, depending on the results obtained within the loop. Such loops are indeterminate—that is, not executed a fixed number of times—by their very nature. Use the following pattern when you write this type of loop in Visual Basic:

```
Do
   Visual Basic statements
Until condition is met
```

A simple example of this is a password fragment in a user control:

```
Dim Password As String
Do
   Password = InputBox("Password please?")
Loop Until Password = "YOUR PASSWORD"
End Sub
```

It's important to remember that the test for equality is strict: typing `your password` would not work. Another point to keep in mind is that the test is done only at the end of the loop, when Visual Basic processes the Until statement.

When you write an indeterminate loop, something must change; otherwise, the test will always fail and you'll be stuck in an infinite loop. To stop an infinite loop during design time, you can use the CTRL+BREAK combination or choose Run|End or use the End tool on the toolbar.

The Relational Operators

Of course, you will usually need ways to check for something besides equality. You do this by means of the *relational operators*. The relational operators are listed here.

Table 4-8: Relational Operators

Symbol	Checks (Tests For)
< >	Not equal to
<	Less than
<=	Less than or equal to
>	Greater than
>=	Greater than or equal to

For strings, these operators test for ANSI order. This means that "A" comes before "B," but "B" comes before "a" (and a space comes before any typewriter character). The string "aBCD" comes after the string "CDE" because uppercase letters come before lowercase letters. The ANSI codes from 0 to 31 are for control combinations and include the BACKSPACE and ENTER keys.

Note

You can make all comparisons in the code attached to a form or control case insensitive by putting the statement `Option Compare Text` *in the Declarations section of the form. Use* `Option Compare Binary` *to return to the default method of comparing strings by ANSI order. The* `Option Compare Text` *uses an order determined by the country that was set when you installed Windows.*

The Do While Loop

You can replace the keyword Until with the keyword While in a loop. (You can always change a Do Until into a Do While by reversing the relational operator.) For example,

```
Do
Loop Until X <> " "
```

is the same as

```
Do
Loop While X = " "
```

These loops test at the bottom so they are executed at least once. To do the test at the top (so the loop may not be executed at all), move the While or Until keyword to the top. For example,

```
Do While Text1.Text <> " "
    'process the nonempty text
Loop
```

will not even start working unless the TextBox is non-empty.

Note

There is also a While/Wend construct that is equivalent to the Do While/Loop form.

Loops with And, Or, Not

When you have to combine conditions in a loop, use the Or, Not, and And keywords. These three keywords work just like they do in English. You can continue a process as long as both conditions are True or stop it when one turns False. However, it becomes increasingly confusing to try to force a combination of the And, Or, and Not operators into loops that they don't seem to fit. For example, suppose you want to continue a process while a number is greater than zero and a text box is empty. It is much easier to say

```
Do While Number > 0 And Text1.Text = ""
```

than to say

```
Do Until Number <=0 Or Text1.Text <> ""
```

although they both mean the same thing.

Conditionals—Making Decisions

Obviously, Visual Basic has a way of choosing which statements to process depending on what the state of the program is. This is done with the If-Then-Else construct. For example, to warn a user that a number must be positive, use a line like this:

```
If X < 0 Then MsgBox "Number must be positive!"
```

You can also use the keywords And, Or, and Not in an If-Then. These let you check two conditions at once.

More often than not, you will want to process multiple statements if a condition is True or False. For this you need the most powerful form of the If-Then-Else, called the Block If-Then. This lets you process as many statements as you like in response to a True condition. The Block If-Then looks like this:

```
If thing to test Then
  lots of statements
Else
  more statements
End If
```

For example, consider the code from the NonNegativeIntegerTextBox form in Chapter 1:

```
If KeyAscii < Asc("0") Or KeyAscii > Asc("9") Then
    KeyAscii = 0
    RaiseEvent BadEntry
End If
```

which did two things in response to a bad key press.

When you use the Block If-Then you do not put anything on the line following the keyword Then; press ENTER immediately after typing it. This bare Then is how Visual Basic knows it's beginning a block. The Else is optional; putting it there (again, alone on a line) means that another block will follow, to be processed only if the If clause is False. However, whether the Else is there or not, the Block If must end with the keywords End If.

Example: What is It?

You can easily use If-Then to determine whether the user has entered a string in the form of a date or a number. The procedure depends on the variant data type combined with two Boolean functions. For example, the built-in function IsDate, which is a Boolean function, tells you whether an expression can be converted to a date. Consider the following code that checks whether the contents of a text box are in the right form to be used as a date:

```
Dim DT     ' DT is a variant
DT = Text1.Text
If IsDate(DT) Then
  ' do whatever you want with the date
Else
  MsgBox "Please enter the text in the form of a
    date!"
End If
```

Similarly, you can use the IsNumeric function to determine whether a variable can be converted to a number. This gives you a quick way of checking for extraneous characters in a string of digits.

Note

There are also IsNull *and* IsEmpty *functions to completely determine the state of a variant variable.*

Example: Message Boxes

Using special-purpose message boxes for displaying information is quite common in a Windows application. The MsgBox statement simply pops up the box, use it in a function and you can detect which button the user clicked. For example:

```
If MsgBox('Do you really want to terminate the program?', vbYesNo)_
= vbYes then End;
```

Note

All message boxes are modal so they must be closed before the application will continue. You can also make a message box system modal so the user will not be able to switch to any of the application. (See below for how to do this.)

The general form is:

```
ReturnValue = MsgBox(prompt [, buttons ] [, title] [, HelpFile] _
[, HelpContextID ])
```

The Prompt Parameter is the string or string expression that you want Visual Basic to display as the text in the message box. It is limited to 1024 characters. You can use the carriage return/line feed combination (vbCRLF) to separate lines if necessary. The Title parameter is a string expression that you want displayed in the title bar of the dialog box. (If you omit this parameter, Visual Basic uses the application name.) The HelpFile and HelpConstantID are used to attach help to the message box (see Chapter 6).

The Buttons Parameter determines the type of message box that appears. There are three different groups of symbolic constants that you can add together. (They are separated by rules in the following table.)

Table 4-9:   Symbolic Constants

Symbolic Constant	Value	Result
vbOKOnly	0	Displays OK button only.
vbOKCancel	1	Displays OK and Cancel buttons.
vbAbortRetryIgnore	2	Displays Abort, Retry, and Ignore buttons.
vbYesNoCancel	3	Displays Yes, No, and Cancel buttons.
vbYesNo	4	Displays Yes and No buttons.
vbRetryCancel	5	Displays Retry and Cancel buttons.
vbCritical	16	Displays Critical Message icon .
vbQuestion	32	Displays Warning Query icon.
vbExclamation	48	Displays Warning Message icon.
vbInformation	64	Displays Information Message icon.
vbDefaultButton1	0	Makes the first button the default.
vbDefaultButton2	256	Makes the second button the default.
vbDefaultButton3	512	Makes the third button the default.

For example, if you set the Button parameter to vbYesNoCancel + vbDefaultButton3, you get a message box that looks like Figure 4-4. Notice that the focus is at the Cancel button.

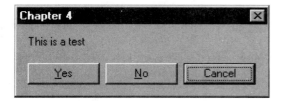

Figure 4-4: A message box at work

Note

If you add a Cancel button to the message box then when the user presses the Esc key, this will have the same effect as if he or she clicked on the Cancel button.

Finally, there is a fourth group of values for the Button parameter that controls the modality of the message box. The default is that the message box is "application modal." This means the user cannot resume working with that application until he or she closes the box. If you add the symbolic constant vbSystemModal (=4096) to the value of the Button parameter, the user will not be able to switch to *any* other application.

As in the simple example given at the start of this section you can test for which button the user clicked. The following table summarizes the return values from the message box. You simply have to test for equality with the appropriate symbolic constant.

Table 4-10:	Return Values from the Message Box	
Symbolic Constant	*Value*	*Button chosen*
vbOK	1	OK
vbCancel	2	Cancel
vbAbort	3	Abort
vbRetry	4	Retry
vbIgnore	5	Ignore
vbYes	6	Yes
vbNo	7	No

Finishing Up with the If-Then

You often need to continue testing within the confines of the original If-Then. This is done with the keywords ElseIf-Then. For example,

```
If Income > 1000000 Then
    Print "Lots of income this year."
ElseIf (Assets + Income) > 2000000 Then
   Print "Income is irrelevant-you're rich."
ElseIf Assets + Income > 1000000 Then
   Print "Need to analyze your income."
Else
   Print "Not rich in any financial way."
End If
```

Now everything is tied together. And just like in the If-Then-Else, Visual Basic activates, at most, one clause and the final Else clause is only activated when all the other cases fail.

Note

A Block If-Then can have essentially as many ElseIf's as you like but only one Else—as the last clause.

Combining the If-Then with Loops

You can use the If-Then to give you a way to write a loop that tests in the middle. For this, you combine the If-Then with a new statement, the Exit Do. Whenever Visual Basic processes the Exit Do statement, it pops you out of the loop, directly to the statement following the keyword Loop.

More generally, Visual Basic allows you to set up a potentially infinite loop at any time; just leave off the tests in a Do loop, an unadorned Do at the top and an equally unadorned Loop at the bottom. Once you've done this, the loop will end only when Visual Basic processes an Exit Do statement. (During program development, you can always end the program prematurely from the Run menu, and you can also use the toolbar or CTRL+BREAK combination.)

Note

There is a version of the Exit *command for leaving a For-Next loop as well; in this case, it takes the form* Exit For.

Select Case

Suppose you were designing a program to compute grades based on the average of four exams. If the average was 90 or higher, the student should get an A; 80 to 89, a B; and so on. This is such a common situation that Visual Basic has another control structure designed exactly for it. It's called the Select Case and is much more flexible than the C/Java equivalent since you can select on any string or numeric expression. To use this command, start with something you want to test.

```
Select Case Average
  Case Is > 90
    Print "A"
  Case Is > 80
    Print "B"
  Case Is > 70
    Print "C"
  Case Else
    Print "You fail"
End Select
```

Users coming from C or Java should note that no break statements are needed because only one clause in a Select statement will be executed.

Using commas allows you give a discrete set of variables and using the keyword To allows you to give a range of values.

```
Select Case YourChoice
   Case 1 To 9
     MsgBox("Usable choice")
   Case -1, 0
     MsgBox("Illegal choice")
End Select
```

The GoTo

The final control structure is, of course, the GoTo. To paraphrase the old joke about split infinitives—modern programmers may be divided into three groups: those who neither know nor care about when they should use the GoTo, those who do not know but seem to care very much, and those who know when to use it.

The most common use of the GoTo statement is for error handling. This is discussed in detail in the section on Error Trapping in Chapter 5.

Routine use of the GoTo leads to spaghetti code: code that is hard to read and harder to debug. On the other hand, there are times when using the GoTo actually makes your code cleaner and easier to understand. In Visual Basic, this situation typically comes up when you are deep inside a nested loop and some condition forces you to leave all the loops simultaneously. You can't use the various forms of the Exit statement because all that does is get you out of the loop you are currently in.

To use a GoTo in Visual Basic, you must label a line. Labels must begin with a letter and end with a colon. They must also start in the first column. You should use as descriptive a label as possible. Here's an example:

```
BadInput:
   'Code we want to process can GoTo here
```

For example, suppose we are using a nested For loop to input data and want to leave the loop if the user enters a 'I am done'.

```
For I = 1 to 10
    For J = 1 to 100
        GetData := InputBox("Data Input", "Enter data,
          ZZZ to end", "")
        If GetData =  "I am done" then
            GoTo BadInput
        Else
            'Process data
        End If
    Next J
Next I
Exit Sub
BadInput:
    MsgBox("Data entry ended at user request")
```

Notice how using an Exit For keyword would be cumbersome here. For
example, it would require extra code in order to break completely out of the
nested loop. Also notice the Exit Sub statement then prevents us from "falling
into" the labeled code.

? "Exit For"
not previously
discussed!

MORE ON VISUAL BASIC'S PROGRAMMING LANGUAGE

Topics in this Chapter

- Arrays
- Types Revisited
- The With Statement
- Enums
- Pointers
- Built-In Functions
- User-Defined Functions and Procedures
- Recursion
- Working with Files
- Working with Running Windows Applications
- The File System Controls
- Sequential Files
- Random-Access Files
- Binary Files
- Sharing Files
- Summary of File-Handling Methods
- Command-Line Information
- Error Trapping

Chapter 5

Chapter 4 showed you the basics of Visual Basic's built-in programming language. This chapter shows you the remaining non-object-oriented features of Visual Basic's language. See Chapters 7 and 8 for Visual Basic's take on object-oriented programming.

First, you'll see a bit more on the type and scope of variables, then a discussion of Visual Basic arrays. Next, there's a brief look at Visual Basic's built-in functions and procedures, including an introduction to using Windows API functions. Following that, there's a section on writing your own functions and procedures. We'll then go a little deeper into the anatomy of a project, illustrating, for example, how to add modules for code alone and true global (Public) code. We end this chapter by showing you how file handling and error trapping are done in Visual Basic.

Arrays

Elements in arrays in Visual Basic are identified by

1. The name of the array
2. The position of the item in the array

In Visual Basic, the name of an array must follow the rules for variable names. For an item in the array, the notation is simply the name of the array followed by a number in parentheses that indicates the position. Array indexes are zero-based by default (the section on Arrays with Index Ranges shows how to go beyond this). For example, the third entry in a string array is accessed via `StringList(2)`.

Arrays can't be open-ended in Visual Basic. While the limits are quite large, you must tell Visual Basic how much memory to set aside for the array before you use it. There are two kinds of arrays in Visual Basic: *fixed arrays*, where the memory allocation never changes; and *dynamic arrays*, where you can change size on the fly. The advantage of a fixed array is that memory is set aside at the beginning of the program; you run a much smaller risk of running out of memory while the program is running. The advantage of dynamic arrays is the flexibility they give. You can change the size in response to what the program has encountered.

Both kinds of arrays may be made visible to the whole application, to a specific form or module, or only within a procedure. To set up a fixed array in the form that will be available to all the procedures in the form or control, place a statement like:

```
Dim Presidents(42) As String
```

in the Declarations section of the form. By default in Visual Basic, this actually sets up a 43-element array for strings visible to every procedure on that form or control. The items would be stored in:

```
Presidents(0), Presidents(1), …, Presidents(42)
```

To set up a dynamic array in a form, place a statement like:

```
Dim Presidents() As String
```

in the Declarations section of the form or control. You then use the ReDim statement inside a procedure to allocate the space:

```
Sub ElectionResults()
' Clinton won so
' set the value of Number
  ReDim Presidents(42) As String
End Sub
```

Note

You can also use the ReDim statement in a procedure without needing a Dim statement in the Declarations section of the form or module first. In this case, the array becomes local to the procedure and space is allocated for that array only while the procedure is active; it disappears as soon as the procedure is exited.

Each time Visual Basic processes a ReDim statement, the information in the array is lost. However, a variation of the ReDim statement can be used to increase the size of a dynamic array while retaining any information already stored in the array. For example, the statement

```
ReDim Preserve NameOfArray(NewSize) As Type
```

can be placed in a procedure to increase the number of entries in the array to `NewSize + 1` without losing data already stored in the array.

Finally, you can set up a local array whose values will be preserved between procedure calls by using the Static keyword. You cannot use a variable inside the parentheses when you do static dimensioning.

Note

Visual Basic has a feature called collections *that can be used as a replacement (and often, an improvement) on arrays. See Chapter 7 for more on the pros and cons of collections and also a way to build "smart arrays" that resize themselves automatically.*

Arrays with Index Ranges

There are two ways to change the bounds used in Visual Basic's arrays:

• The Option Base 1 statement used in the Declarations section of a form (or Standard module; see below) affects all arrays in the form or module. All new arrays dimensioned in that form or module now begin with item number 1. After Option Base 1, Dim Presidents(42) sets aside 42 spots rather than 43.

- Next, Visual Basic allows index ranges in arrays. For example:

```
Dim SalesOfMicrosoft(1986 To 1997)
```

would allow you to store the information about Microsoft's amazing stock growth in an easily accessible form by making the index of the array the same as the year's information being stored. In general, the keyword To marks the range, smaller number first (from 1986 to 1997, in this case), for this way of declaring an array. You can use the To keyword with any statement that declares an array (Dim, ReDim, Static, Private, ReDim Preserve, and so on).and the range can be between any two longs.

Arrays with More than One Dimension

You can also have arrays with more than one dimension; they're usually called *multidimensional arrays*. Just as lists of data lead to a single subscript (one-dimensional arrays), tables of data lead to double subscripts (two-dimensional arrays). For example, suppose you want to store a multiplication table in memory—as a table. You could do this as:

```
Static MultTable(1 To 12,1 To 12) As Integer
Dim I As Integer, J As Integer
For I = 1 To 12
  For J = 1 To 12
    MultTable(I, J) = I*J
  Next J
Next I
```

Visual Basic allows up to 60 dimensions with the Dim statement and 8 with the ReDim statement.

Note

Only the last dimension in a multidimensional array can be changed with Redim Preserve.

Tip

Although you normally use a For-Next loop to iterate through the elements in an array, you can also use the For Each construct whose syntax takes the form:

```
For Each element In the array
    [statements]
    [Exit For]          key word/Phrase   see p 175
    [statements]
Next [element]
```

The advantage is that you need not know the index range for the array. The disadvantage is that this is slower than using the index and you can't be sure of the order in which elements will be accessed. Also, it seems that in the current version of VB you cannot set an array element using the For Each construct but you can read them. Finally, keep in mind when you use this syntax, VB requires the "element" used to iterate in the For Each be a variant even if the array type is not a variant.

The Erase Statement

As your programs grow longer, the possibility that you'll run out of space increases. (Given Visual Basic's rather large limits and Windows 95/NT memory management, it's not likely.) Visual Basic allows you to reclaim the space used by a dynamically dimensioned array. You do this with the Erase command. For example,

```
Erase Presidents
```

would erase the Presidents array and free up the space it occupied. (Note the lack of parenthesis.)

Note

If an array was not dimensioned dynamically (that is, was not dimensioned using the ReDim statement inside a procedure), then the Erase command simply resets all the entries back to zero for numeric arrays, and to the null string for string arrays, or to null for variants. Using the Erase command on a fixed (static) array gives a fast method to "zero out" the entries. (It sets them to the null string for string arrays.)

Variants and Arrays

Variants add a powerful tool to array handling in Visual Basic because you can store an array in a variable of variant type. Some people regard this as a little less than elegant, but since you can't assign one array to another, but you can assign one variant to another, this technique can be very useful. For instance, this gives you a very quick way to swap the contents of two arrays, as the following example shows:

```
Dim I As Integer
ReDim A(1 To 10000) As Long
ReDim B(1 To 10000) As Long
For I = 1 To 10000
  A(I) = I
  B(I) = 5 * I
Next I
Dim Array1 As Variant, Array2 As Variant, Temp As Variant
Array1 = A(): Erase A()
Array2 = B(): Erase B()
Temp = Array1
Array1 = Array2
Array2 = Temp
```

At this point, the variants `Array1` and `Array2` contain the original arrays in reverse order, and the memory for the original arrays has been reclaimed. Since, momentarily, you have two objects instead of one, this technique can be a bit memory-hungry. On the other hand, if you need to swap two arrays, this is a whole lot faster than copying the 10,000 entries one by one (roughly 2.5 times according to our timing tests)!

Note

If you store an array in a variant, use the ordinary index to get it. For example, after you run the above, `Array1(5)` *would have the value* 50?

Occasionally, you need to create an array directly in a variant. Use the Array function whose syntax is:

```
Array(arglist)
```

where the arglist argument consists of an arbitrary list of items separated by commas.

Finally, by using an array of variants you can create the equivalent of non-rectangular arrays or build arrays that combine strings in one row and numbers in another. For example, to build a triangular array of numbers:

```
Dim TriangularArray(1 To 5) As Variant
Dim Row1(1 To 1) As Integer
Dim Row2(1 To 2) As Integer
Dim Row3(1 To 3) As Integer
Dim Row4(1 To 4) As Integer
TriangularArray(1) = Row1()
TriangularArray(2) = Row2()
'and so on
```

Types Revisited

Since variant variables make it easy to avoid dealing with explicit variable types, some programmers, reveling in their freedom from strongly typed languages, are tempted to use them for everything. Most experienced Visual Basic programmers feel this should be avoided. Using variant variables when their special properties are not needed exacts a performance penalty and will, occasionally, lead to subtle bugs. (For example, any variant takes 16 bytes to store—regardless of the type of the data.) It is usually better for the programmer to be in control of the type of his or her variables.

There are, of course, times when variants are useful. You saw how they can be used with arrays to quickly swap the contents of two arrays, and you have seen how useful the built-in IsDate and IsNumeric functions are.

Tip

Using the VarType function combined with an If-Then gives you a way to go beyond the built-in IsDate, IsNumeric functions to build your own IsCurrency function, IsBoolean function, and so on. (Variants can hold any Standard data type except fixed-length strings.)

User-Defined Types

Suppose you want to have a three-dimensional array for employees in a company. The first column is for names, the second for salaries, and the third for social security numbers. This common situation can't be programmed in a multidimensional array except using the variant data type. The problem is that variants use more memory and are slower. For both speed and memory reasons, one (non-object-oriented) idea is to set up three parallel lists—the first for names, the second for salaries, and the third for social security numbers. Having done this, you now would use the same pointer (that is, the row number) to extract information from the three lists.

Traditionally, structured data is not stored in parallel lists but rather in a *user-defined type*. (These are sometimes called *records* or *UDTs*.) Essentially, a record is a type of mixed variable that you create as needed. It usually mixes different kinds of numbers and strings.

Here's the first step: In the Declarations section of the form, enter

```
Type   EmployeeInfo
      Name As String
      Salary As Long
      SocialSecNumber as String
End Type
```

This defines the type. Each of the different parts of the record is called a *field*. From this point on, EmployeeInfo can be treated like any other data type such as single-precision, double-precision, variants, and so on.

Note

User-defined types must be declared Private or Friend (see Chapters 7 and 8) in all Visual Basic component types except code modules. To do this, prefix your declaration with the word "Private" or "Friend."

Now, to set up a variable or an array of "type" EmployeeInfo, all you have to do is declare it using one of Dim, Private, Static ReDim, and so on.

```
Dim YourName As EmployeeInfo
Static YourFriend As EmployeeInfo
ReDim MyNames(1 To 100) As EmployeeInfo 'array of
                                        '100 records
```

To fill the type, you assign values to the various fields using the '.' you have seen for properties:

```
YourName.Name = "Howard"
YourName.Salary = 100000
YourName.SocSecNumber = "036-78-9987"
```

> **Note**
>
> *Because user-defined types are restricted in what they can do in the construction of Visual Basic objects (see Chapter 7), they are often replaced by a user-defined object in VB5.*

The With Statement

You can use the With statement as a convenient method for quickly getting at the parts of a user-defined type. For example,

```
With YourName
   .Name = "Howard"
   .Salary = 100000
   .SocSecNumber = "036-78-9987"
End With
```

lets you avoid some typing and is more efficient.

You can also use the With statement to get at the properties of objects. For example:

```
With txtBox
   .Height = 2000
   .Width = 2000
   .Text = "This is a text box"
End With
```

With statements can be nested if an object has a subobject as a property or VDT. For example:

```
With txtBox
   .Height = 200
   With .Font
      .Bold = True
      .Italic = False
   End With
End With
```

Enums

The newest data type in Visual Basic is the *enum,* which stands for enumerated type. An enum is useful when you want a way to associate constants to a set of related data. For example, it might be convenient to have Sunday associated to 1, Monday to 2, and so on. Enums are also necessary when giving your control properties analogous to BorderStyle—that is, properties with only a fixed number of possibilities. Here's an example of how to declare an enum.

```
Private Enum DaysOfTheWeek
   Sunday = 1
   Monday
   Tuesday
   Wednesday
   Thursday
   Friday
   Saturday
End Enum
```

This would associate the number 1 to Sunday, the number 2 (automatically) to Monday, and so on. You could use this enum in code like this:

```
Dim ComdexWeek As DaysOfTheWeek
ArrivalDate =Tuesday
If ArrivalDate < Monday Then MsgBox("You missed the
   first day.")
```

The point is that Visual Basic automatically and transparently makes the conversion of a variable declared to be an enum of type DaysOfTheWeek to a value, so the If-Then in the above code makes perfect sense. (By the way, once you set up an enum and a variable of that type, Visual Basic automatically (!) displays the constants used in the enum in the IntelliSense List members box.)

Note

The starting value for an enum can be any long integer. If you leave out the starting value, it defaults to 0.

Pointers

There aren't any pointers in the traditional sense of getting directly at memory locations where structured data is stored. So the question is how to imitate them if you need to create data structures like linked lists or trees that use them. There is no perfect solution because you will need to go through some contortions to dispose of the memory allocated.

One way to create analogues to pointers in Visual Basic is to create an array of records and use one or more of the fields in the record to hold the row of the next item. (See Chapter 7 for another way that is a bit slicker and ultimately more powerful, and Chapter 11 for an implementation of linked lists and binary trees using this method.)

If you choose this approach, you need to keep on using ReDim Preserve to build up the object and assign the memory. For example, if you wanted to create a binary tree,

```
Type DataInBinaryTree
   Data As String
   LeftChild As Integer      'row where left child is
   RightChild As Integer     'row where right child is
End Type
```

In this example, the two fields LeftChild and RightChild act as pointers to the row containing the child. To build the tree, for example, you start with an array of records of this type of size 1.

```
ReDim Data(1 To 1) As DataInBinaryTree
```

Each time you need to enter the next item, you have to:

1. Update the counter of the number of items.
2. Use ReDim Preserve to enlarge the array of records.
3. Fill in the "pointer" rows as needed (use a –1 for a pointer to Null).

Note

The only way to reclaim memory from these imitation pointers is to copy the array of records to a new array of records (or a variant)—after eliminating the entry you want to remove.

Built-In Functions

There are hundreds of functions built into Visual Basic. The information about the most common functions is summarized in the three tables that follow. Table 5-1 gives short descriptions of the most common functions that do not have to do with date, time, or string information. Table 5-2 provides short descriptions about the string functions, and Table 5-3 provides information about the date/time functions.

Table 5-1:   Common Functions

Function	Purpose
Abs	Finds the absolute value of a number.
Atn	Finds the arctangent.
Cos	Finds the cosine.
Exp	Raises e (2.7182 . . .) to the given power.
Fix	Returns the integer part of a number.
FV	Future value.
Hex	Gives the hex equivalent.
Int	Returns the integer portion of a number.
Ipmt	Interest paid over time.
IRR	Internal rate of return.
Log	Common logarithm.
MIRR	Modified internal rate of return.
Nper	Time to accumulate (disburse) an annuity.
NPV	Net present value.
Pmt	Pay out for an annuity.
Ppmt	Returns the principal paid out in an annuity payment.
PV	Present value.
Rate	Interest rate per period for an annuity.
Rnd	Calls the random number generator.
Sgn	Returns an integer indicating the sign of a number.
Sin	Returns the sine of the number.
SLN	Straight-line depreciation.

Function	*Purpose*
Sqr	The square root function.
SYD	Sum of years depreciation.
Tan	The tangent of an angle in radians.
Timer	Returns the number of seconds since midnight.

Table 5-2: The Most Common String Functions

Function	*Description*
Asc	Returns the character code corresponding to the first letter in a string.
InStr	Returns the position of the first occurrence of one string within another.
Lcase	Converts a string to lowercase.
Left	Finds or removes a specified number of characters from the beginning of a string.
Len	Gives the length of a string.
Ltrim	Removes spaces from the beginning of a string.
Mid	Finds or removes characters from a string.
Right	Finds or removes a specified number of characters from the end of a string.
Rtrim	Removes spaces from the end of a string.
Str	Returns the string equivalent of a number (the numeral).
StrComp	Another way to do string comparisons.
StrConv	Converts a string from one form to another.
String	Returns a repeated string of identical characters.
Trim	Trims spaces from both the beginning and end of a string.
Ucase	Converts a string to uppercase.

Note

Most of the string functions have a form with the $ (for example Mid$, Left$). These versions return true strings rather than strings inside variants as the ones in Table 5-2 would. For this reason, they will run faster and should be used when time is of the essence.

Table 5-3 gives you the functions for handling date and times.

Table 5-3:	The Date/Time Functions
Function	*Description*
Date	Returns the current date (what is shown in the system clock).
DateAdd	Lets you add a specified interval to a date.
DateDiff	Lets you subtract a specified interval from a date.
DateSerial	Returns a date corresponding to the specified day, month, and year.
DateValue	Takes a string and returns a date.
Day	Tells you what day a string or number represents.
Hour	Tells you what hour a string or number represents.
Minute	Tells you what minute a string or number represents.
Month	Tells you what month a string or number represents.
Now	Returns the current time and date.
Second	Tells you what second a string or number represents.
Time	Tells you the current time in the system clock.
TimeSerial	Returns a variable of date type for the given time.
Weekday	Tells you what day of the week a date corresponds to.
Year	Tells you what year a date corresponds to.

The Logical Operators on the Bit Level

The logical operators (Not, And, Or, and so on) are really functions that work on the bit (binary-digit) level. Suppose you are given two integers, X and Y. Then X And Y make a binary digit 1 only if both binary digits are 1; otherwise, the result is zero. For example, if

X = 7 in decimal   = 0111 in binary

Y = 12 in decimal   = 1100 in binary

then X And Y = 0100 in binary (4 in decimal) because only in the third position are both bits 1. Because And gives a 1 only if both digits are 1, Anding with a number whose binary digit is a single 1 and whose remaining digits are all zero lets you isolate the binary digits of any integer.

For example,

X And 1	Tells you whether the least significant (right-most) binary digit is on. You get a zero if it is not on.
X And 2	Since 2 in decimal is 10 in binary, a zero tells you that the next significant (second from the right) binary digit is off.
X And 255	Since 255 = 11111111, this gives you the low order byte.
X And 65280 =	Since 65280 = 1111111100000000, this would give you the high order bit.

X And $(2^{\wedge}32 - 1 - 255)$

This process is usually called *masking* and is often needed when using the KeyUp, KeyDown event procedures for a control on a form or user control.

User-Defined Functions and Procedures

In Visual Basic, the distinction is that functions can return values and procedures cannot. (We, like many people, use the term *subprogram* if we want to refer to both at the same time.) To add a user-defined subprogram to the current form:

1. Open the Code window by double-clicking anywhere in the form or by pressing F7.
2. Choose Tools|Add Procedure.

The Add Procedure dialog box will pop up, as shown in Figure 5-1.

Set the option button to the type of procedure you want. (For Property procedures, see Chapter 7; for Event procedures, see Chapters 7 and 13.) The Public/Private buttons control the scope of the subprogram—see the section on Standard modules that follows. Once you enter the name, click on OK, and a template for the procedure or function pops up.

Tip

You can also start a new procedure by typing the keyword Function or the keyword Sub followed by the name of the procedure anywhere in the code window and then pressing ENTER or the DOWN ARROW. (Obviously, do this outside an existing Sub or Function.)

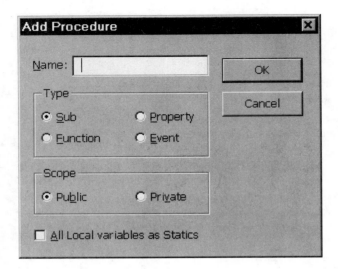

Figure 5-1   The Add Procedure dialog box

Functions

Suppose you want to write a function that would allow you to chop out any substring. To do this, we use Instr to find out where the string is and then use Right, Left, and Mid to do the cutting. Here's the function:

where?

```
Function sCutItOut (sTarget As String, sWhatToCut As _
String) As String
    'local variables
    Dim nPlace As Integer, nLength As Integer

    nPlace = Instr(sTarget, sWhatTOCut)
    nLength = Len(sWhatToCut)
    If nPlace = 0 Then
        sCutItOut = sTarget
    Else
        sCutItOut = Left(sTarget, nPlace-1) & Mid(sTarget, _
        nPlace+nLength)
    End If
End Function
```

?

?

The general form of a Function definition is as follows:

```
Function FunctionName(argument1, argument2, ...) As Type
    statements
    FunctionName = expression
End Function
```

where argument1, argument2 are variables (usually declared as being of a certain type, as in this example). The first line is usually called the *function header*. Function names must follow the same rules as variable names. Visual Basic defaults to sending a memory location, and not a copy of the value (passing by reference); any changes you make to the arguments inside the body of the function will persist.

When you use a function, Visual Basic executes the statements in the function definition; the last value assigned to FunctionName inside the body of the function definition is the one used for the statement involving the FunctionName (argument1, argument2, . . .). The argument entries argument1, argument2, and so on, can be constants, variables, or expressions.

Note

Although you usually use the return value of a function, Visual Basic allows you to simply call a function for its side effects with a statement like:

```
FunctionName (arg1, arg2, arg3)
```

You can usually call a function only when you use the same number of arguments as there are parameters in the function definition. The types must be compatible as well. Visual Basic allows you to create your own subprograms with optional, or a varying number of, arguments. More information is given later in the chapter.

Sub Procedures

The tradition is to use a Sub procedure when you do not want to return a single value. A Sub procedure must have a header that gives its arguments and takes the form

```
Sub SubprocedureName(argument1, argument2, ...)
    statement(s)
End Sub
```

When Visual Basic executes statements of the form

```
SubprocedureName argument1, argument2,...
```

or

```
Call SubprocedureName (argument1, argument2, ...)
```

it passes the memory locations of the data stored in the arguments and executes the code in the body of the procedure. [By the way, these two different conventions for calling procedures can be very frustrating for people coming from other languages. A C programmer, by nature, uses parens and forgets to use a call (or forgets to not use parens), and then beats his or her head against the wall trying to figure out why there are errors calling the sub.]

Caution

Since Visual Basic defaults to sending a memory location and not a value (passing by reference), any changes you make to the parameters inside the body of the procedure will be preserved.

When the End Sub statement is reached, execution continues with the line following the call to the Sub procedure.

Passing by Reference/Passing by Value

There are two ways to pass a variable argument to a procedure or function: passing by value and passing by reference. The default in Visual Basic is to pass information by reference. When an argument variable in a subprogram is passed by reference, any changes to the corresponding parameter inside the procedure will change the value of the original argument when the procedure finishes. When passed by value, the argument variable retains its original value after the procedure terminates—regardless of what was done to the corresponding parameter inside the procedure. Arguments to functions and procedures are always passed by reference unless they are surrounded by an extra pair of parentheses or the ByVal keyword is used in declaring the function or subprogram.

Note

Some programmers like to use the ByRef keyword to indicate that a variable is being passed by reference; however, this is the default behavior and ByRef isn't needed.

Leaving Functions or Procedures Prematurely

You don't have to give every function an explicit value. Sometimes you are forced to exit a function prematurely.

```
Function BailOut (X) As Single
   If X < 0 Then
     Exit Function
   Else
   .
   .
   End If
End Function
```

Use Exit Sub to leave a procedure prematurely. When you leave a function prematurely, it has the last assigned value or the appropriate default value as its return value.

Using Arrays with Procedures

Visual Basic has an extraordinary facility to use both one and multidimensional arrays in procedures and functions. It's easy to send any size array to a subprogram. To send an array parameter to a procedure or function, type the name of the array and include the open parenthesis. For example, assume that DoubleList is a one-dimensional array of double-precision variables. StringArray is a two-dimensional string array, and BigIntegerArray is a three-dimensional array of integers. Then,

```
Sub Example(DoubleList(), StringArray(), _
BigIntegerArray(), X As Integer)
```

would allow this Example procedure to use (and change) an array of double-precision variables, an array of strings, a three-dimensional array of integers, and a final integer variable. Note that just as with variable parameters, array parameters are placeholders; they have no independent existence.

Visual Basic makes this process of dealing with arrays as parameters more practical by including the functions LBound and UBound. LBound gives the lowest possible index and UBound, the highest in an array. For example, you can easily write the following function to find the maximum element in an array.

Listing 5-1:   Function to Find the Maximum Element in an Array

```
Function FindMax(A() As Integer)
  ' local variables nStart, nFinish, I
  Dim nStart As Integer, nFinish As Integer
  Dim nMax As Integer, I As Integer

  nStart = LBound(A)
  nFinish = UBound(A)
  nMax = A(nStart)
  For I = nStart  To nFinish
    If A(I) > nMax Then nMax = A(I)
  Next I
  FindMax = nMax
End Function
```

In general, LBound(*NameOfArray, I*), UBound(*NameOfArray, I*) gives the lower and upper bound for the I'th dimension. For a list (one-dimensional array), the I is optional, as in the preceding example.

For a more serious example of using arrays in procedures, here is the code for a Shell sort, which is one of the best general-purpose sorts for medium-sized arrays.

Listing 5-2:   Shell Sort

```
Public Sub ShellSort(AnArray() As Variant)
  'LOCAL variables are NumOfEntries, Increm, J, Temp
  Dim NumOfEntries As Integer, Increm As Integer, J, Temp
  Dim I As Integer, J As Integer
  Dim BotIndex As Integer, TopIndex As Integer
  BotIndex = LBound(AnArray)
  TopIndex = UBound(AnArray)
  NumOfEntries = TopIndex - BotIndex + 1
  Increm = NumOfEntries \ 2
  Do Until Increm < 1
    For i = Increm + BotIndex To TopIndex
      Temp = AnArray(i)
      For J = i - Increm To BotIndex Step -Increm
        If Temp >= AnArray(J) Then Exit For
        AnArray(J + Increm) = AnArray(J)
      Next J
```

```
        AnArray(J + Increm) = Temp
     Next i
     Increm = Increm \ 2
   Loop
End Sub
```

Note

We used the simplest possible increments (powers of 2) for our implementation. Better sequences, such as 1, 4, 13, 40...are known.

Subprograms with a Variable or Optional Number of Arguments

Visual Basic permits you to have optional arguments in functions and procedures you define yourself. Unlike in Visual Basic 4, optional arguments can be of any type. They still must be the last arguments in a function or procedure. For example, you might have a Sub procedure whose header looks like this:

```
Sub ProcessAddress(Name As String, Address As _
String, City As String, State As String, ZipCode _
As String, Optional ZipPlus4 As String)
```

In this case, the last argument (for a ZipPlus4 code) is optional.

Note

You can have as many optional arguments as you want. They simply must be listed after all the required arguments in the procedure (or function) declaration.

You can also specify a default value for any optional argument, as in the following example:

```
Sub ProcessAddress(Name As String, Address As _
String, City As String, State As String, ZipCode _
As String, Optional ZipPlus4 As String = "0000")
```

which makes the default ZipPlus4 value equal to "0000."

You can also have procedures and functions that accept an arbitrary number of arguments. For this, use the ParamArray keyword with an array of variants, as in the following example:

```
Function AddThemUp(ParamArray VariantNumbers()) As Single
   Dim Total As Single
   Dim Number As Variant
   For Each Number in VariantNumbers()
     Total = Total + Number
   Next
   AddThemUp = Total
End Function
```

Named Arguments

The InputBox function that you have already seen is one of the many Visual Basic built-in functions that supports something called *named arguments*. Named arguments give you a more elegant way of dealing with functions that have many parameters.

Note

Only functions from the Visual Basic for Applications library and user-defined functions support named arguments. As mentioned previously, arguments that can be named show up in bold italic in IntelliSense's QuickInfo feature.

Here's an example of using an InputBox function with named arguments:

```
MyInput   = InputBox(prompt:="Example", _
Default:= "Default string", xpos:=100, ypos:=200)
```

In general, as this example shows, named arguments use a **:=** (colon plus an equal sign), together with the name of the argument. (While the spelling of the argument must match perfectly, case is irrelevant.) Like any argument, you separate named arguments from each other by a comma.

The neat thing about VB5 is that any functions or procedures you create automatically have named arguments. If you are careful when selecting parameter names, using named arguments can be a useful tool to make your code easier to read. This is especially true if you use optional arguments a lot.

Note

Even with named arguments, you can still only omit optional arguments.

Recursion

Recursion is a general method of solving problems by reducing them to simpler problems of a similar type. The general framework for a recursive solution to a problem looks like this:

```
Solve recursively (problem)
  If the problem is trivial, do the obvious
  Simplify the problem
 Solve recursively (simpler problem)
 (Possibly) combine the solution to the simpler
    problem(s) into a solution of the original
    problem
```

A recursive subprogram constantly calls itself, each time in a simpler situation, until it gets to the trivial case, at which point it stops. For the experienced programmer, thinking recursively presents a unique perspective on certain problems, often leading to particularly elegant solutions and, therefore, equally elegant programs. (For example, most fast sorts such as QuickSort are recursive.)

For Visual Basic programmers, besides sorting routines, one common use of recursion is when you need to deal with the subdirectory structure of a disk. For example, if you wanted to delete a file but didn't know where it was, you would need to search on deeper and deeper subdirectories until you had exhausted all the subdirectories on that disk. (See the end of this chapter for the code for a recursive directory search.) For a Web-specific example of recursion, consider the procedure by which a Web crawler searches all the URLs available from a given site.

There are actually two types of recursion possible and both are supported in Visual Basic. The first is where the subprogram only calls itself. This is called *direct recursion*. Using direct recursion in Visual Basic is simple. Call the subprogram the way you would call any subprogram. The second type is called, naturally enough, *indirect recursion*. This occurs, for example, when a subprogram calls another subprogram, which, in turn, calls the first subprogram.

As an example, let's look at the greatest common divisor (GCD) of two integers. (For those who have forgotten their high school mathematics, this is defined as the largest number that divides both of them. It's used when you need to add fractions.) Therefore:

- GCD(4,6) = 2 (because 2 is the largest number that divides both 4 and 6)

- GCD(12,7) = 1 (because no integer greater than 1 divides both 12 and 7)

Around 2,000 years ago, Euclid gave the following method of computing the GCD of two integers, a and b:

- If b divides a, then the GCD is b. Otherwise, GCD(a,b) = GCD(b, a mod b)

(Recall that the mod function gives the remainder after integer division.) For example,

GCD(126, 12) = GCD(12, 126 mod 12) = GCD(12, 6) = 6

Here's the code for a recursive GCD function:

```
Function GCD (P as Long, Q As Long) As Long
  If Q mod P = 0 Then
    GCD = P
  else
    GCD = GCD(Q, P mod Q)
  End If
End Function
```

Here, the pattern is to first take care of the trivial case. If you are not in the trivial case, then the code reduces it to a simpler case, because the mod function leads to smaller numbers. (In this example, there is no need to combine results as there would be in, say, a sorting routine.)

Here's the code for a recursive QuickSort that works with variant arrays. Like most naïve versions of QuickSort, the one we give you here doesn't work very well with arrays that are not randomly arranged.

Listing 5-3:   Recursive QuickSort

```
Sub QuickSort (AnArray(), Start As Integer, Finish As Integer)
  'Local variable PosOfSplitter
  Dim PosOfSplitter As Integer

  If Finish > Start Then
    Partition AnArray(), Start, Finish, PosOfSplitter
    QuickSort AnArray(), Start, PosOfSplitter - 1
    QuickSort AnArray(), PosOfSplitter + 1, Finish
  End If
End Sub
```

```
Sub Partition (AnArray(), Start As Integer, Finish As Integer,_
LocOfSplitter As Integer)
' LOCAL variables are: SplitPos,NewStart,I,Splitter
Dim SplitPos As Integer, NewStart As Integer
Dim I As Integer, Splitter

  SplitPos = (start + finish) \ 2
  Splitter = AnArray(SplitPos)
  SWAP AnArray(SplitPos), AnArray(start) 'get it out of the way
  LeftPos = start                        'needs to be written!
     For I = start + 1 To finish
        If AnArray(i) < Splitter Then
           LeftPos = LeftPos + 1
           SWAP AnArray(LeftPos), AnArray(i)
        End If
     Next i
  SWAP AnArray(start), AnArray(LeftPos) 'LeftPos marks the
                                        'hole
  LocOfSplitter = LeftPos         'This gets passed
End Sub                           'to the original procedure

Sub SWAP(foo,bar)
  temp = foo
  foo = bar
  bar = temp
End Sub
```

Standard (Code) Modules

A Standard (code) module is the place where you put code that you want to be accessible to all code in a project. Standard modules have no visual components. Add a new Standard module by choosing Project|Add Module; add an existing one by using Project|Add File. The convention is that Standard modules have a .bas extension.

The Code window for a Standard module looks much like the Code window attached to a form or control. You can have two types of declarations for variables in the General section of a Standard module:

- For variables visible only to procedures in the Standard module.
- For variables you want visible everywhere in the project.

For the former, use the Private keyword; for the latter, the Public keyword.

```
Private LocalToStandardModule As Integer
Public GlobalToProject As Integer
```

Of course, just as form-level declarations can be superseded by declarations in procedures, public (global) declarations will be superseded by declaring a form- or procedural-level variable.

The Sub and Function procedures in code modules default so that they are available to the whole project. For example, a Standard module attached to the user control form would be usable by all the code in the control. A Standard module attached to a test project could be used by all the forms in the test project. To make subprogram code available only to the code in the Standard module, you must use the Private keyword before the subprogram header. (It is a good idea to use the Public keyword even if, strictly speaking, it isn't needed.) For example:

```
Private ALocalProcedure (Foo As Variant)
Public AGlobalProcedure(Foo As Variant)
```

When you use a Sub or Function procedure inside another procedure, Visual Basic follows very simple steps to determine where to look for it.

1. Visual Basic first looks at procedures attached to the current form or module.
2. If the procedure is not found in the current form or module, Visual Basic looks at all code modules attached to the project.

The second of these options explains why the name of a procedure must be unique throughout all code modules. On the other hand, you can have the same procedure name attached to two different forms; otherwise, forms could not have their own Form_Load procedures.

The DoEvents Function

Usually, you want Windows (and Visual Basic) to constantly monitor the environment for events to respond to. On the other hand, there can be a lot of idle time that you can use, for example, to do time-consuming numeric calculations or sorts. However, you don't want a Visual Basic application to stop responding to events completely. This is something you may want to do when you write a procedure that wastes time, as you saw earlier in this chapter. Obviously, you need a way to tell Visual Basic to periodically respond to events in the environment and return to the calculation when nothing else needs to be done.

The function that does this is called DoEvents. Whenever Visual Basic processes a statement containing this function, it releases control to the Windows operating system to process all the events that have occurred. (Windows keeps track of events in an events queue, and keypresses in the SendKeys queue.) Obviously, you should not use the DoEvents function inside an event procedure if it is possible to re-enter the same event procedure again. For example, a Click event procedure may be called again by the user's clicking the mouse. If you forget about this possibility, your program may be caught in an infinite regression.

Note

The DoEvents function actually gives you the number of forms loaded for the application. Also, DoEvents is needed less for true 32-bit programs, since Windows 95 and NT both do pre-emptive multitasking (see Chapter 14).

First Steps in Using the Windows API

Microsoft Windows consists of libraries of many hundreds of specialized functions. These are called Application Programming Interface (API) functions. Most of the time, VB is rich enough in functionality that you don't need to bother with API functions. But some tasks, like rebooting the user's computer, cannot be done with Visual Basic code. This section introduces API calls; Chapter 12 covers the remaining API calls that VB programmers use on a day-to-day basis.

Note

If you use API functions carelessly, your system may lock up and require you to reboot. You should have the "Save before run" option set when experimenting with API functions.

Another problem is that API functions are cumbersome to use and often require a fair amount of work before the information is usable by your Visual Basic program.

Before using a DLL function within a Visual Basic program, you must add a special declaration to the Declarations section of your code window. For example, if you need to put a control to "sleep" for a while, you would use the Windows API Sleep function. To use this, place the following statement in the Declarations section:

```
Private Declare Sub Sleep Lib "kernel32" _
(ByVal dwMilliseconds As Long)
```

This tells Visual Basic that you will be using the Windows API function Sleep, which is contained in the kernel32 library (Lib stands for library). Since this is a Sub, it doesn't return a value; all you need to do is give it the time to sleep in milliseconds (so 1 second requires passing this API function a value of 1000).

Here's an amusing (if potentially nasty) example of using this API function in a control. Simply add a text box to a user control and use the following code:

```
Private Declare Sub Sleep Lib "kernel32" _
(ByVal dwMilliseconds As Long)

Private Sub Text1_KeyPress(KeyAscii As Integer)
  Sleep (1000) 'wait one second to process keystroke
End Sub
```

This control is guaranteed to drive your users nuts. It will look like an ordinary text box, but every time the user types there will be an agonizing wait of one second before the character appears!

Many of the Windows APIs are functions that return values, using bit masking to tease out the needed information. An example of this is the GetVersion API that returns a long integer that contains information about what version of Windows the user is running.

```
Declare Function GetVersion Lib "kernel32" () As Long
```

The low order byte (i.e., use And with 255) gives the version number as the following amusing example shows (using a Standard EXE).

```
Private Declare Function GetVersion Lib "kernel32" _
() As Long
Private Sub Form_Click()
  Dim WinVersion As Long
  WinVersion = GetVersion() And 255
  Print "Did you know that Microsoft's API says
    Windows 95 is really Windows " & WinVersion
End Sub
```

Note

It is extremely important that the Declare statement for an API function be exactly as Windows expects. Leaving off a ByVal keyword will almost certainly lock your system. Also, names of functions in a 32-bit dynamic-link library (DLL) are case-sensitive, unlike those in the 16-bit version.

Caution

Using an API call means you will have compatibility problems whenever platforms differ in their support for that API function.

Mixed-Language Programming

Using a DLL created with another language such as C is similar to using one of the Windows DLLs. You will need to use a Declare statement to tell Visual Basic about the function you want to use.

Note

Most DLLs expect the values to be passed by value (ByVal) rather than by reference (ByRef). The one usual exception is arrays that are passed by reference.

The full syntax for the Declare statement looks like this for a Sub program in a DLL (one that doesn't return a value):

```
[Public | Private ] Declare Sub name Lib "libname" [Alias " _
aliasname" ][([arglist])]
```

For a function (something that returns a value), use:

```
[Public | Private ] Declare Function name Lib "libname" [Alias " _
aliasname" ] [([arglist])][As type]
```

Most of the elements in a Declare statement (Public, Private, and so on) should be familiar to you. For the new ones, the Lib argument is just book-keeping—it tells Visual Basic that a DLL is being called. The Libname argument is the name of the DLL that contains the procedure you will be calling. The Alias keyword is used when the procedure has another name in the DLL but you don't (or can't) use it (probably because it conflicts with some reserved word in Visual Basic itself). The Aliasname argument is then the name of the procedure in the DLL. The Alias is what you will call it in Visual Basic.

Table 5-4 gives a list of the most common C types, their Windows equivalent, and what you would use in a Visual Basic Declare statement.

Table 5-4: Visual Basic Equivalents for C Types in Declare Statements		
Window Type	*C Type*	*Visual Basic Declare Type*
BOOL	int	ByVal Boolean
BYTE	unsigned char	ByVal Byte
WORD	unsigned int	ByVal Integer
DWORD	unsigned long	ByVal Long
LPSTR	char far*	ByVal String
HANDLE	WORD	ByVal Long
HWND	HANDLE	ByVal Long
HDC	HANDLE	ByVal Long

Working with Files

Visual Basic comes with various functions and methods that interact directly with the underlying file system, the following table summarizes the most useful of these commands that do not deal with reading or writing to an individual file.

Table 5-5: File Commands	
Command	*Function*
ChDir	Changes the default directory.
ChDrive	Changes the logged drive.
GetAttr	Gets attribute information for a file.

Command	*Function*
FileCopy source, destination	Copies a file from the source directory to the target directory.
FileDateTime (pathname)	Returns the date and time a file was created.
FileLen	Returns the length of the file in bytes.
GetAttr	Gets attribute information about the file.
Kill	Deletes a file.
MkDir	Makes a new directory.
Name	Changes the name of a file or moves a file from one directory to another on the same drive.
RmDir	Removes a directory.
SetAttr	Sets attribute information for a file.

As with Windows itself, none of these commands are case sensitive nor is case important in the string you use with them. For example:

```
ChDir "C:\My Documents\Books"
```

changes the current directly to the Books subdirectory of C:\My Documents.

Next, note that as the preceding table indicates, the Name statement can do more than the old DOS REN command; it can copy files from one directory to another directory *on the same drive*. To do this, give the full path name. For example,

```
Name "C:\VB\Sample1.frm" As "C:\EXAMPLES\Sample2.frm"
```

moves the Sample1.frm file from the C:\VB directory to one named C:\EXAMPLES and renames it to be Sample2.frm. As with any file handling function, VB will generate a run-time error if the underlying operating system cannot do what you ask. (See Table 5-11 in the section on "Error Trapping" later in this chapter for a list of the common error codes for file handling.)

Finally, the Kill function accepts wild cards, Name and FileCopy do not. For example:

```
Kill "*.*"
```

deletes all the files in the current directory (not to be done casually!).

Note

VB programmers are not often aware of it but although Windows (and so VB) is not case sensitive for file names it is case retentive. This means Windows does retain the case you use to set the filename up or use with the Name command. This allows programs like Java that are case sensitive for file names to drive VB programmers nuts until they get used to them.

File Attributes

Knowing the various attributes that a file has associated to it is occasionally extremely useful; the GetAttr function returns an integer that encapsulates this information. By using masking techniques to get at the individual bits of this integer, you can determine how the various attributes are set. The following table summarizes the values for the attributes.

Table 5-6: File Attribute Constants

Attribute	*Constant*	*Value*
Normal	vbNormal	0
Read Only	vbReadonly	1
Hidden	vbHidden	2
System	vbSystem	4
Volume	vbVolume	8
Directory	vbDirectory	16
Archive	vbArchive	32

For example, if

```
GetAttrib(FileName) = vbReadOnly + vbHidden  'or just 3
```

then the file is hidden and read-only.

You can also change the attributes of a file directly from VB using the SetAttr function. This function uses the same constants as in Table 5-6 above except, of course, you can't set the volume or directory attributes.

```
SetAttr FileName, attributes
```

For example:

```
SetAttr FileName, vbHidden+ vbReadOnly
```

would hide the file and set it as read-only.

Example: Getting File Info

The following function is one you may find useful. It takes a file name and returns a string that tells you everything you could possibly want to know about the file. The idea used in the code is straightforward: We run through the various possible functions and attributes, adding this information to a string. When we have finished we return the string as the value of the function.

Listing 5-4:   Getting File Info

```
Public Function ReturnInfo(sFileName) As String
   Dim sFile As String
   Dim sTmp As String
   Dim nAttrib As Integer

   sFile = sFileName
   nAttrib = GetAttr(sFile)
   sTmp = sFile & vbCrLf & vbCrLf
   sTmp = sTmp & "Date/Time: " & FileDateTime(sFile) & vbCrLf
   sTmp = sTmp & "Size: " & FileLen(sFile) & " bytes" & vbCrLf
   If (nAttrib And vbReadOnly) = vbReadOnly Then
      sTmp = sTmp & "ReadOnly: X" & vbCrLf
   End If
   If (nAttrib And vbHidden) = vbHidden Then
      sTmp = sTmp & "Hidden: X" & vbCrLf
   End If
   If (nAttrib And vbSystem) = vbSystem Then
      sTmp = sTmp & "System: X" & vbCrLf
   End If
   If (nAttrib And vbArchive) = vbArchive Then
      sTmp = sTmp & "Archive: X" & vbCrLf
   End If
   ReturnInfo = sTmp
End Function
```

(We use this function in the recursive directory search program that you will soon see.)

The Dir Function

This useful function returns the name of a file, directory, or folder that matches a specified pattern or file attribute, or the volume label of a drive or the
empty string if nothing that matches the pattern can be found. For example:

```
Dir$("*.txt")
```

returns a file with the .txt extension in the current directory (or the null string
if one doesn't exist). The full syntax for the Dir$ function is:

```
Dir$[(pathname[, attributes])]
```

where as you might expect the pathname is a string expression that specifies
a file name. You can use both the * and ? DOS wildcards in the pathname. As
indicated by the square brackets, the attributes parameter is optional. but it
can be a numeric expression that uses a combination of one of the vbNormal,
vbHidden, vbSystem, vbVolume, or vbDirectory that you have already seen.
(If you use a file attribute, specify the pathname.) For example:

```
Dir$("Temp*", vbDirectory)
```

will tell you the name of a directory that begins with Temp if one exists.
If you need to find more information using the same pattern, call Dir again
only this time use the empty string. For example, the following code snipped
adds all the *.txt files to a list box named List1

```
Dim sFileName As String
sFileName = Dir$("*.txt)
Do While sFileName <> ""
   List1.AddItem sFileName
   sFileName = Dir$()
Loop
```

(As usual, there is a Dir version that returns a string stored in a variant
instead of a true string.)

Caution

*You cannot be sure of the order returned by the Dir$ or Dir function, nor
can you use these functions recursively without caching the results in an
array for reuse. (See the example program for a directory search that follows for ways around this.)*

Example: Recursive Directory Search

What we want to do in this section is discuss the code needed to activate Figure 5-2. This shows you how you can search a directory or subdirectory recursively for files that match a simple pattern. What you need to do is type a directory in the first text box and then a pattern in the second. Click the start button and the p will display all the files matching that pattern in the list box. You can stop the process at any time (through a judicious use of DoEvents()) and double click on an item (or right click on it) to see a message box that gives all the file attributes.

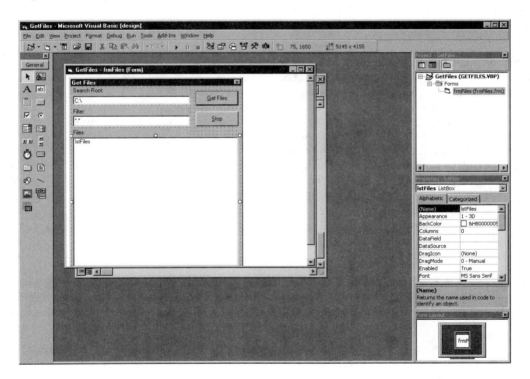

Figure 5-2   The Form for Recursive Directory Search

You have already seen the code needed to analyze a file attribute. The GetFiles_Click procedure is straightforward. It shows the Stop button and then calls the crucial GetFiles routine that does all the work.

```
Private Sub cmdGetFiles_Click()
  'reset stop flag
```

```
            mbStop = False
            'add the stop button
            cmdStop.Visible = True
            'clear list
            lstFiles.Clear
            'call the routine to fill the list
            GetFiles txtRoot.Text, txtFilter.Text
            'remove the stop button
            cmdStop.Visible = False
         End Sub
```

The code for the GetFiles routine is fairly sophisticated since we can't use the Dir function recursively directly. The way around this flaw in the Dir function that we chose is to simply cache the directories we find in an array for use in future calls to GetFiles:

```
'get sub-directories in the current directory
  ReDim sSubDirs(5)  'allocate 5 items
  sTmp = Dir$(sRoot + "*.*", vbDirectory)
  Do While Len(sTmp) > 0
    If Left$(sTmp, 1) <> "." Then  'don't get "." and ".." entries
      If (GetAttr(sRoot + sTmp) And vbDirectory) = vbDirectory Then
        'add the directory name to the array
        sSubDirs(nSubDir) = sTmp
        nSubDir = nSubDir + 1
        If nSubDir = UBound(sSubDirs) Then
          'need to allocate 5 more items
          ReDim Preserve sSubDirs(nSubDir + 5)
        End If
      End If
    End If
    sTmp = Dir$
  Loop
```

Once we have the directories cached we can use GetFiles again:

```
         'search the subdirectories that we found at this level
         For I = 0 To nSubDir - 1
           'recurse into the same routine to get nested levels
           GetFiles sRoot + sSubDirs(I), sFilter
         Next I

         Exit Sub
       GetFilesErr:
         MsgBox Err.Description
       End Sub
```

The .frm file for the GetFiles Example

Here's the full code for the .frm file. (This uses some mouse detection features that we will cover in the next chapter to monitor for right mouse clicks. It also doesn't find hidden or system files.)

Listing 5-5: .frm File for the GetFiles Example

```
VERSION 5.00
Begin VB.Form frmFiles
    BorderStyle        =    4    'Fixed ToolWindow
    Caption            =    "Get Files"
    ClientHeight       =    5910
    ClientLeft         =    4560
    ClientTop          =    2070
    ClientWidth        =    5325
    LinkTopic          =    "Form1"
    LockControls       =    -1    'True
    MaxButton          =    0    'False
    MinButton          =    0    'False
    ScaleHeight        =    5910
    ScaleWidth         =    5325
    ShowInTaskbar      =    0    'False
    StartUpPosition =    2    'CenterScreen
    Begin VB.CommandButton cmdStop
        Cancel         =    -1    'True
        Caption        =    "&Stop"
        Height         =    465
        Left           =    3900
        TabIndex       =    7
        Top            =    825
        Visible        =    0    'False
        Width          =    1335
    End
    Begin VB.TextBox txtFilter
        Height         =    345
        Left           =    75
        TabIndex       =    3
        Text           =    "*.*"
        Top            =    945
        Width          =    3645
    End
    Begin VB.TextBox txtRoot
        Height         =    285
```

```
         Left            =     75
         TabIndex        =     1
         Text            =     "C:\"
         Top             =     315
         Width           =     3645
      End
      Begin VB.ListBox lstFiles
         Height          =     4155
         Left            =     75
         Sorted          =     -1    'True
         TabIndex        =     5
         Top             =     1650
         Width           =     5145
      End
      Begin VB.CommandButton cmdGetFiles
         Caption         =     "&Get Files"
         Default         =     -1    'True
         Height          =     465
         Left            =     3900
         TabIndex        =     4
         Top             =     165
         Width           =     1335
      End
      Begin VB.Label Label1
         Caption         =     "Files:"
         Height          =     240
         Index           =     2
         Left            =     75
         TabIndex        =     6
         Top             =     1380
         Width           =     3645
      End
      Begin VB.Label Label1
         Caption         =     "Search Starting At:"
         Height          =     240
         Index           =     1
         Left            =     75
         TabIndex        =     0
         Top             =     30
         Width           =     3645
      End
      Begin VB.Label Label1
         Caption         =     "Filter:"
         Height          =     240
         Index           =     0
```

```
            Left          =    75
            TabIndex      =    2
            Top           =    705
            Width         =    3645
        End
End
Attribute VB_Name = "frmFiles"
Attribute VB_GlobalNameSpace = False
Attribute VB_Creatable = False
Attribute VB_PredeclaredId = True
Attribute VB_Exposed = False
Option Explicit

Private mbStop As Boolean

Private Sub cmdGetFiles_Click()
  'reset stop flag
  mbStop = False
  'add the stop button
  cmdStop.Visible = True
  'clear list
  lstFiles.Clear
  'call the routine to fill the list
  GetFiles txtRoot.Text, txtFilter.Text
  'remove the stop button
  cmdStop.Visible = False
End Sub


Public Sub GetFiles(sRoot As String, sFilter As String)
  On Error GoTo GetFilesErr

  Dim sSubDirs() As String      'array to hold sub directories
  Dim nSubDir As Integer        'count of sub directories
  Dim I As Integer              'loop index
  Dim sTmp As String            'temp string

  'set the root if it is blank
  If Len(sRoot) = 0 Then
    sFilter = "C:\"
  End If

  'add a trailing "\" is needed
  If Right$(sRoot, 1) <> "\" Then
    sRoot = sRoot & "\"
```

```
End If

'set the filter if it is blank
If Len(sFilter) = 0 Then
   sFilter = "*.*"
End If

'get files in the current directory
sTmp = Dir$(sRoot & sFilter)
Do While Len(sTmp) > 0
   lstFiles.AddItem sRoot & sTmp      'add it to the list
   'this line allows processing of the stop button
   DoEvents
   'check the stop flag and abort if it is set
   'note: this will usually not occur instantly
   If mbStop Then Exit Sub
   sTmp = Dir$
Loop

'get sub-directories in the current directory
ReDim sSubDirs(5)   'allocate 5 items
sTmp = Dir$(sRoot + "*.*", vbDirectory)
Do While Len(sTmp) > 0
   If Left$(sTmp, 1) <> "." Then     'don't get "." and ".." entries
      If (GetAttr(sRoot + sTmp) And vbDirectory) = vbDirectory Then
         'add the directory name to the array
         sSubDirs(nSubDir) = sTmp
         nSubDir = nSubDir + 1
         If nSubDir = UBound(sSubDirs) Then
            'need to allocate 5 more items
            ReDim Preserve sSubDirs(nSubDir + 5)
         End If
      End If
   End If
   sTmp = Dir$
Loop

'search the subdirectories that we found at this level
For I = 0 To nSubDir - 1
   'recurse into the same routine to get nested levels
   GetFiles sRoot + sSubDirs(I), sFilter
Next I

Exit Sub
GetFilesErr:
```

```
      MsgBox Err.Description
   End Sub

   Private Sub cmdStop_Click()
      mbStop = True
   End Sub

   Private Sub Form_Load()
      txtRoot.Text = CurDir
   End Sub

   Private Sub lstFiles_DblClick()
      Dim sFile As String

      sFile = ReturnInfo(lstFiles.Text)
      MsgBox sFile, vbInformation, "File Properties:"
   End Sub

   Public Function ReturnInfo(FileName) As String
      Dim sFile As String
      Dim sTmp As String
      Dim nAttrib As Integer

      sFile = FileName
      nAttrib = GetAttr(sFile)
      sTmp = sFile & vbCrLf & vbCrLf
      sTmp = sTmp & "Date/Time: " & FileDateTime(sFile) & vbCrLf
      sTmp = sTmp & "Size: " & FileLen(sFile) & " bytes" & vbCrLf
      If (nAttrib And vbReadOnly) = vbReadOnly Then
        sTmp = sTmp & "ReadOnly: X" & vbCrLf
      End If
      If (nAttrib And vbHidden) = vbHidden Then
        sTmp = sTmp & "Hidden: X" & vbCrLf
      End If
      If (nAttrib And vbSystem) = vbSystem Then
        sTmp = sTmp & "System: X" & vbCrLf
      End If
      If (nAttrib And vbArchive) = vbArchive Then
        sTmp = sTmp & "Archive: X" & vbCrLf
      End If
        ReturnInfo = sTmp
   End Function

   Private Sub lstFiles_MouseDown(Button As Integer, Shift As
   Integer, X As Single, Y As Single)
```

```
Dim sFile As String
Dim npos As Integer

If Button = vbRightButton Then
   If lstFiles.ListCount > 0 Then
      'need to make the clicked item active
      npos = (Y \ TextHeight(lstFiles.List(0))) + lstFiles.TopIndex
      If npos <= lstFiles.ListCount Then
         lstFiles.ListIndex = npos
      End If
   End If

   sFile = ReturnInfo(lstFiles.Text)
   MsgBox sFile, vbInformation, "File Properties:"
End IfEnd Sub
```

The Shell Function

You can use the Shell function to run any .COM, .EXE, .BAT, or PIF file from within a Visual Basic program. As you just saw some of the basic file-handling programs are built into Visual Basic but many such as the one for formatting a disk are not. While experienced users can move to the Windows desktop and use the Explorer or the Start button to format disks, copy multiple files, or run another program, inexperienced users will need more user friendly ways to accomplish these tasks. For example, you can call the FORMAT.COM program under Windows 95 to format the A: drive with a line like this:

```
X = Shell("C:\WINDOWS\COMMAND\FORMAT.COM A:")
```

Of course, Windows must know where the file you are running is located. It can know this if the file you are shelling to is located in a directory in the path or in the current directory. If you give the full pathname of the application, then you can shell to any program.

When Visual Basic shells to a program, it generates a new iconized window and gives that window the focus. In many situations this is not ideal. For example, the user has to actually press Enter for formatting to occur. You can change this behavior with the general form of the Shell function, as follows:

```
Shell(PathName, WindowStyle)
```

where *Pathname* contains the full pathname of the stand-alone program that you want to execute along with any information needed by the program, and WindowStyle sets the type of window the program runs in. The possible values for WindowStyle are shown in Table 5-7.

Table 5-7: WindowStyle Values		
Symbolic constant	*Value*	*Type of Window*
VbHide	0	Window is hidden but has the focus
VbNormalFocus	1	Normal with the focus
VbMinimizedFocus	2	Iconized with the focus
VbMaximizedFocus	3	Maximized with the focus
VbMaximizedNotFocus	4	Normal without the focus
VbMinimizedNoFocus	6	Iconized without the focus

The Shell function takes named arguments so you can use it in the form:

```
Shell PathName = , WindowStyle =
```

Note

The variant returned by the Shell function identifies the task identification number of the started program (or 0 if the program wasn't successfully started). This information was extremely useful in earlier versions of Visual Basis—it is less useful now. (Previously you could use this value along with the Windows 3.1 GetModuleUsage API call in order to make sure the program you have shelled to finishes before the next Visual Basic statement executes.) For how to start a program and monitor whether it has finished or not from VB, please see Chapter 12.

Working with Running Windows Applications

Sometimes you want to activate a program that is already running on the Windows desktop rather than starting up a new instance of it via the Shell function. VB offers you an amazing number of ways to do this using the power of DDE or more commonly OLE. In this section we want to show you the most primitive and least code-intensive way.

The idea is that you can always send to the active Windows applications any keystrokes you want via Visual Basic. You can even have a Visual Basic project send keystrokes to itself—the obvious key to a self-running demo. The AppActivate statement moves the focus to another project currently running on the Windows desktop; it does not start a program, nor does it change whether the application is minimized or maximized. The syntax for this statement (it takes named arguments) is

```
AppActivate title [, wait]
```

The title argument is a string expression that matches the one in the title bar of the application you want to activate. It is not case-sensitive. The wait parameter is either True or False. Usually you will leave it at the default value of False. (If you set it to True, then whichever application is doing the calling, waits until it has the focus before it activates the new application.)

If the Title parameter doesn't make a match with the whole title bar of an active application, Windows looks for any application whose title string begins with that title and activates it—you cannot control which one gets activated in this case. For example, AppActivate "Exploring" will usually start an instance of the Windows Explorer even though its title bar might be something weird like: "Exploring - HardDisk1_(C:)."

Sending Keystrokes to an Application

Once you've activated another Windows application by using AppActivate, use the SendKeys statement to send keystrokes to its active window. (If no other window is active, the keystrokes go to the Visual Basic project itself. As mentioned earlier this is useful in testing programs and self-running demos.) The syntax for this statement (it also takes named arguments) is

```
SendKeys String[, Wait]
```

If the *Wait* Boolean expression is True (nonzero), Visual Basic will not continue processing code until the other application processes the keystrokes contained in *String* that you sent it. If the Wait expression is False (the default), Visual Basic continues with the procedure immediately after it sends the keystrokes to the other application. The *Wait* parameter matters only when you are sending keystrokes to applications other than your Visual Basic application itself. If you send keystrokes to your Visual Basic application and you need to wait for those keys to be processed, use the DoEvents function that was discussed earlier in this chapter. The value of the String parameter is the keystrokes you want to send. For keyboard characters, simply use the characters. For example,

```
SendKeys "This string is sent via SendKeys", False
```

sends the keystrokes "T", "h", "i", and so on, to the active application, exactly as if the user had typed them on the screen. Since the *Wait* parameter is False, Visual Basic does not wait for these keystrokes to be processed by the active application.

The only exceptions to sending keystrokes by using the actual character is when you need to send either the plus sign (+), caret (^), percent sign (%), brackets ([ ]), tilde (~), an open or close parentheses (( )), or an open or close brace ({ }). The reason is that, as you'll soon see, these have special uses in the SendKeys statement. If you need to send these keys, enclose them in braces. For example, to send "2+2" to the active application, use this:

```
SendKeys "2{+}2"
```

You'll often need to send control key combinations, function keys, and so on, in addition to the ordinary alphanumeric keys (A to Z, 0 to 9). To send a function key, use F1 for the first function key, F2 for the second, and so on. For other keys, such as BACKSPACE, use the following codes:

Key	*What to use*
BACKSPACE	{BACKSPACE} or {BS} or {BKSP}
BREAK	{BREAK}
CAPS LOCK	{CAPSLOCK}
CLEAR	{CLEAR}
DEL	{DELETE} or {DEL}
DOWN ARROW	{DOWN}
END	{END}
ENTER	{ENTER} or ~
ESC	{ESCAPE} or {ESC}
HELP	{HELP}
HOME	{HOME}
INS	{INSERT}
LEFT ARROW	{LEFT}
NUM LOCK	{NUMLOCK}
PGDN	{PGDN}
PGUP	{PGUP}
PRTSCRN	{PRTSC}
RIGHT ARROW	{RIGHT}
SCROLL LOCK	{SCROLLOCK}
TAB	{TAB}
UP ARROW	{UP}

For combinations of the SHIFT, CTRL, and ALT keys, use the codes just given, but place one or more of the following codes first:

Key	Code
SHIFT	+
CTRL	^
ALT	%

To indicate that one (or all) of the SHIFT, CTRL, and ALT keys should be used with a key combination, enclose the keys in parentheses. For example, to hold down CTRL while pressing A and then B (that is, what this book would symbolize as CTRL A+B), use "^(AB)." The string "^AB" would give you the three keystrokes individually. You can also send repeated keys more easily by using the string in the form *Keystrokes*$ *Number%*. There must be a space between the keystrokes and the number. For example, SendKeys "DOWN 5" sends five presses of the Down Arrow to the active application.

As an example of putting all this together, let's suppose Windows Explorer is running. Then the following fragment activates the Windows Explorer and maximizes the window in which it is running by sending the keystrokes needed to open its control box and then choosing the Maximize item on its control box menu:

```
AppActivate "Exploring"
SendKeys "% {Down 4}{Enter}", -1
```

What we are doing in this case is using SendKeys to send the ALT key followed by a press of the SPACEBAR (because the quotes enclose a space). These keystrokes always open the control menu for a Windows application. We then move down four lines to the Maximize menu item and finally send the Enter keystroke in order to choose the Maximize item.

Tip

This technique (using cursor keys instead of the accelerator letters) also works in the international version of Visual Basic where the words on a menu may differ.

Note

SendKeys cannot send keystrokes to a non-Windows application that happens to be running under Windows in a virtual DOS window.

The File System Controls

The file system controls in Visual Basic allow users to select a new drive, see the hierarchical directory structure of a disk, or see the names of the files in a given directory. (The file system controls complement the common dialog boxes you will see in the next chapter.) The file system controls are designed to work together. Your code checks what the user has done to the drive list box and passes this information on to the directory list box. The changes in the directory list box are passed on to the file list box. Figure 5-3 shows the toolbox with the file system controls marked.

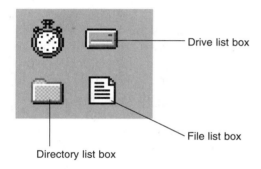

Figure 5-3   The file handling controls

A file list box defaults to displaying the files in the current directory. (Microsoft's suggested prefix for the Name property is *fil*.) You can control the position, size, color, and font characteristic at design time or via code at run time. Most of the properties, events, and methods of a file list box are identical to those of ordinary list boxes. For example, as with all list boxes, when the number of items can't fit the current size of the control, Visual Basic automatically adds vertical scroll bars. This lets the user move through the list of files using the scroll bars. There are five Boolean properties that control what type of files are shown in a file list box: Archive, Hidden, Normal, ReadOnly, and System. The default setting is True for Archive, Normal, and ReadOnly and False for Hidden and System.

It is quite common to use the List, ListCount, and ListIndex properties rather than the Dir function to analyze the information contained in a file list box. For example, suppose the file list box has the default name of File1 and you have already set up a string array for the information contained in the box. Then a fragment like

```
Dim I As Integer
For I = 0 To File1.ListCount -1
   sFileNames(I) = File1.List(I)
Next I
```

fills a string array with the information contained in the file list box named File1. If you need to find out the name of the file that a user selects, you can use File1.List(ListIndex) or the FileName property that, when read, has the same function.

The most important properties for file list boxes are probably Pattern and Path. The Pattern property determines which files are displayed in the file list box. The Pattern property accepts the ordinary file wildcards—the * (match any) and the ? (match a single character). You can set multiple patterns by separating them with commas. The default pattern is set to *.* to display all files. (Of course, the Pattern property works with the attribute properties discussed earlier before Visual Basic displays the files.) When you change the Pattern property, Visual Basic looks to see if you have written a PatternChange event procedure for the file list box and, if so, activates it.

The Path property sets or returns the current path for the file list box, but not for the underlying operating system. To tell the underlying operating system to change the current path from within Visual Basic, you need the ChDir statement. When you change the Path property, Visual Basic looks to see if you have written a PathChange event procedure for the file list box and, if so, activates it.

Changing the FileName property activates the PathChange event or the PatternChange event (or both), depending on how you change the FileName property. For example, suppose you are in the C:\ root directory. Setting

```
File1.Filename ="C:\WINDOWS\*.DLL"
```

activates both the PathChange and PatternChange events.

Note

Remember the Windows convention is that double-clicking a file, not single-clicking, chooses the file. This is especially important when using a file list box, because using an arrow key to move through a file list box would call any Click procedure that you have written. (Arrow movements are functionally equivalent to a single mouse click for a list box.)

Directory List Boxes

A directory list box displays the directory structure of the current drive. (Microsoft's naming convention is to use a *dir* prefix for its Name property.) The current directory shows up as an open file folder. Subdirectories of the current directory are shown as closed folders, and directories above the current directory are shown as nonshaded open folders.

Note

When you click on an item or move through the list, that item is highlighted. When you double-click, Visual Basic automatically updates the directory list box. Directory list boxes do not recognize the DoubleClick event; instead, they call the Change procedure in response to a double-click and reassign the Path property.

The List property for a directory list box works a little differently than it does for file list boxes. While subdirectories of the current directory are numbered from zero to ListCount-1, Visual Basic uses negative indexes for the current directory and its parent and grandparent directories. For example, -1 is the index for the current directory, -2 for its parent directory, and so on. Unfortunately, you cannot use the LBound function to determine the number of directories above a given directory; you must either count the number of backslashes in the Path property or move backward through the items in the directory list box until you get to the top.

As an example of how easy it is to use the Pattern property of the directory list box to change the getFiles program that you saw earlier in this chapter to use a directory list box mostly requires adding the following:

```
Private Sub Dir1_Change()
   cmdGetFiles_Click
   GetFiles Dir1.Path, txtFilter.Text
End Sub
```

and replacing all uses of txtRoot.Text by Dir1.Path

Drive List Boxes

Unlike file and directory list boxes, drive list boxes are pull-down boxes. (Microsoft's naming convention suggests *drv* as the prefix for the Name property.) Drive list boxes begin by displaying the current drive, and then when the user clicks on the arrow, Visual Basic pulls down a list of all valid drives. The key property for a drive list box is the Drive property, which can be used to return or reset the current drive. For example, to synchronize a drive list box with a directory list box, all you need is code that looks like this:

```
Sub drvBox_Change()
   dirBox.Path = drvBox.Drive
End Sub
```

(Notice that if you added a drive box and this code to the second version of getFiles, it would continue to work as expected except that every time you changed drives, the list box would fill up.)

Tying the File Controls Together

As a first example of how powerful the file system controls can be when they begin to work together, put a directory list box and a file list box together on a new project. Now suppose you want a change by the user in a directory list box named dirBox to tell Visual Basic to update the file list box immediately. All you have to do is enter one line of code in the Change event procedure for the directory list box:

```
Sub dirBox_Change()
   File1.Path = dirBox.Path
End Sub
```

To activate this event procedure, the user simply double-clicks on a new directory in the directory list box.

```
Sub dirBox_KeyPress(KeyAscii As Integer)
  If KeyAscii = vbKeyReturn Then
    dirBox.Path = dirBox.List(dirBox.ListIndex)
  End If
End Sub
```

Next, notice that this procedure didn't change the Path property directly because doing so is superfluous. Visual Basic calls the Change event procedure for a directory list box whenever you change the value of the Path property.

When you have all three file system controls on a form, you have to communicate the changes among the controls in order to have Visual Basic show what the user wants to see. For example, let's suppose the user selects a new drive then:

1. Visual Basic activates the Change event procedure for the drive box.
2. The Change event procedure for the drive box assigns the Drive property to the directory box's Path property.
3. This changes the display in the directory list box by triggering the Change event procedure for the directory list box.
4. Inside the Change event procedure, you assign the Path property to the file list box's Path property. This updates the File list box.

Finally, it's important to keep in mind that while the meaning of the Path property for file list boxes and directory list boxes is similar, they are not identical. For directory list boxes, the Path property specifies which directory was selected; for file list boxes, it specifies where Visual Basic should look for files to display

Sequential Files

Sequential files are ordinary text files. They use a Ctrl+Z to mark their end. As far as working with them in VB a useful analogy to keep in mind is that of a recording information on a cassette tape. For example, the operations on sequential files that are analogous to easy tasks for a cassette recorder, such as recording an album on a blank tape, are easy. Those analogous to more difficult tasks, such as splicing tapes together or making a change within a tape, will be more difficult to code. To avoid unnecessary work, use a sequential file only when you know that you will:

- Rarely need to make changes within the file.
- Usually process the information the file contains from start to finish, without needing to constantly jump around within it.
- Usually add to the file only at the end of the file.

Here's a table of some common operations on a cassette tape and the analogous operations on a sequential text file called SampleTextFile in the currently active directory:

Table 5-8: Common Operations on a Sequential File	
Operation	*Visual Basic Equivalent*
Rewind the tape, put the machine in playback mode, and pause.	Open "SampleTextFile" For Input as #1.
Rewind the tape, put the machine in record mode, and pause.	Open "SampleTextFile" For Output as #1.
Add at the end.	Open "SampleTextFile" For Append as #1.
Push Stop.	Close #1.

What follows the Open statement is the name of the file you are working with. The filename must be a string expression whose value is a valid file name, and unless it is in the current directory, you need to provide enough information to identify its path. Under Windows 95, of course, what constitutes a legal file name is much improved over the earlier versions of Windows. You can use up to 255 characters, and spaces are allowed. Case is irrelevant, although it is retained. (You still can't use a \, ? :, ° < , >, or |, however.)

Note

If you want your files to be completely compatible with machines not running Windows 95 or Windows NT, you should follow the rules for filenames that DOS imposes which is that the filename can be at most eight characters with an optional three-character extension following the period.

The characters you can use are A–Z, 0–9, ( ), { }, @, #, $, %, &, !, -, _, ', /, ~.

Lowercase letters are automatically converted to uppercase.

As the table indicates you need a file identifier when working with a file. This is a number between 1 and 511 preceded by the # sign that you will use to identify the file. Each file open at the same time requires a different file number and you can't change this number until you close the file. (The next time you need the file you can open it with a different ID number.)

The easiest way to find an unused file identifier is with the FreeFile function. The value of FreeFile is always the next unused file ID number. Therefore, you can always use a statement like

```
FileNumber% = FreeFile
```

to pick up the next free file number.

When Visual Basic processes an Open statement, it also tells the operating system to reserve a file buffer in the computer's memory. The Close statement usually empties the buffer and tells the underlying operating system to update its file allocation table. But because of Windows's own buffering techniques this may not happen precisely when Visual Basic processes the Close statement.

Tip

The Reset statement, unlike the Close statement, forces the underlying operating system to flush the buffers. Use this statement in critical situations to make it more likely that the underlying operating system file buffer is flushed.

To write to a sequential file use either the Print # or Write # statement. Here is an example of a fragment that sends one piece of information to a file named Sample.Txt:

```
' Writing to a file
Open "Sample.Txt" For Output As #1
Print #1, "TESTING, 1 2 3"
Close #1
```

The comma is necessary, but what follows the comma can be anything that might occur in an ordinary Print statement. And what appears in the file is the exact image of what would have occurred on the screen. In our case the file will contain the word "TESTING," followed by (in order) a comma, a space, the numeral 1, another space, the numeral 2, another space, the numeral 3, and finally the characters that define a carriage return/line feed combination.

Visual Basic uses the Write # statement to send items to a file separated by commas and with quotes around strings. For example,

```
Write #2, "Testing 1,2,3"
```

sends everything (including the quotes and the commas) to the output (or append) file with ID #2.

Caution

If a file in the current directory already exists with the same name as the one you use in the Open for Output statement, it will be erased. Opening a sequential file for output starts a new file; the previous contents of a file with the same name will be lost.

While a file is opened use the Visual Basic statement LOF() (Length Of File) instead of the FileLen function to find out how large the file currently is (including buffered information that may not yet be written to disk). To use this command, place the appropriate file identifier number within the parentheses. To see this command at work (and to confirm what was said earlier about the exact images that Print # gives) try the following Click procedure in a new project:

```
Sub Form_Click()
' a file tester
' demonstrates the 'exact' image property of Print #
   Open "Sample1.txt" For Output As #1
   Open "Sample2.txt" For Output As #2
```

```
    Open "Sample3.txt" For Output As #3
    Print #1,"TESTING, 1,2,3";
    Print #2,"TESTING, 1,2,3"
    Print #3,"TESTING",1,2,3
    Print LOF(1)
    Print LOF(2)
    Print LOF(3)
    Close
End Sub
```

To read information back from a file, you must have already closed it. Then open the file again using the "For Input" version of the Open command with its name :

```
Open "Sample1.txt" For Input As #1
```

More generally you need to use its full pathname if it's not in the currently active directory and give it a file identifier that is not currently being used within the program. (Again, it doesn't have to be the same identifier that it was set up with originally.)

The easiest way to read information up to a carriage return/line feed combination is with the LineInput statement, which picks up everything in a file up to the next carriage return/line feed combination as in the following example:

```
' Reading back a file
Dim ASingleLine As String
Dim FileNumber As Integer
FileNumber = FreeFile
Open "Sample2.txt" For Input As #FileNumber
Line Input #FileNumber, ASingleLine
Close #FileNumber1
```

To pick up individual items when you know their nature and therefore wish to store them in separate variables, use the Input# statement as in the following example:

```
Dim AString As String, B As Integer, C As Integer, D As
Integer
Dim FileNumber As Integer
FileNumber = FreeFile
Open "Sample2.txt" For Input As FileNumber
Input #FileNumber, AString, B, C, D
Close #FileNumber
```

This recovers the numbers as integers (values of integer variables) rather than as strings of numerals (part of a larger string). (You can use variants, of course, if you don't know the nature of the information stored in the file.)

Obviously, For-Next loops are a convenient way to read back information contained in a file but they can only work in the obvious way if you know exactly how many items you want to read back. In general, of course, you will test when you're at the end of a file. The statement in Visual Basic that lets you do this is mnemonic: it's called EOF( ) (End Of File), where the parentheses hold the file ID number. (For sequential files what EOF is actually testing for is the Ctrl+Z [Chr(26) character].)

A general fragment to display the information contained in a sequential file given by a variable named FileName that is set up with Print # statements looks like this:

```
Dim FileName As String
Dim TempString As String
'get the file name somehow
FileNum = FreeFile+
Open FileName For Input As #FileNum
Do Until EOF(FileNum)
   Line Input #FileNum, TempString
   Print TempString
Loop
Close #FileNum
```

Another common use of the EOF statement is to read back the information contained in a sequential file character by character. To do this combine a loop with an EOF test with the

```
StringVariable = Input(NumberOfChars, File Id)
```

statement, where the first entry holds the number of characters and the second holds the file ID. For example: `FileContents   =   Input (LOF(FileID), FileID)`.

Finally, as we mentioned before to add information to the end of an already existing file, use the Append statement:

```
Open FileName For Append As File#
```

This causes three things to occur at once:

- Visual Basic opens the file (if the file doesn't exist, it creates it) and sets up the appropriate buffer.
- Visual Basic locates the end of the file on the disk.
- Visual Basic prepares to output to the file at its end.

THE RICHTEXTBOX CONTROL AND FILE HANDLING

The RichTextBox control to make it easy to send its contents to a file (or conversely, to display the contents of a file inside of one). The following table describes the properties and methods you can use:

NameOfRichTextBox.LoadFile (pathname, filetype)	This loads an .RTF file or text file into the RichTextBox control in one gulp. As usual the pathname is a string expression defining the path and file-name of the file you want to load into the control. The optional filetype parameter controls whether the file is loaded as an RTF file. (The default is that it is, or you can use the symbolic constant rtfRTF.) Use the constant rtfText, to load a text file. (The LoadFile method replaces whatever was in the control with the current contents of the file.)
NameOfRichTextBox.SaveFile (pathname, filetype)	The SaveFile method saves the contents of a RichTextBox control to a file in one swoop. The syntax is similar to that of LoadFile.

Random-Access Files

A *random-access file* is a special disk file arranged by records. This lets you immediately move to the 15th record without having to pass through the 14th before it, which saves a considerable amount of time. Random-access files are a lot less important than they used to be since VB has such awesome database capabilities. Still there are occasionally times when simple random-access file organization is better than using the overhead involved with the full Jet engine.

When you first set up a random-access file, you specify the maximum length for each record. When you enter data for an individual record, you can, of course, put in less information than this preset limit, but you can never put in more.

The command that sets up a random-access file is analogous to the one for opening a sequential file. For example,

```
Open "ARandomAccessFile.RND" As #5 Len = 100
```

opens a random-access file called ARandomAccessFile on the current directory with a file ID of 5, and each record can hold 100 characters. (As in this example the convention is to use an extension like .RND for all random-access files.) Note that, unlike the situation for sequential files, you don't have to specify whether you're opening the file for input, output, or appending. You can have any mixture of random-access and sequential files open at the same time. The only restrictions are set by the underlying operating system. Similarly, you close a file opened for random access by using the Close command followed by the file ID number. As before, the Close command alone closes all open files, regardless of whether they were opened for sequential or random access. Suppose you want to write a random-access file that would keep track of employee records. You start by designing the form. You decide on five categories—Name, SSNumber, Salary, and Miscellaneous. You decide to store the salary as a string of digits. You set up the following limits for each field:

Category	Size
EmployeeName	60
SSNumber	8
Salary	7

Therefore, the total for each record is 75. A random-access file to fit this form is set up (via FileNum = FreeFile, as always):

```
Open "MyCompany.RND" As FileNum Len = 75
```

Each record within a random-access file has a record number. A single random-access file can hold from 1 to 2,147,483,647 (a long) records. Moreover, you don't have to fill the records in order. As you'll see, you can place information in the 15th record without ever having touched the first 14. The disadvantage of doing this, however, is that Visual Basic would automatically set aside enough space for the first 14 records on the disk, even if nothing was in them. To work with a random-access file, first set up a type corresponding to the record. You must use fixed-length strings in order to work within the limitations of a random-access file because of the record length. For example:

```
Type EmployeeInfo
   EmployeeNamer As String*60
   SSNumber As String*8
   Salary As String*7
End Type
```

Now the statements:

```
Dim EmployeeRecord As EmployeeInfo
Get #FileNum, 10, EmployeeRecord
```

would transfer the contents of the 10th record from the random-access file into the record variable EmployeeRecord, automatically filling in the correct components of EmployeeRecord. After filling in the information correctly into the variable EmployeeRecord the statement

```
Put FileNum, 37, EmployeeRecord
```

would send the components of EmployeeRecord to the 37th record of file #FileNum.

The general syntax for the Get and Put command is, as you would expect:

```
Get #FileNumber, RecordNumber, Variable
Put #FileNumber, RecordNumber, Variable
```

Binary Files

Binary files are not a new type of file but a new way of manipulating any kind of file. Binary file techniques let you read or change any byte of a file. Among other features, binary file techniques do not care about any embedded EOFs [CTRL-Z = Chr$(26)] that the file may have.

Caution

If you are moving from VB3 to VB5 without having passed through VB4 be warned binary file-handling techniques have changed from Visual Basic 3; be sure to read the next few sections carefully. Depending on what you are doing, your previous code may be broken and will need to be changed in order to make it work with VB5.

The statement

```
Open FileName For Binary As # FileNum
```

sets up a file to be read with binary techniques. And, just as with random-access files, you can now both read and write to the file. *Now, as long as you are reading back information you are sure was stored as strings,* the easiest way to pick up the information from a text file open in binary file mode is with the Input$(,) function you saw earlier. Because of the automatic conversions Visual Basic 5 makes between Unicode and ANSI strings, this will work transparently for you. (Visual Basic automatically converts ANSI strings to Unicode when data is read back to your application and back to ANSI when strings are written back to a file.) The first slot of the Input$ function still holds the number of characters and the second the file ID number. For example, the following listing gives a module that prints the contents of any text file, regardless of any embedded control characters:

```
Sub PrintAFile(FileName As String)
' example of binary input
Dim I As Integer, FileNum As Integer, Char$
FileNum = FreeFile            ' get free file i.d.
Open FileName For Binary As #FileNum

For I = 1 To LOF(FileNum)
   Char$ = Input$(1,#FileNum)
   Print Char$;
Next I
Close #FileNum
End Sub
```

Using Binary Access in More General (Nontext) Situations

The change between VB3 and VB4 (and continuing to VB5) (and one that will break a lot of previous code, unfortunately!) is

In the 32-bit version of Visual Basic you cannot use the Input$(,) for picking up individual bytes from a file.

Instead, you must use the Get statement with an array of Bytes. The problem is that because of Unicode a character no longer takes up a single byte. Thus, because of Unicode, the procedure is a lot more cumbersome then it was in earlier versions of Visual Basic. (In general, in a Unicode two-byte encoding for an ordinary ANSI string, if the high end byte is 0, the second byte gives the ANSII code. The first step is easy. Next get the bytes out of the file into a byte array using the Get function. The syntax is

```
Get file#, position, ByteArray
```

The number of characters this statement picks up is equal to the size of the byte array given as the last parameter. The second parameter is needed because Visual Basic maintains a file pointer within a file opened for binary access. Each time you pick up a byte, the file pointer moves one position farther within the file. Here's an example of how to use Get for a small enough binary file to fit in memory:

```
Sub BinaryPickUp (FileName As String)
   Dim FileNum As Integer, I As Integer
   ' Example Of Binary Input for a general file!
   FileNum = Freefile                  ' get free file i.d.
   Open FileName For Binary As #FileNum
   Redim ArrayOfBytes(1 To LOF(FileNum) As Byte
   Get #FileNum, 1, ArrayOfBytes
```

(Theoretically this would let you store up to 2^{31} characters—but memory constraints would probably prevent this in most machines.)

Once you have the bytes in memory you will have to decide how you want to manipulate the raw byte information. One possibility is that you can leave them in the array of bytes and then work with them using ordinary array-handling techniques. Another possibility is to:

- Assign the byte array to a string. (This will not do any translations.)
- Use the appropriate "B" character function given in the following table to work with the byte string. (B character functions work similarly to their ordinary namesakes that you saw earlier in this chapter—except that they work with byte strings.)

Table 5-9:	B Character Functions
Function	*Purpose*
AscB	Returns the value given by the first byte in a string of binary data.
InStrB	Finds the first occurrence of a byte in a binary string.
MidB	Returns the specified number of bytes from a binary string.
LeftB, RightB	Takes the specified number of bytes from the left or right end of a binary string.
ChrB	Takes a byte and returns a binary string with that byte.

The Seek and Put Functions

The Seek command is a combined fast-forward and rewind command for binary access. More precisely,

```
Seek filenum, position number
```

moves the file pointer for the file with *filenum* directly to the byte in that position. Any Input or Get would start picking up characters from this location.

The Seek function has another use. Seek (*filenum*) tells you the position number for the last byte read for either a binary or sequential file. (You can also use the Seek function with random-access files. Now it will return the record number of the next record.)

To place information within a file use a modification of the Put command to place the information there. For example,

```
Put #1, 100, ByteArray()
```

would place the contents of the byte array directly into the file with file ID #1 starting at the 100th byte. The number of characters sent to this file is, of course, given by the size of the byte array. The Put command overwrites whatever was there. If you leave a space for the byte position but don't specify it in the Put command, like this:

```
Put #1, , ByteArray()
```

then the information is placed wherever the file pointer is currently located (as set in the last Seek).

Note

You can also use Put with string variables by replacing the ByteArray with a string variable. However, to avoid problems that come from mixing bytes and strings in the same file when doing binary access, you are best off doing this only for text files.

An Example: Encrypting Files

In this section we want to give you a simple way that uses binary file techniques to encrypt a file so that it will be safe from casual probes. It depends on the fact that VB's Rnd function gives a repeatable pattern of pseudo-random numbers if you use a negative seed. What this means is that after each call to say:

```
Rnd(-5)
```

all subsequent uses of the Rnd function give you the same sequence of numbers until you explicitly reseed the random-number generator.

Caution

Since the encryption procedure we give you depends on VB's random-number generator, which is not "cryptographically secure," this code would not withstand more than a few moments' attack by a professional cryptographer. We are confident that a file encrypted with this method will look like gibberish to anyone else!

Once we have a sequence of random numbers we scale them so that they are in the range 0 to 255. We can then use one of the nifty properties of the Xor function to do the encryption—use it twice and you get back to where you started. In other words,

```
A Xor B Xor B
```

always gives you A back again. A routine to use all this to encrypt a file is pretty simple (assuming the file can fit in memory; otherwise, you have to work a little harder). Here it is (the key parameter must be a positive integer):

Listing 5-6:   Encrypting a File

```
Sub Encrypt(FileName As String, Key As Integer)
  Dim FileNum As Integer, I As Integer
  FileNum = FreeFile                        ' get free file i.d.
  Open FileName For Binary As #FileNum
  ReDim ArrayOfBytes(1 To LOF(FileNum)) As Byte
  Get #FileNum, 1, ArrayOfBytes
  Close #FileNum
  NextXorValue = Rnd(-Key)
  For I = 1 To UBound(ArrayOfBytes)
     NextXorValue = 255 * Rnd
     ArrayOfBytes(I) = ArrayOfBytes(I) Xor NextXorValue
  Next
  FileNum = FreeFile
  Open FileName For Binary As FileNum
  Put #FileNum, 1, ArrayOfBytes
  Close #FileNum
  MsgBox "Done with file named " & FileName
End Sub
```

Listing 5-6 gives you the .frm file for a program that incorporates the routine you saw in Listing 5-5, along with a simple GUI interface for choosing the file and making sure that the key is always a positive integer. To decrypt the file, just use the same password and click the button again.

Caution

Fair warning: We want to again caution you against using this routine for mission-critical encryption, it is supplied on an "as-is" basis and we certainly make no guarantees that it will do anything or be bug free. We also know that it can be broken by a good amateur cryptographer fairly quickly. (On the other hand it works much faster than most secure encryption routines, it can encrypt/decrypt something like 400,000 characters a second on a Pentium 166 and that includes the disk i/o time!).

Also, if you use this encryption routine and forget the numerical password that was used to encrypt the file, or if you use the wrong numerical password to try to decrypt the file it will be hard to recover the original file. In particular, there is really nothing we could do to help you get it back if this should happen! (This is not just a problem with our routine: all file encryption techniques are very much two-edged swords.)

Listing 5-7:   .frm File Incorporating Encryption and Decryption

```
VERSION 5.00
Object = "{F9043C88-F6F2-101A-A3C9-08002B2F49FB}#1.1#0"; "COMDLG32.OCX"
Begin VB.Form Form1
    Caption         =     "File Encrypter/Decrypter"
    ClientHeight    =     3195
    ClientLeft      =     165
    ClientTop       =     735
    ClientWidth     =     4680
    LinkTopic       =     "Form1"
    ScaleHeight     =     3195
    ScaleWidth      =     4680
    StartUpPosition =     3    'Windows Default
    Begin VB.TextBox txtKey
        Height         =     495
        Left           =     1920
        TabIndex       =     3
        Top            =     1200
        Width          =     1095
    End
    Begin VB.TextBox txtFileName
        Height         =     495
        Left           =     1920
        TabIndex       =     1
        Top            =     240
        Width          =     2415
    End
    Begin MSComDlg.CommonDialog CommonDialog1
        Left           =     480
        Top            =     2400
        _ExtentX       =     847
        _ExtentY       =     847
        _Version       =     327680
    End
    Begin VB.CommandButton cmdDoIt
        Caption        =     "Encypt/Decrypt"
        Height         =     495
        Left           =     1560
        TabIndex       =     0
        Top            =     2400
        Width          =     1575
    End
    Begin VB.Label Label2
        Caption        =     "Key"
        Height         =     495
```

```
        Left              =    120
        TabIndex          =    5
        Top               =    1200
        Width             =    1455
    End
    Begin VB.Label Label1
        Caption           =    "Label1"
        Height            =    495
        Left              =    1920
        TabIndex          =    4
        Top               =    1320
        Width             =    1215
    End
    Begin VB.Label Fil
        Caption           =    "File Name"
        Height            =    495
        Left              =    120
        TabIndex          =    2
        Top               =    240
        Width             =    1455
    End
    Begin VB.Menu mnuFile
        Caption           =    "&File"
        Begin VB.Menu mnuGetFile
            Caption           =    "Get File"
        End
        Begin VB.Menu mnuExit
            Caption           =    "E&xit"
        End
    End
End
Attribute VB_Name = "Form1"
Attribute VB_GlobalNameSpace = False
Attribute VB_Creatable = False
Attribute VB_PredeclaredId = True
Attribute VB_Exposed = False

Private Sub cmdDoIt_Click()
  Dim Key As Integer
  If IsNumeric(txtKey.Text) Then
    Key = Val(txtKey.Text)
    If Key > 0 Then
      Encrypt txtFileName.Text, Key
    Else
      MsgBox "Please enter a positive integer as a key."
    End If
```

```
     Else
        MsgBox "Please enter a positive integer key"
     End If
     MousePointer = vbDefault
  End Sub

  Sub Encrypt(FileName As String, Key As Integer)
     Dim FileNum As Integer, I As Long
     Dim NextXorValue As Integer
     Dim Start As Single, TheEnd As Single, TimeElapsed As Single
     MousePointer = vbHourglass
     Start = Timer
     FileNum = FreeFile                        ' get free file i.d.
     Open FileName For Binary As #FileNum
     ReDim arrayofbytes(1 To LOF(FileNum)) As Byte
     Get #FileNum, 1, arrayofbytes
     Close #FileNum
     NextXorValue = Rnd(-Key)
     For I = 1 To UBound(arrayofbytes)
        NextXorValue = Int(255 * Rnd)
        arrayofbytes(I) = arrayofbytes(I) Xor NextXorValue
     Next
     FileNum = FreeFile
     Open FileName For Binary As FileNum
     Put #FileNum, 1, arrayofbytes
     Close #FileNum
     MousePointer = vbDefault
     TheEnd = Timer
     TimeElapsed = TheEnd - Start
     MsgBox "Done with file named " & FileName & " in " _
     & TimeElapsed & " seconds."
  End Sub

  Private Sub Form_Load()
    GetFileName
  End Sub

  Private Sub mnuExit_Click()
    End
  End Sub

  Private Sub mnuGetFile_Click()
    GetFileName
  End Sub

  Sub GetFileName()
```

```
On Error Resume Next
CommonDialog1.ShowOpen
txtFileName.Text = CommonDialog1.FileName
End Sub
```

Sharing Files

As more files are available only off networks, it becomes more important to prevent someone from inadvertently working with a file while you are working with it. Visual Basic's file-handling functions can easily be adapted to a networking environment by using the keywords described in the following table.

Keyword	Function
Lock	Prevents access to all or part of an open file.
Unlock	Allows access to a file previously locked.

You can use these functions after you have opened the file, in which case the syntax takes the form:

```
Lock [#]filenumber[, WhatToLock]
```

for the Lock command and

```
Unlock [#]filenumber[, WhatToUnlock]
```

for the Unlock command. Both commands use the file number with which the program opened the file. The WhatToLock (WhatToUnlock) parameter specifies what portion of the file to lock or unlock. For sequential files, Lock and Unlock affect the entire file, regardless of the range specified by the WhatToLock parameter. You use it by giving the Start and End values where they denote the first record (for random-access files) or first byte (for binary access). For example the following code:

```
Open "ABinaryFile" For Binary As #1 Lock #1, 1 To 100
```

would lock the first 100 bytes of the file ABinaryFile. (If you leave off the optional To parameter in the Lock statement, then Lock, locks the whole file.)

Caution

You must use the Lock and Unlock statements in pairs: the arguments must match exactly and be sure to remove all locks with the corresponding Unlock statement before closing a file or quitting your program. Not doing this may foul up the files from that point on.

Summary of File-Handling Methods: The General Form of the Open Statement for Files

The most general form for the Open statement looks like this:

```
Open pathname [For mode] [Access access] [lock] _
As [#] filenumber [Len=reclength]
```

For example, you can use a version of this to control file sharing at the time you open the file using the correct option in the Open command. Here are short descriptions of the parameters possible:

pathname   A string expression that specifies the filename. It may include both directory and drive information.

mode   Specifies one of the file modes you have already seen: Append, Binary, Input, Output, or Random.

access   This specifies what operations are permitted on the open file. There are three possible options: Read, Write, or Read Write. For example:

```
Open #1 For Binary A #1, Access Read
```

will let you read the file but not make any changes to it.

lock   This parameter specifies the operations permitted on the open file by other processes. (Unlike the Access parameter, which controls how *your* program can access the file.) There are four possibilities: Shared, Lock Read, Lock Write, and Lock Read Write, as described in the following table:

Keyword	*Description*
Shared	Other processes can both read and write to the file even while your program is working with it.
Lock Read	No other program can open the file to read it while your program is working with it.
Lock Write	No other program can open the file to write it while your program is working with it.
Lock Read Write	Prevents other programs from working with the file at all while you are working with it..

For example:

```
Open "Foo" For Binary As #256, Access Read, Lock Read
```

would let you read the file but nobody else. (Microsoft suggests reserving numbers larger than 255 for files accessible by other applications.)

filenumber   A valid file number must be in the range 1 to 511, inclusive. (As you have seen, it's best to use the FreeFile function to find the next available file number.)

reclength   This is an integer from 1 to 32,767. For files opened for random access, this number gives the record length. For sequential files, this value is the number of characters buffered by the OS.

Note

In Binary, Input, and Random file modes, you can open a file using a different file number without first closing the file. For sequential Append and Output, you must close a file before you can work with it again in a different mode.

Command-Line Information

Windows Programs still retain the ability to be started from the command line (or from the Run box available off the start menu). The idea is that you can allow a program to start with extra information that can be set by experienced users. (The custom in Windows programming is not to require command-line arguments for inexperienced users!) For example, Figure 5-4 shows the command line options for starting VB itself.

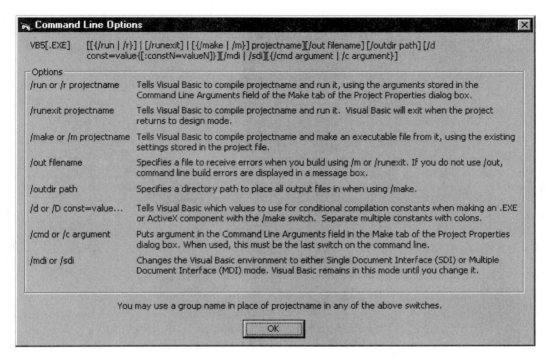

Figure 5-4 Command Line Options for VB

Visual Basic makes it easy to read command-line information. When the user runs your program from the Run box on the Start button or from a DOS Window and uses the line

```
FileExeName info1 info2 info3...
```

then the value returned by the Command function is the string whose value is "*info1 info2….*" You will need to separate out the arguments by looking for the various command-line arguments.

Tip

Since command-line information will only be used by experienced users, you have complete control over the form you require this information to take. If you don't want to waste a lot of code (and coding time!) parsing irregular strings, we suggest enforcing strict conventions on command-line arguments. (Your users will, however, hate you if you require them to be case sensitive as well as being careful in their spacing.)

For example, let's say you wanted to have a Name command-line option. You can require that the experienced user use it in the form:

```
Name=StringWithNameInformation
```

followed by one or more spaces. This makes the code to find out a the name information trivial. For example, the following code fragment stores this information in a string named NameInfo:

```
Dim CommandLineInfo As String, NextChar As String, NameInfo As String
Dim CurrentLocation As Integer
CommandLineInfo = Command()
CurrentLocation = InStr(CommandLineInfo, "Name=") + 5
'since Name= has 5 characters
NextChar = Mid$(CommandLineInfo, CurrentLocation, 1)
Do Until NextChar =  Chr(32) Or CurrentLocation > Len(CommandLineInfo)
   NameInfo = NameInfo + NextChar
   CurrentLocation = CurrentLocation + 1
   NextChar = Mid$(CommandLineInfo, CurrentLocation, 1)
Loop
```

Note that this code is assuming that the user will not use a command-line argument like:

```
Type=Name=Typo
```

and then expect us to think that the value of the command-line option Type was the string:

```
Name=Typo
```

Obviously, if you are going to allow command-line information, you don't want to have to compile the project, try the command line, and then rebuild the EXE each time you made a mistake. As you might expect, Visual Basic gives you a way to provide sample command-line information within the IDE. For this:

1. Choose Project|Project Properties.
2. Go to the Make tab.
3. Fill in the Command-line arguments box as you want. (Don't use quotes unless you want them to be part of the command-line argument you are testing.)

Error Trapping

Regardless of how carefully you debug your own program, it's impossible to anticipate what an inexperienced user may do. If you want your program to "degrade gracefully" and not just roll over after an error, you'll want to prevent fatal errors. The command that activates error trapping is:

```
On Error GoTo...
```

where the three dots stand for the label (line number) that defines the error trap. (See the section on the GoTo in the previous chapter for more on labels.) The labeled code must be in the current procedure. You cannot jump out of a procedure using an On Error GoTo command. On the other hand, the code for an error trap can (and often will) use other Sub or Function procedures.

Since you don't want Visual Basic to inadvertently "fall" into the error-trapping code, it is a good idea to have an Exit (Sub or Function) on the line immediately preceding the label for the error trap.

The On Error GoTo command can occur anywhere in an event, Sub, or Function procedure. Usually, the error-trapping code is inside that procedure. The only exception to this is when one procedure has been called by another. In this case, Visual Basic will look to see if an error trap was enabled in the earlier procedure if one does not exist in the second procedure.

Once you start error trapping with the On Error GoTo command, a run-time error such as a disk not being accessible will no longer bomb the program. The On Error GoTo command should transfer control to a piece of code that identifies the problem and, if possible, fix it.

If the error can be corrected, the Resume statement takes you back to the statement that caused the error in the first place. However, you can't correct an error if you don't know why it happened. Identify the problem by means of the Err object. The Err object has several properties and methods you can use to get information on run-time errors. When a run-time error occurs, the Err object's properties are set with information specific only to the error and you can use the error information to handle the error. You can also Raise errors at run time in your code. The following table summarizes the Err object's main properties and methods.

Table 5-10:	Err Object's Properties and Methods

Property or Method	Description
Number	This is a long integer value specifically identifying an error.
Source	This is a string containing the name of the Visual Basic project.
Description	This is a string containing the error message, if one exists.
LastDLLError	LastDLLError is a long integer that contains the system error code for the last call into a DLL (if the DLL supports returning an error).
Clear	The Clear method resets the Err object.
Raise	The Raise method triggers a run-time error in your code.

When debugging a program, it's helpful to know what the error message for the last error was (for example, to place it in a message box). This would be the string given by:

```
Err.Description
```

Of course, this may be location-dependent so you are better off using the error number. Err.Number is, in fact, the default property for the Err object and the long integer it gives can be used to identify the error. For example, if:

```
ErrorNumber = Err.Number
```

the value of the variable ErrorNumber can help you pick up the type of error. Visual Basic can identify many run-time errors. This table gives some examples of error numbers. (Check the online help for a complete listing.)

Table 5-11:	Error Number Examples

Error Code	Explanation
5	Invalid procedure call or argument
7	Out of memory
13	Type mismatch
52	Bad file name or number (FreeFile may not have been used correctly)

Error Code	Explanation
53	File not found
54	Bad file mode (The code uses two different types of file handling—without closing the file in between)
55	File already open
57	Device I/O error
58	File already exists
59	Bad record length
61	Disk full
62	Input past end of file (You may have put the test for EOF in the wrong place)
63	Bad record number
67	Too many files at the same time
68	Device unavailable
70	Permission denied
71	Disk not ready
74	Can't rename files across different drives
75	Path/File access error
76	Path not found

Tip

An Out of Memory error does not necessarily mean that your application has run out of memory. It is possible for VBA to return this generic error because it cannot determine a more appropriate error. You still need to find out the cause for the error in your code, but you should not try to figure out why your system is low on memory when there is a very good chance that the error has nothing to do with memory.

The way you use this information is simple. Suppose an event procedure will be using the printer. Somewhere in the procedure, before the error can occur, place a statement such as this:

```
On Error GoTo PrinterCheck
```

Now, before the End Sub, add code that looks like this:

Listing 5-8:   An Error Trap

```
Exit Sub
PrinterCheck:
  ErrorNumber = Err.Number
  Beep
  Select Case ErrorNumber
    Case 25
      MsgBox "Your printer may be off-line."
    Case 27
      MsgBox "Is there a printer available?"
    Case Else
      M$ = "Please tell the operator (= program
        author?) that"
      M$ = M$ & vbCrLf
      M$ = M$ & "error number " & ErrorNumber & _
        "occurred."
      MsgBox M$
      End
  End Select

  M$ = "If the error has been corrected click on OK."
  M$ = M$ &vbCrLf
  M$ = M$ & "Otherwise click on Cancel."
  Continue = MsgBox(M$, vbOKCancel)
  If Continue = vbOK Then Resume Else End
```

The idea of this error trap is simple, and the Select Case statement is ideal. Each case tries to give some indication of where the problem is and, if possible, how to correct it. If you reach the Case Else, the error number has to be reported. In any case, the final block gives you the option of continuing or not by using a message box with two buttons. You might want to get into the habit of writing a general procedure that analyzes the error code. The error trap inside a procedure just sends control to the general procedure. If you do this, you can reuse the general procedure in many different projects.

When developing a program, you may want to test how your error handler works. Visual Basic includes the statement

```
Error(errorcode number)
```

which, when processed, makes Visual Basic behave as if the error described by the given error number had actually occurred. This makes it easier to develop the error trap.

Finally, you can define and then raise your own errors in addition to the ones built into Visual Basic. You can even have your functions directly return an instance of the Err object whenever they return variants. Raising your own errors is especially useful when building a control, as you need to provide feedback to the user. Of course, you do not want to overwrite any of Visual Basic's built-in errors. By convention, the way to number your own errors is to follow this prescription:

1. Use the global constant vbObjectError, which defines the range of VB's internal errors.
2. Add 512 to this constant.
3. Start defining your errors with this number.

For example:

```
Const DataNotFound = 1 + vbObjectError + 512

Error.Raise DataNotFound
```

(If your control depends on third-party controls, you have to avoid their error numbers along with VB's intrinsic error codes.)

Resume Revisited

A variant on the Resume command lets you bypass the statement that may have caused the problem. If you use

```
Resume Next
```

or

```
On Error Resume Next
```

VB will do this automatically.

This kind of code is especially important for a user control since the End statement is forbidden. Roughly speaking, use Resume if the error trap clears the error up and Resume Next otherwise.

Visual Basic begins processing at the statement following the one that caused the error. You can also resume execution at any line of code that has been previously identified with a label. For this, use

```
Resume Label
```

Both the Resume and Resume Next commands behave differently if Visual Basic has to move backward to find the error trap in another procedure. Recall that this happens when one procedure is invoked by a previous procedure and the current procedure doesn't have an error trap. In both cases, the statement executed by Visual Basic will not be in the procedure where the error occurred. For the Resume command, Visual Basic will call the original procedure again. For the Resume Next command, Visual Basic will execute the statement after the call to the original procedure. You will never get back to the original procedure.

Suppose the chain of procedural calls goes back even further: Procedure1 calls Procedure2, which calls Function3. Now an error occurs in Function3, but the only error handler is in Procedure1. If there is a Resume command in the error handler in Procedure1, Visual Basic actually goes to the statement that is called Procedure2.

Because this is unwieldy and so prone to problems, it is probably better to rely only on error handlers that occur in a specific procedure. If one procedure calls another, turn off the error handler in the calling routine.

Disabling Error Trapping

If you are confident that you will no longer need an error trap, you can disable error trapping with the statement

```
On Error GoTo 0
```

(although, strictly speaking, the 0 is not needed). Similarly, you can change which error trap is in effect by using another On Error GoTo statement. Be sure to have an Exit command between the error traps. Visual Basic uses the last processed On Error GoTo statement to decide where to go. The On Error GoTo statement will clear the Err object. If you do not use this statement after an error has occurred, it is advisable to use Err.Clear to keep the error from bubbling up to the calling subprogram.

The Line that Caused the Error?

There's one other error-handling function, Erl (Error Line). If you get really desperate and need to find the line that caused the error and Visual Basic isn't stopping the program at that line, you can do the following:

1. Add line numbers before every statement in the procedure. We give you an add-in (see Chapter 15) that will do this automatically.
2. Add the Erl statement to the error trap.

Here's an example of what the code might look like.

Listing 5-9:	Finding the Line that Caused the Error

```
Sub Partition (AnArray(), Start As Integer, Finish As Integer, _
LocOfSplitter As Integer)
   On Error GoTo PartitionErr
   ' LOCAL variables are: SplitPos,NewStart,I,Splitter
   Dim SplitPos As Integer, NewStart As Integer
   Dim I As Integer, Splitter

10   SplitPos = (start + finish) \ 2
20   Splitter = AnArray(SplitPos)
30   SWAP AnArray(SplitPos), AnArray(start)
40   LeftPos = start
50      For I = start + 1 To finish
60         If AnArray(i) < Splitter Then
70            LeftPos = LeftPos + 1
80            SWAP AnArray(LeftPos), AnArray(i)
90         End If
100     Next i
110   SWAP AnArray(start), AnArray(LeftPos)
120   LocOfSplitter = LeftPos
   Exit Sub
PartitionErr:
   MsgBox Err.Description & ' occurred on line ' & Erl
End Sub
```

With information this precise, you can often track down the problem more quickly. We don't recommend this as a common practice, but it may be the only way to debug certain applications or user controls that seem to act differently in various situations.

ADVANCED USER INTERFACE ISSUES

Topics in this Chapter

Chapter 6

Now that you have learned most of the non-object oriented programming techniques needed to work with VB, it's time to turn to the user interface again. To take full advantage of VB's power there are a lot of techniques that you'll need to master. Here are some of the topics that we will cover in this chapter:

- How to work with text selected by the user, including implementing cut and paste features into your programs.
- How to use applications with multiple forms.
- How to control the printer.
- How to use the Windows common controls including the common dialog boxes.
- How to use VB graphics either using the line and shape controls or using the graphics commands to do graphics from scratch.
- How to attach help information to the different parts of your program.
- The first steps in handling resource files to make internationalizing your applications possible.

We even show you ways to insure that the controls on your forms stay in proportion—no matter how the user resizes the form. Finally, since users of your applications and controls will expect you to handle mouse operations in a sophisticated manner, we take that topic up as well.

The Clipboard and Text

The Windows clipboard lets you exchange information between Windows applications and between parts of a windows application. Visual Basic controls, such as text boxes, will automatically implement cut and paste using the standard Windows shortcuts, such as Ctrl+X for cut and Ctrl+V for paste where appropriate (such as between two text boxes). However, to activate menu items for cut and paste requires code. First off, the clipboard can hold only one piece of the same kind of data at a time. If you send new information using the same format to the clipboard, you wipe out what was there before. It is usually safer to make sure that the clipboard is completely free before working with it. To do this, use the Clear method of the Clipboard object:

```
Clipboard.Clear
```

If you need to send text to and from the clipboard, use the two additional methods described in the following table.

Clipboard.SetText StringData	This sends the string information contained in the variable or string expression StringData to the clipboard, wiping out whatever text was there.
StringVariable=Clipboard.GetText	The GetText method takes a copy of the text currently stored in the clipboard and stores it in a string variable. The text contents of the clipboard remain intact until you explicitly clear the clipboard or send new text to it so you can do multiple pasting operations.

You must use the Clipboard object or an object expression that evaluates to it (see Chapter 7) in these methods.

Selecting Text in Visual Basic

When you add a text box, rich text box or a combo box to a Visual Basic form, users can select text following the usual Windows convention like using SHIFT and a direction key. You get at whatever text the user has selected by using three properties of the control. Two of these properties have long integer values and the third is a string.

The SelStart property returns a long integer that gives you the place where the selected text starts. If the value is 0, the user has started selecting text from the beginning of the text or combo box. If the value is equal to the length of the text string—Len(txtBox1.Text), for example—the user wants the code to start working after all the text that's currently in the box. You can specify where selected text starts (for example, in a demonstration program) by setting the value of this property from code. For example, for a text box named txtBox1, a line of code like:

```
txtBox1.SelStart = Len(txtBox1.Text)/2
```

starts the selected text in the middle of the text inside the text box.

The SelLength property gives you the number of characters the user has selected. If SelLength equals 0, he or she has not selected any text. If SelLength is equal to the length of the txtBox1.text string, all the characters in the control were selected. To highlight the first half of the contents of a text box, you would use code like this:

```
txtBox1.SetFocus
txtBox1.SelStart = 0
txtBox1.SelLength = Len(txtBox1.Text)/2
```

Finally, the SelText property is the actual string the user has selected. If the user hasn't selected any text, this is the empty (null) string. This means if you add the following line of code to the fragment just given:

```
Dim FirstHalfOfTtext As String
FirstHalfOfText = txtBox1.SelText
```

then the value of the string variable FirstHalfOfText is what the user selected.

When you assign a new string value to the SelText property, Visual Basic replaces the selected string inside the control with the new string. This means that to allow users to copy selected text all you have to do is combine these properties with the SetText method. For example, for a menu item named Copy and a text box named txtBox1, all you need to do is use code like:

```
Sub mnuCopy_Click()
   Clipboard.SetText txtBox1.SelText
End Sub
```

Or for a procedure that cuts out the selected text, use the following code:

```
Sub mnuCut_Click()
   Clipboard.SetText txtBox1.SelText
   txtBox1.SelText = ""
End Sub
```

The point is that the new line in the Cut procedure resets the value of SelText to the empty string. This has the effect of cutting the selected text out of the text box.

To implement a Paste operation where the user has set the insertion point inside a text box named txtBox1, use the following code:

```
Sub mnuPaste_Click()
   txtBox1.Text = Clipboard.GetText()
End Sub
```

Notice that if the user hasn't selected any text, this code acts as an insertion method. Otherwise, it replaces the selected text.

Note

Some people use the SendKeys statement to send the usual CTRL+C, CTRL+X and CTRL+V combinations to the active control. We don't usually do this although we do occasionally send the undo string (CTRL+Z) via SendKeys to the active control. You can also use an API call (Chapter 12) to undo

The Clipboard and Graphics

Visual Basic 5 can handle a larger class of graphics images inside the clipboard than earlier versions of VB. However, regardless of the type of graphic stored in the clipboard, you are best off trying to determine what type of image is stored there. This is done with the GetFormat method of the Clipboard object, which returns true or false depending on whether the clipboard holds information of the specified type. You use the values described in the following table with the GetFormat method. For example:

```
If Clipboard.GetFormat(vbCFBitmap) Or _
ClipBoard.GetFormat(vbCFDIB) Then
   'clipboard has a bitmap
Else
   'clipboard doesn't have a bitmap
End If
```

The following table lists all the possible clipboard formats:

Table 6-1:   Clipboard Formats

Constant	Value	Description
vbCFText	1	Text.
vbCFBitmap	2	Bitmap (.bmp files).
vbCFMetafile	3	Metafile (.wmf files).
vbCFDIB	8	Device-independent bitmap (DIB). This setting includes both a bitmap and a palette.
vbCFPalette	9	Color palette.
vbCFEMetafile	14	Enhanced metafile (.emf).
vbCFRTF	&HBF01	RichText Format (.rtf).
vbCFLink	&HBF00	DDE conversation information (see the Programmers guide for more on DDE).

(As always, while programming, the Object Browser is the quickest way to get access to these constants.)

To retrieve data from the clipboard, use the GetData method *after* you check that the clipboard has an image and not text. Once you know that an image is inside the clipboard, use the appropriate property of the control to get the image. For example:

```
If Clipboard.GetFormat(vbCFBitmap) Then
   pctBox1.Picture = Clipboard.GetData
End If
```

would place a bitmap in a picture box named pctBox1. (You can also use the format constant in the GetData method but this is rarely necessary because if you leave it out VB will automatically use an appropriate format. There is therefore little reason to use the longer form unless you want to override VB's choice.) To send an image to the clipboard use the SetData method of the clipboard object. For example:

```
Clipboard.SetData pctBox1.Picture
```

The general form for the SetData method is:

```
ClipBoard.SetData Data, Format
```

where the Format parameter is one of the constants given in Table 6-1. (As with the GetData method it turns out that the SetData method is usually smart enough to automatically figure out the appropriate format. So unless you want to override its choice, you can leave the Format parameter out here as well.)

Multiple Form Applications

To this point we have only used a single form in our applications. Most sophisticated interfaces usually require that multiple forms be open at least some of the time. There are two ways to have a multiple form application in VB:

- Add all of the forms at design time.
- Add some or all of them at run time.

This chapter concentrates on the first alternative. We will leave a complete discussion of adding new forms at run time until the next chapter.

First off, just as Visual Basic itself has two possible ways of using multiple forms in its IDE, there are two ways to code a multiple form application with VB. Recall that these two possibilities are:

- SDI (Single Document Interface). Each window exists independently of the others
- MDI (Multiple document interface). There is a single containing window and all other windows sit inside it as *child* windows. (Of course, MDI applications will occasionally use a window that "floats" outside the parent window for things like dialog boxes.)

We first take up the mechanics for adding more forms at design time. This is sufficient for creating and showing forms for an SDI application. The next section takes up the somewhat more sophisticated methods needed for coding an MDI application.

Basics Of Handling Multiple Forms

The easiest way to add another form to your application at design time is simply to choose Project|Add Form.

This brings up a dialog box like the one shown in Figure 6-1. There are obviously a lot of choices! Most of them are self explanatory. For example, Figure 6-2 and 6-3 show the forms for a log-in form and an options dialog box form that uses tabs. (Keep in mind that all the forms that you get this way are simply the interface you will use, they all need code to activate them.

Figure 6-1   The Add Form dialog Box

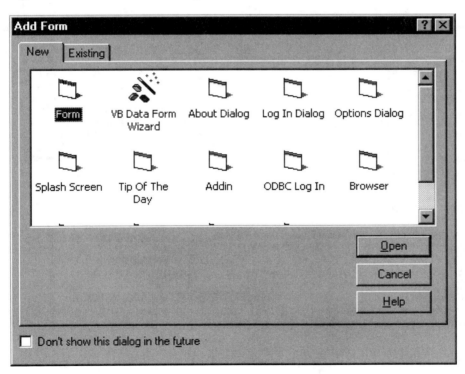

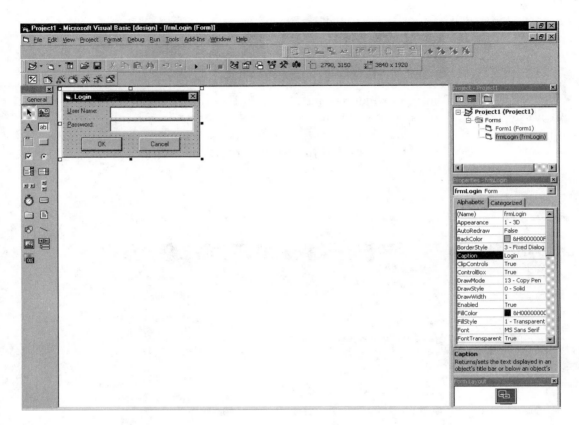

Figure 6-2   A form for a log-in screen

Note that even after you add multiple forms at design time, Visual Basic displays, at most, one form when an application starts running. This is called the *startup form.* Any other forms in your application must be explicitly loaded and displayed via code. (The next section covers the commands to do this.) The startup form is usually the initial form that appears when you begin a new project. If you want to change this:

1.   Choose Project|Project Properties.
2.   Go to the General tab.
3.   Choose the startup form by name. (See Figure 6-4 on page 266 for an example.)

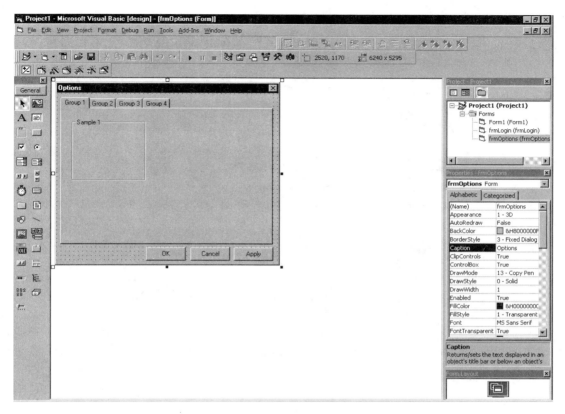

Figure 6-3   A form for an option dialog box

Code for Working with Multiple Forms

Since only the startup form is automatically shown by VB, you need to add the code to your program to handle the display of any additional forms. There are four keywords for working with a form that we describe in this section.

Show

As its name suggests, the Show method shows the form on the screen but a lot more goes on behind the scenes. When you ask VB to Show a form, Visual Basic first checks that the form is loaded into memory. If it is not, then it loads the form automatically. For example, if Form1 is the startup form and you say:

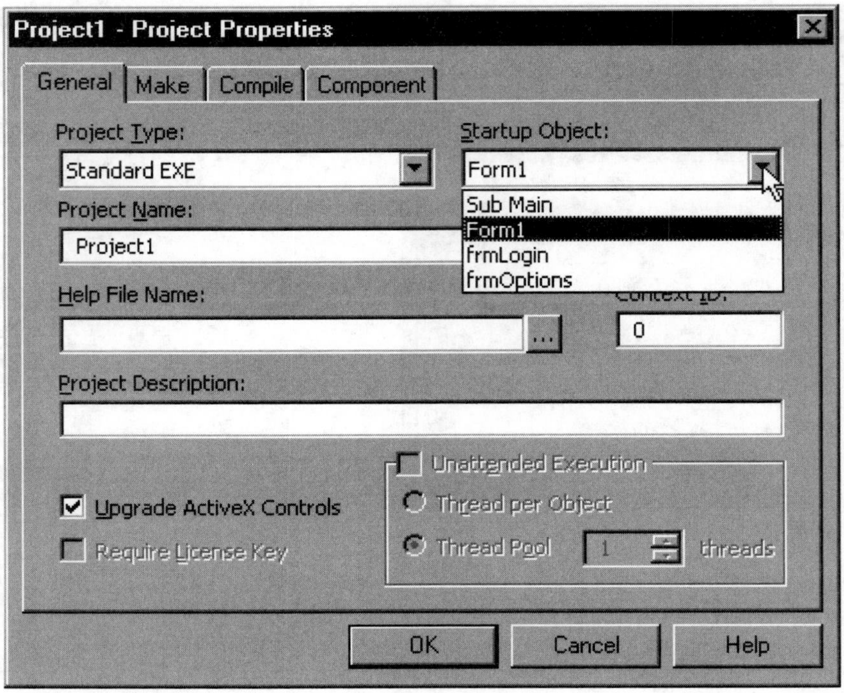

Figure 6-4: Choosing a Startup form

```
Sub Form1_Load()
   Form2.Show
End Sub
```

VB will load Form2 into memory and display it at the location you set for it at design time. The general form for the Show method uses the name you gave the Form at design time:

```
FormName.Show
```

You can also use the Show method to move a loaded form to the top of the desktop if it is invisible or is currently covered by another form.

Caution

Unless you set the AutoRedraw property of the form to be true, covering and uncovering forms can result in information that was displayed on the form being erased. (See the section on "Behind the Scenes with Visual Basic Graphics" for more on the AutoRedraw property.)

Load

You will often want to load forms into memory but not display them automatically. (For example, you can preload forms while a splash screen is up in order to have your application appear to run more quickly down the road. The tradeoff is that you use up more memory. The Load statement tells VB to bring the form into memory but to not display it. (Visual Basic also loads the form into memory whenever you refer to its properties or controls in code.) Its syntax is:

```
Load FormName
```

When Visual Basic loads a form, it sets all the properties of the form to the ones you initially made at design time. If you try to load an already loaded form then VB generates an error. The first time VB loads the form it invokes the Form_Initialize event procedure and then it invokes the Form_Load event procedure.

Unload

The Unload statement removes the form from memory. All information that was contained in any form-level variables will be lost. The syntax for this statement is:

```
Unload FormName
```

After you unload a form using the Unload statement, you can reload the form again (using Load). After reloading a form, VB only calls the Form_Load event procedure and will no longer call the Form_Initialize event procedure. You can follow the load, unload and reload cycle for a form as often as you want.

Hide

The Hide method makes the form invisible but doesn't unload it from memory. While the user can't see any of the controls on the form or the form itself, you can still refer to its properties, methods and events via code. Information stored in form-level variables in a hidden form keep their values and can be accessed. As with loading a form, hiding a form trades response time for memory. The syntax is:

```
FormName.Hide
```

SUB MAIN

If you look closely at Figure 6-4 you see that one of the choices for the startup object is not a form but something called "Sub Main." (This should immediately ring a bell for C, Java and experienced VB programmers.) The idea of a Sub Main is that Visual Basic gives you the option of not showing a form when the application starts running. If you choose the Sub Main option to start your program then you have to explicitly load each form via code. For example, you could choose which form to load depending on the user's screen size (see below) or his or her response to a message box. By combining a Sub Main with a call to Do Events, you can program time-consuming operations that will run only during the computer's "idle time" as in the following sample code:

```
Public Sub Main
   Do While DoEvents()
      'code you want to process during idle time goes
      'here
   Loop
End Sub
```

Life Cycle Events for Forms Revisited

We briefly mentioned the life cycle events for a form in Chapter 3. Recall that at birth these were:

- Initialize, Load, Activate, Got Focus.

At death:

- QueryUnload, Unload, Terminate.

Since you now know you can load and unload forms via code it should be clearer what the differences are between the Initialize and the Load event and between the Unload and Terminate events. The Initialize and Terminate events are called only once no matter how many times you load and unload the form. Use the Initialize event for things like the initial property settings for your form that need to be set only once. Use the Terminate event for the code that absolutely finally cleans up left over details.

Next, before Visual Basic actually unloads a form it triggers the QueryUnload event whose event procedure signature is:

```
Private Sub Form_QueryUnload(cancel As Integer, unloadmode _
As Integer)
```

The parameters that VB passes in this event are very useful. For example, by setting the cancel parameter to be non-zero you stop the form from unloading, as in the following example:

```
Private Sub Form_QueryUnload(cancel As Integer, unloadmode _
As Integer)
   Dim YesNo As Integer
   YesNo = MsgBox("Are you sure you want to leave?", vbYesNo)
   If YesNo = vbNo Then cancel = True
End Sub
```

Next the unloadmode parameter tells you how the user closed the form as described in the following table:

Table 6-2:   The Standard Toolbar Icons

Unload Mode Constant	*Value*	*Description*
vbFormControlMenu	0	The user chose the Close command from the Control menu on the form.
vbFormCode	1	VB Processed the Unload statement for that form in code.
vbAppWindows	2	Windows is shutting down.
vbAppTaskManager	3	The user used the Microsoft Windows Task Manager (Ctrl+Alt+Del once (!)) to try to close the application.
vbFormMDIForm	4	An MDI child form is closing because the MDI parent form is closing. (See below.)

Caution

When VB processes an End statement, all action ceases. The various unloading events are not triggered and you will not be able to give the user a chance to stop the program from ending. For this reason we suggest being very careful in using End statements in your code.

Finally, you should consider explicitly unloading all loaded forms in the QueryUnload procedure for the startup form (or use similar code in the Sub Main if that was how you started the application). The problem is that a multiple form application may look like it is over, in the sense that there are no forms showing, but all of the loaded forms are simply hidden. Remember, for an application with a startup form VB shuts it down only when all forms are unloaded from memory or it processes an End statement.

For an application started from a Sub Main, VB ends the application only when all forms are explicitly unloaded and it processes an End (or the End Sub of the Sub Main). Since DoEvents returns the number of loaded forms, code in the Sub Main often looks like this:

```
Sub Main()
   Do While DoEvents()
      ' code you want to process during idle time
      ' code to load the forms explicitly
      'may also need
     'code for unloading some or all of the forms
   Loop
   'anything else you want to do when all the forms are gone
   End   'not really necessary but is ok here
End Sub
```

Notice that the End statement we used here can't cause any problems. This is because VB will leave the loop only when all forms have been unloaded (which is when the DoEvents function call returns 0), so you know there will be no hidden forms to worry about.

Keeping the Focus in a Form (Modality)

Message boxes require that users close them before they can resume work on the form. This property is often useful for a form as well. For example, you may want to make sure a user has filled in a dialog box you built out of a form before he or she shifts the focus to another form in the application. This property is called *modality* in the Microsoft Windows documentation. You make a form modal by adding an option to the Show method that displays the form. If you have a line of code in a procedure that reads:

```
FormName.Show vbModal
```

then Visual Basic displays the form modally so that no user input to any other form in the application will be accepted until the modal form is hidden or unloaded. For example, a user cannot move the focus to any other form in the application until the modal form is hidden or unloaded. In particular, neither mouse clicks nor keypresses will register in any other form in the application. (The user can always switch to another application in Windows of course.) Usually you have a default command or cancel button on a modal form.

Tip

A dialog box is usually a modal form with a fixed double border.

MDI Applications

One way to make an MDI parent form is simply to choose Project|New MDI Form. The MDI child forms are then any other forms in your project whose MDIChild property is True. At design time, child forms and the MDI parent form look similar—it's hard to tell the differences between them. One way to tell is to look at in the Project explorer at the glyphs (small icons) next to the form names. MDI child forms have an icon that looks like a little form next to a bigger form as shown in Figure 6-5. When you run the project, on the other hand, all the child forms must be explicitly shown (with the Show method) and are displayed within the MDI parent form's boundaries. Moreover, if the child form is minimized, its icon appears inside the MDI parent form, rather than in the Windows desktop. (If you maximize a child form, its caption replaces the caption of the parent form.) When you unload the parent form all of its child forms are automatically unloaded but the QueryUnload event occurs first for the MDI parent form and then for all MDI child forms.

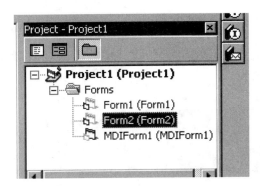

Figure 6-5 Project Explorer with MDI forms

One of the nicest features of Visual Basic's MDI forms is that the menus of the container form change according to which child form has the focus. This lets you work with specific menus for each child form. What happens is that the menu for the child form that has the focus appears on the menu bar of the MDI container form—replacing whatever menu was previously there. In particular, the user only sees the menu for the child form when that child form has the focus.

The MDI Window Menu

Every MDI application should have a Window menu that allows the user to arrange or cascade the child windows. The Window menu should also include a list of the MDI child windows, as shown in Figure 6-6.

Figure 6-6   Menu on a MDI form

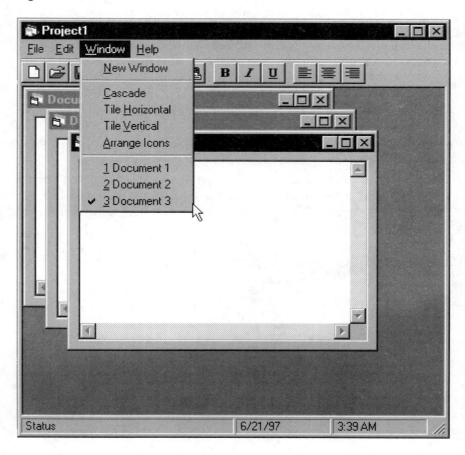

Although the VB application wizard adds the code for the Windows menu automatically and is how we usually do it, it isn't hard to do it yourself. For example, the list of MDI child windows is easy to put on the menu: make sure the WindowList check box on the menu designer is set. Visual Basic will then automatically display the list of the MDI child form captions—and even put a check mark next to the one that most recently had the focus.

If you don't choose to start with the code generated by the VB Application wizard then to activate the Tile, Cascade, and Arrange items on the Windows menu, use code like this:

```
Sub CascadeForms_Click()
   Me.Arrange vbCascade
End Sub
```

This uses the vbCascade constant with the Arrange method applied to the Me object. (The Me object always refers to the current object, only the Parent form would have a Window menu so this will always work correctly regardless of the name you choose for your MDI parent form.) The other constants are vbTileHorizontal, vbTileVertical, and vbArrangeIcons.

Tip

For coding the framework for an MDI application the VB Application Wizard is a real time-saver. It not only adds the code needed to create new child forms at run time using the more sophisticated techniques that you will see in the next chapter, it adds the code to activate many of the normal menus that an MDI application should have. (Such as a Window menu for cascading or tiling the child windows.)

Displaying Information

Now that you have seen how to add multiple forms on an application you will often want to use a secondary form for displaying information. Generally speaking, even if you use a special form to display information, you might want to use a picture box, a multiline text box or a rich text box rather than printing the text directly to that form. For example, both versions of text boxes can have scroll bars which make it easy for the user to look at text that is no longer appearing on the screen. (Trust us, you do not want to write the code that would allow information on a form to "scroll" unless you absolutely have to.)

Note

To position text inside a multiline text box, you need to insert spaces and new-line characters (vbCrLF). Text boxes do not support direct positioning of text.

As the note says, as useful as the various kinds of text boxes are, you are restricted to a line-oriented approach. Even a rich text box does not give you the absolute precision possible with the Print method when applied to a picture box or form. We want to take this up next. The syntax to Print to a form or to a picture box is similar:

```
FormName.Print expressions to print
PictureBoxName.Print expressions to print
```

Where Visual Basic displays the information depends on the current value of two properties of the form or picture box: the *CurrentX* and *CurrentY* properties. CurrentX refers to the horizontal position, and CurrentY to the vertical position, where it will display information. The units used are determined by the scale set up with the various scale methods you saw in Chapter 3. Set the CurrentX and CurrentY properties the same way you'd set any property:

```
ObjectName.CurrentX = Value
ObjectName.CurrentY = Value
```

The value is any numeric expression from which Visual Basic can extract a single-precision value.

Whenever you use the Cls method to clear a form or picture box, Visual Basic resets the CurrentX and CurrentY values to zero. Using the default setting for the various scale properties would mean that the next Print statement puts information in the top left-hand corner of the form or picture box. If you have changed the scale (for example, by resetting the ScaleLeft and ScaleTop properties), Visual Basic will use whatever location on the form or picture box now represented the 0,0 coordinates.

The keys to using CurrentX and CurrentY effectively are the TextHeight and TextWidth properties. These let you determine the width and height of text—before setting the CurrentX and CurrentY properties in order to print the text. For example, here's the kind of code you can use to have a command button that will center the text contained in a single line text box named txtBox1 inside a picture box.

```
Private Sub cmdCenterText_Click()
  Dim WidthOfText As Single
  Dim WidthOfBox As Single
  Dim HeightOfBox As Single
  Dim HeightOfText As Single

  Picture1.Cls
  WidthOfText = TextWidth(txtBox1.Text)
  WidthOfBox = Picture1.Width
  If WidthOfText > WidthOfBox Then
    MsgBox ("Sorry text to wide to center")
    Exit Sub
  Else
    Picture1.CurrentX = (WidthOfBox - WidthOfText) / 2
  End If

  HeightOfText = TextHeight(txtBox1.Text)
  HeightOfBox = Picture1.Height
  If HeightOfText > HeightOfBox Then
    MsgBox ("Sorry text to high to center")
    Exit Sub
  Else
    Picture1.CurrentY = (HeightOfBox - HeightOfText) / 2
  End If
  Picture1.Print txtBox1.Text
End Sub
```

Tip

There is a quick and dirty method of displaying information that works fine with fonts like Courier where all characters have the same width. The ides is that after processing a Print method, Visual Basic moves to the next line. (Setting the new CurrentY value equal to CurrentY plus the height of a line in the current font.) An empty Print statement, therefore, adds a blank line whose height is the height of a line in the current font. If you want to suppress the automatic carriage return, place a semicolon at the end of the Print statement. Next, each time you use a comma in a Print statement, Visual Basic displays the data to the next print zone (set to be the width of 14 characters apart.). The Tab function lets you move to a specific column and start printing there. The Spc function inserts the specified number of spaces into a line starting at the current print position.

Finally, we want to point out that you should not put Print statements in the Form_Load event unless you have either:

- Set the AutoRedraw property of the form to be True

or

- Put a Show method in the Form_Load before the Print statement.

If you fail to do one of these two options, you won't see the information displayed.

Printing

Visual Basic uses the printer that is currently set up as the default printer for Windows. This information is encapsulated in the Printer object. The DeviceName property of the Printer object therefore gives you the name of the default printer. For example:

```
MsgBox "The current default printer is " & Printer.DeviceName
```

might return an image like Figure 6-7.

Figure 6-7   Default printer dialog box

Visual Basic stores all the printers that Windows knows about in what it calls the "Printers collection." (Note the "s," Printer alone is the current Windows default printer, Printers is the collection of all the installed printers.) While we will have a lot more to say about collections in the next chapter, the important point about a collection for us right now is that you iterate through them using the For-Each construct that you saw in the last chapter. You then can change the default printer using the Set command (which we also will have a lot more to say about in the next chapter).

For example, here's the code you need to change the default printer to be WinFax if it is one of the installed printers on your system:

```
Dim APrinter As Printer
For Each APrinter In Printers
   If APrinter.DeviceName = "WinFax" Then
      Set Printer = APrinter
      MsgBox "Just set printer to be WinFax"
      Exit For
   End If
Next
```

Note that code like this can be a little tricky to use in practice since the DeviceName property of the Printer object can be a fairly complicated string (such as "HP DeskJet 870C Series" which is one of our installed printers) and, of course, string matches must be exact unless you use the UCase or LCase functions.

Here's some code that would add all the printer device names to a list box and then let the user double click on one of the names in order to make it the default printer:

```
Private Sub Form_Load()
   Dim APrinter As Printer
   For Each APrinter In Printers
   List1.AddItem APrinter.DeviceName
Next
End Sub

Private Sub List1_DblClick()
   Dim APrinter As Printer
   For Each APrinter In Printers
   If APrinter.DeviceName = List1.Text Then
      Set Printer = APrinter
      MsgBox "Set printer to " & Printer.DeviceName
      Exit For
   End If
   Next
End Sub
```

The idea of this code is straightforward: the Form_Load fills up the list box with the printer names. That way we can check for the name the user selected in the Dbl_Click event procedure for the list box by running through the printers stored in the Printers collection one more time. When we find the match we reset the default printer using the Set command.

Working with the Printer

For working with a printer you need to keep in mind that most of the printer commands in Visual Basic are *page oriented.* This means that Visual Basic calculates all the characters (actually dots) that will appear on a page before it sends the information to the printer. This allows you to have complete control over the appearance of the printed page.

The usual way to send information to a printer is to use the Print method applied to the Printer object. For example, because the Print method is page oriented, you can set the CurrentX and CurrentY properties to precisely position text or even dots on a page just as you do on a form or picture box. The idea is the same:

1. Set The CurrentX and CurrentY properties to where you want them.
2. Then use the Print method applied to the Printer object.

One added bonus is that the twips unit of measurement should map perfectly to the information you print on a page. Twips, after all, are a printer measurement (= 1/20 of a printers point, this book is set in 11-point type). Most Windows printer drivers ensure that an object that is 1440 twips will be one inch when printed.

Next, you control the font properties for printing in the same way as you do for a form or picture box, for example:

```
Printer.Font.Name = "Script"          'Use script font
Printer.Font.Size = 18                '18 point type
```

As with printing to forms and picture boxes, font changes are not retroactive. They affect only text printed after Visual Basic processes the change.

(Semicolons and commas also work the same way in Print statements as they did for forms and picture boxes. The semicolon suppresses the automatic carriage return; the comma moves to the next free print zone—still 14 columns apart. The Tab and Spc functions also work the same. Of course, these commands have the same problems as they do with a form, they only work well for non-proportionally spaced fonts.)

If you check the online help, you'll see that there are 40 properties and 12 methods for the Printer object. Most of the ones that are unfamiliar to you, such as DrawMode, apply to Graphics (see the next section). The vast majority, however, should be familiar to you since you've seen them for forms and picture boxes. The following table summarizes the printer properties and methods we use most often. (If you need some feature we don't cover, check the online help for the Printer object!)

| Table 6-3:   Printer Properties and Methods |

Statement	Description
ColorMode	Lets you determine whether a color printer prints in color or monochrome.
Copies	Lets you set the number of copies to be printed.
Height, Width	These read-only properties give you the height and width of the paper in the printer as reported by Windows. This is measured in twips, regardless of how you set the scale properties.
EndDoc	Tells Windows to release whatever information there is about the page or pages still in memory and sends it to the Print Manager for printing.
KillDoc	Cancels the current print job. (Of course, all the information may already have been sent to the printer so this may not do anything.)
NewPage	Ends the current page and tells the printer to move to the next page. The syntax is simply: Printer.NewPage.
Page	Returns the number of pages printed in the current document. The counter starts over at 1 after Visual Basic processes an EndDoc statement. It increases by one every time you use the NewPage method or when the information you send to the printer with the Print method didn't fit on the previous page.
PrintQuality	Allows you to set the quality of the printed output—if the printer driver supports it. The syntax is: Printer.PrintQuality = *value* where you can use four built-in constants ranging from vbPRPQDraft to vbPRPQHigh. You can also set the value to a specific number of dots per inch if the printer driver supports that resolutions.
Zoom	This neat property (alas not supported by all printer drivers) lets you scale the output. The default is 100 (=100 percent). Setting this property to 200 would double the size of everything, setting it to 50 would halve everything and so on.

You always use these methods with the Printer object. For example:

```
Printer.EndDoc
```

tells VB to release whatever information about the page or pages and sends the information off to the Windows Print Manager for processing.

Tip

If you have a fax program installed as the current printer, it should work in the same way as an ordinary printer. For example, when we use the popular WinFax program with VB, then after VB processes the EndDoc method, WinFax starts up and will happily fax the whole document.

Table 6-4 lists the most common error codes for printing that you will need to trap.

Table 6-4:	Common Printer Error Codes

Error number	*Reason*
396	Tried to reset a page-oriented property such as quality while still on the same page.
482	The generic printer error whenever the printer drive complains.
483	The printer river doesn't support the property you requested (such as color printing).
484	Usually caused by a corrupted printer driver.

Caution

We have found that some errors for printers may turn out to not be trappable. For example, often the Windows printer manager will simply repeatedly pop up its standard message box that says it can't communicate with the printer and do you want to retry the operation. If you hit Cancel in this message box, no error is reported back to VB. We have also found that we may not be notified of the printer error until VB processes the next statement that communicates with the printer.

Finally, the PrintForm method of the Form sends a screen dump of a form to the printer. If your application has more than one form, you have to use the form name:

```
FormName.PrintForm
```

(Or to print the active form from code on it, you can use Me.Printform.)

Because this command does a bit-by-bit dump of the whole form (including captions and borders), it lacks flexibility. Moreover, it is hard to imagine a printer that still has a resolution of only 96 dots per inch, which is what is used in most video drivers. The results of using PrintForm are therefore somewhat crude!

More Controls

Although we do not have the space to cover the many custom controls that are available to you, we want to spend a bit of time on the Windows 95 common controls that are part of every Windows 95 or NT installation.

Microsoft does try to keep a rough count of commercial controls available; the last we heard, there were more than 2,000. The Microsoft ActiveX gallery at Microsoft's Web site (www.microsoft.com\activex\gallery) gives you a hint at what's available—we highly recommend this site.

Common Controls

The first common controls are found in the COMCTL32.OCX file. Since these are not part of the standard VB5 toolbox, you'll need to add them. Go to Project|Components and choose Microsoft Windows Common Controls 5.0. Here are brief descriptions of the common controls.

TabStrip Control

A TabStrip Control, as shown in Figure 6-8, works like the dividers in a notebook or the labels on a group of file folders.

Toolbar Control

A Toolbar Control, as shown in Figure 6-9, contains a collection of Button objects used to create a toolbar that is associated with your control or application. The toolbar can either be aligned to the top of its container, as it is usually used, or placed anywhere on the form to provide a set of buttons or a button group.

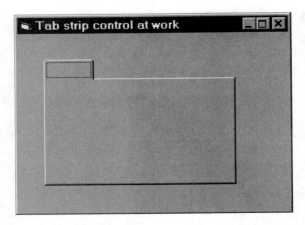

Figure 6-8   TabStrip Control

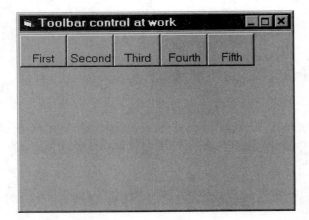

Figure 6-9   Toolbar Control

Note

Getting images on a Toolbar Control requires using an ImageList control to hold the images.

StatusBar Control

A StatusBar Control, as shown in Figure 6-10, provides a window, usually at the bottom of a parent form, through which an application can display vari-

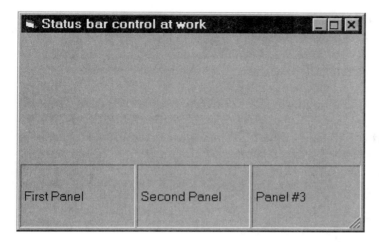

Figure 6-10 StatusBar control

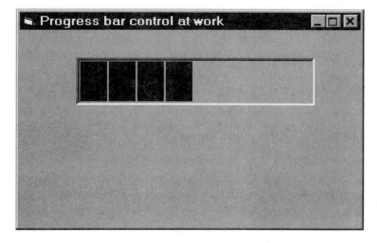

Figure 6-11 ProgressBar Control

ous kinds of status data. The status bar can be divided into a maximum of 16 Panel objects that are contained in a Panels collection. Each panel may have text or a graphic on it that can be added at design time or run time.

ProgressBar Control

The ProgressBar Control, as shown in Figure 6-11, shows the progress of a lengthy operation by filling a rectangle with one or more chunks at a time, from left to right. The amount of fill is determined by the Value property relative to the progress bar's Min and Max properties.

TreeView Control

A TreeView displays a hierarchical list of objects similar to Windows Explorer or the Project Explorer in VB5. Each object is called a *Node*. Each Node consists of a label and an optional bitmap. A TreeView Control is used when you need to display the headings in a document, the entries in an index, the files and directories on a disk, or any other kind of information where seeing it in the form of an outline is helpful. This is the same control used in the Win95 Explorer that displays your system folders including drives, network shares, etc.

ListView Control

The ListView Control displays items using one of four different views: Large Icons, Small Icons, List, or Report. You can arrange items into columns with or without column headings, as well as display accompanying icons and text. This is the control used to display the contents of the folders in the Win95 Explorer.

ImageList Control

An ImageList Control contains a collection of ListImage objects, each of which can be referred to by its index or key. The ImageList Control is not meant to be used alone, but as a way to hold images that other controls, such as the ToolBar, TreeView, and ListView Controls, can use.

Slider Control

A Slider control is a window containing a slider and optional tick marks. You can manipulate the slider by dragging it, clicking the mouse to either side of the slider, or using the keyboard. An example of a Slider control is shown in Figure 6-12.

An Example Using the Common Controls: DateTime

The CD has the full code for a control that extends the StatusBar control. We call it the DateTime control because it simply uses the built-in functionality of the status bar to display the current date and time. In addition, it exposes

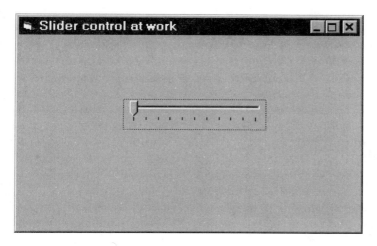

Figure 6-12 Slider Control

a property called ShowKeyboardStatus that, when set to True, widens the DateTime control in order to display the Caps Lock, Scroll Lock and Num Lock status on the keyboard. This demonstrates how to take a complex control and make a simple version of it; one that you may use in its specialized form more often than the basic control. It is easy to imagine doing this with all of the common controls.

Common Dialog Boxes

Working with Windows, you've become accustomed to seeing one of five standard dialog boxes for opening or saving a file, printing, choosing fonts, or setting colors. If your control does any of these operations, users will expect to see the familiar interface at work. This means you will want to build using the common dialog box as your base.

First off, a common dialog control, like a Timer control, has no visible interface. To actually pop up a specific common dialog box requires calling the appropriate method of the common dialog control while the program is running. For example, if you have an Open File item on a File menu and the associated Click procedure is in `OpenFile_Click`, the code to pop up a File Open dialog box using the default name of the control looks like this:

```
Sub OpenFile_Click ()
  ...
  CommonDialog1.ShowOpen
  ...
```

Note

The common dialog boxes take no actions; they accept information only. You will always need to write the code that tells Visual Basic what to do with the information entered and then have this code processed when the user closes the common dialog box.

Working with Common Dialog Boxes

Common dialog boxes are easier to use in principle than in practice. This is because they require a fair amount of initializing to get them to look exactly the way you want. Before you pop up the box, you usually need to initialize the various properties that determine how the common dialog box looks. For example, you might want to set the default in the Print dialog box Print Range to print only page 1. This is done by adjusting the value of the FromPage and ToPage properties of the common dialog control, as shown in the following listing:

```
CommonDialog1.FromPage = 1
CommonDialog1.ToPage = 1
```

All the common dialog boxes allow you to generate an error if the user clicks the Cancel button. Setting up an error trap for this is necessary in most (if not all) cases. To do this, use the following code:

```
[FormName].CommonDialog1.CancelError = True
```

The default is False, so no error is reported when the Cancel button is activated. Set it to True and an error with error number 32755 is generated if the user clicks Cancel or presses Esc. (Again, since nobody would want to use this kind of number in their code—even if they could remember it—use the symbolic constant cdlCancel instead.)

Setting this property to be True and then trapping this error is important because whether the user clicks OK or Cancel, certain values may have changed. Since you only want to use the information when the OK button was clicked, you must have a way to know if the Cancel button was used to close the dialog box.

Here's a general framework for working with a common dialog box that uses an error trap to detect if the Cancel button was pressed:

```
CommonDialog1.CancelError = True
On Error GoTo IsOK
   .
   .
   .
'Make sure the code after the IsOK label
'is always processed
IsOK:
   If Err = 0 Then   'no error so OK clicked
     'code to process data as needed
   ElseIf Err = cdlCancel
     'do nothing cancel invoked
   Else
     'wow you have a real error to handle
   End If
End Sub
```

The File Open and File Save Boxes

The following table gives short descriptions of the most important properties used for these dialog boxes.

Table 6-5:	Properties of the File Open and File Save Boxes

Property	Use
DefaultExt	This sets the default extension for files shown in the box.
DialogTitle	This sets the title bar. In particular, you do not need to use Open and Save if you are using these boxes in other contexts.
FileName	This gives the name and path of the file selected.
FileTitle	This gives the name without the path.
Filter	Changes here show up in the Type box. You can have multiple filters by separating them with the pipe symbol (a Chr(124) |). The format is the string for the description, the Chr(124), the filter, another Chr(124), and so on.
FilterIndex	This is used when you set up many filters using the Filter property.
Flags	This property is used to set various possible options on how the box will look. The values needed are stored in constants that begin with `cdlOFN_`.
InitDir	This specifies the initial directory.
MaxFileSize	This sets the maximum size of the filename including all the path info.

The Flags property is very important in determining the final look and feel of the box. For example, a line of code like:

```
CommonDialog1.Flags =  cdlOFNAllowMultiselect
```

allows the Filename list box to use multiple selections. You can combine more than one flag with an Or and read back the values using bit-masking techniques with the And operator.

Once the user clicks the OK button, you have to write code to read back the information that was entered and take appropriate actions based on these values. For example, `CommonDialog1.FileName` would contain the name of the file chosen.

The Color Choice Box

Here is a table with descriptions of the important properties used for these dialog boxes.

Table 6-6:   Properties of the Color Choice Box

Property	Use
Color	Shows or gets the color.
Flags	As with File Save/File Open, specifies the form of the box.

The symbolic constants for this box begin with `cdlCC`. For example:

```
CommonDialog1.Flags = cdlCCFullOpen
```

would display the whole dialog box (including the one for defining custom colors). When the user clicks the OK button, the value of, for example, `CommonDialog1.Color` is the long integer code for the color selected.

The Font Choice Box

Before we get to the table showing the remaining properties for this box, you'll need to know something about how the Flag property works here. Since you might want to have the font choice box reflect printer fonts only, screen fonts only, or both at once, Visual Basic requires you to set the Flag parameter correctly before it will display the Font box. The symbolic constants used are `cdlCFPrinterFonts`, `cdlCFScreenFonts`, or `cdlCFBoth`. If you don't set the CommonDialog.Flag property to one of these three values and still try to show the Font box, the program generates an error and dies.

There are 14 different Flag property values. As always, you combine them by adding them together.

Here is a table with descriptions of the important remaining properties used for this dialog box.

Table 6-7: Properties of the Font Choice Box	
Property	*Use*
Color	Only used for color printers.
FontBold, FontItalic, FontStrikeThru, FontUnderline	True/False properties. If the `cdlCFEffects` flag is set, you can allow the user to choose these properties.
FontName	Sets or returns the font name.
FontSize	Sets or returns the size of the font.
Max, Min	These change the point sizes shown in the size box. You need to have the `cdlCFLimitSize` flag set before you can use these properties.

Read back the value of the various font properties to see what the user wants. For example, the value of `CommonDialog1.FontName` is the name of the font the user chose. Then have Visual Basic process the code to have the new value go into effect.

The Printer Dialog Box

As before, the Flags property controls how the box appears. For example, if the Flag parameter is `cdlPDAllPages`, then the All option button in the Print Range frame is set. Specifically, this means you will need bit-masking techniques to check out what the user did with the box. Use code like this:

```
If CommonDialog1.Flags And cdlPDAllPages = _
cdlPDAllPages Then
   'all pages button checked
```

Here is a table with descriptions of the remaining properties used for these dialog boxes.

Table 6-8: Properties of the Printer Dialog Box	
Property	*Use*
Copies	Sets or returns the number of copies the user wants.
FromPage, ToPage	What pages are wanted.
HDC	This is the device context number. It is used for API function calls.
Max, Min	Specifies the maximum and minimum pages the user can put in the Print Range frame.
PrinterDefault	Set this to True and the user can click the Setup button to change the WIN.INI file.

The Shape and Line Controls

These two controls let you quickly display simple lines and shapes or print them on a printer. They are different than most other controls because they do not respond to any events: they are for display or printing only. They are also quite sparing of Windows resources.

The Shape control can be used to display rectangles, squares, ovals, or circles. You can also use it to display rounded rectangles and rounded squares. The icon for the Shape control is three overlapping shapes. The Line control can be used to display lines of varying thickness on a form. The icon for the Line control on the toolbox is a diagonal line.

The Shape Control

The Shape control has 20 properties. Usually, you change them dynamically with code while the application is running. The most important properties for the Shape control at design time are described in the following sections.

The Shape Property

This determines the type of shape you get. There are six possible settings.

Table 6-9: Shape Property Settings	
Setting of Shape Property	*Effect*
VbShapeRectangle (=0)	Rectangle (default)
VbShapeSquare (=1)	Square
VbShapeOval(=2)	Oval
VbShapeCircle (=3)	Circle
vbShapeRoundedRectangle (=4)	Rounded rectangle
vbShapeRoundedSquare (=5)	Rounded square

For example, if you add a Shape control in the default size and shape to an ordinary EXE form and write the following in the `Form_Click` procedure, you can see the shapes for yourself.

```
Private Sub Form_Click()
   Static I As Integer
   Shape1.Shape = I
   I = I + 1
   I = I Mod 6 'to prevent error
End Sub
```

The BackStyle Property

This property determines whether the background of the shape is transparent or not. The default value is 1, which gives you an opaque border; BackColor fills the shape and obscures what is behind it. Set it to 0 (Transparent) and you can see through the shape to what is behind it.

BorderWidth

BorderWidth determines the thickness of the line. It is measured in pixels and can range from 0 to 8,192 (rather too large to display on a form).

BorderStyle

Unlike the case for Image controls, the BorderStyle for Shape controls have seven possible settings, as shown in the following table. Having no border

(BorderStyle = 0) prevents the control from being visible unless you modify the FillStyle and FillColor properties.

Table 6-10: BorderStyle Property Settings	
Value of BorderStyle Property	*Effect*
VbTransparent (=0)	No border shown
VbBSSolid (=1)	Solid (default)
VbBSDash (=2)	A dashed line
VbBSDot (=3)	A dotted line
VbBSDashDot (=4)	A dash-dot line
VbBSDashDotDot (=5)	A dash-dot-dot line
VbBSInsideSolid (=6)	Outer edge of border is the outer edge of the shape

Note

If you set the BorderWidth property to greater than 1, then resetting the BorderStyle property has no effect.

(To see these settings in effect, add the line `Shape1.BorderStyle = 1` to the previous demonstration program.)

FillColor, FillStyle

The FillColor property determines the color used to fill the shape in the manner set by the FillStyle property. You can set the FillColor property in the same way as setting any color property, either directly via a hexadecimal code or by using the color palette. The FillStyle property has eight possible settings, as shown in the following table.

Table 6-11:	FillStyle Property Settings

Setting For FillStyle Property	Effect
VbFSSolid (=0)	Solid
VbFSTransparen (=1)	Transparent (default)
VbHorizontalLine (=2)	Horizontal line
VbVerticalLine (=3)	Vertical line
VbUpwardDiagonal (=4)	Upward diagonal
VbDownwardDiagonal (=5)	Downward diagonal
VbCross (=6)	Cross
VbDiagonalCross (=7)	Diagonal cross

The Line Control

The Line control has 15 properties. Usually, you change them dynamically with code while the application is running. The most important properties for the Line control at design time are the BorderWidth property and the BorderStyle property. BorderWidth determines the thickness of the line. It is measured in pixels and can range from 0 to 8,192 (too large to display on most forms). Like the Shape control, the BorderStyle property has six possible settings, but, as before, only the last five are really useful.

The most important properties at run time for the Line control are the X1, Y1, X2, Y2 properties. These govern where the edges of the line appear. The X1 property sets (or tells you) the horizontal position of the left end of the line. The Y1 property sets (or tells you) the vertical position of the left-hand corner. The X2 and Y2 properties work similarly for the right end of the line.

Note

These properties use the underlying scale of the container of the Line control.

Behind the Scenes with Visual Basic's Graphics

To draw on the screen, Visual Basic tells Windows what to display. What this means is that what you can do with Visual Basic's graphics statements depends on the driver programs that Windows uses to control the screen and printer. However, using these driver programs is automatic. You do not have to worry about all the possible hardware combinations a user may have. This is different from what MS-DOS programmers are used to. When graphics are programmed under DOS, part of the program must check to see what kind of graphics board (if any) is installed, and the program must be adjusted accordingly.

However, nothing comes for free. Windows has to do a lot to manage a graphics environment, and this forces tradeoffs. For example, unless you set the AutoRedraw property to True so that Visual Basic saves a copy of the object in memory, you will have to manage the redrawing of graphics yourself. (The jargon says that AutoRedraw controls whether graphics are *persistent* or not.)

Note

Images derived from setting the Picture property of a control or those coming from the Line and Shape controls are always persistent.

There are slight differences between how the AutoRedraw property being set to True works for forms and picture boxes:

- For a resizable form or user control, Visual Basic saves a copy of the entire screen. Thus, when you enlarge the form, no graphics information is lost. This option requires much more memory, instead of leaving AutoRedraw at False since Visual Basic needs to reserve enough memory for a bit-by-bit description of the whole form. However, if your graphics do not currently fit on a form but will when the form is enlarged, choose this option.

- For a picture box, Visual Basic saves an image only as large as the current size of the box. Nothing new will appear even if the box is enlarged later.

Thus, drawing to picture boxes requires less memory than drawing to the form, even if the picture box fills up the form.

A Feature of the AutoRedraw Property

There is one other interesting feature of AutoRedraw: Suppose you change AutoRedraw to False while a program is running. Then you clear the object by using the Cls method. Whatever you drew before you changed the AutoRedraw property will remain, but everything that was drawn after the switch will disappear. This feature can be very useful. To see how it works, start a new Standard EXE project and try the following demonstration program (recall that text is treated as graphics output on a form). For the `Form_Load` procedure, write:

```
Private Sub Form_Load ()
   AutoRedraw = True
   Print "Please click to see a demonstration of
     AutoRedraw."
   Print "These two lines will stay on the screen
     after you double click."
End Sub
```

Now, for the `Click` procedure, add:

```
Private Sub Form_Click ()
   AutoRedraw = False        'keeps old stuff
   Cls
   Print: Print: Print       'third line
   Print "But this line will disappear after you
     double click."
End Sub
```

Finally, the `Double_Click` procedure is simply:

```
Private Sub Form_DblClick ()
   Cls       'Clears line from Click() procedure
End Sub
```

The ClipControls Property and the Paint Event

Visual Basic activates the Paint event each time a part of the form is newly exposed. What happens within the Paint event, in this case, depends on how the ClipControls property is set at design time. If the ClipControls property is set to True (the default) and the AutoRedraw property is False, then Visual

Basic repaints the entire object. If ClipControls is set to False, Visual Basic repaints only the newly exposed areas.

Note

The ClipControls property has a few other features worth noting. Setting ClipControls to True also creates what Microsoft calls a clipping region around non-graphical controls on the object. This means Visual Basic creates an outline of the form and the controls on it in memory. Because the clipping region is created in memory, setting this property to False can reduce the time needed to paint or repaint the object. More time is needed if the object is graphically complex. Clipping regions exclude the Image, Label, Line, or Shape controls.

Tip

If AutoRedraw is set to True, you can speed up your program by setting ClipControls to False.

More on the Paint Event

In any case, if AutoRedraw is False, you need to write the necessary code in the Paint procedure whenever you want to redraw part or all of a form or picture box. Therefore, the least memory-intensive way to handle the problem of graphics disappearing because a user covered a form or picture box is to redraw the image in the form or picture box in the Paint event procedure. Setting AutoRedraw to True uses up memory (if you have it), potentially speeding up the program (although the image may take longer to appear at first). You have to choose what's best for the application. At the extremes, the choice is easy: If the amount of drawing to be done is minimal, using the Paint event procedure is better. In any case, Visual Basic calls the Paint procedure for the object only if the AutoRedraw property of the object is set to False.

Caution

Be very careful about including in the Paint event procedure any commands that move or resize the object. If you include such commands, Visual Basic will just call the Paint procedure again, and you'll be stuck in an infinite regress.

The Refresh Method

You will occasionally need to use the Refresh method when working with graphics. This method applies to both forms and controls. It forces an immediate refresh of the form or control, and will let you see an image develop even when AutoRedraw is True. (If AutoRedraw is set to True, Visual Basic waits for the image to be finished or some other idle time before displaying the image.) If you use the Refresh method, Visual Basic will also call any Paint event procedure you have written for the object. This method is commonly used in the ReSize procedure to redisplay any graphics that are calculated in the Paint event procedure. Also, while Visual Basic handles refreshing the screen during idle time, occasionally you will want to control this process yourself. Whenever Visual Basic processes an ObjectName.Refresh statement, it will redraw the object immediately and generate the Paint event, if the object supports this feature.

Saving Pictures

Finally, Visual Basic makes it easy to save the pictures you've drawn to a form or picture box. The SavePicture statement uses the following syntax:

```
SavePicture ObjectName.Image, Filename
```

The operating system uses the Image property to identify the picture in the form or picture box. If you leave off ObjectName, then, as usual, Visual Basic uses the current form. The syntax for this version of the method is:

```
SavePicture Image, Filename
```

If you originally loaded the picture from a file by assigning an image to the Picture property of the form or picture box, Visual Basic saves the picture in the same format as the original file. (For example, icon files stay icon files.) Otherwise, Visual Basic saves the picture as a bitmap (.BMP) file.

Fundamentals of Programming Graphics

You can draw on a picture box on a form. Using code, you'll take complete control of each dot on the screen or on the printer. Of course, if all you want to do is draw a few shapes on the screen, there is no need to use any of the graphical methods.

Screen Scales

There are six other possible scales besides the default scale, as well as a totally flexible user-defined scale that you'll see in the next section. These scales are set by changing the ScaleMode property at design or run time, as shown in the following table.

Table 6-12: ScaleMode Constants	
ScaleMode Constants	*Units*
vbTwips	Twips (the default)
vbPoints	Points (72 per inch)
vbPixels	Pixels (the number of dots, as reported by Windows)
vbCharacters	Characters (units default as 12 points high and 20 points wide)
vbInches	Inches
vbMillimeters	Millimeters
vbCentimeters	Centimeters

Once you set the ScaleMode property, you can read off the size of the *drawing area*, which is the area inside the form or control or the printable area on the paper. This is reported in the current units when you use the ScaleHeight and ScaleWidth properties. Since both ScaleHeight and ScaleWidth report their results using the units selected by ScaleMode, they are very convenient for resetting form-level or global variables in a Resize event procedure. On the other hand, the Height and Width properties of an object are less useful for graphics except for a user control form. This is because these properties give you the area of the object including the borders and title bar, if there are any. In graphics, you usually care more about the dimensions of the drawing area.

Tip

Use form-level or global variables for the Height and Width properties of the Screen object and recalculate these in the Resize event. Then you can use a percentage of these variables in your code in order to make it easier to have your code independent of the particular monitor and card.

Custom Screen Scales

Regardless of which scale you choose, the drawing area is normally numbered with (0, 0) as the top-left corner. This is obviously inconvenient for drawing tables, charts, graphs, and other mathematical objects. In most of these situations, you want the coordinates to decrease as you move from top to bottom and increase as you move from left to right. For example, mathematics usually uses an X-Y (Cartesian) system, with X measuring distance across from a central point (the origin) and Y measuring distance up or down from the center.

The Scale method sets up new coordinates for forms and picture boxes that you can use in any of the graphics methods. For example:

```
Scale (-100, 100) - (100, -100)
```

sets up a new coordinate system with the coordinates of the top-left corner being (–100, 100) and the bottom-right corner being (100, –100). After this method, the four corners are described in a clockwise order, starting from the top left:

```
(-100, 100)
(100, 100)
(100, -100)
(-100, -100)
```

Now, (0, 0) is roughly the center of the screen. This placement occurs because whenever Visual Basic processes a Scale method that changes to a custom scale, the program automatically finds the pixel that corresponds to your coordinates (by rounding, if necessary).

In general, the Scale method looks like this:

```
Scale (LeftX, TopY) - (RightX, BottomY)
```

where LeftX is a single-precision real number that will represent the smallest X coordinate (left-most), TopY is a single-precision number for the largest Y (top), RightX is the right corner, and BottomY the bottom edge. For example:

```
Scale (-1E38, 1E38) - (1E38, -1E38)
```

gives you the largest possible scale, which means the smallest amount of detail. Large X and Y changes are needed to light up adjacent pixels.

If you use the Scale method with no coordinates, Visual Basic will reset the coordinates back to the default scale of (0, 0) for the top left-hand corner and the units being twips.

Note

Some programmers prefer using a custom scale rather than percentages of the Screen.Height and Screen.Width objects in their code.

Another Way to Set Up Custom Scales

Although the Scale method is the simplest way to set up a custom scale, there is one other way that may be useful. You can specify the coordinates of the top left-hand corner and how Visual Basic should measure the vertical and horizontal scales. You do all this by using combinations of the ScaleLeft, ScaleTop, ScaleWidth, and ScaleHeight properties. For example, after Visual Basic processes:

```
Object.ScaleLeft = 1000
Object.ScaleTop = 500
```

the coordinates of the top left-hand corner of the object are (1000, 500). After Visual Basic processes a statement like this one, all graphics methods for drawing within the object are calculated based on these new coordinates for the top left-hand corner. For example, if you made these changes to a form, then to place an object at the top left-hand corner now requires setting its Top property to 500 and its Left property to 1000.

Similarly, if you set the ScaleWidth to 100 and the ScaleHeight to 200, the horizontal units are 1/100 of the width of the graphics area and the vertical units are 1/200 of the height of the graphics area.

Just as with the Scale method, you can use any single-precision number to reset these four properties. If you use a negative value for ScaleWidth or ScaleHeight, the orientation changes. If ScaleHeight is negative, the coordinates of the top of the object are higher values than those of the bottom. If ScaleWidth is negative, the coordinates of the left side of the object are higher values than those of the right side.

Colors

Visual Basic has quite a few ways to define colors. The easiest, by far, is to use the built-in color constants, such as vbBlack or vbRed. Of course, this restricts you to only eight colors. If you want access to the potentially millions of colors that are available on some graphics adapters, you have two choices.

First you can use the RGB function, whose syntax is:

```
RGB(red, green, blue)
```

The redness, blueness and greenness are set on a scale from 0 to 255. For example:

Color	RGB setting
Black	RGB(0, 0, 0)
Blue	RGB(0, 0, 255)
Cyan	RGB(0, 255, 255)
Yellow	RGB(255, 255, 0)
White	RGB(255, 255, 255)

Next, you can use the hexadecimal code that the RGB function is returning. This is in the form &HBBRRGG, where each two hex digits (00 to FF) give you that color intensity of blue, red, and green on a scale of 0 to 255.

Note

Controls use a data type called OLE_COLOR to pass color codes. This is simply the six hexadecimal digits in the code mentioned above.

Pixel Control

Now you know how colors are assigned and can change the scale of your screen as you see fit. How do you turn a pixel on? The syntax for this method is:

```
PSet(Col, Row) [, ColorCode]
```

Since the color code is optional (as indicated by the square brackets), all you need to do is replace the parameters with the values you want. The value of the first entry determines the column and the second determines the row. After Visual Basic processes this statement, the pixel defined by that point lights up. Obviously, where that point is depends on what scale you've chosen. For example, in the ordinary scale, using the default size for a form, the statement:

```
Pset(2400, 1800)
```

would turn on the center pixel in the default size of a user control on our 800 × 600 but after a ScaleMode=3 command, this would likely cause an overflow run-time error. It is possible to use PSet outside the current limits of the form, but if you exceed the limits on the size of the screen, you'll almost certainly get an overflow run-time error. When you use PSet to turn on a point that is outside the form, Visual Basic records this information but doesn't plot any points. This is where the AutoRedraw property's being set to True can help. Suppose you ask Visual Basic to plot a point that is too large to fit the current size of the form, and AutoRedraw is True for the form. Then the information isn't lost; set the WindowState property to 2 (maximized), and the point will show up.

Tip

In a situation like this where you need to know how many twips correspond to a single pixel, turn to Visual Basic's built-in `TwipsPerPixelX/TwipsPerPixelY` *functions. (Since Windows API functions usually require pixels, these functions are often needed for using API graphics calls.)*

You can use the Point method to determine the color code of any point on the screen. This returns a long integer using the &HRRGGBB& code. The syntax is:

```
object.Point(x, y)
```

where x, y are single-precision values giving the x (the left/right position) and y (up/down position) and vertical (y-axis) coordinates of the point using the ScaleMode property of the Form or PictureBox.

Lines and Boxes

Obviously, if you had to draw everything by plotting individual points, graphics programming would be too time-consuming to be practical. In addition to line and shape controls, Visual Basic comes with a rich supply of graphics tools, usually called *graphics primitives*, that allow you to plot such geometric figures as lines, boxes, circles, ellipses, and wedges with a single statement. The statement:

```
Line (StartColumn, StartRow) - (EndCol, EndRow), ColorCode
```

gives you a line connecting the two points with the given coordinates, using the color specified by ColorCode.

An Example: A Special Effects Control

For example, suppose you wanted to design a Special Effects control that gives you a starburst-like effect that runs continuously when the user clicks in it. To do this, simply set up a user control with a border style property set to Fixed Single. Then add the following code:

Listing 6-1: A Special Effects Control

```
Private Sub UserControl_Click()
   Dim I As Integer, Col As Single, Row As Single
   ReDim CCode(1 To 3) As Integer
   Randomize
   Scale (-100, 100)-(100, -100)
   Do
      X = DoEvents()
      Cls
      For I = 1 To 150
         CCode(1) = 255 * Rnd
         CCode(2) = 255 * Rnd
         CCode(3) = 255 * Rnd
         Col = 100 * Rnd
         If Rnd < 0.5 Then Col = -Col
         Row = 100 * Rnd
         If Rnd < 0.5 Then Row = -Row
         Line (0, 0)-(Col, Row), RGB(CCode(1), CCode(2), _
         CCode(3))
      Next I
   Loop
End Sub
```

There is one subtle point about the code in this control. Since we want the control to work continuously, it is a good idea to have a DoEvents statement in order to allow other events to be processed.

Last Point Referenced

Visual Basic keeps track of where it stopped plotting. This location is usually called the *last point referenced (LPR)*, and the values of the CurrentX and CurrentY variables store this information. If you are continuing a line from the last point referenced, Visual Basic allows you to omit the LPR in the Line method.

When you start any graphics mode with a ScaleMode method or a custom scale, the last point referenced has the coordinates (0, 0) in that scale. For custom scales, this need not be the top left-hand corner. After a Line method, the last point referenced is the end point of the line (the second coordinate pair).

Relative Coordinates

Up to now, you've been using *absolute coordinates*. Each point is associated with a unique row and column. It's occasionally helpful to use *relative coordinates*, where each point is defined by how far it is from the last point referenced. For example, if you write:

```
PSet(12, 100)
```

which makes (12, 100) the last point referenced, then you can write:

```
PSet Step(50, 10)
```

to turn on the point in column 62 (50 + 12) and row 110 (10 + 100). In general, when Visual Basic sees the statement:

```
Step (X, Y)
```

in a graphics method, it uses the point whose coordinates are X units to the right or left and Y units up or down from the last point referenced (depending on whether X and Y are positive or negative).

DrawWidth, DrawStyle

When you draw on the printer or the screen by using the PSet or Line method (or circles—see the section "Circles and Ellipses" later in this chapter), Visual Basic uses dots that are normally drawn one pixel wide. If you need to change the width of points or lines, use the DrawWidth property. The syntax for this method is:

```
Object.DrawWidth = Size%
```

The theoretical maximum size for DrawWidth is 32,767.

If you do not want a solid line, all you need to do is change the DrawStyle property. You can see the effect of DrawStyle only when the DrawWidth is 1. There are seven possible settings when DrawWidth is 1, as shown in the following table.

Table 6-13: DrawStyle Property Settings	
Value of DrawStyle Property	*Description*
VbSolid (default = 0)	Solid
VbDash (1)	Dash
VbDot (2)	Dot
VbDashDot (3)	Dash-dot-dash-dot pattern
VbDashDotDot (4)	Dash-dot-dot pattern
VbInvisible (5)	Transparent—nothing shown
VbInsideSolid (6)	Inside solid (see the next section)

Boxes

A modification of the Line method lets you draw a rectangle. The statement:

```
Line (FirstCol, FirstRow) - (SecCol, SecRow), CCode, B
```

draws a rectangle in the given color code (CCode) whose opposite corners are given by FirstCol, FirstRow and SecCol, SecRow. For example, another way to get a Special Effects control is with code that looks like this:

```
Dim I As Integer
  Scale (-100, 100)-(100, -100)

  For I = 1 To 90 Step 5
    Line (-100 + I, 100 - I)-(100 - I, -100 + I), , B
  Next I
```

Notice that this program leaves off the color code but still keeps the comma to separate out the B. Without this comma, Visual Basic would think the B was the name of a variable rather than the Box command. Leave out the comma, and Visual Basic would think you're asking for a line connecting

```
(5*I, I)-(639-5*I, 199-I)
```

with color code the current value of B. (Since an uninitialized numeric variable has value 0, you'd probably get a color code of 0.)

The width of the line defining the boundary of the box is determined by the current value of DrawWidth for the object on which you are drawing. When you have a fairly wide line for the boundary, you can see the effect of using the "inside solid" (DrawStyle = 6). Using the InsideSolid line makes a boundary of the box that is half inside, half outside.

Filled Boxes

You can arrange for the variant on the Line method that gives boxes to also fill the box. Use BF rather than B, and you get a filled box. Therefore,

```
Line (FirstCol, FirstRow) - (SecCol, SecRow), CCode, BF
```

will yield a solid rectangle whose opposite corners are given by FirstCol, FirstRow and SecCol, SecRow.

FillStyle, FillColor

Boxes (and circles—see the next section) are usually empty or solid, but Visual Basic allows you seven different patterns to fill boxes as well as using no fill pattern at all. To do this, you need to change the FillStyle property of the form or picture box, using properties from the following table.

Table 6-14: FillStyle Property Settings	
Value of FillStyle Property	*Description*
vbFSSolid = 0	Solid
vbFSTransparent (default =1)	Transparent
vbHorizontalLine (=2)	Horizontal line
vbVerticalLine (=3)	Vertical line
vbUpwardDiagonal (=4)	Upward diagonal
vbDownwardDiagonal (=5)	Downward diagonal
vbCross (=6)	Cross
vbDiagonalCross (=7)	Diagonal cross

Once you have changed the FillStyle property from its transparent default (FillStyle = 1), you can use the FillColor property to set the color used for FillStyle. This property has the syntax:

```
Object.FillColor = ColorCode
```

where, as usual, you can set the color code in any of the four ways mentioned previously.

Circles and Ellipses

Normally, to describe a circle in Visual Basic, you give its center and radius. The following fragment draws a circle of radius 0.5 units, starting at the center of the screen:

```
Scale (-1, 1) - (1, -1)
Circle (0, 0), 0.5
```

The last point referenced (CurrentX, CurrentY) after a Circle method is always the center of the circle. You can also add a color code to the Circle method. For example,

```
Circle (0, 0), 0.5 , CCode
```

would draw a circle of radius 0.5 in the color code indicated here by the variable CCode.

To draw a sector or an arc, you have to tell Visual Basic which angle to start at and which angle to finish at. You do this using radian measure, which you may have seen in high school. (It is also used in the trigonometric functions in Visual Basic.) Radian measure isn't very difficult. It measures angles by what percentage the radian measure would give of the circumference of a circle of radius 1. For example, all the way around a circle of radius 1 is 2π units. It is also 360 degrees, so 360 degrees is equal to 2π radians. One-half of a circle of radius 1 is 180 degrees and π units. Therefore, 180 degrees is π radians. Similarly, one-quarter of a circle (90 degrees) is $\frac{\pi}{2}$ radians, and so on. To go from degrees to radians, multiply by $\pi/180$; to go back, multiply by $180/\pi$. (Since π is roughly 3.14159, 360 degrees is roughly 6.28 radians.) In any case, the statement:

```
Circle (XRad, YRad), Radius, CCode, StartAngle, EndAngle
```

draws an arc of the circle starting at the angle given in radians by StartAngle and ending with EndAngle. (The Circle method does not, unfortunately, support named arguments.) To get a sector, use negative signs.

There are a few peculiarities of these methods that you should be aware of. The first is that, although mathematics allows negative angles, Visual Basic does not. The negative sign only serves to indicate, "Draw a sector rather than an arc." The second is that if you want your arc to start with a vertical line pointed due east (that is, 0 degrees = 0 radians), you shouldn't use –0 for the StartAngle or EndAngle. Instead, use $-2*\pi$ (= –6.28 . . .). The final peculiarity is that angles in the Circle method can only have values between -2π (–6.28 . . .) and 2π (6.28 . . .).

Ellipses and the Aspect Ratio

You convert the Circle drawing method to an ellipse drawing command by adding one more option. This also lets you override Visual Basic's default settings if you need to adjust the aspect ratio for your monitor. The syntax for this method is:

```
Circle [Step] (XCenter, YCenter), radius, , , , aspect
```

The four commas must be there even if you are not using the color code and angle options that you saw earlier. (Step is optional, of course.) This version of the Circle method lets you change the default ratio of columns to rows. (It's really an Ellipse command.) If the aspect parameter is less than 1, the radius is taken in the column direction and the ellipse is stretched in the horizontal direction. If the aspect parameter is greater than 1, the radius is taken in the row direction and the ellipse is stretched in the vertical.

The PaintPicture Method

One problem with earlier versions of Visual Basic is that there was no quick way to paint a picture at a specific place on a form or picture box. (You had to use the BitBlt API call.) Visual Basic has now added a version of this API call directly to its language. This new method is called PaintPicture. It has many uses, for example, it lets you do simple animation quite effectively within Visual Basic. The simplest version of the syntax for PaintPicture looks like this:

```
object.PaintPicture picture, x1, y1, width, height
```

The object can refer to any form, picture box, or the printer. (If you leave it out, Visual Basic assumes you mean the form.) The picture parameter gives the source of the graphic to be drawn. (For example, it could be the Picture property of a Picture Box.) Finally, the x1 and y1 parameters give the coordinates of the upper left-hand corner where you want the picture to appear (using the scale of the object parameter).

To see the PaintPicture method at work, add a Picture box with the default size and width to the form. Assign the Picture property of the Picture box to any bitmap you might have. (Use Paint to make one, for example.) Now try the following code:

```
Private Sub Form_Click()
   Dim I As Integer, J As Integer
   Dim NumberOfCols As Integer, NumberOfRows As
      Integer
   Picture1.Visible = False
   NumberOfRows = Form1.ScaleHeight / Picture1.Height
   NumberOfCols = Form1.ScaleWidth / Picture1.Width
   For I = 1 To NumberOfRows
      For J = 1 To NumberOfCols
         Form1.PaintPicture Picture1.Picture, (J - 1) _
* Picture1.Width, (I - 1)*Picture1.Height, _
Picture1.Width
      Next J
   Next I
End Sub
```

What this code does first is figure out the number of copies of the picture we can place on the form. For example, if the picture box was 400 twips high and the form was 4400 twips high, we can have 11 rows. (A similar calculation is made for the columns.) Next comes the crucial line:

```
Form1.PaintPicture Picture1.Picture, (J - 1)* _
Picture1.Width, (I - 1)* Picture1.Height, _ Picture1.Width
```

which paints multiple copies of the picture on the form.

Finally, the full version of PaintPicture has the following syntax (it doesn't use named parameters, unfortunately):

```
object.PaintPicture picture, x1, y1, width1, _ height1, _
x2, y2, width2, height2, opcode
```

The first three parameters you have already seen—they are all required. All the remaining parameters are optional. However, if you want to use an optional argument, you must specify all the optional arguments that would appear before it. (No empty commas allowed!)

The optional width1 and height1 parameters are single-precision values that let you set the width and height of the resulting picture. The optional x2 and y2 parameters let you specify single-precision values that give the left/right (x) and up/down (y) coordinates of a clipping region within the original picture. The optional width2 and height2 parameters are single-precision values that give the coordinates of a clipping region within the original picture.

The optional opcode parameter is a Long integer that is used only with bitmaps. This parameter will affect how the picture blends with whatever image was at the location. Its uses are highly specialized, so we don't cover it here.

Tip

You can flip a bitmap horizontally or vertically by using negative values for the destination height (height1) or the destination width (width1) arguments.

The Picture Object

The designers of Visual Basic 5 decided that it would be convenient to have a generic object to store pictures. So just as VB has a Printer or Clipboard object, it now has a *Picture* object that you can use as a container for pictures. The Picture object makes it easier to manipulate bitmaps, icons, metafiles enhanced metafiles, GIF, and JPEG images.

The only tricky thing is that you must use the Set keyword and not an = sign to assign a picture to the Picture object as you did for the Printer object. For example:

```
Dim APicture As Picture
Set APicture = LoadPicture("Smile.bmp")
Set Picture1.Picture = APicture
```

Tip

You can use an array of Picture objects to keep a series of graphics in memory without needing to use (multiple) controls to store them. This saves resources and can also make your program run faster, since getting and setting properties of a control is fairly time-consuming.

Once you have a Picture object you can find out its height and width using the read only Height and Width properties of the Picture object. Note that VB returns the size information in a scale mode called HiMetric. HiMetric units measure how large the image is—regardless of the screen resolution or size. 1000 HiMetric units is always one centimeter, so if

```
Picture.Height = 10000
```

then you know the picture is 10 centimeters high (=3.92 inches) regardless of whether the image is displayed on a 14" or 31" monitor. (You can use the ScaleX and ScaleY methods to convert HiMetric units into the scale you need if this is necessary.)

Finally, the Type property of the Picture object lets you know what kind of image is currently stored in the Picture object. The Type property uses the constants described in the following table.

Table 6-15:	Type Property Constants	

Constant	Value	Description
vbPicTypeNone	0	Picture is empty
vbPicTypeBitmap	1	Bitmap (.bmp files)
vbPicTypeMetafile	2	Metafile (.wmf files)
vbPicTypeIcon	3	Icon (.ico files)
vbPicTypeEMetafile	4	Enhanced Metafile (.emf files)

Z-Order: How Visual Basic Displays Information

At this point we have covered all the methods Visual Basic uses for displaying information. We now need to go under the hood a little bit. Visual Basic actually paints the display for your application in three layers. The back (bottom) layer is where you draw information directly on the form using the graphical methods. The middle layer contains the graphical controls (lines, shapes, picture boxes, and the image control). The top layer contains the non-graphical controls like command buttons, list boxes, and check and option buttons. Certain controls, such as labels, have a FontTransparent property that lets information from the layers below shine through.

Within each layer you can control the order in which controls appear. For example, if you use an MDI form, you can control which one is on top after you use the Arrange method. Or, if you overlap two command buttons, you can specify which one appears on top.

You can do this in two ways. At design time you can use the Bring To Front and Send To Back options from the Edit menu to specify the initial ordering of what's on top. To change it dynamically while the program is running, you need the ZOrder method. Its syntax is:

```
[object.]ZOrder [position]
```

The position parameter can be 0 or 1. If it is 0 or omitted, the object named moves to the front. If it is 1, the object moves to the back. If you omit the object name, the current form moves to the top.

Form Resizing Problems and Screen Resolution Problems

One of the problems you have with coding a VB application is that your users will not necessarily have the same size screen as you. They will also have an annoying habit of resizing your forms to a size other than what you intended. This in turn will play havoc with your carefully arranged control locations as you can see in Figure 6-13 and Figure 6-14 which take a carefully constructed form and then maximizes it. The only practical solution involves a fair amount of code which we want to show you in this section.

Let's take up the problem shown in Figures 6-13 and 6-14 first and leave the problem of dealing with different screen resolutions to the next section. What we need to do is sometimes described as making a container *elastic*.

Figure 6-13   A non-maximized form

Note

It is possible to buy an elastic container control. For example, VideoSoft has a shareware control called Elastic that is worth checking out.

Using a third party elastic control does have some definite costs, and we don't only mean the cost of the control. For example, using an elastic control inside a user control form might enlarge the footprint of your control too much.

Figure 6-14 The form from Figure 6-13, maximized

If you choose to write the code to make your forms elastic yourself, the trick is to get out of the habit of thinking of controls as having a fixed size. Instead, think of them as having certain proportions relative to the size of the form. To see what we mean, let's start with a simple example: you want to write the code that will guarantee that the command button will always show up centered at the bottom of the user control form with the same proportions it had when you started out.

Here are the relative dimensions on a 640 ↔ 480 video display of a form with a default size command button.

Object	Height	Width
Command button	495	1215
Form	4140	6690

Thus, the ratio of the heights of the command button to the form is 495/4140, and that of the widths, 1215/6690. Given this information, you can use the Move method in the Resize event to make sure the command is always centered on the bottom of the form and has the correct proportions:

```
Sub Form_Resize()
   Dim TheHeight As Single, TheWidth As Single
   TheHeight = (495/4140)*ScaleHeight
   TheWidth = (1215/6690)*ScaleWidth
   Command1.Move ScaleWidth/2 -(TheWidth/2),_
ScaleHeight - TheHeight, TheWidth, TheHeight
End Sub
```

The key line:

```
   Command1.Move ScaleWidth/2 -(TheWidth/2),_
ScaleHeight - TheHeight, TheWidth, TheHeight
```

moves the command button exactly where you want it and also resizes it appropriately.

Note

If you haven't set the AutoRedraw property to True, you will want to have the Paint event procedure call the Resize event procedure.

Of course, this is rather cumbersome to do by hand if you have many controls on a form. However, Visual Basic gives you a way to iterate through every control on your form using what it calls the Controls collection. As with the Printers collection you saw earlier in this chapter, we can iterate through all the controls on the form using the For Each construct. We will also need the Count property, which will return the number of items in the collection. Once we have the Controls collection and its count it is not hard to see how to automate the process we just described.

1. Set up a type called ProportionsForAControl in the Declaration section of a code module:

```
Type ControlProportions
WidthProportions As Single
HeightProportions as Single
TopProportions As Single
LeftProportions as Single
End Type
```

2. Set up a form-level array of these records:

    ```
    Dim ArrayOfProportions() As ControlProportions
    ```

3. In the Form_Initialize event, use the Controls.Count property to redimension the ControlProportionsArray array we are using to hold the proportion information. (If you add a control by using a control array using the techniques described in the next chapter, you will need to update the information.)

4. Fill the array with the correct values by iterating through the Controls collection to get the proportions of all the controls on the form.

5. Use the information now contained in the ControlProportions Array in the UserControl_Resize procedure to resize all the controls on the form whenever the form is resized.

One final point you need to aware of in the code that follows is that we had to avoid checking the size of invisible controls, such as Timers or Common Dialog controls. We do this using On Error Resume Next; you could also directly check the type of the control using the techniques from the next chapter. Here's the complete code for one version of a generic resize routine for your forms and user control forms that follows the above outline.

Listing 6-2: Generic Resize Routine

```
Private Type ControlProportions
  WidthProportions As Single
  HeightProportions As Single
  TopProportions As Single
  LeftProportions As Single
End Type
Dim ArrayOfProportions() As ControlProportions

Sub InitResizeArray()
  On Error Resume Next
  Dim I As Integer
  ReDim ArrayOfProportions(0 To Controls.Count - 1)
  For I = 0 To Controls.Count - 1
    With ArrayOfProportions(I)
      .WidthProportions = Controls(I).Width / ScaleWidth
      .HeightProportions = Controls(I).Height /
```

```
            ScaleHeight
        .LeftProportions = Controls(I).Left / ScaleWidth
        .TopProportions = Controls(I).Top / ScaleHeight
    End With
  Next I
End Sub

Sub ResizeControls()
  On Error Resume Next
  Dim I As Integer
  For I = 0 To Controls.Count - 1
    With ArrayOfProportions(I)
        'we will move the controls to where they should be
        'resizing them proportionally
        Controls(I).Move    .LeftProportions * ScaleWidth, _
                            .TopProportions * ScaleHeight, _
                            .WidthProportions * ScaleWidth, _
                            .HeightProportions * ScaleHeight
    End With
  Next I
End Sub

Private Sub Form_Initialize()
  InitResizeArray
End Sub

Sub Form_Resize()
  ResizeControls
End Sub
```

Note

It is easy to imagine further improvements that prevent the form from being made too small to display the controls in a useful manner. We will leave this improvement to you. (Our code just keeps on shrinking things as the form shrinks, this eventually leads to a very silly looking form.)

Screen Resolution Problems

The generic resize code we just showed you does go a long way towards solving the problem of keeping the controls in proportion as the user resizes your form at run time. What it doesn't do is solve the problem that a form designed for a 640x480 screen will look like a postage stamp on a monitor using a resolution of 1280x1024. We want to take this problem up next.

First off, if you right click in the Form Layout Window, VB does have a tool that gives you an indication of where you form will appear in different screen resolutions. In all honesty this is not usually sufficient information to make a professional looking application. Instead, you really have to check your application at various resolutions!

Once you know how you want the default appearance of your application at the various possible screen resolutions, you'll need to find the user's screen resolution at start-up time and either modify the form appropriately or offer the user a choice of form (and control sizes inside the form—use the generic resize code for this(!). We obviously feel that the best choice is to let you user choose what looks best on their screen. For example, a form that takes up a quarter of the screen real estate might be acceptable on a laptop but would look awfully silly on a 21" monitor running 1280x1024.

The Screen object lets you get at the user's screen resolution easily. For example:

```
Screen.Width / Screen.TwipsPerPixelX
```

is the resolution in pixels for the width of the screen as currently set in Windows, and

```
Screen.Height / Screen.TwipsPerPixelY
```

is the resolution in pixels for the height of the screen as currently set in Windows.

Knowing this information lets you set the size of each form accordingly. For example, you could have code like this in the Form_Load:

```
UserScreenHeight = Screen.Height / Screen.TwipsPerPixelY
Select Case UserScreenHeight
   Case 480
     '640X480 resolution
   Case 600
     '800x600 resolution and so on.
End Select
```

Monitoring Mouse Activity

Windows, and, therefore, Visual Basic, constantly monitors what the user is doing with the mouse. Up to this point, all we have used are the Click and

Double Click events. These detect whether the user clicked the mouse once or twice in a form or control. The next few sections show you how to obtain and use more subtle information. Was a mouse button pressed? Which button was it? Is the mouse pointer over a control? Did the user release a button, and if so, which one? Did the user move the mouse out of one form and into another? Exactly where inside the form is the mouse? Visual Basic can detect all these events. Of course, as with all Visual Basic operations, you must write the event procedures that determine how Visual Basic will respond to the event.

Mouse Event Procedures

There are three fundamental mouse event procedures:

Table 6-16: Fundamental Mouse Event Procedures	
Name	*Event That Caused It*
MouseDown	User clicks one of the mouse buttons.
MouseUp	User releases a mouse button.
MouseMove	User moves the mouse pointer.

In many ways, these procedures are analogous to the KeyUp, KeyDown event procedures. For example, as with those event procedures, you use bit-masking to determine if the user was holding down the SHIFT, ALT, or CTRL key at the same time he or she pressed or released a mouse button.

Only forms and picture boxes return where the mouse pointer is in terms of their internal scales. For the other controls, it's necessary to calculate this information by using the scale of the surrounding container—a method that may or may not be practical.

Controls recognize a mouse event only when the mouse pointer is inside the control; the underlying form recognizes the mouse event in all other cases. However, if a mouse button is pressed and held while the mouse pointer is inside a control or form, that object captures the mouse. This means that no other Visual Basic object can react to mouse events until the user releases the mouse button, regardless of where the user moves the mouse.

All mouse event procedures take the same form and use the same parameters:

```
Object_MouseEvent(Button As Integer, Shift As _
Integer, X As Single, Y As Single)
```

If the object was part of a control array, then, as usual, there is an optional first Index parameter:

```
ObjectInControlArray_MouseEvent(Index As Integer, _
Button As Integer, Shift As Integer, X As Single, _
Y As Single)
```

As the next sections show, bit-masking lets you use the Button argument to determine which mouse button was pressed. Similarly, you can find out if the user was holding down any combination with the SHIFT, ALT, or CTRL keys by bit-masking, using the Shift parameter. Finally, X and Y give you the information you need to determine the position of the mouse pointer, using the internal coordinates of the object, if they exist (forms and picture boxes).

The MouseUp/MouseDown Events

To see this event procedure at work, start up a new project. Double-click to open the Code window and move to the MouseDown event procedure. Now enter the following:

```
Sub Form_MouseDown(Button As Integer, Shift As _
Integer, X As Single, Y As Single)
   Circle (X,Y), 75
End Sub
```

This simple event procedure uses the positioning information passed by X and Y. Each time you click a mouse button, a small circle is centered exactly where you clicked—namely, at CurrentX = X and CurrentY = Y, of size 75 twips. If you add a MouseUp event procedure that looks like:

```
Sub Form_MouseUp(Button As Integer, Shift As _
Integer, X As Single, Y As Single)
   Dim CCode As Integer
   Randomize
   CCode = Int(15*Rnd)
   FillStyle = 0
   FillColor = QBColor(CCode)
   Circle (X,Y), 75
End Sub
```

then each time you release the same button, Visual Basic fills the circle with a random color. On the other hand, even though you may have two or even three mouse buttons, Visual Basic will not generate another MouseDown event until you release the original mouse button. This prevents you from filling some circles and leaving others empty when using these two procedures.

Suppose, however, you wanted to make some circles filled and some empty. One way to do this is to use the added information given by the Button argument. For example, suppose the user has a two-button mouse. You can easily write code so that pressing the correct mouse button gives the user a filled circle; pressing the wrong one gives only a colored circular outline. The Button argument uses the lowest three bits of the value of the integer, as shown here:

Button	*Value of Button Argument*
Left (primary)	vbLeftButton
Right (secondary)	vbRightButton
Middle	vbMiddleButton

Visual Basic will tell you about only one button for the MouseUp/MouseDown combination. You cannot detect if both the left and right buttons are down simultaneously, for example. Thus, you can rewrite the MouseUp event procedure to allow both filled and empty circles using the left/right buttons:

```
Sub Form_MouseUp(Button As Integer, Shift As _
Integer, X As Single, Y As Single)
   Dim CCode As Integer
   Randomize
   CCode = Int(15*Rnd)
   Select Case Button
     Case vbLeftButton, vbMiddleButton
        Circle (X,Y), 75, QBColor(CCode)
        FillColor = &HFFFFFF&
     Case vbRightButton
        FillStyle = 0
        FillColor = QBColor(CCode)
        Circle (X,Y), 75
   End Select
End Sub
```

If you want a pop-up menu in response to a right mouse click, use a line of code like this:

```
If Button = vbRightButton Then PopUpMenu MenuName
```

You can also let the user combine the keyboard with a mouse. For example, you can have the SHIFT-right mouse button combination drop down a special menu. This uses the SHIFT argument in the MouseUp or MouseDown event procedure. Here's a table of the possible values for the lower three bits of the Shift parameter:

Table 6-17: Possible Values for Lower Three Bits of Shift Parameter		
Action	*Bit Set and Value*	*Symbolic Constant*
SHIFT key down	Bit 0: Value = 1	VbLeftButton
CTRL key down	Bit 1: Value = 2	VbRightButton
ALT key down	Bit 2: Value = 4	VbMiddleButton
SHIFT+CTRL keys down	Bit 0 and 1: Value = 3	VbLeftButton + vbRightButton
SHIFT+ALT keys down	Bit 0 and 2: Value = 5	VbLeftButton + vbMiddleButton
CTRL+ALT keys down	Bit 1 and 2: Value = 6	VbRightButton + vbMiddleButton
SHIFT+CTRL+ALT keys down	Bits 0, 1, and 2: Value = 7	VbLeftButton + vbRightButton + vbMiddleButton

At the present time, most people seem to be writing code for the SHIFT key by using a Select Case statement, as follows:

```
Select Case Shift
  Case vbShiftMask
    Print "You pressed the Shift key."
  Case vbCtrlMask
    Print "You pressed the Ctrl key."
  Case vbShiftMask + vbCtrlMask
    Print "You pressed the Shift + Ctrl keys."
  Case vbAltMask
    Print "You pressed the Alt key."
```

and so on.

Microsoft suggests not using this kind of code, reserving the possibility of using the higher order bits for something else, and using the And operator to isolate the first three bits before proceeding. You can do this as follows:

```
Shift And 7
Select Case Bits
  Case vbShiftMask
    Print "You pressed the Shift key."
  Case vbCtrlMask
    Print "You pressed the Ctrl key."
  Case vbShiftMask + vbCtrlMask
    Print "You pressed the Shift + Ctrl keys."
  Case vbAltMask
    Print "You pressed the Alt key."
```

The line Shift And 7 (binary pattern of 7 = 111) eliminates any information that may eventually be contained in the higher order bits, letting the program concentrate on the information contained in the lowest three bits. You might also want to apply the same prevention against future problems for the Button argument.

The MouseUp/MouseDown event procedures work similarly for picture boxes, the only difference being that, as you've seen, you must use the control name of the picture box (and the index if the picture box is part of a control array), as shown here:

```
Sub CntrlName_MouseDown(Button As Integer, Shift As _
Integer, X As Single, Y As Single)
```

The MouseMove Event

Visual Basic calls the MouseMove event procedure whenever the user moves the mouse. This is the most powerful of the mouse event procedures because, unlike the MouseUp/MouseDown event pair, you can use it to analyze completely the state of the mouse buttons. For this event procedure, the Button argument tells you whether some, all, or none of the mouse buttons are down.

You should not get into the habit of thinking that the MouseMove event is generated continuously as the mouse pointer moves across objects. In fact, a combination of the user's software and hardware determines how often the MouseMove event is generated. To see the MouseMove event at work, start a new project and enter the following MouseMove event procedure:

```
Sub Form_MouseMove(Button As Integer, Shift As _
Integer, X As Single, Y As Single)
  DrawWidth = 3
  PSet (X,Y)
End Sub
```

Now run the project and move your mouse around the form at different speeds. As you can see, the dots are more tightly packed when you move the mouse slowly than when you move it rapidly. This happens because Visual Basic relies on the underlying operating system to report mouse events, and such events are generated frequently but not continuously. Because the MouseMove event procedure is not called continuously, the dots are relatively sparse when the mouse is moved rapidly.

Nonetheless, since the MouseMove event procedure will be called relatively frequently, any code inside this event procedure will be executed often. For this reason, you will want to tighten the code inside the MouseMove event procedure as much as possible or provide a flag to prevent repetitive processing. For example, use integer variables for counters and do not recompute the value of variables inside this procedure unless the new value depends on the parameters for the event. Always remember that accessing object properties is much slower than using a variable.

Dragging and Dropping Operations

To move a control as you are designing the interface in your Visual Basic project, hold down the left mouse button and then move the mouse pointer to where you want the control to end up. A gray outline of the control moves with the mouse pointer. When you are happy with the location, release the mouse button. The Microsoft Windows documentation calls moving an object with the mouse button depressed *dragging* and calls the release of the mouse button *dropping*. Visual Basic makes it easy to program this potential into your projects. You can even drag and drop from one form to another if your project uses multiple forms.

Controls permit two types of dragging. These correspond to two different values of the DragMode property. The default is to not allow you to drag controls around except under special circumstances. (As always, you'll need to write the code for these special circumstances; see the next section.) This is called manual dragging, and the DragMode property will have the value of 0. Changing the value of this property to 1, Automatic, means that the user may drag the control around the project. Regardless of the setting for the DragMode property, the control will actually move only if you write the code using the Move method to reposition it, as shown in the next example.

For this example, start up a new project and add a single command button to it. Set the DragMode property of that command button to 1, automatic.

The event that recognizes dragging and dropping operations is called the DragDrop event, and it is associated with the control or form where the drop occurs. Thus, if you want to drag a control to a new location on a form, you write code for the form's DragDrop event procedure. For example, to allow dragging and dropping to move the single command button around the form in this example, use the following:

```
Sub UserControl1_DragDrop(Source As Control, X As _
Single, Y As Single)
   Source.Move X, Y
End Sub
```

or if you are using a standard form, the code would look like this:

```
Private Sub Form_DragDrop(Source As Control, X As _
Single, Y As Single)
   Source.Move X, Y
End Sub
```

Since the type of the Source parameter is a control, you can refer to its properties and methods by using the dot notation, as in the preceding example. If you need more information about what type of control is being dragged before applying a method or setting a property, use the If TypeOf Control Is... statement.

If you run this example, you will notice that the object remains visible in its original location while the gray outline moves. You cannot use the DragDrop event to make a control invisible while the dragging/dropping operation takes place, because this event procedure is called only after the user drops the object. In fact, the DragDrop event need not move the control at all. You often use this event to allow the user to just initiate some action. This is especially common when dragging from one form to another. The reason is that the only way a similar control can appear on a new form in Visual Basic is if you created it on another form to place an invisible control of the same type on the new form at design time, to make the control part of a control array, or to use object variables. The top left corner of the control will be placed where the mouse button was released.

To change the gray outline that Visual Basic uses during a drag operation, set the DragIcon property of the control at design time. To do this, select the DragIcon property from the Properties box. Now click the three dots to the left of the Settings box. This opens up the Load Icon dialog box for choosing icons. You can also assign the drag icon of one object to another:

```
FirstControl.DragIcon = SecondControl.DragIcon
```

The final possibility is to use the LoadPicture function. For example:

```
Control.DragIcon=LoadPicture("C\VB\ICONS\MISC\CLOCK01.ICO")
```

If you design a custom icon, a common practice is to reverse the colors for the drag icon. An Icon Editor program makes this easy to do.

The following table summarizes the events, methods, and properties used for dragging and dropping.

Table 6-18: Events, Methods, and Properties Used for Dragging and Dropping

Item	Description
DragMode property	Allows automatic dragging (vbAutomatic) or manual dragging (vbManual).
DragIcon property	Changes from the gray rectangle to a custom icon when dragging.
DragDrop event	Associated with the target of the operation; generated when the source is dropped on the target control.
DragOver event	Associated with any control the source control passes over during dragging.
Drag Method	Starts or stops dragging when DragMode is set to manual.

Manual Dragging

If you have left the value of the DragMode property at its default value of zero, then you must use the Drag method to allow dragging of the control. The syntax for this method is:

```
Control.Drag TypeOfAction
```

The TypeOfAction is an integer value from 0 to 2, as shown here:

```
Control.Drag vbCancel 0        Cancel dragging
Control.Drag vbBeginDrag 1     Begin dragging
Control.Drag vbEndDrag 2       Drop the control
```

If you omit the TypeOfAction argument, the method has the same effect as the statement Control.Drag 1. That is, Visual Basic initiates the dragging operation for the control.

One way to use the flexibility this method gives you is to allow expert users to drag and drop controls, but make the default that users cannot do this. For example, use the CTRL+MouseDown combination to allow dragging to take place. You can do this by beginning the MouseDown event procedure with the following:

```
Sub CntrlName_MouseDown(Button As Integer, Shift As _
Integer, X As Single, Y As Single)
   If (Shift And 7) = vbCtrlMask Then
     CntrlName.DragMode = vbAutomatic
  .
  .
End Sub
```

Another example of where you might want to use this method is in self-running demonstration programs. You can use a value of 1 to start the dragging operation and a value of 2 to drop the control. This lets you show off dragging and dropping operations.

The DragOver Event

All Visual Basic objects, except menus and timers, will detect if a control is passing over them. You can use the DragOver event to allow even greater flexibility for your projects. This event lets you monitor the path a control takes while being dragged. You might consider changing the background color of the control being passed over. The event procedure template for forms is:

```
Sub Form_DragOver(Source As Control, X As Single, Y _
As Single, State As Integer)
  .
  .
End Sub
```

For controls, this event procedure template takes the form:

```
Sub CtrlName_DragOver([Index As Integer,]Source As _
Control, X As Single, Y As Single, State As Integer)
  .
  .
End Sub
```

As usual, the optional Index parameter is used if the control is part of a control array. The Source is the control being dragged, but the event procedure is associated with the control being passed over. The X and Y parameters give you the CurrentX and CurrentY values in terms of the scale of the object being passed over for forms and picture boxes and the underlying form for all other controls. The State parameter has three possible values:

Table 6-19: State Parameter Values	
Value of State Parameter	*Description*
VbEnter 0	Source is now inside target.
VbLeave 1	Source is outside the target.
VbOver 2	Source moved inside target.

An Example: A Circular Command Button

We want to put everything you have seen so far about pixel graphics and mouse detection to work by showing you how to build a "circular" command button. To make it simple, we'll simply use a solid red circle.

The way this button works is:

1. The user control form contains a red circle.
2. Using the MouseUp event, we determine if the user clicks inside the circular area.
3. Then we raise the Click event for the control.

Actually, the hard part of programming this control is remembering the tiny bit of math that is needed to check that the user clicks inside the circle. To make the math a little easier, we use a custom scale method that puts the center of the user control at coordinates (0, 0). To do this, we use the following Scale statement:

```
Scale (-ScaleWidth / 2, ScaleHeight / 2)-(ScaleWidth _
/ 2, -ScaleHeight / 2)
```

The idea is that the usual scale of a form runs from 0 to ScaleWidth and 0 to ScaleHeight. We make it more symmetrical by moving half the units to their negatives. Next, we need a little geometry (sorry!). Geometry tells us if all the points inside a circle of radius r satisfy the equation:

```
x*x + y*y <= r*r
```

We use the x and y parameters of the MouseUp event to check that this condition is true. This is summarized in Figure 6-15.

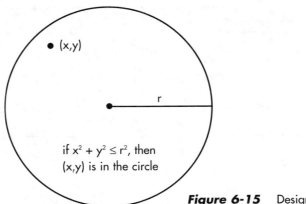

Figure 6-15   Designing a circular button

While the whole code is on the CD in the CH6 directory (CircleButton.vbp), here is what you'll need to follow along. First, set the AutoRedraw property of the control to True so the user of the control can see our red circle all the time. Next, we have the module level declarations for one variable and the custom Click event:

```
Private mRadius As Single 'for the radius
Public Event Click()
```

Here is the code in the MouseUp event that uses the algebraic test described above to test where the button was clicked:

```
Private Sub UserControl_MouseUp(Button As Integer,_
Shift As Integer, X As Single, Y As Single)
  Scale (-ScaleWidth / 2, ScaleHeight / 2)- _
(ScaleWidth / 2, -ScaleHeight / 2)
  If Button = vbLeftButton And (X * X + Y * Y _
<=mRadius * mRadius) Then RaiseEvent Click
End Sub
```

Tip

There is actually a faster way to do this kind of checking for where you are in a graphic, in our case, assuming the color of the circle is different than the color of the rest of the user control. (This is a natural assumption but you can check for this in code, of course.) Simply check the color at the point (X,Y) using the built-in Point method.

Finally, we need the code to make sure we keep a circle when the user resizes the control at design time. This must be placed in the Resize event of

the control. We use a bare Scale command in order to set the scale mode back
to the default scale before recalculating the scale of the circle:

```
Private Sub UserControl_Resize()
  Scale 'reset scale back
  Cls
  FillColor = vbRed
  FillStyle = vbSolid
  If ScaleHeight < ScaleWidth Then
    mRadius = ScaleHeight / 2
  Else
    mRadius = ScaleWidth / 2
  End If
  Scale (-ScaleWidth / 2, ScaleHeight / 2)- _
(ScaleWidth / 2, -ScaleHeight / 2)
  Circle (0, 0), mRadius
End Sub
```

Note

*Because of how VB draws circles, you might want to slightly reduce the
value of the mRadius variable to, say, 0.98 of its current value. This will
help prevent the circle from looking flattened.*

To test the control, you can add a new project and use code like this:

```
Private Sub UserControl1_Click()
  MsgBox "You clicked in the circle"
End Sub
```

If you did everything right, then you'll see the message box only if you click
inside the circle.

Note

*The version of this control on the CD adds a shading feature to the
perimeter of the circle so the circle looks pressed in when you click it.*

OLE Drag and Drop

Unlike the usual mouse operations that you just saw, OLE drag and drop is
the ability to transfer *data* by dragging an object that contains the data from

one place to another. OLE Drag and Drop often seems like magic: certainly we were amazed the first time we dragged a file with a doc extension to Word and Word automatically opened it!

While OLE drag and drop it is based on some very sophisticated programming being done for you "under the hood," it is often easy to use it in VB. For example:

1. Create a document using your favorite word processor (or WordPad even), add fancy fonts, different point sizes and so on.
2. Save it to the desktop in rich text format using the name Test.rtf.
3. Start up a new VB project and add a rich text box to a form.

Now:

1. Start the project and leave it running (minimize VB if necessary so that you can see the Windows desktop).
2. Drag the Test.rtf file from the desktop to the RTF control in the form.

Pretty impressive, isn't it? Notice how even the mouse pointers change automatically. (If you don't see the embellished text show up in the rich text box, go back to VB and make sure that OLEDragMode and OLEDropMode for the rich text box are both set to automatic.)

As you might expect, the OLE drag and drop methods, events and properties have similar names to those for ordinary mouse drag and drop. Automatic OLE drag and drop, as you have just seen, is trivial. The control presumably knows what to do with the data it is being fed. If it doesn't know what to do with the data or if you need finer control of the process then you will need to work harder.

One reason manual OLE drag and drop can get complicated very quickly is that the number of possible data formats you may need to work with can be very large. However the ideas for coding manual OLE drag and drop aren't hard:

- Coding manual OLE drag and drop means you will need to write code in one or more of the OLE drag and drop events in order to get things to work the way you want.

We will take up these events shortly but first we want to give you an overview of how the various standard VB controls can work with OLE drag and drop.

Controls and OLE Drag and Drop

Almost all Visual Basic controls support OLE drag and drop to some extent.
The following controls support OLE drag and drop both automatically and
manually. For the automatic mode all you need to do is check that the
OLEDragMode and OLEDropMode properties of the control are set to
Automatic. (They are true by default for a rich text box, for example, but are
off by default for a text box.)

- Data-Bound Grid
- Image Box
- Masked edit box
- Picture box
- Rich text box
- Text box

The following controls only provide automatic support for OLE drag operations. This means that you can take data out of them but not put data into
them automatically. To enable automatic dragging of data out of these controls, set their OLEDragMode property to Automatic.

- Combo box
- Data-Bound Combo box
- Data-Bound list box
- Directory list box
- File list box
- List box
- List View
- Tree View

The following controls will always need code for OLE drag and drop since
they support only manual OLE drag and drop.

- Check box
- Command button
- Drive list box

- Frame
- Label
- Option button

Tip

To check if a custom control supports OLE drag and drop and whether it does so automatically or manually, check the Properties window (or use the Object Browser) for OLEDragMode and OLEDropMode properties. Essentially all Visual Basic components (including forms) support manual OLE drag and drop.

Working with OLE Drag and Drop

There are few subtleties about the OLE drag and drop events because in OLE drag and drop you are moving *data* around and not objects. In fact, the key to working with OLE Drag and Drop via code is a predefined Visual Basic object called the DataObject. The DataObject is simply a container for the data being transferred from the source component to the target component. It can hold multiple kinds of data at the same time as long as they are of different types. You work with the DataObject in much the same way as you do with the Clipboard object. For example, the DataObject has Clear, GetData, GetFormat and SetData methods that work much as they did for the Clipboard object.

Let's start with coding a simple yet typical example of coding OLE drag and drop. We will let the user drag a set of file names form Explorer to a Visual Basic list box. The list box will then display the file names. To make this happen all we will need to do is write code in the OLEDragDrop event. This event is triggered when data is dropped onto the target control. *It is an event of the target control and not the source control.*

The signature for the OLEDragDrop event is:

```
Private Sub object_OLEDragDrop(data As DataObject, effect As Long,_
    button As Integer, shift As Integer, x As Single, y As Single)
```

The button, shift, x and y parameters work the same as for ordinary mouse events, so we won't bother with them here. As mentioned before the key for manual OLE drag and drop is to work with the data parameter, which is a *DataObject*. For our sample application:

1. Add a list box to a new Visual Basic project.
2. Set the OLEDropMode property of the list box to 1—Manual.
3. Write the following OLEDragDrop event procedure for the list box:

```
Private Sub List1_OLEDragDrop(Data As DataObject, Effect As Long, Button _
As Integer, Shift As Integer, X As Single, Y As Single)
  Dim FileName
  If Data.GetFormat(vbCFFiles) Then
    For Each FileName In Data.Files
       List1.AddItem (FileName)
    Next FileName
  Else
    MsgBox "Not a list of file names, sorry!"
  End If
End Sub
```

Let's go through this procedure line by line since it illustrates so well the ideas needed for coding OLE Drag and Drop. First off, we need to check the type of the data being dragged to the list box. This is done exactly as you did for working the Clipboard object: use the GetFormat method. (Only now, of course, we are applying it to the DataObject rather than the Clipboard object.) The next line uses the vbCFFFiles constant in the GetFormat method to check whether the DataObject contains a list of files. More precisely the call to GetFormat(vbCFFFiles) returns true if and only if the data contains a bunch of file names. (For example, file names that were selected in Windows Explorer.)

Next, if the user did select a bunch of file names, the Files property of the DataObject lets us get at the list because its Files property (Data.Files in this case) returns a *collection* of the file names that the user had selected. Once the file name information is in a collection we are home free: as you saw earlier in this chapter, you can run through the items in a collection using the For Each statement. We do this and at each step we simply add the next file name the list box.

Note

The OleDragDrop event is triggered only if the OLEDropMode property of the control is set to 1 (Manual).

The following table summarizes the other parameters in the OLEDragDrop event.

Table 6-20: OLEDragDrop Event Parameters	
Parameter	*Description*
Effect	This long integer is set by the target component to tell the source what it is doing to the data. The source can then decide what to do in its OLECompleteDrag event. The possible settings are: vbDropEffectNone (the target cannot accept the data), vbDropEffectCopy (the target copied the data), vbDropEffectMove (the data was moved). (The protocol is that the source and not the target removes the data from the Data object after receiving this message.)
Button	Indicates the state of the mouse button for the dragging operation. Works the same as for ordinary mouse operations, so the left button is bit 0, the right button is bit 1, and the middle button is bit 2.
Shift	Indicates the state of the SHIFT, CTRL, and ALT keys as in ordinary mouse operations.
x, y	These parameters let you get at the current location of the mouse pointer where the user dropped the data. These are always expressed in terms of the coordinate system set by the ScaleHeight, ScaleWidth, ScaleLeft, and ScaleTop properties of the target object.

Summary of OLE Drag and Drop

The following table summarizes the properties and events with which you will need to work in order to go further with OLE drag and drop.

Table 6-21: OLE Drag and Drop Properties and Events	
Item	*Description*
OLEDragMode	This property of the source object is how you enable automatic or manual dragging of data out of the control. Note that if the control supports manual but not automatic OLE dragging, it won't have this property. Instead it will have only the OLEDrag method and the OLE drag-and-drop events.
OLEDropMode	This property specifies how the target control will respond to the drop.
OLEDragDrop	This target event is triggered when a data source object is dropped onto a target.
OLEDragOver	This target event is triggered when a source object is dragged over a target that can accept an OLE drop. You can give the source feedback by changing the Effect parameter.
OLEGiveFeedback	This very useful source event is where you can put code that will give the user feedback that an OLE drag and drop is in process. It is triggered by a change in the Effect parameter made in the target's OLEDragOver event.
OLEStartDrag	This source event is triggered when the OLE drag and drop process starts. You can specify here what the source will allow to be done with the data. (For example, it could not allow moving of data, just copying.)
OLESetData	This source event is one place where you put the code to store the data that will be sent in the Data Object. (Usually you do this in the StartDrag event unless it is time consuming to get the data. For example, you can use this to load the data to be transferred out of a file or to do a recalculation in a spreadsheet before making the data available.
OLECompleteDrag	This is the event that is triggered in the source by the target to tell it the data was dropped on the target.

Notice that like mouse events, there are OLE drag and drop events and methods for both the source and the target. Finally, there is only one relevant method, called OLEDrag. This method is a method of the *source* object. Once you call this method on the source object (usually in a standard mouse event procedure, VB triggers the OLEStartDrag event in the source.

A File OLE Drag and Drop Example

What we want to do in this section is show you how to code an application that has two versions of OLE drag and drop at work.

- It will have a list box that you can drag files from Internet Explorer. You will then see the full path name in the list box.
- It will have a text box that will let you use OLE drag and drop on the information in the list box. If you drag the data from the list box, it will show up in the text box. However, if you hold down the control key while dragging, it will display the contents of the file. (Well, actually only the first 32,000 characters because of the limits of a multiline text box.)

To start out:

1. Add a list box and make sure multiselect is 0 (none), set its OLEDragDrop property to Manual.
2. Add a multiline text box and add vertical scroll bars, set its OLEDragDrop property to Manual.

Since we want the list box to accept a list of file names we need to put the code in its OLEDragDrop event. The idea is that we check if the data is of type vbCFFiles and then run through the file names that are stored in the Files collection of the Data object. Here's the code:

```
Private Sub List1_OLEDragDrop(Data As DataObject, Effect _
As Long, Button As Integer, Shift As Integer, X As _
Single, Y As Single)
   Dim FileName
   List1.Clear
   If Data.GetFormat(vbCFFiles) Then
     For Each FileName In Data.Files
        List1.AddItem (FileName)
     Next FileName
```

```
    Else
      MsgBox "Not a list of file names, sorry"
    End If
End Sub
```

In this case we decided to separate out the setting the formats for the data from storing the data. As we mentioned before, this is common when the data might take a while to get. (The SetData event is triggered only when the OLEDragdrop event happens on the target, so by putting the data collection in SetData, you may save yourself some work if the operation was cancelled. Here's the code:

```
Private Sub List1_OLEStartDrag(Data As DataObject,
AllowedEffects As Long)
    Data.SetData , vbCFText
    Data.SetData , vbCFFiles
End Sub
```

The SetData event of the source looks like this:

```
Private Sub List1_OLESetData(Data As DataObject,
DataFormat As Integer)
    Dim Temp As String
    If DataFormat = vbCFFiles Then
        Data.Files.Add List1.Text
    ElseIf DataFormat = vbCFText Then
      For I = 0 To List1.ListCount - 1
        Temp = Temp + vbCrLf + List1.List(I)
      Next I
      Data.SetData Temp, vbCFText
    End If
End Sub
```

The idea here is that we add only the file name that is currently selected if we are transferring the data contained in the file or we store all the file names in a string where the items are separated by carriage return line feeds. The code for the text box OLEDragDrop event must check if the user held down the Ctrl key. We also use an auxiliary routine called TextInFile to get the data out of the file but otherwise the code is straightforward:

```
Private Sub Text1_OLEDragDrop(Data As DataObject, Effect As Long_
, Button As Integer, Shift As Integer, X As Single, Y As Single)
    Text1.Text = ""
    If Shift And vbCtrlMask = vbCtrlMask Then
      Dim FileName
      FileName = Data.Files.Item(1)
```

```
        Text1.Text = TextInFile(CStr(FileName))
    Else
        Text1.Text = Data.GetData(vbCFText)
    End If
End Sub
```

This simple example can be jazzed up a great deal more. For example, we haven't used the fact that the source can specify what effects it wants to allow or the target can send information to the source for us in the OLEGiveFeedback event of the source. For example, suppose we have a form level boolean variable called FileViewingAllowed. If this is false we don't want the user to be able to use the Ctrl+Drag feature to move the contents of the list box. We can do this by modifying the OLEStartDrag event as follows:

```
Private Sub List1_OLEStartDrag(Data As DataObject, _
AllowedEffects As Long)
    Data.SetData , vbCFText
    Data.SetData , vbCFFiles
    If FileViewingAllowed then AllowedEffects = _
vbDropEffectCopy Else AllowedEffects = vbDropEffectNone
End Sub
```

Changing the AllowedEffects parameter will also tell the control what to do. For example, if you set it to vbDropEffectMove then when you drag the data in a rich text box to another rich text box it will be moved and not copied.

Next, we could have the target give feedback back to the source. For example, suppose the file is larger than the 32,000 character limit or there was no data in the file, it would be polite to tell the source this. We can do this by changing the code in the OLEDragOver event as follows:

1. We check the file length of the file whose data is going into the text box.

2. If the length is too large we change the Effect parameter in the OLEDragOver event.

3. This triggers the OLEGivefeedback event of the source.

4. We then change the mouse pointer to the vbNoDrop in the OLEGiveFeedBack event to be vbNoDrop.

5. We then change the mouse pointer back to the default in the OLECompleteDragEvent of the source.

The Code for the OLE Drag and Drop Example

Here's the form file code that includes all the features we have discussed.

Listing 6-3:   Form File Code for OLE Drag and Drop

```
VERSION 5.00
Begin VB.Form Form1
    Caption         =    "OLE Drag Drop For Files"
    ClientHeight    =    4860
    ClientLeft      =    45
    ClientTop       =    330
    ClientWidth     =    3750
    LinkTopic       =    "Form1"
    OLEDropMode     =    1   'Manual
    ScaleHeight     =    4860
    ScaleWidth      =    3750
    StartUpPosition =    3   'Windows Default
    Begin VB.TextBox Text1
        Height        =    2292
        Left          =    0
        MultiLine     =    -1   'True
        OLEDropMode   =    1    'Manual
        ScrollBars    =    2    'Vertical
        TabIndex      =    1
        Top           =    2280
        Width         =    3615
    End
    Begin VB.ListBox List1
        Height        =    1035
        Left          =    0
        OLEDragMode   =    1    'Automatic
        OLEDropMode   =    1    'Manual
        TabIndex      =    0
        Top           =    720
        Width         =    3495
    End
End
Attribute VB_Name = "Form1"
Attribute VB_GlobalNameSpace = False
Attribute VB_Creatable = False
Attribute VB_PredeclaredId = True
Attribute VB_Exposed = False
Dim FileViewingAllowed As Boolean

Private Sub Form_Load()
  FileViewingAllowed = True
End Sub
Private Sub Form_Resize()
  List1.Width = ScaleWidth
```

```
   Text1.Width = ScaleWidth
End Sub

Private Sub List1_OLECompleteDrag(Effect As Long)
   Screen.MousePointer = vbDefault
End Sub

Private Sub List1_OLEDragDrop(Data As DataObject, Effect As Long, _
Button As Integer, Shift As Integer, X As Single, Y As Single)
Dim FileName
List1.Clear
If Data.GetFormat(vbCFFiles) Then
   For Each FileName In Data.Files
     List1.AddItem (FileName)
   Next FileName
Else
   MsgBox "Not a list of file names, sorry"
End If
End Sub

Function TextInFile(ByVal sFileName) As String
   Dim FileNumber As Integer
   FileNumber = FreeFile
   On Error GoTo AnError
   Open sFileName For Input Access Read Lock Read _
Write As #FileNumber
   Dim TempString As String, NextLine As String
   Do Until EOF(FileNumber) Or Len(TempString) > 32000
     Line Input #FileNumber, NextLine
     If TempString <> "" Then TempString = TempString & vbCrLf
     TempString = TempString & NextLine
   Loop
   Close #FileNumber
   TextInFile = Left$(TempString, 32000)
Exit Function
AnError:
   MsgBox Err.Description
End Function


Private Sub List1_OLEGiveFeedback(Effect As Long, DefaultCursors As Boolean)
   If Effect = vbDropEffectNone Then
     Screen.MousePointer = vbNoDrop
   End If
End Sub
```

```
Private Sub List1_OLESetData(Data As DataObject, DataFormat As Integer)
  Dim Temp As String
  If DataFormat = vbCFFiles Then
     Data.Files.Add List1.Text
  ElseIf DataFormat = vbCFText Then
    For I = 0 To List1.ListCount - 1
      Temp = Temp + vbCrLf + List1.List(I)
    Next I
    Data.SetData Temp, vbCFText
  End If
End Sub

Private Sub List1_OLEStartDrag(Data As DataObject, AllowedEffects As Long)
  Data.SetData , vbCFText
  Data.SetData , vbCFFiles
  If FileViewingAllowed Then AllowedEffects = vbDropEffectCopy Else
AllowedEffects = vbDropEffectNone
End Sub

Private Sub Text1_OLEDragDrop(Data As DataObject, Effect As Long, _
Button As Integer, Shift As Integer, X As Single, Y As Single)
  Text1.Text = ""
  If Shift And vbCtrlMask = vbCtrlMask Then
     Dim FileName
     FileName = Data.Files.Item(1)
     Text1.Text = TextInFile(CStr(FileName))
     If Text1.Text = "" Then Effect = vbDropEffectNone
  Else
     Text1.Text = Data.GetData(vbCFText)
  End If
End Sub

Private Sub Text1_OLEDragOver(Data As DataObject, Effect As Long, _
Button As Integer, Shift As Integer, X As Single, Y As Single, _
State As Integer)
  If Shift And vbCtrlMask = vbCtrlMask Then
     If FileLen(Data.Files.Item(1)) > 32000 Then
       Effect = vbDropEffectNone
     End If
  End If
End Sub
```

A Database Example Using OLE Drag and Drop

Although we don't cover much of VB's awesome database capabilities in this book, we couldn't resist showing you the following example. Like the previous example, the code illustrates how to have two different data formats in the DataObject and also how to have multiple formats for different controls work with each other. The idea is that we will store both a file name and the text representation of the file name in the DataObject. What we will do is use OLE drag and drop to let you drag any Access (.mdb) database to a list box. The list box then displays all the tables in the database. We then will add another form with another list box. If you drag one of the items listed in the first list box to the second list box, it will automatically display all the fields in that table. So start up a new project, add a list box to the form and:

- Set the list box OLEDragMode to be 1—Automatic.
- Set its OLEDropMode property to be 1—Manual.
- Add the DAO reference using Project|References -> "Microsoft DAO 3.5 Object Library."

The code for the list box OLEDragDrop event will be triggered when you drag an .mdb database to the list box. Without getting too much into the intricacies of VB database programming, what this code does is find all the table names in the database and store this information in the list box. Here's the code:

```
Dim db As Database 'used for the database name

Private Sub List1_OLEDragDrop(Data As DataObject, _
Effect As Long, Button As Integer, Shift As Integer, _
X As Single, Y As Single)
  On Error GoTo errh
  Dim t As TableDef
  Dim sDatabase As String

  sDatabase = Data.Files.Item(1)
  Set db = OpenDatabase(sDatabase)
  List1.Clear

  For Each t In db.TableDefs
    If (t.Attributes And dbSystemObject) = 0 Then
      List1.AddItem t.Name
    End If
  Next
  Caption = "Tables - " & sDatabase
```

```
   Exit Sub
errh:
   MsgBox Err.Description
End Sub
```

On the other hand, the code for the StartDrag event has to allow you to drag a table to the second form and find out the field names. The code for this procedure looks like this:

```
Private Sub List1_OLEStartDrag(Data As DataObject, _
AllowedEffects As Long)
   Data.Clear
   Data.SetData , vbCFFiles
   Data.Files.Add db.Name
   Data.SetData List1.Text, vbCFText
End Sub
```

Notice how we clear the information from the DataObject before starting. Then we set the first possible format that can be stored in the DataObject to be file names (vbCFFiles). We then add the name of the database to the list of files. Next, we set another possible format for the stored data: simple text. Finally, we place the text for the current table as text in the DataObject as well. (This is actually a very common technique: store a file name in the Data.File collection and store the name of the file in the text.)

Now, we add a second form to the project and add a list box to that form. The code for the OLEDragDrop event for the list box in the second form again uses some database features of VB that we don't have space to explain but the idea is simple. We use the text stored in the DataObject to title the second form and we use the filename stored to start working with the actual database.

```
Private Sub List1_OLEDragDrop(Data As DataObject, _
Effect As Long, Button As Integer, Shift As Integer, _
X As Single, Y As Single)
   On Error GoTo errh

   Dim fld As Field
   Dim db As Database
   Dim sDatabase As String
   Dim sTable As String

   sDatabase = Data.Files.Item(1)
   sTable = Data.GetData(vbCFText)
   List1.Clear
   Set db = OpenDatabase(sDatabase)
```

```
For Each fld In db.TableDefs(sTable).Fields
   List1.AddItem fld.Name
Next fld

Caption = "Fields - " & sTable

   Exit Sub
errh:
   MsgBox Err.Description
End Sub
```

The CD contains the full source code for this example. (You'll need to hold down the CTRL key to drag between the list boxes.)

Help Systems

Writing the Help files for your application is hardly as much fun as coding it. Hooking it up correctly is easy but tedious. Nonetheless, if your online help doesn't have the look and feel of a Windows help system, users will have to learn too much (and you'll probably be working too hard to teach them). Both the Professional and Enterprise editions of Visual Basic come with the Windows Help compiler to make it possible to create a help system for your applications. They also come with some tools (see Appendix A) that can make the tedium a little easier.

Roughly speaking, the way you use the Help compiler is simple: You prepare a rich text file that contains certain formatting codes that the Windows Help compiler translates into jumps, definitions, and so on.

However, we don't recommend doing it this way. This is because it is *much* easier to create a help system using one of the many third-party tools out there—we guarantee that the money you spend for a good help tool will save you hours of work.

Tip

Our favorite commercial tool for building help systems is RoboHelp from Blue Sky Software (www.blue-sky.com). There are also a couple of tools supplied with VB that can take some of the drudgery out of writing Help files. (See Appendix.)

In any case, a help system should also include the standard menu to which users are accustomed. The Help menu should certainly have Contents,

Search, and About items. The Search item should lead to the list of keywords through which the user can search. These keywords will connect to the topics that you write. Various parts of your application (like Visual Basic itself) should have context-sensitive help. This way, all users know that if they press F1, they can get help about a specific item on a form.

You use the HelpFile property of the Application object to associate a (compiled) Help file with your application. You create context-sensitive help by setting the HelpContext of the form or component. Once you assign the value of the HelpContext property for the form or component, you have to tell the Help compiler how to *map* the HelpContext property to specific topics in your help file.

The Help project file contains the information needed for the Help compiler to do its job in associating context numbers with help topics. The Help project file must be an ordinary ASCII file. The custom is to use .HPJ as the extension on all Help project files. The Help compiler changes this to .HLP for the compiled version. The Help project file lists all the topic files and can optionally add bitmaps or a map between context strings and context numbers. You can also assign two context strings to the same topic by modifying the project file.

To map Help context numbers to specific topics for context-sensitive help, place the topic after the keyword [MAP], followed by white space (press the SPACEBAR or TAB), followed by the Help context numbers. Here's a sample of what you might have in the [MAP] section of the Help project file if you are doing it by hand instead of using one of the third-party tools.

```
[MAP]
first_context_string      5      ;5 is context number
                                 ;Comments follow semicolons
second_context_string    10      ;10 is context number
third_context_string     15      ;15 is context number
```

The point is that the context number is passed by the Visual Basic program as the value of the HelpContext property.

Finally, if you need to call the Windows Help engine directly you can either user the ShowHelp method for the CommonDialog control or a Windows API call. (The API call is more flexible, so we suggest using it. We cover it in Chapter 12.)

Tip

If you want a Help button to appear in a common dialog box, add the cdlOFNHelpButton constant to the Flags property of the dialog box control.

Resource Files and Internationalization

While we don't have space to cover the intricacies of writing VB code that supports Chinese Windows NT (although rest assured, it is possible), we do want to say a little bit about the basics of internationalizing your code. First off, Windows maintains a LocaleId that describes what country and language the user set. This in turn determines how Windows (and so VB) displays things like currency, dates and times. You can access the LocaleId using a Windows API call or as the value of the Ambient.LocaleID property of a user control. In both cases you need to do bit-masking techniques to find out both the language (English) and the version (for example, U.S. English or British English).

The next step in internationalizing an application is to get away from hard coding in strings like:

```
MsgBox "Hello"
```

Can you imagine going through your code and changing all occurrences of "Hello" to "Bonjour"?

The way around this is that Visual Basic lets you store strings in what is called a resource file. For example, strings can then be identified by a resource ID. Roughly speaking your code might look like this:

```
Greeting = LoadResString(2)
MsgBox   Greeting
```

More generally, you can then load the specific string you want from the file depending on the value of the LocaleID. Resource files can even include icons, bitmaps and constants as well as text.

Adding Resources to a Project

You create a resource file using a text editor and resource compiler. The Professional and Enterprise editions of VB come with a resource compiler. It can be found in the \Tools\Resource\Rc32 directory on your VB CD (see Appendix). Consult the documentation supplied with the resource compiler (the file named Resource.txt file in that directory) to see how to build and then compile the resource text file that you create with your favorite text editor. The compiled resource file has a .res file name extension. To add the resource file to your project, simply:

- Choose Project|Add File.
- Pick the correct resource file to load.

Tip

Microsoft is making a new utility called the Resource Editor available on the VB Owners site. http://www.microsoft.com/vstudio/. This utility makes it much easier to create and use resources in your application.

There are three Visual Basic functions for retrieving the data stored in the resource file.

Table 6-22:   VB Functions for Retrieving Data from Resource Files

Function	*Description*
LoadResString	Gets a resource string.
LoadResPicture	Gets an image, such as a bitmap, icon, or cursor.
LoadResData	Gets the information as a Byte array. This is used for audio files or for any other information that isn't obviously a picture or a string.

For example, a line like:

```
Picture1.Picture  = LoadResPicture(20)
```

would use the picture with resource identifier 20.

We don't recommend hand coding all the calls to LoadResString, LoadResPicture and LoadResData. Instead, if you run the VB Application Wizard and tell it that you will be using a resource file, it will automatically generate the code for using a resource file for you. It does this by means of this rather nifty Sub program:

Listing 6-4:   VB Application Wizard Generated Code for Using a Resource File

```
Sub LoadResStrings(frm As Form)
    On Error Resume Next

    Dim ctl As Control
    Dim obj As Object
    Dim fnt As Object
    Dim sCtlType As String
    Dim nVal As Integer

    'set the form's caption
    frm.Caption = LoadResString(CInt(frm.Tag))

    'set the font
    Set fnt = frm.Font
    fnt.Name = LoadResString(20)
    fnt.Size = CInt(LoadResString(21))

    'set the controls' captions using the caption
    'property for menu items and the Tag property
    'for all other controls
    For Each ctl In frm.Controls
        Set ctl.Font = fnt
        sCtlType = TypeName(ctl)
        If sCtlType = "Label" Then
            ctl.Caption = LoadResString(CInt(ctl.Tag))
        ElseIf sCtlType = "Menu" Then
            ctl.Caption = LoadResString(CInt(ctl.Caption))
        ElseIf sCtlType = "TabStrip" Then
            For Each obj In ctl.Tabs
                obj.Caption = LoadResString(CInt(obj.Tag))
                obj.ToolTipText =
LoadResString(CInt(obj.ToolTipText))
            Next
        ElseIf sCtlType = "Toolbar" Then
            For Each obj In ctl.Buttons
                obj.ToolTipText =
LoadResString(CInt(obj.ToolTipText))
            Next
        ElseIf sCtlType = "ListView" Then
            For Each obj In ctl.ColumnHeaders
                obj.Text = LoadResString(CInt(obj.Tag))
            Next
        Else
```

```
            nVal = 0
            nVal = Val(ctl.Tag)
            If nVal > 0 Then ctl.Caption = LoadResString(nVal)
            nVal = 0
            nVal = Val(ctl.ToolTipText)
            If nVal > 0 Then ctl.ToolTipText = LoadResString(nVal)
         End If
      Next
End Sub
```

It is very easy to adapt this code for your own use. Why? Well, because the idea of this code is that we fill properties like the tag property of the control with various integer values and use those to pull out the correct resource. If you make each country a fixed distance apart in their resource IDs (U.S. 2-100, France 102 to 200, Germany 202-300 for example—1 is not an allowable resource ID by the way), you can:

- Use the LocaleId to find the country.
- Use this to set the correct value for the property.

While the actual code for this needs a Windows API, the pseudo-code for this is simple:

```
Select Case LocalId
   Case US
     Shift = 0
   Case France
      Shift = 100
   Case Germany
      Shift = 200
```

and so on.

VISUAL BASIC OBJECTS

(AND AN INTRODUCTION TO OBJECT-ORIENTED PROGRAMMING)

Topics in this Chapter

- Introduction to OOP

- The Vocabulary of OOP

- How to Objectify Your Programs

- The Object Browser

- Manipulating Objects Built into Visual Basic

- Creating New Objects at Run Time

- Creating a New Class Module

Chapter 7

If you have read this far (or were familiar enough with some version of VB to jump right to here) then you are pretty comfortable with manipulating most of VB5's built-in objects. We now want to teach you the techniques that VB5 uses for creating new, *reusable* objects as well as some more advanced techniques for manipulating VB's built-in objects. Fair warning: If you are an experienced VB programmer you may need *to change the way you think about VB programming in order to take full advantage of these new techniques.*

First a confession: for us, it was hard at the beginning to see why the new techniques were worthwhile: Why? Because, just as you take quite usable pictures with a simple point-and-shoot camera, we could build reasonably useful programs with VB5 by sticking to the old event-driven approach to VB programming. However, we are now convinced that to take full advantage of the amazing powers that were added to VB5, we needed to go beyond the "point-and-shoot" approach to working with VB's built-in objects, we really needed to change the way we thought and worked. For example, you can't really build truly reusable controls without using this new way of thinking nor can you use VB5 to build the kind of large-scale projects that were once the domain of C++ without these techniques.

This is why the purpose of the next two chapters is to teach you what you need to know about this new way of thinking, usually called *Object Oriented Programming* (or OOP) in order to become fully productive with VB5. We will do this in a practical way by stressing the techniques that you as a VB programmer will use to solve real problems on a day to day purpose. We will try hard not to fall into the trap of discussing everything from an abstract point of view and being needlessly complete. (There are dozens of books out there that teach the "theory" of object-oriented programming if you are interested.) Still, there is a fair amount of terminology needed to make sense of OOP, so we'll start by showing you the necessary concepts and definitions. After this, you'll start to see how VB5 implements its version of OOP. (The next chapter shows you more advanced techniques that you can use in VB's approach to OOP.)

Finally, it is worth keeping in mind that Object-Oriented Programming seems to be well on its way to becoming the dominant programming paradigm. OOP is rapidly replacing the structured programming techniques developed in the early '70s. This means your boss may someday insist that you need to learn Java or C++. If you master the techniques we show you here than moving to these languages will be much, much easier.

Introduction to OOP

Here's a question that, on the surface, seems to have nothing to do with programming: How did companies like Compaq, Dell, Gateway, Micron Technologies, and the other major personal computer manufacturers get so big, so fast? Most people would probably say they made good computers and sold them at rock-bottom prices in an era when computer demand was skyrocketing. But dig a little deeper—how were they able to this? How could they manufacture so many models so fast and respond to the changes that were happening so quickly?

Well, a big part of the answer is that these companies farmed out a lot of the work. They bought components from reputable vendors and then assembled them. They almost never invested time and money in designing and building power supplies, disk drives, motherboards, and other components. In a nutshell, what the personal computer manufacturers were doing was buying "prepackaged functionality." When they bought a power supply, they were buying something with certain properties (size, shape, and so on) and a certain functionality (smooth power output, amount of power available, and so on). Compaq showed the power of this approach; when they moved from engineering all of the parts in their machines to buying many of the parts, they dramatically improved their bottom line. Their stock has gone up more than 10 times since they made the changeover.

Object-Oriented Programming (OOP) springs from the same idea. Your program is made up of objects, with certain properties of the objects and certain operations that the objects can perform. The current state of an object may change over time, but you always depend on the objects in your program to not interact with each other in undocumented ways. Whether you build an object or buy it might depend on your budget or on the time you have available. But, basically, as long as the objects satisfy your specifications as to what they can do and how they respond to outside stimuli, you don't much care how the functionality is implemented. In OOP-speak, you say you only care about what the objects *expose*. So, just as PC manufacturers don't care about the internals of a power supply as long as it does what they want, the users of your control won't care how the control is implemented as long as it does what they want it to.

The key to being most productive in OOP is to make each object responsible for carrying out a small set of related tasks. (To do this successfully also means that the object has to be responsible for maintaining information about its internal data.) If an object needs to do something that isn't its responsibility, it needs to have access to an object that can do that task. The first object then asks the second object to carry out the task using a more generalized version of the function and procedures that you are familiar with from procedural programming. (In Visual Basic you have seen a lot of these generalized function calls at work already—they are nothing more than the methods or properties of a control.) In OOP jargon, what people say is that client objects are supposed to send *messages* to server objects.

Note

The standard joke to check whether you really understand OOP's way of thinking is the following: Question: How many OOP programmers does it take to change a light bulb? Answer: none, a properly OOP-designed light socket would accept a ChangeBulb message.

Caution

How the term messages is used in OOP is only distantly related to the way the term "messages" is used in Windows programming. For example, the "message" used for API functions such as SendMessage that communicate between the windows in your programs is not an OOP-like message. (See Chapter 12 for more on API calls and Windows messages.)

In particular, an object should never directly manipulate the internal data of another object. All communication between objects should be done only via messages. By designing your objects to handle a specific set of messages and then leaving it to the "black box" to manipulate their internal data, in order to respond to the messages you maximize reusability and minimize debugging time. *In VB5, this means that you should only manipulate the objects you create by changing properties or calling methods.* No public (global) variables should be inside the VB5 objects you create.

Next, just as with modules in VB, you will not want an individual object to do too much. Both design and debugging are simplified when you build small objects that perform a few tasks, rather than overly complicated objects with complex internal data that need hundreds of properties and methods to manipulate them.

The Vocabulary of OOP

The most important OOP term is *class*. A class is usually described as the template or blueprint from which the object will be made. Each object is said to be an *instance* of the class. For example, suppose you were designing a program for doing personal management in a company. You would certainly have a class called Employee. Each instance of the Employee class would correspond to a specific employee.

Note

Since a class is a template for objects, many people like to think about classes as cookie cutters. Objects are the actual cookies. The dough, in the form of memory, will need to be allocated as well. Visual Basic 5 is pretty good about hiding this "dough preparation" step from you. As you will soon see, you simply use the New keyword to obtain memory. (At some point, the analogy breaks down: You usually have to reclaim the memory you used to reuse it—you'll see how to do this later as well.)

Encapsulation

Encapsulation is the key concept in working with objects in all versions of OOP—including the one in VB5. Formally, encapsulation is nothing more than combining data and behavior in one package and hiding how the data is implemented from the user of the object. Encapsulation insists that data inside objects only be manipulated by messages. (Remember in VB this means by setting properties and calling methods.) The data in an object is stored in its *instance fields*. (Other terms you will see for the gadgets that store the data are *member variables* and *instance variables*. All three terms are used interchangeably, which you choose is a matter of taste; we will usually use instance fields.)

For example, let's return to the design of an object-oriented program for doing personal management in your company. You would certainly have a class called Employee. Each instance of the Employee class would correspond to a new employee. The instance fields in an Employee class might be things like:

- Name
- Date hired
- Current salary

and (as in this case) the current values of these instance fields for a specific object define the object's current state.

The functionality built into in an object is a fancy way of saying what it can do. This corresponds to its methods in VB. For example, you might have a RaiseSalary method in an Employee class that takes a certain percentage as a parameter. Notice that the RaiseSalary method would obviously manipulate the Current Salary instance field but that it is possible that a single method like RaiseSalary might work with more than one instance field. The RaiseSalary method might look at a person's sales as well as their current salary!

Caution

At the risk of repeating ourselves once too often, we cannot stress enough that the key to making encapsulation work is to make sure that the other parts of your programs can never access the instance variables (fields) in a class. Programs should interact with this data only through the object's properties and methods. Encapsulation requires this. Keeping data private is the only way to give an object its "black box" behavior (or data hiding, as it is sometimes called). Data hiding is critical to successful reuse and reliability.

Inheritance

For an example of inheritance at work, let's return to an object-oriented approach to designing a program for dealing with payroll and similar issues in your business. When you have an OOP language that allows inheritance, you would start with an Employee class and specialize this to get a Manager class, an Executive class, and so on. Classes like Manager would inherit from an Employee class. (They certainly share many properties such as having a hire date, a salary, and so on.)

OOP terminology says that a class that builds on another class *extends* it. The general concept of extending a base (or *parent*) class is called *inheritance*. The inheritance relationship denotes specialization. In traditional OOP, if a class A extends class B, class A inherits methods from (hence, extends) class B, but has more capabilities. In traditional inheritance little if any code needs to be written in the child class to gain access to the power of the parent class. What this means is that the extended class starts out with all the properties of its parent. You then pick and choose which methods of the parent class to override by changing their behavior.

For example, (alas) if employees get a 4 percent raise, managers might automatically get a 6 percent raise. In addition to overriding existing methods and properties of the parent class to give them new functionality, you can even introduce new methods in your child classes that have no counterpart in the methods contained in the parent. For example, a Manager class might have a Secretary property.

Visual Basic 5 does not support inheritance in the classic OOP sense. (Actually, it is not just VB5; any language that uses VBA 5.0 will not support classic style OOP inheritance.) However, when you create a control from an existing control, the process gives the *appearance* of using inheritance. One would think that the specialized text box you saw in Chapter 1 inherits from an ordinary TextBox. But, under the hood in VB5, there is no parent-child relationship between the two. Instead, as you saw in Chapter 1, the user control form for the modified text box *contains* an ordinary textbox. Containment (sometimes called *aggregation*) is one of the main tools that VB uses to get the benefits of inheritance.

Note

The reason that the designers of the VBA language that underlies VB5 did not want to include the more usual OOP version of inheritance is that there is always a tension between inheritance and encapsulation. If Object B inherits properties and methods of Object A and you change Object A, you may inadvertently break B's functionality. (This is sometimes called the problem of the fragile base class.)

Visual Basic 5 gets around the fragile base class problem by using a concept called an *interface* to replace true inheritance. As you will see in the section on "Polymorphism" that follows and in the next chapter, interfaces give you most, if not all, of the functionality you want out of inheritance without risking the problem of fragile base classes. Of course, nothing is free. As you will see in the next few chapters, using interfaces (often combined with containment) for inheritance requires much more coding than is needed when you use classic OOP style inheritance. Luckily, for control creation, VB5 comes with a Control Interface Wizard (see Chapter 13) that does much of the routine coding that VB5's interfaces require for doing interface style inheritance. It is also easy enough to write a VB Add-in (see Chapter 15) to automate the process of coding interface style inheritance for more general situations.

Note

Sometimes using inheritance is called subclassing. *Purists, therefore, do not like it when people use the word subclassing for the process of creating a new control out of an existing one in VB5 or using interfaces to simulate inheritance because VB5 doesn't support inheritance. We aren't purists.*

Polymorphism

Traditionally, polymorphism (from the Greek "many faces") means that inherited objects know what methods they should use depending on where they are in the inheritance chain. For example, when a motorcycle and a car (both inheriting from an abstract "Vehicle" class) get a "right turn" method they would use different methods to accomplish this task. As another example, the Employee parent class and, therefore, the Manager class both have a method for changing the salary of their instances. But things being the way they are, the RaiseSalary method probably works differently for Manager objects than Employee objects. The way polymorphism would work in this classic situation where a Manager class inherited from an Employee class is that an Employee object would know if it was a plain old employee or really a manager. When it got the word to use the RaiseSalary method,

- If it were a manager, it would call the RaiseSalary method in the Manager class rather than the one in the Employee class.
- Otherwise, it would use the usual RaiseSalary method.

The point is that the object knows which method to use based on the message it got. This means you don't need to know what class an object ultimately belongs to when you send it a message.

Note

People often use polymorphism to describe what happens when you use the Move method on a control. After all the Move method behaves differently for different controls. This type of behavior is not considered true polymorphism by OOP theory. (It is called name overloading or ad-hoc polymorphism.) OOP theory restricts the use of the term polymorphism for behaviors that must be resolved dynamically at run time. When you say Text1.Move or Command1.Move this is done statically at compile time since the compiler knows exactly where to go to find the code for the Move method of the TextBox or Command Button.

How Visual Basic Deals with Polymorphism: A First Look at Interfaces

Of course, Visual Basic does not have inheritance so polymorphism works a little differently in VB than in the classic version just described. However, the last sentence of the previous section remains the key:

You don't need to know what class an object belongs to when you send it a message. All you need to know is the name of the message and its parameters.

(The name and parameters of a method is usually called its *signature*.)

What VB5 does is to use its notion of *interface* to implement this key part of polymorphism. An interface is nothing more than a contract between the class and the user of the class that says: "I have a method with this signature; if you call me and pass me the name and the parameters indicated in the methods signature, I will use my version of the method and you won't have to worry."

One advantage to interfaces is that they make talking to the instances of your classes possible in the most efficient manner. If you call a method to change a property of a control or class, Visual Basic can find out at compile time (*early bind* is the technical term) what code to call in your control or class. This works at compile time roughly as follows:

1. Visual Basic looks to see if your object says it supports the method in one of its interfaces. (*Implements* is the term for supporting an interface.)

2. If your object does expose this method in one of its interfaces, then at compile time, Visual Basic looks in the code for the object and generates code that says "Go to this method."

Now, compare this to what happens if you don't give your objects an interface that makes a contract that you will support a method.

1. Since your code hasn't promised it will support the method, at compile time Visual Basic is smart enough to not go looking for what may or may not be there yet.

2. So, at compile time, Visual Basic generates a lot more code. This code politely asks the object if it supports the method with the signature you specified and would it mind running the method if it does?

This kind of code has two features that make it slower to execute:

1. It needs error trapping in case you were wrong, and

2. In any case, since VB can't know at compile time where to "jump" to the location of the method inside the object, it has to rely on a more indirect method for the object to send it the location information at run time.

(By the way, this whole process is called *late binding* and is significantly slower than early binding. We will give you some examples of how much slower it is a little later on in this chapter.) On the other hand, late binding allows true polymorphic behavior since it must be done dynamically at run time.

Another advantage of the interface approach to inheritance is that objects that support interfaces can make multiple contracts—support multiple interfaces—without the complexity of managing multiple inheritance chains (one of the real pains in C++!).

Finally, only when you build a reusable class do you need to do a lot of coding for the interfaces yourself. When you use VB5 to build an ActiveX server (Chapter 14) or an ActiveX control (Chapter 13), the interfaces needed for the users of your control are created for you automatically. Visual Basic 5 hides the required ActiveX interface code (and there would be a lot of it!) so you probably don't have to worry about the interfaces that make a control or ActiveX server. You will also need to worry about the interface code when you use interfaces to do inheritance.

Note:

For more on interfaces and polymorphism, please see the next chapter.

How to Objectify Your Programs

In the traditional "structured" procedure-oriented programming, you identify what needs to be done and then you either

1.   Break the task to be accomplished into subtasks, and these into smaller subtasks, until the subtasks are simple enough to be implemented directly (this is the *top-down approach*).

or

2.   Write procedures to solve simple tasks and combine them into more sophisticated procedures, until you have the functionality you want (this is the *bottom-up approach*).

Most programmers, of course, use a mixture of the top-down and bottom-up strategies to solve a programming problem. The usual way for discovering procedures turns out to be pretty much the same as the rule for finding methods in OOP: Look for verbs, or actions, in the problem description. There are two important differences between OOP and procedure-oriented programming.

1.   In OOP, you first isolate the classes in the project. Only then do you look for the methods and properties of the class.

2.   Each method or property is associated with the class that is responsible for carrying out the operation, and methods do not exist independently of a class.

So, the obvious question is: How do you find the classes?

Tip

A good rule of thumb is that classes are the nouns in your analysis of the problem. The methods in your objects correspond to verbs that the noun does. The properties are the adjectives that describe the noun.

You saw this with the object-oriented approach to a personal management program. Employees are one of the obvious nouns, things like RaiseSalary are the methods. Of course, the "noun-verb-adjective" correspondence to classes, methods, and properties is only a first step. Only experience can help you decide which nouns, verbs, and adjectives are the important ones when building classes and controls in VB5.

As another example, suppose you want to design a program to manage your checking account using an object-oriented approach. Some nouns are:

- Accounts
- Checks
- Check registers
- Deposit Slips

These nouns may lead to the classes Account, Check, CheckRegister, DepositSlip, and so on. Next, look for verbs. Accounts need to be *opened* or *closed*. Checks need to be *added* to the register. The check register needs to be *reconciled*. Deposit slips need to be *totaled*. With each verb, such as "add," "reconcile," and "total," you have to identify the one object that has the major responsibility for carrying it out. For example, the deposit slip has the major responsibility for totaling itself up. Thus, Total should be a method of the DepositSlip class.

Finally, one rule is the same as with modular programming, just as modules should be simple, classes should be too. Object-oriented programming is much easier when the classes you build are themselves not overly complex. A single class that is both simple in its internal structure and has limited relationships to other classes is much easier to grasp by the programmer or to put together in a team approach to OOP.

Summarizing Class Relationships

In traditional OOP, there are three standard relationships between classes:

- use
- containment ("has–a"—sometimes called aggregation)
- inheritance ("is–a")

The *use* relationship is the most obvious and also the most general. For example, the CheckRegister class uses the Account class, since a check register needs to know what account it is working with. But the DepositSlip class does not use the Check class, since deposit slips have nothing to do with checks. Often a class uses another class if it manipulates objects of that class. More generally however, a class A uses a class B if:

- a method or property of A sends a message to an object of class B,

or

- a method or property of A creates, receives, or returns objects of class B.

Tip

Try to minimize the number of classes that use each other. The point is, if a class A is unaware of the existence of a class B, it doesn't care about any changes to B. (And this means that changes to B do not introduce bugs into A!)

The *containment* relationship is easy to understand; Containment simply means that instances of class A contain objects of class B. For example, a CheckRegister object could contain Check and DepositSlip objects. Of course, containment is a special case of use; if an A object contains a B object, then at least one method of the class A will make use of that object of class B type.

Finally, the third relationship, inheritance, was described above. Since it isn't really used in VB5 in the classic form, we won't say anything more about it except to repeat that Visual Basic often uses containment ("has a") along with its interface approach to get the benefits inheritance. (See the next chapter.)

Tip

What you should do in an object-oriented approach to Visual Basic is to think of a fourth relationship between classes to add to the classic three; we usually call it "supports a." The idea of "supporting a" corresponds to Visual Basic's notion of an interface.

These relationships between classes are so important in OOP that a whole industry has sprung up to explain how to make diagrams that make class relationships clearer. One common (high tech) trick for finding (and documenting) the classes in your program is to start with a stack of index cards. You brainstorm on individual index cards the various possible classes, use one card for each class. Make sure the index card lists the name of the class together with its responsibilities and the other classes it uses. You can use the back of the card for the instance fields. (Hence the name *CRC cards* for them. CRC stands for *class, responsibility, and collaboration*.)

The other possibility is to use a diagram approach. Figure 7-1 shows a diagram for an order-taking system using the Booch-Rumbaugh unified notation. Here's what this diagram means:

- The RushOrder class is a subclass of the Order class (indicated by the line with the usual arrow).
- The Order class is sending a "charge" message to the Account Class (indicated by the ▶).
- The Item class is contained in the Order class (indicated by the ◇).

Note

Visual Basic Enterprise Owners can get a free copy of "Visual Modeler" which is a joint production of Microsoft and Rational Software (the home of Booch and Rumbaugh) by going to Microsoft's Web site. Visual Modeler has tools for producing class diagrams that use the unified notation. You'll have to register your copy of VB Enterprise before you will be allowed access to the page (http://www.microsoft.com/vstudio/owner).

While we won't use class diagrams or index (CRC) cards to model class relationships in this book, you should definitely use either (or both) of these aids if it makes it easier for you to think about the relationship between your classes! (And if you have the Enterprise edition of VB, check out Visual Modeler for use in more complex projects as well.)

What About Individual Objects?

Suppose you have decided on the classes in your project and will soon be working with objects that are specific instances of each class. The key to working with a specific object in OOP is to identify the "three whats" of an object. The three key questions to ask yourself are:

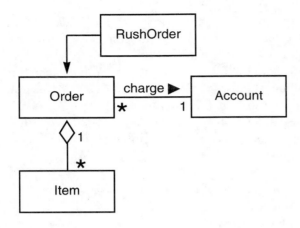

Procedural Programming

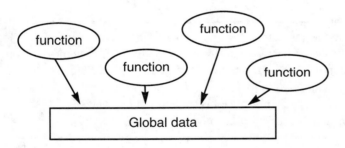

Figure 7-1 A class diagram

1. What is the object's state?
2. What is the object's identity?
3. What is the object's behavior?

Each object stores information about what it currently looks like and often how it got that way. This is what is usually called the object's *state*. An object's state isn't fixed, but any change in the state of an object must be because of messages that were sent to the object. Note also that the current state of an object does not completely describe it. Each object also has a distinct *identity*. This means that despite two objects appearing to be in the same state and looking, feeling, and reacting the same, they are still *different* objects. In VB5, the identity of an object is usually visible through the object's Name property unless it is part of a control array (see later in the chapter). For example, each text box on a form is different. Although they may look and work the same, they may even have the same event procedures with identical code in them. Finally, all objects that are instances of the same class share a family resemblance by potentially behaving the same. This means that all objects that are instances of the same class will (potentially) respond to the same messages.

These three characteristics can obviously influence each other. For example, the state of an object will certainly influence its behavior. (If a note in an object-oriented e-mail system was "unread," it may send out a caution message before allowing itself to be discarded. Conversely, if a note was read, you should be able to discard it more easily and so the response to a "discard" message would be different.) Note that depending on the state of an object, the response to a specific message may be so different as to make you think that the object is not responding to that message! For example, if you disable a text box, it will respond very differently than another textbox that is still enabled. (However, the key point is that its *potential* responses remain the same.)

Advantages To OOP

On the surface, the OOP approach that leads to classes and their associated methods and properties is much like the structured approach that leads to modules. Properly designed classes not only provide a convenient clustering mechanism for methods, properties, and data, they do it in a more natural way. The reason is that each cluster (class) will correspond to a natural division point in the problem analysis.

This leads to another advantage to class modules that you won't see in the kinds of programs we can show you in a book; example programs in books like this are typically small. And, for small programs, the breakdown into procedures used in structured programming works very well. Experience has shown, however, that there are lots of problems when you try to scale up techniques that work with smaller programs to much larger program—those that require many months or even man-years of programming time.

The clustering mechanism inherent in the class approach makes OOP ideal for projects that involve teams of programmers. The encapsulation that is built into OOP classes helps you as well. Other team members don't have to worry about data contamination since classes hide their data representations from all code except their own properties and methods.

Finally, any VB programmer knows (and uses to his or her advantage) probably the most significant advantage to OOP. (Although you may never have thought of VB in these terms.)

- Classes are factories for making objects whose state can diverge over time.

Sounds too abstract, sound like it has nothing to do with VB programming? Well this is exactly what the toolbox is! Each control on the toolbox is a factory for making objects that are instances of a specific class. Suppose the toolbox wasn't based on a bunch of little class factories waiting to churn out new text boxes and command buttons in response to your requests. Can you imagine how little fun VB would be if you needed a separate code module for each text box? The same code module can't be linked into your code twice and it therefore would require fairly convoluted coding to have a way for a module to make two identical text boxes whose states can diverge over time.

Because of the existence of the toolbox, VB has always been object-based but you had to use the objects that other people built for you. VB5 is the first version of VB that lets you build the class (factories) that can churn out all the kinds of objects (such as specialized controls) that you want.

The Object Browser

In Chapter 2, you saw how to use the Object Browser (shortcut is F2) to look at the built-in constants in Visual Basic. The Object Browser can do far more. It:

1. Makes it easier to navigate among the procedures and functions you added to your project.
2. Lets you see information about constants, enumerations, functions and sub programs at a glance

Even more importantly, the Object Browser:

- Gives you complete access to the classes and other objects that you can use in your VB5 projects (including the ones you build).

More precisely, objects that are usable in Visual Basic are usually collected into *type libraries*. These type libraries contain descriptions of the constants, events, properties, and methods of the class. A type library can be as sophisticated as the one in Excel or as simple as the one underlying a user-defined

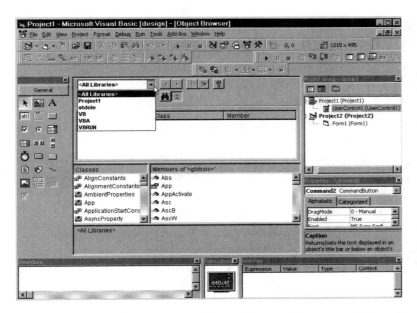

Figure 7-2 The Object Browser with initial libraries showing, including the current project

class or control. The Object Browser uses the information from the type library for its display.

Tip

If you are using the MDI interface for VB5, you can move back to the Object Browser by using Ctrl+Tab. If you want to hide it simply right click and choose hide from the context menu.

For example, as shown in Figure 7-2, every control project starts out with the ability to browse itself (listed as Project1 in Figure 7-2) along with the VB (Visual Basic) type library, the VBA (Visual Basic for Applications) type library, the VBRUN type library (the Visual Basic Virtual machine), the stdole (the OLE library that handles communications between controls and their containers), or all of them at once. There are also type libraries for Excel, Access—most anything you might imagine.

Figure 7-3 shows the Tools|References dialog box on a typical machine. As you can see, there are dozens of type libraries available to VB5. All you have to do is check off the box for the library you want to browse and then you will

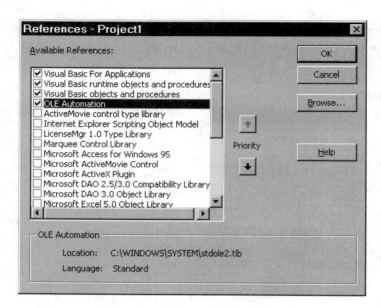

Figure 7-3 The References dialog box

be able to select it from the Libraries drop-down list box at the top of the Object Browser.

In general, you use the Libraries/Projects drop-down list box to choose from the available object libraries, including the ones referenced in the current Visual Basic project. Once you choose a library, the left-hand Classes pane gives you access to all the classes in the library and the right-hand pane gives you access to all the *members* of the class highlighted in the left-hand pane. (Members is a fancy name for the constants, events, properties, and methods of the class.) Properties have little letter icons, methods have green icons whose identity escapes us, events have a yellow lightning bolt icon, and constants have gray boxes to their left. The bottom pane gives you the signature of the member if it is a method. It also gives you a more or less useful description of the member.

Tip

If you are browsing the code that you created, simply double-click on any bold-faced item in the Members pane and you will immediately be taken to where the code for that member is located in the Code window. (Boldface is how the Object Browser indicates that there exists code for that member.)

The context menu for the Object Browser has one especially useful item. If you choose Group Members from the context menu, all of the members of each type will be grouped together instead of intermixed.

Navigating in the Object Browser

First off, like many list boxes in Windows, typing a letter highlights the first object whose name begins with that letter in the pane that has the focus. The Object Browser also has a search facility. Simply type anything in the text box below the library box on the left and press ENTER and the Browser will display a list of every item whose name contains those characters.

Next, the descriptions in the bottom pane of the Object Browser often have hyperlinks. These are underlined in green. Simply click on one to go to that item.

Adding Your Own Descriptions for Class Members

The object browser will also use the information you add when it displays information about the objects, methods, properties constants and enumerations of the current project. For all your code (including the classes you build and your user controls), it would be courteous if you added the kind of descriptions to your members that you have seen the Object Browser display for the built-in type libraries. For this you can either:

1. Click on the member you want to document.
2. Choose Tools|Procedure attributes.

or

1. Open the Object Browser and choose the current project.
2. Highlight the name of the object whose members you want to document.
3. Right-click on the member of the class you want to document and select Properties.

For example, for a function named Cut on your main form you will see a dialog box like the one shown in Figure 7-4. Enter a description of the function in the middle text box. As you can see, this box has a text box for a description of the Property. The description shows up in the bottom pane of the Object Browser and also in the bottom of the Properties window if you were documenting a property. The Name Drop-Down List Box gives you

Procedure Attributes   ☒

Name: │Cut   ▼│   ┌─────────┐
                                              │   OK   │
Description: └─────────┘
┌────────────────────────────────┐ ▲   ┌─────────┐
│   │   │ Cancel │
│   │ ▼   └─────────┘
└────────────────────────────────┘   ┌─────────┐
                                              │ Apply │
Project Help File: Help Context ID: └─────────┘
┌────────────────────┐   ┌──────────────┐   ┌─────────┐
│   │   │ 0   │   │Advanced >>│
└────────────────────┘   └──────────────┘   └─────────┘

Figure 7-4 Procedure Attributes dialog box

quick access to the attributes of all the properties, methods, and events currently defined. You fill in the Help Context ID for associating context-sensitive help to the member (most commonly for a property). Finally, while you can only see the value for the Project Help File, you cannot set it here. You set it in the General tab in the Project|Properties dialog box.

If you click on the Advanced button shown in Figure 7-4, the Procedure Attribute dialog box "grows" to look like Figure 7-5. We want to go over the less obvious features in the full version of this dialog box one by one.

Tip

If you aren't used to an Apply button like the one in Figure 7-5, this simply applies what you have set but doesn't close the dialog box—unlike the OK button, which applies what you have done and closes the dialog box. It is a good idea in your own dialog boxes to add an Apply button with similar functionality for any possible repetitive action. For example, it used to drive one of the authors mad when early versions of Word could only insert one symbol per use of the Insert Symbol dialog box.

Procedure ID

Many applications that use ActiveX Control have some knowledge of the standard events and properties a control or object can expose. This combo box lets you choose one of these standards. In most cases these settings are

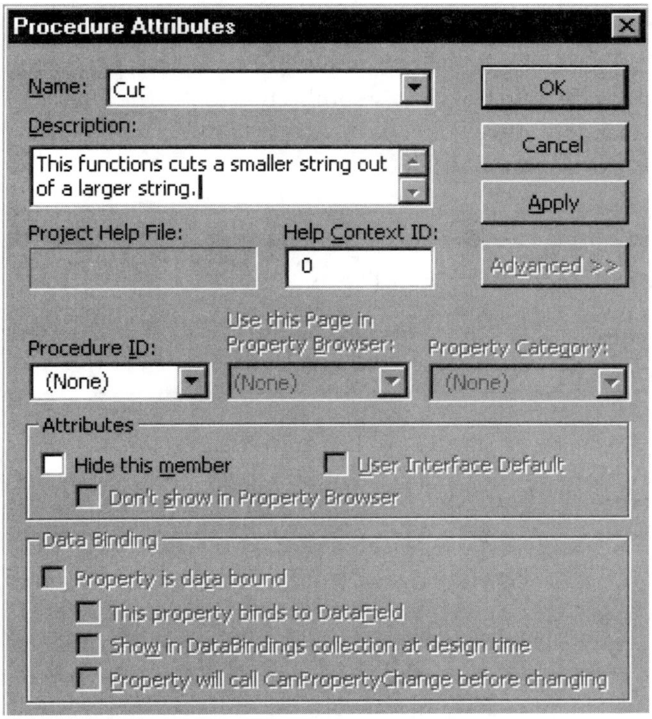

Figure 7-5 The Full Procedures Attributes dialog box

advisory, not proscriptive. For example, calling something a BackColor property in this combo box doesn't make it behave the way a BackColor property should. You still need to write the code to do this. This box simply tells the user of your procedure, function, or property to expect some standard behavior from your member.

Note that for a property in a control that you build, choosing the Default option in this combo box makes that property the default property for your control. This makes it act like the Text property of a textbox or the Caption of a label control. (Although, as we mentioned before, we rarely use default properties and so, most often, do not provide them for our classes and controls.)

Use this Page in Property Browser

This is important when using Property Pages (see Chapter 13). Setting this option adds an ellipsis button to the property in the Properties window. VB will load the custom property page when the user clicks on the ellipsis.

Property Category

As you have seen, the Properties Window has the ability to display properties either alphabetically or by categories. Use this combo box to set the category. You can use one of the supplied ones, such as Behavior, or add your own by typing in the name in this combo box.

Attributes

These check boxes allow you to set things like whether the property is a design-time or run-time property. The three check boxes are described in the following table.

Table 7-1: Property Attribute Check Boxes	
Hide This Member	This gives you a property that is not visible to the outside world, although it can still be accessed with code. If you check this box, Visual Basic will not show the property in the Properties window ever and will only show it in the Object Browser if you choose Show Hidden Members from the Object Browser's context menu. Think of this option as telling the user of your control that this is a secret property and they should use it at their own risk.
Don't Show in Property Browser	This simply determines if VB shows the property in the Properties window. The property will still always show up in the Object Browser and you can continue to write code to work with it
User Interface Default	This determines which property is highlighted in the Properties window when the user presses F4 with focus in your user control. It also sets the event that VB displays in the Code window when you double-click the control. Obviously, there can be only one default property and one default event.

Tip

You can make a property of a control settable or readable only at run time, but this requires code. See the section on the Ambient object in Chapter 13.

Data Binding

These check boxes (grayed in Figure 7-5) are used with the VB data control. (Being data bound is not enough to make a control able to read and write data from a database, you also need a data control to orchestrate the connection between the data bound control and the database.)

Manipulating Objects Built into Visual Basic

The key to working with objects in Visual Basic are variables of the special *object* type. For example, when you use the Me keyword to refer to the current object, you are using an object variable. You saw object variables in the last chapter when we dimensioned something "As Printer" or in the generic resize code when we dimensioned something "As Control." As you might guess based on their use in the last chapter, you declare an object variable with the same Dim, Private, Public, Static keywords that you've already seen. Thus, you can have local, form level, or public (global) object variables. Microsoft suggests using an appropriate 3-letter prefix for object variables. Here are some examples:

```
Dim frmHelpForm As Form
Dim txtTextInfoBox As TextBox
Public cmdOKButton As CommandButton
Dim fntCourier As Font
```

Generally, the name to use for an object variable of a given control type is the name you see in the top of the Properties window. For user controls, it is the value of the Name property you give the control at design time (which is yet another reason not to leave it at the default value of UserControl1).

There are a few general types of object variables for use in situations where you need to refer to objects of many different types. For example, there is the

```
Dim ctlAnyControl As Control
```

Control type that gives you a way to refer to any control that you saw in the generic resize code. Similarly,

```
Dim objVeryGeneral As Object
```

Finally, objects can also be stored in a variable declared to be of Variant data type.

```
Dim anyThing As Variant
```

Set

When you want to make an object variable refer to a specific object of that type in your VB5 code, use the Set keyword (just as we did in the last chapter when we changed the default printer using Set). For example, if your project had a command button named Command1, your code would look like this:

```
If Command1.Enabled Then Set cmdAButton = Command1
```

In particular, you cannot use an assignment statement to make an object variable equal to, say, a text box. Code like this:

```
Dim txtNoGood As TextBox
txtNoGood = Text1
```

will simply give you an error message.

Tip

The Set command can also be used to simplify lengthy control references.

Here's an example:

```
Set fntInner = frmHelp.picInfo.Font
```

Now you can write

```
fntInner.Size = 18
```

instead of

```
frmHelp.picInfo.Font.Size = 18
```

Caution

It is important to note that the Set command does not make a copy of the object, as an ordinary assignment statement would. Instead, the Set command points the object variable to the other object. This can lead to subtle bugs. The problem is that if you change a property of an object variable that is Set to another object, the property of the original object changes as well. For example, if you use:

```
Set frmMain.Font = txtLastName.Font
```

then executing

```
txtLastName.Font.Size = 18
```

will also change the font size of frmMain because they both point to (share) the same font object. (See the section in the next chapter on "Cloning" for more on how to make a copy of an object.)

Speeding Up Programs with Control References

Always use the most specific object variable you can find when using Set. Your programs will run faster as a result.

For example, code with this statement

```
Dim txtFoo As TextBox
Set txtFoo = Text1
```

will always run faster than

```
Dim ctlFoo As Control
Set ctlFoo = Text1
```

which, in turn, will always run faster than

```
Dim objFoo As Object
Set objFoo = Text1
```

In particular, when you use variant variables to hold objects instead of object variables, this slows your program down the most (and probably makes it harder to debug). The reason was touched upon earlier: It has to do with late binding versus early binding. If you say that an object is a text box, then VB knows where to find its text property at the time the code is compiled. If you say that a text box is only an object, VB has to use late binding to find out where the Text method is located in the compiled code. If you run a simple program that assigns a string to the Text property of a text box using:

```
Dim Foo As Object
```

or

```
Dim Foo As TextBox
```

you will find that the second choice (early binding) is about 10 percent faster. If you had chosen to use:

```
Dim Foo As Variant
```

then the early binding (Dim Foo as TextBox) it is about 11 percent faster

The Is Keyword

You can use the Is keyword in an If-Then to test if two object variables refer to (have been Set to) the same object. Suppose FirstControl and SecondControl are two control object variables. A line of code like

```
If FirstControl Is SecondControl Then
```

lets you test whether these object variables refer to the same object. (It is a wise programmer who always checks if changing the properties of one object variable will also, perhaps inadvertently, change the properties of another object!)

To check that an object variable has not yet been Set to anything, use the reserved word Nothing. Just as 0 is the value of an uninitialized numeric variable, Nothing is the value of an uninitialized (i.e. not yet Set) object variable. For example:

```
If objThing Is Nothing Then . . .
```

By the way, don't try to use:

```
If objThing = Null Then . . .
```

it won't even compile. Null and Nothing are different. Null is a special kind of variant, Nothing simply means that the object variable is not yet set to point to any location in memory.

Manipulating Objects via Code

It is quite common to need a general procedure that manipulates properties of forms or controls or even the forms and controls themselves. First, properties of forms and controls can only be passed by value. For example, consider the following simple Sub procedure:

```
Sub ChangeText (ByVal X As String, Y As String)
   Y = X
End Sub
```

If you call it using the following code:

```
Call ChangeText(Form1.Caption, Y$)
```

then the current value of Y$ is the new caption for Form1.

Tip

If you set the Tag property of the form or control to contain information otherwise not available at run time, you can write a general procedure using this technique to analyze the Tag property. This lets you find out information about the control that would otherwise not be available at run time.

On the other hand, you will often want to affect the properties of a form or control by using a general procedure. For this, you have to pass the form or control as a parameter by reference. To do this, declare the argument to the procedure to be of one of the object types. (You could use variants, too, of course, but, as mentioned earlier, this should be avoided unless absolutely necessary because it is slower and creates harder-to-debug code.)

If you often find yourself writing code to center a form on the screen, why not use the following general procedure?

```
Public Sub CenterForm(AForm As Form)
   AForm.Move (Screen.Width - AForm.Width)/2, _
(Screen.Height - AForm.Height)/2
End Sub
```

Then, whenever you are in a procedure attached to a specific form, you can simply say

```
CenterForm Me
```

to center the form on the screen. (You could also think about making CenterForm a custom property of a form—see later in the chapter for more on this.)

Similarly, you can have a Sub or Function procedure that affects a property of a control. A first approximation to a general procedure to change the caption on a control might look like this:

```
Sub ChangeCaption (X As Control, Y As String)
   X.Caption = Y
End Sub
```

Notice that this procedure used the general Control type. However, suppose you tried to use this procedure in the form of

```
Call ChangeCaption(Text1, "New text")
```

where Text1 was the name of a text box. Then Visual Basic would give you a run-time error because text boxes do not have a Caption property.

There are two ways around this. The simplest, as far as code goes, is to use the On Error Resume Next statement, as in the following:

```
Sub ChangeCaption (X As Control, Y As String)
   On Error Resume Next
   X.Caption = Y
End Sub
```

However, this kind of code requires being sure that no other error is being inadvertently handled. (In a one-line procedure, this is a good bet—in a more complicated procedure, you might have to be more careful.)

A more robust way to proceed is to use a version of the "If-Then" that lets you check the type of an object. There are two ways to do this, the first is to use a version of the If-Then that uses the *TypeOf* keyword as in the following example:

```
Sub ChangeCaptionOrText (X As Control, Y As String)
   If TypeOf X Is TextBox Then
     X.Text = Y
   Else
     X.Caption = Y
   End If
End Sub
```

The general framework looks like:

```
If TypeOf Control Is ControlType Then
   .
.Else
   . .
End If
```

where the ControlType parameter is the same as that used in declaring an object variable (Form, Label, TextBox, and so on).

Next, you will often find yourself using an empty If clause for clarity. For example, if you wanted to play it safer:

```
Sub ChangeCaption (X As Control, Y As String)
   If TypeOf X Is TextBox Then
     '   Do Nothing
   Else
     X.Caption = Y
   End If
End Sub
```

although you can use:

```
If not (TypeOf X Is TextBox) Then
```

Since there is also no version of the Select Case for controls, you may need the If-Then-ElseIf version of this control structure:

```
If TypeOf X Is...Then
   . .
ElseIf TypeOf X Is...Then
   .
ElseIf TypeOf X Is...Then
   .
Else
   .. .
End If
```

Using TypeName

Visual Basic 5 allows you to use the TypeName function to determine the type of an object as well as the type of a variable. For example:

```
Private Sub Command1_Click()
   Dim Foo As CommandButton
   Set Foo = Command1
   Print TypeName(Foo)
End Sub
```

prints the string CommandButton. Just be careful you have done the Set first before the test. If you used the following:

```
Private Sub Command1_Click()
   Dim Foo As CommandButton
   Print TypeName(Foo)
End Sub
```

you'll see the string Nothing and not the string CommandButton. In general the TypeName function returns the string equivalent of what you use in the If TypeOf structure.

Next, keep in mind that since the TypeName function

- takes a variant,
- variants can hold any Visual Basic type including an object,
- and returns an ordinary string,

the TypeName function is both powerful and flexible. Strings, after all, can be used in every VB control structure. For example:

```
ObjectType = TypeName(Foo)
Select Case ObjectType
   Case "TextBox"
      'do what you want to Foo assuming it's a text box
   Case "CommandButton"
      'do what you want assuming it's a Command button
'and so on
```

Of course, we had to be careful, for example, to check for the string "TextBox" and not the string "textbox." (Although, a judicious use of, for example, the UCase function, would eliminate even this problem.)

The following table summarizes what TypeName returns for generic VB types.

Table 7-2: What TypeName returns for generic VB types

Variant Variable Holds	String returned
Byte value	Byte
Integer	Integer
Long integer	Long
Single-precision floating-point number	Single
Double-precision floating-point number	Double
Currency value	Currency
Decimal value	Decimal
Date value	Date
String	String
Boolean value	Boolean
An error value	Error
Uninitialized	Empty
No valid data	Null
An object	Object
An object whose type is unknown	Unknown
Object variable that doesn't refer to an object	Nothing

If you stored an array in a variant, then TypeName returns the type followed by the empty and close parenthesis such as Double().

Creating New Objects at Run Time

You can create objects four ways in Visual Basic. One is by using a built-in class that comes with Visual Basic. For example, Visual Basic comes with a very useful *collection class* for dealing with groups of objects. A collection is, in many ways, a better array than arrays themselves. You'll see a lot more about collection later in this chapter. Each time you make a new collection as an instance of the collection class, you will be creating a new object. Next, as you have already seen in Chapter 1, you can create a new user control, add that to the toolbox, and use it as a class just like Visual Basic's built-in control classes. Each time you click on the user control tool, you get a new instance of your control. Next, Forms are classes in VB so you can use an existing form as a template for new copies of the form. You can also add custom properties and events to an existing form. Then, you can use that more specialized form as a class (template) for new form instances (objects!). Each new instance of the specialized form class will have the new properties and events that you added to the prototype.

Finally, you can use a special type of module called a Class module. Class modules become the factory for making new instances of that class. Class modules can't be seen but if you think of them as nonvisual controls at first, then you won't go too far wrong. Class modules have the advantage that, if you are using the Professional or Enterprise edition of Visual Basic, they can be compiled separately and used by other Windows applications as a convenient library of code because other applications will be able to make instances of your classes-even applications that don't support ActiveX controls. (See Chapter 14 for more on this.)

In general, a Class module object contains the code for the custom properties, methods and events that objects created from it will have. Each Class module you create gives you, naturally enough, a single class (template) for building new instances of that class. You can then create new instances of the class in any code module or form in your project. You can even build new instances of one class inside another so you can use containment. You can have as many Class modules in a project as you like (subject only to operating system constraints, of course), and Class modules can be added both to user control projects and Standard EXE projects, although you will often find yourself compiling them into separate ActiveX DLLs (see Chapter 14).

For example, we got tired of adding the necessary timer code to some of our samples so that we could give you timings. We decided, therefore, to make a reusable class out of the timing code, as you'll soon see. Next, Visual Basic has no convenient way to deal with the individual bits of a value except by writing the masking functions as needed. It makes sense to encapsulate the functionality for bit-twiddling into a class module. (See this example later in this chapter for how to do this.) Finally, we want to show you a smart array class that is halfway between a collection and a usual array for situations where collections are too slow and arrays too much of a pain!

Collections

We first want to turn to one of the neatest and most useful Visual Basic objects you can create at run time—a *Collection* object. A Collection object is an object whose parts can be referred to individually as needed, and you still can refer to the object as a whole when necessary. It looks and works like a very smart version of an ordinary array.

Note

Collections are examples of what are sometimes called dictionaries *or* associative arrays *in other languages.*

Here's a hint of what a collection can do:

- You'll never have to use a construct like Redim Preserve with a collection. The collection automatically resizes itself to accept more elements.

- Even better, a collection automatically shrinks itself when you remove an element. No more manually "compactifying" an array by finding the "empty entries" and copying higher numbered entries into the holes.

- They can be keyed for quick lookup.

Of course, collections aren't perfect. While small collections are essentially cost-free, large collections have definite costs. If you need to deal with many thousands of items, arrays are often a better choice. The reason is that in this situation using a collection instead of an array will take up a lot more memory and may also slow your program down considerably. As with all programming gadgets, the choice to use a collection should come because you need to use collections' special (and nifty) properties like automatic compactification and keyed access. It shouldn't be made to save you a few lines of code if the cost of slowing your program down five-fold.

Built-In Collections

You have already seen two of Visual Basic's built in collections: The Controls collection holds all the controls on a specific form; the Printers collection holds all the printers that Windows knows about. Visual Basic also has built-in collections that give you information about all the forms loaded in a Forms collection that holds all the loaded forms. The Count property of a collection tells you how many items are in the collection. For example, Forms.Count is the number of forms you have loaded.

You can access individual forms or controls by saying, for example,

Forms(0), Forms(1), and so on. Unfortunately, although the count starts at 0, Forms(0) is not necessarily the start-up form. The order of the Forms, Controls, or Printers collection is unpredictable. Since the index for a built-in collection starts at 0, to get all the loaded forms we could use:

```
For I = 0 Forms.Count-1
   'do something with Forms(I)
Next I
```

The For-Each Loop

Although you can always use a For-Next loop to iterate through a collection like the Forms collection, there is a better way to do so. As you saw in the last chapter, Visual Basic uses a loop structure called the For-Each to iterate through a collection. The framework for the For-Each structure takes the following form:

```
For Each Element In TheCollection
Next
```

The Element counter must be dimensioned to be of a compatible type. For example, you could say:

```
Dim Foo As Control
For Each Foo In Controls
```

or

```
Dim Foo As Object1
For Each Foo In Controls
```

but you couldn't say:

```
Dim Foo As Printer1
For Each Foo In Controls
```

Here's an example that prints the captions of all the loaded forms in a project in the Immediate window.

```
Dim frmForm As Form
For Each frmForm In Forms
   Debug.Print frmForm.Caption
Next
```

Notice how we didn't even have to worry whether the collection starts at 0 or 1 when you use For-Each.

Tip

The For-Each structure not only makes your code clearer when you need to iterate through all the elements in a collection, it is faster than using a loop that begins, for example: `For I = 0 To Forms.Count   -1.`

Building Your Own Collections

You will often want to build your own collections. The items in a collection (usually called its *members* or *elements*) can be of any type, and you can mix types in a collection if you need to. (See the next chapter for how to build a collection that will accept only entries of a specific type.)

Since a collection is an object, you must create it as an instance of a built-in class in Visual Basic. The class you need is called, naturally enough, the Collection class. For example,

```
Dim MyCollection As New Collection
```

creates a new collection as an instance of the Collection class. As you might expect if you use the TypeName function on an object that holds a collection, the string returned is simply: "Collection."

Just as with the Forms, Controls, or Printers collection, the Count property of each collection you create tells you the number of items in a collection. *However, collections you create are one-based; the first element in a user created collection has index 1 and not index 0 like the built-in collections.* (Collections you create start out with no elements, so the Count is 0.)

Each element in a collection can be referred to by its index, just as you saw in the built-in collections. This means that the following gives you one way of dealing with all the elements in a collection

```
For I = 1 To NameOfCollection.Count
   work with NameOfCollection(I)
Next I
```

but

```
For Each Foo In NameOfCollection
   work with Foo
Next
```

is preferable since it runs faster and also you don't have to worry about the difference between zero- and one-based collections.

Caution

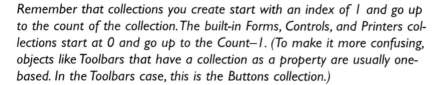

Remember that collections you create start with an index of 1 and go up to the count of the collection. The built-in Forms, Controls, and Printers collections start at 0 and go up to the Count–1. (To make it more confusing, objects like Toolbars that have a collection as a property are usually one-based. In the Toolbars case, this is the Buttons collection.)

The Add Method

Once you create the collection by using the New keyword, use the Add method to add items to it. For example,

```
Dim VBVersions As New Collection
Dim Foo As String
Foo = ("Visual Basic 3.0")
VBVersions.Add Foo
Foo = ("Visual Basic 4.0")
VBVersions.Add Foo
Foo = ("Visual Basic 5.0")
VBVersions.Add Foo
```

In general, the Add method has the following syntax (it supports named arguments, by the way):

```
CollectionObject.Add item [, key as string] _
[, before As Long] [, after As Long]
```

In particular, you can (and probably should) use something like the following modified version of the above example:

```
Dim VBVersions As New Collection
Dim Foo As String
Foo = ("Visual Basic 3.0")
VBVersions.Add Foo, Old
Foo = ("Visual Basic 4.0")
VBVersions.Add Foo, Last year's model
Foo = ("Visual Basic 5.0")
VBVersions.Add Foo, "The Present"
```

and now you can simply say,

```
Print "The best way to create ActiveX controls is " & _
VBVersion ("The Present")
```

Here's another example of using Add that also uses the With keyword to simplify the object references.

```
Dim Presidents As New Collection
Dim Foo As String
With Presidents
  Foo = "George Washington"
  .Add Foo, "Didn't lie"
  Foo = "Thomas Jefferson"
  .Add item := Foo, key:= "Smartest?"
End With
```

Now you can access Thomas Jefferson by

```
Presidents.Item("Smartest?")
```

or

```
Presidents("Smartest?")
```

Caution

The match to the string in the key must be perfect, although case doesn't seem to matter. For example, using:

```
Presidents.Item("smart")'
```

and

```
Presidents("didn't")
```

won't work.

Finally, here's an example of combining the built-in Controls collection with a user-defined collection to store information about all the text boxes on a form. We will also use the Name property of the control as the key.

```
Dim AllTextBoxes As New Collection
Dim Foo As Control
For Each Foo in Controls
  If TypeOf Foo = TextBox Then
    AllTextBoxes.Add Foo, Foo.Name
  End If
Next
```

Now you can access the TextBoxes by their name. (Although, as it turns out, this little program has a subtle bug. If you used a control array of text boxes, the key would not be unique since all control array elements have the same name. This leads to a run-time error.) To fix it just add an OnErrorResumeNext statement.

Here are short descriptions of the Add method parts.

Collection Object

This is any Collection object or object variable that refers to a user defined collection. You cannot use the Add method on the Forms, Controls, or Printers collections.

item

This is required. Since the information will be held in a variant variable, it can be an expression of any type. (As mentioned previously, you can mix types in a collection.)

key

The key parameter is optional. It must be a string expression, and within the collection it must be unique up to case or you'll get a run-time error. You can't change the key except by removing the previous value, a smarter collection object would have a rekey property.

before, after

These optional parameters are usually numeric expressions that evaluate to a (long) integer. The new member is placed right before (right after) the member identified by the before (after) argument. If you use a string expression, then it must correspond to one of the keys that was used to add elements to the collection. You can specify before or after positions, but not both. Generally speaking, you will not want to use indices to add to a collection as you are better off keying an entry. (This is because the numerical index you set for an entry can change over time without you being aware of the change. Also, as you will see in the timing test below using indices is a *very* slow method to access collection entries.)

The Item Method

The Item method is the default method for a collection; it is how you refer to (or return) a specific element of a collection. Its syntax is:

```
CollectionObject.Item(index)
```

but since it is the default method for a collection, you can just say:

```
CollectionObject(index)
```

(We confess: This is one of the few cases where we use the default method for an object so that we can code with the shorter form.)

The index parameter specifies the position of a member of the collection. It is a long integer (you can have lots of elements in a collection) and goes to the number of items in the collection. For example,

```
MyCollection.Item(1)
MyCollection(1)
```

are both the first item in the collection.

However, as we mentioned before, we rarely use the Item method with a numeric index. After all, the index may change over time as you add and remove elements form a collection. A better way is to use a *key* to access the elements in a collection. This key is a string that you set up at the time you add the element to the collection (see the next section). Using a key rather than an index is much more useful; you can easily associate a useful mnemonic to the item for the key and then you always know what you are getting back. The syntax for accessing a collection member using a key is simply:

```
MyCollection.Item(StringKeyGoesHere)
MyCollection(StringKeyGoesHere)
```

Caution

If you must use an integer as a key, be sure to use the CStr function; otherwise, VB is sure to get confused between the index and the key.

The Remove Method

When you need to remove items from a collection, use the Remove method. It, too, supports named arguments, and its syntax is

```
CollectionObject.Remove index
```

where, as you might expect, the index parameter is used to specify the element you want removed. If the index is a numeric expression, then it must be a number between 1 and the collection's Count property. If it's a string expression, it must exactly match a key to an element in the collection. As with the Add method, you cannot use the Remove method to remove objects from the Printers, Forms, or Controls collections.

Timings

We said that using For-Each is faster than a For-Next loop. We did some timings and the results surprised even us. First off, adding elements to a collection is roughly twice as long as adding them to an array. (For 20,000 items we got .28 versus .55 seconds.)

Next, we tried iterating through a large collection (with 20,000 items) by using the For-Next and then the For-Each loop. We also built an array with the same 20,000 items and also used the For-Next and For-Each constructs. Here's what we found:

Situation	Time it took
Collection iterating with For-Each	.11
Collection iterating with For-Next	35.26 (!)
Array iterating with For-Each	.06
Array iterating with For-Next	.11

The moral of the story is:

- Never use For-Next for a collection and never use For-Each for an array.

(And, since VB has the UBound and LBound functions, it's hard to imagine where you would need to use For-Each for an array.)

The Nothing Keyword and Reclaiming Memory

Once you create a new object like a collection, you have used up some memory and resources. When you are done with the object, you must release the memory that was used by the object. This is done by setting the object variable to the keyword Nothing that you saw earlier to test if an object variable had not yet been set to anything. For example,

```
Dim colSample As New Collection
'code to work with the collection
'would then be used but eventually you need to say:
Set colSample = Nothing
```

In particular, there is no Clear method for a collection class. If you need to clear out everything in a collection.

- Set it to Nothing.
- Then make a new one.

You can reuse the name after you release its memory in the Set command:

```
Dim colSample As New Collection
'code to work with the collection
'would then be used but eventually you need to say:
Set colSample = Nothing
' now you can say again
Set colSample = New Collection
```

(Notice that we didn't use Dim again on the colSample variable—that wouldn't be allowed by VB.)

Caution

Since object variables merely point to the object, it is possible for several object variables to refer to the same object. When several object variables refer to the same object, then you must set all of them to Nothing in order to release the memory and system resources associated with the object.

Memory may be released automatically, for example, after the last object variable referring to the object goes out of scope. However, relying on this is sloppy and not guaranteed to work. If you create an object instance as the value of a local object variable inside a procedure, set it to Nothing before the Sub is exited; don't rely on Visual Basic to clean up after you! (See the next chapter for more on how to make sure (or alas, debug) code releases all its object references.)

Tip

A good place to clean up object references that you made in a form is by setting them to nothing is in the QueryUnload event of the form or the Terminate event of the control or class (see below for more on this event).

The Form as a Class

The first case we want to show you of creating a new object at run time is when you want to use the form you designed as a template to create new instances of itself. The form may or may not contain controls on it. Once you create these new instances of your original form, they exist independently.

Changing any property of a new instance of your original form has no effect on the original form.

For example, a word processing program might want to be able to create identical windows for use by different documents. More generally, when one has an MDI (multiple document interface application), your "child" windows will often need to be cut from the same cookie cutter (although, over time, their contents will almost surely diverge).

Assume you have a form named Form1 in your project already. Then the statements

```
Dim frmAnotherInstance As Form1
Set frmAnotherInstance = New Form1
```

create a new instance of Form1. You can also combine the two statements into one:

```
Dim frmAnotherInstance As New Form1
```

but most people find the two-statement version clearer and easier to understand.

This new instance starts out with the same properties as the original Form1 at the time the code is executed. In particular, it will have copies of all the controls that were on Form1 in exactly the same places. However, a new form instance isn't yet visible. To make it visible, you have to use the Show method. Then, you have to move it away from its parent form using the Move method or changing a property like Left or Top. For example,

```
Dim frmAForm As New Form1
Dim frmBForm As New Form1
frmFirstForm.Show
frmSecondForm.Show
frmFirstForm.Move Left - 199, Top + 100
frmSecondForm.Move Left - 399, Top + 200
```

shows two copies of the original Form1. The locations are determined by the value of the Left and Top properties of the original Form1. (We needed to use the Move method to prevent the child forms from stacking one on another because instances inherit *all* the properties of their parent—including their initial location properties.)

Note

You do not use the New keyword to create new controls. Only forms in VB5 are classes (templates for new objects). (To see the method for creating new controls at run time in VB5, see the section on "Control Arrays" that follows.)

One final point: creating a new instance of a Form at run time via a call to New is completely different than adding another form to a project at design time and then using Load or Show to bring the second form into memory. Every form you add at design time is a new cookie cutter. When you use the New keyword to create a new one, you are stamping out the form cookies. In this case, the new form is an instance of what you made it look like at design time. When you create another instance of a form using New, you have *cloned* an object at run time.

Adding Properties and Events to Forms

You use the same ideas for adding properties to all three ways of creating classes in VB5, although the terminology is confusing at first. However, if you think about it the right way, the terminology actually makes sense. Let's start off with the obvious question: What are the most basic things you will want to be able to do with a new property?

- Get its current value.
- Assign a new value to it.

For the first situation, you use a special type of procedure called a Property Get procedure. For the second, you use a Property Let procedure (or a Property Set procedure, if the value is itself an object).

Tip

One good way to remember the distinction between Property Gets and Property Lets is that a Let statement will let you make an assignment in Visual Basic, so it is natural to use it for assigning to properties.

For example, suppose you want to add a custom property to a form that will tell you whether a form name is centered. Also, you want setting this property to be True to automatically center the form. Here's what you need to do. Set up a Private variable in the declarations section of the form to enforce encapsulation.

```
Private CheckCentered As Boolean
```

Then add the following property procedures to the form:

```
Public Property Let CenterForm(X As Boolean)
   CheckCentered = X 'get the current state of the
                        'property
   If X then
     Me.Move (Screen.Width - Me.Width)/2, _
     Screen.Height - Me.Height)/2
   End If
End Property
```

The first line of code uses the Private variable to store the current value of the property. Now you can use a line of code such as

```
Me.CenterForm = True
```

to center the form (or any instance of it). From another form or code module, you can use a line of code like

```
CustomForm.CenterForm = True
```

to center the form named CustomForm.

Of course, it might be useful to know if a form is centered. For this, we need to use a Property Get procedure that returns a Boolean:

```
Public Property Get CenterForm() As Boolean
   CenterForm = CheckCentered
End Property
```

The one line of code in this procedure uses the current value of the CheckCentered (Private) Boolean variable that we are using to hold the information about the current value of the property and assigns it as the value of the Property Get procedure. (Property Get procedures are similar to Function procedures in that you assign a value to them inside the body of the property procedure.)

Note

You may be wondering: Why all this bother? Why not query or assign the variable CheckCentered directly? The point is that you are trying to give objects as much "black box" behavior as you can. You would not want another object in your project to query the CheckCentered instance variable directly. Since, in our example, this variable was declared Private, you couldn't. Making the CheckCentered variable Public to allow someone to query the instance variable directly to check if a form is centered defeats encapsulation. At the risk of sounding overly repetitive: Never use Public variables for property access!

General Property Procedures

Property Let and Property Get procedures work in tandem, as do Property Set and Property Get. The value returned by the Property Get procedure is of the same type as the one used in the assignment for the Property Let or Set. In general, the number of arguments for a Property Get is also one less than that of the corresponding Property Let or Set. The difference between Let and Set is explained later. (The last argument is the one that will be changed.) A Property Get procedure that you write without a corresponding Property Let procedure gives you a read-only property, since you have no way to change it.

The full syntax for a Property Let procedure template looks like this:

```
[Public | Private][Friend] [Static] Property Let
     name [(arglist)]
     [statements]
     [name = expression]
     [Exit Property]  if need be
End Property
```

- Use Public to make the Property Let procedure accessible to every procedure in every module.

- Use Private to make the Property Let procedure accessible only to other procedures in the form, class module, or user control where it is declared.

- Use the new Friend keyword to make the property available to any part of the project. (See the next chapter for more on the Friend keyword.)

The other Visual Basic keywords work as they would in any procedure. Use the Static keyword if you need all the Property Let procedure's local variables preserved between uses. The Exit Property keywords give you a way to immediately exit from a Property Let procedure, and so on. The name of the Property Let procedure must follow standard procedure-naming conventions, except that the name will be the same as the corresponding Property Get or Property Set procedure in the same module.

The full syntax for a Property Get procedure template looks like this:

```
[Public | Private][Friend][Static] Property Get name _
[(arglist)][As type]
     [statements]
     [name = expression]
```

```
    [Exit Property]   if need be
End Property
```

> **Note**
>
> *The name and type of each argument in a Property Get procedure must be the same as the corresponding arguments in the corresponding Property Let procedure, if it exists. The type of the value returned by a Property Get procedure must be the same data type as the last argument in the corresponding Property Let procedure, if it exists.*

The last type of Property procedure is the Property Set statement. Its syntax is:

```
[Public | Private][Friend] [Static] Property Set name _
[(arglist)]
     [statements]
     [Exit Property]    'if need be
     [statements]
End Property
```

This is used when the value you are setting is an object itself. For example, if you wanted to add a custom Font property, you would need a Property Set because Font is itself a Visual Basic object.

Adding Events to a Form Instance

Just as you can add custom properties to forms, you can add custom events to a form class and then create a new instance of the form that will expose that event. For example, suppose we want to have a new instance of a form with the added functionality that whenever someone presses any key with the focus in the form, we raise an event. To see this at work, we are going to create three forms.

The original form is automatically added to a Standard EXE. We will add a line of code to this form that says that instances of our form can raise an event. However, it turns out, if you run the application with this form as the start-up form, the first form can't actually raise the event. This seems so weird, at first, that it deserves a bit of explanation. The reason is that the first form instance was created before you added the code for raising the event. The first instance of the form was, after all, created in the design environment before you added any code. For this reason, we will use another form as the start-up form.

What it turns out we need is a new instance of the first form. This new instance will be created using code that tells the new form instance that it should notify anyone who asks about its custom event. All we need is to create (remember, *instantiate* is the buzzword) a slightly modified version of the original form, which has an "event-raising" capability.

Finally, we need a start-up form to manage the creation of the form from Step 2. This "manager" form will:

1. Create the second instance of the original form—the one that has the ability to send out events to objects that care to listen for them. (Having the ability to listen to events requires code as well!)

2. Have an event handler that is triggered when the form from Step 2 sends out its custom event to all who ask.

Note

This kind of curious behavior where you have to distinguish the instance of an object at design time from additional instances of it created at run time will be important when you go deeper into the control creation process.

Let's go through the needed steps one by one.

1. Start up a Standard EXE.
2. For the First form, change its caption to read "No Keys."
3. Set this form's KeyPreview property to True.
4. Add the following code to the Declarations section of the No Keys form:

```
Public Event NoKeyPresses(Key$)
```

This line tells VB that instances of the form will have the potential to raise an event that accepts a single string parameter. Now, make the KeyPress event for the No Keys form read.

```
Private Sub Form_KeyPress(KeyAscii As Integer)
   RaiseEvent NoKeyPresses(Chr(KeyAscii))
End Sub
```

This line says that instances of the form will have the ability to raise the NoKeyPresses event when someone presses a key inside of it. The string equivalent of that key will be sent out along with the event notification.

Now, we want to create the form that will manage everything, so:

5. Choose Project|Add Form.

6. Change the name of the new form to ManagerForm.

7. Add the following Declaration to the General section of this Form:

```
Public WithEvents Foo As Form1
```

This is the key line. It tells VB that the second form will be referring to an instance of the first form that can send out events. Now make the Form_Load of the ManagerForm read as follows:

```
Private Sub Form_Load()
   Set Foo = New Form1 'create an instance of Foo
   Foo.Caption = "Please don't press any keys inside  of
me."
   Foo.Show
End Sub
```

The first line in this code actually creates the instance of Form1 named Foo. However, because we declared Foo using the WithEvents keyword in the ManagerForm, this new instance has the needed event signaling ability. The remaining lines of code justify position Foo so it isn't hidden by its parent.

Finally, you may have noticed that once you added the line

```
Public WithEvents Foo As Form1
```

the IDE automatically added a Foo object to the Object list box in the Code window for the Manager form. The Foo object has a NoKeyPresses event. We can now write the code in the Foo_NoKeyPresses event:

```
Private Sub Foo_NoKeyPresses(Key$)
   MsgBox "You pressed an " & Key$ & _
          ". No keypresses allowed in this form!"
End Sub
```

8. Now set the Start-up Object in Project|Properties to ManagerForm.

That's it. If you run the application and click in the Foo form (the one with the clever caption) to give it focus, then press a key, VB will pop up the message box, thus proving that the Foo form is sending out an event.

Creating a New Class Module

You create a new Class module at design time by choosing Project|Add Class Module. This gives you a screen like Figure 7-6: Choose the Class Module item in Figure 7-6 to get started. (The Class Builder option in Figure 7-6 leads to a Wizard that is occasionally very useful. We will cover the Class Builder later in this section.)

Once you have a Class module, you use the New keyword to create new instances of it in code elsewhere in your project. for example, if MyClass is the name of a Class module in your project,

```
Dim FirstInstance As New MyClass
```

would create a new instance of it. Note that, unlike, modules each instance of a class module has its own data. There is no way to have static data in a class module. As with adding custom properties of a form:

Figure 7-6   The Add Class screen

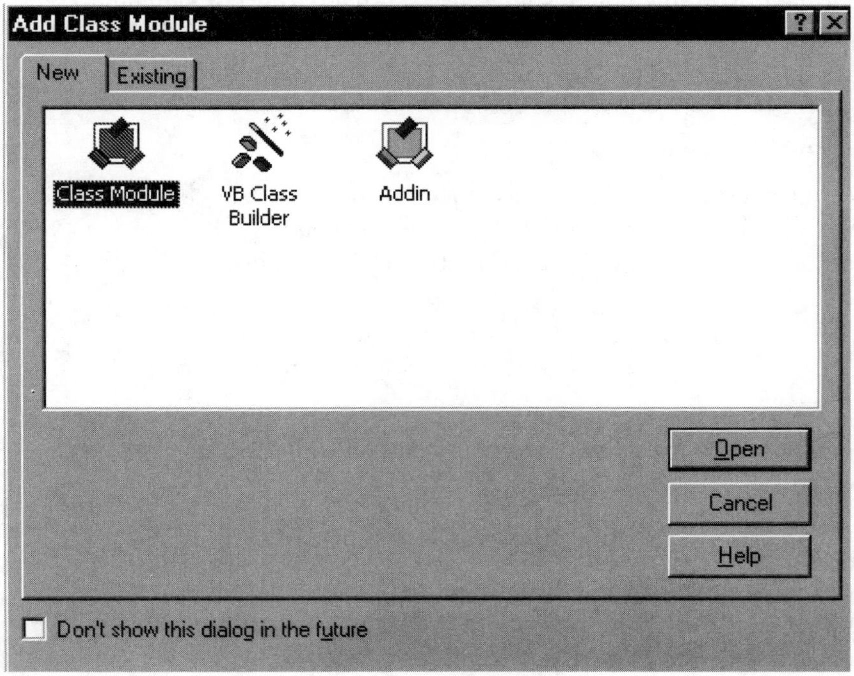

- Use Property procedures to define the properties of your class.
- Use Public Sub and Function procedures for its methods.

You can also raise events in a Class module, we will give you an example of this shortly. (This is actually somewhat unusual; most of the time though if you are going to raise events in a control, you might as well go all the way and make a control out of the class module.)

Each Class module can respond to only two events: Initialize and Terminate. As their names suggest, these events are triggered when someone creates an instance of your class or terminates it. Use the Initialize event to give the instance fields in your classes their initial data. In particular the Initialize method is called when you make a new instance of a class and the Terminate method is called when you set the instance to Nothing.

Note

While the Initialize event lets you give initial data to your instance vari-ables, it can't take parameters. This means that, compared to constructors in languages like Java or C++, the Initialize event in VB is crippled. If you need to send parameters to a class module in order to set its initial state, the custom is to add a Create *method to the class module with whatever parameters are necessary. Then call the* Create *method explicitly immedi-ately after the call to New that creates the class.*

The Terminate event for a Class module is triggered when all references to the class are Set to Nothing or when the object falls out of scope. This means that objects declared in procedures as the values of local variables would be automatically garbage collected—but, it is not good to rely on this. We feel strongly that *you should set any objects (that includes collections) that you may have created inside the class to Nothing in the Terminate event for that class as well.*

Caution

The Terminate event is not triggered if the application stops because of the End statement. This means that necessary cleanup may not take place if you use End statements promiscuously. In particular, don't ever use an End statement until you are sure that all the memory for objects you create has been released.

Properties of Class Modules

There are only two: Name and Instancing. The Name property is standard: It's what you use in the Dim statement:

```
Dim Foo As MyClass
```

then MyClass had better be the value of the Name property of the class.

As with naming any VB objects, people have strong opinions about the conventions you should use for the name of your classes. Some people get terribly out of joint if you don't prefix class names with a capitol C: CTimingClass, CEmployee, etc. (We don't.) The value of the Name property is also the return value of the TypeName function when you use it on an object that has been set to an instance of your class.

The second property is called *Instancing* and you may be wondering where it is—it probably isn't showing up in your Properties Window. (Well at least it won't if you confined yourself to building a Standard EXE.) This property only applies when you create other types of VB Projects such as ActiveX Controls (see Chapter 13) or ActiveX DLL's (see Chapter 14) or ActiveX EXE servers (see Chapter 14). The next chapter has more on the Instancing property and so all we want to say here is that this property controls who can make objects from your classes. Since a Standard EXE isn't used by any other program, Instancing is set to be Private automatically.

Class Modules and User-Defined Types

You can think of a class module as a user-defined type with properties and methods added, but, in fact, user-defined types and class modules have only an uneasy coexistence. One reason is that user-defined types can only be Private or Friend inside a Class module. This usually won't cause problems since you shouldn't have any Public data in a Class module anyway. However, in keeping with a more object-oriented approach to VB, we suggest replacing most uses of a user-defined type inside a class to hold the Private data by other VB objects such as classes or collections. There are two reasons for this, other than aesthetics:

1. The user-defined type can't be the value of a public property anyway.

2. Using a Visual Basic object (and, therefore, a Property Set) gives you more freedom. This is because the class or collection that holds the property data will now have a much richer structure.

Class Modules and Error Handling

Suppose someone tries to set a property to an illegal value. You need to send the appropriate error information back to the calling code. (See Chapter 6 for more on error handling.) The terminology used for this is that you need to *raise* an error and you do this with the Raise method of the Error object.

For a simple example of using the Raise method, here's some code from the SmartArray class you will see shortly. This code checks to see that you have not tried to access an array element that does not exist using a private instance variable called mItemsInArray.

```
Property Get ItemsAt(I As Integer) As Variant
   If I < 1 Or I > mItemsInArray Then
      Err.Raise 1 + vbObjectError, "SmartArray", _
      "Tried to access an  non-existent element"
   Else
      ItemsAt = mHiddenArray(I)
   End If
End Property
```

Here's the general syntax for the Raise method:

```
Error.Raise number, source, description, helpfile, help-
context
```

and Table 7-3 explains what the parameters mean.

Table 7-3:	Raise method parameters
Argument	*Description*
number	This required long integer between 0 and 65,535 identifies the error. You can create your own numbers or use one of Visual Basic's built-in error numbers. If you create your own error number you should add the number to the vbObjectError constant.
source	This optional parameter is a string expression that you can use to describe the object. The convention is to use the value of the TypeName function on the class. Be sure to specify the source otherwise VB defaults to using the ID of the current Visual Basic project.
description	This optional parameter is a string expression that should describe the error.

helpfile	This optional parameter should be the fully qualified path to the Microsoft Windows Help file in which help on this error can be found. (If you leave this out, Visual Basic uses the fully qualified drive, path, and file name of the Visual Basic Help file.)
helpcontext	This optional parameter gives the context ID for the help topic. (If you leave it out, VB uses the context ID for the error corresponding to the Number property used, if it exists.)

Examples of Class Modules

In the next few sections we want to give you three examples of class modules. We will show you:

- A timer class that is useful for benchmarking.
- A bit/byte class for working with individual bits.
- A smart array class that is useful when you need some of the power of collections but not all of them.

A Timing Class

When you are writing a book you need to do a lot of timings. We got tired of adding the code by hand and decided to make a reusable class out of it. This class is simple, it needs:

- A StartMe method.
- An EndMe method.
- A read-only property DisplayTimeElapsed that returns a string with the time elapsed.
- A read-only property TimeElapsed that returns a single with the time elapsed.

We use two instance fields to store the data:

```
Private mTimeStarted As Single
Private mTimeEnded As Single
```

As a first attempt we simply used the Timer function that returns the number of seconds since midnight. For example, the code in StartMe method looks like this:

```
Public Sub StartMe()
   mTimeStarted = Timer
End Sub
```

and the one in the EndMe looks the same. Then we tried this code to figure out the TimeElapsed property:

```
Public Property Get TimeElapsed() As Single
   TimeElapsed = mTimeEnded - mTimeStarted
End Property
```

Unfortunately, this code has a subtle bug: If you use our timing class around Midnight, the Timer function will reset itself so that you will get a silly result (a negative time elapsed). The easiest way around this is to use a day that has 86,400 seconds, together with the Mod function:

```
Public Property Get TimeElapsed() As Single
   Dim Temp As Single
   Temp =  mTimeEnded - mTimeStarted
   If  Temp > 0 Then
     TimeElapsed = Temp
   Else
     TimeElapsed = Temp + 86400
   End If
End Property
```

(Notice that given the encapsulation inherent in a class module means nobody would even notice the bug fix, since this property is still returning a value of the same type.)

Here's the complete code for the Timing class:

```
Option Explicit

Private mTimeStarted As Single
Private mTimeEnded As Single

Public Sub StartMe()
   mTimeStarted = Timer
End Sub

Public Sub EndMe()
   mTimeEnded = Timer
End Sub
```

```
Public Property Get TimeElapsed() As Single
   Dim Temp As Single
   Temp = mTimeEnded - mTimeStarted
   If Temp >= 0 Then
      TimeElapsed = Temp
   Else
      TimeElapsed = Temp + 86400
   End If
End Property
Public Property Get DisplayTimeElapsed() As String
   DisplayTimeElapsed = Format$(TimeElapsed, "###.###")
End Property
```

Note

We admit that even with the bug fix we just made, our class will only successfully time events for up to 24 hours. Also, given the accuracy inherent in VB's Timer function, timings will only be accurate to about 1/18 of a second. See Chapter 12 for a way to modify this class to be both more accurate and to allow (although we can't imagine why) timings over a period of up to 46 days.

A Bit/Byte Class

We want to create a class that lets you manipulate the byte equivalent of a zillion bits (actually, we will allow the number of bits to be long). Then, we want to be able to work with any individual bits in the various bytes. For example, our class should have:

- A read-only property called getBit. This property tells us whether a specific bit is on.

- Write properties called turnBitOn and turnBitOff that can turn an individual bit on. (Notice that a property that merely switched the current state of a bit couldn't do this.)

So, the first question is, how to store the information in the class. For simplicity's sake, we will use an array of Booleans for the bytes. (This is not quite the most space efficient because VB does not implement the Boolean type in a single bit but rather in an integer.)

Anyway, to start building the BitClass Module, add a Class module to a Standard EXE. First you need the Private array to hold the bits:

```
Private BitArray() As Boolean
```

Next, you need the property that resizes the array correctly, depending on the size it is sent.

```
Public Property Let MakeBitSet(N As Long)
   ReDim BitArray(1 To N)
End Property
```

Now, we need the three Property procedures. They are pretty simple: getBit reads off the current value in the array and returns this as the value of the property; TurnOnBit makes a specific bit True; and TurnOffBit makes a specific bit False.

```
Public Property Get getBit(whichBit As Long) As _
Boolean
   getBit = BitArray(whichBit)
End Property

Public Property Let turnOffBit(N As Long)
   BitArray(N) = False
End Property

Public Property Let turnOnBit(N As Long)
   BitArray(N) = True
End Property
```

One of the reasons to implement a bit class is that it lets us program one of the standard benchmarks called the Sieve of Eratosthenes. This is a method discovered more than 2,000 years ago for listing all the *primes*. (A prime is a number like 7 that can only be divided by itself and 1.)

The idea behind the Sieve is that you make a list of all the integers:
2 3 4 5 6 7 8 9 10 11 12 13 14 15 16 17 18 19 20 21 22 23 24 25 26.

Now you cross out all the multiples of 2 (except 2, of course):
2 3 4 5 6 7 8 9 ~~10~~ 11 ~~12~~ 13 ~~14~~ 15 ~~16~~ 17 ~~18~~ 19 ~~20~~ 21 ~~22~~ 23 ~~24~~ 25 ~~26~~.

Now strike through all the remaining multiples of 3:
2 3 4 5 6 7 8 9 ~~10~~ 11 ~~12~~ 13 ~~14~~ ~~15~~ ~~16~~ 17 ~~18~~ 19 ~~20~~ ~~21~~ ~~22~~ 23 ~~24~~ 25 ~~26~~

and so on. You continue this process until you have gaps that can't be struck through by using the preceding numbers. (For example, 5 is a prime because you can't get to it by striking out multiples of 2 or 3.)

We will imitate this process by flipping a bit instead of striking through the number. To make the Sieve more of a benchmark, we also flip all the bits to

True first. The code works as follows. First, we have the routine that makes the bit class the right size and turns on all the bits. The key parts of this code look like this:

```
Dim testArray As New BitArray
testArray.BitSet = Size
For I = 1 To Size
  testArray.turnOnBit = I
Next I
```

Next, we have the code that imitates the crossing-out procedure described above. (We only have to go up to when I*I < =Size because every nonprime number has a factor smaller than its square root.)

```
I = 2
  Do While I * I <= Size
    If testArray.getBit(I) Then
      K = 2 * I
      Do While K <= Size
        testArray.turnOffBit(K)
        K = I + K
      Loop
    End If
    I = I + 1
  Loop
```

Finally, we count the number of bits that are still on.

```
For I = 2 To Size
    If testArray.getBit(I) Then Count = Count + 1
Next I
```

That's it, the Count variable holds the number of primes.

Note:

By the way, compiling this in VB5 native mode gives roughly five-fold improvement over VB4's P-code.

More precisely on the machine we tried it on (a P166 with 80 megs of RAM) we got:

VB4	35.92 seconds
VB5(compiled code)	6.92 seconds

The Full Code for a Sieve Example

The following form adds a Click procedure to a command button and a text box to enter the size to use for the bit array, but is otherwise quite straightforward.

Listing 7-1: Sieve Example

```
VERSION 5.00
Begin VB.Form frmSieve
    BorderStyle     =    4   'Fixed ToolWindow
    Caption         =    "Sieve Test"
    ClientHeight    =    2565
    ClientLeft      =    3795
    ClientTop       =    2685
    ClientWidth     =    4410
    LinkTopic       =    "Form1"
    MaxButton       =    0   'False
    MinButton       =    0   'False
    PaletteMode     =    1   'UseZOrder
    ScaleHeight     =    2565
    ScaleWidth      =    4410
    ShowInTaskbar   =    0   'False
    Begin VB.TextBox Text1
        Height      =    330
        Left        =    2925
        TabIndex    =    0
        Top         =    1305
        Width       =    1200
    End
    Begin VB.CommandButton Command1
        Caption     =    "Start Sieving"
        Default     =    -1  'True
        Height      =    492
        Left        =    1230
        TabIndex    =    1
        Top         =    1875
        Width       =    1740
    End
    Begin VB.Label Label1
        Alignment   =    2   'Center
        Caption     =    "Enter the ending number:"
        Height      =    330
        Left        =    135
```

```
        TabIndex          =    2
        Top               =    1335
        Width             =    2550
    End
End
Attribute VB_Name = "frmSieve"
Attribute VB_GlobalNameSpace = False
Attribute VB_Creatable = False
Attribute VB_PredeclaredId = True
Attribute VB_Exposed = False
Private Sub Command1_Click()
  Dim testArray As BitArray
  Dim Size As Long, Foo As Variant
  Dim I As Long, Count As Long, K As Long

  Foo = Text1.Text
  If Not IsNumeric(Foo) Or Val(Foo) < 0 Then
   MsgBox ("Enter a positive number please")
   Text1.Text = vbNullString
   Text1.SetFocus
   Exit Sub
  End If

  Screen.MousePointer = vbHourglass
  Size = Val(Text1.Text)
  'start the timer
  theTime = Timer

  'set the array size
  Set testArray = New BitArray
  testArray.MakeBitSet = Size



  'turn all bits on
  For I = 1 To Size
   testArray.turnOnBit = I
  Next I

  'set the values in the array
  I = 2
  Do While I * I <= Size
    If testArray.getBit(I) Then
     K = 2 * I
     Do While K <= Size
       testArray.turnOffBit = K
       K = I + K
     Loop
```

```
      End If
      I = I + 1
   Loop
'count the set bits
   For I = 2 To Size
      If testArray.getBit(I) Then Count = Count + 1
   Next I
   Screen.MousePointer = vbDefault

   'print out the results on the form
   Cls
   Print "There are " & Count & " primes up to " & Size & "."
   Print "Total time taken was " & Timer - theTime & " seconds."

   'destroy the class instance
   Set testArray = Nothing

End Sub
VERSION 1.0 CLASS
BEGIN
   MultiUse = -1  'True
END
Attribute VB_Name = "BitArray"
Attribute VB_GlobalNameSpace = False
Attribute VB_Creatable = False
Attribute VB_PredeclaredId = False
Attribute VB_Exposed = False
Private BitArray() As Boolean

Public Property Let MakeBitSet(N As Long)
   ReDim BitArray(1 To N)
End Property

Public Property Get getBit(whichBit As Long) As Boolean
   getBit = BitArray(whichBit)
End Property

Public Property Let turnOffBit(N As Long)
   BitArray(N) = False
End Property

Public Property Let turnOnBit(N As Long)
   BitArray(N) = True
End Property
```

A Smart Array Class

Collections are great but there are times when they simply introduce too much overhead. In this section we want to show you a "smart array" class that will automatically:

- expand itself when the user tries to add an entry if room in the array has run out, and
- compress itself when you remove an entry.

The version of the class we build here accepts variants, we will leave it to you to make the changes so the smart array accepts a more restricted range of types or even a single type. Also, so as not to complicate the code, we will assume that our array class always starts at index 1.

To build the class we start with the instance fields that are used internally:

```
Private mHiddenArray() As Variant
Private mItemsInArray As Integer
Private mCurrentSize As Integer
Private mIncrement As Integer
```

The mHddenArray holds the data. The mIncrement variable lets us add more than one slot a time. This is convenient since ReDim preserve is a relative time-consuming operation. The mItemsInArray and mCurrentSize variables are used to determine when we need to resize the array. Here's the Initialize event:

```
Private Sub Class_Initialize()
  mItemsInArray = 0
  mCurrentSize = 5
  mIncrement = 5
  ReDim mHiddenArray(1 To 5)
End Sub
```

Here's the code to resize the array when needed:

```
Property Let ItemAt(I As Integer, Foo As Variant)
  Dim NewSize As Integer
  NewSize = Int((1.1 * mCurrentSize) + mIncrement)
  If I < 1 Or I > NewSize Then
    Err.Raise vbObjectError + 2, "SmartArray", _
    "Tried to insert at an illegal index"
```

```
      Exit Property
   End If
   If mItemsInArray + 1 > mCurrentSize Then
      ReDim Preserve mHiddenArray(1 To NewSize)
      mCurrentSize = NewSize
   End If
   If VarType(Foo) = vbObject Then
      Set mHiddenArray(I) = Foo
   Else
      mHiddenArray(I) = Foo
   End If
   mItemsInArray = mItemsInArray + 1
End Property
```

Again to avoid constantly having to use ReDim Preserve we resize the array that is stored in the mHiddenArray instance field in chunks. We increase the size of the array by 10 percent + 5 units whenever the array needs to be resized. Notice in the code above how we raise an error if the user tries to insert an item at a nonexistent spot. Finally, notice the extra code to take into account the fact that we may be trying to place an Object in the array. (Remember objects require the Set statement rather than an assignment statement.)

Here's the Property Get that is the counterpart of the Property Let you just saw:

```
Property Get ItemAt(I As Integer) As Variant
   If I < 1 Or I > mItemsInArray Then
      Err.Raise 1 + vbObjectError, "SmartArray", _
      "Tried to access an  non-existent element"
   ElseIf VarType(mHiddenArray(I)) = VbObject Then
      Set ItemAt = mHiddenArray(I)
   Else
      ItemAt = mHiddenArray(I)
   End If
End Property
```

Next, we want our smart array to look and feel as close to an ordinary array as possible. For example, we would obviously like it if we could say:

```
SmartArray(I) = Foo
```

Instead of saying:

```
SmartArray.ItemAt(I) = Foo.
```

For this we need to make the ItemAt property the *default* property of the SmartArray class. To do this:

1. Open the Object Browser with F2.
2. View the members of the SmartArrayClass by choosing the Project from the libraries drop-down list box.

Right click on the itemAt property in the right-hand box of the browser.

3. Choose properties from the context menu. You should see the Properties Dialog box we discussed earlier. Click on the Advanced Button to go to the Advanced Properties Dialog Box.
4. Drop-down the Procedure ID button and choose Default.

That's it.

Note

Our smart array class works roughly twice as slowly as a usual array for most of its operations. This is because of the extra code that was needed to check whether to resize the array. [There is also a (small) extra overhead of a class module.]

Here's the full code for the SmartArray class.

Listing 7-2:   Full code for SmartArray class

```
VERSION 1.0 CLASS
BEGIN
  MultiUse = -1  'True
END
Attribute VB_Name = "SmartArray"
Attribute VB_GlobalNameSpace = False
Attribute VB_Creatable = True
Attribute VB_PredeclaredId = False
Attribute VB_Exposed = False
Attribute VB_Ext_KEY = "RVB_UniqueId" ,"3390DB7701A4"
'a smart array class that automatically expands
' and compresses itself

Option Explicit
```

```
'data for instance fields

Private mHiddenArray() As Variant
Private mItemsInArray As Integer
Private mCurrentSize As Integer
Private mIncrement As Integer

'checks if an item can safely be gotten
'before getting it

Property Let ItemAt(I As Integer, Foo As Variant)
  Dim NewSize As Integer
  NewSize = Int((1.1 * mCurrentSize) + mIncrement)
  If I < 1 Or I > NewSize Then
    Err.Raise vbObjectError + 2, "SmartArray", _
    "Tried to insert at an illegal index"

    Exit Property
  End If
  If mItemsInArray + 1 > mCurrentSize Then
    ReDim Preserve mHiddenArray(1 To NewSize)
    mCurrentSize = NewSize
  End If
  If VarType(Foo) = vbObject Then
    Set mHiddenArray(I) = Foo
  Else
    mHiddenArray(I) = Foo
  End If
  mItemsInArray = mItemsInArray + 1
End Property
Property Get ItemAt(I As Integer) As Variant
Attribute ItemAt.VB_UserMemId = 0
  If I < 1 Or I > mItemsInArray Then
    Err.Raise 1 + vbObjectError, "SmartArray", _
    "Tried to access an  non-existent element"
  ElseIf VarType(mHiddenArray(I)) = vbObject Then
    Set ItemAt = mHiddenArray(I)
  Else
    ItemAt = mHiddenArray(I)
  End If
End Property

Public Property Let IncrementSize(ByVal Size As Integer)
  If Size > 0 Then mIncrement = Size
```

```
End Property

Public Sub RemoveItemAt(I As Integer)
  If I < 1 Or I > mItemsInArray Then
    Err.Raise 3 + vbObjectError, "SmartArray", "Tried to
remove a non-existent element"
    Exit Sub
  Else
    Dim J As Integer
    For J = I + 1 To mItemsInArray
      mHiddenArray(J - 1) = mHiddenArray(J)
    Next J
    mItemsInArray = mItemsInArray - 1
  End If
End Sub

Private Sub Class_Initialize()
  mItemsInArray = 0
  mCurrentSize = 1
  mIncrement = 5
  ReDim mHiddenArray(1 To 5)
End Sub
```

Using the Class Builder Wizard

Now that you have seen what class modules look like under the hood, you are in a better position to take advantage of the Class Builder Add-In. Like most Wizards, how much the Class Builder helps you write the code you need varies from problem to problem. (It is particularly good in coding the kinds of specialized collections you will see in the next chapter.)

The Class Builder also uses an Explorer type interface to show the hierarchy of the classes in your project. It can also give you a list of all the members (properties, events, and methods) of an individual class. What we want to do in this section is lead you through a sample session with the Class Builder to create the classes you might need for a computer chess game. We will need classes for:

- the board location (cell);
- the chess pieces;
- the players; and
- two collections, one for the whole board and another for the pieces.

So start up a Standard Exe and from the Add-In menu, choose the Class Builder Utility. Figure 7-7 shows you the initial screen of the Class Builder looks like:

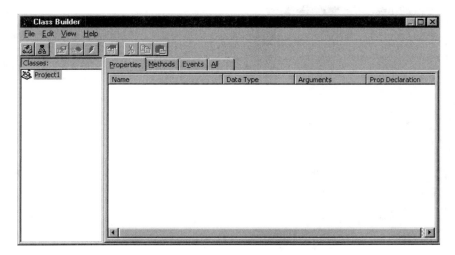

Figure 7-7   The Initial screen on the Class Builder

Now:

1. Select View|Options in the Class Builder and check both of the Code Generation options given there as shown in Figure 7-8. Then click on OK.

Figure 7-8   Class Builder options

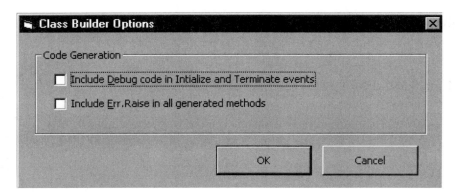

2. Now click the "Add New Class" button on the far left of the toolbar (or choose File|New|Class. A screen like Figure 7-9 opens up

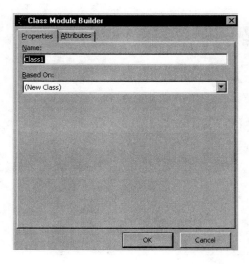

Figure 7-9   Class Module Builder main screen

3. Enter "Cell" for the name and click and leave the Based On at the default value of New Class. (See the next chapter for how to use this item for inheritance.)

4. Repeat steps 2 and 3 only this time enter "Player" for the next class name. However be sure to check the "This is a Top Level Object" checkbox before adding this class. (Otherwise the class will be below Cell in the class hierarchy.)

5. Repeat Step 4 and enter "Piece" for the last class name.

Now we want to add some properties to our classes. You can add a property to any class that you have selected in the left box of the Class Builder. For example:

1. Click the "Cell" class in the left box in the Class Builder.

2. To add a property, the easiest way is click the third toolbar button from the left. This brings up a screen like Figure 7-10. (You can also use the context menu when the focus is in the Properties tab.)

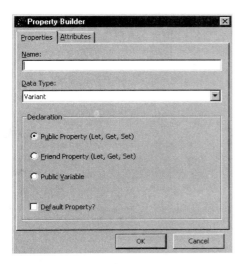

Figure 7-10   The Property Builder

- Now enter "CurrentPiece" for the name of the property and select "Piece" from the drop-down list of possible data types. Leave everything else at their default values.

- Now repeat the process to add the properties shown in the following table:

Class	Property Name	Data Type	Other
Cell	X	Integer	
Cell	Y	Integer	
Piece	Color	Byte	
Piece	CurrentCell	Cell	
Piece	Name	String	Default Property
Player	Name	String	Default Property
Player	Color	Byte	

Now we want to add a method to the Piece class called "Move." To do this, use the fourth Tool. (Or select the Methods Tab, right click and choose New Method.) You'll see the Method Builder Screen as in Figure 7-11.

Enter Move for the name of this method.

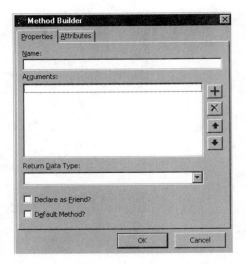

Figure 7-11   The Method Builder Screen

- Click the Plus button to add an argument with the name "X" and type Integer.
- Click the Plus button to add an argument with the name "Y" and type Integer.
- Select "Boolean" from the Return Data Type drop-down list.

Click OK. Now we are ready to add the two collections we need. Click the second tool from the left. You'll see the Collection Builder as shown in Figure 7-12.

Figure 7-12   The Collection Builder

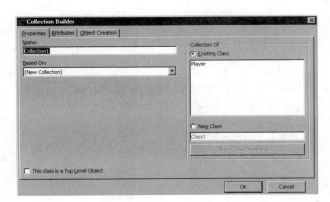

- Enter "Cells" for the name of the collection and select "Cell" in the Collection Of list on the right. Now click on OK.

Caution

Some versions of the Class Builder have a bug that requires you to save your work first if you want to create another collection. To play it safe, save the work that you have done so far. To do this choose File|Update Project from the main menu of the Class Builder. This will add the code that the class builder has created so far—more than one collection at a time.

- Now add another collection named Pieces. Make it a collection of Pieces by choosing Piece in the right-hand box. Also make sure the Top-Level Object box is selected. That should do it for our chess model. All we need to do now is select File|Exit and the Class Builder will generate all the code for you. The Class Builder will also create the fairly complex code to allow you to enumerate through these specialized collections. (See the next chapter for more on this.) It will also generate some debug code to help you keep track of object creation and termination. Here's an example of the kind of code the Class Builder generated for the Piece class. Notice how the Class Builder includes some comments that tell you how to use the code. (The lines with a # like #If DebugMode are used with conditional compilation. See Chapter 9 for more on this useful debugging technique.)

Listing 7-3: Code generated by Class Builder for Piece class

```
VERSION 1.0 CLASS
BEGIN
  MultiUse = -1  'True
END
Attribute VB_Name = "Piece"
Attribute VB_GlobalNameSpace = False
Attribute VB_Creatable = True
Attribute VB_PredeclaredId = False
Attribute VB_Exposed = False
Attribute VB_Ext_KEY = "SavedWithClassBuilder" ,"Yes"
Attribute VB_Ext_KEY = "Top_Level" ,"Yes"
'set this to 0 to disable debug code in this class
```

```
#Const DebugMode = 1

#If DebugMode Then
    'local variable to hold the serialized class ID that
was created in Class_Initialize
    Private mlClassDebugID As Long
#End If
Private mvarColor As Byte 'local copy
Private mvarCurrentCell As Cell 'local copy
Private mvarName As String 'local copy
Public Property Let Name(ByVal vData As String)
    On Error GoTo NameLetErr

'used when assigning a value to the property, on the left
side of an assignment.
'Syntax: X.Name = 5
    mvarName = vData
    Exit Property

NameLetErr:

    Call RaiseError(MyUnhandledError, "Piece:Name Property
Let")
End Property

Public Property Get Name() As String
Attribute Name.VB_UserMemId = 0
    On Error GoTo NameGetErr

'used when retrieving value of a property, on the right side
of an assignment.
'Syntax: Debug.Print X.Name
    Name = mvarName
    Exit Property

NameGetErr:

    Call RaiseError(MyUnhandledError, "Piece:Name Property
Get")
End Property

Public Property Set CurrentCell(ByVal vData As Object)
    On Error GoTo CurrentCellSetErr

'used when assigning an Object to the property, on the left
side of a Set statement.
'Syntax: Set x.CurrentCell = Form1
```

```
    Set mvarCurrentCell = vData
    Exit Property

CurrentCellSetErr:
    Call RaiseError(MyUnhandledError, "Piece:CurrentCell
Property Set")
End Property

Public Property Get CurrentCell() As Cell
    On Error GoTo CurrentCellGetErr

'used when retrieving value of a property, on the right side
of an assignment.
'Syntax: Debug.Print X.CurrentCell
    Set CurrentCell = mvarCurrentCell
    Exit Property

CurrentCellGetErr:
    Call RaiseError(MyUnhandledError, "Piece:CurrentCell
Property Get")
End Property

Public Property Let Color(ByVal vData As Byte)
    On Error GoTo ColorLetErr
'used when assigning a value to the property, on the left
side of an assignment.
'Syntax: X.Color = 5
    mvarColor = vData
    Exit Property
ColorLetErr:
    Call RaiseError(MyUnhandledError, "Piece:Color Property
Let")
End Property

Public Property Get Color() As Byte
    On Error GoTo ColorGetErr

'used when retrieving value of a property, on the right side
of an assignment.
'Syntax: Debug.Print X.Color
    Color = mvarColor
    Exit Property

ColorGetErr:
    Call RaiseError(MyUnhandledError, "Piece:Color Property
Get")
End Property
```

```
Private Sub Class_Initialize()
    #If DebugMode Then
        'get the next available class ID, and print out
        'that the class was created successfully
        mlClassDebugID = GetNextClassDebugID()
        Debug.Print "'" & TypeName(Me) & "' instance " &
mlClassDebugID _
& " created"
    #End If
End Sub

Private Sub Class_Terminate()
    'the class is being destroyed
    #If DebugMode Then
        Debug.Print "'" & TypeName(Me) & "' instance " &
CStr(mlClassDebugID) _
& " is terminating"
    #End If
End Sub

#If DebugMode Then
    Public Property Get ClassDebugID()
        'if we are in debug mode, surface this property
that consumers can query
        ClassDebugID = mlClassDebugID
    End Property
#End If
```

Control Arrays

Finally, we want to end this chapter by showing you how to add new controls to a form at run time. It would be logical if you could also use the New keyword to create controls at run time; unfortunately, that isn't the way it works. Visual Basic 5 still uses the older (and somewhat clumsier) method of control arrays to create new controls of a specific type. (You may have discovered control arrays inadvertently if you gave two controls of the same type the same control name, or tried to copy a control using the Edit menu. If you did, then you saw a dialog box that looks like the one shown in Figure 7-13.

Any time you use the same control name more than once while designing a Visual Basic form or a user control form, VB5 asks you whether you really want to create a control array. Click the Yes button (or press ENTER), and you now can add more controls of the same type while the application is running. Each new control in a control array is called an *element* of the control array.

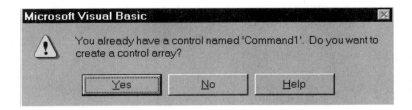

Figure 7-13   Message box to create control array

Since both controls now have the same name, Visual Basic needs a way to distinguish them. You do this with the Index property. When you ask Visual Basic to create a control array, Visual Basic gives the first control an Index property of 0 and the second control an Index property of 1. Like any properties of Visual Basic objects, you can change them at design time using the Properties window. In fact, if you assign any number to the Index property of a control at design time, Visual Basic automatically creates a control array. This lets you create a control array without having to use two controls at design time.

Note

Create the control array first before writing any event procedures for its first element. (Although you do not have to create all the elements in the control array before coding them, this is one of the big advantages to the index parameter.)

Suppose you want to work with the Click event procedure for an element of the command button control array created as in Figure 7-12. Suppose you gave it the control name of cmdInArray. When you move to the Code window by, say, double-clicking one of these, the command buttons in the control array, your code event template looks like this:

```
Private Sub cmdInArray(Index As Integer)

End Sub
```

Notice how, instead of having no parameters, as the Click event procedure ordinarily does, this event procedure now uses a new parameter, Index As Integer. This index parameter is the key to the smooth functioning of control arrays. If you want to use the Click procedure for any element of the control array, call it with the appropriate index parameter:

```
cmdInArray_Click(0)      'applies to the original command
                         'button

cmdInArray_Click(1)      'applies to the second one
```

For example, add the following code to the event procedure template shown here:

```
Private Sub cmdInArray_Click (Index As Integer)
   If Index = 0 Then
     MsgBox "You clicked button 0"
   Else
     MsgBox "You clicked button 1"
   End If
End Sub
```

or even more simply:

```
Private Sub cmdInArray_Click (Index As Integer)
   MsgBox "You clicked button " & Index
End Sub
```

When you click one of the command buttons, VB5 calls this event procedure and passes the index parameter to the procedure. In this way, the event procedure can use the index to determine what to do.

If you inadvertently added a control to a control array at design time, you can remove it by changing the control name or deleting the control. However, once Visual Basic creates a control array, you must change all the control names or delete all the controls that were in the array in order to eliminate the control array. At that point, you can reuse the name.

Finally, we think it is worth noting the difference between an array of controls and a control array. An array of controls is simply a usual VB5 array that happens to contain control objects rather than numbers; a control array is a dynamic object used to create new controls at run time.

Adding and Removing Controls in a Control Array

You must create a control array at design time, but, after that, you can add new elements to the control array while the application is running. Use a variation of the Load command that can also be used to load a new form in an application with multiple forms. For example, suppose you want to add three more command buttons to the example control array created in the previous section. To do this when the start-up form loads, you only need to add the following code to the Form_Load event procedure for the start-up form:

```
Private Sub Form_Load()
  Dim I As Integer

  For I = 2 To 4
    Load cmdInArray(I)
    cmdInArray(I).Caption = "Command Button #" & I
  Next I
End Sub
```

Note

Whenever VB5 loads a new element of a control array, the object is invisible—the visible property is set to False. All other properties (except the Tab Index and Control Array Index) are copied from the object that has the lowest index in the array.

This means that newly created controls in a control array default to being stacked one on top of the other. Because of this, you'll often find yourself applying the Move method to controls in a control array after you tell VB5 to load them.

You can use the Unload statement to remove any element of a control array that you added at run time. You cannot use the Unload statement to remove the original elements of the control array that you created at design time. For example, if you add the

```
Private Sub Form_Click()
  Static I As Integer

  If I < 4 Then
    Unload cmdInArray(I + 2)
    I = I + 1
  Else
    Exit Sub
  End If
End Sub
```

each click on an empty place in the form removes the next command button in the control array, but no routine like this can remove the initial element in the control array.

You must be careful, of course; you can only load or unload an element of a control array once. If you try to load or unload a control array element twice in succession, Visual Basic gives a run-time error you can trap (Err = 360).

ADVANCED OBJECT-ORIENTED PROGRAMMING

Topics in this Chapter

- Inheritance
- Problems with Delegation for Inheritance
- Interfaces
- Making a Copy of an Object (Cloning)
- Persistence
- Under the Hood: A Bird's-Eye View of COM (=ActiveX)

Chapter 8

The last chapter introduced you to the basic principles of object orient-ed programming. This chapter covers more advanced issues. The first part of this chapter covers what you need to do in Visual Basic to deal with its lack of true inheritance. As you will see, some of these workarounds are quite elegant, others are clumsy beyond belief. The next part of this chapter is an introduction to the subtle issues involved with making a copy of (or *cloning,* as it is usually called) an object. Cloning an object is related to the question of how to package the current state of an object so that you can store it on a disk drive or send it over the net. (This is usually called *persistence.*) We take that up next. The final part of this chapter is a short introduction to the principles behind Visual Basic object model—Microsoft calls this *COM,* which stands for the common object model.

Inheritance

You saw how useful collections were in the last chapter. One problem they had was that they were not *type safe.* By this we mean that collections hold variables of the generic *variant* type, and variants, as you know, can hold any-thing. This is not what you want for safe programming. If you use a collection and inadvertently store an object of the wrong type in it, your program may fail at a crucial time when you try to call a function that needs a reference parameter of a certain type.

What would be better than Visual Basic's generic collection class is to have specialized collections that can hold only objects of a single type. For example, we could have a StringCollection class that can hold only strings, or an IntegerCollection that can hold only integers and so on. Specialization, of course, is what inheritance is all about. What we need to do is have a new class that works just like a collection except we need to change properties like the Add and Item method, so that they are type safe. The Count property, on the other hand, is just fine the way it is. For example, the Add method for a StringCollection class should only be able to add strings to the more specialized collection. (This is usually called *overriding* the parent method.) In pseudo-code a string collection would look like:

```
String Collection Inherits (Specializes) Ordinary Collection
      Add method only accepts strings
      Item method only return strings
      every thing else the same
End String Collection
```

The trouble is that Visual Basic doesn't yet support true inheritance (or *implementation inheritance,* as it is sometimes called.) Instead you need to use what is called *delegation inheritance*. The idea of delegation inheritance is that we replace the "is-a" relationship that is the hallmark of true (implementation) inheritance by the "has-a" that marks containment. In the case of a specialized collection class what we do is add a private instance field that is an ordinary collection. We use this private collection to get at the functionality we need. More generally we *delegate* to an object contained in our object what we want done.

Here's an example of the kind of code you need. First add a class module and set the Class name to be StringCollection. Then add a private instance field that we will use for the delegation process:

```
'A String collection class
Private mCollection As Collection 'for delegation
```

Then you need to have the Initialize and Terminate events to set up and reclaim the memory that is used for the private collection:

```
Private Sub Class_Initialize()
   Set mCollection = New Collection
End Sub
```

```
Private Sub Class_Terminate()
   Set mCollection = Nothing
End Sub
```

This kind of code will always be necessary when you do inheritance by delegation. You will always need to reclaim the memory you set up for the private object(s) used in the delegation process. Next, we need to write the code for the various members of our specialized collection we want to expose to the outside world. For consistency's sake we will use the same Add, Remove, and Count names that an ordinary collection uses. We want our Add methods to only accept strings but otherwise delegate everything to the Add method of the private collection. The simplest way to deal with this is simply to use the following one-liner:

```
Sub Add(Item As String)
   mCollection.Add Item
End Sub
```

This shows you delegation at work: we are delegating the Add method to the private instance field that is itself a collection. In practice, of course, the Add method for a collection is much more sophisticated. As you know from the last chapter it can take optional parameters for the key and the before and after positions. Since we know that the position of an item in a collection is not something that is of much use in a collection, we decided our Add method won't use the before and after parameters. The optional key parameter is, of course, the real point of a collection, but we feel that a key shouldn't be optional, so we make it required. Here's all the code required for this:

```
Public Sub Add(Item As String, Key As String)
   mCollection.Add Item, Key
End Sub
```

Similarly, we don't believe you should be able to remove items by their index so we insist that the index be the key. We can do that by making the parameter be a string rather than a variant:

```
Public Sub Remove(Item As String)
   mCollection.Remove Item
End Sub
```

Now you won't have to worry about the subtle bug of using a numeric key and having the collection class think it is an index. (Since the parameter we pass to the internal collection is always a string.) Finally, there's the Count property, which simply reports the current value of the Count property of the internal collection, and the Item property, which gets at the Items. Here's the count code:

```
Public Function Count() As Long
   Count = mCollection.Count
End Function
```

The Item code is on the CD. We now have a type safe string collection that you can use in the project by saying:

```
Dim Foo As New StringCollection
```

Note

At this point all our utility classes will need to be added to a specific project via Project|Add Class Module. It is possible to compile the class module in such a way that it can be used as an "object factory" by your projects without having to add the source code to your project each time. See Chapter 14 for how to do this.

Improving the StringCollection Class

There are two problems remaining with the string collection class. The first is that you probably want the Item property to be the default property of the class. For this, you need to get to the Advanced Procedure Attributes dialog box shown in Figure 8-1. You can get to this either by using the Object Browser or simply by:

1. Placing the cursor in the Item method.
2. Choosing Tools|Procedure attribute.
3. Clicking the Advanced tab.
4. Choosing the Item property from the Name combo box.
5. Choosing Default from the Procedure ID drop-down list box.

The more serious problem is that you can't yet use the For-Each construct to iterate through our string collection. This is where true inheritance would be a great help, we would get the For-Each for free since we didn't override it. Instead, we need to resort to pure black magic. Here's what you need to do to add the ability to use a For-Each on the items in the string collection:

1. Add the following code to the class module:

   ```
   Public Function NewEnum As IUnknown
      Set NewEnum = mCollection.[_NewEnum]
   End Function
   ```

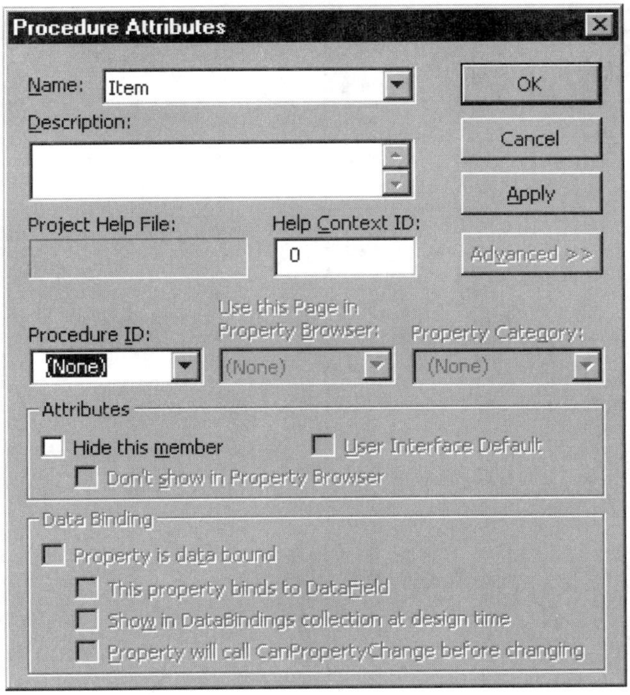

Procedure Attributes

Name: Item

Description:

OK

Cancel

Apply

Project Help File: Help Context ID: 0

Advanced >>

Procedure ID: (None)

Use this Page in Property Browser: (None)

Property Category: (None)

Attributes

☐ Hide this member   ☐ User Interface Default
☐ Don't show in Property Browser

Data Binding

☐ Property is data bound
☐ This property binds to DataField
☐ Show in DataBindings collection at design time
☐ Property will call CanPropertyChange before changing

Figure 8-1   The Advanced Procedure Attributes dialog box

2.   Now the magic happens. We need to set the Procedure ID for
     this code to be –4 (yes, that's a –4) as shown in Figure 8-2.

And then the magic happens and you can use For–Each on the type safe
collection.

Note

*Obviously "and then magic happens" is not a great way to code. The end
of this chapter has a short section that explains a little bit about what is
going on under the hood in this code. But to be quite honest, a full explanation of what is going on under the hood would take a book roughly as
long as this.*

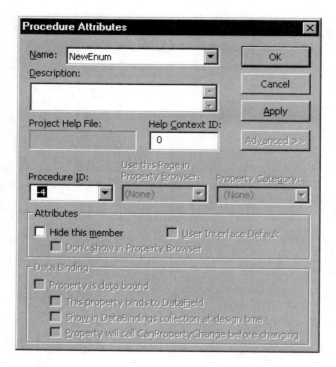

Figure 8-2   Magic Spell for making For-Each work

Problems with Delegation for Inheritance

Let's suppose we are trying to come up with an object-oriented approach to a personnel management system. There will be a base class of Employee and specialized classes like Manager, Programmer, Secretary and so on. All these classes are supposed to inherit from (specialize) the Employee class. How can we code an Employee class in VB? We might have private instance fields for things like Salary, Name, Social Security Number, Date Hired and such:

```
Private mName As String
Private mSalary As Currency
Private mDateHired As Date
Private mSocialSecurityNumber As String
```

The first problem we come up against is the standard one: the Initialize event for a Visual Basic class doesn't allow us to use parameters. What we would like to do is set the private instance fields like the Employee's social security number, date hired, and name in the Initialize event. Unfortunately, we can't do this so we adopt the standard convention of having a Create procedure that will take this information as its parameters

```
Public Sub Create(Name As String, Salary As Currency, _
SocialSecurityNumber As String, DateHired As Date)
   mName = Name
   mSalary = Salary
   mDateHired = DateHired
   mSocialSecurity = SocialSecurityNumber
End Sub
```

The Name, Social Security number, and Date Hired we will assume are read-only properties. They should only be settable in the Create routine. This means they will have Property Gets but no associate Property Lets:

```
Public Property Get EmployeeName() As String
   EmployeeName = mName
End Property

Public Property Get DateHired() As Date
   DateHired = mDate
End Property

Public Property Get SocialSecurityNumber() As String
   SocialSecurityNumber = mSocialSecurityNumber
End Property
```

Next, let's take up the EmployeeSalary property we want to allow a way to reset the person's salary so we have to have both a Property Get and a Property Let:

```
Public Property Get EmployeeSalary() As Currency
   EmployeeSalary = mSalary
End Property

Public Property Let EmployeeSalary(ByVal NewSalary As _
Currency)
   mSalary = NewSalary
End Property
```

Finally, for illustration purposes we will add a method called RaiseSalary that allows you to raise a person's salary by a fixed percentage but does a little bit of error checking as well:

```
Public Sub RaiseSalary(ByVal PercentageIncrease As Single)
  Dim YesNo As Integer
  YesNo = vbYes
  If PercentageIncrease > 0.1 Then
    YesNo = MsgBox("Do you really want to raise this
person's salary by " _
    & (100 * PercentageIncrease) & "%?", vbYesNo)
  End If
  If YesNo = vbYes Then mSalary = (1 +
PercentageIncrease) * mSalary
End Sub
```

Okay, now we have an Employee class and we want to make a Manager class. The only difference will be that the Manager class will have a Secretary instance field. Immediately we have a problem. If we use delegation, the class then has to start out as:

```
'Manager class
Private mEmployee As Employee
```

Now we add the private instance field for a Secretary that will also be of type Employee:

```
Private mSecretary As Employee
```

and add Property Get and Property Set to return and set references to the secretary:

```
Public Property Get Secretary() As Employee
  Set Secretary = mSecretary
End Property

Public Property Set Secretary(ByVal Secretary As Employee)
  Set mSecretary = Secretary
End Property
```

So far, so good. But now we run into a problem: Members like the HireDate and Name properties are ReadOnly by design, we can't set them by calling the Create routine like we did before because the mEmployee instance field is private.

```
'won't work!!!!
mEmployee.Create(EmployeeName = Name, . . .)
```

Going back and changing the original Employee class to make the Name a read/write property is not a great idea. Properties like Name or HireDate should be settable only once. (Ideally in the Initialize procedure for the class, because of VB's inadequacies in this area, in our Create procedure.)

Well, we can certainly make a Create routine for the Manager class that takes Employee parameters. We can then build up the Employee part of a Manager's internal structure first and pass that as a parameter:

```
Public Create (Employee As Employee, Secretary As Employee)
   Set mEmployee = Employee
   Set mSecretary = Secretary
End Sub
```

But how do we build up the Employee and Secretary objects for use in this new version of the Create routine? We would need to resort to code like this:

```
Dim Tom As New Employee
Dim SallyAsEmployee As New Employee
Dim SallyAsManager As New Manager
Tom.Create"Tom ",50000,"023-23-3456",#1-1-97#
SallyAsEmployee.Create"Sally", 100000,"098-88-2233",#1-1-93#
SallyAsManager.Create SallyAsEmployee, Tom
```

This kind of kludgy code would be necessary because we need to have SallyAsEmployee as the value of the private mEmployee instance field inside the Manager class. If all this ugliness wasn't enough of a turn-off, there is a much more serious problem:

- We need to use the SallyAsEmployee object whenever we are collecting Employees into a structure such as an array.

If you tried the following:

```
Dim MyCompany As Employee(1 To 100)
Set MyEmployee(1) = SallyAsManager
Set MyEmployee(2) = Tom
```

you would get an error message because SallyAsManager *is not of type Employee, she is of type Manager.* And, since she is not an instance of the Employee class, she can't be placed inside an array that holds employees. At this point you might be tempted to forget about using delegation to get inheritance but all is not lost. Visual Basic has a much more sophisticated way to do delegation involving the interfaces we mentioned briefly in the last chapter, we take that up next.

Interfaces

The problem is that we want Sally to be able to exhibit her "Employeeness" when she need to expose employee information (like being put into an array of Employees) and her "Managerness" when she needs to be treated as a manager. The ability to present multiple "faces" to the world is one of the things Interfaces allow you to do. Multiple (inter)faces are also the key to polymorphism and early binding in VB. Every class in VB always has one interface that comes from its own nature. Think of this as the default (inter)face that a class presents to the world: a manager class has a Manager interface. You don't have to do anything to make VB expose the default interface to the world. To expose "Employeeness" in a Manager class, though, requires some work.

So, what is an Interface? Essentially, an interface is a class that provides a framework for one of the faces that other objects can present to the world. For example, to start the process of cleaning up the object model for the Personnel Management program, we will need to set up an interface called IEmployee. This interface will allow Sally to be part of an array that holds employees. (The convention is that interfaces that will be implemented in multiple kinds of classes always begin with a capitol I).

All the employee objects will have the potential to expose this (inter)face to the outside world—regardless of whether they are managers, secretaries, programmers, or the CEO. As you can see in figure 8-3, the convention for drawing figures that show interfaces is that you use "lollypops" for the various interfaces that an object can expose to the outside world.

Note

Figure 8-3 is actually a much simplified view of what is going on under the hood, classes in VB come with lots of other interfaces automatically supplied. Moreover the one we call the Manager interface would actually be called the _Manager interface. These interfaces are used by COM and allow COM, for example, to have both early and late binding. See the end of this chapter for more on these COM interfaces.

The first step in using an Interface is easy, just add the Implements keyword:

```
'Manager class with Employee (inter)face to the world
Implements IEmployee
```

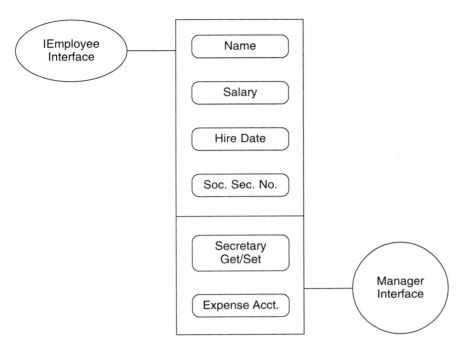

Figure 8-3 Exposing Multiple Interfaces

The next step is the most important, we need to add the IEmployee framework to the Manager class. This requires adding *every member of the IEmployee interface to the Manager* class. Every member means every member, no exceptions are allowed. Once you put the keyword Implements you are entering into a "contract" that you will support all the members of the IEmployee interface and VB will not run your code if you fail to fulfill all the elements of the contract.

What Is an Interface?

But what is an Interface? The answer is easy:

- In Visual Basic an interface is simply a class.

You actually have two ways to build the classes you will use for Interfaces. The most common one is to have a class with only a framework and no actual code. In this case the framework consists of only the signatures for the members:

```
'Class IEmployee
Option Explicit

Public Sub Create(Name As String, Salary As Currency, _
SocialSecurityNumber As String, DateHired As Date)

End Sub

Public Property Get EmployeeName() As String

End Property

Public Property Get DateHired() As Date

End Property

Public Property Get SocialSecurityNumber() As String

End Property

Public Property Get EmployeeSalary() As Currency

End Property

Public Property Let EmployeeSalary(ByVal NewSalary As
Currency)

End Property

Public Sub RaiseSalary(ByVal PercentageIncrease As Single)

End Sub
```

Note

The other method is to (unlike languages like Java) use code in the members of your interface instead of skeletons only. These concrete interfaces are most often used when you are combining inheritance by delegation with an interface.

Let's use the abstract class to build our personnel management system rather than delegation since it seems so silly to have a concrete IEmployee class inside a Manager class—it is conceptually easier to think of the IEmployee class as giving you "employeeness." So start up a new project and:

1. Add a class module with the name IEmployee.

2. Add the abstract members given in the above code.

Now we want to make some classes that Implement the IEmployee interface. Let's have a Programmer Class and a Manager class and a Secretary class. All three of these classes will implement the IEmployee Interface. For example, to build the Programmer class for this model:

1. Add a class module called Programmer to the project that has the IEmployee class in it.

2. Add the lines:

   ```
   'A programmer Class implements the IEmployee Interface
   Implements IEmployee
   ```

Now some IDE magic happens:

1. Drop down the Object dialog box. Notice there is an Item called IEmployee (see Figure 8-4).

2. Choose this item.

Now if you go to the Procedure list box you will notice all the members of the IEmployee interface ready for you to fill in the skeletons. (See Figure 8-5.)

The next step is to systematically go through the Procedure list box and select them one by one. This will make VB add the skeletons for all the members you will need to add. (See Figure 8-6.)

Notice however that the skeletons for the members of the IEmployee interface that are showing up in the Programmer class are a bit different from what you might expect. Here is what the framework looks like for the Create event that is shown at the top in Figure 8-6. (We are using the underscore line continuation character because the whole declaration is too long to fit on one line in this book.)

```
Private Sub IEmployee_Create(Name As String, _
Salary As Currency, SocialSecurityNumber As String, _
DateHired As Date)
```

This has two unusual elements in the signature:

1. It is Private not Public.

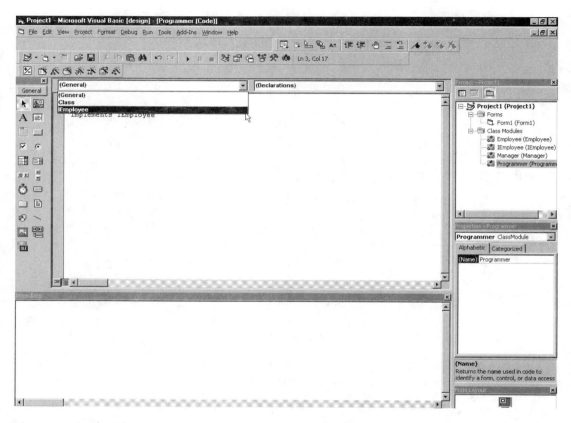

Figure 8-4   The Object Drop Down for implementing an interface

2. It has the funny IEmployee_Create name rather than the
    Create name that you might expect.

We will take up these points a little later but so that we can actually test the
code we want to build up the needed code to make some of these objects.
Make the Programmer class look like this (or use the Programmer.cls in the
CH8 directory on the CD). First we need the Instance fields and the assignment statements as in the original Employee class:

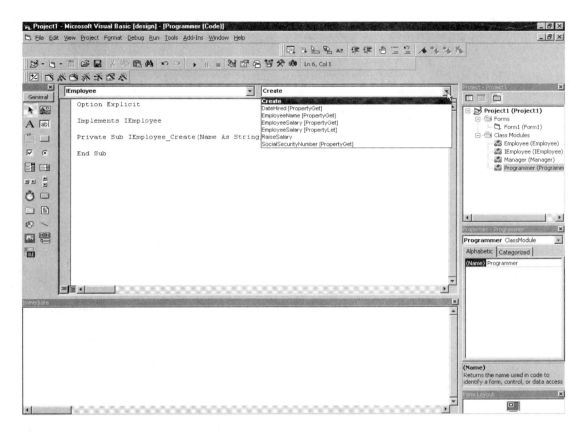

Figure 8-5   The Procedure Drop Down for implementing an interface

```
Private mName As String
Private mSalary As Currency
Private mDateHired As Date
Private mSocialSecurityNumber As String

Private Sub IEmployee_Create(Name As String, Salary As _
Currency, SocialSecurityNumber As String, DateHired As Date)
  mName = Name
  mSalary = Salary
  mDateHired = DateHired
  mSocialSecurityNumber = SocialSecurityNumber
End Sub
```

Here's what the whole Programmer class looks like:

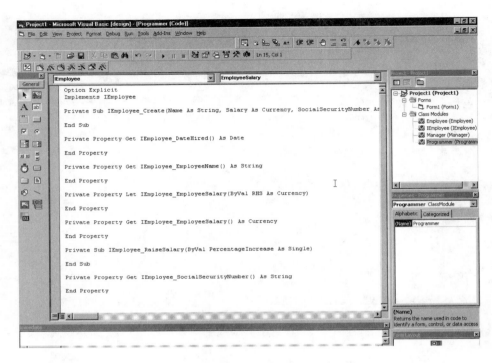

Figure 8-6   The Code Window for implementing an interface

Listing 8-1   The Programmer Class

```
'A programmer class that will implement the Employee interface
Option Explicit
Implements IEmployee

Private mName As String
Private mSalary As Currency
Private mDateHired As Date
Private mSocialSecurityNumber As String
'now we will flesh out the skeletons
Private Sub IEmployee_Create(Name As String, Salary As
Currency, SocialSecurityNumber As String, DateHired As Date)
  mName = Name
  mSalary = Salary
  mDateHired = DateHired
  mSocialSecurityNumber = SocialSecurityNumber
End Sub
```

```
Private Property Get IEmployee_DateHired() As Date
   IEmployee_DateHired = mDateHired
End Property

Private Property Get IEmployee_EmployeeName() As String
   IEmployee_EmployeeName = mName
End Property

Private Property Let IEmployee_EmployeeSalary(ByVal RHS As Currency)
   IEmployee_EmployeeSalary = RHS
End Property

Private Property Get IEmployee_EmployeeSalary() As Currency
   IEmployee_EmployeeSalary = mSalary
End Property

Private Sub IEmployee_RaiseSalary(ByVal PercentageIncrease As Single)
   Dim YesNo As Integer
   YesNo = vbYes
   If PercentageIncrease > 0.1 Then
     YesNo = MsgBox("Do you really want to raise this person's salary by " _
     & (100 * PercentageIncrease) & "%?", vbYesNo)
   End If
   If YesNo = vbYes Then mSalary = (1 + PercentageIncrease) * mSalary
End Sub

Private Property Get IEmployee_SocialSecurityNumber() As String
   IEmployee_SocialSecurityNumber = mSocialSecurityNumber
End Property
```

Notice that all the members of the IEmployee interface show up with the IEmployee_ prefix and all are Private. Do the same for the Manager class and the Secretary class (or pull them off the CD). Okay, so now we have the classes. The obvious but important questions are:

- How to we create some objects of these types?

Making objects of IEmployee type is trivial, you simply use an Object variable:

```
Dim EmployeeData As IEmployee
```

Getting at the employeeness of one of our programmer or manager objects is a little trickier. For example:

- How do we actually get at the "Employee" (inter)face that objects of type Manager, Programmer, and Secretary will be able to expose?

For example, how can we call the Create routine in order to initialize their state? As long as IEmployee_Create is private you can't use:

```
Sally.IEmployee_Create "Sally", 10000000, "987-65-432", #1/1/70#
```

To get around this you have two choices. The first is to change the IEmployee_Create member to be Public in all three classes. Then you *can* simply call it as in the following:

```
Dim Sally As New Manager
Sally.IEmployee_Create "Sally", 10000000, "987-65-432", #1/1/70#
```

This is probably the simplest and cleanest solution.

Some people would argue that this is not such a great solution because it (philosophically) breaks encapsulation. They say that you should only access IEmployee members through IEmployee objects and Managers objects are not IEmployee objects so don't even think about writing code like we just did. We think this is kind of silly especially when you consider the alternative. (Again, all this is forced on us because VB doesn't have true inheritance.)

```
Dim Sally As New Manager
Dim TempVariable As IEmployee
Set TempVariable = Sally
TempVariable.Create "Sally", 10000000, "987-65-432",
#1/1/70#
```

The idea is that we have to use a temporary variable of IEmployee type in order to expose the members of the IEmployee interface to us. As in the above code, Visual Basic always allows you to Set an object implementing an interface to an object that is Dim'ed as being of that interface type.

While we think this criticism is silly in this specific case and don't particularly like the code given above, the idea of using temporary variables that are of type IEmployee is a vital one. In fact, the general method at getting at the "employeeness" of an object that implements IEmployee is:

- You assign your object variable to a (temporary) object variable that is of the IEmployee type or that is used as a parameter of IEmployee type.

For example, consider the following Sub:

```
Sub ReportInfoOn(AnEmployee As IEmployee)
  Dim Message As String
  Message = AnEmployee.EmployeeName & "'s" & " salary is "
  Message = Message & AnEmployee.EmployeeSalary
  MsgBox Message
End Sub
```

Now when we make a call like:

```
ReportInfoOn Sally
```

we automatically get the benefit of having Sally show her "employee" face to the world. Sally gets passed to a parameter of type IEmployee and then VB (well, COM actually) will be able to "see" the members in the Employee interface. And, since she is showing her employee face, lines like:

```
AnEmployee.EmployeeName & "'s" & " salary is "
```

are perfectly acceptable and do what we want. Next, add the following line to the above code:

```
Message = Message & ". My type is " & TypeName(AnEmployee)
```

and run the example again. You should see something like Figure 8-7. Notice that although Sally is exposing her "employeeness" in this example VB still knows she is a manager.

Next, try to run the program but change the parameter in the ReportOnInfo from:

```
AnEmployee As Employee
```

to:

```
AnObject as Object
```

If you now try:

```
ReportInfoOn Sally
```

you will get the famous error #438, "Object doesn't support this property or method" as shown in Figure 8-8. The (important) point is that you can only access the members of an interface when the object is showing that face to the world. When we change the parameter to be of type object, the fact that Sally had an IEmployee interface is never used.

You may say that you are unlikely to use an Object parameter for an Employee but consider the following code:

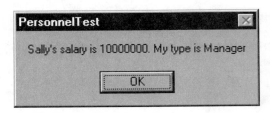

Figure 8-7   Type is preserved

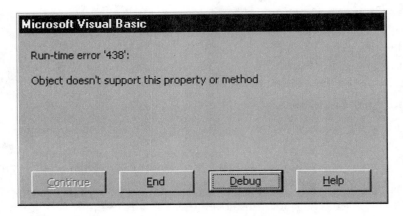

Figure 8-8   Passing a bad object as a parameter

```
Sub MySecretary(AManager As Manager)
    Dim Message As String
    Message = "Hi I'm " & AManager.EmployeeName
    Message = Message & ". My secretary is " &
AManager.Secretary.EmployeeName
    MsgBox Message
End Sub
```

This looks like it should give a nice message box like Figure 8-9 but it doesn't. Instead, it gives you an error message like Figure 8-10. The reason is very important to keep in mind:

- As long as an object is of type Manager the private IEmployee properties and methods are hidden.

As before, to get at the Employee information you have to make methods public or use a temporary variable like this:

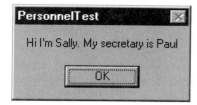

Figure 8-9 Getting the secretary

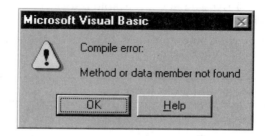

Figure 8-10 What you really get

```
Sub MySecretary(AManager As Manager)
    Dim Message As String, Foo As IEmployee
    Set Foo = AManager
    Message = "Hi I'm " & Foo.EmployeeName
    'now I can use the Employee name method!!
    Message = Message & ". My secretary is " & _
AManager.Secretary.EmployeeName
    MsgBox Message
End Sub
```

Tip

Another alternative is to design the classes so that they have a property that returns an IEmployee object. Use this property to get access to the "employeeness" of the object once and for all. You can even make it the default property of the class to save some typing (although we don't recommend this):

```
Public Function MyEmployeeness() As  IEmployee
    Dim TempData as IEmployee
    Set TempData = Me
    Set MyEmployeeness = TempData
End Function
```

A Sorting Example

One of the most powerful uses of interfaces is to allow you to abstract out properties of your code. Sorting is a good example of this. If you think about it, you can see that the essence of sorting is to have a "compare method". As long as you have a compare method, you can sort the object. We can use this observation to write a totally generic sorting routine.

First we need a Sortable interface. To make it as simple as possible we also insist that the object that implements the ISortable interface have a swap method and methods to give us the number of items to sort. Here's the ISortable interface.

Listing 8-2   The ISortable Interface

```
'A sortable interface ISortable
'allows you to sort anything once you implement methods
' for getting and setting elements at positions,  swapping them  and
'comparing them. Could sort records on a disk for example

Public Property Get GetItemAt(index As Integer) As Variant
    'use variants to allow anything to be sorted.
    'could add an OfType method to this interface to allow conversions
End Property

Public Sub SetItemAt(index As Integer, foo As Variant)
    'need element access
End Sub

Public Property Get IsLessThanAtIndex(A As Integer, B As Integer) As Boolean
    'need to compare two items at different indices
End Property

Public Property Get LowerBound() As Integer
    'sorts need to start somewhere
End Property

Public Property Get UpperBound() As Integer
    'sorts need to end somewhere
End Property

Public Sub Swap(I As Integer, J As Integer)
```

```
' swaps the items - need not be physically swapped
End Sub
```

Most of the methods we decided to add to this interface were designed to make the Sort routines easier to code. We have methods to get the elements at a specific place, to swap them, or to find the upper bound for the limits of the loops needed in the Sort routine. For example, we could use all this to have a SortIt class that looks like this (we used a simple "ripple" sort so as not to get bogged down in implementation details of the sort):

```
Option Explicit
Private Bottom  As Integer
Private Top As Integer
Private I As Integer
Private Temp As Variant
Private J As Integer

' use Ripple sort as a test
' shows that all one needs is the methods in the
ISortable interface
Public Sub Sort(foo As ISortable)

    Bottom = foo.LowerBound
    Top = foo.UpperBound
    For I = Bottom To (Top - Bottom)

        Temp = foo.GetItemAt(I)
        For J = I + 1 To Top
            If foo.IsLessThanAtIndex(J, I) Then
                foo.Swap I, J
            End If
        Next J
    Next I
End Sub
```

The key, of course, is that the Sort routine takes a parameter of type ISortable. This means we can call the Sort routine generically. For example, here's a class that extends an Integer array to a new class so that it can be sorted by implementing all the members of the ISortable interface. (For illustration purposes we use the initialize event to fill up the array with 20 random values). The key routine is the one that does the obvious comparison.

Listing 8-3 Class Sortable by Implementing All Members of the ISortable Interface

```
Implements ISortable
Option Explicit

Private Temp As Variant
Private Data() As Integer

Private Property Get ISortable_GetItemAt(index As Integer) As Variant
    'lets the sortable stuff be generic by returning variants
    ISortable_GetItemAt = Data(index)
End Property

Private Sub ISortable_SetItemAt(index As Integer, foo As Variant)
    Data(index) = foo
End Sub

Private Property Get ISortable_IsLessThanAtIndex(A As Integer, _
B As Integer) As Boolean
    If Data(A) <= Data(B) Then
       ISortable_IsLessThanAtIndex = True
    Else
       ISortable_IsLessThanAtIndex = False
    End If
End Property

Private Sub Class_Initialize()
    ReDim Data(1 To 20)
    Dim I As Integer
    For I = 1 To 20
     Data(I) = 20 - I
    Next I
End Sub

Private Property Get ISortable_LowerBound() As Integer
    ISortable_LowerBound = LBound(Data)
End Property
```

```
Private Property Get ISortable_UpperBound() As Integer
    ISortable_UpperBound = UBound(Data)
End Property

Private Sub ISortable_Swap(I As Integer, J As Integer)
    Temp = Data(I)
    Data(I) = Data(J)
    Data(J) = CInt(Temp)
End Sub
```

Now we get to the fun stuff. Suppose we want to be able to sort all the forms in a project by their width. We can do this by making a form array class that implements ISortable! We can do this without having to store the actual forms in an array by using an integer that points to the various forms in the Forms collection. For example, we could store all the forms in the Forms collection via:

```
Private Sub Class_Initialize()
    ReDim Data(1 To Forms.Count)
    Dim I As Integer
    For I = 1 To Forms.Count
      Data(I) = I - 1  ' use an integer array to keep
                       ' track of the forms
    Next I
End Sub
```

Now we can write the needed compare routine by using the Data array as follows:

```
Private Property Get ISortable_IsLessThanAtIndex(A As _
Integer, B As Integer) As Boolean
'as a test uses the width of the form for the comparison
    If Forms(Data(A)).Width <= Forms(Data(B)).Width Then
      ISortable_IsLessThanAtIndex = True
    Else
      ISortable_IsLessThanAtIndex = False
    End If
End Property
```

Here's all the code for the class that lets us sort the forms:

Listing 8-4   Complete Code for Class that Enables Us to Sort

```
Option Explicit

Implements ISortable  'so need the ISortable_ methods!

Private Temp As Variant  ' to store possible switches
Private Data() As Integer

Private Property Get ISortable_GetItemAt(index As Integer) As Variant
    ISortable_GetItemAt = Data(index)
End Property

Private Sub ISortable_SetItemAt(index As Integer, foo As Variant)
    Data(index) = foo
End Sub

Private Property Get ISortable_IsLessThanAtIndex(A As Integer, _
B As Integer) As Boolean
'as a test uses the width of the form for the comparison
    If Forms(Data(A)).Width <= Forms(Data(B)).Width Then
       ISortable_IsLessThanAtIndex = True
    Else
       ISortable_IsLessThanAtIndex = False
    End If
End Property

Private Sub Class_Initialize()
    ReDim Data(1 To Forms.Count)
    Dim I As Integer
    For I = 1 To Forms.Count
      Data(I) = I - 1  ' use an integer array to keep track of the forms
    Next I
End Sub

Private Property Get ISortable_LowerBound() As Integer
    ISortable_LowerBound = LBound(Data)   'actually always 1
End Property

Private Property Get ISortable_UpperBound() As Integer
    ISortable_UpperBound = UBound(Data) ' always forms.count + 1
    End Property

Private Sub ISortable_Swap(I As Integer, J As Integer)
    'rather than swap the forms in the collection swap their numbers in the
```

```
' forms collection. Easier!
Temp = Data(I)
Data(I) = Data(J)
Data(J) = Temp
End Sub
```

Finally, to test the routine just add a few forms of different sizes to the project (or load the SortExample from the CH8 directory). The kind of code you then need to get the example off the ground needs to create a class of the type that implements ISortable. For example, here's what we do in the cmdFormTest_Click procedure to get us started:

```
Dim TestForm As New FormArray
Dim SortModule As New SortIt
Dim SortingObject As ISortable
Set SortingObject = TestForm
SortModule.Sort SortingObject
```

Again, notice the use of a temporary parameter of type ISortable that we use to pass to the sorting routine (SortIt) an object of the correct type. Once this code is processed the forms have been sorted by size in the sense that the integers that represent the forms are in their correct order. To see the results of the sort, we use code like this:

```
For I = 1 To Forms.Count
    Forms(SortingObject.GetItemAt(I)).Top = 1000 * I
    Forms(SortingObject.GetItemAt(I)).Left = 1500 * I
Next I
```

which moves the Forms in the order indicated by the sorting routine. (See Figure 8-12.) Here's the rest of the code for the cmDFormTest_Click.

```
Private Sub cmdFormTest_Click()
    Dim TestForm As New FormArray
    Dim SortModule As New SortIt
    Dim SortingObject As ISortable
    Set SortingObject = TestForm
    SortModule.Sort SortingObject
    Dim I As Integer

    For I = 1 To Forms.Count
        Forms(I - 1).Show
    Next I

    For I = 1 To Forms.Count
```

```
        Forms(SortingObject.GetItemAt(I)).Top = 1000 * I
        Forms(SortingObject.GetItemAt(I)).Left = 1500 * I
    Next I
End Sub
```

Here's the full code we need for the form sorting test:

Listing 8-5   Full Code for Form-Sorting Test

```
Private Sub cmdIntegerTest_Click()
    Dim TestInteger As New IntegerArray
    Dim SortModule As New SortIt
    Dim SortingObject As ISortable
    Set SortingObject = TestInteger
    SortModule.Sort SortingObject
    Dim I As Integer
    Cls
    For I = 1 To 20
        Print SortingObject.GetItemAt(I)
    Next I
End Sub

Private Sub cmdStringTest_Click()
    Dim TestString As New StringArray
    Dim SortModule As New SortIt
    Dim SortingObject As ISortable
    Set SortingObject = TestString
    SortModule.Sort SortingObject
    Dim I As Integer
    Cls
    For I = 1 To 20
        Print SortingObject.GetItemAt(I)
    Next I
End Sub

Private Sub Form_Load()
  Load Form2
  Load Form3
  Load Form4
End Sub
```

Making a Copy of an Object (Cloning)

One of the problems you will often run into is how to make a copy of an object. You know that the Set keyword won't do it:

```
Set Object1 = Object2
```

since this kind of code simply makes the Object1 variable point to the area of memory used by Object2 variable. If you change the state of Object 1 then the state of Object 2 will change as well.

A *clone* (sometimes called a *deep* copy), on the other hand, is an object that starts out the same but has the ability to diverge over time. (Dolly's clone will certainly diverge over time from Dolly.) Cloning an object is never easy. It is up to the designer of the class to supply a clone method if he or she wants to. It is easier to implement a clone in some classes than in others. For example, it is almost trivial to clone one of our smart arrays from Chapter 7. Just add a clone method to the original class as follows:

```
Public Function CloneMe() As SmartArray
   Dim TempArray As New SmartArray, I As Integer
   For I = 1 To mItemsInArray
      TempArray.ItemAt(I) = Me.ItemAt(I)
   Next
Set CloneMe = TempArray
End Function
```

Notice that we could even simplify the key line to:

```
TempArray(I) = Me.(I)
```

and that all the other necessary manipulations, such as adjusting the size of the TempArray, are handled automatically by the SmartArray class.

Okay, that was pretty easy, let's try to add a CloneMe method to our StringCollection class. The first step in adding a Clone Function to one of our specialized collections is easy:

```
Public Function CloneMe() As New StringCollection
   Dim TempCollection As New StringCollection, Item As _
Variant
   For Each Item in mCollection
      TempCollection.Add Item
   Next
   Set CloneMe = TempCollection
End Function
```

At this point TempCollection has a copy of all the items in the internal collection used for the String Collection. Or does it? Actually, this code won't even run. There are two very serious problems with this code. The first one is that we would be trying to add variants to a string collection. That one is easy to fix with the CStr function:

```
Public Function CloneMe() As New StringCollection
   Dim TempCollection As New StringCollection, Item As
Variant
   For Each Item in mCollection
     TempCollection.Add CStr(Item)
   Next
   Set CloneMe = TempCollection
End Function
```

Unfortunately we are still not done. Remember in the original design of the string collection we overrode the Add method so that it requires a key? Well, this line:

```
TempCollection.Add CStr(Item)
```

isn't following that rule so it won't even compile. We need to have some way of extracting the key from an item.

Oops, there's no way to do that without changing our string class to be not *a collection of strings* but a collection of "keyed string objects." That is, we would need to set up a class to hold our strings as data but that also allowed us to get the key as a property of the class. Of course, we would have to be very careful to keep the keys unique. The moral of the story is that cloning even as simple a class as our string collection class is highly non-trivial.

Tip

A class with only cloneable private instance fields is easy to clone. For example, if the private instance fields are one of the basic types such as strings or a numeric type, it is trivial to clone the object. Simply copy the private data to the clone. If the private instance fields are objects themselves, then they must support the cloning operation otherwise you are in for a difficult (probably impossible) time. For example, if the designers of the Collection class in Visual Basic had added a clone method to the collection class, cloning our StringCollection class would have been trivial.

Persistence

Persistence can be thought of as a special case of cloning. (Some people would say vice versa.) Only now instead of making a clone within a running project you want to store the clone in a disk file or in a stream of bytes that you can send over the net. Some objects in Visual Basic, such as ActiveX controls, come with the ability to persist their state fairly easily, for other objects you have to roll your own.

First, if you can't clone the object don't even bother to try to make its state persist. So, just as with cloning if all of the data in the instance fields for your object are one of the simple data types such as strings or integers, persistence is no harder to do than cloning. You merely have to write the data out to a file and then read it back in. Your objects simply have to have methods for writing and reading back the information. For example, for a simple employee class with only the instance fields like HireData, Salary and the like, you can do something as trivial as:

```
Sub PersistMe(FileName As String)
   Dim FileNumber As Integer
   FileNumber = FreeFile
   Open FileName For Output As #FileNumber
   Write #FileNumber, mName
   'etc etc
```

This kind of naive way of achieving persistence works very well until instance fields are objects—even if they are cloneable objects. For example, consider the case that a manager is sharing a secretary with another manager. If you proceed naively, you will end up with two copies of the secretary's data stored on your disk or sent over the net. This may not seem so bad but imagine a sophisticated OOP system where one object was used by millions of other objects. You would not want to write a million copies of that shared object's data to your disk or send a million copies of the same byte stream over the net!

The solution is ultimately to think of the information not being stored in a simple "flat" sequential file but rather in a database table (or tables). You can then use the ability of the database to make joins to eliminate redundancy where necessary. Moreover, you can use VB's database ability (through, for example, the Jet engine) to store the persisted information easily and efficiently. For example, the table used for an employee database might look like Table 8-1.

Table 8-1	Table for an Employee Database					
Employee Number	*Name*	*Type*	*Salary*	*HireDate*	*Social Security Number*	*Secretary*
1	Bill	Manager	10000000	1/1/70	123-45-6789	3
2	Steve	Manager	5000000	1/1/75	123-46-6789	3
3	Harry	Secretary	1000000	1/1/70	123-47-6789	Null
4	Sally	Manager	1000000	1/1/70	123-48-6789	Null
5	Dave	Programmer	1000000	1/1/70	123-49-6789	Null
6	Gary	Programmer	1000000	1/1/70	123-05-6789	3

The idea, of course, is that we use the database capabilities to avoid redundancy.

Note

COM itself comes with sophisticated methods for achieving persistence but these are not available very easily to VB programmers.

Under the Hood: A Bird's Eye View of COM (=ActiveX)

First off, COM and ActiveX are really two names for the same technology. Microsoft uses ActiveX because it has more of a marketing pizzazz. (The older version of this technology was called OLE.) We prefer calling it COM since it is really about a way of doing objects—the *common object model*.

On the surface, COM is designed to solve what seems like an insoluble problem:

- How can a stream of bytes stored on a disk or sent over the net provide functionality to your machine?

Before we can even hope to give you even a rough idea of how this is possible we need to go deep into the underpinnings of how a computer works. The idea of a so-called "Von Neumann" computer (which are all the computers you ever deal with) is that the memory of your computer holds bits (on-off) and these bits can be combined into bytes. Two bytes, in turn, can be combined into "words." Each byte (or sometime word) is either data or an instruction to the machine. The convention for an executable program under DOS (and Windows too, for that matter) is that the first byte of a program was the starting instruction, so the operating system could simply "jump" to this memory location to start a program.

The trouble is that in an object-oriented world (COM, remember, stands for the common object model), the code you work with isn't so much an executable as an "object factory" that provides objects (services) to other parties. Your hard disk is filled with these object factories. When you have a line like:

```
Dim ExcelApp As New Excel.Application
```

how can you get at the many services that Excel can provide you? How do you even know what they are? The answer that COM comes up with is made up of two parts:

- A standard way analogous to "jumping" to the first byte to find out what services an object factory can supply.
- An identifier that is "unique across space and time" to identify object factories uniquely.

Let's take up the second point first since it is easier. You think that the name of rich text box is "RichTextBox," after all, that is what the TypeName function returns. Well, it ain't true. This is a human understandable version of its name. Its real name is:

```
{3B7C8860-D78F-101B-B9B5-04021C009402}
```

No matter what language you are running Windows on, no matter what machine you look at, if they have Microsoft's rich text box control, this *GUID* (globally unique identifier) is the name of the rich text box control. GUIDs are generated by an algorithm that is guaranteed to give you a different one no matter how many classes people create.

Note

One of the things that setting "binary compatibility" for a control does is make sure that the new version of the control uses the same GUID as the old. If it didn't then nobody would know that the new control was supposed to replace the old.

Anyway, your *registry* stores the GUIDs along with the names of the files that can create objects of that type. (You can look in HKEY_CLASSES_ROOT to see all these GUID's—see Chapter 12 for more on the registry.) Roughly speaking, when you add a rich text box to a form, VB does the following:

1. It looks in the registry for the GUID for the richtx32.ocx.
2. This will tell it where the file for the OCX was stored on your machine.
3. It then loads the code.

However, we have put off the really hard question: GUIDs combined with the registry let you get the code into memory, they don't have anything to do with how the object factory can provide (or tell you) about any services it can offer you. How can you ever find out what services (properties and methods in this case) the rich text box has?

The way COM deals with this very difficult problem is a sophisticated generalization of the "jump to the first byte and everything will happen automagically" approach used for an executable. Instead of using the first byte, COM specifies that every COM object must have three special places in its code to which other objects can go. These three places are the starting point for functions that:

1. Specify what services the code can provide.
2. Add to a counter so that the object factory knows how many people are using its services.
3. Subtract from the counter used in step 2. When a calling program finishes with the object factory, the "reference count" is correct. When the reference count is zero, COM knows the object factory is no longer in use and the memory can be reclaimed.

The way Step 1 works is that every COM object has a function called QueryInterface to which COM always knows how to jump. QueryInterface tells you about all the interfaces that the object factory can provide.

Note

What QueryInterface really does is give you a way of getting at the locations of the other interfaces so you can ask them what they do.

In fact, the jargon says that QueryInterface returns a pointer to a table of other functions. The pointer lets you get at the information in this table since a pointer is simply a memory location. Steps two and three are called the AddRef and Release functions. In sum:

- A COM (ActiveX) object is simply any object factory that supports QueryInterface, AddRef, and Release functions in a standard way.

The key, though, for people who use COM is that the QueryInterface function gives you a pointer to a table of interfaces that the object supports. For example, when we have lines like:

```
Dim Sally As New Manager
Dim TempData As IEmployee
Set TempData = Sally
```

1. COM will call the QueryInterface function on the Manager object factory.
2. See if one of the interfaces that the Manager object factory supports is IEmployee.
3. If this is the case, COM returns a "pointer" to this interface. VB can use this pointer to get at the functions in the IEmployee interface.

Finally, the COM specification also uses GUIDs to identify interfaces, that's why you can't change the interface contract. If you did, the GUID would no longer identify the object uniquely!

Note

COM is a very difficult subject to get into, and even at Microsoft, people who understand all of its ins and outs are at a premium. The standard reference is Craig Brockschmidt's "Inside OLE2," Microsoft Press, 1995. This book is essentially unreadable unless you have a strong C/C++ background and isn't easy even then. A gentler introduction to the underlying technologies for COM/ActiveX may be found in David Chapell's "Understanding ActiveX and OLE," Microsoft Press, 1996, which we recommend highly.

WHO'S ON FIRST?

We can't resist ending this rather heavy chapter with a comic interlude (with apologies to Abbott and Costello). The convention that all COM interfaces begin with a capitol I must have inspired many versions of the famous Abbott and Costello routine "Who's on first." Here's the start of our version:

Once upon a time in a rainy kingdom, the King calls his chief Wizard, whose name is Paul, in for an audience.

The King: Paul, you are in charge of my language institute. You know I have a great love for that subject, before I became the King, I worked with my friend, the other Paul, on inventing the BASIC language for making spells easier. You have been working on making my language an even more powerful language for deep and darker spells.

Paul: Yes, we have added a nifty new word called Implements that allows us to create new faces in your language that we can reveal to the world.

The King: What kind of faces will you now reveal to the world? What is the most powerful face?

Paul: ICantTellYou

The King: What do you mean you can't tell me? I am the king. I can have your head. Tell me the name of the most powerful faces you are creating.

Paul: IToldYou, ICantTellYou

The King: (*losing patience*) How dare you be so rude, I can have your head. All right, what face is your team leader and wise man Matt working on?

Paul: IDontKnow

The King: What do you mean you don't know, what sort of team leader are you? I want a complete list of the faces you are working on.

Paul: IToldYou, ICantTellYou, ILikeYouThough

The King: (*interrupting*) I don't care if you like me, I can have your head, you are lucky all I am doing is demoting you to peon and taking you away from ruling the language institute. This is your last chance, what are the faces you and your team are working on?

Paul: (*confused*) IToldYou, ICantTellYou, IDontCare, IAmFullyVested.

TESTING AND DEBUGGING

Topics in this Chapter

- On to Debugging
- Debugging in Code

Chapter 9

To this point we have described the perfect world where code didn't need to be tested because it was always assumed to be bug-free. This chapter moves into the real world of buggy code! We cover general techniques for testing and debugging (later chapters cover techniques that are specific to the type of project covered in those chapters).

Testing requires both organized and extensive execution of the code you have written. Make sure that all code paths in your control are tested by having them all processed by the host application. This has to be done by running an exhaustive set of scenarios on the code. Realistically, though, testing is one aspect of a project that is never really finished, so you also must know when good enough is good enough and just ship it. (The SendKeys statement you saw in Chapter 5 can help automate the process as can use of a product like Microsoft Test.)

On to Debugging

Visual Basic is certainly one of the best development environments available when it comes to debugging. One important reason is an extraordinarily useful feature usually called *edit and continue*. After you stop a program in midstream, putting the IDE in what is usually called *break* mode, the edit and continue feature lets you examine and even modify your code and then continue execution from the stopping point or some other point.

Note

You can put a program in break mode either by hitting a breakpoint (see later in the chapter for more on this feature), using a Stop statement in code, or by pressing CTRL+BREAK.

Of course, only breakpoints and the Stop statement give you precise control of what line was being executed when the program stopped.

Tip

When you are in break mode, you can often find the value of a variable by holding the mouse cursor over the variable for a moment. This depends on the variable being in context (VB-speak for the variable being in the scope of the code that was executing when you broke execution). As shown in Figure 9-1, if the variable is in context, a little box will pop up showing the current value of the variable. (You can even highlight an expression and use this feature.)

Figure 9-1   Variable Info in Break mode

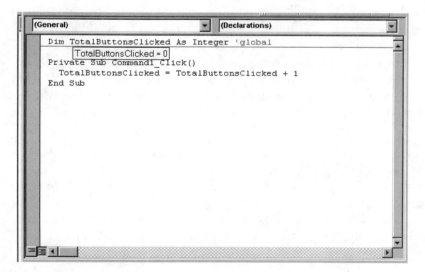

CTRL+BREAK

Pressing CTRL+BREAK (usually) stops the execution of your application and puts Visual Basic into break mode. The IDE will also highlight the current line of executable code if a line of code is executing. However, if the application is not currently executing any code, it will simply go into break mode and no line will be highlighted.

An obvious but important question is, how can your application be running but no code is executing? The most common cause of this is that the application is waiting for input perhaps from the user or another application or module (such as a DLL). If you stop a program in this state, the IDE regards the active form as being in the current scope. So, if you were in this state and entered:

```
Print Caption
```

in the Immediate window, it would display the current form's caption.

Tip

Almost everybody we know uses the ? shortcut for the Print keyword when working in the Immediate window. Just type ? caption and press RETURN and its value will be printed out.

Run/Restart

As you know, pressing F5 is used to run an application from the beginning. However, if you are in break mode, pressing F5 actually makes the application continue from the current line. The way to restart a program from the beginning when you are in break mode is to use SHIFT+F5. (You can also use the equivalent tools on the Standard or Debugging toolbars.)

End

There is no shortcut key for this. It is available on the Run menu and the Debug toolbar. Using the End tool immediately stops the program.

More on the Immediate Window (Debug Window)

If the Immediate window isn't visible, choose View|Immediate window or press CTRL+G. (Although Immediate window is its official name, most people, including us, call it the Debug window or the I-Pane.)

In Visual Basic, you can do more with the Debug window than ever before. For example, in Visual Basic 4.0, you could not execute one of your own procedures unless you were in break mode. With Visual Basic, you can execute any available procedure in your code or VBA simply by typing the proper call statement.

Another thing you can do now is load a form, although the designer for that form must be closed for this to be possible. Of course, the form may not act entirely correctly if it is dependent upon the application to be in a particular state when it is loaded. The really weird thing in this case is that the form is running but the rest of the application is still in an uncompiled, non-running state.

The Debug window is primarily used to evaluate variables and expressions. We use it extensively in break mode after a run-time error has occurred in order to fix the problem code. For example, a common problem is trying to access a character in a string by using a function like Mid with an invalid index such as a negative number, zero or something larger than the length of the string. For example, consider the following code:

```
Function GetMiddleInitial(sName As String) As String
   GetMiddleInitial = Mid$(sName, InStr(sName, ".") - 1, 1)
End Function
```

The problem is that this code assumes the name passed to it will have a period after the middle initial. If it doesn't, a run-time error of "Invalid Procedure Call" will occur and the line of code will be highlighted. At this point, you can evaluate the parts of your code line. For example, if you had passed in John Doe, you would see that InStr(sName, ".") is 0 and thus, subtracting 1 yields –1. This, however, is an invalid index for accessing the characters of a string variable. At this point, you would simply add the following code to the procedure and run it again:

```
If InStr(sName, ".") Then
   GetMiddleInitial = Mid$(sName, InStr(sName, ".") - 1, 1)
End If
```

The ability to do this in break mode makes debugging very efficient.

Tip

A word of caution is needed here. If you make many changes that you want to keep, we suggest you stop the application and save the code before continuing. It is not possible to save your changes while in break mode, so if you happen to crash your application or system, you will lose everything you did while in break mode.

Breakpoints

A breakpoint is a line where you want execution to stop right before Visual Basic is going to process it. To set a breakpoint, go to an executable line of code and press F9 or left-click in the left margin. A (red) dot, as shown in Figure 9-2, will appear in the margin of the line. This dot indicates that the breakpoint has successfully been set.

Figure 9-2   A line with a breakpoint set

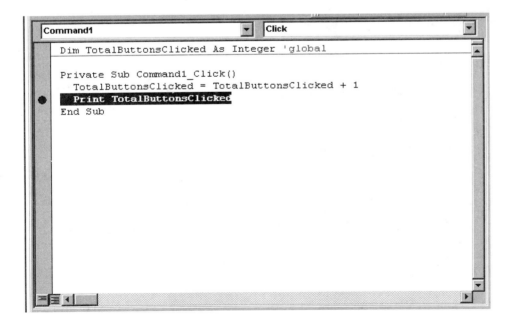

Note

Setting a breakpoint is probably the most common and useful method of stopping code execution. One disadvantage to it, though, is that breakpoints do not persist across programming sessions; you will need to set them up each time you reload the project. (See the section on the Assert method for another way to handle breakpoints that avoids this problem.)

Advanced Breakpoints and Watch Items

There are other ways to tell Visual Basic to break at a certain time that are quite powerful in certain situations. The most common is to use the *watch feature* of the IDE. This, in turn, depends on a concept called a *Watch Point*. As the name suggests, a Watch Point lets you tell the IDE to watch what is going on and stop when something you specify happens. To create a Watch Point, select Debug|Add Watch and the dialog box shown in Figure 9-3 will appear. Notice the Context frame that currently shows (All Procedures). If you drop down the Procedure list box shown in Figure 9-3, you will see a list of all the procedures in the module. This lets you take into account local behavior of a variable if this is necessary. You can also drop down the Module box to change the Module from the current one to some other module in the project.

Figure 9-3   Add Watch dialog box

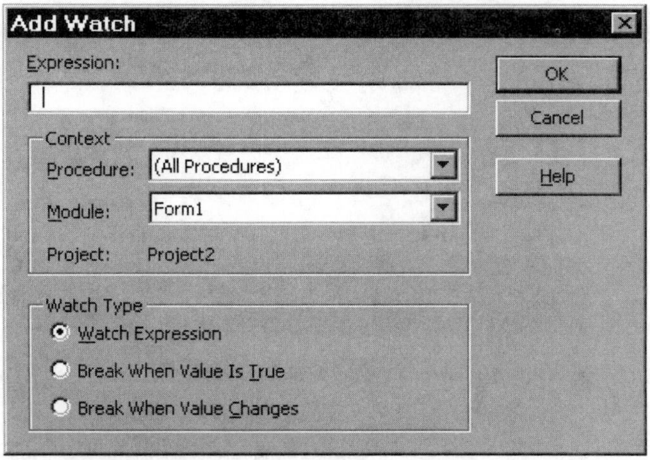

Add Watch

Expression:

Context
Procedure: (All Procedures)
Module: Form1
Project: Project2

Watch Type
⦿ Watch Expression
○ Break When Value Is True
○ Break When Value Changes

OK
Cancel
Help

Next notice that in Figure 9-3, there are three watch types, we describe them next:

Watch Expression

Choosing this simply displays the value of whatever expression you have in the Expression field in the Add Watch dialog box of the Watch window. An example of this was shown in Figure 9-3. Note that Visual Basic defaults to placing what you have highlighted in the Expression box. You can combine this feature with the single step mode to watch the state of an expression continuously.

You can only watch expressions that are in the current scope. For example, if Total was a form level variable, you could watch it while any code attached to the form was evaluating. If Counter was local to a procedure, you could only see its value when you were executing code in that procedure. Try this: Start up a simple form with a command button and put a Static integer counter in the command button Click event and then add the code `Counter = Counter + 1` to this event procedure. Add Counter as a watch expression. Start the form running. At this point, the Counter variable is out of scope so you simply see an <<Out Of Context>> in the Watches window, as shown in Figure 9-4.

Figure 9-4   Watches window out of context variable

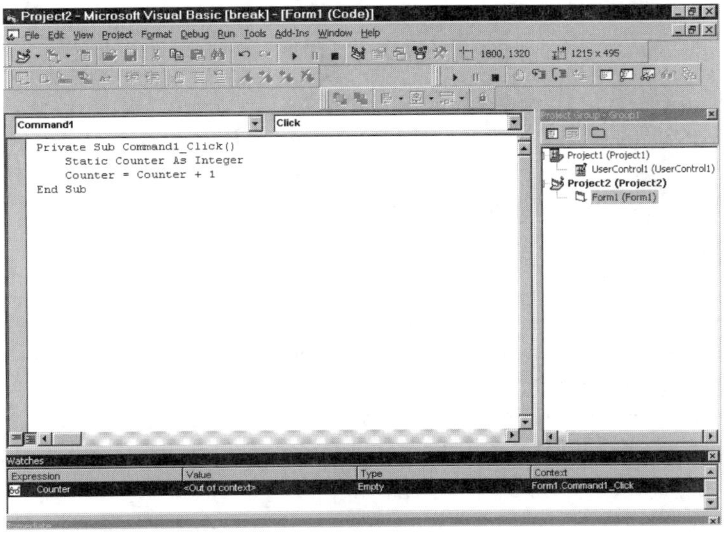

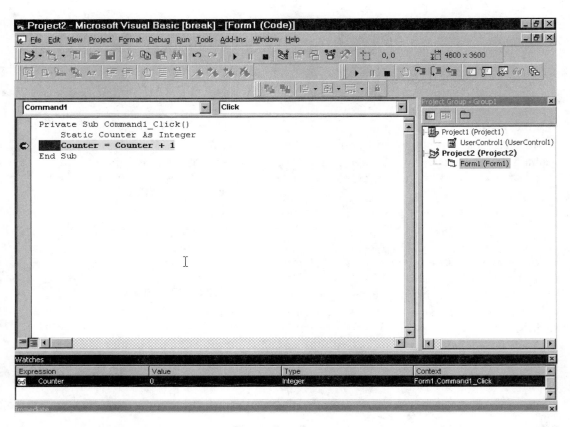

Figure 9-5   Watches window in context

Notice, as in Figure 9-4, that even if a variable is out of context, the Watches window shows you the context of the variable. If you put a breakpoint at the `Counter = Counter + 1` line and start the program again, you can see that the Watches window shows you that the counter is, indeed, initialized to zero. Figure 9-5 illustrates this.

Tip

When you have to debug a class module, you might want to add all the relevant (private) module level instance variables to the Watch window with the (All Procedures) setting. This techniques is the best way we know to get a clear picture of the state of a specific instance of the class. (See Chapter 11 for a detailed example of debugging a class module.)

Break When True

This method lets you stop the program and go into break mode when an expression becomes True. This is quite useful when you want to break inside a loop. For example, you can enter a variable or an expression like Text1.Enabled or I = 3, and when the expression becomes True (nonzero), Visual Basic will stop the program at the line *following* the one that made the expression True.

Break When Expression Changes

The third method lets you make Visual Basic stop executing a program when a value changes. For example, suppose you are having trouble with a particular flag being reset at a time when you do not want it to be. This is probably caused by an event firing when you didn't expect it. The Break When Expression Changes statement is the watch type that will let you stop the program when a property value changes. You can use it to see where, and probably why, the expression changed so you can ensure that it changes only as you intend.

Stepping Through Code

Pressing F8 allows you to step through the code, that is, execute it on a line-by-line basis. If you use F8 instead of F5 to start a program, you can start stepping through your code from the beginning line (usually in the Form_Initialize, Form_Load events or the Sub Main procedure). You can also use F8 to step through the code one line at a time, starting from the current breakpoint. Stepping through code is extremely useful for checking your logic on a line-by-line basis.

Since you often want to consider a call to another procedure as one step, the IDE has the SHIFT+F8 combination as well as the F8 key. SHIFT+F8 will step over subprocedures. For example, suppose you make Sub Main the start-up code instead of the Form_Initialize, then in the following code, you might even add numbering in the code to illustrate the order of the execution.

```
Sub Main()
  Dim i As Integer
  For i = 0 to 10
    Debug.Print MySub(i)
  Next
End Sub
Function MySub(i As Integer) As String
  Debug.Print I am in Mysub
  MySub = "Item Number " & i
End Function
```

Pressing F8 would step into MySub every time through the loop and, therefore, would require two more uses of F8 to get out of the loop. Using SHIFT+F8 would execute the line in Sub Main with the call to MySub, but you would never have to move through the lines of MySub individually.

Tip

If you inadvertently step into a subroutine, you can simply press SHIFT+CTRL+F8 to step "out" and return to the line after the call.

The final way to use the IDE's stepping features is to choose "Run To Cursor" off the Debug menu or use the shortcut CTRL+F8. As the name suggests, you use this by moving the cursor to a place in your code, then pressing CTRL+F8. The IDE will execute all the code up to that line. One example of where this feature is useful is when you want to run to the end of a loop. Simply click on the line after the Next statement (in our example code) and press CTRL+F8. All of the code in the loop will be executed and you will stop at the line immediately after the loop.

Note

Statements such as GoTo, Exit Sub, or Exit For may cause execution to bypass your cursor location, so you want to make sure this type of code is not present when you use this feature.

Set Next Statement

Pressing CTRL+F9 on an executable line in the current procedure will make it the next statement to execute. This is extremely useful after you have modified a line of code and want to execute it again. Make sure that all variables have the value you expect them to at this point so the code executes as expected.

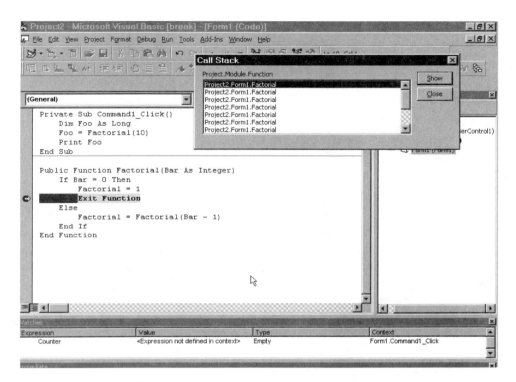

Figure 9-6   The Call Stack window for a recursion

Call Stack

The Call Stack dialog box (an example of which is shown in Figure 9-6) is very useful when you need to figure out how you got to where you are. It will show you every function call in the current path of code execution. One common example of where this is helpful is when you are debugging a recursive program where it is not readily apparent that it was recursive in the first place. The call stack will be full of the same calls over and over again, which is a very good indication of a recursion in place.

Debugging in Code

In addition to the built-in debugging features in the IDE, it is possible to add code to your application to aid in debugging. The following are the statements used specifically for debugging.

Stop Statement

This is a line of code that stops execution when it is hit, which is very useful when you need a breakpoint to persist across debugging sessions. Make sure not to leave any of these in the finished code as they will produce a run-time error. Also consider using the newer Assert statement described later instead.

MsgBox Statement

Placing MsgBox statements in your code is probably the oldest method of debugging because they produce visual notification of what the application is doing. Make sure to remove them as well.

Caution

One thing to be aware of when using message boxes to debug is that they sometimes don't interact well with other Windows events. For example, if you add a MsgBox call to a control's MouseDown event, you may not get the MouseUp and Click events. (Professionals say that message boxes "consume" extra Windows messages. The result is that you may not get events that would normally be fired.)

Debug.Print

This is not as visual as a MsgBox but also not as intrusive. The output simply goes to the Debug window in the IDE. You can see all the things you printed to the Debug window simply by scrolling through the window. These statements are ignored by the compiler and, therefore, have no impact on the execution of the final control.

Assert

The idea of the new Assert method of the Debug object is borrowed from the C language. This method can be an extremely useful debugging tool once you get used to the idea of using it routinely. It is simply a statement to the IDE that "I claim this statement is True. If it is not, stop the program at that point and tell me." This means you can use a line of code like:

```
Debug.Assert TestExpression
```

and you will have an automatic breakpoint when TestExpression first becomes False. In particular, you can use:

```
Debug.Assert False
```

for the equivalent of a Stop statement. (The advantage to using the Assert method instead of a Stop statement is that since it belongs to the Debug object, it has no effect on the final OCX.)

Conditional Compilation

Visual Basic has the ability to compile different branches of your code depending on the state of various flags. This is usually called *conditional compilation*. The advantage to conditional compilation is that code that is excluded by using conditional compilation is not in the final executable file. In particular, it has no size or performance effect. For example, to include "debug code," as it is usually called, your code needs to include a block like the following:

```
#If InDebug Then
    'Place statements that will be used only under
    'debugging here.
    '
#Else
    'Place non-debug statements here
#End If
```

(Notice the similarity to an ordinary If-Then-Else. There is even an #ElseIf if you need it.)

Note

The Option Compare statement doesn't affect the tests in an #If. Visual Basic always uses case-insensitive comparisons in an #If.

You can define your own compiler constants at any point by defining an ordinary constant. Here's an example:

```
#Const InDebug = True
```

Notice that you use the # to define a conditional compiler constant. Conditional compiler constants defined in code belong to the form control or module in which they appear—they cannot be global (public) in scope.

Note

If you need to define conditional compiler constants that affect the whole project, choose Project|Project Properties and fill in the appropriate line of the Make tab. (Separate multiple compiler constants by colons.)

Debugging and Error Handlers

Having an active error handler (see Chapter 5) can make debugging confusing and more difficult. After all, getting in a situation where you are dividing by zero is probably a bug and you shouldn't use an error handler to replace weeding out the bad code. The problem is that the active error handler will prevent you from even knowing that such a bug was in your code. The cure for this is to do some of your testing and debugging with all error handlers inactive. To do this:

1. Go to the Tools|Option dialog box.
2. Click on the General tab.
3. Check the "Break on all errors" check box.

Once this option is checked, the IDE will disable all error handlers and go into break mode when any error is encountered. This is certainly more convenient than commenting out all the error handling code!

If this is too drastic, check the "Break on unhandled errors," which will only take you to break mode when you don't explicitly handle the error.

Tip

The remaining option on this tab "Break in class module" is especially useful when you are debugging a class module or control. (Or, for that matter any code that refers to objects—even if those objects come from outside Visual Basic.) The problem is that when you use an object, it may generate an error. You may not want this error silently handled by the object. It is often more useful, if the object you are referring to generates an error, to know about it at the place in your VB code that called the object. When this option is checked, Visual Basic breaks at the code that referenced the object that gave the error. (However, usually all Visual Basic can do is report a generic error. This is because it doesn't know enough about the internal makeup of the object it calls to do much else. Visual Basic will most often use Err.Number = 440 for any error in an object outside itself.)

OPTIMIZATION AND PROFILING

Topics in this Chapter

- Starting the Optimization Process
- Perceived Speed versus Real Speed
- Local Code Optimizations
- Reducing the EXE Size
- Reducing Your Application's Memory Requirements While It's Running
- The Visual Basic Code Profiler (VBCP)

Chapter 10

You have your VB code running. Is it running as fast as it could? Probably not, but the real questions you should always ask are: Does it matter? Do your *users* care?

> We *should* forget about small efficiencies, say about 97% of the time: Premature optimization is the root of all evil. Yet we should not pass up opportunities in that critical 3%.
>
> —Donald Knuth [1]

The end of this chapter will show you how to identify that critical (and often elusive) three percent that Knuth was talking about. We will do this by introducing you to one of the least well known tools that VB ships with: the VBCP ("Visual Basic Code Profiler"). (Profilers make it easy to determine bottlenecks in your code by letting you see how much time certain code took to execute.)

However, we'll start off with ways to make your users *think* that your application is running faster than it really is. Most of these techniques depend on preloading data and graphics while the user is concentrating on some other

---

1. From his famous article "Structured Programming with Go To Statements" in *Current Trends in Programming Methodology*, Vol. 1. Edited by R. Yeh. (Prentice Hall, 1977). Donald Knuth is the author of the monumental series of books called *Fundamental Algorithms*. (Algorithms are the methods that one uses to solve problems like how to sort data or search through lists.)

activity. Next, you'll see techniques that are risk free and relatively painless to implement but using them will speed up your code. (Most of them are also considered as better programming style by experienced VB programmers as well.) For example, using integers instead of variants in loop counters is always a win, occasionally a big win. Not repeatedly assigning to or reading from a property of a control is also usually a (very) big win. Once you get used to these techniques, they become second nature. It is these kinds of techniques that often are all you need to improve the speed of that crucial three percent to acceptable levels.

Having said that, we do need to point out the big wins for improving the code may come from changing the way you deal with the data and require changing the *algorithm* you are using. Doing a linear search on an ordered list is absurd. One sorting method can literally be 1000 times faster than another on a large array. The trouble is that choosing the fastest algorithm—the fastest method for solving your problem—depends on the problem and data with which you are working. There is no perfect algorithm, for example some of the slower sorts are actually faster if the data you will be working with is in some special form. We will have to leave the problem of fast algorithms and good data structures for VB programming to another book. (Chapter 11 shows you how to implement the data structures that you can dig up out of books like the one by Knuth in pure VB. You can also usually trust commercial libraries to make a good, if not perfect, choice in the algorithms they give you.)

Starting the Optimization Process

The programmers guide supplied with VB says the following:

> It is a common misconception that optimization is a process that takes place at the end of the development cycle. To create a truly optimized application, you must be optimizing it while you are developing it. You choose your algorithms carefully, weighing speed against size and other constraints; you form hypotheses about what parts of your application will be fast or slow, large or compact; and you test those hypotheses as you go.

There is a lot of truth in this. There will almost always be a trade-off between size and speed, for example. But the main point they seem to be making is misleading at best and false at worse. We think the guide is confusing two kinds of optimization—we like to call them "local" optimization versus "global" optimization. The algorithm you chose to sort an array is a local choice. Your code should simply have a call like this:

```
ProjectSortingLibrary.Sort ThisArray()
```

When you are developing your project you shouldn't care what sorting algorithm you have in the ProjectSortingLibrary.cls (or more likely what kind of sorting algorithm is in the sorting library that was given to you.) Object oriented code is modular by its very nature. In a properly designed object oriented program, you should be able to plug the code for a new sorting algorithm into the sorting library class without the user of the class knowing it ever happened. The messages remain the same, the new sort algorithm still sorts after all. Even for equally quick algorithms there may be two choices and one works better in your specific case but why worry about it at the beginning? (For example, quick sort and tree sort are equally fast but using tree sort takes extra memory. On the other hand, if you have the data stored in a fairly balanced binary tree (see the next chapter) already, then tree sort is the right choice since you have done all the work already.)

What the guide *is* right about is that the "global" structure of your project is worth thinking about before you start coding. After all, it is not easy to change the class design—the global structure—of your project down the road. It is worth spending some extra time at the design stage to make sure that the classes you are building are easy to optimize!

In the first draft of this chapter, we wrote:

- Before optimizing a program it has to be as bug-free as possible.

However, in the spirit of what is correct in the programmers guide, we want to change this to read:

- Before optimizing a program (on the local level) it has to be as bug-free as possible.

Of course, we are not even sure that you should be writing code when you are thinking about optimizing code at the global level—paper and pencil, index cards for the classes, and a dash of pseudo-code often can't be beat. We feel pretty strongly that worrying about whether you are using the right sorting algorithm in a program that isn't yet working the way it is supposed to is counterproductive at best and just stupid at worst. Your program doesn't work yet, you have tons of debugging code embedded in the project and you are thinking about optimizing it on a line-by-line or call-by-call basis?

> **Note**
>
> *This doesn't mean that you shouldn't be thinking about writing code that is easy to optimize nor does it mean that you shouldn't avoid silly slow-downs like using variants for loop counters.*

Next, and perhaps most important ask yourself—twice:

- Is it really necessary to optimize this program?

As we said before, the rule should be that you only optimize a program if its speed or resource requirements are unacceptable *to the user*. (You can usually optimize for speed or resource requirements, it is unlikely that you can do both.)

This works both ways—you can't assume everyone has a Pentium II with 64 MB of RAM! For a machine with 64 MB of RAM, having lots of large arrays around in your code or relying on OLE automation is not usually a problem. For a machine with 8 MB of RAM, either of these techniques may result in unacceptable delays. In any case, from bitter experience, we know how easy it is to fall into the trap that Knuth points out. Optimizing for optimization's sake often results in code that is *much* harder to maintain or code that is filled with subtle bugs that don't show up in routine testing (or more likely both).

Perceived Speed versus Real Speed

There is always a question of perceived speed versus real speed. The VB team worked extraordinarily hard at making forms display faster—and they succeeded. The start-up form in VB5 displays many times faster than it did in earlier versions of VB. However, you still need to have the Visual Basic Virtual Machine loaded before that form will show up. Since msvbvm50.dll is a 1.3 MB file, this can take some time. If this file isn't currently in memory, your users will *think* that there was a long wait for the start-up form to show up even though what they were really waiting for the msvbvm50.dll file to load. There is no way around this, you obviously need the VB run-time DLL loaded. There is, however, a trick you can occasionally use to make it *seem* like the problem has gone away.

OPTIMIZING THE DEVELOPMENT (AND MAINTENANCE) PROCESS

Programmers sometimes forget that there is another side to the optimization process: optimizing *the time you and your colleagues spend now and will spend in the future on the code*. Your predecessor may have used a lot of tricky code in order to get a few percent improvement only to leave a nightmarish maintenance problem for you. Using API calls may speed up your program a bit but they make your program easier to crash and harder to debug.

Writing code is sometimes a lot like buying stereo equipment: the last one percent of improvement often costs 10 times what the first 99 percent did. You *may* be able to hand code a spell checker that works faster than one supplied as a commercial control, but it might take you a month to find out you couldn't or that after all that hard work you got a whopping three percent improvement in your application.

On the other hand, if you are using a large third-party control or library for a simple task it may be that coding it in VB5 from scratch is the better choice. If all you need is a simple editor, using a text box or a rich text box will make your project run a lot faster than using a third-party custom editing control with a 100 properties and a few 100k byte footprint. (Visual Basic 5.0 has been improved so much that you may find that operations that you previously used outside tools for can be done more efficiently with VB's own tools and controls.)

- Load a compiled VB project when the user starts up Windows.

(It doesn't even have to do anything.) The point is that people do not notice when their machine takes a few extra few seconds to boot up! By having a compiled VB project in the user's start-up directory, you know that all 1.3 MB of the VB run-time DLL is happily sitting in memory and therefore subsequent VB programs will be perceived as loading much faster. (This trick works especially well when you are working in an office environment and using VB for custom projects for that office.)

Don't forget little things like changing the mouse pointer to an hourglass while the code is in the midst of a time-consuming operation. If the operation is *really* going to take a lot of time, consider programming a progress indicator to show the user that something is happening. (Make the progress bar sufficiently granular: the Windows 95 Find New Hardware progress bar is notorious for not doing this. It often seems like it is not moving when it is just working away on plug and pray.)

Tip

When you change the mouse pointer there are a few points to keep in mind:

- *You need to make sure to reset the mouse pointer in the event of a run-time error that causes your code to jump to an error handler and then exit the procedure. This is best done with a global error handler routine that displays the error and resets the mouse pointer (See Chapter 5 for more info on error handlers).*

- *In a multitasking environment, such as Windows 95 or Windows NT, the hourglass shows up only when the focus is in your application. If they move away, they stop getting any visual feedback that your application is still working. There is not much you can do about this except to consider using something more substantial that just a pointer change to notify the user that your application is busy.*

Simplify Your Start-Up Form

Simple splash screens are the way to go. The more complicated a form is, the longer it takes to load. You certainly don't want the Form_Initialize and Form_Load of the start-up form to be very complicated. When VB loads a form for the first time, all the code in the Form_Initialize and Form_Load events will be processed before the user will see the form. The code in the Form_Initialize event has to be processed but you can change VB's default behavior of code in the Form_Load event:

1. Use the Show method in the Form_Load.
2. Follow the call to show by a call to DoEvents to force the form to finish painting itself.

Here's what the Form_Load for a start-up splash screen form might look like when the main form is called frmMain:

```
Sub Form_Load()
    Show                'or Me.Show-to display start-up form.
    DoEvents            'Ensure start-up form is painted.
    Load frm.Main       ' Load main application form.
    Unload Me           ' Unload start-up form.
    frm.Main.Show       ' Display main form.
End Sub
```

Also, Visual Basic loads code from .BAS modules only when you call a procedure in them. Therefore don't call a lot of module code from your start-up form. Finally, calling in-process DLLs (see Chapter 14) are just as fast as calling code that is an actual part of the application. You might want to think about breaking out the nonvisual parts of your application into DLLs and then calling them as needed instead of loading all of them at once.

Don't Do Work Unless You Have To

For example, you are loading a Treeview control at load time, perhaps you need only to populate the first few levels? Can you wait for the user to click on a node before you populate the children of that node? (This is how the Win95 File Explorer works with its folders.)

Get Data in Appropriate Chunks

If what you are trying to do is get everything out of a sequential file, then using code like this:

```
Input(#FileNumber, LOF(FileNumber) )
```

work a whole lot faster than reading a file back line by line. On the other hand, if what you need is just the first few lines of a file, a line-by-line approach is better and will seem faster to the user. (E-mail programs are best when they give you the option of getting either the whole messages or only the headers, for example.) Also, while we are on the subject of getting information off a disk (or from the Net): if you need to go to disk to load several small files, get them all at once. The user won't notice the extra time (or will blame it on their hard disk). The same holds true for downloading files from the Net. For small files, making multiple requests from a server is much more time consuming than making one request for a medium-size .zip file and then decompressing it on the client.

Use Idle Time Wisely

If you use Sub Main to start your application then you can take full advantage of idle time. (In the time someone takes to decide on which menu item they want to click on, a Pentium might be able to add 10,000 numbers together.)

But be sure to have enough DoEvents in your code to make sure that the user doesn't perceive a slowdown in response time if you choose this route. (But be careful that the user doesn't re-enter the loop or shut your application down when you release control to him or her by the DoEvents call!) Code like this works great:

```
Static I As Long
If I Mod 1000 = 0 Then
    DoEvents() 'but remember to stop them from ending the
              'program or reentering
    I = 0
End If
I = I + 1
'back to doing what you wanted to do in idle time
```

For the extra cost of a few integer operations, your user will never notice that their machine is plugging away in idle time. (The programmers guide advocates going this one step further by using a timer control in the form. The idea is that you can do a piece of the work each time the timer goes off. We are not sure whether this is as good an idea as simply using a Sub Main together with the DoEvents command inside the code module as in the fragment indicated above.)

Note

As more applications become true 32 bit, Windows 95 and Windows NT preemptive multitasking feature makes idle time hand-holding code less necessary than it was in Win 3.1 days.

Allow the User to Cancel Time-Consuming Operations

We want to end the section on changing how your user perceives your application with one final technique you might want to consider.

- Give the user a way to cancel time-consuming operations.

This is actually harder (and often more dangerous) to do then you would think. For example, once your code starts a large file I/O operation, VB gives you no way of making it stop. On the other hand, there *is* a way to give users the option of stopping an operation when you are in the middle of a time-consuming loop. We feel that this should be done rarely since it involves some tricky coding and may lead to lots of unforeseen (and perhaps untestable) problems as the user tries to stop your code at various stages of the loop. Here are some things to consider before you choose to allow this option:

- Will breaking out of the loop early mean the application is at a loss for vital data?
- Can the user perform potentially harmful operations during the needed DoEvents call? (Such as exiting the application or starting another operation inside the same application.)
- Does the user need to be able to redo the operation they just cancelled?
- Does the user need to be able to restart the operation from the point they cancelled it?

Keeping all these questions in mind, here are the steps you can take to add this feature to your code.

1. Add a module-level cancellation flag variable to the module.
2. Add a line of code to initialize the flag prior to entering the loop.
3. Add the test of the flag into the loop code logic.
4. Add a DoEvents to the loop to allow some other code to set the cancellation flag.
5. Add code somewhere else in the application, such as a keyboard handler or button to set the cancellation flag.

Here is an example of this code in a form module.

```
Private mbCancel As Boolean

Private Sub cmdCancelOperation_Click()
  mbCancel = True
End Sub

Private Sub LongOperation(sFile As String)
```

```
   Dim sTmp As String
   Dim f As Integer
   mbCancel = False
   f = FreeFile
   Open sFile For Input As #f
   Do While (Not mbCancel) And (Not Eof(f))
      Line Input #f, sTmp
      Debug.Print sTmp
      DoEvents
   Loop
   Close #f
End Sub
```

Local Code Optimizations

In this section, we want to show you some simple techniques that make your code run faster and won't complicate your code or make it harder to maintain. (In most cases this coding style will actually make your code clearer and *easier* to maintain.) Once you get sufficiently used to them to make them routine, they have no downside.

Note

To drive home the point we will always supply you with timings (using our Timing class from Chapter 7) based on multiple iterations of simple sample code.

Before we begin, though, it is worth stressing that loops are where the pain and gain is most often to be found. You can see this most clearly with what are called loop invariants. If something doesn't change inside the loop, it should be set outside the loop. Consider the following code:

```
Dim I As Long
For I = 1 To 100000
    If Len(Foo) = 0 Then
        ' lots of stuff we used
        TheCount = TheCount + 1

    'let's assume Foo doesn't change
Next I
```

and:

```
Dim I As Long
Bar = Len(Foo)
For I = 1 To 100000
    If Bar  = 0 Then TheCount = TheCount + 1
Next I
```

The latter code takes the loop invariant Len(Foo) out of the loop. The result is that the Len function is called only once—resulting in a 300 percent improvement! (Admittedly, this is a toy example but the point about keeping loop invariants outside of your loops is a real one.)

By the way, just as we did in the code above, don't compare strings to null; check if their length is 0. Not only is:

```
If Len(Foo) = 0 Then …
```

more readable and less error prone than:

```
If Foo = "" Then …
```

It is, surprisingly, also faster. We tried the following two programs:

```
For j = 1 To 10
  For I = 1 To 100000
    If Foo = "" Then TheCount = TheCount + 1
  Next I
Next j

For j = 1 To 10
  For I = 1 To 100000
    If Len(Foo) = 0 Then TheCount = TheCount + 1
  Next I
Next j
```

and found the second one to be 22 percent faster than the first. The reason for this is that VB stores the length of a string directly before the actual string in memory, so comparing this easily retrievable value with zero is much more efficient than loading the string and " " into memory and comparing them.

Next, collections are great—but, as you saw in Chapters 7 and 8 they will slow your program down if not used wisely. Collections work best in a situation where you have a unique key, they should not be used as substitute for an array—even the smart array class that you saw in Chapter 7 is often a better choice if you need to iterate through items frequently.

Finally, use longs and integers as much as possible. (Long arithmetic is just as fast (and sometimes even faster) as integer arithmetic on Pentium class processors. Avoid the single and double type unless you are dealing with decimals. Avoid the currency type completely unless you need the complete accuracy it provides. (Recall that the currency type avoids any round-off error since these variables use scaled integers.) The following table lists the arithmetic speeds for the numeric data types from fastest to slowest.

Table 10-1: Arithmetic Speeds for Numeric Data Types

Numeric data types	Speed
Long	Fastest
Integer	.
Byte	.
Single	.
Double	.
Currency	Slowest

Don't Use Variants Unless You Have To

Consider the simplest possible loop code:

```
Dim I As Variant
For I = 1 To 1000000
   'I is a variant here
Next I
```

as opposed to:

```
Dim I as Long
For I = 1 To 1000000
   'I is a long
Next I
```

The first loop, which uses a variant for the counter, takes around 50 percent longer (.39 versus .27 in the design-time environment.)

There is also a speed-up when you choose the string version of a function that comes in both a variant form and a string form (for example Mid$ versus Mid), although the differences may not be significant. We modified the above code as follows:

```
For I = 1 To 10000
   Temp = Mid("Hello", 1, 1)
Next I
```

as opposed to:

```
Dim I As Integer
For I = 1 To 10000
   Temp = Mid("Hello", 1, 1)
Next I
```

and finally used the correct type for everything:

```
Dim I as Long, Temp As String
For I = 1 To 10000
   Temp = Temp +  Mid$("Hello", 1, 1)
Next I
```

Here the difference was less dramatic—variants for everything took 2.36 seconds, using the correct types took 2.25 seconds—around a five percent improvement. (Using Mid instead of Mid$ took 2.27 versus 2.25 seconds or at most a one percent improvement, by the way.)

Finally, VB5 lets you type the optional arguments to procedure instead of forcing you to use variants. Take advantage of this new feature!

Don't Make Repeated Use of Property Values:

Consider the following two examples:

```
Dim I As Integer
For I = 1 To Len(Text1.Text)
   YourText =  Mid(Text1.Text, I, 1)
Next
```

and:

```
Dim I As Integer, YourText As Text
YourText = Text1.Text
For I = 1 To Len(YourText)
   YourText =  Mid(YourText, I, 1)
Next
```

When we filled a text box with 1000 characters, the former code took 16.37 seconds and the latter took .51 seconds, a mere 3500 percent improvement! (This is actually a special case of the suggestion to eliminate loop invariants.)

The converse is also true: to build up the Text property of a text box, accumulate the information into a temp variable and do one assignment:

```
Dim I As Integer
For I = 1 To Len(MyText)
   Temp = Temp & vbCrLf & Mid(MyText, I, 5)
```

```
Next I
Text1.Text =   Temp
```

runs many times faster than:

```
Dim I As Integer
For I = 1 To Len(MyText)
   Text1.Text = Text1.Text & vbCrLf & Mid(MyText, I, 5)
Next I
```

Code Optimizations That Aren't (Or Are To Be Avoided!)

The programmers guide says you should pass by value instead of by reference into procedures and functions whenever possible because passing by value is faster. Well, we tried it and we couldn't detect any significant change. (Which isn't to say that you should be careful to pass by value if that is what is indicated.) Passing by reference when you need to pass by value can lead to some subtle bugs. This is especially true in recursive procedures.

Next, the manual recommends:

- Replace procedure calls with inline code.

This is usually a horrible decision—one almost guaranteed to make your code harder to maintain.

Optimization for Dealing with Objects

A Visual Basic program is made up of cooperating objects. There are the intrinsic VB objects, custom ActiveX controls, in-process DLLs and possible out-of-process ActiveX servers. (See Chapter 14 for more on these.) The rule is simple:

- Calls to in-process components are almost always faster than calls to out-of-process components, which in turn are faster than calls to remote objects.

This means you should use a cross-process call (to an ActiveX server) only when you need their special properties (like the ability to be multithreaded) or, if you want to break up an extremely time-consuming process into pieces that will be handled by many remote systems. (See Chapter 14 for more on ActiveX servers.) Of course, in-process DLLs must be 32 bit and can't use modal forms but that is usually a small price to pay for their speed advantage. To demonstrate this we made a DLL and an EXE that simply add up the first 100,000 integers and then returns that value. We found that even for this simple example that the EXE (out-of-process) server was about 50 percent slower than the in-process server.

Next, remember that no matter which kind of objects you use:

- Choose early binding over late whenever possible. (See Chapters 7 and 8 for more on early binding versus late binding.)

Reducing the EXE Size

It is nice to think in an age of bloatware that it is possible to optimize an application for size. This is especially useful when applications are delivered over the Net. One idea that VB'ers may try (yes, even after waiting so long for native EXE compilation) is to go back to the tried and true p-code compiler. The p-code version of your application is usually significantly smaller. For example, when we compiled the VisData sample supplied with VB we found that the p-code version was 425k, while the native EXE version was 868k. And, when running them we found the difference in speed hardly noticeable. (By the way, compiling into native code takes about five times as long as compiling into p-code.)

(Cynically speaking.) Of course, the best way to optimize an application for size is to not have your apps suffer from "creeping featuritis." (Did you know that Word 97 has three times as many functions as Word 2.0c did in 1992? How many do you use? Did you know it's about 10 times larger as well?) For example, as we mentioned earlier, don't use a control like HighEdit's amazing word processor in a control if all the functionality that you need is in VB's rich text box. Don't use a rich text box if all the functionality you need can be gotten out of a multiline text box and so on.

Finally, we want to end with an obvious point that can too easily be forgotten in the rush to optimize your application:

- Variable names, comments, and blank lines don't affect your EXE size.

In other words:

- Keeping your code readable doesn't cost you anything.

Next, internationalizing your apps in the era of the Internet is great but resource files may not be the best way to do so. It may be better to recompile the application using the correct bitmaps and strings rather than trying to embed a giant resource file into your application. (Resource files are compiled into the application and so increase its footprint.)

Finally, don't use the same image as the Picture property of more than one control. (The problem is that each image will be compiled into the EXE. Use code at run time to share images instead.)

Tip

The Visual Basic Code Profiler described at the end of this chapter can help you remove "dead" code that may be bloating your application.

Reducing Your Application's Memory Requirements While It's Running

This is related to the problem of building a smaller EXE but, in practice, the solution demands quite different techniques. The smallest EXE, after all, can suddenly demand unlimited resources. Most of the memory requirements for a running application come from three different sources:

- The (large) arrays the application is using

The cure for this is to use dynamic arrays whenever possible. Then, you can use the Erase method to reclaim the memory they used. (For a fixed array, the Erase method only "zeros" out the data. For a dynamic array, you actually get back the memory you were using.)

Note

As always, don't use variants unless you need to. Each number you store in a variant takes 16 bytes, compared to two for an Integer, four for a long or eight for a Double. A variant string is always 16 bytes longer than the comparable string variable. For example, storing an array of 10,000 strings in variants will not only slow your program down, it means that your EXE is taking up an extra 160,000 bytes.

Next, consider

- The memory requirements for a form and its controls.

Here the trade-off is between response time and memory used: Keeping forms loaded at all times obviously makes your application snappier; it will also increase the memory requirements considerably. This is especially true if you have set the AutoRedraw property of the form to be True since this requires VB to keep a bit-by-bit image of the form in memory at all times. (You might also consider setting clipping regions to minimize the memory requirements for your forms.)

Next, what kind of controls you placed on the form can cost you: control arrays loaded as needed will use less memory than adding controls at design time that are left invisible until run time. Image controls use less resources than picture boxes, labels less than text boxes. The shape controls are particularly sparing of Windows resources.

Finally,

- Consider the memory requirements for the images you are using.

If time is not a problem consider loading image data from the user's disk as needed. This will, of course, be much slower than building the information into the program and keeping it in memory all the time but it also means information won't be loaded into memory until it is needed. Note that while a resource file increases the disk footprint of your application, the information contained in it is not loaded into memory until the code calls for it. Next, if you need the same image repeatedly in different places at design time, place it in only one of the objects. As we mentioned before, pictures added at design time are compiled into the EXE. Use code at run time to share the picture, (the new Picture object in VB5 is great for this).

Finally, the .gif, .rle, and .wmf formats take up a lot less space than bitmaps. (But all image formats take up a lot of memory. The exception is formats that use a "lossy" compression scheme like the one used in the .jpeg format.)

The Visual Basic Code Profiler (VBCP)

Okay, you have a nice bug-free program and its time to find that three percent that Knuth was talking about. Both the Professional and Enterprise versions of VB include a nifty utility called the Visual Basic Code Profiler (VBCP) to help you do just that. The profiler may be found in the TOOLS\ Unsupprt\VBCP directory on your VB CD.

The Visual Basic Code Profiler helps you zero in on Knuth's goal by showing you:

1. Which code gets executed the most.
2. How long a line or function takes to execute.

Moreover, you can log this information while you are running your test suites and analyze it at any time.

It is important to remember, however, that timing is relative, not absolute. In a multitasking operating system, it is possible for code timing to be distorted by events external to the application. With this in mind, we advise multiple timing runs to obtain an average performance.

To use the code profiler you have to install it as an Add-In. To do this:

1. Copy the Visual Basic Code Profiler DLL (vbcp.dll) to the Windows\System directory (or any directory in your path).
2. Register the DLL using RegSvr32 by entering the following in the Run box off the Start menu:

```
RegSvr32 vbcp.dll
```

Next:

1. Open up the VBADDIN.INI file found in your \Windows directory.
2. Go to the section marked [Add-Ins32].
3. Add the following line at the end of this section:

```
VBCP.VBCPClass=0
```

Then, the next time you load Visual Basic:

1. Choose Add-Ins|Add-In Manager.
2. Check the VB Code Profiler box.

Note

The Visual Basic Code Profiler assumes that the application you want to profile has all its components in the same directory. If a project is spread across several directories, simply copy all of the necessary files into a single directory and try again.

Most people think of a profiler as simply a tool for performance tuning. The Visual Basic profiler actually can help you with three common problems. It can:

1. Do code profiling (of course).
2. Check code coverage, which also helps in the testing process.
3. Find dead code.

Using the Profiler

The way the profiler works is that it adds timing and hit code to your source code. This lets it keep track of things like how long a function took to execute or how many hits a specific function or line of code got. (Be sure to click on the Remove Profiler code option in Figure 10-1 when you are done or your source code will be filled with lots of extraneous lines of code.) Figure 10-1 shows you the opening screen of the code profiler. As you can see, you can profile Line Timing, Function Timing, Line Hit Count, and Function Hits.

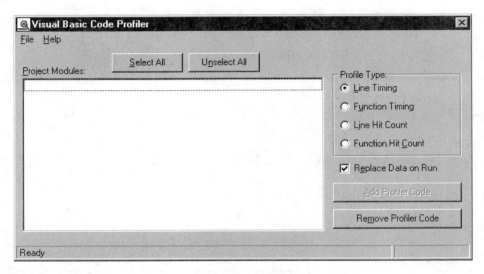

Figure 10-1   The opening screen of the profiler

Note

While the profiler does make a backup so that it can restore your original code, we suggest making your own backup of the source code before running the VBCP on it.

The steps for using the profiler are:

1. Save your project. You have to save the project before you can profile it and the profiler will insist that you save any changes that you have made as well—it pops up a message box telling you if the file is "dirty." (Dirty is jargon for a file with unsaved changes.)

2. Make sure that only the modules you want to profile are checked in the Project Modules box. You *must* include the start-up module or form. (The default is that all the code will be profiled.)

3. Then click the "Add Profiler Code" button.

The VBCP will then add the code it needs to do the kind of profiling you specified for the modules you selected. Then, after the profiler has added the code and reports that it is Ready in its status bar:

1. Close the profiler (optional).
2. Return to your application.

As you can see in Figure 10-2 for one of the sample files supplied with VB, the profiler added lots of lines that begin VBCP_Update to your source. It uses these lines to do its profiling.

Now run your application through its testing suite. (You can run it from the IDE or make an EXE/DLL and run that.) In all cases the VBCP collects the type of profiling information you selected as you test the application. Moreover, it collects the information and stores it in the form of a Jet .mdb database file.

Figure 10-2   The code window for a profiled application

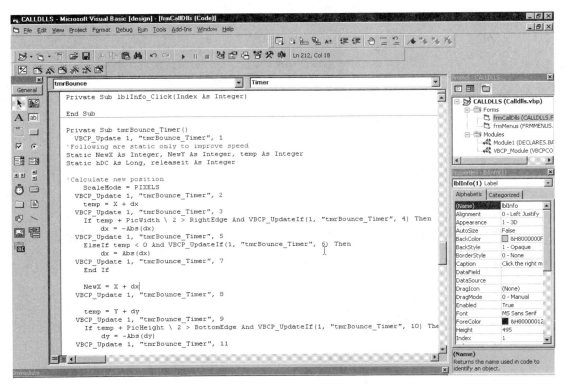

Tip

You can run and stop an application that is being profiled as many times as you like. However, if you would like the information collected from a new profiler session to be added to the information collected in previous session(s), make sure you uncheck the "Replace Data on Run" option in Figure 10-1. This allows you to merge the data from many testing sessions together as you need.

Finally, the data the profiler collects may be seen by selecting the File|View Results function. The result is shown in a grid that can be seen in Figure 10-3 for about the simplest application possible—a message box in the Form_Load. Notice the headings for the columns in Figure 10-3, as you will soon see you can sort the grid by the results that will show up up in one or more columns. You can also filter the data to make the most sense out of it. Finally, you can also export the data as a tab-delimited file for easy import into Excel (or, for that matter, any tool that can handle tab-delimited files). That way your boss will be impressed with the graphs you can produce about your code's efficiency.

A Sample Session for Performance Tuning

We want to work through a sample session that uses the profiler. This will enable us to show you how to find and correct a non-obvious performance flaw in a simple application. We will actually use one of the samples supplied with Visual Basic, so:

Figure 10-3   The grid for results in the code profiler

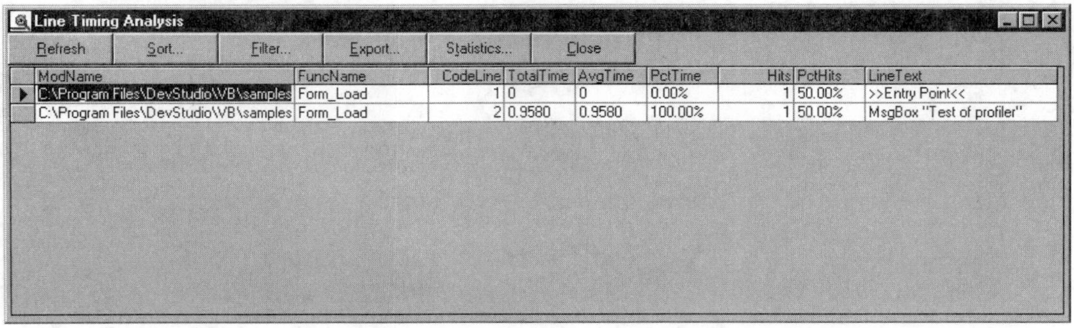

ModName	FuncName	CodeLine	TotalTime	AvgTime	PctTime	Hits	PctHits	LineText
C:\Program Files\DevStudio\VB\samples	Form_Load	1	0	0	0.00%	1	50.00%	>>Entry Point<<
C:\Program Files\DevStudio\VB\samples	Form_Load	2	0.9580	0.9580	100.00%	1	50.00%	MsgBox "Test of profiler"

Line Timing Analysis

Refresh   Sort...   Filter...   Export...   Statistics...   Close

1. Load the \SAMPLES\CompTool\CALLDLLS\CALLDLLS.VBP project.
2. Load the VB Code Profiler from the Add-Ins menu.

Now, make sure all the check boxes for the different modules in this application are selected in Figure 10-4.

Now:

1. Select "Line Timing."
2. Hit the "Add Profiler Code button and return to VB."
3. Run the CALLDLLS application and click the BitBlt button.
4. Click the BitBlt button again when the ball has traveled across the form once.
5. Close the application.
6. Return to the VBCP and select "File/View Results." (Your screen should look like Figure 10-5.)

Now we want to find out which lines were hit most often. For this:

- Click the Sort button on the Results form of the profiler, a screen like Figure 10-6 should pop up.

Figure 10-4   The opening screen for profiling the CALLDLLS project

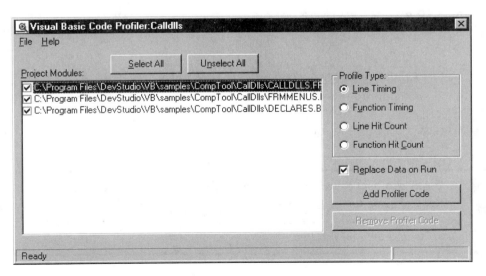

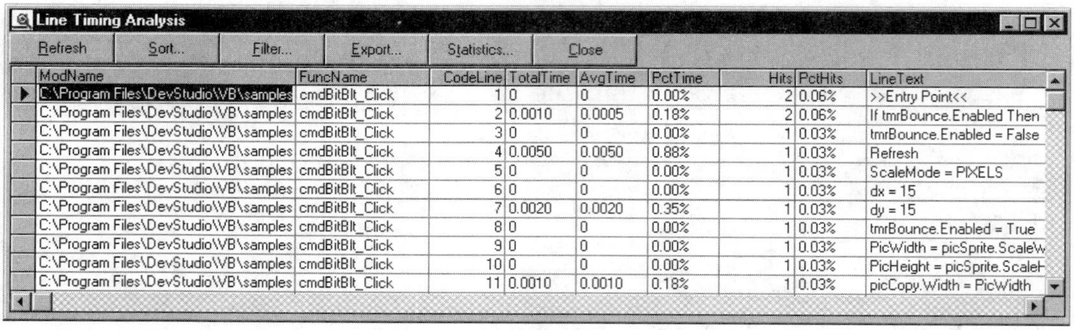

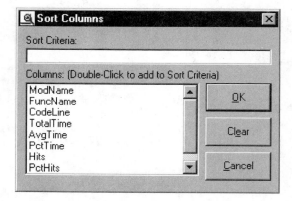

Figure 10-5   Results grid for profiling the CALLDLLS project

Figure 10-6   The Sort Columns dialog box

Now:

- Double click on the Hits item. The Sort Order dialog box shown in Figure 10-7 should pop up.

Choose a descending sort.

Tip

You can also hold down the control key while clicking in the Hits column instead of going through the Sort dialog box. The sort dialog box has the advantage of allowing you to use multiple sorting criteria like sorting first on Hits and then on PctTIme.

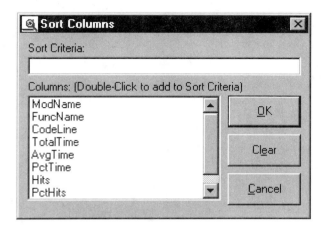

Figure 10-7 Sort Order dialog box

The results are shown in Figure 10-8. As you can see, the tmrSysInfo_ Timer event is where the action is. In fact, consecutive lines of this event procedure are all hit equally often—a generally bad sign.

Here's what the relevant code for this event procedure looks like:

```
If fraInfo(RES_INFO).Visible Then
    For intX = 1 To 3
        lblR(intX).Visible = True
        lblResInfo(intX).Visible = True
        shpBar(intX).Visible = True
        shpFrame(intX).Visible = True
    Next intX
Else
```

Figure 10-8 Sorting by hit count

ModName	FuncName	CodeLine	TotalTime	AvgTime	PctTime	Hits	PctHits	LineText
C:\Program Files\DevStudio\VB\samples	tmrSysInfo_Timer	12	0.0330	0.0001	5.79%	306	8.59%	shpFrame(intX).Visible = Fals
C:\Program Files\DevStudio\VB\samples	tmrSysInfo_Timer	8	0.0230	0.0001	4.04%	306	8.59%	For intX = 1 To 3
C:\Program Files\DevStudio\VB\samples	tmrSysInfo_Timer	9	0.0320	0.0001	5.61%	306	8.59%	lblR(intX).Visible = False
C:\Program Files\DevStudio\VB\samples	tmrSysInfo_Timer	10	0.0390	0.0001	6.84%	306	8.59%	lblResInfo(intX).Visible = Fals
C:\Program Files\DevStudio\VB\samples	tmrSysInfo_Timer	11	0.0320	0.0001	5.61%	306	8.59%	shpBar(intX).Visible = False
C:\Program Files\DevStudio\VB\samples	tmrSysInfo_Timer	2	0.0100	0.0001	1.75%	102	2.86%	If fraInfo(RES_INFO).Visible
C:\Program Files\DevStudio\VB\samples	tmrSysInfo_Timer	23	0.0070	0.0001	1.23%	102	2.86%	If Width <> shpBar(3).Width
C:\Program Files\DevStudio\VB\samples	tmrSysInfo_Timer	14	0.0140	0.0001	2.46%	102	2.86%	GlobalMemoryStatus YourMe
C:\Program Files\DevStudio\VB\samples	tmrSysInfo_Timer	1	0	0	0.00%	102	2.86%	>>Entry Point<<
C:\Program Files\DevStudio\VB\samples	tmrSysInfo_Timer	15	0.0250	0.0002	4.39%	102	2.86%	lblInfo(6).Caption = "Physical
C:\Program Files\DevStudio\VB\samples	tmrSysInfo_Timer	16	0.0090	0.0001	1.58%	102	2.86%	Width = shpFrame(1).Width

```
    For intX = 1 To 3
        lblR(intX).Visible = False
        lblResInfo(intX).Visible = False
        shpBar(intX).Visible = False
        shpFrame(intX).Visible = False
    Next intX
End If
```

The problem with this code is obvious (in hindsight) We are setting the Visible properties of the controls whether this is needed or not.

Now we want to attempt a fix for this local problem. So we need to remove the profiling code from the CALLDLLS module. Do this by:

1. Making sure that only its box is checked in the main profiler screen.

2. Clicking on the remove Profiler Code button.

Now go back into the code window in VB and move to the code for the tmrSysInfo_Timer event procedure. Add the lines marked with a * in the comments to the original code:

```
Static bVisible As Boolean     '*

If fraInfo(RES_INFO).Visible <> bVisible Then      '*
    bVisible = fraInfo(RES_INFO).Visible      '*
    If fraInfo(RES_INFO).Visible Then
        For intX = 1 To 3
            lblR(intX).Visible = True
            lblResInfo(intX).Visible = True
            shpBar(intX).Visible = True
            shpFrame(intX).Visible = True
        Next intX
    Else
        For intX = 1 To 3
            lblR(intX).Visible = False
            lblResInfo(intX).Visible = False
            shpBar(intX).Visible = False
            shpFrame(intX).Visible = False
        Next intX
    End If
End If     '*
```

Now:

1. Save the modified project.
2. Add profiling code to this module again.
3. Repeat the test.

Look at the new profile. Notice that the problem lines do not even appear in the list of most active lines. Also notice that the line:

```
If fraInfo(RES_INFO).Visible <> bVisible
```

takes only as much time as the lines in the For/Next loop did previously. This means that we have eliminated lines in a For/Next loop that were executing three times for every time the procedure was called. We eliminated 12 lines that set a property (property setting is very expensive, as you saw earlier).

Code Coverage

Testing for code coverage is done by choosing either the Line Hit or Function Hit count options in the main screen of the profiler. (There is no need for timing data when you are checking for code coverage.) Code coverage has two purposes:

- Checking for dead code—code that can safely be removed.
- Checking that your test suite is really exercising all possible code pathways.

The first step for both these problems is finding out which code wasn't hit by your testing. Then you can start thinking about whether it is dead code or whether your test suite needs to be improved!
For this:

1. Run your test suite.
2. Choose View Results.
3. Click on the Filter button. This pops up a screen like Figure 10-9.
4. Set the Filter property to Hits=0.
5. Click on OK.

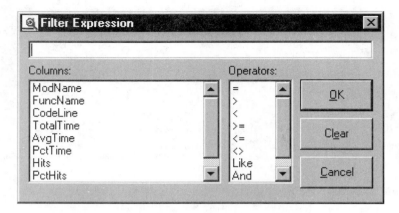

Figure 10-9 The Filter dialog box

The Result box of the profiler will now show only the results that satisfy the filter.

Other Features of the Profiler

The profiler has a few other feature you may find useful. If you want a quick count of the number of modules, functions, or lines of code that you were profiling:

- Click on the Statistics button in the main profiler screen.

This pops up a message box like Figure 10-10.

Finally, as we mentioned before, the data from the profiler can be exported as a tab-delimited file for import into a spreadsheet. You can export not only the entire database but also filtered and sorted data from the analysis

Figure 10-10 Profiler Statistics

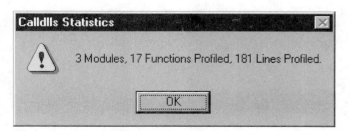

grid. In addition, you can import the data into Microsoft Access, which will make it easy to create reports and forms to view the data any way you like.

Note

If you would like to see other functionality added to the profiler, you should send e-mail to Dave (Daveje@microsoft.com) with your suggestions. (He wrote it.) You may also want to check out NuMega's VB tools suite, which includes an advanced code profiler (www.numega.com).

DATA STRUCTURES: VB DOES POINTERS!

Topics in this Chapter

- A Simple Example
- Binary Trees
- Debugging the Binary Tree Code

Chapter 11

A sophisticated program has to organize the information with which it works. Ideally, one wants to do this in a way that makes dealing with the information both easy and efficient. Do you need keyed access? Then a collection is a great choice. Do you need to iterate through the items? A simple array may be your the best choice. *Data structures* is the fancy term used by computer scientists for gadgets like arrays and collections that are used for organizing information—they are, after all, ways of *structuring* information.

Keep in mind that there is no perfect data structure. As you saw in Chapter 7, collections are great when you need keyed access, they are not the best choice when you need to constantly iterate through the items. For example, storing all the bits for an image prior to modifying them in an image processing program in a collection would be a dumb idea. Or, while collections are great when you can identify an element by a key, they are not so great if you add the requirement that you need to search by part of a key.

It is worth repeating: *there is no perfect data structure.* Often there is a trade-off between speed and the memory used for the data structure. Sometimes, there a trade-off between ease of coding and performance. Data structures that work well if data will be entered "randomly" may be terrible if the data will be entered in already sorted form. We could continue the list of trade-offs for a long, long time. This is why the typical computer science curriculum spends at least one whole semester going through the coding and, of course, the pluses and minus of the standard kinds of data structures. (Computer scientists often find themselves trying to invent the better mouse-trap—a better data structure—for a specific problem.)

Obviously, we can't hope to cover in one chapter what an academic course would cover in one semester. Data structure textbooks are often nearly as long as this book is, after all! What we can do, though, is show you the techniques that you need to *implement* any data structure in VB. That way you will be able to easily adapt the code from any one of the standard data structure textbooks for your needs. Finally, while adapting code from a textbook isn't going to be hard after reading this chapter, debugging the code you write for a data structure often poses peculiar and frustrating problems. For this reason, we end this chapter with a detailed debugging session that analyzes a buggy version of the rather sophisticated data structure that we use as our main example.

A Simple Example

Before we move on to the main example in this chapter we want to start with a much simpler example of a data structure. We hope that this will make it easier to master the fundamental techniques involved. Linked lists are, as the name suggests (see Figure 11-1), a way of structuring data so that each item points to its successor. This makes inserting and removing items easy. You merely splice into or remove the link of the chain at the appropriate place.

Figure 11-1 A linked list

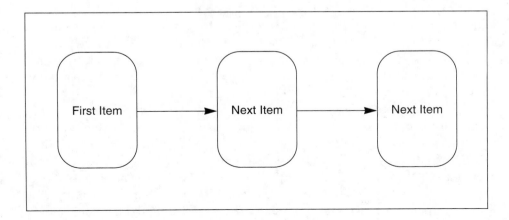

Simple linked lists are actually not all that useful except in unusual circumstances: one obvious disadvantage of a simple linked list is that the only way to get to the last link is to "walk" through all the links starting from the first one. The further away you are from the first (or root) the longer it takes to get there. Also, finding the parent of a link to start the splicing in to or removing of a link means walking through the links from the root and so on. (There are modifications of linked lists that, at the cost of some extra memory used and slightly more code, get around some of these problems.) Nonetheless, a linked list class is a good way to become comfortable with the techniques you need to build more sophisticated and thus, ultimately, more useful, data structures.

The problem, as you can see in Figure 11-1, that we need to solve is how to "point" to the link that follows a link. This is the reason why traditionally, programming data structures is done using the notion of a pointer. (A pointer for those who have never programmed with them before is simply a way of identifying—pointing—to an area of memory.) A linked list implementation in a language that supported pointers would say that a link consisted of the data and a "pointer" to the next link. More precisely, the pointer would be a way of getting at the specific area of memory that contained the next link. (See Figure 11-2.)

Figure 11-2   Pointers

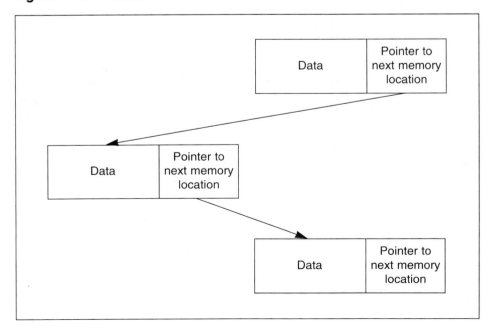

The trouble is that since pointers are memory locations, once you have access to the computer's memory, you can easily write data to the wrong place. Real programmers, of course, are supposed to be careful enough not to lose memory or cause a memory leak by forgetting to reclaim the memory they had set aside. Given the number of memory leaks and bugs that programs written in languages like C that depend on pointers always seem to have, this seems often more of a dream than a reality. Nonetheless, there has always been a somewhat "macho" attitude among certain programmers:

- Real programming languages have pointers, VB, therefore, is a "toy" language since it doesn't do pointers.

Of course this is silly for many, many reasons but still, it was true that versions of Visual Basic prior to VB4 had to imitate pointers to strucutres by storing all the data in an array. (You did have a way at getting at the memory location for variables using VarPtr, for example.) You then used the index of the array element as a pointer. For example, to make a link you created a type:

```
Type Link
   MyData As String
   NextLink As Integer
End Type
```

Then you would create an array of that type:

```
Dim LinkedList Link()
```

trusting to Redim Preserve to expand and contract the array as needed.

To actually use this array you would use the NextLink field of the Link data type to tell you in what array position the next link could be found. The trouble with using arrays and array indices to imitate pointers is that, as you saw in Chapter 7, arrays require extra code in order to remove an element in the middle of an array and reclaim the space. For example, here are the steps for removing a link containing a specific piece of data for a linked list built using an array of "Links."

- Find out which array element contains the data.
- Find out which array entry is pointing to this entry.

For example, suppose the data you were looking for was in the 500'th element of the array:

```
LinkList(500).MyData
```

You now have to find out the "Pointer" (index array) for which:

```
LinkedList(Pointer).NextLink = 500
```

Note that this Pointer is unlikely to be 499 since links can change over time. Now, if we wanted to delete this node, what we had to do was:

- Make that element point to the element that the 500th link used to point to:

  ```
  LinkedList(Pointer).NextLink = LinkList(500).NextLink
  ```

- "Compactify" the array to reclaim the space by removing the 500th element, *moving everything down and rewriting all the "pointers" (array indices) to reflect the new positions.*

The kicker, of course, was the step needed to reclaim the space and rewrite all the pointers. People argued that if the whole point of a linked list was to make it easy to remove and add links, this was certainly not all that easy! The solution for a pointer-based system is easier:

- Adjust the pointers to reflect the correct areas of memory for the predecessor and successor links,
- Reclaim the memory used for the deleted link by telling the operating system it was free. (One line of code was all reclaiming memory usually took.)

We guess that the critics of the old version of VB have a point—in the sense that while writing code for compactifying the array of links and changing all the array indices (pointers) by reducing them by one isn't hard, it isn't very elegant.

Linked Lists In "Modern" VB

So, having admitted that VB (even VB5) lacks traditional pointers, why do we find the whole question funny? The reason is that pointers are not the issue, *references* are. *VB5 has the Set keyword which lets you refer to an object. And it is references that make data structures possible, memory locations pointers are simply a way to get references to other objects.*

Note

The irony of the story is that the Set keyword and the ability to make object references is not a feature added to VB5, VB4 has the same ability to use the Set keyword to refer to an object. We also think it is worth noting that the widely acclaimed Java programming language uses exactly the same idea of object references to do its data structures. It also doesn't have traditional "memory" pointers. Yet, nobody accuses Java of being a "toy language," curious isn't it?

Okay, how do we use VB's notion of a reference (via the Set keyword) to do a linked list? Here's the code for a hypothetical Link class that uses a Property Set to give the ~~pointer~~ reference to the next link:

```
Private mData As String
Private mNextLink As Link

Public Property Set NextLink(ALink As Link)
   Set mNextLink = ALink
End Property
```

Then we can use the following Property Get in order to access the next link.

```
Public Property Get NextLink()
   Set NextLink = mNextLink
End Property
```

Of course, we need some way to set and get the data stored in the link:

```
Public Property Let MyData(Data As String)
   mData = Data
End Property

Public Property Get MyData() As String
   MyData = mData
End Property
```

Not much to it, is there? The idea is that you can always get and set the next link using the NextLink property since it has both a Property Set and Property Let associated to it.

Finally, we need to set the private instance object variable used for the mNextLink pointer to Nothing in the Terminate event of the Link class. This step is essential whenever you have a data structure that uses VB's object variables and Set to refer to them.

- You must reclaim the memory used for private instance fields that are objects in the Terminate event for the object.

```
Private Sub Class_Terminate()
   Set mNextLink = Nothing
End Sub
```

Building the LinkedList Class

The next step is to build the "LinkedList" class that manipulates the actual link objects that are instances of the Link class. The LinkedList class is responsible for creating new links, adding, or deleting them. Note that the LinkedList class doesn't need an array or a collection to store all the current existing links. This would be terribly inefficient. Instead, all it needs to do is maintain a reference to the root link. Using that reference it can "walk" through all the links in the current linked list.

```
Private mRootLink As Link
```

Then, we add a special CreateRootLink method to the class for creating the root link:

```
Public Sub CreateRootLink(TheData As String)
   Set mRootLink = New Link
   mRootLink.MyData = TheData
End Sub
```

As we mentioned in Chapter 7, this kind of technique is necessary because VB has no way to give parameters in the Initialize method for a class. (The program that asked the LinkList class to create an instance of itself would have to know enough to call this CreateRootLink routine.)

Next, we need a method to add a link before a given link. This will depend on a member function in the LinkedList that gets at the parent link, which we will call FindParent: (You'll see the code for FindParent in a moment.)

```
Public Sub AddLinkBefore(ALink As Link, TheData As String)
   Dim NewLink As New Link

   Dim ParentLink As Link
   Set ParentLink = FindParent(ALink)

   If ParentLink Is Nothing Then
     'going before root link
     ' so swap the info

     NewLink.MyData =  mRootLink.MyData
```

```
      Set mRootLink.NextLink  = NewLink
        mRootLink.MyData = TheData
   Else
      Set ParentLink.NextLink = NewLink
      NewLink.MyData = TheData
    Set NewLink.NextLink = ALink
   End If
End Sub
```

Of course, this pushes off answers to these questions regarding other code:

- How do we get a reference to the parent link?
- How do we get at a reference to the link used as a parameter in the AddLinkBefore procedure?

Let's take up the question of how to find a link given a piece of data. One way to deal with this is to insist that the data stored in a link be unique. This is a pretty natural assumption for a linked list. If we do this then it is easy to create a function that returns a reference to the link containing specific data. Notice how the following code that does this uses the mRootLink instance field to start the walk through the links:

```
Public Function FindLink(TheData As String) As Link
   Dim TempLink As Link
   Set TempLink = mRootLink
   Do Until TempLink.MyData = TheData Or TempLink Is Nothing
      Set TempLink = TempLink.NextLink
   Loop
   Set FindLink = TempLink
End Function
```

Next, we need the code to find the parent link.

Note

There is actually a version of a linked list called a doubly linked list that maintains a reference to the parent of a link inside the link itself. This makes finding the parent link trivial. The downside to using a doubly linked list is:

- *You will use up more memory for the extra reference for the parent (16 bytes per link).*
- *The insertion code becomes a little more complex since you have to adjust both backward and forward pointers.*

> • *The deletion code becomes even more involved since you not only have to remember to adjust forward and backward pointers you have to remember to delete the reference to the parent link or you will have a memory leak. (Otherwise the reference count for the parent link will always remain at least one.)*

In our case, rather than going back and building a doubly linked list class what we will do is simply call a helper function called FindParent. The way this function works is that it

- Takes the link of the parent for whom you are looking.
- Starts at the root link and walks through the linked list.
- Returns the link it finds or nothing for the root link.

Here's the code:

```
Private Function FindParent(ALink As Link) As Link
   Dim TempLink As Link, ParentLink As Link
   Set ParentLink = Nothing
   Set TempLink = mRootLink
   Do Until TempLink Is Nothing Or TempLink Is ALink
      Set ParentLink = TempLink
      Set TempLink = TempLink.NextLink
   Loop
   Set FindParent = ParentLink
End Function
```

Notice that since we are assuming the data is unique we could have made it the parameter. (Instead of using the link that would be returned by a function like the FindLink function you just saw.) The advantage to what we did is that this code works regardless of whether data is unique or not. (But this does beg the question of how to find a link if the data in it is not unique.) We will leave it to you to write the code to add a link after a given link, it is not much different that what you have already seen.

Deleting a link isn't much more difficult. The only complication comes if what we are trying to do is delete the root link. This requires some extra work that we encapsulate in another (private) procedure called DeleteRootLink:

```
Public Sub DeleteLink(ALink As Link)
   Dim ParentLink As Link
   Set ParentLink = FindParent(ALink)
   If ParentLink Is Nothing Then
      Call DeleteRootLink
```

```
   Else
      Set ParentLink.NextLink = ALink.NextLink
      Set ALink = Nothing
   End If
End Sub
```

Notice that we are setting ALink to Nothing only after we changed its parent link to point to the successor of the link that we are deleting. If we didn't do this, we wouldn't have any way of getting at its child. One of the consequences of not maintaining a central "store" like a collection for all the links in the linked list is that you can get at the next entry only via a reference to its parent.

If we have done everything right, the combination of these two actions should remove all references to the ALink object and so VB will call the Terminate event in the Alink object. This, in turn, will free up the dangling reference to the successor link given by the mNextLink instance field in the link class.

Here's the code to change the root link:

```
Private Sub DeleteRootLink
   If mRootLink.NextLink Is Nothing Then
      MsgBox "Can not delete root link if no other links exist"
    Exit Sub
   Else
    Set mRootLink = mRootLink.NextLink
   End If
End Sub
```

At this point we will leave it to you to write a front end to manipulate the links by allowing you to insert or delete new links. However, we do want to end this section by correcting one design flaw in the original Link class whose instances the LinkedList class is designed to manipulate. To understand what the design flaw is, imagine that you compile the project containing both these classes into either an in-process DLL or an EXE server. Now suppose the Instancing property of these classes is set so that other applications can create a linked list class. You do not want the client class to be able to create new links or to change any of the data in a link. For this reason, we would make four changes to the Link class:

- Make it Public Not Creatable.
- Change the Property Let MyData property to Friend so that only the linked list class can change the data in a link.
- Do the same for the Property Set NextLink member.
- Add reasonable error handling.

Binary Trees

Keeping data in a sorted array is great if what you want to do is search through the array at some later date. Using the well-known binary search technique of dividing the array in half and searching only one half means that essentially any size sorted array can be searched instantly. The pseudo-code is something like:

```
Do Until Item Is Found
  If Item < Item In Middle, Look in first half of list
Else Look In second half
  Repeat process with list consisting of the correct half
Loop
```

Using binary search on a sorted array with 10,000,000 entries takes less than 25 iterations until the item is found. (Of course, sorting an array that large will require a very fast algorithm like a QuickSort algorithm.)

On the other hand, in many cases, you don't really want to sort the items, you sort them only so that you can search through them quickly using binary search! (Notice that a collection won't work if you need to search by partial keys.) It should come as no surprise that computer scientists have long searched for techniques that let you store information in such a way that:

- You can search through it as quickly as if it were sorted.
- You don't necessarily have to sort it.

(Of course, a nice added bonus would come if you could sort the items quickly down when needed.)

Surprisingly enough such a data structure exists, it's called a *binary tree*. Of course, as we have stressed before, there is no such thing as a free lunch. Binary trees are fairly hard to program, deleting items is a particular pain as you will see. Most importantly:

- Unless you use very sophisticated methods (not described here), binary trees only work well if the data entered is in random order.

If someone entered data into a binary tree in sorted order, the standard binary tree as described here would be a disaster!

Introduction to Binary trees

To understand a binary tree, suppose you have a list of names:

Greg, Gary, Hannah, Dave, Gene, Michael, Shara, Saul, Rebecca, Deborah, Esther, Alyssa, Emma

Start by putting the first name in the center of a piece of paper:

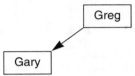

Since Gary Comes before Greg alphabetically we place an arrow pointing to the left with Gary's name:

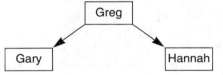

Hannah's name comes after Greg's so we place an "after" arrow—an arrow pointing to the right:

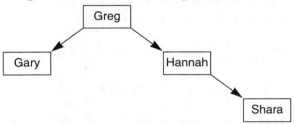

Shara comes after Greg and after Hanna so the picture looks like this:

Dave comes before Greg and Gary so the picture looks like this:

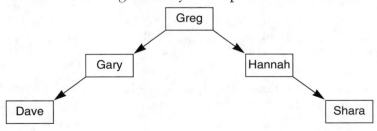

Gene comes before Greg but after Gary so the picture now looks like this:

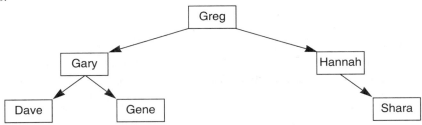

Finally, the whole picture looks like this:

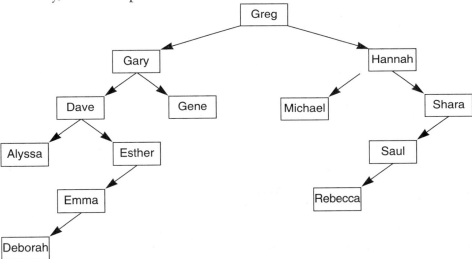

It's called a *binary tree* because we only have two choices to make and it is supposed to look like a tree if you turn it upside down. (And, because "binary bush," which is what it really looks like, sounded too funny to the computer scientists who invented it.) The idea, of course, is that when you insert a new name, you follow the "branches" in the right order until you get to an empty place. Then you put the data there.

It's a good idea to learn some of the standard terminology for binary trees. Each item in the tree is called a *node*. Just as for a linked list, the node at the top is called the *root* (or root node). The nodes that the arrows point to are called the *left child node* and *right child node* and one speaks about the *parent* node for a specific child node. In our example, Greg is the root node and has two children nodes. Greg's left child is Gary, his right child is Hannah. A node that has no children is called a *leaf*. When you enter the data you are said to have *loaded* the tree. As you will see, adding a new node to a binary tree is usually very quick. For example, it takes only five comparisons to add Deborah's name to the tree.

Finally, you should note that a binary tree is inherently a recursive object. You can think of any node as defining a smaller version of the current tree. The obvious examples are that the left child of any parent starts what is called the *left subtree* and the right child of any parent starts the *right subtree*. In fact, here is the recursive pseudo-code to add a node to a binary tree that uses the notion of a left and right subtree:

```
LoadTree(TheTree, CurrentNode, ItemToAdd)
   If the CurrentNode Is Empty
     add new node there
   Else
       If the ThingToAdd is less than the contents of
the current node
          LoadTree(LeftTree,LeftChild,ItemToAdd)
       Else
         LoadTree(RightTree, RightChild,ItemToAdd)
       End Inner If
   End Outer If
End LoadTree
```

Implementing a Binary Tree

As before we will build the binary tree using two classes: one for the nodes and the other a class to manipulate them. The class for the nodes starts out much like the class for a link does. We have instance fields for the data and two object variables for the references that we will use to point to the child nodes:

```
Private mMyData As String
Private mRightChild As TreeNode
Private mLeftChild As TreeNode
```

The property procedures to get and set the data are standard except that the ones to set the properties are declared as Friend for the same reasons as before:

```
Friend Property Let Data(TheData As String)
   mMyData = TheData
End Property

Public Property Get Data() As String
   Data = mMyData
End Property
```

The property procedures for getting and setting children are what you might expect. they simply get the information stored in the private instance objects variable mRightChild and mLeftChild. Again, we made the set properties Friend rather than Public:

```
Public Property Get LeftChild() As TreeNode
   Set LeftChild = mLeftChild
End Property

Friend  Property Set LeftChild(ANode As TreeNode)
   Set mLeftChild = ANode
End Property
Public Property Get RightChild() As TreeNode
   Set RightChild = mRightChild
End Property

Friend Property Set RightChild(ANode As TreeNode)
   Set mRightChild = ANode
End Property
```

The Terminate event simply sets all the relevant object variables used for the references to nothing:

```
Private Sub Class_Terminate()
   Set mRightChild = Nothing
   Set mLeftChild = Nothing
End Sub
```

The BinaryTree Class

The class for the actual nodes (called treeNode.Cls in the CH11 directory on your CD) was pretty simple, the class for the BinaryTree class that manipulates the nodes is not. However, it starts out much like the LinkedList class does with an instance field for the root:

```
Private mRootNode As TreeNode
```

We will again use the mRootNode to hang the whole tree on. This means we again do not need an array or collection for all the nodes. Everything will be retrieved by starting with the root node and then walking through the tree.

Next, we need a procedure to initialize the tree. Again, we have the problem that we can't use the Initialize event for this because VB5 does not allow parameters to be passed to the Initialize event. Instead, we use a procedure called MakeRootNode that looks like this:

```
Public Sub MakeRootNode(TheData As String)
  Set mRootNode = New TreeNode
  mRootNode.Data = TheData
End Sub
```

As you can see it makes an new instance of the node class for the root node but leaves the right and left children set to Nothing. We also add a convenience Property Get to the BinaryTree class that returns a reference to the root node.

```
Public Property Get RootNode() As TreeNode
  Set RootNode = mRootNode
End Property
```

Now it's on to the procedure to load the tree. This will take two parameters: the data you want to add and a reference to the current node. This allows us to call the procedure recursively. You need to call this procedure with something like:

```
LoadATree(ATree.GetRootNode, TheData)
```

to start the process. The code will then change the parameter (pass by reference!) to reflect the new position. Otherwise the following code follows the recursive outline we discussed earlier pretty well. We keep track of:

1. The ParentNode.
2. What direction we took from the parent node to get to the current node.

Keeping this information in mind we can use code like the following to make the new node:

```
Public Sub LoadATree(TheData As String, CurrentNode As _
TreeNode)
  Dim ParentNode As TreeNode
  Dim Direction As String
  Do
    Set ParentNode = CurrentNode
    If TheData < CurrentNode.Data Then
      Set CurrentNode = CurrentNode.LeftChild
      Direction = "Left"
    Else
      Set CurrentNode = CurrentNode.RightChild
      Direction = "Right"
    End If
  Loop Until CurrentNode Is Nothing
  Set CurrentNode = New TreeNode
```

```
   CurrentNode.Data = TheData
   If Direction = "Left" Then
      Set ParentNode.LeftChild = CurrentNode
   Else
      Set ParentNode.RightChild = CurrentNode
   End If
End Sub
```

(It would be a little more efficient to use Booleans for the Direction valve. We'll leave that change to you.) At this point we have the tree loaded so we can start asking what good it is!

Using a Binary Tree

Well, first, we can search through the tree. This can be done (for random data) roughly as fast as for an ordinary sorted array. Here's the code for searching the tree for specific data. (Again, we are assuming the data added to the tree is unique.) The idea is that you use recursion to call the TreeSearch routine on either the left tree or the right tree. To start the search process you tell the routine to start working at the root of the tree. Here's the code:

```
Public Function TreeSearch(MyNode As TreeNode, _
TheKey As String) As TreeNode
   Do Until (MyNode Is Nothing)
      If TheKey = MyNode.Data Then
         Set TreeSearch = MyNode
         Exit Function
      End If
      If TheKey > MyNode.Data Then
         Set MyNode = MyNode.RightChild
         TreeSearch MyNode, TheKey
      Else
         Set MyNode = MyNode.LeftChild
         TreeSearch MyNode, TheKey
      End If
   Loop
   Set TreeSearch = MyNode
End Function
```

This function returns either a reference to the correct node or a reference to Nothing—the reserved object variable.

How fast is tree search? The answer is that it completely depends on the shape of the tee. If you have a tree that is as "bushy" as possible, one where essentially every node has both a left and a right child, then tree search is just as fast as the standard binary search The trouble is, as we mentioned earlier, that if the tree isn't very bushy, tree search deteriorates. For example if the data was ordered as it was entered into the tree, the tree looks like this:

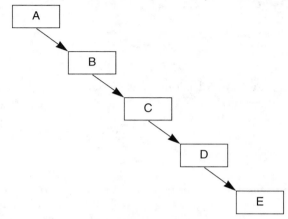

Given this shape, tree search is the slowest search of all! You end up walking through every element in the tree instead of cutting the number in half at each level.

Note

Trees that are as bushy as possible are sometimes called balanced trees. Computer scientists have come up with ways to rebalance unbalanced trees but they are quite sophisticated and we have to refer you to a book on data structures for the techniques that are known for doing this.

Tree Sort

One of the most amazing things about a binary tree is that if you look at it right, it's sorted! Here's what we mean.

1. Suppose you go as far left as you can, that's obviously the smallest element in the tree.
2. It's parent is obviously the next smallest entry.
3. From the parent, if you can go right, do so and then go as far left again as you can, that's obviously the third smallest element.
4. If the parent from Step 2 doesn't have a right child, move up to the grandparent of the node from step 1 and repeat the process.

(This is usually called an *in-order transversal*.)

Here's some code that translates this recursive description and simply adds the next item in alphabetical order to a list box. (We will use this in our routine that puts everything together a little later on in this chapter.)

```
Public Sub TreeSort(MyNode As TreeNode)
   Dim NextNode As TreeNode
   If MyNode Is Nothing Then
    ' do nothing
    Else
      TreeSort MyNode.LeftChild
      Form1.List2.AddItem MyNode.Data
      TreeSort MyNode.RightChild
   End If
End Sub
```

How fast is tree sort? The answer is that, just as for tree search, it completely depends on the shape of the tee. As with tree search if you have a tree that is as "bushy" as possible, one where essentially every node has both a left and a right child, then tree sort is about as fast a sort as one can ever get.

Deleting Items in a Binary Tree

We have said repeatedly that nothing comes for free. One of the places you pay for the power of binary trees is in the code needed to delete a node from a binary tree. There is no good way to do this. Every method you try will require lots of special case code in order to reassign all the needed pointers—oops, we meant references. Ironically, the pseudo-code for deletion isn't hard, here are the easy cases:

1. If the node has no children simply delete it.
2. If the node has only one child, attach the pointers of the parent of the node to be deleted to the sole child.

The procedure to delete a node with two children is more complicated, it involves finding a "foster" parent. One way to do this is to find the node whose data comes immediately before the node you want to delete. You get this node by going left from the node to be deleted and then as far right as you can.

Unfortunately, translating this simple pseudo-code into actual code is a little tricky. Let's take the first case given above—it's obviously the easiest. The trick to remember is that you need to set all the relevant references to nothing. Here's one possible way to do this:

```
If NodeToGo.RightChild Is Nothing And NodeToGo.LeftChild _
Is Nothing Then
      ' no children
      If MyParent.LeftChild Is NodeToGo Then
         Set MyParent.LeftChild = Nothing
      Else
         Set MyParent.RightChild = Nothing
      End If
' more cases to follow in the ElseIf clauses for deletion
' with children
```

Notice how we are zeroing out the correct reference in the parent node. Here's the kind of code you need to delete a node with a single (left) child that would follow the previous fragment:

```
ElseIf (NodeToGo.RightChild Is Nothing) And Not _
(NodeToGo.LeftChild Is Nothing) Then
      If MyParent.LeftChild Is NodeToGo Then
         Set MyParent.LeftChild = NodeToGo.LeftChild
      Else
         Set MyParent.RightChild = NodeToGo.LeftChild
      End If
      Set NodeToGo.LeftChild = Nothing
```

Next, notice in both these cases we would need some special case code for the root node and we also need to have a way of finding the parent of the node to be deleted. This can be done in two ways:

- By changing the node class to include a pointer to the parent of a node.
- By writing a little function that gives us the parent:

```
Public Function FindParent(ANode As TreeNode) As TreeNode
  Dim ParentNode As TreeNode, ChildNode As TreeNode
  Dim Found As Boolean

    Set ChildNode = mRootNode
    Do Until Found
      If ANode.Data = ChildNode.Data Then
        Found = True
        Set FindParent = ParentNode
      ElseIf ANode.Data > ChildNode.Data Then
        Set ParentNode = ChildNode
        Set ChildNode = ParentNode.RightChild
      Else
```

```
              Set ParentNode = ChildNode
              Set ChildNode = ParentNode.LeftChild
           End If
      Loop
End Function
```

The advantages to not maintaining a reference to the parent are:

- You save the 16 bytes per node for the parent reference.
- The code for the binary tree becomes much easier. With a reference to a parent node you have to be very careful to set all the appropriate references to Nothing.

The real problem comes when you try to delete a node with two children. We still need to distinguish between the root node and a non-root node but let's forget that problem for a moment and assume we are trying to delete a non-root node. We obviously need a helper function that finds the next entry as described in the pseudo-code above. It looks like this:

```
Private Function FindNextEntry(NodeToGo As TreeNode) As
TreeNode
     Dim TempNode As TreeNode
     'go left
     Set TempNode = NodeToGo.LeftChild
     'now go right as far as we can
     Do Until TempNode.RightChild Is Nothing
        Set TempNode = TempNode.RightChild
     Loop
     Set FindNextEntry = TempNode
End Function
```

Now we want to show you the code to delete a node that has two children that doesn't happen to be the root node. The easy part is calling the FindNextEntry routine and the FindParent routine, the hard part is dealing with all the special cases! For example, we described the procedure as go left and then go right, but suppose you can't go right. Then you are, in effect, replacing the node to be deleted with its left child. We can check for this special case by looking at the parent of the entry that we found using the FindNextEntry function. If the Parent is the node we want to delete, we know we are in this special case. Similarly, we need to distinguish between cases depending on whether the replacement node we found by going left and then going right (i.e., with FindNextEntry) has a left child or not. Having alerted you to all the special cases, here's the code:

```
Private Sub DeleteWithTwoChildren(NodeToGo As TreeNode, _
MyParent As TreeNode)
    Dim TempNode As TreeNode, TempParent As TreeNode
    Set TempNode = FindNextEntry(NodeToGo)
    Set TempParent = FindParent(TempNode)
    If TempParent Is NodeToGo Then
        ' strange case left child is it - can't go right
        If MyParent.LeftChild Is NodeToGo Then
            Set MyParent.LeftChild = TempNode
        Else
            Set MyParent.RightChild = TempNode
        End If
        Set TempNode.RightChild = NodeToGo.RightChild
        Exit Sub
    End If
    If Not (TempNode.LeftChild Is Nothing) Then
        'set tempnode child to correct place since
        'replacement has node dangling
        Set TempParent.RightChild = TempNode.LeftChild
    Else
        Set TempParent.RightChild = Nothing
    End If
    ' now swap TempNode for NodeToGo
    If MyParent.LeftChild Is NodeToGo Then
        Set MyParent.LeftChild = TempNode
    ElseIf MyParent.RightChild Is NodeToGo Then
        Set MyParent.RightChild = TempNode
    End If
    Set TempNode.LeftChild = NodeToGo.LeftChild
    Set TempNode.RightChild = NodeToGo.RightChild
End Sub
```

The Full Code for the BinaryTree Class

Here's the complete code for the binary tree class, including the special code
that allows you to delete the root node.

Listing 11-1:   The Complete Code for the Binary Tree Class

```
Option Explicit
Private mRootNode As TreeNode

Public Sub LoadATree(TheData As String, CurrentNode As _
TreeNode)
```

```
      Dim ParentNode As TreeNode
      Dim Direction As String
      Do
        Set ParentNode = CurrentNode
        If TheData < CurrentNode.Data Then
            Set CurrentNode = CurrentNode.LeftChild
            Direction = "Left"
          Else
            Set CurrentNode = CurrentNode.RightChild
            Direction = "Right"
          End If
      Loop Until CurrentNode Is Nothing
      Set CurrentNode = New TreeNode
      CurrentNode.Data = TheData
      If Direction = "Left" Then
        Set ParentNode.LeftChild = CurrentNode
      Else
        Set ParentNode.RightChild = CurrentNode
      End If
End Sub

Public Sub TreeSort(MyNode As TreeNode)
    Dim NextNode As TreeNode
    If MyNode Is Nothing Then
      ' do nothing
      Else
        TreeSort MyNode.LeftChild
        Form1.List2.AddItem MyNode.Data
        TreeSort MyNode.RightChild
      End If
End Sub

Public Function TreeSearch(MyNode As TreeNode, _
TheKey As String) As TreeNode
    Do Until (MyNode Is Nothing)
        If TheKey = MyNode.Data Then
          Set TreeSearch = MyNode
          Exit Function
        End If
        If TheKey > MyNode.Data Then
          Set MyNode = MyNode.RightChild
          TreeSearch MyNode, TheKey
        Else
          Set MyNode = MyNode.LeftChild
          TreeSearch MyNode, TheKey
        End If
```

```
      Loop
      Set TreeSearch = MyNode
End Function

Public Function FindParent(ANode As TreeNode) As TreeNode
   Dim ParentNode As TreeNode, ChildNode As TreeNode
   Dim Found As Boolean

   Set ChildNode = mRootNode

      Do Until Found
         If ANode.Data = ChildNode.Data Then
            Found = True
            Set FindParent = ParentNode
         ElseIf ANode.Data > ChildNode.Data Then
            Set ParentNode = ChildNode
            Set ChildNode = ParentNode.RightChild
         Else
            Set ParentNode = ChildNode
            Set ChildNode = ParentNode.LeftChild
         End If
      Loop

End Function
Public Sub MakeRootNode(TheData As String)
   Set mRootNode = New TreeNode
   mRootNode.Data = TheData
End Sub

Public Property Get RootNode() As TreeNode
   Set RootNode = mRootNode
End Property

Public Sub DeleteNode(NodeToGo As TreeNode)
   Dim MyParent As TreeNode
   Set MyParent = FindParent(NodeToGo)
   If MyParent Is Nothing Then
     Call DeleteRootNode
     Exit Sub
   End If

   If NodeToGo.RightChild Is Nothing And
NodeToGo.LeftChild Is Nothing Then
        ' no children
        If MyParent.LeftChild Is NodeToGo Then
```

```
            Set MyParent.LeftChild = Nothing
         Else
            Set MyParent.RightChild = Nothing
         End If
      ElseIf (NodeToGo.RightChild Is Nothing) And Not _
(NodeToGo.LeftChild Is Nothing) Then
         If MyParent.LeftChild Is NodeToGo Then
            Set MyParent.LeftChild = NodeToGo.LeftChild
         Else
            Set MyParent.RightChild = NodeToGo.LeftChild
         End If
         Set NodeToGo.LeftChild = Nothing
      ElseIf Not (NodeToGo.RightChild Is Nothing) And _
(NodeToGo.LeftChild Is Nothing) Then
         If MyParent.LeftChild Is NodeToGo Then
            Set MyParent.LeftChild = NodeToGo.RightChild
         Else
            Set MyParent.RightChild = NodeToGo.RightChild
         End If
         Set NodeToGo.RightChild = Nothing
      Else
          Call DeleteWithTwoChildren(NodeToGo, MyParent)
      End If
      Set NodeToGo = Nothing
   End Sub


Private Sub DeleteRootNode()
   Dim TempNode As TreeNode
   If mRootNode.RightChild Is Nothing And _
mRootNode.LeftChild Is Nothing Then
        MsgBox "Nothing in tree left, shutting down program"
        End
   End If
   If mRootNode.RightChild Is Nothing And _
Not (mRootNode.LeftChild Is Nothing) Then
         Set mRootNode = mRootNode.LeftChild
   ElseIf Not (mRootNode.RightChild Is Nothing) And _
mRootNode.LeftChild Is Nothing Then
         Set mRootNode = mRootNode.RightChild
   Else
      Set TempNode = FindNextEntry(mRootNode)
      Dim TempParent As TreeNode
      Set TempParent = FindParent(TempNode)
      If TempParent Is mRootNode Then
         Set TempNode.RightChild = mRootNode.RightChild
```

```
            Set mRootNode = TempNode
         Else
            Set TempParent.RightChild = TempNode.LeftChild
            Set TempNode.LeftChild = mRootNode.LeftChild
            Set TempNode.RightChild = mRootNode.RightChild
            Set mRootNode = TempNode
         End If
      End If
End Sub
Private Sub DeleteWithTwoChildren(NodeToGo As TreeNode, _
MyParent As TreeNode)
      Dim TempNode As TreeNode, TempParent As TreeNode
      Set TempNode = FindNextEntry(NodeToGo)
      Set TempParent = FindParent(TempNode)
      If TempParent Is NodeToGo Then
         ' strange case left child is it - can't go right
         If MyParent.LeftChild Is NodeToGo Then
            Set MyParent.LeftChild = TempNode
         Else
            Set MyParent.RightChild = TempNode
         End If
         Set TempNode.RightChild = NodeToGo.RightChild
         Exit Sub
      End If
      If Not (TempNode.LeftChild Is Nothing) Then
         'set tempnode child to correct place since
         'replacement has node dangling
         Set TempParent.RightChild = TempNode.LeftChild
      Else
         Set TempParent.RightChild = Nothing
      End If
      ' now swap TempNode for NodeToGo
      If MyParent.LeftChild Is NodeToGo Then
         Set MyParent.LeftChild = TempNode
      ElseIf MyParent.RightChild Is NodeToGo Then
         Set MyParent.RightChild = TempNode
      End If
      Set TempNode.LeftChild = NodeToGo.LeftChild
      Set TempNode.RightChild = NodeToGo.RightChild
End Sub

Private Function FindNextEntry(NodeToGo As TreeNode) _
As TreeNode
      Dim TempNode As TreeNode
      'go left
```

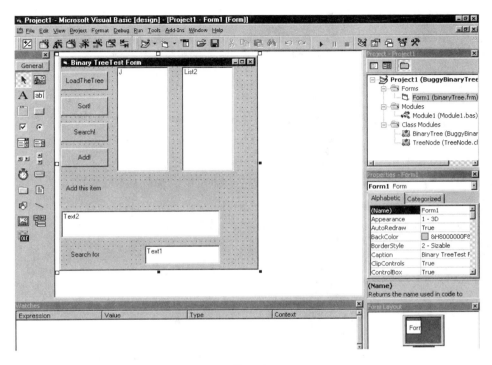

Figure 11-3 BinaryTree Demonstration Form3+--

```
    Set TempNode = NodeToGo.LeftChild
    'now go right as far as we can
    Do Until TempNode.RightChild Is Nothing
       Set TempNode = TempNode.RightChild
    Loop
   Set FindNextEntry = TempNode
End Function
```

A Demonstration Program for Binary Trees

Figure 11-3 shows you the form that we used to build a demonstration program to show off all the features we added to our binary tree class. You can add items to the list box, sort the tree (they will be shown in the second list box) or delete items by double clicking on them in the first list box. As you can see by looking at the form file that follows we made most of the items in Figure 11-3 invisible until you click on the Load button.

Here's an example of the code we used to load the tree when you click on the Load command button:

```
Private Sub cmdLoadTree_Click()
   Dim CurrentNode As TreeNode
   Set TestTree = New BinaryTree
   TestTree.MakeRootNode List1.List(0)
   For I = 1 To List1.ListCount - 1
       Set CurrentNode = TestTree.RootNode
       TestTree.LoadATree List1.List(I), CurrentNode
   Next I
   MsgBox "I'm done"
   cmdSearchTree.Visible = True
   cmdSortTree.Visible = True
   Label1.Visible = True
   txtSearchText.Visible = True
   txtItemToAdd.Visible = True
   cmdAdd.Visible = True
   Label2.Visible = True
   Me.Height = 6100
End Sub
```

This code inside the For-Next loop can work because we wrote the LoadATree routine in the BinaryTree class to automatically (pass by reference!) change the CurrentNode parameter to reflect the new position in the tree.

Next, the cmdAdd_Click routine calls the TreeSearch routine to decide whether it can add the item or not. If this returns Nothing then we know we should add the item to the list box and to the tree, otherwise we shouldn't.

```
Private Sub cmdAdd_Click()
   Dim CurrentNode As TreeNode
   Set CurrentNode = TestTree.RootNode
   If TestTree.TreeSearch(TestTree.RootNode,
txtItemToAdd.Text) Is Nothing Then
      List1.AddItem txtItemToAdd
    TestTree.LoadATree txtItemToAdd.Text, CurrentNode
   Else
      MsgBox "Item already in tree"
      txtItemToAdd.Text = ""
   End If
End Sub
```

The Full Form Code for the BinaryTree Test Form

Here's the form file:

Listing 11-2: The Full Form Code for the Binary Tree Test Form

---

```
VERSION 5.00
Begin VB.Form Form1
    AutoRedraw       =    -1   'True
    Caption          =    "Binary TreeTest Form"
    ClientHeight     =    2940
    ClientLeft       =    60
    ClientTop        =    345
    ClientWidth      =    5025
    LinkTopic        =    "Form1"
    LockControls     =    -1   'True
    ScaleHeight      =    2940
    ScaleWidth       =    5025
    Begin VB.TextBox txtItemToAdd
        Height           =    735
        Left             =    0
        TabIndex         =    8
        Text             =    "Text2"
        Top              =    3840
        Visible          =    0    'False
        Width            =    4095
    End
    Begin VB.CommandButton cmdAdd
        Caption          =    "Add!"
        Height           =    495
        Left             =    0
        TabIndex         =    7
        Top              =    2160
        Visible          =    0    'False
        Width            =    1215
    End
    Begin VB.ListBox List2
        Height           =    2790
        Left             =    3120
        TabIndex         =    6
        Top              =    0
        Visible          =    0    'False
        Width            =    1335
    End
```

```
Begin VB.CommandButton cmdSearchTree
    Caption             =    "Search!"
    Height              =    495
    Left                =    0
    TabIndex            =    4
    Top                 =    1480
    Visible             =    0     'False
    Width               =    1215
End
Begin VB.TextBox txtSearchText
    Height              =    495
    Left                =    2160
    TabIndex            =    3
    Text                =    "Text1"
    Top                 =    4800
    Visible             =    0     'False
    Width               =    1935
End
Begin VB.CommandButton cmdSortTree
    Caption             =    "Sort!"
    Height              =    495
    Left                =    0
    TabIndex            =    2
    Top                 =    800
    Visible             =    0     'False
    Width               =    1215
End
Begin VB.ListBox List1
    Height              =    2790
    ItemData            =    "binaryTree.frx":0000
    Left                =    1440
    List                =    "binaryTree.frx":0007
    TabIndex            =    1
    Top                 =    0
    Width               =    1335
End
Begin VB.CommandButton cmdLoadTree
    Caption             =    "LoadTheTree"
    Height              =    495
    Left                =    0
    TabIndex            =    0
    Top                 =    120
    Width               =    1215
End
Begin VB.Label Label2
    Caption             =    "Add this item"
```

```
            Height        =      495
            Left          =      120
            TabIndex      =      9
            Top           =      3120
            Visible       =      0      'False
            Width         =      3855
         End
         Begin VB.Label Label1
            Caption       =      "Search for"
            Height        =      495
            Left          =      240
            TabIndex      =      5
            Top           =      4920
            Visible       =      0      'False
            Width         =      1455
         End
      End
   End
   Attribute VB_Name = "Form1"
   Attribute VB_GlobalNameSpace = False
   Attribute VB_Creatable = False
   Attribute VB_PredeclaredId = True
   Attribute VB_Exposed = False
   Option Explicit
   Dim I As Integer
   Dim TestTree As BinaryTree

   Private Sub cmdAdd_Click()
    Dim CurrentNode As TreeNode
    Set CurrentNode = TestTree.RootNode
    If TestTree.TreeSearch(TestTree.RootNode, _
   txtItemToAdd.Text) Is Nothing Then
       List1.AddItem txtItemToAdd
       TestTree.LoadATree txtItemToAdd.Text, CurrentNode
    Else
       MsgBox "Item already in tree"
       txtItemToAdd.Text = ""
    End If
   End Sub

   Private Sub cmdSortTree_Click()
     List2.Clear
     List2.Visible = True
     TestTree.TreeSort TestTree.RootNode
   End Sub

   Private Sub cmdSearchTree_Click()
```

```
   Dim TheNode As TreeNode, MyParent As TreeNode
   Set TheNode = TestTree.TreeSearch(TestTree.RootNode, _
txtSearchText.Text)

  If TheNode Is Nothing Then
    MsgBox "Failure"
  Else
    MsgBox "Success"
    Set MyParent = TestTree.FindParent(TheNode)
    Dim MyParentIs As String
    If MyParent Is Nothing Then
      MyParentIs = "Nothing"
    Else
      MyParentIs = MyParent.Info
    End If
    MsgBox "My parent is " & MyParentIs
  End If
End Sub

Private Sub cmdLoadTree_Click()
  Dim CurrentNode As TreeNode
  Set TestTree = New BinaryTree
  TestTree.MakeRootNode List1.List(0)
  For I = 1 To List1.ListCount - 1
      Set CurrentNode = TestTree.RootNode
      TestTree.LoadATree List1.List(I), CurrentNode
  Next
  MsgBox "I'm done"
  cmdSearchTree.Visible = True
  cmdSortTree.Visible = True
  Label1.Visible = True
  txtSearchText.Visible = True
  txtItemToAdd.Visible = True
  cmdAdd.Visible = True
  Label2.Visible = True
  Me.Height = 6100
End Sub

Private Sub List1_DblClick()
  Dim TempNode As TreeNode
  Set TempNode = TestTree.TreeSearch(TestTree.RootNode,
List1.Text)
  TestTree.DeleteNode TempNode
  List1.RemoveItem (List1.ListIndex)
  List2.Clear
```

```
   cmdSortTree_Click
End Sub

Private Sub List2_DblClick()
   Dim TempNode As TreeNode
   Set TempNode = TestTree.TreeSearch(TestTree.RootNode, _
List2.Text)
End Sub
```

Debugging the Binary Tree Code

In Chapter 9 we showed you the basic debugging techniques, in this section we want to work through a debugging session using a buggy version of the Binary Tree project. (You can find the BuggyBinaryTree.cls file in the CH11 directory on the CD.) We suggest you load it in order to work along with us.

First, when you are debugging a sophisticated program involving objects you need to make sure that all objects are set to Nothing and no dangling references remain. One useful technique for this is:

1. Add a global counter called, say, gRefCount to a BAS module. Make this a watch item.

2. Modify the Initialize and Terminate events in the node class to add and subtract one for the global reference count.

For example:

```
Private Sub Class_Initialize()

   Set mRightChild = Nothing
   Set mLeftChild = Nothing
   gRefCount = gRefCount + 1
End Sub
```

We also find it helpful to have a message box that pops up when we are in the Terminate event so it looks like this in the BuggyBinaryTree program:

```
Private Sub Class_Terminate()
   MsgBox "Am in terminate event for " & mMyData

   Set mRightChild = Nothing
   Set mLeftChild = Nothing
```

```
    gRefCount = gRefCount - 1
End Sub
```

Debugging the Load Procedure in the BuggyBinaryTree Project

Run the buggy version of the binary tree demo program. To the initial entry of J add an item with data = "A" and data = "Z." You should see a message box that says you are in the Terminate event for A! (See Figure 11-4). This is certainly strange, obviously somehow the reference to the node containing "A" is being lost.

The next thing we tried to do was start the program up again and do it in the other order, adding "Z" first and then "A." Surprisingly enough this worked as seen in Figure 11-5.

Obviously, we have come across a peculiar bug. If we try a few more examples, adding, for example, a "B" and then an "X" we see that adding the "X" tells us that we are in the Terminate event for Z. At this point we began to

Figure 11-4   A weird situation

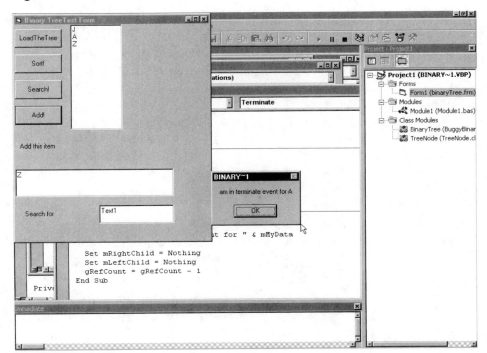

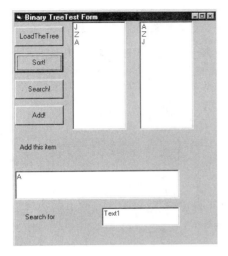

Figure 11-5 Everything seems to be okay

suspect the trouble was in the code for loading the tree. Now the amazing powers of the Watch Window in VB 5 can help you.

1. Make the mRootNode object variable a watch variable with "All module scope." (Make the watch window a bit larger than you might usually.)
2. Set a breakpoint in the LoadATree routine. (See Figure 11-6.)

Now run the program. Since loading the root node doesn't actually use the LoadATree procedure, we need to put an "A" in the text box and click on the Add item. You should hit the breakpoint as shown in Figure 11-7.

Notice in the Watch Window that the mRootNode object variable has a little + sign next to it. This is because the Watch Window is able to peer inside objects! If you click on it your screen will look like Figure 11-8. Notice how you can see the internal structure of the object variable.

Step through the program (use Shift+F8 to make it quicker). After the code in this is processed, the Watch window will now look like Figure 11-9. Notice that the mLeftChild and LeftChild members of the mRootNode objects now have little plus signs next to them:

If you expand one of these objects you will see (as shown in Figure 11-10) that the left child of the root is indeed pointing to "A."

Okay, continue the process by continuing the program and then adding a "Z." Your Watch window will look like Figure 11-11. If you look at Figure 11-11, you can see that the mLeftChild of the root node is pointing to itself. This is obviously wrong and so we need to look at the code to find out what went wrong.

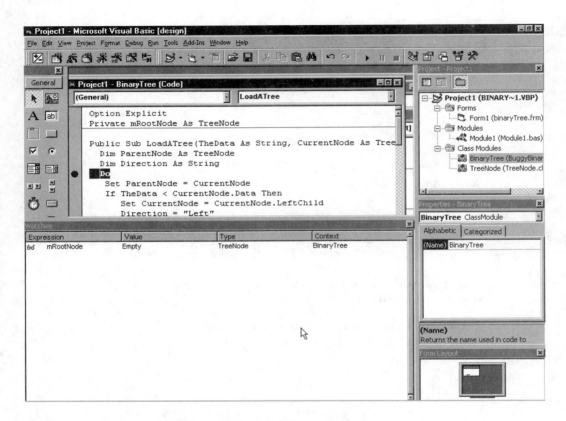

Figure 11-6   First steps in debugging the LoadATree procedure

Here's the code in the buggy version of LoadATree:

```
Public Sub LoadATree(TheData As String, CurrentNode As
TreeNode)
   Dim ParentNode As TreeNode
   Dim Direction As String
   Do
     Set ParentNode = CurrentNode
     If TheData < CurrentNode.Data Then
        Set CurrentNode = CurrentNode.LeftChild
        Direction = "Left"
      Else
        Set CurrentNode = CurrentNode.RightChild
        Direction = "Right"
      End If
Loop Until CurrentNode Is Nothing
```

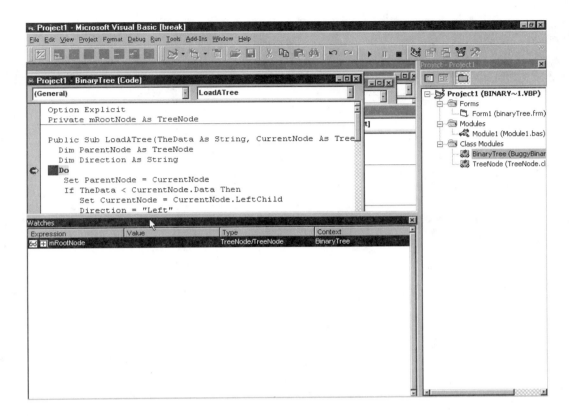

Figure 11-7 The breakpoint hit

```
    Set CurrentNode = New TreeNode
    CurrentNode.Data = TheData
    If Direction = "Left" Then
       Set ParentNode.LeftChild = CurrentNode
    Else
       Set ParentNode.LeftChild = CurrentNode
    End If
End Sub
```

Staring at this for a second and knowing that the problem is in the left child, we can see that we made the usual kind of typo in the following clause:

```
If Direction = "Left" Then
    Set ParentNode.LeftChild = CurrentNode
  Else
    Set ParentNode.LeftChild = CurrentNode
End If
```

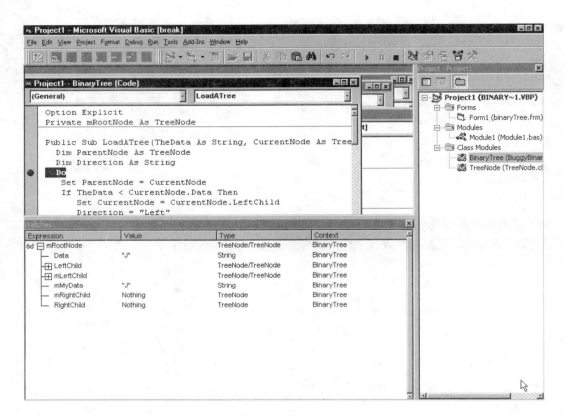

Figure 11-8   mRootNode object variable viewed

Obviously, the second Set ParentNode line should be:

```
set ParentNode.RightChild = CurrentNode!
```

If you run the program with this change it should load the tree correctly. (You can check this with the Watch window and the Sort button, for example.)

Deletion Routines: Reference Counting

Okay, now that we have the tree loaded it's time to test (and debug) the main part of the deletion routines. The controller code is given here:

```
Public Sub DeleteNode(NodeToGo As TreeNode)
    Dim MyParent As TreeNode
    Set MyParent = FindParent(NodeToGo)
    If MyParent Is Nothing Then
        Call DeleteRootNode
```

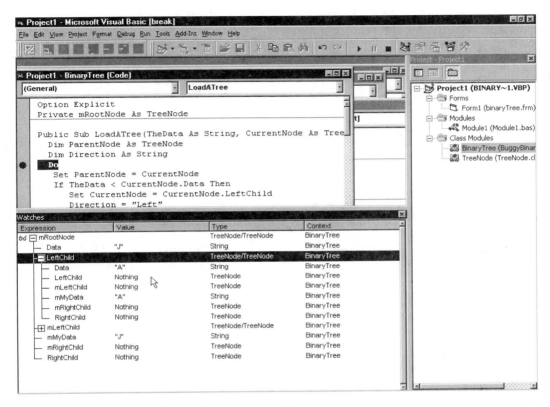

Figure 11-9 mRootNode viewed with a node added

```
        Exit Sub
    End If

    If (NodeToGo.RightChild Is Nothing) And Not _
(NodeToGo.LeftChild Is Nothing) Then
        If MyParent.LeftChild Is NodeToGo Then
            Set MyParent.LeftChild = NodeToGo.LeftChild
        Else
            Set MyParent.RightChild = NodeToGo.LeftChild
        End If
        Set NodeToGo.LeftChild = Nothing
    ElseIf Not (NodeToGo.RightChild Is Nothing) And _
(NodeToGo.LeftChild Is Nothing) Then
        If MyParent.LeftChild Is NodeToGo Then
            Set MyParent.LeftChild = NodeToGo.RightChild
        Else
```

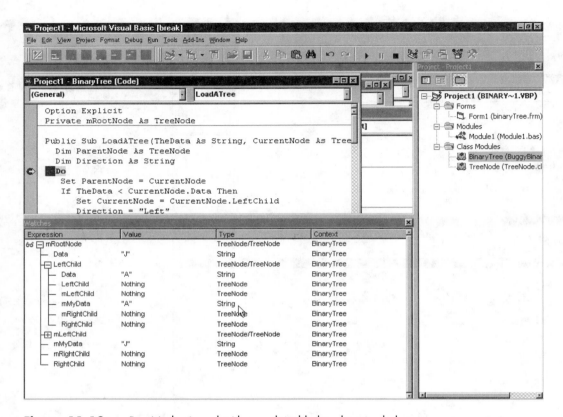

Figure 11-10   mRootNode viewed with a node added and expanded

```
                    Set MyParent.RightChild = NodeToGo.RightChild
            End If
            Set NodeToGo.RightChild = Nothing
        Else
            Call DeleteWithTwoChildren(NodeToGo, MyParent)
        End If
        Set NodeToGo = Nothing
    End Sub
```

To test this routine continue to have the mRootNode object variable as a watch item but also add the global reference counter (gRefCount) as a watch item. Make sure that the scope of the watch for this global variable is set to be all modules. We used as data for the tree: J, A, M, C, E, F, K. This gives us a tree like Figure 11-12.

If you sort the tree and then double click on the line containing E in the first list box, everything works okay. You see a message box saying you are in

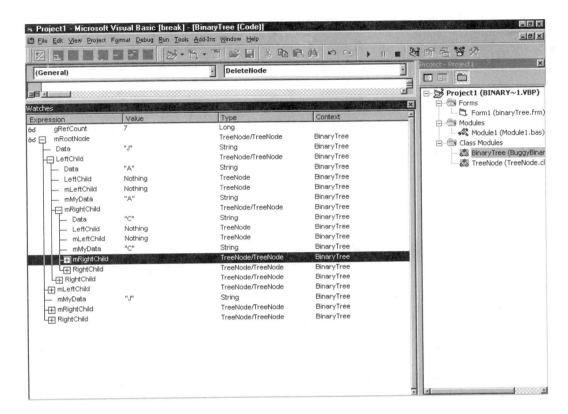

Figure 11-11   mRootNode viewed with the bug revealed

the Terminate event for E and if you check the Watch Window you will see that the gRefCount variable is giving you six, as it should. If you double click on F however, you see that you get an error message saying "Object variable or With block variable not set." (See Figure 11-13.)

This error message almost always means that the object variable you are using is set to Nothing when you meant to refer to an existing object. We need to find out why this happened. We know F has no children so that helps us isolate the part of the code that is causing the problem. So, keep the watch items as before and place a breakpoint at the Set MyParent line in the DeleteNode routine. Run the program again. delete the E node by stepping through the program. Try to delete the F node. Add the MyParent object variable to the Watch window. Look at it. (See Figure 11-14). Everything seems to be okay. MyParent is "C" as it is supposed to be.

Continue stepping through the code, keeping an eye on the watch window.

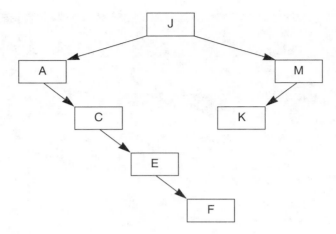

Figure 11-12   A demo tree

Somehow we ended up in the FindNextEntry routine! Figure 11-15 shows you the Calls stack that got us where we are. As you can see in Figure 11-15, we seem to have ended up in the DeleteWithTwoChildren routine when we know the node "F" has no children.

If you look at the code, you see the problem, somehow since we thought we had nothing to do if the node had no children, we neglected to put any code in to deal with this situation. So, let's be naive and simply add a line that says:

```
If (NodeToGo.RightChild Is Nothing) And NodeToGo _
LeftChild Is Nothing) Then Exit Sub
```

since we assume the rule is that if the node has no children, we have nothing to do to! If you do this and run the program you will quickly see that there is

Figure 11-13   An error message

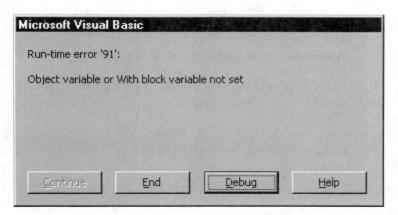

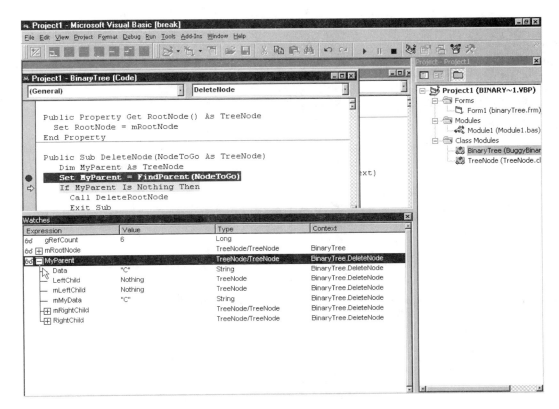

Figure 11-14 Watching during node deletion

a problem. Nodes with no children seem to get deleted erratically, if at all. The reference count is never right, the Terminate event doesn't seem to get called when it is supposed to (since the message box doesn't show up when

Figure 11-15 The Calls window

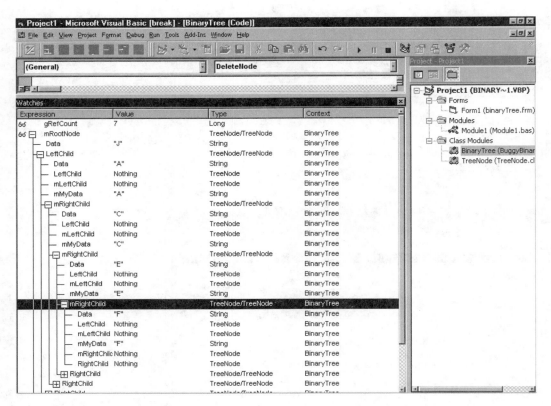

Figure 11-16   Drilling down to hunt for a deleted node

we think it should) and so on. This kind of problem usually means that there are some dangling references that we need to clear up.

To try to get a better handle on this, run the program again and try to delete the F node. You can see that something is wrong because you don't see the terminate message box and the reference count is seven instead of six. We need to drill down in the Watch window to see if we can find what references are dangling. For this, place a breakpoint at the line we added and make sure that the mRootNode object variable is being watched. Drill down until you get to the node for E as shown in Figure 11-16. Now we are really confused because the left child pointer of E is pointing to F, yet we thought the F node was already deleted. Welcome to the joys of dangling references!

The problem turns out to be that although the outline said we didn't have to do anything if a node had no children, this is not quite right in our implementation. The point is that since the parent of a node maintains a reference to its children, we need to make sure these references are set to Nothing as well. Here's the code that you need to use instead of that naïve Exit Sub call:

```
If NodeToGo.RightChild Is Nothing And NodeToGo.LeftChild _
Is Nothing Then
        ' no children reset parent pointers!
        If MyParent.LeftChild Is NodeToGo Then
          Set MyParent.LeftChild = Nothing
        Else
          Set MyParent.RightChild = Nothing
        End If
```

UNDER THE HOOD: API CALLS AND THE REGISTRY

Topics in this Chapter

Chapter 12

C hapter 6 had a short introduction to using the Windows API; this chapter tries to cover the rest of what a working VB programmer needs to know. We will also show you what you need to know about the Windows *Registry*. (The Registry is where Windows stores essentially all the information it needs for proper functioning.)

Before we begin though, we want to point out that it is possible to write endlessly about the Windows API and for almost as long about the Windows Registry. They are exceptionally complicated, usually maddening, and can be painful to work with. For example, the definitive book on the Windows API for Visual Basic programmers is around 1600 pages.[1] Appleman's book is a important reference that every serious Visual Basic programmer will want to own but it is hardly something you will want to read from cover to cover. We won't try in this chapter to give you the Reader's Digest condensed version of Appleman's 1600+ pages—that would be impossible. Instead, we want to:

- Make sure you understand the mechanics of using the various kinds of API calls.

- Give you a handle on the 20 or so API calls that a VB programmer uses on a daily basis.

---

1. Dan Appleman's *Visual Basic 5.0 Programmer's Guide to the Windows API*, Ziff-Davis Press, 1997.

We will also show you how to use an Add-In that we wrote that makes using the Windows API a little easier. It lets you search the needed Declares using the equivalent of VB's Like operator. (Although Add-Ins are explained only in Chapter 14, we do supply the source code in the CH12 directory of the CD.)

Similarly, there are a half a dozen or so books on the Windows Registry that start around 400 pages and go up from there. We can't hope to cover everything that these specialized books do in this chapter either. (We recommend *Inside The Windows 95 Registry* by Ron Petrusha (O'Reilly Press). It has some very useful chapters addressed directly to VB programmers.) Most of the time, VB programmers use the Registry only to save the current settings of an application. This can be done completely in VB without any API calls. We will show you the VB commands needed for doing this. Next, we give you a little program that lets you save various VB configurations to the Registry. That way you can start up VB in different configurations depending on the project you are using. For example, you can have a special configuration for debugging and another one for "hacking." This program demonstrates how to use the API calls that let you completely control the Registry.

Tip

When using API calls in VB, the Microsoft "Developers Network" and the Microsoft's "Knowledge Base" become even more valuable than they usually are. (The Knowledge Base is available as part of a Developer Network subscription. A sample probably came with your copy of VB.) These resources contain quite a lot of useful code that (at your own risk, of course), you are free to use. A searchable version of the knowledge base may be found at Microsoft's web site (www.microsoft.com). You can either subscribe to the Developer Network on CD (which includes the Knowledge Base) or use the free on-line version of both. Both the CD and on-line version are searchable.

Should You Use the Windows API?

It may seem strange to begin a chapter on using the Windows API by telling you that most of the time it isn't necessary to use it! However this is something that you should always keep in mind. The 32-bit Windows API consists of literally thousands of functions. In some sense, Windows itself is a result of the cooperation of these API functions. It should therefore come as no surprise that API functions allow you take complete control of Windows. If you want to flash a window, there's an API call for that. Do you want to add images instead of text to a menu bar? There a way to do this. Make text display in a circle on a form? There a way to do that. In fact, it is hard to imagine anything a fanatic API programmer couldn't get Windows to do. And, pretty much anything a C/C++ API programmer can do with the Windows API, a Visual Basic programmer can do as well. (Occasionally, a third party tool like Desaware's [www.desaware.com] great "SpyWorks" tool might be necessary to use some of the more exotic API functions.)

Given that Windows API calls are so powerful and therefore so seductive, why do we suggest that you forget about 95 percent of the Windows API calls that are so carefully documented in an API references like Microsoft's SDK or Appleman's book? The reason is that experience has shown that a Visual Basic programmer doesn't need to bother with them, most of the powers you need from them are already built into VB. For example, there is an API call to get the current directory, but VB has a perfectly good CurDir function that does what you need and is easier to use. Of the remaining 5 percent of API functions, you will use most of them only once in a very long while. What is left is about 20 API calls that you will use pretty much on a daily basis. This chapter will, of course, explain how to use these 20 or so API functions. For example, here are some things you may need to do frequently that are simply impossible to do using pure VB:

- You can't shut down and restart Windows.
- You can't find out how much free disk space is available.
- You can't get a timer more accurate than 1/18 of a second.
- Find out if the machine is running Windows 95 or NT.
- Start a program (like with Shell) but *know* when it finishes.

But the point to keep in mind is that *most* of the time there is a way completely within VB to accomplish your goal. After all, one reason why VB programmers are so much more productive than C/C++ Windows programmers is *because* VB and its controls encapsulate the functionality of the API so well. For example, there is an API function to play a multimedia audio file—there's actually a whole library of API functions for working with multimedia. It's not particularly difficult to use these API calls but why bother? Most of the time you are better off using the multimedia control. Why? Because the multimedia control has so much more power—and in most multimedia applications you will need this extra power. Writing lots of API calls in order to recover most of the functionality of the multimedia control is pretty silly. Why reinvent the wheel? What do you think the people at Microsoft who wrote the multimedia control did? The answer is that they encapsulated the most useful of the multimedia API calls and wrapped them into a nice user interface!

However, the extra overhead needed for a control like the Multimedia OCX does lead to one more time when you might consider using API calls:

- When you need only a limited subset of a control's functionality and the footprint of your application needs to be as small as possible.

A good example of this is the choice between using Microsoft's SysInfo control versus using the GetSystemInfo API call.

Are there any other times that API calls make sense? We can think of one more:

- Where it is so much faster or easier to use the API call that you feel that the extra time saved is worth making your code a bit more complex and a bit harder to maintain and debug.

A good example of this is that there is an API call that lets you search a list box for a string or part of a string essentially instantly. We may not bother using this API call for a list box that contains 10 or 20 items but we would certainly use it for a list box that contains a hundred items. (Actually what we would do is make a searchable list box once and for all by extending the ordinary list box using this API call. You can do this using the techniques from Chapter 13.)

Finally, another common use of the Windows API is for making graphical special effects, such as fading an image, animation, or fancy font changes. This is a highly specialized area and we won't cover it here. We do want to point out that the PaintPicture function that was added to VB in Version 4 may turn out to do most or all of what you want. Before turning to API calls, you might want to master this neat VB function.

Note

Keep in mind that once you start using API calls, VB's great debugging tools become less valuable. (They can't do much with the "black box" that an API call gives you.) For debugging a program that uses API calls extensively, you may need to compile your program with the "Create Symbolic Debug Info" option that is available on the Compile Tab of the Project|Properties dialog box. Then you can use a C/C++ debugger like the one supplied with VC++ 5.0. We also recommend getting third-party debugging aids like the great ones from NuMega Technologies (www.numega.com) if you start using API calls extensively.

In sum:

- Your code will be a lot easier to maintain and debug if you avoid API calls unless absolutely necessary.

An Overview of the Win API Libraries

The core Windows API is divided into three dynamic link libraries. There is a fourth library that is used for multimedia and another one where the Registry functions are stored. What follows are short descriptions of the three main libraries along with the names you use to refer to them in a Declare statement.

Windows Management (user32)

This library has the basic windows management functions. This library also has the keyboard and mouse handling functions. (See below for an example of using this library to read or reset the keyboard state.) The clipboard functions are here as well as are the ones for managing dynamic data exchange. (The libraries for ActiveX are contained in the stdole library and are not considered part of the Windows API, although they are obviously vital to the proper functioning of Windows.)

Tip

Keep in mind when deciding where to look for API functionality that, although controls sit in Form windows, from the point of view of Windows most controls are windows. This means they can be managed separately from the Form that contains them. You can, for example, even move a control from one form to another using an API call.

(The forms that are not windows in the sense of the Windows API are those without a Handle property. See the section on Windows Messaging for more on Window's handles. The Line and Shape and Image controls are the most common examples of controls without a "Windows handle.")

Graphic Device Interface (gdi32)

This library acts as the interface to the display and printers. The gdi32 library is where you go for the fancy graphics effects that are only possible with API calls. You can control fonts, drawing, and do quite sophisticated image manipulation with these functions. The user32 library and the gdi32 library work hand in hand to control what the user sees on his or her screen.

System Services (kernel32)

This library contains the routines that handle memory, files, and Windows 95 and NT's ability to (seem to) run more than one program at the same time (see Chapter 14 for more on the operating system's multiprocessing ability). This library also handles communicating with the various kinds of dynamic libraries that may be in memory at a given moment. Since VB programmers are shielded (thankfully) from having to worry about memory management, the most common use of this library in VB is for file and disk handling. We give some examples of these uses below.

Getting the Right Declare Statement

First, before we can show you these techniques, we need to bring up the unpleasant point that VB comes with little or no documentation on what the various API functions do or how to use them. All VB has is an API Viewer Add-In that lets you get at the syntax and constants needed for a specific Declare statement more easily. The API viewer won't help you find out what API function (Declare statement) to use. (If you need something we don't cover here turn to the Knowledge Base or Appleman's book.)

Chose Add-Ins|API Viewer to bring the API viewer up. The API Viewer lets you copy Declare statements, along with the constants and user defined types needed to use an API call, into the ClipBoard or directly into your VB program. Figure 12-1 gives you a picture of what the API viewer looks like.

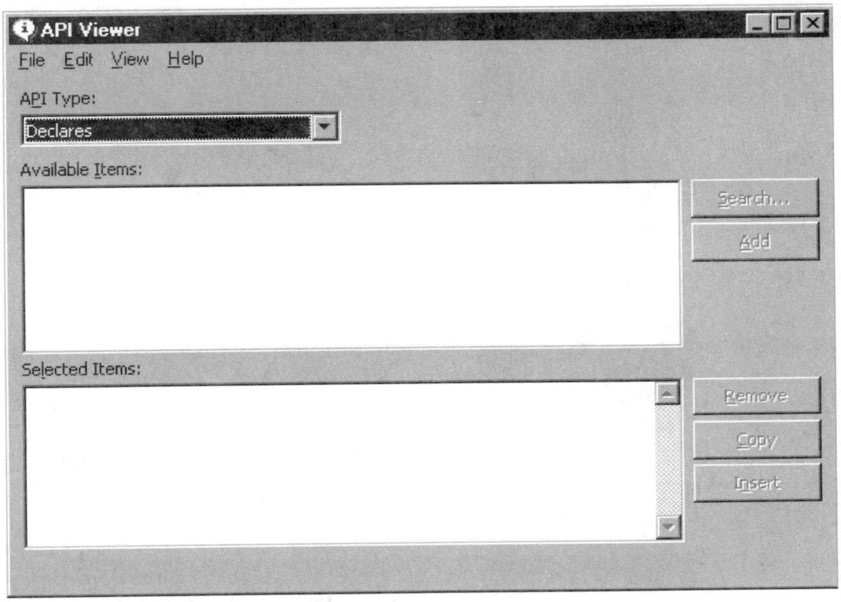

API Viewer

File Edit View Help

API Type:

Declares

Available Items:

Search...

Add

Selected Items:

Remove

Copy

Insert

Figure 12-1   The API Viewer

Caution

It is absolutely vital that you use the correct parameters in a Declare statement. Leaving off something as seemingly innocuous as a ByVal modifier will almost certainly crash your program. We strongly recommend using the API viewer program or our Add-In (see below) to copy the Declare statement directly into your code.

The first step in using the API viewer is to tell it where to find the information. For this:

- Open the File menu
- Open the file called Win32api.txt that may be found in the WinAPI subdirectory of your VB directory.

The first time you load this file, the API viewer will ask you whether you want to convert this file to a database, as shown in Figure 12-2. If you have the extra 1.5 megs or so of hard disk space that the database version of Win32api.txt will take, we recommend doing this. Having the API file in data-

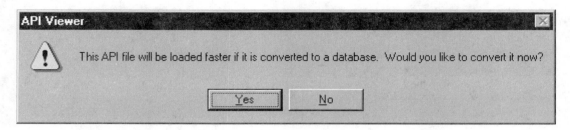

Figure 12-2   Message box to convert API file to a database

base form speeds up the searching process considerably. (This will also let you use our API search Add-In that is described below.)

The API viewer search facilities are primitive. At first glance, it doesn't seem to have a search feature at all, instead it uses the stupid search facilities

Figure 12-3   Inserting an API Declare

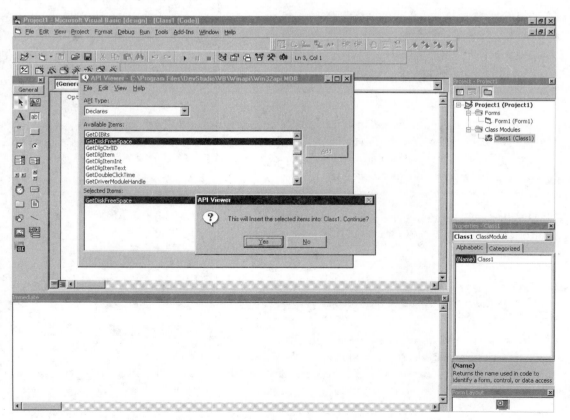

that come standard with a list box. If you type a letter it goes to the first item that begins with that letter. If you type another letter it doesn't do an incremental search it goes to the first item that begins with that letter. *You can change this behavior by choosing View\Line Item.* Once you select this item, you can use incremental search.

Using the API viewer is simple. For example, suppose you want to use the GetDiskFreeSpace API:

1. Find it in the list of Declares.

2. Click the Add button.

3. Then click the Insert button.

The API viewer will pop up a nice message box telling you where it will insert the Declare (see Figure 12-3). It will be pasted at the current location of the cursor in your VB project. The convention is to make all API declares Public in a Code (.bas) module. You can also have them as Private in a Form or Class module. The API viewer inserts a Declare on one long line, but most people use underscores to break it up so they can see the whole declare more easily.

Tip

Many of the API functions that get information begin with Get, as in our example of GetDiskFreeSpace. (The naming conventions for APIs often leave something to be desired.)

Still, it would have been a lot more useful to have a full search facility built into the API viewer. For example, suppose all you could do was vaguely remember that the API call for getting the amount of free disk space had the word "Free" in it. There's no way to search for text *inside* a string using the API viewer. We decided that this feature was too useful not to have it available for our (and your) use. So we wrote our own API Add-In that lets you search inside the Declares using the same wildcards as VB's Like operator. (We also give you the source code.) All you have to do to use our Add-In is (see Chapter 14 for more on using Add-Ins):

1. Change the API32.txt file to a database (.mdb) file as described above.

2. Leave this .mdb file in the WinAPI subdirectory below where VB is stored.

3. Copy the APISearch.DLL file from our CD to the VB. It may be found in the CH12\APISearch directory on the CD.

4. Register the Add-In.

You can do this by using the regsvr32 program that may be found on the Tools directory of your VB CD. (You should copy regsvr32 to your C:\Windows directory, it's a very useful program to have in your path.) This can be done by typing regsvr32, followed by the full path name where you put the APISearch.DLL in the Run dialog box available off the Start menu. For example:

```
regsvr32 "c:\program files\vb\APIsearch.dll"
```

After you have done this you have to go to the file called VBADDIN.INI file in your \Windows directory and add this line at the end of it:

```
APISearch.Connect=1
```

Then you can start VB and check off the API search option in the Add-Ins|Add-In Manager. At this point the APISearch Add-In is ready to use. It uses the same kind of "fuzzy" search wildcards that VB's own Like operator uses. For example by using *Free, you could have searched for all Declares that have the word Free embedded in them. Figure 12-4 is a picture of what you will see if you use our APISearch Add-In to look for Free.

Figure 12-4   Using our API searcher

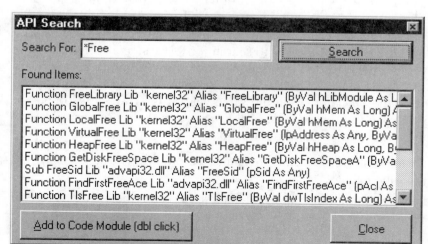

The Anatomy of a Declare Statement

What we want to do in this section is explain the terms used in an API Declare that may not be familiar to you. First, API calls can be either functions or subroutines. As with ordinary VB programming the function version returns a value, the sub version will not. Some API calls come in both flavors; however, you can only declare one flavor per program. As with any function in VB, you can use the function version as a sub program by throwing away the return value or simply not bothering to get it in the first place.

The General framework for an API declare is:

```
[Public | Private] Declare Sub|Function Name Lib "libname" _
[Alias "aliasname"] [([arglist])] [As Type]
```

Here's an example:

```
Private Declare Function SendMessage Lib "user32" Alias _
"SendMessageA" (ByVal hwnd As Long, ByVal wMsg As Long, _
ByVal wParam As Long, lParam As Any) As Long
```

API declarations are often *long;* luckily, VB now allows you to use the underscore with API declarations.

The *name* parameter is required and is how you will refer to the API call in your VB program. In our example, the name we will use is SendMessage. Note that *unlike VB itself, API names are case sensitive: "sendmessagea" won't work.* The keyword *Lib* must always be there. Following the Lib keyword is the name of the library (user32 in our example). Libraries can, as we mentioned in Chapter 6, be from any DLL, not just one of the standard Windows ones. The Alias keyword is optional. You use this keyword when you don't want to (or can't use) the official API name. In our example, the official name of the API call that we are using is SendMessageA. Aliases are necessary when the name of the API call is an illegal name in VB. (Beginning with an underscore is the most common.) In this case, the Alias is simply a convenience because Windows 16 programmers are used to calling this function SendMessage.

Note

Many API calls come in an "A" flavor or a "W" flavor. The letter indicates that it will work with Unicode strings. The version of SendMessage we gave is the ASCII version and this is indicated by the "A". Also, if you happen to know it, you can use the numeric version of the function's ordinal order in the DLL in the Alias clause by using a # instead of the human readable version. (We don't know why you would do this, however.)

The parameters for a Declare can be passed by value or by reference (the default). As we said before it is *essential* that you not change the method for parameter passing given in the API declare. The type names are as you expect, except the "As Any" parameter that you saw in SendMessage means that you can send any Visual Basic type to that particular API call—it does not mean only variants are allowed.

Tip

You can change a declaration using As Any via the Alias keyword to be type safe. For example:

```
Private Declare Function SendMessageByString Lib _
"user32" Alias "SendMessageA" (ByVal hwnd As Long, _
ByVal wMsg As Long, ByVal wParam As Long, _
lParam As String) As Long
```

and then VB will enforce you using a string as the parameter when you call SendMessage.

Finally, just as with ordinary VB functions and subprograms, you can pass arrays or have optional arguments as parameters in an API Declare.

Getting Information Out of an API Call

There are basically three techniques that you will need to use to get information back from an API call. There are:

- Techniques for getting numeric information back via variables passed into the API call by reference.
- Techniques for getting string information back via a *string buffer variable* passed by reference.
- Techniques for getting back information when it is stored in a user-defined type. (Usually called a *structure* in deference to the tender sensibilities of the C/C++ crowd.)

We'll start with an example of getting the free disk space. This is an example of getting numeric information out of an API call. We then will give examples of the other two techniques.

Example: Getting Free Disk Space

As we mentioned above, here's the Declare for the GetDiskFreeSpace API:

```
Declare Function GetDiskFreeSpace Lib "kernel32" Alias _
"GetDiskFreeSpaceA" (ByVal lpRootPathName As String, _
lpSectorsPerCluster As Long, lpBytesPerSector As Long, _
lpNumberOfFreeClusters As Long, lpTtoalNumberOfClusters _
As Long) As Long
```

Obviously this is going to be pretty useless without some documentation. Well, just to show you how useful the Internet can be, Figure 12-5 gives you what you can get by doing a search at Microsoft's Web site for GetDiskSpaceFree. (We could have restricted the search to just look at the Visual Basic knowledge base if we had wanted to.)

Figure 12-5   Searching for information at Microsoft's Web site

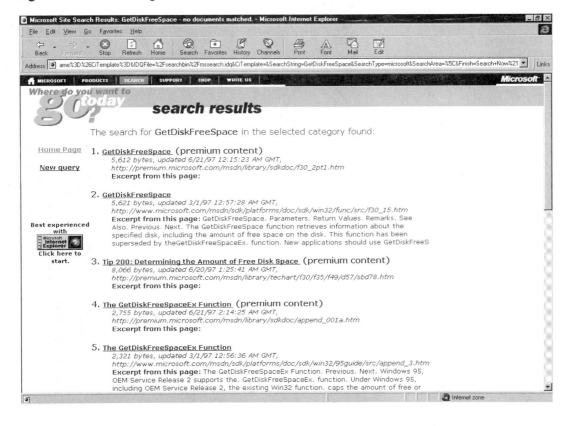

Note

Premium content just means that you have to register to use it. Microsoft doesn't charge for this information and lets you use it freely although, of course, they make no guarantees about its accuracy and the disclaimer is full of the usual legal mumbo jumbo: "You have a royalty-free right to use, modify, reproduce and distribute the Sample Application Files and source code (and/or any modified version) in any way you find useful, provided that you agree that Microsoft has no warranty, obligations or liability for any Sample Application Files or source code."

The key item for a VB programmer was item #6 (although you could have used the information in some of the other article). Here's what the abstract says:

6. <u>How To Find and View the Amount of Free Disk Space on a Drive</u>

10,297 bytes, updated 7/1/96 12:00:00 AM GMT,
http://www.microsoft.com/kb/articles/q153/0/91.htm

Excerpt from this page: From Visual Basic, it is possible to use the Win32 API function GetDiskFreeSpace to find and view the amount of free disk space on a specified drive. The code sample below shows this in practice. MORE INFORMATION Sample Code 1. Start a new proje...

If you click on this link you will be taken to a knowledge base article that tells you how to get the free disk space using this API. This article also gives you the full source code for an example program to do this.

The answer to getting the free disk space turns out to be that you:

1. Give the API function the name of the drive.
2. Multiply the other parameters together.

Sometimes the knowledge base articles are too informative. You would have to examine the source code given in this article to see that is what you really needed to do to get the free disk space. On the other hand, the source code they give is quite straightforward:

Listing 12-1:   Getting Free Disk Space

```
Dim info As DiskInformation
Dim lAnswer As Long
Dim lpRootPathName As String
Dim lpSectorsPerCluster As Long
Dim lpBytesPerSector As Long
Dim lpNumberOfFreeClusters As Long
Dim lpTotalNumberOfClusters As Long
Dim lBytesPerCluster As Long
Dim lNumFreeBytes As Double
Dim sString As String
lpRootPathName = "c:\"
lAnswer = GetDiskFreeSpace(lpRootPathName, _
lpSectorsPerCluster, _ lpBytesPerSector, _
lpNumberOfFreeClusters, lpTotalNumberOfClusters)
lBytesPerCluster = lpSectorsPerCluster * lpBytesPerSector
lNumFreeBytes = lBytesPerCluster * lpNumberOfFreeClusters
sString = "Number of Free Bytes : " & lNumFreeBytes & vbCr & vbLf
sString = sString & "Number of Free Kilobytes: " & _
(lNumFreeBytes / 1024) & "K" & vbCr & vbLf
sString = sString & "Number of Free Megabytes: " & _
Format(((lNumFreeBytes / 1024) / 1024), "0.00") & "MB" _
MsgBox sString
```

Note they even are nice enough to convert the answer to megabytes for you. It is obvious how to modify this information for your own use. You simply have to change the value of the string that gives the drive. Finally, notice that although the return value of the API call was a long, it wasn't the amount of free space as you might naively have hoped, instead you have to multiply some parameters together.

This is perhaps the most common way of using an API call: pass by reference allows the API call to change the value of its parameters to reflect *part* of the required information. You then get the needed information by combining the parameters in sometimes obvious, sometimes arcane, ways.

Tip

The values returned by API calls are often simply error flags. For example, the value returned by GetDiskFreeSpace is non-zero if the drive information was successfully obtained and zero otherwise. The Knowledge Base article that we quoted would probably have been better with the insertion of an If-Then, as in the following code:

```
lAnswer = GetDiskFreeSpace(lpRootPathName, _
lpSectorsPerCluster, lpBytesPerSector, _
lpNumberOfFreeClusters, lpTotalNumberOfClusters)
If lAnswer  = 0 Then
   ' or raise an error
   MsgBox "Error accessing drive"
Else
   'what they have
```

instead of proceeding as if no error condition can ever happen.

Getting String Information from an API Call

The GetDiskFreeSpace API call returned its information by changing the value of the long variables passed by reference to it. The results of passing by reference is usually the key to getting string information back from an API call. The trick here is that you have to supply a "buffer" for the information. The buffer must be a string variable already filled with enough blanks so that it is big enough to hold the information that will be returned. (API calls, unlike VB itself, cannot resize strings on the fly.) The value returned by the API call is then how many characters you need to take out of the buffer variable.

A good example of this technique is when you need to work with the API function that tells you where the \Windows directory may be found. If you get the Declare off the API viewer you will see that it is:

```
Declare Function GetWindowsDirectory Lib "kernel32" _
Alias "GetWindowsDirectoryA" (ByVal lpBuffer As String, _
ByVal nSize As Long) As Longlacle off the
```

The steps for using this API are:

1. Create a string variable that currently holds enough characters for the worse possible case. (In this case, 255 characters is certainly enough.)
2. Call the API.
3. The return value of the API call is the number of characters sent back.

Therefore:

- Use the Left function with the value returned from Step 3 in order to get the \Windows directory

Here's some sample code:

```
Dim Foo As String
Foo = Space(255)
Foo = Left(Foo, GetWindowsDirectory(Foo, 255))
MsgBox "The windows directory is " & Foo
```

Another sample of this technique (and also an example of how inconsistent the API naming conventions are), is a similar API function called GetTempPath that will tell you what directory Windows is using as its \Temp directory. This kind of information is useful since you often need a place to stash temp files. The Declare is:

```
Private Declare Function GetTempPath Lib "kernel32" _
Alias "GetTempPathA" (ByVal nBufferLength As Long, _
ByVal lpBuffer As String) As Long
```

and, as you can see, the order is reversed for this API call: You give the size first and the buffer after. Here's some code that uses this API call:

```
Foo = Space(255)
Foo = Left(Foo, GetTempPath(255, Foo))
MsgBox "A place to store temp files  is " & Foo
```

What we recommend that you make a class that wraps the most common API file handling calls. For example, this class might start out:

Listing 12-2:   Class to Wrap the API Calls

```
'Class to wrap the API calls
Option Explicit

Private Declare Function GetWindowsDirectory Lib "kernel32" _
Alias "GetWindowsDirectoryA" (ByVal lpBuffer As String, _
ByVal nSize As Long) As Long
Private Declare Function GetTempPath Lib "kernel32" Alias _
"GetTempPathA" (ByVal nBufferLength As Long, ByVal _
lpBuffer As String) As Long

Public Property Get WindowsDirectory() As String
  Dim Foo As String
  Foo = Space(255)
  WindowsDirectory = Left(Foo, GetWindowsDirectory(Foo, 255))
End Property

Public Property Get TempDirectory() As String
  Dim Foo As String
```

```
Foo = Space(255)
TempDirectory = Left(Foo, GetTempPath(255, Foo))
End Property
```

Tip

We recommend wrapping API calls into utility classes that you compile into ActiveX DLLs (dynamic link libraries). See Chapter 14 for more on this technique.

Using Structures

The final method of getting information out of an API call depends on the API call returning (at least so far as VB is concerned) a user defined type. A good example of this is the API call that lets you determine when a file was created (or cheat and change the time that Windows *thinks* the file was created.) This actually requires a fair amount of work. The problem is that any time you use an API call to work with a file, you need to have something called a *file handle*. The only way to get a file handle is through another API function. Then you have to be sure to close the handle through the use of a third API function. Here are the steps for working with GetFileTime. (Set FileTime is similar, and we will leave it to you to make the necessary changes.)

First add the Declare for the GetFileTime call:

```
Private Declare Function GetFileTime Lib "kernel32" _
(ByVal hFile As Long, lpCreationTime As Any, lpLastAccessTime _
As FILETIME, lpLastWriteTime As Any) As Long
```

Now add the Declares to get the needed file handle and to close them. It turns out that you get a file handle by using the CreateFile API with an OPEN_EXISTING constant:

```
Private Declare Function CreateFile Lib "kernel32" _
Alias "CreateFileA" (ByVal lpFileName As String, _
ByVal dwDesiredAccess As Long, ByVal dwShareMode As Long, _
ByVal lpSecurityAttributes As Any, ByVal _
dwCreationDisposition As Long, ByVal dwFlagsAndAttributes _
```

```
As Long, ByVal hTemplateFile As Long) As Long
Private Declare Function CloseHandle Lib "kernel32" _
(ByVal hObject As Long) As Long
```

Here are the constants we need:

```
Const GENERIC_READ = &H80000000
Const GENERIC_WRITE = &H40000000
Const OPEN_EXISTING = 3
Const FILE_ATTRIBUTE_NORMAL = &H80
```

(You could work with other kinds of files by using a constant other than FILE_ATTRIBUTE_NORMAL—or even combine them with the Or operator to take care of multiple cases.)

Next we need the user defined type for the FILETIME structure:

```
Private Type FILETIME
    dwLowDateTime As Long
    dwHighDateTime As Long
End Type
```

Now it turns out that you need another API function along with yet another structure in order to translate the FILETIME structure into a more useful form. The API call is:

```
Private Declare Function FileTimeToSystemTime Lib _
"kernel32" (lpFileTime As FILETIME, _
lpSystemTime As SYSTEMTIME) As Long
```

and the structure you need is:

```
Private Type SYSTEMTIME
    wYear As Integer
    wMonth As Integer
    wDayOfWeek As Integer
    wDay As Integer
    wHour As Integer
    wMinute As Integer
    wSecond As Integer
    wMilliseconds As Integer
End Type
```

Now that we have all the preliminaries in place, the actual work can be done in the following sub, which we use to set the instance fields such as mYear and mMonth in the class. The trick is that we simply pass by reference the correct structures and the API call fills them with the correct information.

Listing 12-3:   Sub for GetFileTime

```
Private Sub WhenAccessed()
  Dim FilePointer As Long
  Dim L As Long
  Dim TempLong As Long
  Dim LastAccess As FILETIME
  Dim TheTime As SYSTEMTIME
  If mFileName = "" Then
    MsgBox "Please set a file name"
    Exit Sub
  End If
  '  Open the file to get a file handle
  FilePointer = CreateFile(mFileName, GENERIC_READ Or _
GENERIC_WRITE, 0&, 0&, OPEN_EXISTING, FILE_ATTRIBUTE_NORMAL, 0&)
  TempLong = GetFileTime(FilePointer, 0, LastAccess, 0)
  TempLong = CloseHandle(FilePointer)

  ' Convert the time to system time
  TempLong = FileTimeToSystemTime(LastAccess, TheTime)

  '  Set the instance fields
  mYear = TheTime.wYear
  mMonth = TheTime.wMonth
  mDay = TheTime.wDay
  mHour = TheTime.wHour
  mMinute = TheTime.wMinute
  mSecond =TheTime.wSecond
End Sub
```

We can then use combine these values with the DateSerial and TimeSerial functions to get human useable results by having two read-only properties:

```
Public Function GetDate() As Date
   GetDate = DateSerial(mYear, mMonth, mDay)
End Function

Public Function GetTime() As Date
   GetTime = TimeSerial(mHour, mMinute, mSecond)
End Function
```

(See the CD for a full implementation of this class.)

Windows Messaging

The SendMessage API that we showed you a little while ago is probably the most powerful API call. For example, most events in VB are triggered in response to Windows sending out a message to the control. Moreover, almost all objects that you see under Windows can be sent a message that interrupts, so to speak, their normal train of thought. In particular, any VB control that has a hWnd property can be sent a message using SendMessage and your program won't continue execution until the message is processed. (The return value of SendMessage is non-zero if the message was successful; you can disregard it and use SendMessage as if it were a Sub if you want to.)

Note

Handles are the generic term used in Windows development for a way of identifying an object. You have already seen how to use a file handle in the GetFileTime API. The hWnd property returns the window handle. The window handle is a long integer that identifies that window uniquely in the current session of Windows. As we said before, any control with an hWnd property can be sent a message and is, as far as Windows is concerned, as much a Window as its parent form.

Tip

In addition to file handles and windows handles (and process handles, see below) there are also device context handles that identify things like printers. The device handle is the value of the hDc property of any object that has this property. For example the Printer object has a device context handle that you can pass to the SelPrint method of a Rich Text Box in order to print the contents in a "WYSIWYG" (what you see is what you get) fashion. Here's some code that shows this off:

```
Dim Handle As Long, Length As Long
Handle = Printer.hDC
Length = Len(RichTextBox1.Text)
RichTextBox1.SelStart = 0
RichTextBox1.SelLength = Length
Printer.Print()
RichTextBox1.SelPrint (Handle)
Printer.EndDoc
```

Using SendMessage lets you send a control a message that asks it do to something that the designers of VB may have left out. For example you can:

- Undo the last action in a text box (instead of needing to change the focus and use SendKeys).
- Stop a control from repainting itself.
- Search a list or combo box incrementally.

Although the details are tedious, using SendMessage is almost trivial: you simply call SendMesssage with the appropriate message constant. All the various flags are given as constants in the API viewer. For example, to tell a text box to undo the last action, you send the WM_UNDO flag. You can even check if you *can* undo the last action in a text box by first passing the EM_CANUNDO parameter and seeing what you get back. Here's some code that undoes the last action in a text box named Text1 using SendMessage:

```
CONST EM_CANUNDO = &HC6
CONST WM_UNDO = &H304
Dim TextHandle As Long, Temp As Long
TextHandle = Text1.hwnd
  If SendMessage(TextHandle, EM_CANUNDO, 0&, 0&)   Then
    Temp = SendMessage(TextHandle, WM_UNDO, 0&, 0&)
  End If
```

Here's another example of where you might want to send a message to a control you often want to stop a control repainting itself temporarily. (TreeView controls are notorious for repainting themselves too frequently.) This can be done with SendMessage as well using code like the following:

```
Public Const WM_SETREDRAW   = &HB
Public Const REDRAWOFF  = 0&
Public Const REDRAWON  = 1&

SendMessage object.hWnd, WM_SETREDRAW, REDRAWOFF, 0&
```

Use:

```
SendMessage object.hWnd, WM_SETREDRAW, REDRAWON, 0&
```

to turn redrawing back on.

Searching a list box or a combo box for a specific piece of text requires sending the control a SendMessage with:

- LB_FINDSTRING for a list box (LB_FINDSTRINGEXACT for a complete match).

- CB_FINDSTRING for a combo box (CB_FINDSTRINGEXACT for a complete match).

Using these constants determines whether a string is a substring of an item in the list or combo box. The search is not case sensitive.

For example, the CD has a project called SearchableListBox. The idea is that you can type in the text box and then the matching item in the list box will be highlighted. It depends on the following txtSearch.Change procedure:

Listing 12-4   Procedure for txtSearchChange

```
Private Sub txtSearch_Change()
    Dim TempString As String
    Dim TheHandle As Long
    Dim Position As Long

    TempString = txtSearch.Text
    TheHandle = lstBox.hwnd
    If Len(TempString) = 0 Then
        'nothing to find
        lstBox.ListIndex = 0
    Else
      'set the list index to the matching entry
     'or back to first entry if nothing found
        Position = SendMessage(TheHandle, LB_FINDSTRING, -1, _
TempString)
        If Position = -1 Then
           lstBox.ListIndex = 0
        Else
            lstBox.ListIndex = Position
        End If
    End If
End Sub
```

Finally, before we leave SendMessage we want to mention that VB5 allows you to intercept and modify and Windows messages *before* they get to a control. This can be done using the new AddressOf operator combined with the SetWindowsLong API call. This technique is called *subclasssing*. We won't cover subclassing in this book since we feel that this is a technique that is rarely needed by VB programmers. Appleman's book is a good place to start if you feel you need to subclass a control. We do want to warn you that subclassing makes debugging your programs within VB almost impossible and can lead to spectacular program crashes as messages don't get to where they are supposed to. If you need to subclass a control, we suggest getting a tool like the one in Desaware's "SpyWorks." (This also comes with a useful tutorial on the ins and outs of subclassing.) Using a control (or DLL) like the ones that come in SpyWorks for subclassing lets you continue to benefit from VB's great IDE while diverting messages away from their intended target.

The Registry

It might be an exaggeration to say that the Registry is where Windows stores *all* the information it needs for its proper functioning—but it wouldn't be much of one. For example, as you saw in Chapter 8, the Registry contains the information needed to match up a GUID (globally unique identifier) with the executable file that can create instances of a class. It contains most of the information that programs store in order to save their state. It contains information about the users who can log in to the system. The list can go on and on.

Tip

A corrupted Registry is one of the most common reasons for Windows to behave erratically. There are some great shareware tools (try www.hotfiles.com) that make backing up the Registry a snap. We strongly suggest backing up your Registry before you start testing any programs that use any of the functions that allow you to manipulate the Registry data.

Figure 12-6 shows you what the Registry looks like, courtesy of the RegEdit program supplied with Windows. As you can see, the Registry looks a bit like a tree node control. You can expand any node by clicking on the + sign. (It is sometimes easier to think of it as a file system with each of the five keys described in Table 12-1 being directories.)

Table 12-1: The Registry Roots	
Key	*Description*
HKEY_CLASSES_ROOT	This contains two types of information. The associations for file name extension like .vbp with Visual Basic and the location of the files associated with GUIDS.

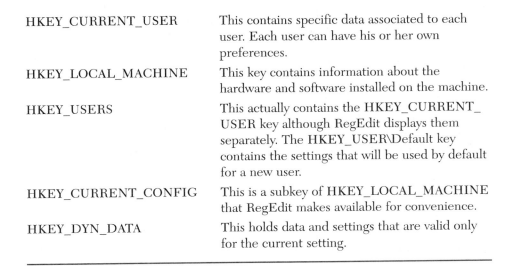

HKEY_CURRENT_USER	This contains specific data associated to each user. Each user can have his or her own preferences.
HKEY_LOCAL_MACHINE	This key contains information about the hardware and software installed on the machine.
HKEY_USERS	This actually contains the HKEY_CURRENT_USER key although RegEdit displays them separately. The HKEY_USER\Default key contains the settings that will be used by default for a new user.
HKEY_CURRENT_CONFIG	This is a subkey of HKEY_LOCAL_MACHINE that RegEdit makes available for convenience.
HKEY_DYN_DATA	This holds data and settings that are valid only for the current setting.

Figure 12-6   The collapsed Registry tree

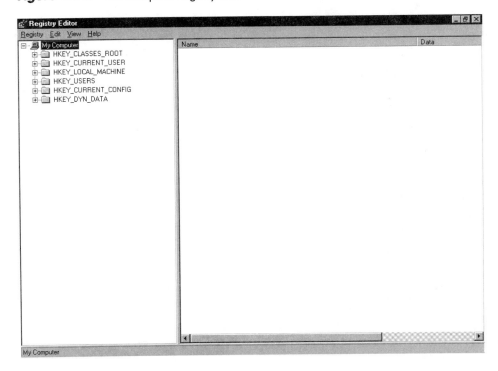

For example, Figure 12-7 shows you what happens if you drill down in HKEY_CLASSES_ROOT using RegEdit's Find command in order to view the information associated with the RichTextBox control. As you can see, there is the totally inscrutable CLASID along with the name of the file (in the Inprocserver32 key). This indicates that the OCX—like all OCX—will work "in-process." (See Chapter 14 for more on what this means.)

Working with VB's Registry Functions

You will often want to save the state of an application so that it can start up in a similar fashion to the way it was the last time. For example, you might want the user's window to be in the same place and have the same size as it did in the previous session. VB5 comes with four functions that let you work with the registry and are the most common ways to save the state of an application. They are described in the following table (all work with a registry key that identifies that node):

Figure 12-7   The Registry entry for the RichTextBox

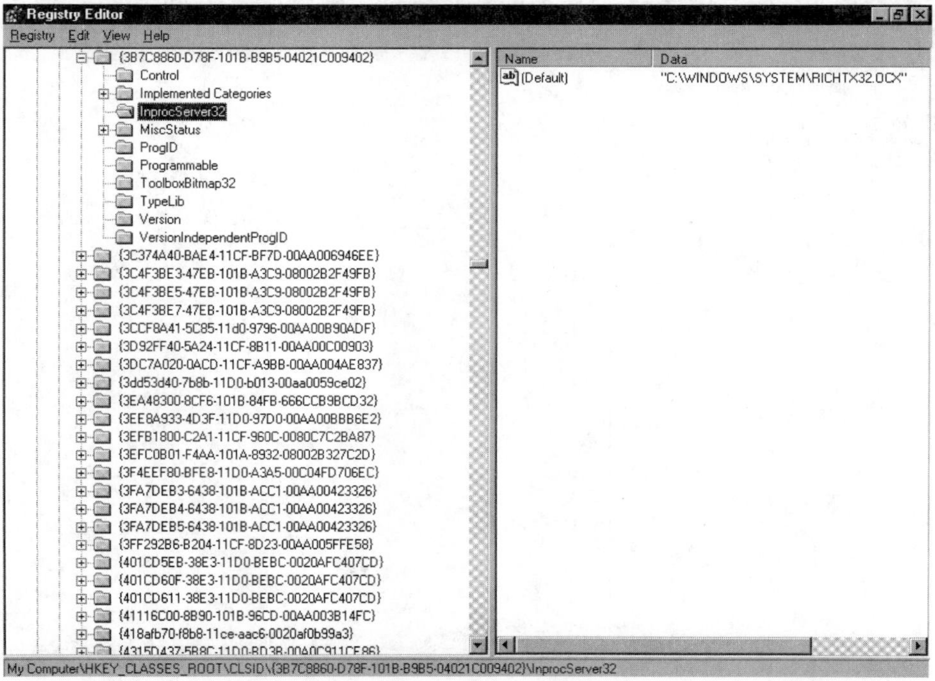

Table 12-2: Registry Functions	

Registry Function or Statement	*Description*
GetSetting function	Retrieves a specific registry setting.
SaveSetting statement	Saves or creates a specific registry setting.
DeleteSetting statement	Deletes a specific registry settings.
GetAllSettings function	Returns an array containing multiple registry settings.

The GetAllSettings, which returns an array, is rarely used.

For example, here is all the code that you would need to make the height and width of a form persist so that the program will start up with the same dimensions it had previously:

```
Option Explicit

Private Sub Form_Load()
  Dim MyHeight As Integer, MyWidth As Integer
  MyHeight = GetSetting("TestRegistrySettings", "Startup", _
"Height", CStr(Screen.Height / 2))
  MyWidth = GetSetting("TestRegistrySettings", "Startup", _
"Width", CStr(Screen.Width / 2))
  Me.Height = MyHeight
  Me.Width = MyWidth
End Sub


Private Sub Form_Unload(Cancel As Integer)
  SaveSetting "TestRegistrySettings", "Startup", "Height", _
CStr(Me.Height)
  SaveSetting "TestRegistrySettings", "Startup", "Width", _
CStr(Me.Width)
End Sub
```

Figure 12-8 shows you where this information is stored in the Registry. As you can see, these functions store information in the following location:

```
HKEY_CURRENT_USER\Software\VB and VBA Program _
Settings\appname\section\key
```

As the example code above shows, the general form for these functions and statements is:

```
SaveSetting application name, section name, key, value
Value = GetSetting(application name, section name, _
key[,default  value]
```

and all the parameters must be strings. For example, in the above sample code we gave a default size of half the screen's current height and width.

The DeleteSetting function has the following syntax:

```
DeleteSetting application name, section name, key
```

The Registry API functions

Obviously the various Registry setting functions supplied with VB are quite limited in what they can do, they can only work with one location after all. To take full control of the Registry you need to use the API calls that are contained in advapi32.dll. The most common of these are described in the following table:

Figure 12-8   Saving a setting

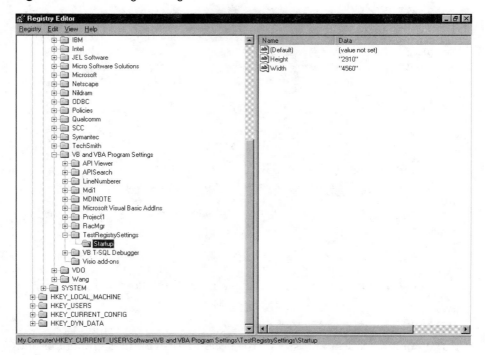

Table 12-3:	The Registry Functions
Function	*Description*
RegCloseKey	Closes an open key.
RegCreateKeyEx	Creates a new key.
RegDeleteKey	Deletes a key.
RegDeleteValue	Deletes a value.
RegEnumKeyEx	Enumerate the subkeys of a given key.
RegEnumValue	Enumerates the values for a key.
RegFlushKey	Ensures that changes to a key have been written to disk.
RegLoadKey	Loads registry information that had been saved to a file.
RegOpenKeyEx	Opens a key.
RegQueryInfoKey	Obtains information about a key.
RegQueryValueEx	Retrieves value data.
RegReplaceKey	Replaces registry information with data in a file.
RegRestoreKey	Restores registry information with data in a file.
RegSaveKey	Saves registry information to a file
RegSetValueEx	Sets a value for a key.

As you will see in the example in the next section, these functions are somewhat difficult to use because they contain some rather strange types that need to be converted into a useable form. For example, numbers may not be in standard format, there can be a lot of binary data and so on.

Example: VBSchemes

We want to use the registry functions described in the previous table for a fairly sophisticated program that saves what we call "schemes". These are specific settings for VB such as SDI versus MDI, sizes of the various win-

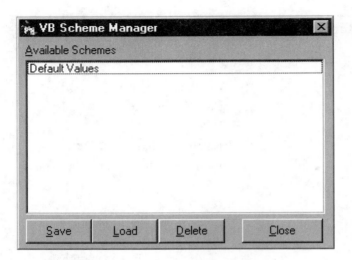

Figure 12-9   Screen for VBSchemes

dows, and their locations. Figure 12-9 shows you the form we built for this program.

The idea of this program is that you:

- Compile it to be an executable.
- Run it right after you shut VB down in order to save the previous state.
- Run it with a command line switch to restore a previously saved scheme as shown in Figure 12-10.

The program uses a code module (Schemes.bas) for the API calls. After the necessary Declares, constants, and type definitions, we have Sub Main, which is the startup object for this app. Sub Main is pretty straightforward—it basically looks at the command line. If there is one, it checks for that name in the VBSCHEMES key defined by:

```
Global Const VBSCHEMESKEY = "Software\Microsoft\Visual _
Basic\5.0\Schemes"
```

Then it calls the CopyVBSettings routine:

```
Sub Main()
    Dim rc As Long
```

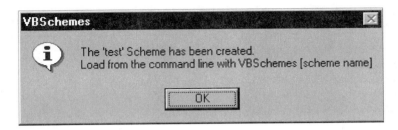

Figure 12-10 How to use VBSchemes

```
'process the command line if there is one
If Len(Command$) > 0 Then
  If UCase$(Command$) = "DEFAULT" Then
    ClearVBSettings
    rc = Shell("vb5.exe", vbNormalFocus)
  Else
    If CopyVBSettings(VBSCHEMESKEY & "\" & Command$, _
VBREGKEY) Then
      rc = Shell("vb5.exe", vbNormalFocus)
    Else
      MsgBox "'" & Command$ & "' Scheme not found!", _
vbCritical
    End If
  End If
  Else
    frmSchemes.Show
  End If
End Sub
```

Most of the work is done in the CopyVBSettings function, which looks for a specific scheme and then copies this information to VB's own UI registry setting. This location is stored in the VBREGKEY constant:

```
Global Const VBREGKEY = "Software\Microsoft\Visual _
Basic\5.0"
```

The key to the following code may be found in the call:

```
UpdateKey HKEY_CURRENT_USER, sTarget, Left$(sKeyName, _
lKeyName), bData, lDataLen, lType
```

This function lets you copy a key to a target. We will describe this function next. First though, here's the code for CopyVBSettings:

Listing 12-5:   CopyVBSettings

```
Function CopyVBSettings(sSource As String, sTarget As _
String) As Boolean
   On Error GoTo CopyVBSettingsErr

   Dim lhCLSIDKey As Long
   Dim sKeyName As String
   Dim lrc As Long
   Dim idx As Long
   Dim lKeyName As Long
   Dim lType As Long
   Dim bData() As Byte
   Dim lDataLen As Long

   'Open the clsid key to scan it's subkeys
   lrc = RegOpenKey(HKEY_CURRENT_USER, sSource, lhCLSIDKey)
   If lrc <> ERROR_NONE Then
      Exit Function
   End If

   ' reset index for key enumeration
   idx = 0

   Do
      lKeyName = 2000
      lDataLen = 6000
      sKeyName = String$(lKeyName, 0)
      ReDim bData(6000)
      lrc = RegEnumValue(lhCLSIDKey, idx, sKeyName, _
lKeyName, 0, lType, bData(0), lDataLen)
      ' if we ran out of keys
      If lrc = ERROR_BADKEY Or lrc = ERROR_ACCESS_DENIED Then
         lrc = 0
         GoTo Done
      ElseIf lrc = ERROR_MORE_DATA Then
         GoTo IncrementIndex
      ElseIf lrc <> ERROR_NONE Then
         ' any other error
         RegCloseKey lhCLSIDKey
         GoTo Done
      End If

      UpdateKey HKEY_CURRENT_USER, sTarget, Left$(sKeyName, _
lKeyName), bData, lDataLen, lType
```

```
IncrementIndex:
    ' increment index
    idx = idx + 1
  Loop
  RegCloseKey lhCLSIDKey

Done:

  CopyVBSettings = True

  Exit Function

CopyVBSettingsErr:
  MsgBox Err.Description
End Function
```

The UpdateKey function uses the RegCreateKeyEx function to create the key and then uses the RegSetValueEx to write the values. Here's the code for this function:

Listing 12-6: The UpdateKey Function

```
Public Function UpdateKey(KeyRoot As Long, KeyName As
String, SubKeyName _
As String, SubKeyValue() As Byte, lDataLen As Long, _
lType As Long) As Boolean
  Dim rc As Long                    ' Return Code
  Dim hKey As                       ' Handle To A Registry Key
  Dim hDepth As Long
  Dim lpAttr As SECURITY_ATTRIBUTES   ' Registry Security Type

  lpAttr.nLength = 50
  lpAttr.lpSecurityDescriptor = 0
  lpAttr.bInheritHandle = True


  '_____
  '- Create/Open Registry Key...
  '_____
  rc = RegCreateKeyEx(KeyRoot, KeyName, 0, REG_SZ, _
        REG_OPTION_NON_VOLATILE, KEY_ALL_ACCESS, lpAttr, _
        hKey, hDepth)       ' Create/Open //KeyRoot//KeyName
```

```
  If (rc <> ERROR_SUCCESS) Then GoTo CreateKeyError
  ' Handle Errors...

  rc = RegSetValueEx(hKey, SubKeyName, 0, lType, _
VarPtr(SubKeyValue(0)), lDataLen)

  If (rc <> ERROR_SUCCESS) Then GoTo CreateKeyError
  ' Handle Error
  '_____

  '- Close Registry Key...
  '_____

  rc = RegCloseKey(hKey)                      ' Close Key

  UpdateKey = True                            ' Return Success
  Exit Function                               ' Exit
CreateKeyError:
  UpdateKey = False                 ' Set Error Return Code
  rc = RegCloseKey(hKey)            ' Attempt To Close Key
End Function
```

You can find the rest of the code on the CD. One noteworthy point of the code we give you is that we "wrap" a bunch of the Registry API calls to make them easier to use. You can freely use these wrappers in your own code. An example of this is:

Listing 12-7:   Cover Function for RegEnumKey

```
'Cover function for RegEnumKey
'(easier to use version of RegEnumKeyEx)
Function EnumKey(ByVal hKey As Long, ByVal iSubKey As Long, _
stSubKey As String) As Long
  Const cchMax = 1024

  Static rgchValue As String * cchMax
  Dim i As Integer
  Dim regerr As Long

  regerr = RegEnumKey(hKey, iSubKey, rgchValue, cchMax)

  If regerr = 0 Then
    i = InStr(rgchValue, Chr$(0))
    If i <> 0 Then
```

```
      stSubKey = Left$(rgchValue, i - 1)
    Else
      stSubKey = rgchValue
    End If
  Else
    stSubKey = ""
  End If
  EnumKey = regerr
End Function
```

INI Files

INI files were the old way of storing information about a program. In most cases nowadays the Registry is a better choice. The one exception is when you need to have a file that is easy for the user to change. (INI files are ordinary text files.) A good example of this is the INI file used by Visual Basic for its Add-Ins. You work with INI files using the API functions that are described in the following table. (All of these APIs may be found in kernel32.)

Table 12-4: INI API Functions

API Function	Description:
GetPrivateProfileInt	Retrieves an integer data setting
GetPrivateProfileSection	Retrieves data for an entire section
GetPrivateProfileString	Retrieves a string
WritePrivateProfileSection	Writes data for an entire section from a private initialization file
WritePrivateProfileString	Sets a string into the INI file

For example, if you use the Add-In template (see Chapter 14), it comes with the following function:

```
Sub AddToINI()
    Dim ErrCode As Long
    ErrCode = WritePrivateProfileString("Add-Ins32", _
"MyAddIn.Connect", "0", "vbaddin.ini")
End Sub
```

As you might expect looking at this code, the Declare for WritePrivateProfileString is:

```
Declare Function WritePrivateProfileString& Lib _
"kernel32" Alias "WritePrivateProfileStringA" _
(ByVal lpApplicationName As String, ByVal _
lpKeyName As Any, ByVal lpString As String, ByVal _
lpFileName As String)
```

Example: The VB Add-In Viewer

To show off the INI file API calls, we wrote a little application that displays the information contained in the Add-Ins32.Ini file. Figure 12-11 shows you this application at work.

The basic work is done in the Form_Load, which fills up the list box using a call to get GetWindowsDirectory to find out where the VBADDIN.INI file is located.

Figure 12-11   The VBADDIN.INI Manager

Listing 12-7:   Form_Load

```
Private Sub Form_Load()
 On Error GoTo Form_LoadErr

 Dim sWinDir As String * 255
 Dim nLenWinDir As Long
 Dim sFile As String
 Dim sLine As String

 nLenWinDir = GetWindowsDirectory(sWinDir, 255)
 If IsNull(Mid(sWinDir, nLenWinDir, 1)) Then
    'WIN NT adds a null to the end of the string so we
    'remove it when saving the path name
    sFile = Left$(sWinDir, nLenWinDir - 1)
 Else
    sFile = Left$(sWinDir, nLenWinDir)
 End If
 sFile = sFile & "\VBADDIN.INI"

 'open the ini file and get the current addins
 Open sFile For Input As #1
 While Not EOF(1)
    Line Input #1, sLine
    If Left$(sLine, 1) <> "[" And Len(sLine) > 0 Then
       lstAddIns.AddItem sLine
    End If
 Wend
 Close #1

 Exit Sub
Form_LoadErr:
 MsgBox Err.Description, vbInformation
End Sub
```

On the other hand, if you try to delete a key you need to use the appropriate API call. For example, here's the code to delete a key:

```
Private Sub cmdDelete_Click()
   Dim sTmp As String
```

```
    If lstAddIns.ListIndex < 0 Then Exit Sub
    sTmp = Left$(lstAddIns.Text, Len(lstAddIns.Text) - 2)
    If MsgBox("Delete '" & sTmp & "'?", vbQuestion + _
vbYesNo, Me.Caption) = vbYes Then
        'delete the AddIn from the INI file by setting its
        'value to null
        WritePrivateProfileString "Add-Ins32", sTmp, _
vbNullString, "VBADDIN.INI"
        lstAddIns.RemoveItem lstAddIns.ListIndex
    End If
End Sub
```

Note

The code to add an Add-In uses a DLL that gives "type lib info" that is supplied with VB. This DLL lets you get at the same kind of information that
the Object Browser shows. In this case we use it simply to check whether
the item you are trying to add is an Add-In.

Some Useful API calls

Now that you have seen all the basic techniques for manipulating API calls
we want to end this chapter with a potpourri of the API calls that we have
found most useful. (If we have forgotten one that you think especially important we hope you will E-mail one of us so that we can think about adding it
in future editions of this book!)

Shutting Down (and Restarting) Windows

Occasionally you will need to force a reboot of Windows. An example of this
would be in a Password protected program where you may want to shut
Windows down for the unfortunate non-user. The API call that does this is:

```
Declare Function ExitWindowsEx& Lib "user32" _
(ByVal uFlags As Long, ByVal dwReserved As Long)
```

The dwReserved is reserved. At the present time you simply set it to zero.
The following table describes the possible parameters (as always, you can
combine parameters where appropriate using the Or operator).

Table 12-5: Parameters for dwReserved	
Parameter	*Type/Description*
EWX_FORCE	Terminate processes that do not respond.
EWX_LOGOFF	Terminates processes, then log off.
EWX_SHUTDOWN	Actually shuts powers off to the system if the system supports advanced power management.
EWX_REBOOT	Reboots the system.
EWX_SHUTDOWN	Shuts the system down.

For example:

```
TerminateAll = ExitWindows(EWX_FORCE Or EWX_SHUTDOWN, 0)
```

Getting and Setting the Keyboard State

Finding out the status of the shift, and num luck keys is often useful. The API call that lets you do this is:

```
Private Declare Function GetKeyState Lib "user32" _
(ByVal nVirtKey As Long) As Integer
```

The nVirtKey parameter uses Virtual key code constants, you can find them with the API viewer. (They all begin with VK_ and have the same values as what are used in the KeyDown/KeyUp event procedures.). For example, here's a function that you can use to find out the current status of one of the keys:

```
Public Function GetToggleState(KeyCode As Integer) As Boolean
   Dim KeyState As Integer
   ' Determine the current state of the toggle key
   KeyState = GetKeyState(KeyCode)
   Select Case KeyState
     Case 1
       GetToggleState = True
     Case Else
       GetToggleState = False
   End Select
End Function
```

Setting the keyboard status is a little trickier. The idea is that the current status of the keyboard is stored in a string of 255 characters called a *keyboard map*. You have to use the Mid$ function to go in an change the appropriate key in this string. The two API calls you need are:

```
Private Declare Function GetKeyboardState Lib "user32" _
(ByVal pbKeyState As String) As Boolean
Private Declare Function SetKeyboardState Lib "user32" _
(ByVal lppbKeyState As String) As Boolean
```

Here's a class that encapsulates all this:

Listing 12-8:   Class for Key State Manipulation

```
'Class for key state manipulation
Option Explicit

Private Declare Function GetKeyState Lib "user32" _
    (ByVal nVirtKey As Long) As Integer
Private Declare Function GetKeyboardState Lib "user32" _
    (ByVal pbKeyState As String) As Boolean
Private Declare Function SetKeyboardState Lib "user32" _
    (ByVal lppbKeyState As String) As Boolean

Private Const VK_CAPITAL = &H14      ' Shift Lock
Private Const VK_NUMLOCK = &H90      ' Num Lock
Private Const VK_SCROLL = &H91       ' Scroll Lock

Public Function GetToggleState(KeyCode As Integer) As Boolean
   Dim KeyState As Integer
   ' Determine the current state of the toggle key
   KeyState = GetKeyState(KeyCode)
   Select Case KeyState
     Case 1
       GetToggleState = True
     Case Else
       GetToggleState = False
   End Select
End Function

Public Sub SetToggleState(KeyCode As Integer)
   Dim KeyboardMap As String * 256
   Static ChangeState As Boolean
   Dim OK As Boolean
```

```
' Get the current keyboard state
KeyboardMap = Space$(256)
OK = GetKeyboardState(KeyboardMap)

' Change the state of the requested key in the keyboard map
'the key we need to change is one more than the VK code
If ChangeState Then 'or If GetToggleState(KeyCode)
   Mid$(KeyboardMap, KeyCode + 1, 1) = "1"
Else
   Mid$(KeyboardMap, KeyCode + 1, 1) = "0"
End If
' need to actually put the new key state map into effect
OK = SetKeyboardState(KeyboardMap)
ChangeState = Not ChangeState
End Sub
```

Figure 12-12 shows you a form that you can use to test this class module. If we keep the command buttons in a control array named cmdToggle, then we can use the following code to monitor the status:

```
Sub ShowStatus()
   bNumLock = AKeyClass.GetToggleState(VK_NUMLOCK)
   If bNumLock Then
      cmdToggle(0).Caption = "Num Lock On"
   Else
      cmdToggle(0).Caption = "Num Lock Off"
   End If
   bCapsLock = AKeyClass.GetToggleState(VK_CAPITAL)
   If bCapsLock Then
```

Figure 12-12   A keystatus demonstration form

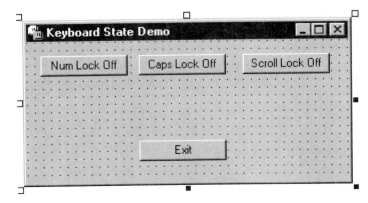

```
      cmdToggle(1).Caption = "Caps Lock On"
   Else
      cmdToggle(1).Caption = "Caps Lock Off"
   End If
   bScrollLock = AKeyClass.GetToggleState(VK_SCROLL)
   If bScrollLock Then
      cmdToggle(2).Caption = "Scroll Lock On"
   Else
      cmdToggle(2).Caption = "Scroll Lock Off"
   End If
End Sub
```

Here's the rest of the code needed to make this work. (We set the Form_KeyPreview property to be true so that you could see the effects of changing the keys via keystrokes.)

```
Option Explicit
Private Const VK_CAPITAL = &H14
Private Const VK_NUMLOCK = &H90
Private Const VK_SCROLL  = &H91
Dim AKeyClass As KeyClass
Dim bCapsLock As Boolean
Dim bNumLock As Boolean
Dim bScrollLock As Boolean

Private Sub Form_Load()
   Set AKeyClass = New KeyClass
   ShowStatus
   Show
End Sub


Private Sub Form_KeyUp(KeyCode As Integer, Shift As _
Integer)
   ShowStatus
End Sub


Private Sub cmdToggle_Click(Index As Integer)
Dim Caption        As String
Dim KeyCode        As Integer
' Set the virtual key code based on the command
' button that was clicked
   Select Case Index
     Case 0
        AKeyClass.SetToggleState (VK_NUMLOCK)
        ShowStatus
     Case 1
```

```
    AKeyClass.SetToggleState (VK_CAPITAL)
    ShowStatus
  Case 2
    AKeyClass.SetToggleState (VK_SCROLL)
    ShowStatus
  Case 3
    ' Exit from program
    Unload Me
  End Select

End Sub

Private Sub Form_QueryUnload(Cancel As Integer, _
UnloadMode As Integer)
  Set AKeyClass = Nothing
  End
End Sub
```

Note

VB4 came with a control that let you set and get the keyboard state. Although not part of the standard installation, most editions of VB5 still have this OCX. You can find it in Tools\Controls\keyst32.ocx on the VB CD. As always, the advantage to rolling your own via the API is that you save the overhead of an OCX.

More Accurate Timings

The Timer function in VB is only accurate to about 1/18th of a second. There's a simple API call that gives you a much more accurate timer. It also has the advantage that it rolls over roughly every 49 days rather than every 24 hours. The declaration for this function is:

```
Private Declare Function GetTickCount Lib "kernel32" () As Long
```

and it returns the number of milliseconds since Windows was last started. If you divide this by 1000 you would get seconds, by 60 * 1000 minutes and so on. Here's the obvious code to use:

```
MillisElapsed = EndTime - StartTime
Seconds = (MillisElapsed / 1000 * 60)
Minutes = (MillisElapsed / 1000 * 60 * 60)
Days = MillisElapsed / (1000& * 60 * 60 * 24)
```

> **Tip**
>
> *Many systems have the ability to do high performance timings that go way beyond what even GetTickCount can do. You can find out if your system has this ability with the QueryPerformanceCounter API call in kernel32. If it returns a non-zero value, then you have a high performance timer.*

Accessing the Help System

The ShowHelp method of the common dialog control gives you access to the Windows help system. It lacks a few features and so many VB programmers like to encapsulate the necessary API calls to access WinHelp into a class. Here's the API call that you need:

```
Private Declare Function WinHelp Lib "user32" Alias "WinHelpA" _
(ByVal hwnd As Long,  ByVal lpHelpFile As String, _
ByVal wCommand As Long,  ByVal dwData As Long) As Long
```

Many people like to make them type safe:

```
Private Declare Function WinHelpString Lib "user32" _
Alias "WinHelpA" (ByVal hwnd As Long, ByVal lpHelpFile _
As String, ByVal wCommand As Long, ByVal dwData As _
String) As Long

Private Declare Function WinHelpStruct Lib "user32" _
Alias "WinHelpA" (ByVal hwnd As Long, ByVal lpHelpFile _
As String, ByVal wCommand As Long, dwData As Any) As Long
```

The idea is that you send the WinHelp API call the name of the help file along with a parameter that tells it what to do. All the constants begin with HELP_. Here are the most common ones:

```
Const HELP_CONTEXT = &H1
Const HELP_QUIT = &H2
Const HELP_INDEX = &H3
Const HELP_CONTENTS = &H3&
Const HELP_HELPONHELP = &H4
Const HELP_SETINDEX = &H5
Const HELP_SETCONTENTS = &H5&
Const HELP_CONTEXTPOPUP = &H8&
Const HELP_FORCEFILE = &H9&
Const HELP_KEY = &H101
Const HELP_COMMAND = &H102&
Const HELP_PARTIALKEY = &H105&
```

Then after you set up a bunch of property procedures to get and set the following instance fields:

```
Private mHelpFileName        As String
Private mhWnd                As Long
Private mContextID           As Long
Private mHelpKeyWord         As String
```

You can then use add a method to a class module to actually call the Help engine. It might look like this:

```
Public Sub Action(WhatAction As Long)
   Select Case WhatAction
      Case HELP_QUIT, HELP_INDEX, HELP_CONTENTS, HELP_HELPONHELP
         Call WinHelp(mhWnd, mHelpFileName, WhatAction, 0)
      Case HELP_KEY, HELP_PARTIALKEY
         Call WinHelpString(mhWnd, mHelpFileName, _
WhatAction, mHelpKeyWord)
      Case HELP_CONTEXT, HELP_CONTEXTPOPUP
         Call WinHelp(mhWnd, mHelpFileName, WhatAction, mContextID)
   End Select
End Sub
```

Sophisticated Shelling

In the old 16-bit days of VB you could use the return value of the Shell command to determine when whatever program you shelled to ended. This is no longer possible in Win 32. Instead, if you need to know when a shelled program ends, you must use the CreateProcess() API function to begin the shelled program rather than the Shell() function. The idea is that the CreateProcess() API function gives you a process handle. You can than pass this process handle to the WaitForSingleObjectAPI call. Note that calling the WaitForSingleObject() API function makes your Visual Basic program stop everything until Windows notifies it that the shelled process has finished.

Note

Recall that a process can be thought of as a "virtual computer" with its own memory and data. Windows 95 and 32 are called multiprocessing because they have the ability to run multiple processes at what appears to be the same time, although, of course, what is actually going on is that the operating system is interrupting the process periodically to give time to another process. (See Chapter 14 for more on multiprocessing.)

You need the following Declares. (As with any handle you need to release it using CloseHandle after you are done with it.)

```
Private Declare Function WaitForSingleObject Lib "kernel32" _
(ByVal hHandle As Long, ByVal dwMilliseconds As Long) As Long

Private Declare Function CreateProcessA Lib "kernel32" (ByVal _
lpApplicationName As Long, ByVal lpCommandLine As String, ByVal _
lpProcessAttributes As Long, ByVal lpThreadAttributes As Long, _
ByVal bInheritHandles As Long, ByVal dwCreationFlags As Long, _
ByVal lpEnvironment As Long, ByVal lpCurrentDirectory As Long, _
lpStartupInfo As STARTUPINFO, lpProcessInformation As _
PROCESS_INFORMATION) As Long

Private Declare Function CloseHandle Lib "kernel32" (ByVal _
hObject As Long) As Long
```

Then you need the following structures:

```
Private Type STARTUPINFO
    cb As Long
    lpReserved As String
    lpDesktop As String
    lpTitle As String
    dwX As Long
    dwY As Long
    dwXSize As Long
    dwYSize As Long
    dwXCountChars As Long
    dwYCountChars As Long
    dwFillAttribute As Long
    dwFlags As Long
    wShowWindow As Integer
    cbReserved2 As Integer
    lpReserved2 As Long
    hStdInput As Long
    hStdOutput As Long
    hStdError As Long
End Type
Private Type PROCESS_INFORMATION
    hProcess As Long
    hThread As Long
    dwProcessID As Long
    dwThreadID As Long
End Type
```

Here are the constants you need:

```
Private Const NORMAL_PRIORITY_CLASS = &H20&
Private Const INFINITE = -1&
```

Now the actual code is trivial:

```
Public Sub StartProgram(ProgramName As String)
   Dim proc As PROCESS_INFORMATION
   Dim start As STARTUPINFO
   Dim ReturnValue As Long

   start.cb = Len(start)

' Start the shelled application:
   ReturnValue = CreateProcessA(0&, ProgramName, 0&, 0&, 1&, _
   NORMAL_PRIORITY_CLASS, 0&, 0&, start, proc)

'Wait for the shelled application to finish:
   ReturnValue = WaitForSingleObject(proc.hProcess, INFINITE)
'get rid of the handle
   ReturnValue = CloseHandle(proc.hProcess)
End Sub
```

Keeping a Window on Top All the Time

If you want a VB form window to be on top all the time *regardless of whether that VB application is active*, use the SetWindowPos API call in user32. The Declare for this API call looks like this:

```
Private Declare Function SetWindowPos Lib "user32" _
(ByVal hwnd As Long, ByVal hWndInsertAfter As Long, _
ByVal x As Long, ByVal y As Long, ByVal cx As Long, _
ByVal cy As Long, ByVal wFlags As Long) As Long
```

where x is the new x (left/right) coordinate, y the new y (up/down) coordinate, cx is the width of the window and cy is the height. *All these coordinates are taken using pixels.* You also need two constants:

```
Const HWND_TOPMOST = -1
Const SWP_SHOWWINDOW = &H40
```

For example, as Figure 12-13 shows, the Form window activated by the code that follows remains on top—even though that window is inactive! (You can tell that it is inactive because its title bar is grayed and the Word window below it has its title bar highlighted.)

Figure 12-13   A window always on top

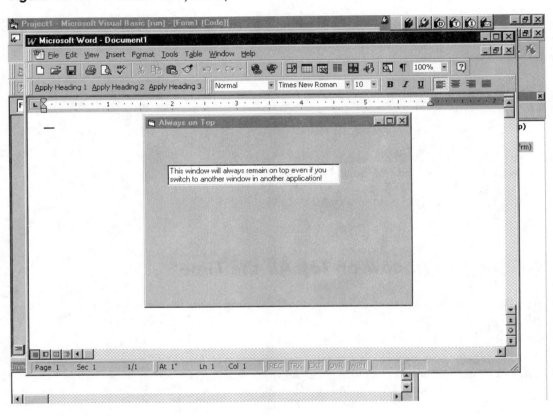

Listing 12-9:   Keeping a Window on Top

```
Option Explicit

Private Declare Function SetWindowPos Lib "user32" (ByVal hwnd As Long, _
    ByVal hWndInsertAfter As Long, ByVal x As Long, ByVal y As Long, _
    ByVal cx As Long, ByVal cy As Long, ByVal wFlags As Long) As Long

Const HWND_TOPMOST = -1
Const SWP_SHOWWINDOW = &H40


Private Sub Form_Load()

  Dim TempValue As Long
  Dim MyWidth As Long, MyHeight As Long
  Dim MyTop As Long, MyLeft As Long


  MyWidth = (Screen.Width / 2)
  MyWidth = MyWidth / Screen.TwipsPerPixelX
  MyHeight = Screen.Height / 2
  MyHeight = MyHeight / Screen.TwipsPerPixelY
  MyTop = MyTop / Screen.TwipsPerPixelY

  TempValue = SetWindowPos(Me.hwnd, HWND_TOPMOST, 0, 0, _
 MyWidth, MyHeight, SWP_SHOWWINDOW)
End Sub
```

ACTIVEX CONTROLS

Topics in this Chapter

Chapter 13

Although you can certainly choose File|Make .ocx and get a reusable ActiveX control from the simple samples we have already shown you, the controls you have seen so far really can't do much. The purpose of this chapter is to show you what you need to know in order to build full-featured controls. (Of course just making a full-featured ActiveX control is usually not enough; Chapter 20 shows you what goes into setting up and distributing your controls.)

The Anatomy of a User Control

As far as the user interface of your control goes, you will usually use the techniques from Chapter 3 and Chapter 6 to "paint" the needed constituent controls onto the user control form. These constituent controls can be any controls on your system for which you have the appropriate license. In particular, they can be other custom controls that you have already created. Also, as you saw in Chapter 6 you can use graphics code on a Picture Box (or even on the user control form) to brighten up the user interface of your ActiveX control. As an example of how you use constituent controls Figure 13-1 is the way your screen would look if you were designing the address control that we will discuss later in the next chapter. Notice that this user control has 15 (!) constituent controls (7 text boxes, 7 labels, and one command button).

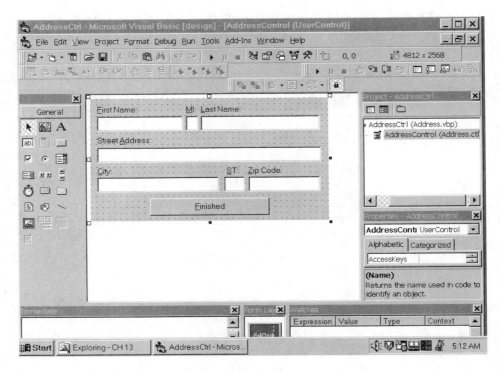

Figure 13-1   The Address Control at design stage

After you build the interface of your control, you have to decide on which members (properties, events, and methods) of your control you want to expose to its users. The visibility is controlled by your use of the Public, Private, or Friend access specifier in the relevant code. For example, the possible events your user control can raise to anyone who uses the control are those declared with the Public keyword (or no keyword, since Public is the default for a user control). For example, placing

```
Public Event BadKey()
```

or

```
Event BadValue(bSetToLimit As Boolean)
```

in the Declarations section of your user control would give you the ability to raise these two events to the user of your control. (You can also have Private or Friend custom events in a control but these are uncommon.) In general, the distinction is:

- Public events give the developer using your control (simply referred to as the user from now on) the opportunity to react to something.
- Private events give your control the opportunity to react to something.
- Friend events give the other components of your user control project the opportunity to react to something but not the user of your control (relatively rare).

As with class modules, the properties of your control come from the Property Procedures you write. More precisely, a Public Property Get/Property Let or Public Property Set/Property Let combination becomes a property that the user of your control can both read and write to. Unless you change VB5's defaults, the Public Properties are exactly the same properties of your user control that are visible in the Properties window of the VB5 IDE when the user of your control adds an instance of that control to their form. (See the next section for how to change this.) Similarly, when you use a Public Property Get procedure without the corresponding Property Set/Let procedure in the code for your control, you have a user-readable read-only property. (It is also possible, as you will soon see, to create read/write properties that can be set only at design time or only at run time.)

Finally, the methods that a user of your user control can call are exactly the same Public functions and procedures you write. Any Private functions and procedures you write will never be seen by the user of your control. This lets you hide whatever code was needed to carry out the tasks of the control and furthers encapsulation. In particular, if you come up with a better way to carry out an internal task, you probably won't break any existing code. The user of the control never sees internal implementation details.

Writing the Code

As with writing any procedures, the Tools|Add Procedure dialog box is probably the most convenient method to get the templates for the members of your control into the Code window, (although you can always simply start typing in the Code window anywhere outside an existing procedure or function).

For example, open up the Add Procedure dialog box and add a Public Property procedure named ExampleProperty. The IDE will automatically generate the following templates:

```
Public Property Get ExampleProperty() As Variant _
End Property
Public Property Let ExampleProperty(ByVal vNewValue _
As Variant)
End Property
```

Notice that the IDE, by default, created both the Property Let and the Property Get. The default parameter for a Property procedure is a variant named vNewValue and this parameter is passed by value and not by reference. Obviously, you will often need to change these defaults for the Property procedures you write.

If you chose to add a public event named TestEvent using this dialog box, you would simply get the following declaration in the General object of your user control:

```
Public Event TestEvent()
```

As with Property procedures, you would have to add any parameters you want to this template by hand.

Finally, since methods are nothing but the Public Subs and Functions of your user control, there's no special box in the Add procedure dialog box for them. Simply write the code and use the appropriate identifier (or none, since Public is the default).

Once you have created the header for one of the members of your control, you should think about changing its attributes. For a control this goes beyond specifying what the user will see in the Object Browser; you can set the description of a property that the user of the control sees in the Properties window—or even if he or she can see the property in the Properties windows at all. The process is identical to what you saw in Chapter 7, either work through the Object Browser or more simply:

- Place the cursor in the name of the member you want to document
- Choose Tools|Procedure Attributes.

Figure 13-2 is an example of what you see for a property named SampleProperty. As you can see, this box has only room for a description of the Property and the Help Context ID (used for associating context-sensitive help).

For the members of the controls you code you will often need to work with the Advanced Procedure Attributes dialog box. So click on the advanced button in Figure 13-2 to go to the screen shown in Figure 13-3 on page 612. For

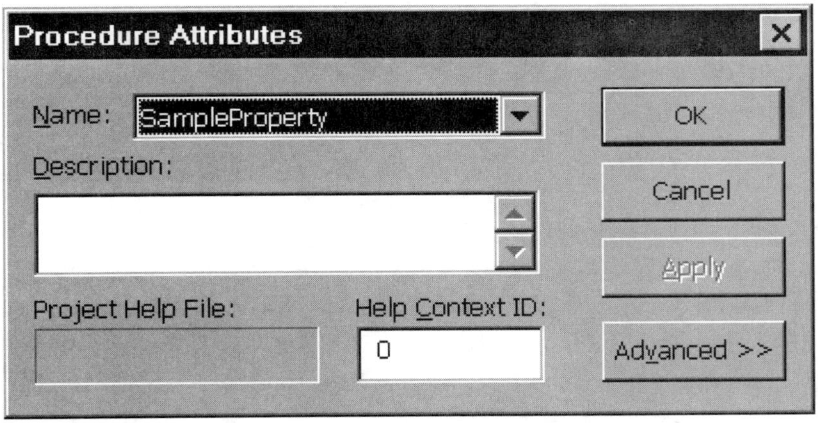

Procedure Attributes ✕

Name: SampleProperty ▼

Description:

▲
▼

Project Help File: Help Context ID:
0

OK

Cancel

Apply

Advanced >>

Figure 13-2   Procedure Attributes dialog box

an ActiveX control, choosing the Default option in the Procedure ID combo box makes that property the default property for your control. This box also can be used to tell the user of your ActiveX control that your event or property is one of the standard ones.

Caution

These settings are advisory, not proscriptive. For example, calling something a BackColor property in the Procedure Attributes combo box doesn't make it behave the way a BackColor property should. You still need to write the code to do this. This box simply tells the user of your control to expect some standard behavior from your member.

The Use this Page in Property Browser drop-down list box is important when working with Property Pages (see the section on them later in this chapter). Setting this option adds an ellipsis to the property in the Properties window. This in turn will tell VB to load the custom Property Page selected when the user clicks it. The Property Category drop-down list box is there because as you know the Properties window in VB5 has the ability to display properties either alphabetically or in categories. Use this combo box to set the category. You can use one of the supplied ones like Behavior or add your own by typing in the name in this combo box.

The Attributes check boxes allow you to set things like whether the property is a design-time or run-time property. The three check boxes are described in Table 13-1.

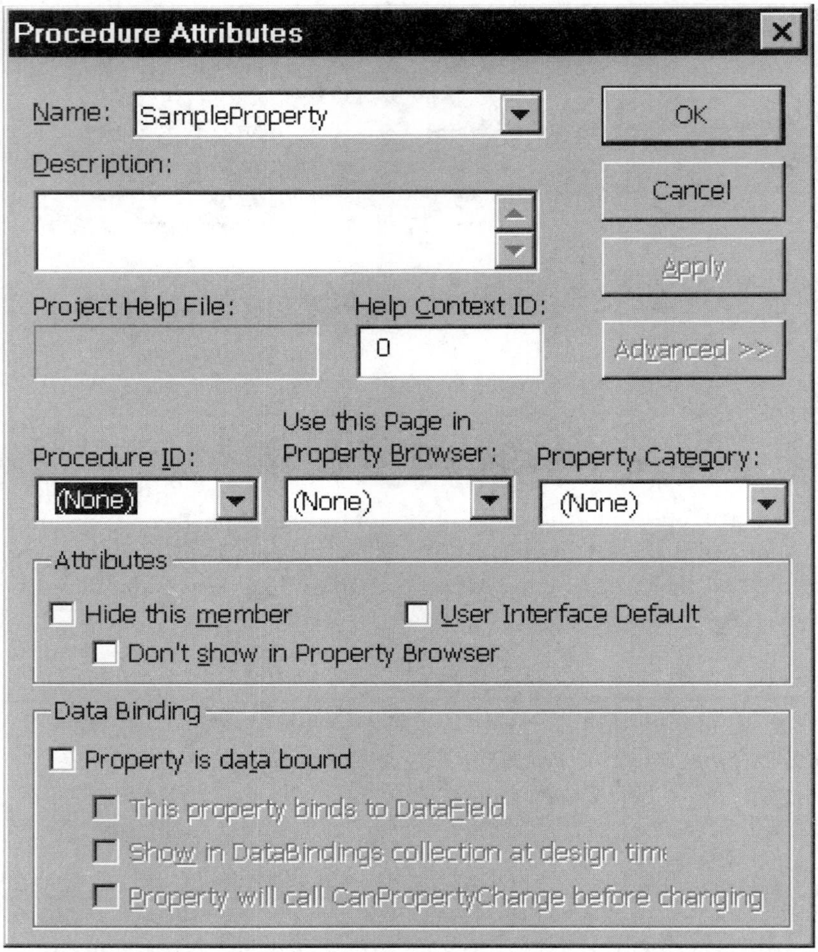

Procedure Attributes   ☒

Name: SamplePropery   ▼   OK

Description: Cancel

                                 ▲
                                 ▼   Apply

Project Help File: Help Context ID:

                        0   Advanced >>

                   Use this Page in
Procedure ID: Property Browser: Property Category:
(None)   ▼   (None)   ▼   (None)   ▼

┌─ Attributes ──────────────────────────────────┐
│ ☐ Hide this member   ☐ User Interface Default │
│   ☐ Don't show in Property Browser   │
└──┘

┌─ Data Binding ────────────────────────────────┐
│ ☐ Property is data bound   │
│   ☐ This property binds to DataField   │
│   ☐ Show in DataBindings collection at design time │
│   ☐ Property will call CanPropertyChange before changing │
└──┘

Figure 13-3   The full Procedure Attributes dialog box

Note

You can make a property settable or readable only at run time but this requires code. See the discussion on the Ambient object later in this chapter.

Finally the data binding options check boxes are used when you want to make your control data aware or data bound. Since we don't cover data access in this book, we will leave this option to a future volume.

Table 13-1:	Attribute Check Boxes
Hide This Member	This gives you a property that is not visible to the outside world, although it can still be accessed with code. If you check this box, VB5 will not show the property in the Properties window ever and will only show it in the Object Browser if you choose Show Hidden Members from the Object Browser's context menu. Think of this option as telling the user of your control that this is a secret property and they should use it at their own risk.
Don't Show in Property Browser	This simply determines if VB5 shows the property in the Properties window. The property still will always show up in the Object Browser and you can continue to write code to work with it.
User Interface Default	This determines which property is highlighted in the Properties window when the user presses F4 with focus in your user control. It also sets the event that VB5 displays in the Code window when you double-click the control. Obviously, there can be only one default property and one default event.

Mapping Properties, Methods, and Events

Consider the address control from Figure 13-1. It should obviously be able to raise a "Finished" event that the user of the control can work with when the end user clicks on the Finished button. This event must, equally obviously, be connected somehow to the Click event of the command button that we put on the user control form.

We need a way to connect these two events. To do this, suppose the Finished command button inside the user control form has the name cmdFinished. Then, here's what you need to have in your code to connect the Finished custom event with the intrinsic Click event for the constituent command button.

1. Put the following declaration for the Public Finished event in the Declarations section of the user control:

```
Public Event Finished()
```

(Again, the keyword Public is optional since it is the default.)

2. Next you need the code that actually connects the two events. There's not much to it:

```
Private Sub cmdFinished_Click()
   RaiseEvent Finished
End Sub
```

However, short as this code is, it does have some points worth noting. For example, notice that the cmdFinished_Click event is marked as Private. This means that the user of the Address control will never see it. He or she will have no way to write an event procedure for the Click event of the button. However, Windows doesn't care about the code you write. It still triggers the Click event for the cmdFinished button when the end user of the Address control clicks on it.

So what happens? Well, because of the key RaiseEvent line in this event procedure, a click on this button simply raises the (Public) Finished event of the user control—which is what we want. As you can see, it is natural to call what we just did a *map* between the Click event of the command button and the custom Finished event of the user control and to call the whole process *mapping*.

After you design the interface for your control, you should start thinking about how you want to map the methods, events, and properties (members) of your control to the methods, events and properties of the constituent controls. Although we will have more to say about the whole topic of mapping the members of your user control later on in this chapter when we discuss the Control Interface Wizard, it is still a good idea to get the basics down pat. This is because, while the Control Interface Wizard automatically generates a lot of the code needed for mapping the members of your user control, it may not be able to do it all. Moreover, as a general rule, if you don't understand what the Wizard does, you will be completely at the Wizard's mercy. We don't recommend this for the Control Interface Wizard—good as it is! (By the way, it may seem somewhat ironic in an age of computers, but a piece of paper with two columns marked user control Members and Constituent Control Members is often the best way to keep things straight whether you write the mapping code yourself or use the Control Interface Wizard.)

Mapping Properties

Mapping properties is a little more subtle than mapping events, so let's go through another example for this, again using the Address Control. Notice that all the labels in the Address Control have their own ForeColor property. Suppose we decide that all the labels inside our control should have the same ForeColor property. We want the user of the control to have the ability to set this property, and it should affect all the labels inside the user control. To do this, we need to *map* a ForeColor property of the user control to all the ForeColor properties of the labels.

For this we first need a Public Property Let procedure to allow the user of the control to set the ForeColor property for the control. The code for this procedure must, in turn, set the ForeColor for all the labels in our control. Here's the code for this:

```
Public Property Let ForeColor(ByVal New_ForeColor As OLE_COLOR)
    Dim i As Integer
    For i = 0 To 6
       lblLabels(i).ForeColor = New_ForeColor
    Next
    UserControl.ForeColor() = New_ForeColor
    PropertyChanged "ForeColor"
End Property
```

Let's go through the above code line by line. First, because of the Public access specifier, the user of this control can see this property. Since it is a Property Let, he or she can assign to this property. This property takes as a parameter an unsigned long integer for the color. (OLE_COLOR is a built-in data type for color codes.)

Next, we have a loop that runs through all the labels on the form. (Notice the advantage of using a control array of labels!) In each case, the loop assigns the current value of the ForeColor property parameter to the ForeColor of the individual labels. This has the effect of changing the colors of all the constituent labels whenever the user of the control sets the ForeColor property of the user control. The next two lines are the key. First we have:

```
    UserControl.ForeColor() = New_ForeColor
```

Here we are giving the new value to the ForeColor property of the user control, based on the parameter passed to the Property Let Procedure.

Next, in the line:

```
    PropertyChanged "ForeColor"
```

you see a method you haven't seen before, the PropertyChanged method. Think of this as a flag that tells VB5 that the user of the control activated code made a change in a property value.

Caution

If you fail to include the call to the PropertyChanged method using the name of the property that you have changed in code, your user control and the form designer that is using it will get out of sync. For example, leave it out and the Properties window for the form that uses your user control will have no way to update itself. Also, you won't be able to save the current state of the user control to the .frm file for the project. (See below for how to save and restore the state of your user control.)

Next, let's analyze the associated Property Get procedure. As with any Property Let/Get pair, the associated Property Get has one fewer parameter (i.e., none, in this case) and returns the type of the missing parameter. So its header looks like this:

```
Public Property Get ForeColor() As OLE_COLOR
```

and the one line of code needed is simply:

```
ForeColor = UserControl.ForeColor
```

What this line of code does is check the current setting of the ForeColor property of the user control. Notice because of the line:

```
UserControl.ForeColor() = New_ForeColor
```

in the Property Let procedure, these are in sync whenever the user assigns to the ForeColor property of the control.

ATTRIBUTES

If you look at the code for your control in a standalone editor, as opposed to the editor in the IDE, you will often see lines containing the keyword Attribute. Attributes are things like the description of the property (what shows up at the bottom of the Properties window). More often than not, attributes are the things that you set via dialog boxes in the IDE, as in the section on Procedure Attributes dialog box that you just saw.) The code for the various attribute settings is hidden from you in the IDE and it is not a good idea to mess with it by loading the .ctl file in a standalone Code Editor (where it will be visible).

For example, here's the code for the above Property Get as you would see it in a standalone editor:

```
Public Property Get ForeColor() As OLE_COLOR
   Attribute ForeColor.VB_Description = _
"Returns/sets the foreground color used
to display text and graphics in an object."
   ForeColor = UserControl.ForeColor
End Property
```

What the Attribute line does, in this case, is tell VB5 to embed the description for the method inside the method. This setting corresponds to what you enter in the Description text box in the Property Attributes dialog box. (One case where you might change these hidden lines with an editor is if you are a terrible typist and decide to run these kind of lines through a spelling checker.)

Managing the State of a User Control

Once you have created the Property procedures that define your custom properties, changes to the properties are done when VB5 processes the code in your Property Lets and Property Sets.

Tip

One way to see this at work is to use the debugging techniques described in Chapter 9 to stop execution whenever VB5 is processing code inside a Property Let. Then change that property via the Properties window. You would see that VB5 really does go to the Property Let anytime you change a property.

There are two ways to change a property via code. The most common is indirectly via a change to one or more of the instance variables in your control. This works because the Property procedures themselves have code that reads off the current state of the instance variables that they are concerned with inside themselves. Thus, whenever the Property procedure code is processed, you would see the change. Notice that there can be a lag between the change in the instance variables and its effect on the property.

Occasionally, you need to make sure that changes are made directly to a property without waiting for the Property Let to be called at some future time. You would want to do this if changing one property affected other properties that were showing in the Properties window. For example, a little later on in this chapter you will see an IntegerTextBox. This control is an extension of the one you saw in Chapter 1 because, among other things, it has MinValue and MaxValue properties that determine how large or small the value that the end user enters can be. Suppose we wanted to add a Range property to this control. The Range property would let you automatically set up a symmetric range. For example, if you set the Range to be 50, the MinValue would automatically be −50 and the MaxValue would automatically be +50. We obviously want any change in the Range property to be immediately reflected in what shows in the Properties window for the MinValue and MaxValue properties. The first step in doing this is to directly change the MinValue and MaxValue properties, as in the following code:

```
Public Property Let Range(ByVal vNewValue As Variant)
   If vNewValue <= 0 Or Not (IsNumeric(vNewValue)) Then
      MsgBox "Range must be positive!"
   Else
      'change MinValue and MaxValue properties directly
      MinValue = -vNewValue
      MaxValue = vNewValue
      'update the instance variable
      m_Range = vNewValue
      PropertyChanged "Range" 'always necessary
   End If
End Property
```

The key to this synchronization process is the lines that directly change the MinValue and MaxValue properties:

```
MinValue = -vNewValue
MaxValue = vNewValue
```

The Life Cycle of a User Control

When you change a property of a user control on a form, you certainly want this information to be preserved in the .frm file. (In the language of Chapter 8 we need to have the object persist.) Similarly, if a user loads a .frm file, you need to have your user control use the information about its properties that were preserved in the .frm file. Or, to take it from another angle, we certainly want the Properties window to reflect any changes we make to the properties in the various Property procedures. The key to all this is putting the right code in the "life-cycle" events of your user control. Since the details of the life cycle for a user control are a bit strange, we will concentrate on what you need to get your controls up and running. First, though, here again are the lifestyle events for a user control in the order in which they occur:

At birth: Initialize, InitProperties, ReadProperties, Resize

At death: WriteProperties, Terminate

You would most likely use the InitProperties event to read off data from the instance variables to set the initial state of your control. Next, recall in the Property procedure code above there was a call to the PropertyChanged method. The general syntax for this method is:

```
PropertyChanged PropertyName
```

where the PropertyName is a string expression for the name of the property (for example, the line PropertyChanged "Range" in the above code). What the PropertyChanged method does is notify whatever object is using the control that a property value has been changed. In Visual Basic, this immediately triggers the WriteProperties event. You must write the code in the WriteProperties event to save the current values of the properties. Here is a typical example (taken from the IntegerTextBox example given below) of what a WriteProperties event procedure looks like.

```
Private Sub UserControl_WriteProperties(PropBag As PropertyBag)
   On Error Resume Next
   Call PropBag.WriteProperty("MinValue", m_MinValue, m_def_MinValue)
   Call PropBag.WriteProperty("MaxValue", m_MaxValue, m_def_MaxValue)
   Call PropBag.WriteProperty("Value", m_Value, m_def_Value)
End Sub
```

Before we go through this code line by line, we want to emphasize: Every control you create must have code that looks like this.

(In general, you will have one PropBag.WriteProperty statement for each Public writable property in your control.)

Having said how important this type of code is, let's go over it line by line to make sure you understand it. First, the parameter for a WriteProperties event is a PropertyBag object. You haven't seen these VB5 objects yet, but think of a property bag as simply a container that holds property names, their current values, and, possibly, a default value. Some people like to think of it as a specialized collection but, in fact, how PropertyBags are implemented is completely irrelevant. All you have to know is you can take out and put in the current state of a property into a property bag and hence make your controls persist. (Just as the OOP theory would want you to do.)

Next, notice the On Error Resume Next statement. This is absolutely necessary when writing out property values to a PropertyBag. The reason is that certain environments do not let you write out properties from the design environment. (Visual Basic 5 does, but remember people may use your user control in many different environments.) You must catch this error; otherwise, any program that uses your control in one of these nonstandard environments will crash.

Next, we have the lines that write out the properties. The syntax, in general, is:

```
PropBag.WriteProperty(DataName, Value[, DefaultValue])
```

The DataName parameter is simply a string that gives the name of the property. (Think of this as the key for the specialized property bag collection.) The Value parameter is simply the current value of the property. Finally, the DefaultValue parameter is a default value for the property.

You may be wondering, why bother with a default value? One reason is that, otherwise, the .frm file could grow absurdly big. If you supply a default value for a property, VB5 will write out the value of your property only when the value you want VB5 to save is different from the default.

The mirror image to the WriteProperties event and the WriteProperties method are the ReadProperties Event and the ReadProperties method. The syntaxes are also parallel. For example,

```
Sub UserControl_ReadProperties(PropBag As PropertyBag)
```

and

```
UserControl.ReadProperty(DataName[, DefaultValue])
```

The idea is that you use the appropriate number and kind of ReadProperty methods to restore the previous state of the control, such as the ReadProperty event for the IntegerTextBox. (Notice how this code parallels the code in the WriteProperty event.)

```
Private Sub UserControl_ReadProperties(PropBag As PropertyBag)
    On Error Resume Next
    m_MinValue = PropBag.ReadProperty("MinValue", m_def_MinValue)
    m_MaxValue = PropBag.ReadProperty("MaxValue", m_def_MaxValue)
    Value = PropBag.ReadProperty("Value", m_def_Value)
End Sub
```

Presenting the Best Face to the User of Your Control

There are two aspects to presenting the best face to the user of your control. The first is trivial but should not be neglected. Would a Finance Control be as professional looking if this (Figure 13-4) wasn't the icon for it?

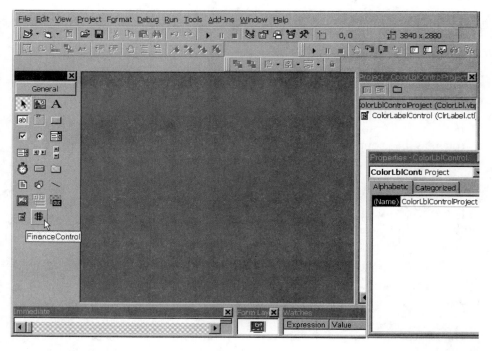

Figure 13-4   The icon for a Finance Control

The bitmap for the icon the user sees on the toolbox is simply the value of the ToolboxBitmap property. Once you assign this property and compile the control into an OCX, the bitmap is made part of the OCX file so you don't have to supply it separately to the user of your control.

Note

There are many tools for creating bitmaps. You can even use the Paint program supplied with Windows. The \Tools directory on the VB CD also has one (see Appendix).

If you use Microangelo (or any other shareware product, for that matter) for longer than the trial period, we hope you will be willing to pay the small license fee required to the creator.

The second and most important issue is to insure the proper sizing of your control and its constituent controls. If you don't make the constituent controls that are inside the form behave properly, your control will look unprofessional. The place to make the code look the way a user would expect it to is in the UserControl_Resize event. For example, suppose you start out with a PictureBox that is supposed to fill up the whole user control form, as shown in Figure 13-5. (We use the Globe.wmf file supplied with Access.)

Now, place this control on a test form and start enlarging it. The result, as shown in

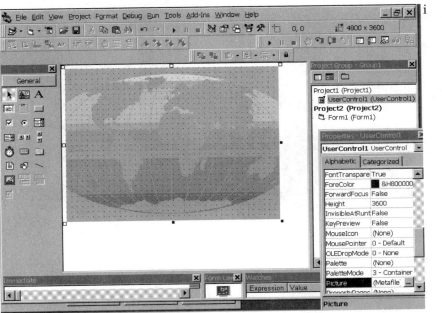

Figure 13-5   A Picture Box at design time

Figure 13-6, is less than ideal. (To make it more dramatic, we changed the BackColor property of the user control form to Blue, which shows up in Black in Figure 13-6.)

The problem is that the constituent PictureBox control that is inside the user control is not resizing itself properly in response to changes in the size of the containing user control form. The way to fix the bad behavior shown in Figure 13-6 is in the UserControl_Resize event. This event is triggered whenever the user of your control resizes the control (that is, the user control form). For example, to fix up the display shown in Figure 13-6 requires only two lines of code:

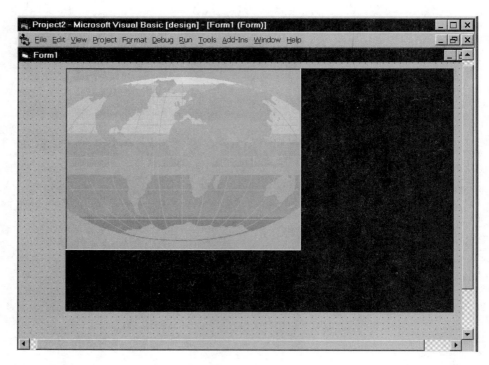

Figure 13-6   Resize problems at design time

```
Private Sub UserControl_Resize()
  'stretch to width and height of the control
  Picture1.Width = Width
  Picture1.Height = Height
End Sub
```

Now, the constituent picture box will always be as wide and as high as its container.

Tip

For an ordinary form, you would use ScaleHeight and ScaleWidth in similar code. The reason is that ScaleHeight and ScaleWidth give the internal area of an ordinary form—without the title bar and such. Height and Width give the actual height and width, including the title bar. Since user control forms do not have a title bar, it doesn't matter which you choose.

The above code works fine when you have a single constituent control, but what happens if you have lots of them inside your user control like our address control? In this case, you need to preserve the proportions of the controls inside the user control form. Luckily you can simply use the generic resize code from Chapter 6 with minor modifications.

A Full-Blown Example: An Integer Text Box

Although we have a few more points to cover about user controls, we have covered enough so that you can understand the code for an IntegerTextBox that:

- Accepts only integers
- Has a minimum and maximum possible acceptable value as custom properties
- Resizes itself properly

Let's go through the main point of the control. The full code of the control will be found in the CH 13 directory on the CD. Note that you have already seen the ReadProperties and WriteProperties event codes, so we won't repeat them in this section.

First, we have the general declarations. They look like this:

```
Option Explicit

Public Event BadValue(bSetToLimit As Boolean)
Public Event BadKey()
'Default Property Values:
Const m_def_Value = 0
Const m_def_MinValue = 0
Const m_def_MaxValue = 1000
'Property Variables:
Dim m_Value As Integer
Dim m_MinValue As Integer
Dim m_MaxValue As Integer
```

Besides the Option Explicit to enforce good programming habits, we have the declaration for the two Public events, one for a bad keystroke and the other if the value the end user enters (or pastes) is too large. The Constants give us some reasonable defaults for the MinValue and MaxValue properties.

The first code you write for a control will almost always be in the Initialize event. Ours simply looks at the form level constants to set up the Initial values. (These values, in turn, could be changed by the ReadProperties event code that you already saw.) The code for the Initialize event looks like this:

```
'Initialize Properties for User Control
Private Sub UserControl_InitProperties()
  m_Value = m_def_Value
  m_MinValue = m_def_MinValue
  m_MaxValue = m_def_MaxValue
End Sub
```

Next, here's the simple code we chose to use for the Resize event:

```
Private Sub UserControl_Resize()
  'stretch to width of control
  txtValue.Width = Width
  'set to fixed height
  Height = 330
End Sub
```

Notice that we decided to have the text box that is the only constituent of the user control to have a fixed height but its width will always be as large as the user control container.

Next, here's the code for the Change event. At this point, it should be pretty straightforward. The idea is simply to check whether what has been entered is bigger than the current settings of the m_MinValue and m_MaxValue instance variables:

```
Private Sub txtValue_Change()
  Dim bSetToLimit As Boolean
  'check the value for proper range
  If Val(txtValue.Text) < m_MinValue Then
    'raise the event

    RaiseEvent BadValue(bSetToLimit)
    If bSetToLimit Then
      'reset to the min value
      txtValue.Text = m_MinValue
    Else
      'reset to previous value
      txtValue.Text = m_Value
    End If
```

```
  ElseIf Val(txtValue.Text) > m_MaxValue Then
    'raise the event
    RaiseEvent BadValue(bSetToLimit)
    If bSetToLimit Then
      'reset to the max value
      txtValue.Text = m_MaxValue
    Else
      'reset to previous value
      txtValue.Text = m_Value
    End If
  End If
  'set the value var
  m_Value = Val(txtValue.Text)
End Sub
```

The KeyPress event needs to be a little more sophisticated than the one you saw in Chapter 1. We want to allow the end user of the control to use the Backspace key as well as a negative sign if it is in the first position in the text box. (This occurs when the value of txtValue.SelStart is 0. You could allow trailing spaces if you want by first using the LTrim function before checking for the minus sign.)

```
Private Sub txtValue_KeyPress(KeyAscii As Integer)
  'minus sign only at first character
  Dim GoodEntry As Boolean
  'backspace allowed
  If KeyAscii = Asc(vbBack) Then Exit Sub
  ' need to check for minus  sign only at beginning

  Select Case txtValue.SelStart
    Case 0
      If KeyAscii = Asc("-") Or (KeyAscii >= _
      Asc("0") And KeyAscii <= Asc("9")) Then
        GoodEntry = True
      End If
    Case Else
      If (KeyAscii >= Asc("0") And KeyAscii _
<= Asc("9")) Then
        GoodEntry = True
      End If
  End Select
  If Not GoodEntry Then
    KeyAscii = 0
    RaiseEvent BadKey
  End If
End Sub
```

Then we have the code for the three custom properties. Here's the code for the Value property. It simply reads off the current state of the m_Value instance variable.

```
Public Property Get Value() As Integer
   Value = m_Value
End Property
```

The associated Property Let procedure updates the value of the m_Value instance variable after checking that the bounds haven't been breached. (We pop up a message box if it has.) The code looks like this:

```
Public Property Let Value(ByVal New_Value As Integer)
   If New_Value < m_MinValue Then
     MsgBox "Minimum Limit Exceeded!"
     m_Value = m_MinValue
   ElseIf New_Value > m_MaxValue Then
     MsgBox "Maximum Limit Exceeded!"
     m_Value = m_MaxValue
   Else
     m_Value = New_Value
   End If
   txtValue.Text = m_Value
   PropertyChanged "Value"
End Property
```

The Property Procedures for the MinValue and MaxValue properties are similar:

```
Public Property Get MinValue() As Integer
   MinValue = m_MinValue
End Property

Public Property Let MinValue(ByVal New_MinValue As _
Integer)
   If New_MinValue > m_MaxValue Then
     MsgBox "Minimum cannot exceed Maximum!"
   Else
     m_MinValue = New_MinValue
     PropertyChanged "MinValue"
   End If
End Property

Public Property Get MaxValue() As Integer
   MaxValue = m_MaxValue
End Property

Public Property Let MaxValue(ByVal New_MaxValue As _
```

```
Integer)
   If New_MaxValue < m_MinValue Then
     MsgBox "Maximum cannot be less than Minimum!"
   Else
     m_MaxValue = New_MaxValue
     PropertyChanged "MaxValue"
   End If
End Property
```

Interacting with the User of Your Control

One of the things the code in your user control has to know is whether the control is being used at design time or run time. After all, you may want to only allow setting certain properties at design time or run time. This is done by checking the current state of the UserMode of the Ambient object in your code. The value of Ambient.UserMode value is True if we are in design time and False otherwise. For example, suppose you add a timer to a user control that will change the background color periodically. We don't want the label to change color when it is in design mode. So our Timer event has to look like this:

```
Private Sub Timer1_Timer()
   On Error Resume Next
   Static nColor As Integer
   If Not Ambient.UserMode Then Exit Sub 'don't
                              ' execute in design mode

   If nColor = 15 Then
     nColor = 0                          'start over again
   Else
     nColor = nColor + 1                 'increment it
   End If
   lblLabel.ForeColor = QBColor(nColor)   'set the forecolor
End Sub
```

Tip

Use similar code in Property Procedures to give design-time or run-time properties. Simply check the state of the Ambient.UserMode property before executing the code in the Property procedure.

What is going on under the hood is actually kind of interesting so we want to spend a little more time on the Ambient keyword. First off, what the Ambient property is really doing is returning an AmbientProperties Object. This object, in turn, has properties like the UserMode property that you can query to find interesting information about the container in which your control is sitting. In addition, the AmbientProperties object lets you check for suggested values for some of the more common properties. For example, you can use the value of Ambient.BackColor or Ambient.ForeColor to find out what the container is suggesting for the back color and forecolor of your control. You can use the Ambient.DisplayName value to see if the container has a suggested name for the control. The value of the Ambient.LocaleID property is a long integer that follows Windows conventions in telling you the language and country of the user. (We suggest looking at the online help for more information on this useful object.)

Extender Object

The Extender object is often more useful than the AmbientProperties object. This object gives you access to certain properties, methods, and events that come from the container control. For example, if you have a label or text like object, perhaps you want the default caption or text to be the same as the name the user gives to the current instance of your user control. Notice that this is a value given in the Properties window of the form designer and it is not immediately clear how to access this information. Through the wonder of the Extender object, all you have to do is query the current value of the Extender.Name property!

Table 13-2 lists the most useful Extender properties.

Note

You cannot be sure all the environments that are using your control will provide the Extender properties, methods, and events described in the following tables. For example, browsers would not normally provide a property like the Extender.Left property to tell you how far from the left edge of the container you are.

Table 13-2:	Extender Properties

Extender Property	*Description*
Name	Gives the name the user of your control gave the current instance.
Visible	Tells if the instance of your user control is currently visible.
Parent	Gives the name of the container for your control on the user's form (usually the name of the form, but could be a picture box or a frame, for example).
Cancel	Used for buttonlike objects. Tells you whether your control is the default Cancel button for the container.
Default	As with Cancel, this property tells you if the user control is the default button for the container.
Container	Returns a read-only object that represents the visual container of the control.
DragIcon	A read/write property that specifies the icon to use when your user control is dragged someplace.
DragMode	This read/write property tells you whether you are in manual or automatic mode for dragging.
Enabled	This read-only property tells you if the instance of your control is currently enabled.
Height	A read/write property that returns an integer that gives the height of the control in the container's scale units.
HelpContextID	A read/write property that specifies the context ID in the associated Help file that should be used when the user of the object presses the F1 key when the instance of your control has the focus.
Index	A read-only property that specifies the position in a control array this instance of the control occupies.
Left	A read/write property that specifies the position of the left edge of the control relative to the left edge of the container. (Uses the scale of the container of your control.)
TabIndex	A read/write property that gives the tab order for your control.
TabStop property	This read/write property specifies whether your control can be tabbed to.
Tag	Gives the value of the Tag property that the user gave the instance of your control.

Table 13-2:	Extender Properties (continued)

Extender Property	Description
ToolTipText	A read/write property that gives exactly what the name implies.
Top	This read/write property specifies the position of the top edge of the instance of your control relative to the top edge of the container. (As with the other size properties, uses the scale of the container.)
Width	This read/write property gives the width of the instance of your user control in the container's scale units.

The Extender object also has some methods your control can use. The most useful are described in the following table.

Table 13-3:	Extender Methods

Method	Description
Drag	Use this method to begin, end, or cancel someone trying to drag your control.
Move	Lets you move the instance of your control around.
SetFocus	Sets the focus to your control.
Zorder	Lets you change the Z-order for your control (see Chapter 6).

Next, we have the Extender events that you can work with.

Table 13-4:	Extender Events

Event	Description
DragDrop	This event is raised when another control on the form is dropped on your control.
DragOver	This event is raised when another control on the form is dragged over your control.
GotFocus	This event is triggered when your control gets the focus.
LostFocus	This event is raised when your control loses the focus.

An Example: The Guaranteed-to-Drive-Your-User-Crazy Command Button

We want to show off the powers of the Extender object with a custom command button that you will probably not want to use in your projects. Why? Well, anytime the mouse gets near it, it runs away.

The full code is on the CD, the code that make it behave the way it does needs to be in the MouseMove event. Although the code is a little complicated, the idea is actually simple: Any time the mouse gets inside our control, we move it to a new location. (If need be, we make it appear on the opposite edge of the containing form.) There are two ways to do this. The first is to do what we did and directly reset the UserControl.Extender.Left and the UserControl.Extender.Top properties. The second is to call the UserControl.Extender.Move method.

Here's the mouse move procedure that makes our control so cruel:

```
Private Sub Command1_MouseMove(Button As Integer,_
Shift As Integer, X As Single, Y As Single)
  Dim l As Single
  Dim t As Single
  l = UserControl.Extender.Left
  t = UserControl.Extender.Top

  Const Unit = 100

  'see what direction they moved in from
  If X < (BTN_WIDTH / 2) Then
    'they are on the left half of the button
    l = l + Unit
    If Y < (BTN_HEIGHT / 2) Then
      'they are on the top half of the button
      t = t + Unit
    Else
      t = t - Unit
    End If
  Else
    l = l - Unit
    If Y < (BTN_HEIGHT / 2) Then
      'they are on the top half of the button
      t = t + Unit
    Else
      t = t - Unit
    End If
```

```
   End If

   'check the left setting
   If (l + BTN_WIDTH) < (Unit * 4) Then
     'went off the left side of the screen
     l = UserControl.Extender.Container.ScaleWidth - _
     BTN_WIDTH
   ElseIf (l + Unit) >
UserControl.Extender.Container.ScaleWidth Then
      'went off the right side of the screen
      l = 0 'ScaleWidth + Unit
   End If

   'check the top setting
   If (t + BTN_HEIGHT) < (Unit * 4) Then
     'went off the top of the screen
     t = UserControl.Extender.Container.ScaleHeight - _
     BTN_HEIGHT
   ElseIf (t + Unit) >
UserControl.Extender.Container.ScaleHeight Then
      'went off the bottom of the screen
      t = 0 'ScaleHeight + Unit
   End If

   'now set the new left and top
   UserControl.Extender.Left = l
   UserControl.Extender.Top = t
End Sub
```

Using the Control Interface Wizard

To give the user of your control the ability to fine-tune the control for specific use may require exposing dozens of members. Of course, as you saw earlier in this chapter, exposing the members of the constituent controls that make up your user control is not conceptually difficult; it just requires writing lots of routine code.

For example, every member you want to make public needs to be distinguished from every member you want to keep private, and, regardless of the scope, both may require writing two routine Property procedures. Also, once you have a lot of constituent controls in your user control, it becomes more complicated to *map* the members correctly. (As you saw in the last chapter, mapping simply refers to how members of the user control pair up with members of the constituent controls.) For example, if you have five labels and a caption property for your control, do you want to map the caption property of your user control to the caption property of the first label, the second? Perhaps you don't want to map it to the caption property of a label at all!

Of course, you could write all the needed code by hand following the models from the last chapter, but the process is tedious, at best. Even the most experienced VB developer would not willingly do what is required if there was an easier way. And, there is. The Control Interface Wizard that comes with VB5 (on the Add-Ins menu) writes a lot of the necessary code automatically. Even the most experienced control developers (including those at Microsoft!) use the Control Interface Wizard to build the functionality into their controls. Then, they tweak the resulting code by hand to finish off their control.

This section walks you through using the Control Interface Wizard and the necessary hand tweaking in two realistic situations. The first is a simple banner control. The second control is the address control whose interface you saw in Figure 13-1. Since the address control uses multiple controls inside the user control form in order to provide more functionality and a richer user interface, mapping the members is more difficult, but also more important.

In both cases, we take you through the steps needed to use the Wizard. After each step, we explain what is going on behind the scenes given the choices we made. After all, all of the Wizards that come with VB5 are there to simplify generating the needed code. If you don't understand the code generated by a Wizard, you will never be able to take full advantage of VB5.

Building a Simple Banner Control

This control is simple in the sense that it has no visible controls on it. It consists of a timer control that is invisible at run time and the user control form itself that is used to display the text. We will create this control from scratch. For this follow these steps:

1. Load VB5 and start up a new ActiveX Control project.
2. Set the AutoRedraw property of the user control form to True. This way, the text will persist if the control is covered or moved.

3.   Double-click the Timer control in the Toolbox. Using a Timer control lets us set the rate at which the banner moves.

4.   Set the Interval property of the timer to 100 (milliseconds). This gives our control a default value other than the usual 0 (meaning inactive) that timers start out with.

Once you have created the user control form for the banner control, you are ready to run the Control Interface Wizard. Load the Control Interface Wizard from the Add-Ins menu. Figure 13-7 shows the opening screen of the Wizard.

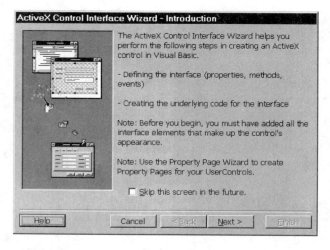

Figure 13-7   Opening screen of the Wizard

Click Next to go to the "Select Interface Members" step, as shown in Figure 13-8. As you can see, this screen is divided into two list boxes. The left one, called Available names, lists all the methods, properties, and events of all the constituent controls on your user control. For example, if you scroll down you can see methods like the Cls method of the form or the Timer event of the Timer control. The right list box, called Selected names, lists the members of the constituent controls that the Wizard will make public (or *expose*, as it is usually called). For example, you probably want the user to be able to set the BackColor property of the form.

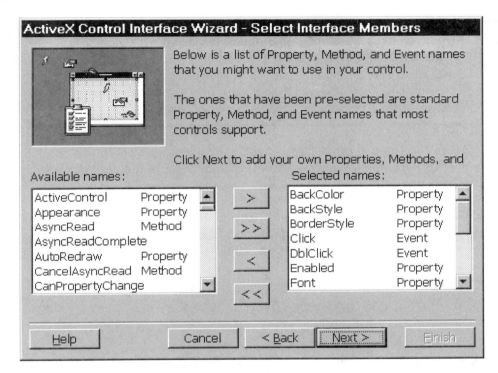

Figure 13-8   Select Interface Members screen of the Wizard

On the other hand, we do not want the user able to change the BackStyle property of our user control. (Recall the possible values are Opaque and Transparent. Why would you want a Transparent banner?) Do this by double-clicking on the BackStyle property. Double-clicking in the Wizard moves any item to the other list.

Note

Any member you remove from the Selected names list becomes Private to your control. Removing these items tells the Wizard to not add the code needed to expose them.

Now, remove the keyboard events from the Selected names list by double-clicking them: KeyDown, KeyPress, KeyUp. These events are not needed because this control doesn't use the keyboard.

Tip

In addition to double-clicking, which moves the item to the other pane immediately, you can use the ordinary click, SHIFT + click or CTRL + click methods to select, respectively, one name, a continuous list of names, or a discontinuous group of names from a pane. Then press either the ← or → buttons to move the selected items to the other pane.

Move the Interval property from the Available names list to the Selected names list by double-clicking it. Once it is in the Selected names list, we know it will be exposed (made Public). This property needs to be exposed so the user can set the interval for the control to scroll the text.

Click Next to go to the Create Custom Interface Members screen, as shown in Figure 13-9. (A *custom interface member* is Wizard-speak for any property, event, or method that is special to your control.)

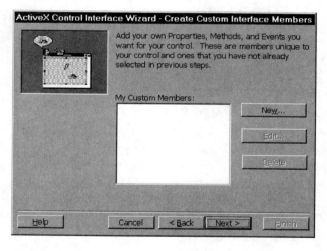

Figure 13-9   Create Custom Interface Members

We want to add our own member called Caption. This will be a string property that the user can set for the text that the banner displays. (We could have called it BannerText or some such name but it is easier for your users if you use the obvious VB equivalent of the property.) Notice that we need to add a custom property for this because the user control itself does not have a caption property. (User controls are essentially forms without title bars—no title bar, no caption!)

To do this, click New. The Add Custom Member dialog box, shown in Figure 13-10, pops up.

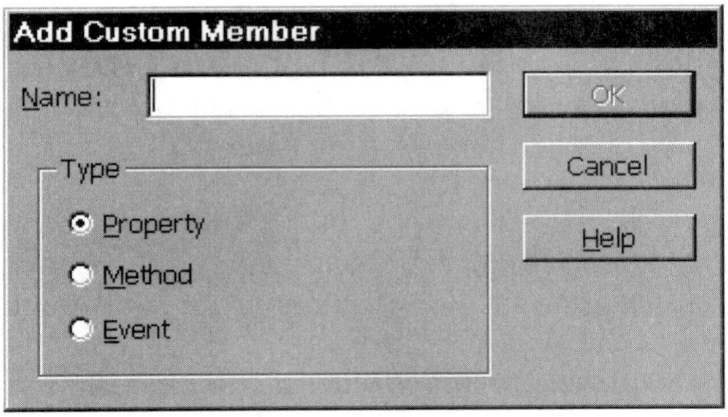

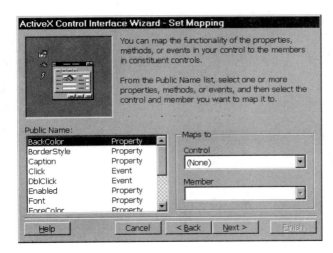

Figure 13-10   Add Custom Member dialog box

Add a Property called Caption and click on OK.

Click Next to go to the Set Mapping step, as shown in Figure 13-11 The
Set Mapping page of the Wizard is where you tell the Wizard which properties, methods, and events of the user control are to be tied to properties of its
constituent controls. For example, the Timer event of the user control has to
be associated to the Timer event of the Timer control.

Figure 13-11   Set Mapping dialog box

Note

*The contents of the Public Name list box in this screen are exactly the names
you had in the Selected names box in the step shown in Figure 13-11. This
is why you won't, for example, see a BackStyle property listed here.*

Make sure the focus is at the top of the list of Public Names and press SHIFT+END to select the entire list. Now hold down the CTRL key and click on the Interval and Caption items in order to deselect them. The point is that these two properties need to be mapped differently than all the rest of the Public Names.

Now, in the Maps to frame, select UserControl in the Control drop-down. This will map all of the selected items to the equivalent member of the user control itself. For example, the BackColor of the banner control will come from the BackColor of the user control form.

We now need to tell the Wizard what to do with the Caption and Interval properties that do not yet have a home. Let's take up the Caption property first. For this:

1. Make sure only the Caption property is selected in the Public Name box.

2. Select None in the Control drop-down list. This is because the Caption property is not going to correspond to any property of the constituent controls.

3. Click Next to go to the Set Attributes step, as shown in Figure 13-12. This is where we set up the custom caption property. This screen tells us that this is where we can clean up the loose ends of "unmapped members."

Figure 13-12   Set Attributes screen

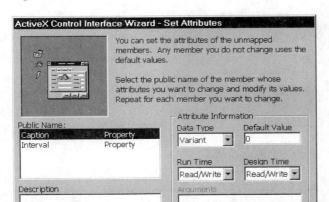

4. Select String in the Data Type drop-down.

5. Type in This is a Banner! in the Default Value field. Leave the other drop-down boxes alone. We want our Caption property to be both readable and writable at run time and design time.

Next, we need to map the Interval property. For this:

6. Click Back to go back to the Set Mapping screen.

7. Click on Interval to set its mapping.

8. Choose Timer1 from the Control drop-down box.

9. The Interval Property pops up in the Member drop-down list box. (In general, the Member box contains a list of all the members of any constituent control you are mapping your Public names to. For a timer, this is only the Enabled and Timer members. However, since the Wizard automatically puts the default property of the control you are mapping to, the Interval property is listed here.)

That's it. Click on Finish to go to the Finish Screen, shown in Figure 12-13, where you are given the opportunity to see the summary report, shown in Figure 13-14. (The summary report contains nothing you don't already know.)

Figure 13-13   Finished screen for the Wizard

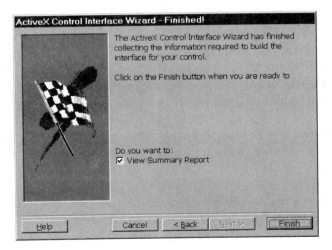

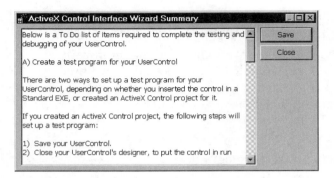

Figure 13-14   Summary screen for the Wizard

What the Wizard Did

After you click on Finish and close the Wizard, the Wizard goes off and performs its wizardry. It creates all of the code needed to expose the properties, events and methods to the user of our user control. It also adds code to set the default values when the control is initialized. Take a look at what the Wizard created. We apologize for the length of the code, but we hope this will convince you that you would never want to write all this code yourself. The elements that go into this kind of code were explained in earlier chapters, so we won't do it again here. Note that the Wizard uses m_ to indicate its module level variables rather than a simple m as we usually do. It also leaves off the Public modifier for events, since this is the default.

Caution

The Wizard adds lots of comments beginning with `"WARNING!"` *These comments are used by the Wizard to know what it did previously when you run it another time in order to add or change something. If you change or remove any of these comments, you risk confusing the Wizard so that it may not perform as expected the next time you run it. In particular whenever you tweak code by hand that the Wizard creates, you will probably not be able to use the Wizard again. We actually suggest not trying to run the Wizard again once you have your control working the way you like. You are better off putting in any of the final touches on it by hand. If you do need or want to run the Wizard again, make sure you have saved and backed up your control to a different location. This way, you can go back to where you were before running the Wizard the second time.*

```
'Default Property Values:
Const m_def_Caption = "This is a Banner!"
'Property Variables:
Dim m_Caption As String
'Event Declarations:
Event Click() 'MappingInfo=UserControl,UserControl,-1,Click
Event DblClick() 'MappingInfo=UserControl,UserControl, _
-1,DblClick
Event MouseDown(Button As Integer, Shift As Integer, _
X As Single, Y As Single)
   'MappingInfo=UserControl,UserControl,
   -1,MouseDown
Event MouseMove(Button As Integer, Shift As Integer, _
X As Single, Y As Single)
   'MappingInfo=UserControl,UserControl,-1,MouseMove
Event MouseUp(Button As Integer, Shift As Integer, X As _
Single, Y As Single) 'MappingInfo=UserControl,UserControl,
                     '-1,MouseUp


'WARNING! DO NOT REMOVE OR MODIFY THE FOLLOWING COMMENTED LINES!
'MappingInfo=UserControl,UserControl,-1,BackColor
Public Property Get BackColor() As OLE_COLOR
   BackColor = UserControl.BackColor
End Property

Public Property Let BackColor(ByVal New_BackColor As OLE_COLOR)
   UserControl.BackColor() = New_BackColor
   PropertyChanged "BackColor"
End Property

'WARNING! DO NOT REMOVE OR MODIFY THE FOLLOWING COMMENTED LINES!
'MappingInfo=UserControl,UserControl,-1,ForeColor
Public Property Get ForeColor() As OLE_COLOR
   ForeColor = UserControl.ForeColor
End Property

Public Property Let ForeColor(ByVal New_ForeColor As OLE_COLOR)
   UserControl.ForeColor() = New_ForeColor
   PropertyChanged "ForeColor"
End Property

'WARNING! DO NOT REMOVE OR MODIFY THE FOLLOWING COMMENTED LINES!
'MappingInfo=UserControl,UserControl,-1,Enabled
Public Property Get Enabled() As Boolean
   Enabled = UserControl.Enabled
```

```
End Property

Public Property Let Enabled(ByVal New_Enabled As Boolean)
  UserControl.Enabled() = New_Enabled
  PropertyChanged "Enabled"
End Property

'WARNING! DO NOT REMOVE OR MODIFY THE FOLLOWING COMMENTED LINES!
'MappingInfo=UserControl,UserControl,-1,Font
Public Property Get Font() As Font
  Set Font = UserControl.Font
End Property

Public Property Set Font(ByVal New_Font As Font)
  Set UserControl.Font = New_Font
  PropertyChanged "Font"
End Property

'WARNING! DO NOT REMOVE OR MODIFY THE FOLLOWING COMMENTED LINES!
'MappingInfo=UserControl,UserControl,-1,BackStyle
Public Property Get BackStyle() As Integer
  BackStyle = UserControl.BackStyle
End Property

Public Property Let BackStyle(ByVal New_BackStyle As
Integer)
  UserControl.BackStyle() = New_BackStyle
  PropertyChanged "BackStyle"
End Property

'WARNING! DO NOT REMOVE OR MODIFY THE FOLLOWING COMMENTED LINES!
'MappingInfo=UserControl,UserControl,-1,BorderStyle
Public Property Get BorderStyle() As Integer
  BorderStyle = UserControl.BorderStyle
End Property

Public Property Let BorderStyle(ByVal New_BorderStyle As
  Integer)
  UserControl.BorderStyle() = New_BorderStyle
  PropertyChanged "BorderStyle"
End Property

'WARNING! DO NOT REMOVE OR MODIFY THE FOLLOWING COMMENTED LINES!
'MappingInfo=UserControl,UserControl,-1,Refresh
Public Sub Refresh()
```

```
      UserControl.Refresh
End Sub

Private Sub UserControl_Click()
    RaiseEvent Click
End Sub

Private Sub UserControl_DblClick()
    RaiseEvent DblClick
End Sub

Private Sub UserControl_MouseDown(Button As Integer,
    Shift As Integer, X As Single, Y As Single)
    RaiseEvent MouseDown(Button, Shift, X, Y)
End Sub

Private Sub UserControl_MouseMove(Button As Integer,
    Shift As Integer, X As Single, Y As Single)
    RaiseEvent MouseMove(Button, Shift, X, Y)
End Sub

Private Sub UserControl_MouseUp(Button As Integer,
    Shift As Integer, X As Single, Y As Single)
    RaiseEvent MouseUp(Button, Shift, X, Y)
End Sub

'WARNING! DO NOT REMOVE OR MODIFY THE FOLLOWING COMMENTED LINES!
'MappingInfo=Timer1,Timer1,-1,Interval
Public Property Get Interval() As Long
    Interval = Timer1.Interval
End Property

Public Property Let Interval(ByVal New_Interval As Long)
    Timer1.Interval() = New_Interval
    PropertyChanged "Interval"
End Property

Public Property Get Caption() As String
    Caption = m_Caption
End Property

Public Property Let Caption(ByVal New_Caption As String)
    m_Caption = New_Caption
    PropertyChanged "Caption"
End Property
```

```vb
'Initialize Properties for User Control
Private Sub UserControl_InitProperties()
  Set Font = Ambient.Font
  m_Caption = m_def_Caption
End Sub

'Load property values from storage
Private Sub UserControl_ReadProperties(PropBag As PropertyBag)

  UserControl.BackColor = PropBag.ReadProperty("BackColor",
    &H8000000F)
  UserControl.ForeColor = PropBag.ReadProperty("ForeColor",
    &H80000012)
  UserControl.Enabled = PropBag.ReadProperty("Enabled", True)
  Set Font = PropBag.ReadProperty("Font", Ambient.Font)
  UserControl.BackStyle = PropBag.ReadProperty("BackStyle", 1)
  UserControl.BorderStyle =
    PropBag.ReadProperty("BorderStyle", 0)
  Timer1.Interval = PropBag.ReadProperty("Interval", 0)
  m_Caption = PropBag.ReadProperty("Caption", m_def_Caption)
End Sub

'Write property values to storage
Private Sub UserControl_WriteProperties(PropBag As PropertyBag)

  Call PropBag.WriteProperty("BackColor",
    UserControl.BackColor, &H8000000F)
  Call PropBag.WriteProperty("ForeColor",
    UserControl.ForeColor, &H80000012)
  Call PropBag.WriteProperty("Enabled", UserControl.Enabled,
    True)
  Call PropBag.WriteProperty("Font", Font, Ambient.Font)
  Call PropBag.WriteProperty("BackStyle",
    UserControl.BackStyle, 1)
  Call PropBag.WriteProperty("BorderStyle",
    UserControl.BorderStyle, 0)
  Call PropBag.WriteProperty("Interval", Timer1.Interval, 0)
  Call PropBag.WriteProperty("Caption", m_Caption,
    m_def_Caption)
End Sub
```

Activating the Banner

We still need to add some code to make the control actually act as a banner. The following code lets the text scroll from right to left at the desired interval:

```
Private Sub Timer1_Timer()
  Static nPos As Integer
  Static msBanner As String

  If Not Ambient.UserMode Then Exit Sub   'design mode
                                'so no scroll in design mode
  If Len(msBanner) = 0 Then
    msBanner = Caption & Space(Len(Caption))
    While TextWidth(msBanner) < (Width * 2)
      'pad with spaces to fill the whole control twice
      msBanner = msBanner & " "
    Wend
    nPos = 1
  End If

  'move left the corrected number of positions based on
  'the character width of the current left most character
  nPos = nPos + ((TextWidth("W") \ TextWidth(Mid$(msBanner,_
  nPos, 1)))))
  'check for being past the end of the string and reset if so
  If nPos > Len(msBanner) Then nPos = 1
  'shift it to the right
  m_Caption = Mid$(msBanner, nPos) & Left$(msBanner, nPos)
  RefreshCaption
End Sub
```

Since the caption is drawn directly on the user control itself, we need to write code to do this. We need to do this from a lot of places, so it is best to encapsulate it in a subroutine.

```
Sub RefreshCaption()
  'print the caption
  UserControl.Cls: UserControl.Print m_Caption
End Sub
```

Now, we need to add the RefreshCaption call to some spots in the code the Wizard generated. Basically, any Property Let routine that changes the user control needs to also reset the caption, such as the Property Let associated to the BackColor, ForeColor, Font, and Caption properties. Add a call to the sub, above the PropertyChanged call, as in the following example.

```
Public Property Let BackColor(ByVal New_BackColor As OLE_COLOR)
  UserControl.BackColor() = New_BackColor
  RefreshCaption
  PropertyChanged "BackColor"
End Property
```

Just a few more code changes and we'll be done. In order to make the control look a little nicer in its default state, let's add some defaults of our own to the UserControl_InitProperties event. We need to replace the subroutine that the Wizard created with the one given next. This code will make the control start off with a border, a red background, blue text, and a bold Courier font.

```
'Initialize Properties for User Control
Private Sub UserControl_InitProperties()
  'set the defaults
  BackColor = &HFFFF00
  ForeColor = &HFF&
  BorderStyle = 1
  UserControl.FontName = "Courier New"
  UserControl.FontBold = True
  m_Caption = m_def_Caption
End Sub
```

Now, in order to make the control properly display the caption when we place one on a form, we need to add the RefreshCaption call to the resize event of the user control, as in:

```
Private Sub UserControl_Resize()
  RefreshCaption
End Sub
```

Finally, to make it even neater, let's add code to resize the font when the user of the control resizes it.

```
Private Sub UserControl_Resize()
  Static sglLastHeight As Single
  Dim sglCurrHeight As Single
  Dim nFont As Single

  If sglLastHeight = 0 Then
    'initialize it
    sglLastHeight = Height
  End If

  nFont = UserControl.FontSize
  sglCurrHeight = Height

  'resize the font to match the control size
  If (sglLastHeight <= sglCurrHeight) And (TextHeight("A") _
< sglCurrHeight) Then
    'they enlarged it
    While TextHeight("A") <= sglCurrHeight
      nFont = nFont + 0.25
      UserControl.FontSize = nFont
    Wend
  Else
    'they reduced it
    While (TextHeight("A") >= sglCurrHeight) And (nFont >
1.25)
      nFont = nFont - 0.25
      UserControl.FontSize = nFont
    Wend
  End If
'save the current height to compare against next time
  sglLastHeight = Height
  RefreshCaption
End Sub
```

Building an Address Control

Now, we are going to move on to a more complex control that requires more programming and a greater use of the Control Interface Wizard in order to add and map its own custom properties, events, and methods. This control has a much more substantial user interface, as shown in Figure 13-15. Notice that this control has fifteen constituent controls. The idea, of course, is that anytime you need to allow a user to enter an address in a VB project or on a Web page, you can use this ActiveX control rather than recoding it from scratch.

This control uses two control arrays: one for the various text boxes and the other for the labels. As you will see, using control arrays considerably simplifies the code for the control.

Given the complexity of the user interface, you might want to load the form for the user control from the CD. The control in its raw state is named

Figure 13-15   The designer for the Address Control

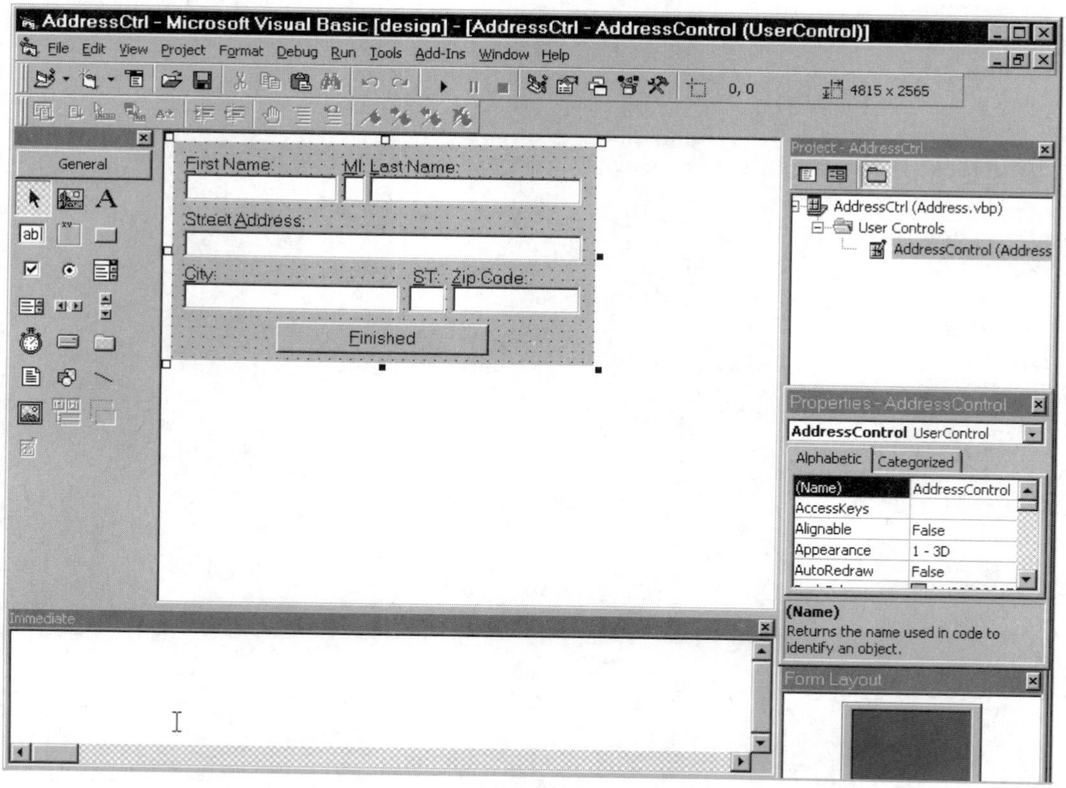

AddressFirstStage.vbp and may be found in the CH13 directory of the CD. Of course, the AddressFirstStage.vbp is currently unusable because it does not expose any members. The user of this control in its current state couldn't do anything useful with it. Therefore, it's time to use the Control Interface Wizard to make our job easier.

Load the AddressFirstStage.vbp control project into VB5 and start up the ActiveX Control Interface Wizard from the Add-Ins menu. Click Next to go to the Select Interface Members step. At this step:

1. Click the DOUBLE LEFT ARROW button to move all of the default selections to the Available names list. If we stopped at this point, we would be exposing nothing to the user of the control.

2. Double-click the following member items from the Available names list in order to move them to the Selected names list:

    BackColor, BorderStyle, Change, Enabled, Font, and ForeColor

These are the properties, events and methods we want to expose to the user. We now want to add a few custom members to our Address Control. The tricky thing here is that since our Address Control has so many constituent controls of the same type, we need to be careful about what member of our control gets mapped to what member of one of the eight constituent controls. So, click Next to go to the Create Custom Interface Members step. Now:

1. Click New and add a property called DataFont.
2. Click New and add a property called DataBackColor.
3. Click New and add a property called DataForeColor.
4. Click New and add a property called FirstName.
5. Click New and add a property called LastName.
6. Click New and add a property called MI.
7. Click New and add a property called Address.
8. Click New and add a property called City.
9. Click New and add a property called State.
10. Click New and add a property called Zip.
11. Click New and add a method called ClearAll.
12. Click New and add an event called Finished.

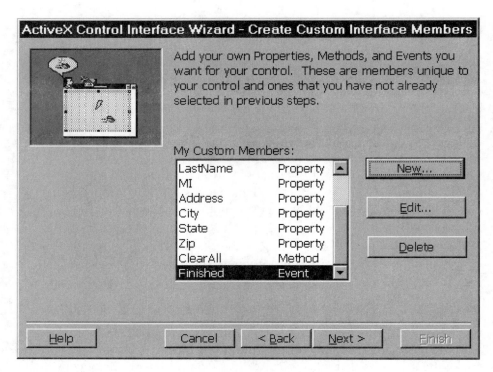

Figure 13-16   Custom Interface Members for the Address Control

The result is shown in Figure 13-16.

The idea is to present the user of the control with a property like FirstName but map that to the Text property of the appropriate text box. This is the role of the Set Mapping screen in the Control Interface Wizard. So click on Next to take you to the Set Mapping screen, as shown in Figure 13-17. Notice that the Public Name box lists all the names we had in the Select names box in the second screen of the Wizard, plus all the custom members we just created.

Mapping the Members

This is where we tell the Wizard how to map the various members we have selected so it will know what code to generate in order to do the mapping. The following table shows how to map the members.

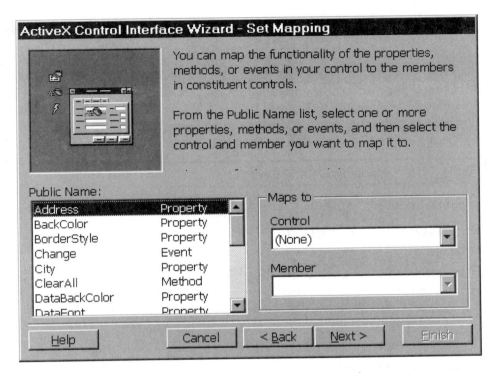

Figure 13-17   The Set Mapping screen for the Address Control

Table 13-5:	Mapping Members	
Member Name	*Maps to Control*	*Maps to Member*
Address	Control = "txtData(3)"	Member = "Text"
BackColor	Control = "UserControl"	Member = "BackColor"
BorderStyle	Control = "UserControl "	Member = "BorderStyle"
Change	Control = "txtData(0)"	Member = "Change"
City	Control = "txtData(4)"	Member = "Text"

The ClearAll method does not really map to any member of the constituent controls or the user control form, so we need to leave it unmapped. Any unmapped members like this one will need hand-tweaked code to make it work correctly. For this, simply map the ClearAll property to the user control but leave the Member box blank.

Next, since we have used control arrays for the text boxes, we will simply map the various Data properties to `txtData(0)` and fix the code later by adjusting the control array index, if necessary. (This kind of trick can save you a lot of time when using the Control Interface Wizard.) The mappings we use for the data properties are described by the following table.

Table 13-6: Mapping Data Properties		
Member Name	*Maps to Control*	*Maps to Member*
DataBackColor	Control = "txtData(0)"	Member = "BackColor"
DataFont	Control = "txtData(0)"	Member = "Font"
DataForeColor	Control = "txtData(0)"	Member = "ForeColor"

Next, make the mapping described in the following table.

Table 13-7: Mapping		
Member Name	*Maps to Control*	*Maps to Member*
Enabled	Control = "UserControl "	Member = "Enabled"
Finished	Control = "cmdFinshed"	Member = "Click"
FirstName	Control = "txtData(0)"	Member = "Text"
Font	Control = "UserControl "	Member = "Font"
ForeColor	Control = "UserControl "	Member = "ForeColor"
LastName	Control = "txtData(2)"	Member = "Text"
MI	Control = "txtData(1)"	Member = "Text"
State	Control = "txtData(5)"	Member = "Text"
Zip	Control = "txtData(6)"	Member = "Text"

That's it. Click Next to go to the "Finished" step and click Finish.

Tweaking the Code

The Wizard creates a lot of the code needed for our address control. However, because of the many constituent controls and the fairly complex mapping, we need to go in and modify the code slightly to get it working correctly. We will start at the top of the code module and work our way down, making additions and corrections as we go. You can see that the Wizard did a tremendous amount of work for us. Even where we need to add code of our own, the Wizard often provided a template for adding what we need.

In order to set the individual subcontrol property values, we need to add a loop that walks through all of the labels in the `lblLabels` control array. For example, for the Font objects, the Wizard generated this code:

```
Public Property Set Font(ByVal New_Font As Font)
   Set UserControl.Font = New_Font
   PropertyChanged "Font"
End Property
```

We need to replace this with:

```
Public Property Set Font(ByVal New_Font As Font)
   Dim i As Integer
   For i = 0 To 6: Set lblLabels(i).Font = _
   New_Font: Next
   Set UserControl.Font = New_Font
   PropertyChanged "Font"
End Property
```

in order to be sure that the fonts are changed for all the elements in our control array. (The ease of adding this kind of code is one of the main reasons why control arrays are so useful when making a user control.)

Do the same thing for the ForeColor property. Replace:

```
Public Property Let ForeColor(ByVal New_ForeColor _
As OLE_COLOR)
   UserControl.ForeColor() = New_ForeColor
   PropertyChanged "ForeColor"
End Property
```

with

```
Public Property Let ForeColor(ByVal New_ForeColor _
As OLE_COLOR)
   Dim i As Integer
   For i = 0 To 6: lblLabels(i).ForeColor = _
   New_ForeColor: Next
```

```
UserControl.ForeColor() = New_ForeColor
PropertyChanged "ForeColor"
End Property
```

Next, you'll need to modify the DataBackColor, DataForeColor and DataFont properties. For this, replace:

```
Public Property Let DataBackColor(ByVal
    New_DataBackColor As OLE_COLOR)
    txtData(0).BackColor() = New_DataBackColor
    PropertyChanged "DataBackColor"
End Property
```

with

```
Public Property Let DataBackColor
    (ByVal New_DataBackColor As OLE_COLOR)
    Dim i As Integer
    For i = 0 To 6: txtData(i).BackColor() = _
    New_DataBackColor: Next
    PropertyChanged "DataBackColor"
End Property
```

and replace:

```
Public Property Let DataForeColor
    (ByVal New_DataForeColor As OLE_COLOR)
    txtData(0).ForeColor() = New_DataForeColor
    PropertyChanged "DataForeColor"
End Property
```

with

```
Public Property Let DataForeColor
    (ByVal New_DataForeColor As OLE_COLOR)
    Dim i As Integer
    For i = 0 To 6: txtData(i).ForeColor() = _
    New_DataForeColor: Next
    PropertyChanged "DataForeColor"
End Property
```

Finally, replace:

```
Public Property Set DataFont(ByVal New_DataFont _
As Font)
    Set txtData(0).Font = New_DataFont
    PropertyChanged "DataFont"
End Property
```

with

```
Public Property Set DataFont(ByVal New_DataFont _
As Font)
   Dim i As Integer
   For i = 0 To 6: Set txtData(i).Font = _
   New_DataFont: Next
   PropertyChanged "DataFont"
End Property
```

Creating a Member from Scratch— The ClearAll Method

The Wizard did not know how to handle the ClearAll method because we did not map it to anything, so we need to replace the function it created. For this, replace:

```
Public Function ClearAll() As Variant
   ClearAll = UserControl.()
End Function
```

with

```
Public Sub ClearAll()
   Dim i As Integer
   For i = 0 To 6: txtData(i).Text = _
   vbNullString: Next
End Sub
```

Mapping Common Properties

Properties like ForeColor should be set once for all the constituent controls when the user of the control works with the property. For all of the constituent controls to reflect the single value entered by the user for the ForeColor, DataBackColor, and DataForeColor properties of the user control, replace the following lines in the UserControl_ReadProperties sub:

```
UserControl.ForeColor = _
PropBag.ReadProperty("ForeColor", &H80000012)
txtData(0).BackColor = _
PropBag.ReadProperty("DataBackColor", &H80000005)
txtData(0).ForeColor = _
PropBag.ReadProperty("DataForeColor", &H80000008)
```

with

```
ForeColor = PropBag.ReadProperty( _
   "ForeColor", &H80000012)
DataBackColor = _
PropBag.ReadProperty("DataBackColor", &H80000005)
DataForeColor = _
PropBag.ReadProperty("DataForeColor", &H80000008)
```

This works directly with the property rather than with the private variable and, thus, makes the change we want.

Creating Property Pages

If you played around with the Windows 95 custom controls briefly described in Chapter 6, you saw they all have a property called Custom. If you clicked on this, you saw a screen that let you set the properties of the control more easily. For example, Figure 13-18 shows you the Property Pages for the Tab Strip Control. In general, a property page makes it easier for the user of your control to use it, so you should seriously consider adding one for any control that has complex properties to set. The purpose of this section is to show how to build custom property pages using VB5.

A property page is attached to a user control as the value of its PropertyPages property. Visual Basic 5 comes with three standard property pages called StandardFont, StandardColor, and StandardPicture. For example, start up a user control and go to the PropertyPages property and click on the three dots. This will open up a screen like Figure 13-19.

Figure 13-18   Property Pages for the Tab Strip Control

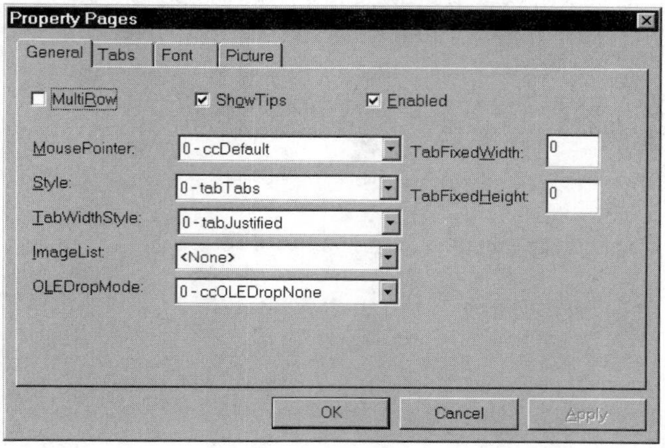

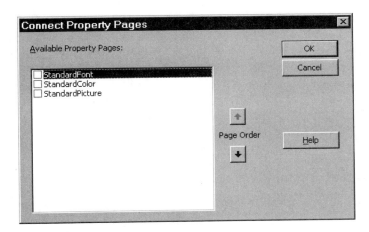

Figure 13-19   The Connect Property Pages dialog box

Choose the StandardPicture page and click on OK. At this point, your control designer doesn't look very interesting. However, if you add a Standard EXE to give a form to test the user control on and close the control designer, you will notice a new (custom) property listed for the user control, as shown in Figure 13-20.

If you click on the three dots, you'll see the StandardPicture property page, as shown in Figure 13-21

Of course, this property page can't do anything because there is no code behind it. We'll show you the code needed to activate a property page shortly.

Tip

If a control has a property page, then right-clicking on the control and clicking on Properties brings up the property page.

Finally, you can have multiple property pages by clicking off the appropriate check boxes in the Connect Property Pages dialog box. The arrow keys on this dialog box let you order them.

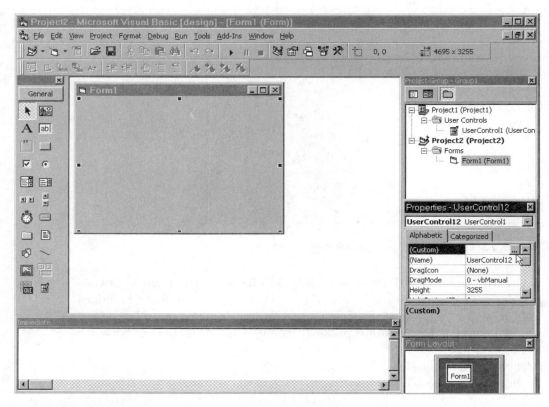

Figure 13-20   A (Custom) property

Figure 13-21   The StandardPicture property page

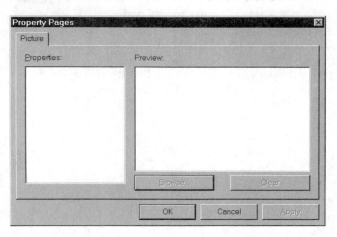

Building a Simple Property Page

Let's start with a fairly simple example of creating a property page. To show you how to do this, let's create a control that has a property whose value is potentially a list of items. Rather than require the user to type in a long list of items separated by commas in the Properties window, we will create a property page that contains a list box with those values in it. All the user of the control has to do is select from this box using the ordinary Windows techniques for list box selection.

First, we need to create the control. This control is going to be a list box that only displays a subset of a group of possible values. For example, lets say you want to make a control that lists the days of the week for users to select from. Sometimes, you want all the days available; other times, you want just weekdays or weekend days. The property page will show a list of all the days and allow the user to select which days to display. Start up a new ActiveX project in Visual Basic 5 using the CtrlGroup so that you also have the test form. Now,

1. Add a standard list box control to the user control.
2. Set the following properties to the user control.

Table 13-8:   Controls and Properties for a Simple Property Page

Constituent control	Property	Value
User Control	Name	DayListControl
List1	IntegralHeight	False
List1	Left	0
List1	MultiSelect	1 – Simple
List1	Top	0

The user control form looks like Figure 13-22.

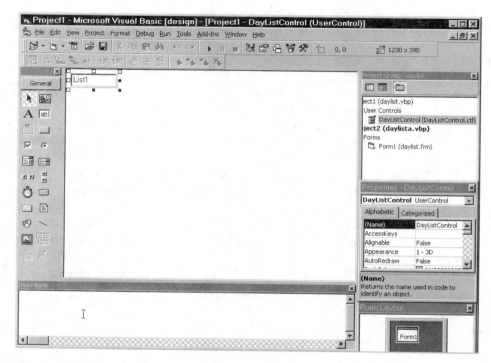

Figure 13-22   DayListControl in design time

Writing the Code for the DayList Control

Double-click the user control and add the usual code to the Resize event in order to keep the list box the same size as the surrounding user control form.

```
Private Sub UserControl_Resize()
   List1.Width = Width
   List1.Height = Height
End Sub
```

Save the control project and call it DayList.

Now, we are ready to add the ListValues property that will tell the list box which values to display when it is loaded in an application or HTML page. Internally, this will be a semicolon delimited string. To add this read/write property, we need to add the appropriate Property Get/Let procedures along with a private variable for data transfer. To do all this, add the following code to the General section of the code for the user control.

```
Dim msDays As String

Public Property Get Days() As String
   Days = msDays   'a semi-colon delimited list
End Property

Public Property Let Days(sData As String)
   Dim nEnd As Integer
   Dim nStart As Integer

   msDays = sData

   'clear out any previous items
   List1.Clear

   'add the current items to the list box by walking through the
   'delimited string and pulling out each item. This loop
   'assumes
   'that each item is followed by a ";" including the final one
   nStart = 1
   nEnd = InStr(msDays, ";")
   While nEnd > 0
      List1.AddItem Mid$(msDays, nStart, nEnd - nStart)
      nStart = nEnd + 1
      nEnd = InStr(nStart, msDays, ";")
   Wend

End Property
```

Next, we want to add the controls to read and write the properties back from the PropertyBag.

```
Private Sub UserControl_ReadProperties(PropBag As PropertyBag)
   'Load property values from storage
   Days = PropBag.ReadProperty("Days", msDays)
End Sub

Private Sub UserControl_WriteProperties(PropBag As PropertyBag)
   On Error Resume Next
   'Write property values to storage
   Call PropBag.WriteProperty("Days", msDays)
End Sub
```

Finally we need some code to initialize the control:

```
Private Sub UserControl_Initialize()
  msDays = Days
End Sub
```

Close the user control designer so the control will be available for use in the test project. Now the DayList user control is ready to test. If you don't already have a test project, select File|Add Project and add a Standard EXE project to VB5. Add the new DayListControl and place one on the test form of the project, as shown in Figure 13-23.

Notice that the Property window contains the Days property. Try setting it to something like `Monday;Wednesday;Thursday;`. If you have done everything correctly up to this point, the list should display "Monday," "Wednesday," and "Thursday." The problem is that users will have to type out the words, spell them correctly, use the right delimiter, etc., so this is not very user friendly.

Figure 13-23   The Test form for the DayList Control

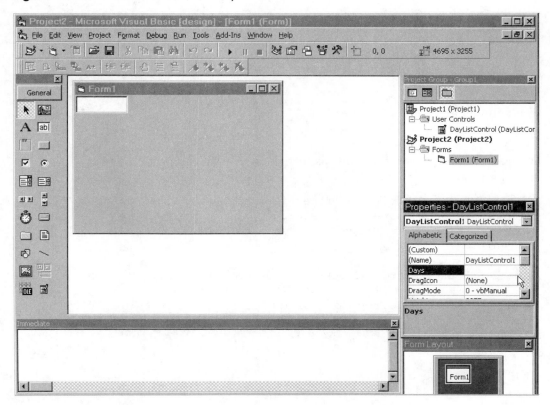

Adding the Property Page

Now, we are ready to create a Property page that allows users to set this property simply by picking days from a list. To do this, we will add a Property page that allows the user to set the Days property from it. For this:

1. Make sure that the current project is the user control.
2. Select Project|Add Property Page on the main menu bar. The Add Property Page screen shown in Figure 13-24 will show up.

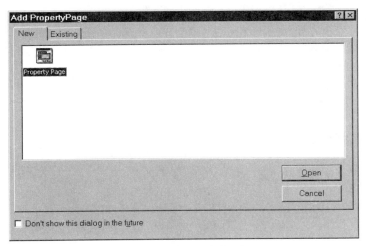

Figure 13-24   Add Property Page dialog box

Choose PropertyPage and click on Open. You should have a Property page displayed on your screen, as shown in Figure 13-25. Notice your Project window should include a Property Pages item on the same level as the user control item.

The Property page designer looks like an ordinary form designer. The only clue is in the title bar. This is because a Property page is really just an ordinary form. In particular, that means you need to design it the same way you design any form. For our Property page:

1. Set the Name property of the Property page to DaysProp.
2. Set the Caption property of the Property page to Day List.
3. Add a List Box Control and call it 1stDays. Enlarge it to show the days of the week.

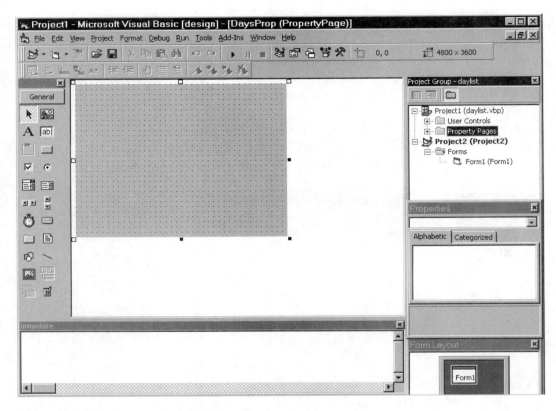

Figure 13-25   Property Page in design mode

4.   Add the days of the week to the List property of 1stDays.

5.   Set the MultiSelect property of 1stDays to 1—Simple.

Tip

Use Ctrl + Enter to separate the lines in the List box.

Your Property page designer should look like Figure 13-26.

Activating the Property Page

We need to add the code to activate the Property page. Before we do that, however, we need to tell the user control it now has a Property page. For this:

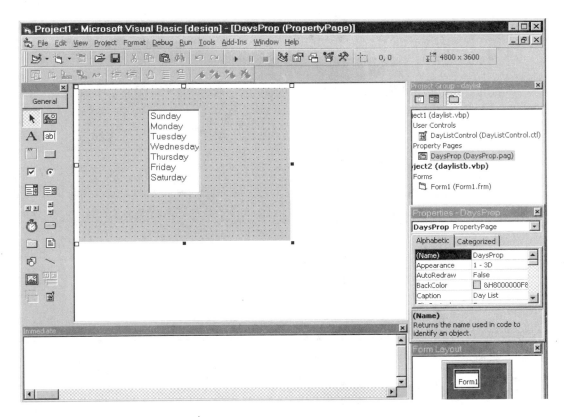

Figure 13-26   Property Page designer in progress

1. Open up the Connect Property Pages dialog box by double-clicking in the PropertyPages property of the user control.

2. DaysProp should show up, in addition to the standard three Property pages that VB5 comes with. Choose it.

We need to know whether the user clicks inside the list box on the Property page. The way to do this in VB5 is by working with the value of the Changed property. For this, open a Code window for the Property page and add the three procedures that we discuss next to the Property page code.

```
Private Sub lstDays_Click()
   Changed = True
End Sub
```

This tells us that when the user clicks in the list box, the Property page has changed. (Changed is a built-in property of a Property page that returns or sets a value to tell you whether a property on a Property page has changed.)

Next, we need a procedure to apply the changes after the user makes them. This is done with the ApplyChanges event procedure that, like Changed, is one of the standard procedures that a Property page has. The code will build up the delimited string from what the user selected in the Property page and then assign it to the Days:

```
Private Sub PropertyPage_ApplyChanges()
   Dim i As Integer
   Dim sTmp As String

   'build the delimited string from the selected items
   For i = 0 To lstDays.ListCount - 1
     If lstDays.Selected(i) Then
        sTmp = sTmp & lstDays.List(i) & ";"
     End If
   Next
   SelectedControls(0).Days = sTmp
End Sub
```

Note

`SelectedControl(0)` *is the currently selected control on the form. If the user selects more than one control,* `SelectedControl(0)` *is the primary control in the group. None of our Property page code deals with the controls in a multiselected group.*

Finally, we need the standard SelectionChanged() procedure of a Property page. This event gets triggered when the user changes anything in the Property page. This code tells us which items were selected by assigning the value of the appropriate entry in the Selected array that is associated with any list or combo box. Here is the code needed for this event.

```
Private Sub PropertyPage_SelectionChanged()
   Dim i As Integer

   'select the items that are in the string
   For i = 0 To lstDays.ListCount - 1
     If InStr(SelectedControls(0).Days,
          lstDays.List(i) & ";") > 0 Then
        lstDays.Selected(i) = True
     End If
   Next
End Sub
```

Testing the Completed Property Page

Now the property page is ready to test. Reload Form1 of the EXE project we added earlier. It should still have Monday, Wednesday, and Thursday in it. Right-click the user control and select properties. The property page you just created with the three days selected is as shown in Figure 13-27.

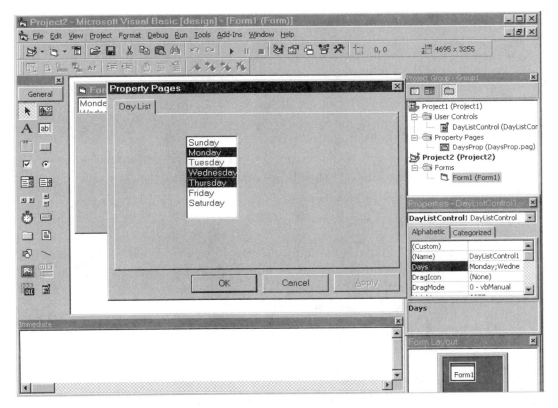

Figure 13-27   The DayList property page at work

Now we need to check that our property page really works. For this:

1. Make sure the DayList property page and Form1 are visible on your screen, as in Figure 13-27.

2. Click on some other day or days.

3. Then click Apply and OK.

You should see the list on Form1 change to the newly selected items and the Days property list in the Properties window will be updated as well. This is clearly much easier for the user than typing in a delimited string of entries to use our control!

Polishing Up Our Property Page

There are many more ways to embellish our Property page. This section will describe a few of them. First, you may have noticed that even though we created a custom Property page for the Days property, the results are still displayed in the Properties window as a delimited string that users might try to edit directly. If you want to prohibit the user of your control from doing this, you need to set an attribute of the property. To do this:

1. Load the user control code window.
2. Open the Tools menu and select Procedure Attributes.
3. Click Advanced. This brings up a screen like Figure 13-28.
4. Check the check box titled "Don't show in Property Browser."
5. Click on OK to close the dialog box.

Another possibility is to leave the Days property listed in the Properties window but allow users to load the custom property page from this line of the Properties window. This is also done by setting another attribute on the Procedure Attributes dialog box. In this case:

1. Select the user control code window.
2. Click the Tools menu and select Procedure Attributes.
3. Click Advanced.
4. Uncheck the check box titled "Don't show in Property Browser" if it is still checked.
5. Select DaysProp from the "Use this Page in Property Browser" list.
6. Click on OK to close the dialog box.

Now, when you go back to designing with the DayList Control and work with the Properties window for the control, you'll see that the Days property shows nothing until you select it. When you select this property, you will

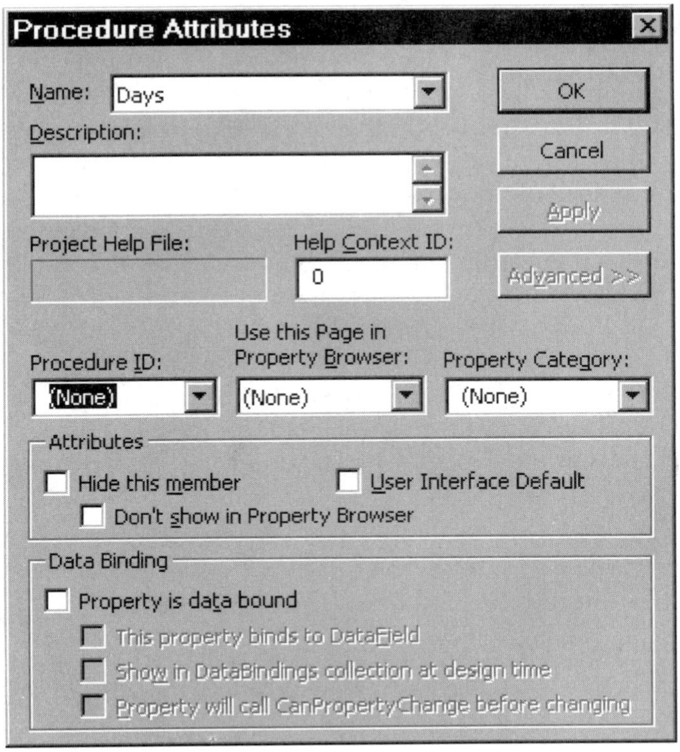

Procedure Attributes ✕

Name: Days ▼ | OK

Description: | Cancel

| Apply

Project Help File: Help Context ID: | Advanced >>
0

Use this Page in
Procedure ID: Property Browser: Property Category:
(None) ▼ | (None) ▼ | (None) ▼

┌─ Attributes ───────────────────────────
│ ☐ Hide this member   ☐ User Interface Default
│   ☐ Don't show in Property Browser

┌─ Data Binding ─────────────────────────
│ ☐ Property is data bound
│   ☐ This property binds to DataField
│   ☐ Show in DataBindings collection at design time
│   ☐ Property will call CanPropertyChange before changing

Figure 13-28   Advanced Procedure Attributes screen

notice a little button to its right with the usual three-dot ellipsis that indicates
a dialog box is waiting for you. Click the ellipsis and VB5 loads the custom
Property page you created and displays it again.

Note

*What we just did does not prohibit the user of the control from typing
directly into the Properties window, but at least the Property page is there
if needed.*

If you want to, you can also add usability features to the Property page,
such as buttons for None and All, so the user does not have to click every
entry to select them all.

The Property Page Wizard

If you create a custom control with a lot of exposed properties, VB5 comes with a Property Page Wizard that makes the job of creating property pages a bit easier. However, the current version can only create text boxes and check boxes. Thus, you will need to add things like list boxes and combo boxes by hand if your property page design calls for them. Still, it is often easier to use the Wizard to reduce the amount of busywork that you would otherwise need to do. To show how the Wizard works, let's go through a typical session using it.

First, we need to create a simple control and add some properties to it in order to have something to work with. To do this, start with a simple text box and run the Control Interface Wizard to expose some properties. We will then place those properties on the Property pages we create. So, start up a new ActiveX Control project.

1. Add a text box to the user control.
2. Load the Control Interface Wizard from the Add-Ins menu.
3. Click Next to go to the Select Interface Members step.
4. Move the Locked and MaxLength properties from the Available names list to the Selected names list.
5. Move the BackStyle property from the Selected names list to the Available names list, because it does not apply to a text box.
6. Click Next to go to the Create Custom Interface Members step.
7. Click New to create a custom member.
8. Enter P1 in the Name field.
9. Click New again. Enter P2 in the Name field, make sure the Property button is clicked, and then click OK.
10. Click Next to go to the Set Mapping step.
11. Select the entire list of Public Names by going to the top of the Public Names and using Shift/End.
12. In the Control drop-down, select Text1.
13. Click Next to go to the Set Attributes step. As shown in Figure 13-29, we have only two custom properties to set attributes for.

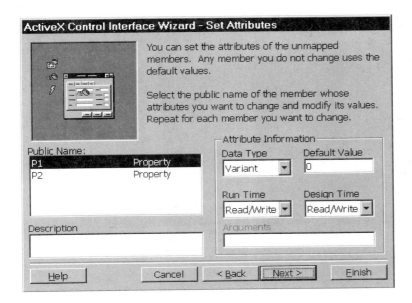

Figure 13-29 Set Attributes dialog box

14. With P1 selected in the Public Names list, select String in the Data Type drop-down list.

15. Enter abcd in the Default Value field.

16. Select P2 in the Public Names list.

17. Select Boolean in the Data Type drop-down list.

18. Click Next, then Finish to make the Wizard do its job.

The result is a simple control with lots of properties of various types. Now we are ready to create a set of Property pages for this control using the Wizard. Save your control before we go on.

Using the Property Wizard

We now have a control to show off the Property Wizard. Start up by choosing Add-Ins|Property Page Wizard. You'll probably see an introductory screen like Figure 13-30. (If not, you will see a screen like Figure 13-31.)

Click Next to go to the first functional screen in the Wizard, as shown in Figure 13-32. Notice in Figure 13-32 that the Wizard detects that you have

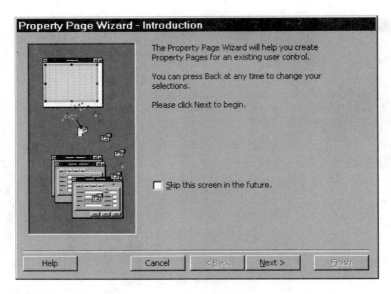

Figure 13-30 Introductory screen for the Property Wizard

Figure 13-31 Select the Property Pages screen
in the Property Wizard

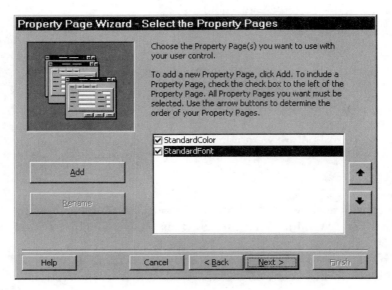

Property Page Name   ☒

Enter new page name: ┌──────────┐
                                                  │   OK   │
                                                  └──────────┘
                                                  ┌──────────┐
                                                  │ Cancel │
                                                  └──────────┘

┌──┐
│PropertyPage1   │
└──┘

Figure 13-32   Property Page Name dialog box

some properties of type Color and Font and, therefore, selects the Standard
pages for these types of properties. Properties of type Font, Picture, and
OLE_COLOR are automatically placed on the standard pages for you. To use
them, select the pages in the PropertyPages property of the user control. The
Wizard will do this for you if you leave these boxes checked on this screen.

We now want to add a Property page. For this, click the Add button. A dialog box like Figure 13-33 pops up to give the name of the property page.

Let's call our property page General. So enter General for the new name

Figure 13-33   Select the Property Pages screen completed

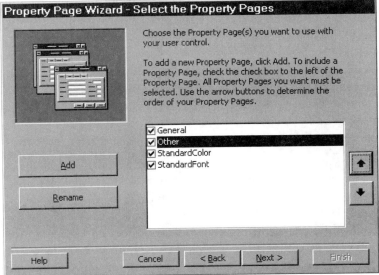

of the Property Page and click OK to confirm the new name. Notice that the Select Property Pages screen adds the General page with a checkmark. Next, follow the procedure to add a property page named Other.

To rearrange the order the user will see the Property pages, select the page that you want to move by clicking the Up and Down arrows keys. See if you can get them in this order: General, Other, StandardColor, StandardFont.

We now want to add the appropriate properties to the Property pages we created. For this, click Next to go to the Add Properties step, as shown in Figure 13-34. This screen is where you place the properties you want on each particular page. You cannot place properties on any of the three Standard pages. They are simply here for reference to give you a somewhat clearer view of your final Property page collection.

There are numerous ways to get a property onto a page at this step. The most obvious is to:

1. Select a page.
2. Select a property.
3. Then click the single right-arrow button to move the property to the current page.

However, since this Wizard supports "drag and drop," an easier way is to simply drag the desired property from the Available Properties list to either the current page or the tab of the desired page and drop it. (There's a neat hand icon when you drag and drop, as shown in Figure 13-35.)

Tip

It is a good idea to add the properties in the order you want them to be displayed on the final Property pages, otherwise the Wizard will lay them out in the order you added them.

Using either technique, place the P1 and P2 properties on the Other page and the other 3 properties on the General page. Click Next, then click Finish to have the Wizard create the Property pages you have set up.

Now that the Wizard has created the Property pages, it is time to see what they look like. To do this, add a form to the control project and place a user control on it. Then you can either right-click and choose Properties, or select the Custom property in the Property Browser and click the little "Ö" button. The result will look like Figure 13-36.

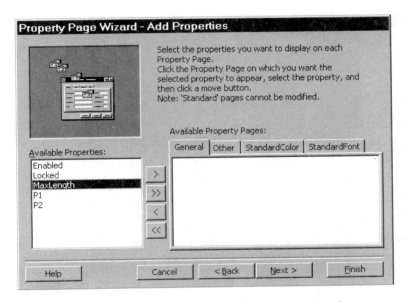

Figure 13-34 Add Properties page in the Property Wizard

Figure 13-35 Drag and Drop in the Add Properties page

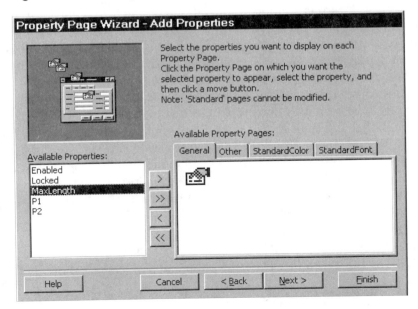

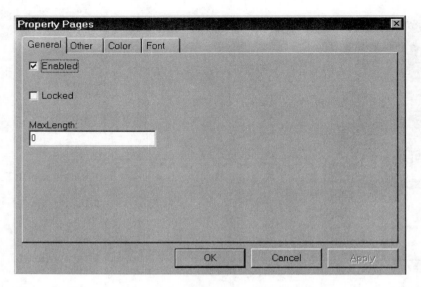

Figure 13-36   Property Pages that the Wizard created

Polishing Up the Wizard's Results

The Property Page Wizard is a simple utility intended to help you get started with building Property pages. It will remove a lot of the tedium of writing the code needed to hook up the properties. It will not, however, produce sophisticated Property pages with controls such as list boxes, option buttons, or frames without you massaging its output by hand.

There is a lot you can do to enhance Property pages and make them easier to use. As you have seen with our simple DayList example, lots of properties have values that come from a set list of possibilities. If you use the Property Page Wizard, these properties will be displayed simply as multiple text boxes because it is impossible for the Wizard to determine what the predefined list of possible values is. It is fairly easy to convert a text box property to a drop-down combo. To do this with the P properties from the previous example, simply follow these steps:

1. Load the Other property page.
2. Delete the text box under the P1 caption and add a combo box in its place.
3. Set the Name property to cboP1.

4. Add some items to the List property, such as A, B, C.
5. Open the code module for the property page.
6. Replace all occurrences of txtP1 with cboP1.
7. Add the following code:

```
Private Sub cboP1_Click()
    Changed = True
End Sub
```

Now load Form1 again and right-click the user control and choose Properties to display the Properties pages. Select the Other page and notice that, instead of a text box, the user now has a drop-down combo box from which to choose a value.

Testing Controls

First, the control must do the basic tasks for which it was designed. For example, does an extension of a text box still accept text? Does it still allow cut and paste using the standard Windows conventions? If a control is designed to be a numeric-only TextBox, you need to verify that it does not accept any non-numeric characters from the keyboard or by pasting from the clipboard. Verifying this is simply a matter of knowing those tasks and trying each one. For example, our original version of the modified TextBox in Chapter 1 had a bug because it allowed the user to paste in negative numbers. This was found simply by trying to paste a negative number into it and discovering that it worked without raising an error after this action.

Secondly, as with any code you must test the so-called *negative cases*. These are cases where you expect the control to fail but you want to verify that, even in failure, it produces an expected result such as a meaningful error message. For example, with a numeric TextBox, suppose we have a maximum value property. You would certainly want to enter a value outside the range and have the control issue an appropriate error, as opposed to simply beeping or failing silently. Next, you will again want to test at the *boundary cases*. For the numeric text box, you will want to test it with exactly the minimum and the maximum values to make sure that they are accepted.

Finally, as you have seen, controls can neither be tested nor run in the traditional way you run a Visual Basic application. Controls must work "in the process" of another application. This usually means that you add the control to a form or forms that are part of a Standard EXE project. As you saw way back in Chapter 1 the most common way to test your control is:

1. Add a Standard EXE project to your current session. This gives you a form on which to place the control you are testing.

2. Close the designer for the user control. This puts the control in what is usually called run mode. (You can always tell you are in run mode by looking for the enabled icon of your user control on the toolbox.)

3. Completing Step 2 allows you to place an instance of your user control on the test form (or forms) from Step 1 and then start the test project.

Note

Your control should not produce any untrapped run-time errors that could cause the host application to fail. The samples and templates shipped with this book could have significantly more error handling code—they are really designed to serve as starting points for you, i.e. proofs of concept.

Unless the control was coded with some of the debugging techniques listed above, it will be nearly impossible to determine if you are executing every code path. This is where tools such as the Visual Basic Code Profiler (Chapter 10) would come in handy to produce a report of code coverage to show which code was executed or not.

Platform Testing for Controls

The next phase of testing involves using the control in all of the host applications in which it is intended to be used. Controls can be used in Visual Basic itself, other applications such as Microsoft Access or Excel, and the most important host of late, Internet Explorer. Testing here requires that you first build an OCX using the File|Make *ProjectName.*OCX command. This command pops up the dialog box shown in Figure 13-37. (You should then click on the Options button to go to a dialog box for setting versioning information, as shown in Figure 13-38.) When you make an OCX out of your control, Visual Basic creates a binary executable file with the extension .ocx *and* it registers the control for use on your system. For example, if you have Visual

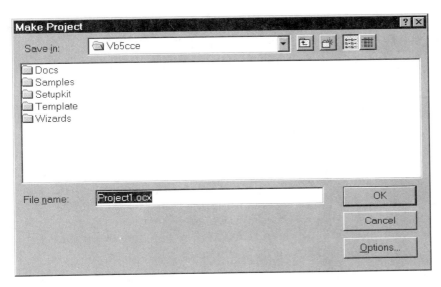

Figure 13-37   Make Project dialog box

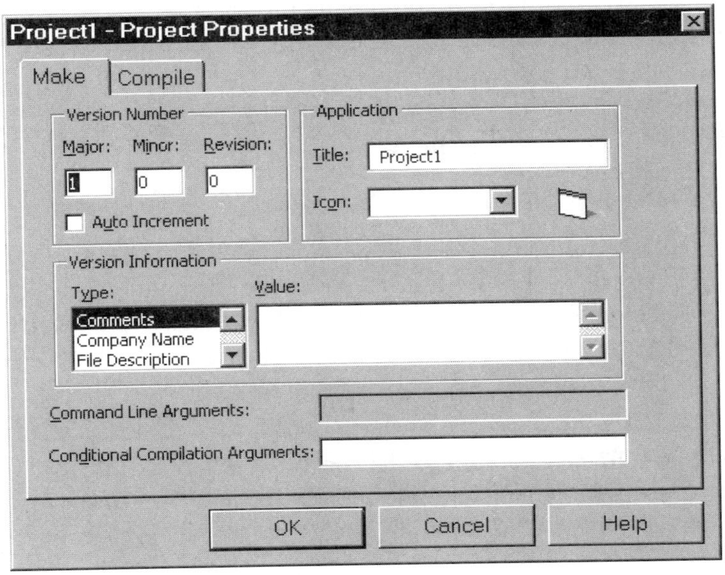

Figure 13-38   Project Properties dialog box

Basic 4.0 on your system, the new control should appear in the list of available controls when you choose Tools|Custom Controls.

On the other hand, if you copy the OCX file to another system that has an OCX hosting application such as Office 97 or Internet Explorer, then you will have to register the control on that system. This can be done in the Setup program for the control (see Chapter 20).

Testing in Internet Explorer

Testing your user control in Internet Explorer 3.01 or later involves a few more steps. We are going to run through a session using the free ActiveX Control Pad utility that makes it easy to manipulate ActiveX controls in Internet Explorer. (A version of the ActiveX control pad is available on the CD that comes with this book or for the latest version go to Microsoft's Web site.)

So assuming that you have already made the OCX file and installed the ActiveX Control Pad on your system, follow these steps:

1.   Load the Control Pad.
2.   Place your edit cursor at the beginning of a line in the Body of the new HTML page. (Failure to do this may cause the Control Pad to insert the control data in an undesirable location that will most likely lead to errors.)
3.   Select Edit|Insert ActiveX Control and select the control you want to test from the list. An example of what you will see is shown in Figure 13-39.

The control may have a strange name if you did not properly name it when you created it in the first place (see the tip that follows). The name that you will see in the ActiveX Control Pad will be the description of the class for the control itself. If you did not put this in the Project Properties dialog box.

Tip

To give a control a user-friendly name, load the control project, press F2 for the Object Browser, choose the name of the control project in the main drop-down and the control in the "Classes" list. Then, right-click the control name and choose Properties. This will display a Members Options dialog box, as shown in Figure 13-40 (for the Banner Control), that allows you to enter a description that ends up being the friendly name of the control. Now isn't that intuitive?

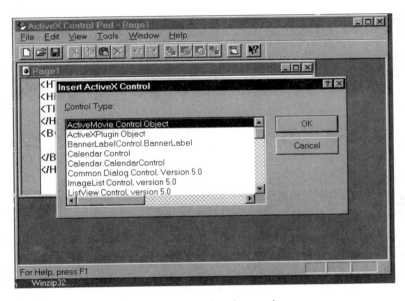

Figure 13-39   The ActiveX Control Pad at work

Figure 13-40   The Member Options dialog box inside the IDE

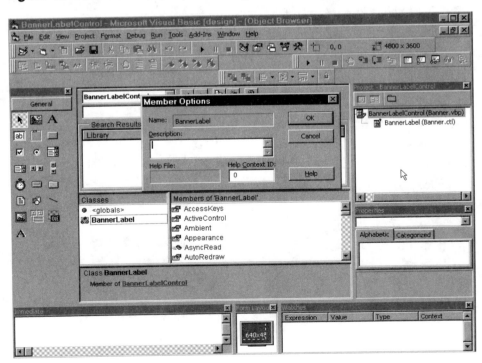

Inserting a Control with the ActiveX Control Pad

After you have selected the desired control, choose OK and your screen should look like Figure 13-41, with a couple of overlapping windows. The currently active window is the property sheet for the control.

Note

Set properties in the ActiveX Control Pads Properties window by highlighting a property and typing in the box next to the Apply button. Then click on Apply. If this control has a custom property page, you can get to it by right-clicking in the control and choosing the last Properties item.

Partially obscured in Figure 13-41 are windows (see Figure 13-42) for the visual representation of the control (analogous to the user control form) and one for the HTML code.

Figure 13-41   The ActiveX Control Pad at design time

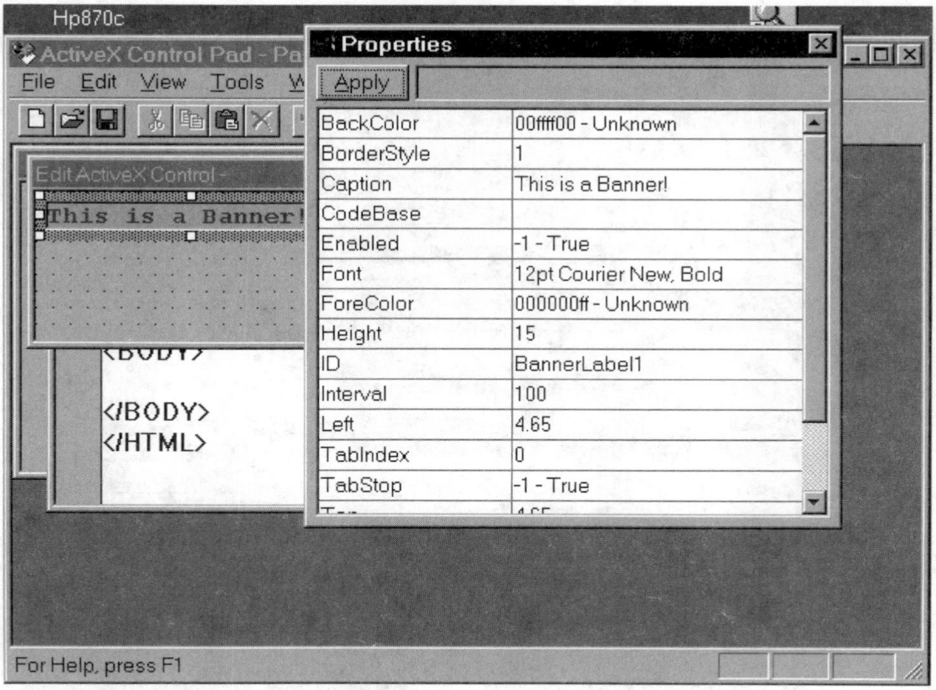

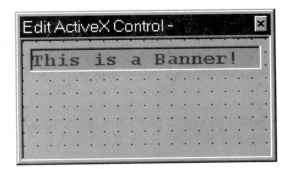

Figure 13-42   The user control form in the ActiveX Control Pad

Once you have set the properties as you like, close the "Edit ActiveX Control" dialog and the needed information to use the ActiveX control will be added to the HTML page you are creating, an example of which is shown for a calendar control in Figure 13-43. (This information consists of the totally inscrutable ClassID property plus the lines needed to set the properties of the controls.)

Figure 13-43   The ActiveX Control Pad with needed HTML Object tag

```
ActiveX Control Pad - [Page1]
 File  Edit  View  Tools  Window  Help

<HTML>
<HEAD>
<TITLE>New Page</TITLE>
</HEAD>
<BODY>


<OBJECT ID="Calendar1" WIDTH=417 HEIGHT=312
 CLASSID="CLSID:8E27C92B-1264-101C-8A2F-040224009C02">
  <PARAM NAME="_Version" VALUE="458752">
  <PARAM NAME="_ExtentX" VALUE="8805">
  <PARAM NAME="_ExtentY" VALUE="6604">
  <PARAM NAME="_StockProps" VALUE="1">
  <PARAM NAME="BackColor" VALUE="12632256">
  <PARAM NAME="Year" VALUE="1996">
  <PARAM NAME="Month" VALUE="12">
  <PARAM NAME="Day" VALUE="30">
</OBJECT>

For Help, press F1
```

Now:

1. Save the HTML page.
2. Load Internet Explorer 3.01 or greater. (You don't need an active Internet connection, so do not log on to your service provider as you usually do. We're just going to connect to the page on our local machine instead of connecting to one on a remote machine.)
3. Choose File|Open and enter the path name where you saved the HTML page from Step 1. This will probably display a dialog box, as shown in Figure 13-44, informing you of a potential safety violation because the page you are loading contains an ActiveX Control. Select OK and then Yes and the page should load, displaying the control.

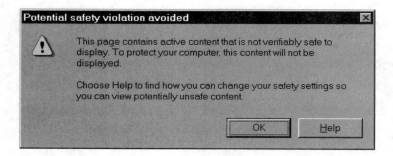

Figure 13-44   Security Warning dialog box

Scripting Your ActiveX Control

Of course, if you followed the previous steps, the page doesn't do much except what it is programmed to do in its initial state—because you don't have any code hooked up to it. (For example, the Banner Control would work fine but all it would say is "This is a banner!") To test your control, you have to know how to add some simple VBScript code to interact with the control.

Note

VBScript is a simple subset of the VBA language that uses only variants. It should take someone who has gotten this far about 15 minutes to master it. The Microsoft Web site (www.microsoft.com/vbscript) has sufficient documentation on it for an experienced programmer and there is a version of both the VBScript DLL and the docs on the CD.

Go back to the ActiveX Control Pad and select Tools|Script Wizard. This will load a dialog box like the one shown in Figure 13-45. Notice that this dialog box has two treeview lists and a code or list window.

Suppose you have registered the Address Control from Chapter 9 and want to test it with some simple script code. Follow the steps given previously, only this time add an instance of our Address Control to an HTML page in the ActiveX Control pad. Now start up the Script Wizard again:

Figure 13-45   The Script Wizard in the ActiveX Control Pad

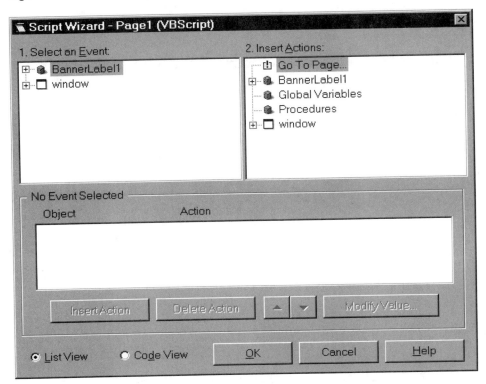

1. Select "Code View."
2. Expand the Address Control in the left-hand pane by clicking the "+" to the left of its name.
3. Click on one of the events shown below the control.

For example, our Address Control has Change and Finished events. If your control has not exposed any events, there will not be any for you to test so you will not be able to continue with this process on that particular control. When you clicked on an event name, you should have noticed that the Code window now looks like Figure 13-46 and has code something like:

```
Sub AddressControl1_Finished()
```

in it. Below this line, simply enter:

```
If AddressControl1.FirstName = "William" Then
  MsgBox "Everybody calls him Bill though!"
End If
```

Figure 13-46   Address Control in ScriptWizard

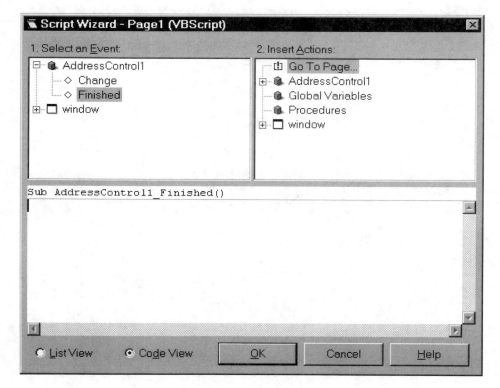

Caution

Don't put in an End Sub. An annoying peculiarity of the control pad's Scripting Wizard is that it adds the End Sub automatically but doesn't display it!

Now click the OK button and the code will automatically be inserted into the HTML page. Save the HTML page and go back to Internet Explorer. If you still have the page loaded, click the Refresh button on the toolbar and the page will reload. If not, simply reload the page using its location as described above.

Click on the Finished button (or do whatever is needed to fire the particular event you chose to test). In our case, enter "William" into the First Name field so the message box will pop up. If you followed all these steps, substituting your control and its events for our event and it worked, you should pat yourself on the back But you aren't done. You still need to repeat the steps described above for all of the events your control has exposed!

OBJECT FACTORIES-ACTIVEX SERVERS: ACTIVEX DLLs, AND ACTIVEX EXEs

Topics in this Chapter

- Processes
- ActiveX DLLs
- ActiveX EXEs
- Multithreading

Chapter 14

To this point you have seen how to create objects using Visual Basic in two different ways:

- Instances of classes that are part of a standard EXE project.
- Instances of an ActiveX control that you create and then add to the toolbox.

Visual Basic can build projects whose classes will be factories for creating objects in two more ways. The purpose of this chapter is to explain these two other kinds of object factories. Finally, along the way, you will learn more about *processes* and what (and how to do) *multithreading* in Visual Basic.

These two types of object factories are examples of what are usually called *ActiveX servers*. ActiveX servers depend on the COM technology that you learned about in Chapter 8. Technically, an ActiveX server is any executable code that supports the standard ActiveX interface IUnknown and which you can also program through a special COM interfaces called IDispatch. (This ability used to be called OLE automation.) Technically speaking, therefore, an ActiveX control is also an ActiveX server but we, like most people, use the term *ActiveX component* to encompass all three kinds of object factories and use the term ActiveX server for the object factories discussed in this chapter.

Note

The objects created by these ActiveX server "object factories" can be used not only by other Visual Basic applications, they can also be used in Office 97 applications. They can even be used in programs written in most Windows 95/NT enabled languages such as Visual J++, Visual C++, and Delphi 3.

Processes

The fastest typist in the world types around 200 words per minute. This translates into roughly 0.1 second per keystroke. To a processor running at 200 million cycles a second, 0.1 second is a long period of time. For example, if you run the following code:

```
TimeStarted = Timer
TimeTaken = Timer
Do Until TimeTaken - TimeStarted >= 10
   I = I + 1
   TimeTaken = Timer
Loop
MsgBox "I counted to " & I / 100 & " in 1/10 of a second"
```

you can get a sense of how many operations your machine can do in .1 second. Notice this includes the time spent on the call to the Timer function and the time spent in managing the loop. (This program reports a count of around 625 on a Pentium 166 running in the IDE, by the way.) It obviously makes sense to try to take advantage of all this idle time.

Modern operating systems, such as Windows NT and to a lessor extent, Windows 95, take advantage of this idle time through what is usually called *preemptive multitasking* (*preemptive multiprocessing* is another term for this).

Note

For simplicity's sake, we assume that you have only one CPU and do not take into account operations that can go on without the use of the CPU such as some disk I/O operations. We also do not take into account problems involved with multitasking "legacy" Windows 3.1 or DOS programs.

Preemptive multiprocessing works roughly as follows:

- The operating system assigns each program a slice of memory for its code and data.

- The operating system insures that these different memory slices do not interfere with each other. For example, it prevents one application from writing data to the part of memory assigned to another.

- After giving a program some time (and this might be unimaginable small by human time standards), the operating system stops that program and puts it into suspended animation.

- It then restarts one of the other programs and gives it a "slice" of time. (Which is why the whole process is sometimes called *time slicing.*) The method it uses to pick which program to start from the list of suspended programs is somewhat complicated. It also is different under Windows NT than under Windows 95.

Each piece of memory can be thought of as a virtual computer and is usually referred to as a *process* (see Figure 14-1). The point is that the switching between processes happens transparently to the user. Multiprocessing gives the user the *impression* that multiple programs are running simultaneously. Although, of course, this is actually impossible for a machine with only a single CPU. (It is actually quite tricky to have more than one program truly running at the same time even when you have multiple CPUs—but that is another question entirely.)

Figure 14-1 Processes

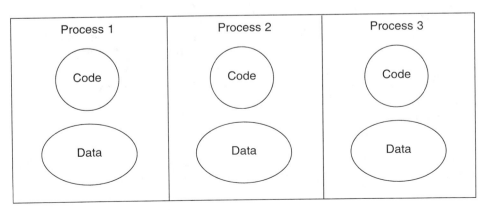

Your computer's memory

Process 1	Process 2	Process 3
Code	Code	Code
Data	Data	Data

Note

*It's called preemptive multitasking because the operating system can
(and does) interrupt each program without asking its permission. In
cooperative multitasking the program must relinquish control.
Cooperative multitasking was the only kind of multitasking possible in
Windows 3.1 and is still necessary for legacy programs running under
Windows 95. (A periodic call to Do Events is, of course, the way earlier
VB programs relinquished control.)*

In-Process versus Out-Of-Process

How can controls blend so seamlessly into VB? For all practical purposes a
control you add to the toolbox seems as much a part of VB as the intrinsic controls like text boxes and command buttons that are shipped as part of VB's executable. The answer is that anything you add to the toolbox runs in the *process*
of VB. An ActiveX control that is part of an application runs in the process of
that application. *For all practical purposes there is no difference between the
response time of code executing in process and code that is part of the application itself.* Of course, there is a downside to this, the process has to "grow"
to encompass any objects that are running "in-process" (see Figure 14-2).

Note

*Figure 14-2 is conceptually correct, but it is not correct as far as the physi-
cal memory of your machine is concerned. The operating system is smart
enough to share code when it knows that it is safe. It is the data that is
stored separately. The operating system acts as if there is a separate copy
of the code in each process but it doesn't actually keep multiple copies in
memory. For example, no matter how many applications are using common dialog controls there is only one physical copy of the COMDG32.OCX
file in physical memory. This type of sharing is called dynamic linking and
applications that can be used this way are called DLLs. (DLL stands for
dynamic link library.) The key point is that all DLLs (and controls are special cases of DLLs) run in process.*

Next, suppose that it isn't a control that you are adding to the toolbox. Instead
you go to Project|Properties and add a reference to one of the items listed

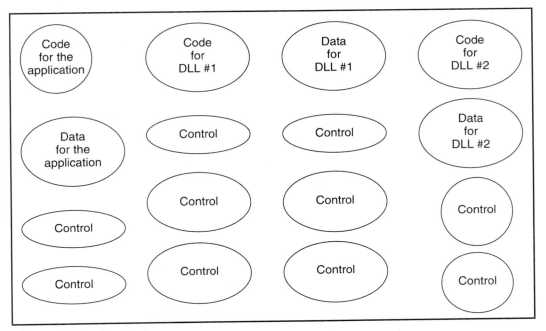

Figure 14-2 Running in-process

there. When you do this, you are essentially saying that you will want to create objects using that resource. Now you will have two possibilities. You can:

- Add a reference to a DLL and then ask it to create objects.
- Have these objects be created in the process of your application.

On the other hand, you can:

- Have these objects created out of the process of your application.

This occurs when you add a reference to a stand-alone application. An application that can make objects available to another application that is not running in its own process is called *an out of process server*. (The ones that VB can make are called *ActiveX EXEs.*)

But, we previously said that the operating system maintains a barrier between processes. How can you have code in one application that creates and then manipulates objects that are not in its process? We are asking the

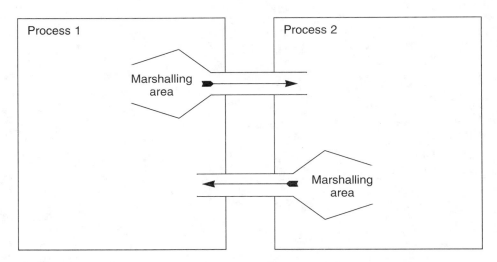

Figure 14-3   Marshalling data across the process boundaries

operating system to break the rigid process barriers that it is trying so hard to keep up.

The answer is that the operating system can relax its process barriers for certain special requests. Obviously these requests must be handled in a way that they minimize the risk of cross process contamination. The process needed is usually called *marshalling*. Similarly, after the request is received by the out of process object, the results have to be marshalled again in order that it can be sent back across the process barrier to the original application. (Think of marshalling as being like the way cells in your body can get nutrients and waste products across their cell walls.)

Of course, to prevent contamination, the marshalling process only allows you to send *messages* and the needed parameters across the process barrier. You can not use marshalling to actually go and mess with the data and code in another process!

Note

For those who are interested, ActiveX (OLE) solves the cross process barrier by creating a proxy object inside the calling process called a stub. The stub has the same signatures as the out of process object you are using including exposing the same interfaces. When you call a member from an object created out of process, OLE collects the needed parameters using the stub's interfaces. It then uses the out of process object by calling the matching member there getting the results and sending them back to the stub.

As you can imagine, the marshalling process needed for communicating across the process barrier takes time. (For an example of how much more time, see the section on ActiveX EXEs at the end of this chapter.)

The Instancing Property

For most purposes, the class modules that will be part of your ActiveX servers are coded the same way as class modules in a stand-alone application. For example, you will certainly want to document the members of your classes using the Properties Attributes dialog box. (Actually, since your servers can be used to create objects by other applications, good information in the Object Browser is even more important than it is for the classes in a stand-alone application.)

The one significant new feature that you need to become fully familiar with is the *Instancing* property of a class in a server. The Instancing property determines how the classes in your server actually creates objects. We want to go over the possible settings for this important property for classes that are common to both kinds of ActiveX servers in detail in this section.

Note

There are two settings that are available only for out of process (ActiveX EXEs). We will cover them in the section on ActiveX EXEs later on in this chapter. Also, this property is not available for classes that are part of stand-alone applications and has only one possible setting for class modules that are part of ActiveX controls.

Private

This is the default. The objects created as instances of private classes can only be created by the project that they are a part of. This is the only possible setting for classes in a standard EXE. As a general rule, mark classes to be Private in a server if they are "helper" classes that are only to be used internally. The TypeLib information in a Private class will not be visible in the Object Browser even after you have added a reference to the server that contains it.

PublicNotCreatable

This setting lets other applications use objects of the class but doesn't let the other applications create them. This is why it is the ideal setting for data structures where you may have a utility class that you want exposed but only the controlling class should be able to create the utility class. (Like a Linked List class and its helper Node class from Chapter 12.) The Object Browser can see the type library information for these kinds of classes as well. This is the only other possible setting for a class in an ActiveX control project.

MultiUse

This allows applications to create as many objects of that class as it would like. Although you don't have to actually set it, a user control is obviously a MultiUse object factory—having a control on the toolbox that could be used only once would be sort of funny. (There is a setting called SingleUse discussed below that applies to ActiveX EXEs only.)

GlobalMultiUse

This is a fun and occasionally very useful setting that like MultiUse allows you to create as many objects of that type as you want. The neat feature is that after you add a reference to an ActiveX DLL or ActiveX EXE that has the Instancing property set to GlobalMultiUse you *don't have to create an instance of the class using New. You can use the members of the class simply by calling them by name.* For example, for all practical purposes the members of an in process DLL with GlobalMultiUse set can be used as if those functions were built into VB.

As an example of where we used this nifty feature all the time in writing this book is that we made the TimingClass from Chapter 7 into a GlobalMultiUse class. We then added a reference to it (see below for how to do this). At that point we could simply have code like:

```
StartTimingMe
For I = 1 To 100
  'do something
Next
EndTimingMe
MsgBox DisplayElpasedTime
```

and the code works just as if VB had these timing functions built in.

Caution

Since members in GlobalMultiUse classes become part of the "name space" used by VB, you have to be careful not to have any conflicts with names reserved by VB or that are already in use by global servers higher up in the References dialog box. For example, if you do inadvertently give a member of a GlobalMultiUse class a name that is in use by the VB or VBA libraries, it will be shadowed by the intrinsic function and not be available in the same way that the other members of your GlobalMultiUse object are.

ActiveX DLLs

At the beginning of this chapter we said that an ActiveX DLL is an object factory that runs in the calling process of the application. In this section, we want to go over the special points that you will need to know when using, testing, and (alas) debugging ActiveX DLLs. First, creating an ActiveX DLL is as simple as choosing ActiveX DLL from the New Projects dialog box. You can also go to the Project|Properties dialog box and change the type of your project to an ActiveX DLL after the fact.

To test and where necessary debug a DLL in the development environment works much like it did for an ActiveX control. (Not surprising: ActiveX controls are, of course, special cases of ActiveX DLLs.) You need to add another Standard EXE project to build a Project Group. For example to show off how neat GlobalMultiUse objects are, do the following:

1. Start up an ActiveX DLL.

2. Select the Project in the Project Explorer and change its name to GlobalMultiUseDemo.

3. Set the Instancing property of the class in the DLL project to 6—GlobalMultiUse.

4. Add the following code to the class:

```
Public Sub HelloWorld()
  MsgBox "Hello world!"
End Sub
```

Now we need to add another project in order to test this DLL. For this:

1. Choose File|Add Project and choose Standard Exe.

2. Go To Project|References and you should see an item marked GlobalMultiUseDemo (see Figure 14-4). Check it off.

4. Make the Form_Load for Project1 look like this:

```
Sub Private Sub Form_Load()
  HelloWorld
End Sub
```

Don't hit the Run button yet. (If you do nothing will seem to happen). There is one last step to take in testing a DLL project built this way. The problem is that we started with a DLL project, so Visual Basic thinks it's the start-up project. (Its name is highlighted in the Project Explorer for this reason.) We need to make the test project the start-up project. For this:

1. Right click on the line that says Project1.

2. Choose "Set As Start Up" from the context menu that pops up.

Figure 14-4   GlobalMultiUse Demo

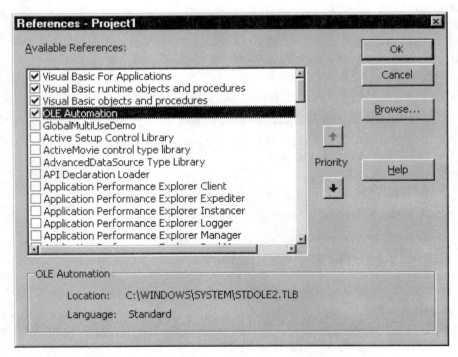

(And yes, we also think it is terrible that this functionality is only available form the context menu.)

3. Run the Project.

That's it. You should see a message box that says HelloWorld, proving that the "HelloWorld" is now as much a function in VB as the Print function.

Registration Issues

When you make a project group to test a DLL, VB temporarily adds the needed information to the registry so that you can see it in the References dialog box. This is necessary so that you can test and debug the DLL. If you want to use a DLL permanently, you:

1. First have to compile it into a DLL.
2. Then you need to run a program called regsvr32 to register it.

(The rgsvr32 program can be found in the \Tools\RegUtils directory on the VB CD.) You can run rgsvr32 from the DOS prompt or the Run box off the Start menu. For example, Figure 14-5 shows what the Run dialog box looks like to register the GlobalTiming DLL.

Tip

To unregister a DLL (or an EXE) use the /U switch. For example:

```
regsvr32 /U myapp.dll
```

Figure 14-5   Registering the Global Timer

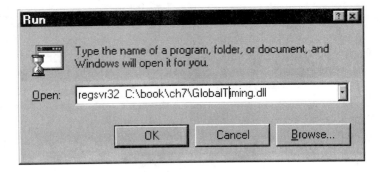

ActiveX EXEs

Of course, on the surface, changing a stand-alone application with some class modules or an ActiveDLL to an ActiveX EXE is no more complicated than flipping an item on the Project|Properties dialog box and recompiling. (ActiveX EXEs can be registered by simply running the EXE—you don't even need regsvr32.) This hardly seems to require the pages of text that will follow. In practice, there are lots of subtleties involved in knowing when to *choose* an ActiveX EXE over an in-process DLL for your object "factory." In particular, ActiveX EXEs are the only way to make truly multithreaded objects in Visual Basic. (See below if you don't know what the term multi-threaded means.) There are also additional techniques needed when debugging an out of process server. The rest of this chapter covers these vital issues.

Disadvantages of ActiveX EXEs

It may seem strange to start a section on ActiveX EXEs with a description of their disadvantages but it is vital that you keep in mind, that, as we mentioned earlier:

- When you ask an ActiveX EXE to create an application, the object created will run out of the process of the calling application.
- Communicating between processes is slow.

How slow? The answer is *dramatically* slower. On the CD in the CH14 directory you have the source code for a word counter class and two project files. One project gives you an ActiveX DLL and the other an ActiveX EXE. There is also a simple project group you can use to test the DLL version and a project for the ActiveX EXE. (The easiest way to test the EXE is to start up another instance of VB as described later in this chapter.)

The objects that can be created by the classes in these two servers are pretty simple: they simply expose one method that returns an integer. This integer gives the number of "words" in a string that you send to the method as a parameter. (For illustrative purposes, we made the code very simple: We assume each word is separated from the next by a single space and there are no multiple spaces inside the string.)

```
Public Function WordCount(sText As String) As Integer
  Dim sTmp As String
  Dim nCount As Integer
  sTmp = GetWord(sText)
  Do While Len(sTmp) > 0
    nCount = nCount + 1
    sTmp = GetWord(sText)
  Loop
  WordCount = nCount
End Function

Private Function GetWord(sText As String) As String
  Dim nPos As Integer
  nPos = InStr(sText & " ", " ")
  GetWord = Left$(sText, nPos - 1)
  sText = Mid$(sText, nPos + 1)
End Function
```

Okay, we want to run a program that simply creates an object as "manu-factured" by the DLL and the ActiveX EXE. We then use both to count the number of words in the string "This is a test" 1000 times. This requires com-municating with the objects created by the two kinds of servers 1000 times. Here's what we found:

ActiveX EXE	7.738 seconds
ActiveX DLL	.27 seconds

A simple calculation shows that the ActiveX EXE is almost 30 times slower. Given this amazing disparity you may be wondering, "Why bother with ActiveX EXEs?" Well, first off, sometimes you don't have any choice. Certainly, appli-cations like Word or Excel are not going to be exposed as DLLs. (On the other hand why parts of Office, such as the shared spell-checker do not let you cre-ate objects that encapsulate their functionality in process is, of course, another question. This is even more of a shame since so often these shared components *are* DLLs. Unfortunately, you usually have to go through an Office application running out of process in order to create objects of these types.)

But, since you are developing the application, you have the source code. The question really is:

- Why shouldn't you simply maintain two versions of the source: One for a DLL and the other for a standalone EXE application?

Use the EXE when you need to run the code as a stand-alone application and use the DLL when you want to make its objects available to the another application as efficiently as possible.

Actually, the short answer to this question is that this is often a very good choice. For example, the Data Form Wizard and the VisData Add-In share a lot of common code. However, the VisData application needed to be able to run as a stand-alone application, so it was made into an EXE. The Data Form Wizard, like all Wizards, is an in-process DLL.

The remaining part of the answer to the question is that there are actually times when using an out-of-process ActiveX EXE is the *right* choice. We take that up next.

When to use an ActiveX EXE?

Sometimes what gets lost in the dramatic results of how slow an ActiveX EXE is compared to an in-process DLL is:

- The code in each runs equally fast.

It's easy to forget that it's the *communication* between the processes that is slow. That is, using the properties and methods of the objects created by the ActiveX EXE is what takes time (because of the overhead of the marshalling process mentioned earlier). This leads us to the first situation where an ActiveX EXE is appropriate. Imagine agent software that cruises the Net. This agent program might keep track of stock prices or some other useful pieces of information. The information it retrieves might be of use to more than one program currently running on a machine. While these applications may be interested, what they do is mostly mind their own business. Periodically, however, they might ask the ActiveX EXE to send them the data. Or the ActiveX EXE can notify the interested application that something dramatic has happened.

Notice that we don't expect the communication to occur frequently between the agent program and the applications that are consumers of this information. Given this, the time spent in cross-process communication is irrelevant. If you only want to find out a stock price every 15 minutes, you really don't have to be concerned with cross-process communication overhead! Now that we know that the time issue is irrelevant for an "agent" server, there are two advantage to using an ActiveX EXE.

- It is often better to have one program managing scarce communication resources rather than having the operating system negotiate among the competing in-process DLLs that all want to use the same resource (a communication port or a TCP/IP stack in the case of an agent) using its multiprocessing ability.

- If you have the Enterprise edition of VB5, the ActiveX EXE can actually lie on another machine. This potentially gives you access to unprecedented computing power if you can break up the computation into multiple pieces that can be run on different machines and reintegrated by the process on your machine that created all the remote objects.

There is, however, one final advantage of an ActiveX EXE that is often the most important. This is because ActiveX EXEs can be *multithreaded*. The next section explains why this is often a powerful tool that you will want to take advantage of.

The Instancing Property for an ActiveX EXE

Classes in ActiveX EXEs have one additional kind of instancing: single use. On the surface, SingleUse objects are quite wasteful. If you set the instancing property of a class in an ActiveX EXE to SingleUse, then any time someone asks for an instance of that class, the operating system will start up another process containing the server. Usually, you would use one of the two possible single use settings only when you have lots of Public Not Creatable objects in the server and want a new "conductor" class to orchestrate their creation. The two possible single use settings are SingleUse or GlobalSingleUse. (GlobalSingleUse works like GlobalMultiUse as far as increasing the name space of the project that uses the class.)

Multithreading

Recall from the beginning of this chapter that you can think of a *process* as being a virtual computer that the operating system sets up for an application. Inside that process, you have your application's executable code and its data. DLLs that are used by your application can also be though of as living in the same process. (As we mentioned earlier, certainly the data for any DLLs you use does live in-process. The executable code for the DLL is shared in practice.) The process (virtual computer) does its thing and what it does can't crash any other process. (Well, most of the time under Windows 95 and pretty much all of the time under NT.) The operating system periodically *time slices between the processes* in order to give the impression that your machine is doing two things at once.

A *multithreaded* application carries the idea of a multiprocessing operating system to the next level. As you know, you can be cruising new Web pages while downloading a file from a previous page or you can be printing a document while continuing to enter text in your word processor. Both of these kinds of applications take advantage of multithreading. Think of a thread as being a way to break down a single process into multiple smaller processes (see Figure 14-6).

Figure 14.6   Multiprocessing and multithreading

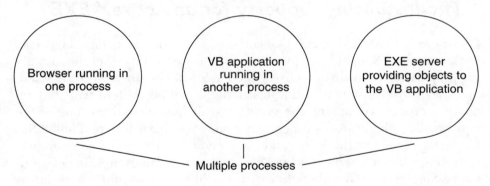

Browser running in
one process

VB application
running in
another process

EXE server
providing objects to
the VB application

Multiple processes

A multithreaded process like the browser above,
"under the microscope"

Thread 1—
Browsing
a page

Thread 2—
Downloading
a file

Thread 3—
Printing
a page

Of course since multithreading occurs within the *same* process, you run the risk of having one thread contaminate the data of other threads that are working in that process. For example, a multithreaded application could conceivably be trying to print a file while another thread is changing it. Visual Basic has no way of knowing this, so you must carefully code any multithreaded server (actually this is true no matter what language you use) in order to prevent re-entrant problems. (As old-time VB programmers knew to do when they used Do Events!)

As far as VB goes:

• You can only write multithreaded ActiveX EXEs.

(Actually, there is a trick that will let you write a VB application that gives the impression of being multithreaded—you'll see it shortly.)

Note

In VB5, a multithreaded ActiveX EXE may not have a user interface. More precisely, in VB a multithreaded ActiveX server EXE cannot have any user interaction.

So, after you remove all the UI components from your server (this includes forms, message boxes, and input boxes) then all you have to do is:

1. Go to the Project|Properties dialog box.
2. Select the Unattended Execution checkbox (see Figure 14-7).

Once you have removed the user interface elements and checked off this box, then every time another application creates an object from the ActiveX EXE, the operating system will give that object its own thread.

For example, suppose you have a FileHandling ActiveX EXE with two classes: one named PrintingFile to print files (with various format options) and the other named EncryptingFile to encrypt files (again with various options). If you set the Unattended Execution box for this server, then an application can now create a PrintingFile object and an EncryptingFile object and they will run in separate threads in the server.

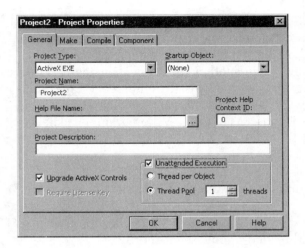

Figure 14-7   The Project Properties dialog box
for a multithreaded server

Caution

*We need to repeat that it is up to the programmer of the multithreaded
server to write the code to handle synchronization problems like one
thread trying to print a file that the other thread is encrypting. (The obvious way of dealing with this particular problem is to lock the file when it is
use by the other object. Other synchronization problems may be harder to
solve.) The general problem of synchronizing methods in a multithreaded
program so that they don't contaminate each other is not something VB
programmers need to worry about—yet.*

Note

*In VB, you should also note that each thread gets its own copy of the glob-
al data of the server. This helps with some synchronization problems.
Threads can not pass global data between themselves. This means the
data stored in global variables can not be used to communicate among
threads and so will not contaminate each of the various threads. Similarly,
static variables exist for the life of the thread, not the application. (This is
sometimes called the apartment model for multithreading and helps prevent contamination between the code running in each thread.)*

What about the other two options: Thread per object and Thread Pool? To understand these options recall that an ActiveX EXE or DLL can be set to either MultiUse or SingleUse. As you know, when you set the Instancing property on an ActiveX EXE to MultiUse, the server can create multiple objects *without* the operating system needing to make new instances of the server for each new object. The Thread per object and Thread Pool option buttons are only relevant for MultiUse ActiveX EXEs.

- Checking off the Thread per Object option means that an ActiveX EXE with its Instancing property set to MultiUse will create a new thread for each object request.
- Checking off and then setting a Thread Pool number means that you are telling the operating system what is the maximum number of threads you will tolerate for this particular ActiveX EXE. (Each thread carries with it some overhead cost.) After the maximum number that you set is reached, Visual Basic starts placing new object instances in existing thread instances.

We recommend never setting a Thread Pool unless you find performance degrading too much.

Note

Although you can set an ActiveX DLL to Unattended Execution, this doesn't make it multithreaded in VB5. Instead, this works with multithreaded applications written in other languages that have the VB created DLL in their process space. Setting a DLL to Unattended Execution means that objects are created in the threads supplied by the calling application. It is unlikely that you will be using this feature in VB5 very often!

How to Make a VB Application Look Multithreaded

If you look at the documentation, you would say this can't be done. The documentation clearly states that the only VB projects that can be multithreaded are non-UI-based ActiveX EXEs set for unattended execution. However, there is a trick to make a VB application *seem to be multithreaded:*

- Create an ActiveX EXE whose various objects can do the job(s) that you want to multithread.
- Set the ActiveX EXE up for multithreading by the method you have just seen.
- Create an object from the server of the type that handles the job you want to run in a separate thread.

The thread *in the EXE server* will now do whatever it was that you wanted to multithread.

Of course, you can't use this trick if you need to communicate a lot with the "thread"—performance would suffer too much. On the other hand, this trick works great if what you are doing is something like printing or encrypting a file. After all, these kinds of task require communicating only once with the server. (And, of course, you know that you can code the server so that these tasks can be safely done in a multithreaded fashion. For example, locking the files ensure that there are no re-entry problems.)

Testing and Debugging an ActiveX EXE

The most effective ways to both test and debug an ActiveX EXE depend on VB 5.0's ability to have multiple copies of itself running in *different* processes. By using another instance of Visual Basic, you can actually debug the ActiveX EXE running out of process.

Note

You will need to set the Error Trapping method to "Break In Class Module" in the Tools|Options General tab prior to running this example.

To show you the testing and debugging process at work we will use a modified version of the WordCounter server called BuggyWordCounterEXE. You can find it in its own directory in the CH14 directory on the CD. So load this project into VB and start it running. Now:

1. Load another copy of Visual Basic 5.0.
2. Open a standard EXE type project.
3. Go to Project References and check off the BuggyWordCountEXE reference (see Figure 14-8).

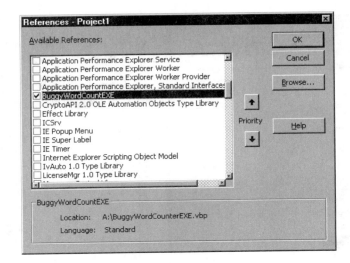

Figure 14-8   The Reference dialog box for testing an ActiveX EXE

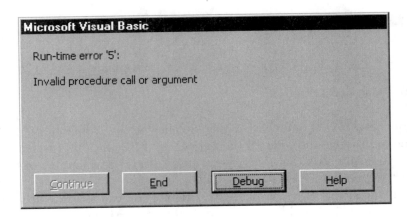

Figure 14-9   An error message box

Now:

1. Add a command button to the form.
2. Enter the following code into the Click event procedure:

```
Dim Foo As New BuggyWordCount
MsgBox Foo.WordCount("This is a test")
```

Run the application. You should get an error message like the one shown in Figure 14-9.

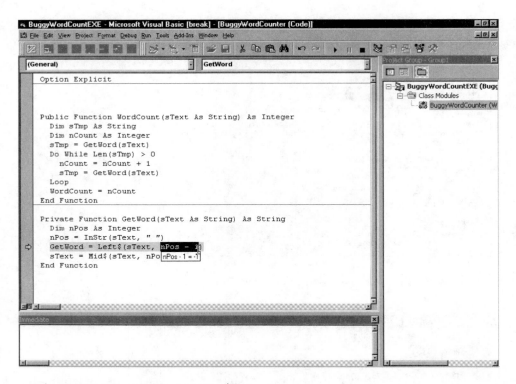

Figure 14-10   Using Instant Watch

We obviously need to find out what's wrong. So click on the Debug button and you will be returned to the code for the ActiveX EXE! Using VB's Instant Watch feature you can check that the value of nPos–1 is –1—which it obviously shouldn't be (see Figure 14-10).

Similarly, looking at the value of the sText variable, you can see that it is "This" without a space. The problem is that in the buggy version of the word counter, the crucial line:

```
nPos = InStr(sText, " ")
```

doesn't add the extra space to the sText parameter. Now, for the really nifty point: *Edit and Continue still works.* By changing the line back to be:

```
nPos = InStr(sText & " ", " ")
```

setting the next statement (Ctrl+F9) back to this line and continuing the program, you can see that the out-of-process instance of VB will work correctly.

Finally, since a multithreaded EXE application can't have a user interface, it is sometimes hard to debug the various threads when you are checking for re-entrant problems. One useful trick is to set up *another* EXE processor that the first server will send information to. The second server can display any information about the state of the threads of the server you need for debugging purposes. This requires adding a fair amount of code to your server, of course. You need to:

- Create an instance of the debugging object in the class you are trying to debug.
- Add the code to every event procedure and every member that sends the information to the debugging server.

(It is possible to write an Add-In [see Chapter 15] that can do most of this automatically.)

Notice to do this you will need to have *three* instances of VB running!

1. The VB instance that creates objects from the multithreaded ActiveX EXE.
2. The VB instance for the multithreaded ActiveX EXE.
3. The instance of VB that will create the objects used for logging. (And this instance can, of course have a UI.)

WRITING VB ADD-INS

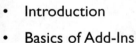

Topics in this Chapter

Chapter 15

Introduction

The designers of Visual Basic 5 decided to expose most of the functionality of VB's IDE to the programmer. This means you can write an Add-In that adds code to a project or extends VB's IDE in many ways. For example, the Class Builder is an Add-In, as is the Code Profiler. Add-Ins give you the ability to add functionality that does not already exist to the Visual Basic IDE. For example, you probably find it tedious to set the tab order of the controls on a form. Visual Basic 5 ships a sample Add-In called TabOrder (discussed later in this chapter) that makes this process quite easy. Even more is possible. As you will see in this chapter, you can write an Add-In that blasts code into a project—just like the Profiler did. You can also write Add-Ins that, like the Class Builder, can add new class modules to your project. You can write Add-Ins that automatically add a Copyright splash screen and make it the start-up form. You can save, rename, or add new projects to a running instance of VB. The possibilities for Add-Ins are limited only by your imagination.

Just as a sample of what you can do, in this chapter you will see the code for two full-featured Add-Ins. We built these because:

- We got tired of going through the contortions necessary to make a backup of a project. (Save the first form with a new name, save the second form with a new name, save the project file with a new name, etc., etc.) So we wrote an Add-In that does all this automatically.
- We needed a quick way to add and remove line numbers from procedures for last-ditch debugging.

If there is a boring, repetitive task that reoccurs when you work with VB, you can probably write an Add-In to make it automatic! Finally, there are many ways to actually connect the Add-In into VB. They will all be discussed later on in this chapter.

Basics of Add-Ins

Add-Ins are possible because Visual Basic exposes most of the functionality of its IDE through what the documentation for VB refers to as the *extensibility interface* or *extensibility model.* By sending the right messages to the objects in the IDE through the extensibility interface, your Add-In can add, remove, modify, and monitor all of the objects in VB's IDE. This includes its windows, its menus and toolbars (*command bars* is the term used to refer to both together), the projects, the controls, the references, and the code of the current project or project group. (Modifying code through the extensibility interface is one of the reasons that Wizards are possible, after all.). This is why a reasonable formal definition of an Add-In is:

- An ActiveX DLL or an ActiveX EXE that manipulates the VBIDE object.

Add-Ins may also be either modal or non-modal, depending upon how you want them to interact with the user.

Writing Add-Ins is not conceptually very difficult—under the hood, an Add-In is simply a program that manipulates the objects that make up VB's IDE—the devil is in the details. Writing an Add-In requires becoming comfortable with a whole new (and very large) set of objects and dozens of their member functions. (The properties of the VBIDE object are often other objects of course, such as the Code Module object that holds the actual code.)

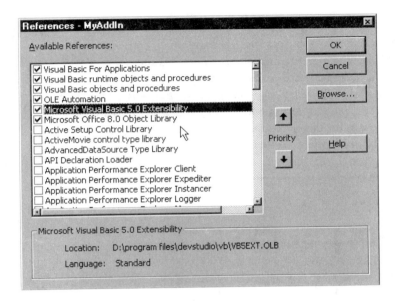

Figure 15-1   The Project I References dialog box for an Add-In

First Steps in Creating an Add-In

To start the process of creating an Add-In the usual procedure is to:

- Choose the Add-In template from the New Project dialog box.

This will automatically add a reference to the VBIDE and Microsoft Office 8.0 Object libraries (as shown in Figure 15-1).

Of course, you can add the references by hand if you aren't using VB's Add-In template. We don't recommend doing this: It is much easier to follow the usual standards for Add-Ins if you use the supplied template.

Next, as you will soon see, the key step for your code is that your Add-In has to implement an interface called the IDTExtensibility interface. We feel that one of the best ways to understand the steps necessary for building an Add-In is to work through the different members of this interface. We will do this right after we discuss the extensibility model. However, we do want to remind you here, that, as you know from Chapter 8, implementing an interface may require a fair amount of code. One extra bonus of using the Add-In templates supplied with VB is that they automatically add the skeletons for the members of this interface to your code.

Tip

The name you choose for the class module that implements the IDTExtensibility interface is very important. It becomes the name that is registered as the main connection class for the Add-In. We suggest using a name like "Connect" or "Wizard" depending on whether it is an Add-In or a Wizard (see the next chapter). (Connect is the name used by the Add-In template.) If you do use this name then your application will be registered as "MyProject.Connect" where MyProject would, of course, be replaced by the name you chose for the project.

Add-In—DLL or EXE?

If you plan to interact with the components in a project within the IDE, running the Add-In in process as a DLL will be much faster (about 20 times). To see the difference, try this little test.

1. Load a standard EXE project into VB.
2. Load the Visual Data Manager from the Add-Ins menu.
3. Using File|Open Database|Microsoft Access, open the Biblio.MDB file located in the Visual Basic directory.
4. Choose Utility|Data Form Designer.
5. Type a form name in the top field.
6. Choose "Publishers" in the Recordsource drop-down list.
7. Choose all fields by clicking the >> button.
8. Click the "Build the Form" button and watch the form get built.
9. Close VisData.

This uses the VisData Add-In which is running as an out-of-process EXE server. Now try the VB Data Form Wizard, which runs in process.

1. Choose Project|Add Form from the main menu.
2. Select "VB Data Form Wizard" from the list of forms available.

3. Click "Next" to get to Database Type step.
4. Click "Access", then "Next."
5. Browse to find the Biblio.MDB file, then click "Next."
6. Choose "Single Record" and click "Next."
7. Choose "Publishers" in the Recordsource drop-down list.
8. Choose all fields by clicking the >> button.
9. Click the "Finish" button and watch the form being built.

Notice that the form for the database was built in a fraction of the time it took to build the same form using the VisData utility application. The only difference in the code between these two applications is that VisData is an ActiveX EXE running out of process and the Data Form Wizard is an in-process DLL. You can see how being in process makes the interaction with forms and controls much quicker. The only downside to using a DLL is that they must be registered with a utility such as regsvr32.exe (found in the \Tools\Regutils directory on the Visual Basic CD) and they cannot be run as stand-alone applications. VisData was written as an EXE so that it could be run stand-alone. The moral is:

- Unless there is a special reason for doing so, all of your Add-Ins should be DLLs!

The Extensibility Interface

The extensibility interface lets you access almost everything about the current instance of VB's IDE. It contains objects that represent essentially everything that the user is working on in the IDE. This includes the projects, components, modules, controls, and the actual code. You can, for example, find the name and signatures of every method in a code or in a class module. There are therefore a lot of objects, properties, methods, and events in this model.

The best way to get a handle on the extensibility object model is to play with the various objects contained within it. For example, as we said in the introduction, later on in this chapter you will see an Add-In for adding and removing line numbers from code. (As a last resort for debugging!) The code for the Add-In contains lines that when expanded look like this:

```
Set modModule = VBInstance.SelectedVBComponent.CodeModule
```

The idea is that we want to make an object that can refer to the currently selected code. We then can get access to an individual line of the selection through code like this:

```
modModule.CodePane.GetSelection lStartLine, lStartCol, _
    lEndLine, lEndCol
```

(Well, not quite: We used Set and With wherever possible to simply the references in the actual code, of course.)

A Hands-On Approach to the Extensibility Interface

While we will shortly provide you with diagrams that describe the extensibility model, we feel that before you start dealing with the level of abstraction given by diagrams, the best way to get a handle on it is to walk through some of the extensibility interface using VB's own browse and watch capabilities. (This will also give you a sense of the riches that await you if you master the VBIDE object). For this:

1. Start up a new VB Add-In project.

2. Open up the Connect class.

3. Add a breakpoint at the following line in the IDTExtensibility_OnConnection event (see Figure 15-2). (Notice that the template even suggests that this is a good place to set a breakpoint!) This event is triggered when the Add-In is connected to a project, for example through the Add-In Manager:

    ```
    Debug.Print VBInst.FullName
    ```

4. Go to the Immediate window (CTRL+G) and enter the following line (see Figure 15-3):

    ```
    AddToINI
    ```

    This executes the AddToINI routine that you can find in the Add-In.BAS code module. What this routine does is add the current project as an Add-In project to the VBAddIn.INI file. (See Chapter 12 for more on the WritePrivateProfileString API function.) Remember to hit the ENTER key.

5. Run the project and leave it running.

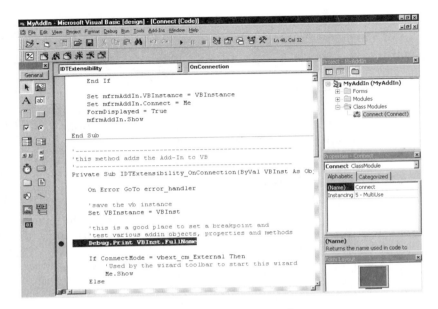

Figure 15-2   A breakpoint set in the Connect class

Figure 15-3   Adding to the INI file

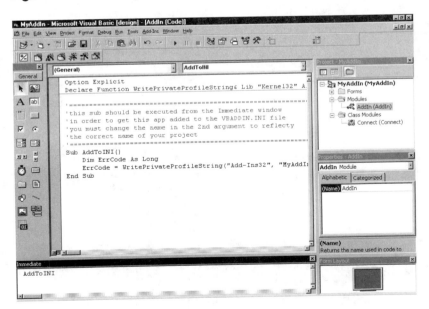

At this point, the Add-In is registered on your system. (If you look at the vbadd.ini file in the [Add-Ins32] section you would see a line that says: MyAddIn.Connect = 0.) Now:

- Start up another instance of Visual Basic 5.0.

Add a command button to the form. Add a simple "You clicked me" message box to the Click event for the command button.

```
Sub Command1_Click()
   MessageBox "You clicked me"
End Sub
```

Next, we want to add the code for a simple class module. So add a class module to the project. Now, add the code for one simple property and one simple method (see Figure 15-4):

```
Public Property Get TestProperty() As String
   TestProperty = "test property"
End Property
```

Figure 15-4   Code for a simple class module

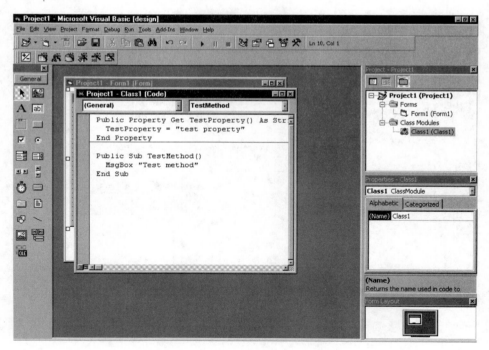

```
Public Sub TestMethod()
  MsgBox "Test method"
End Sub
```

Now, we want to use the Add-In Manager to hook in the simple Add-In that has the breakpoint set. That way we can use it to examine our simple project. For this:

- Select Add-Ins|Add-In Manager and you should see "My Add-In" in the list. Check it and click the OK button. This will trigger the OnConnection Event and you should immediately be stopped at the breakpoint we set in the OnConnection event.

Now we can use the magic of the Watch window to peek at all the parts of our little sample application. For this:

1. Open up the Watch window and make it as large as you can.
2. Add the VBInst object variable to the Watch window (use SHIFT+F9 or Debug|Add Watch). See Figure 15-5.

Figure 15-5   The Add Watch window for the VBInst object variable

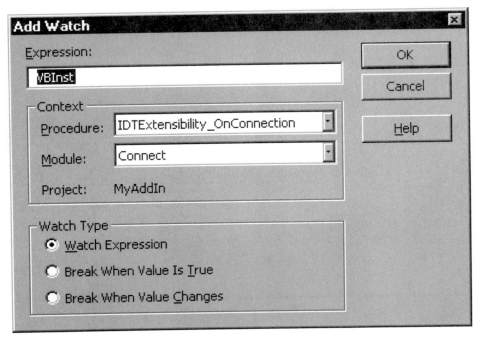

Your Watch window should now look like Figure 15-6. Click on the + sign in the Watch window to view all the members of the VBInst object variable. Your screen will look like Figure 15-7.

Okay, we want to show off some of what the VBInst object will let you manipulate. We need to drill our way down until we can see some information in the ActiveVBProject (which is our sample after all). So:

1. Click on the + sign in the ActiveVBProject, as shown in Figure 15-7.

2. Click on the + sign next to VBComponents.

Figure 15-6   Watch window for VBInst unexpanded

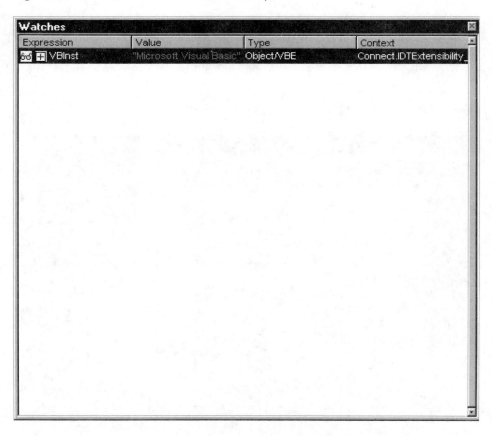

Your screen will look like Figure 15-8. Notice the count is two. This is because our simple project has a form and a class module. At this level the Components count is essentially telling us about the number of items you see in the Project Explorer. (At other levels of detail, the Component count may refer to the number of ActiveX controls on a form. We'll have more on the Components collection later in this chapter.) Next, notice in Figure 15-8 there are objects marked Item1 and Item2 with + signs next to them. These are the two items in the Components collection and correspond to the form and the class module. Once you expand these items, you will be able to see the information about the form and the class module that are exposed by the IDTExtensibility model.

Figure 15-7   Watch window for VBInst first expansion

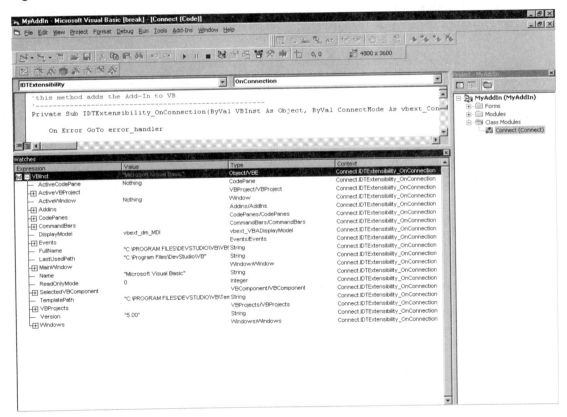

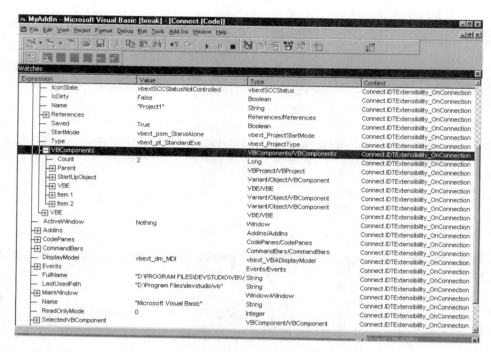

Figure 15-8   Looking at components

Caution

While watching the VBInst object variable, it is easy to get into an infinite regress like some of Escher's famous drawings. This is because, as you can see in Figure 15-8, many sub-objects still maintain a reference to the VBE object. If you click on the VBE object you will see another copy of the whole tree (and theoretically, of course, you could repeat the process like in the famous Escher print of a magnifying globe.)

Okay, now click on the + signs next to both Item1 and Item2 in order to expand them. Your screen should look like Figure 15-9. Notice the Name property shows "Form1" and "Class1" since we didn't change the default names for the form or class module. As you might imagine when we start writing code, it is easy to drill down to this level in order to access or change the names used for the parts of your project.

Now, we can continue the process of drilling down another level or two. Click on the + sign next to the CodeModule item for Form1. Your screen should look like Figure 15-10. Notice that CountOfLines is 3—because the

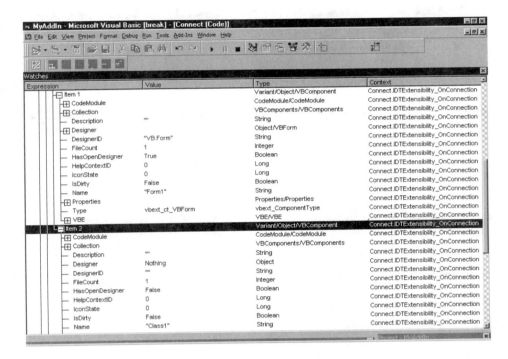

Figure 15-9 The items in our sample project exposed

Click event procedure for our command button has exactly three lines! There were no declarations, so CountOfDeclarationLines is 0. (You will soon see how to get at the actual text in lines of code via the extensibility model by drilling further down this tree.)

Now, expand the Designer item inside the same Form item. The result looks like Figure 15-11.

Expand the ContainedVBControls item shown in Figure 15-11 and (finally) click on the Item1 item that is now exposed. Your screen should look like Figure 15-12. Notice that we now know we had a command button on our form!

Collapse the ActiveVBProject back. Now for a quick look see at what is in the class module:

1. Expand the ActiveVBProject again.

2. Expand the VBComponents item.

3. Expand Item2 this time.

4. Expand the Code Pane item.

5. Expand the Members item. You should see objects marked Item1 and Item2, as shown in Figure 15-13.

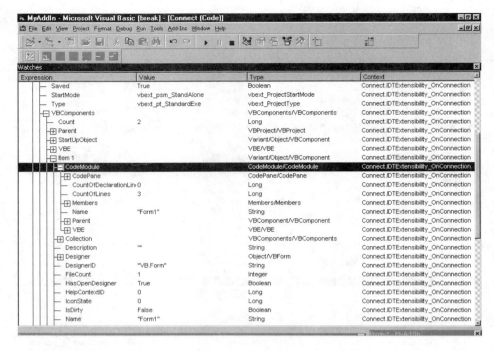

Figure 15-10 The CodeModule item for the form expanded

Figure 15-11 The Designer item expanded

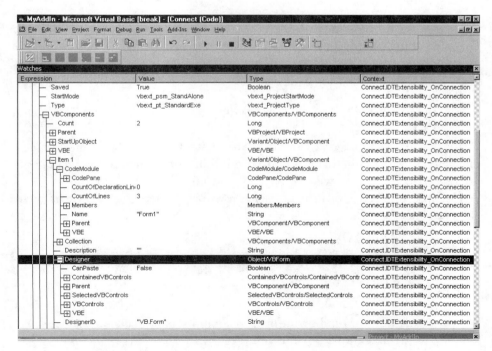

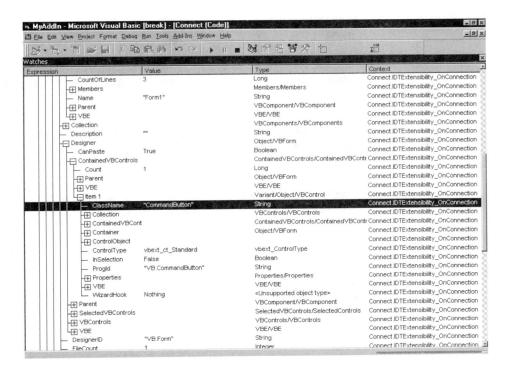

Figure 15-12   The ContainedVBControl item expanded

Figure 15-13   The class module code module expanded

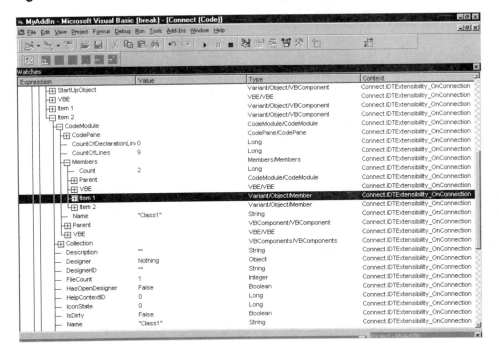

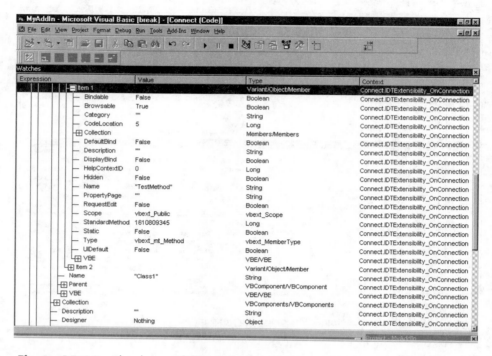

Figure 15-14   The class module's method exposed

Finally, expand the Item1 object. Your screen will look like Figure 15-14. Notice that you can see the name of the method ("TestMethod"). The fact that this is a Public method may be seen by looking at the Scope line and the fact that it is a method may be seen by looking at the Type line.

All this may have seemed cumbersome and time consuming to get at via the Watch window, but the point is that everything you can get at via multiple clicks in the Watch window can also be accessed (and manipulated) via code.

Tip

The Object Browser is incredibly useful when working with the Extensibility model. There are literally thousands of objects, methods and constants to keep track of. (Even Dave, who wrote most of the Add-In's that ship with VB5, is constantly referring to the Object Browser for syntax and explanations of the required member functions.)

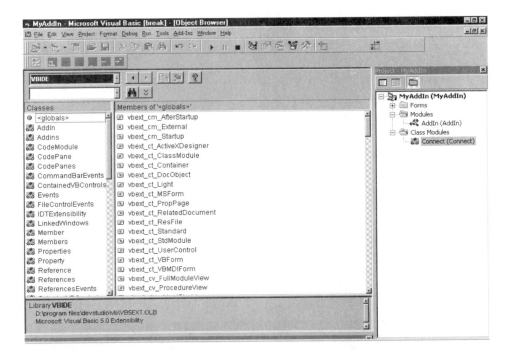

Figure 15-15   The VBIDE library in the Object Browser

Figure 15-15 shows you the opening screen of the Object Browser for viewing the VBIDE library. (Of course, as useful as the Object Browser will be, you first need to get the big picture—that's the purpose of the next section.)

Overview of the VBIDE Objects

The easiest way to understand the objects that go into the extensibility model is to break them down by function. As the previous trip using the Watch window indicated, there are objects that:

- Encapsulate the user interface so that you can manipulate it.
- Objects that encapsulate all the projects and files in the current instance of VB so that you can manipulate them.

- Objects that correspond to the forms and the components on them so that you can manipulate individual forms and the components on those forms.

- Objects that allow you to respond to events in the VB instance.

- Objects that allow you to manipulate all the source code in the current instance.

- Objects that allow you to work with Add-Ins that are hooked into the VBIDE.

Most of these objects are accessed by working with either the VBE object or the VBForm object. We strongly recommend stopping and using the Object Browser to look at all the members of these two objects. What you start with is shown in Figures 15-16 and 15-17.

Figure 15-16   The VBE class

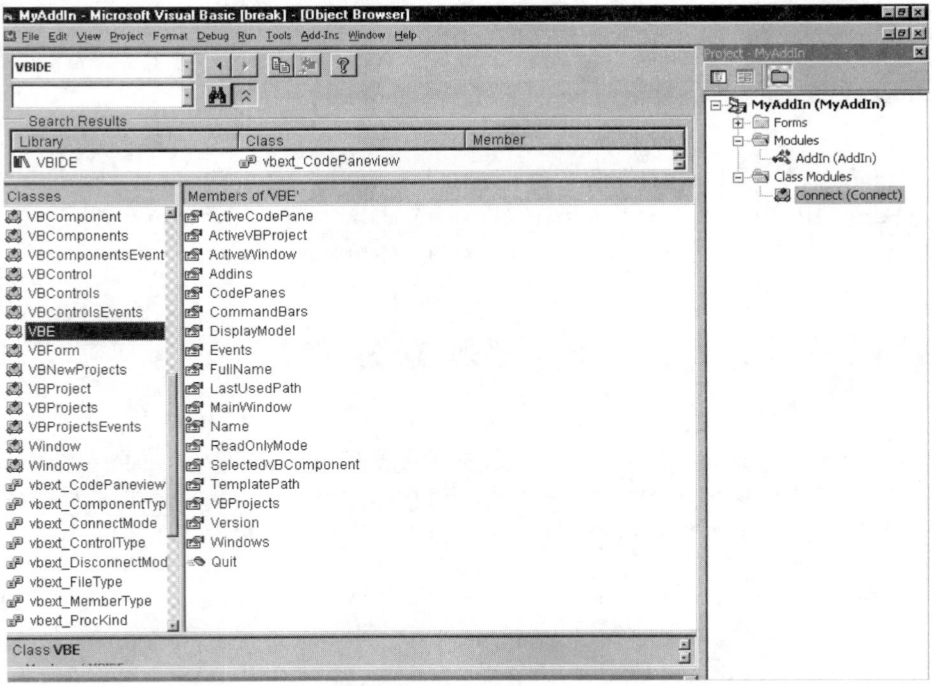

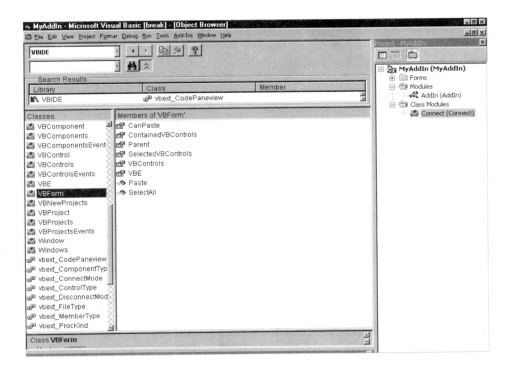

Figure 15-17   The VBForm class

Note

When coding an Add-In, the VBInstance object variable always refers to the instance of the Visual Basic IDE that the Add-In is working with. It is an object of type VBE.

For example, in a nicely self-referential sort of way, the VBE class has members that let you get at the current Add-Ins that are hooked into the current VB instance. (This is how the Add-In Manager can do its work, for example.) This is the VBInstance.AddIns collection and its individual elements (call Add-In, obviously). For example, after getting a specific Add-In via a call to VBInstance.AddIns collection, the Add-In.Connect method lets you connect or disconnect that specific Add-In.

Objects that Encapsulate the Interface

These are gotten at via properties of the VBInstance root object. For example:

```
VBInstance.CodePanes
```

is the collections of all code windows. (A CodePane is a specific element of the CodePanes collection and represents a single code window.) You use this group of objects to customize the user interface. For example, you can add new menu items or even create a new menu or toolbar. You can also use these objects to open, close or move windows within the IDE.

Note

The extensibility model distinguishes between the code window (called a CodePane Object) and the actual code (called a CodeModule object). You can see a CodePane but you cannot manipulate the code in it, you can manipulate the code in a CodeModule object but you can't see it. You will immediately see any code added via the CodeModule in the CodePane so it is not necessary to write code to keep the two in sync.

The following diagram shows you how the VBE class may be broken down to get at these objects. Each indentation level corresponds to another dot:

```
VBE Object (VBInstance gives a reference to the current instance)
    Command Bars Collection (all the menus and toolbars)
        Command Bar (a specific menu or toolbar)
    Windows Collection (all the Windows in the IDE)
        Window (a specific window)
            Windows collection (the windows inside a specific Window object)
    CodePanes Collection
        CodePane (an individual code window)
```

Objects You Use to Manipulate the Projects in the Current Instance of VB

These are some of the objects we had to manipulate in order to write our backup application that you will see at the end of the chapter. You use these objects to add, remove, or rename projects. You can also use these

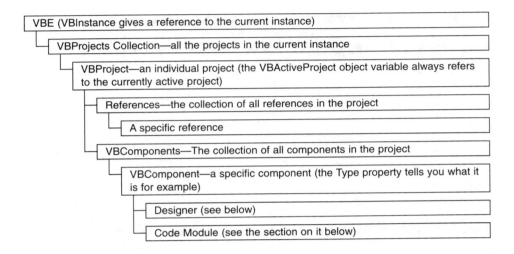

objects to programmatically change project properties and add and remove references.

The key point is that a VBComponent can be a form, class module, code module, user control form, or property page form—in addition to being an ActiveX control. It depends on the level of detail you are looking at. Probably, the most difficult concept to get used to when working with the extensibility model is that:

- In order to deal with a form, you need to access the Designer property of the VBComponent object associated to that form.

The Designer property of a VBComponent object is how you get at the design characteristics of an individual component. (Individual Designer objects will, of course, have different properties.) Figure 15-18 uses the magic of the Watch Window to show you some of what the Designer object of a Form object exposes. Looking back at Figure 15-8, you can see that our simple form has two items, one for the form and one for the code.

Next, keep in mind also that in order to manipulate the code in your project, you need to go a level deeper than you might expect—to the *CodeModule* property of the appropriate *VBComponent* object. You can see this in Figure 15-18 if you open the CodeModule object in Item2. (Notice that Item2 is of type VBComponent as well.)

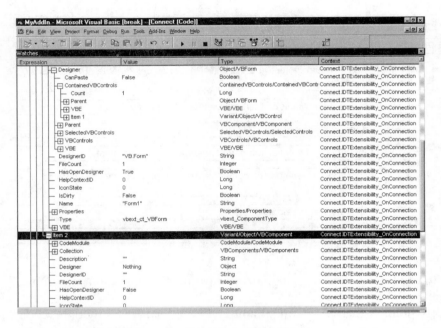

Figure 15-18 The Designer property for a Form object

Objects that Allow You to Manipulate a Form

This group of objects helps you control and manipulate the various kinds of form designers used in VB. This includes the ones used for Form design, ActiveX control design, ActiveX Documents, and Property Pages. You can use these objects do to things like manipulate the size, shape and location of existing controls on a form or to add new controls to a form.

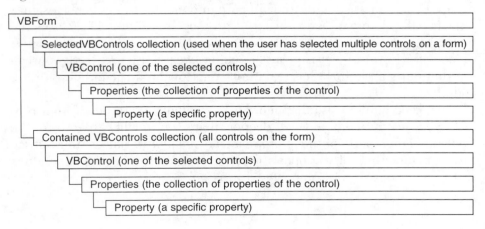

Objects that Allow You to Respond to Events

These are all members of the VBE.Events object. You can use this to respond to events like the user selecting a menu item or selecting a control.

```
VBE (VBInstance gives a reference to the current instance)
  └─ Events
        ├─ CommandBarEvents (toolbar and menu clicks)
        ├─ FileControlEvents
        ├─ ReferencesEvents
        ├─ SelectedVBControlsEvents
        ├─ VBComponentEvents
        ├─ VBControlsEvents
        └─ VBProjectEvents
```

All the Event objects can be analyzed to find out the actual event. For example, if you look at the Object Browser for the FileControl events you'll see things like AfterCloseFile, which is triggered when a file is closed, or AfterAddFile, which occurs when a file is added to the current project.

The CodeModule Object

This, of course, is one of the most useful classes of objects. As we said earlier, you need to drill down through the appropriate VBComponent object in order to gain access to it. Using the CodeModule object you can actually add, remove, or modify code in an existing project. Add-Ins like the Control Interface Wizard take full advantage of this power!

The CodeModule object has the following properties summarized in Table 15-1. (Use the Object Browser to check out the signatures for these properties.)

Table 15-1   CodeModule Object Properties

Property	Description
CodePane	The Window in which the code is located.
CountOfDeclarationLines	The number of declaration (Dim) lines in the code module.
CountOfLines	The number of actual lines.

Table 15-1: CodeModule Object Properties (continued)	
Property	*Description*
Lines	This is how you get at specific lines of code.
Members	This is a collection of all the properties, methods, and events in the code module. The individual members are called, obviously, Member (For example, you can get at the name of a procedure from Member.Name.)
Parent	Returns the object containing the code module.
ProcBodyLine	Returns the first line of a procedure.
ProcCountLines	Returns the number of lines in a procedure.
ProcOfLine	Returns the name of the procedure that contained a specified line.
ProcStartLine	Returns the line in the Code Pane where the procedure starts.

For example, here's a modified version of a snippet of code from our add-line number Add-In that uses these properties extensively:

```
Set modModule = VBInstance.SelectedVBComponent.CodeModule
modModule.CodePane.GetSelection lStartLine, lStartCol, _
lEndLine, lEndCol
sProc = modModule.ProcOfLine(lStartLine, vbext_pk_Proc)
```

Essentially, what these three lines do is:

- Get the current code module.
- Get the currently selected procedure in the code pane associated to the current code module.
- Find out the name of the procedure.

Table 15-2 gives you the methods you can apply to a CodeModule object. (Use the Object Browser to check out the full signature needed for these methods.)

Table 15-2: CodeModule Object Methods	
Method	*Description*
AddFromFile	Lets you add information from a file at the current line.
AddFromString	Inserts the text above the first line in the module.
CreateEventProc	Lets you create an event procedure from scratch.
DeleteLines	Allows you to delete a specified number of lines from a specific place.
Find	Lets you find out if a string is inside the current module. (Returns a Boolean, not the location.)
InsertLInes	Unlike AddFromString, lets you insert at a specific line.
ReplaceLine	Lets you replace lines of code with other lines of code.

Analyzing the Add-In Template

We want to work through a line-by-line and member-by-member analysis of the Add-In template. The first line in it is, naturally enough, the line saying what interface this class module will implement:

```
Implements IDTExtensibility
```

The next lines of code are for the data members. Notice, as we discussed earlier, that in all the code that follows how the VBInstance object variable will be used to refer to the current instance of VB.

```
Public FormDisplayed        As Boolean
Public VBInstance           As VBIDE.VBE
Dim mcbMenuCommandBar       As Office.CommandBarControl
Dim mfrmAddIn               As New frmAddIn
```

Next, there is the declaration for the one basic event that an Add-In will expose:

```
Public WithEvents MenuHandler As CommandBarEvents
```

This is used for the command bar event handlers. (Remember, command bar is a general term: it applies to both toolbars and menu bars.) Next, we have the Hide and Show methods for the Add-In. The Hide method is straightforward, it simply flips the FrmDisplayed object variable to False and hides the actual form (mfrmAddIn) that is used for the Add-In.

```
Sub Hide()
    On Error Resume Next

    FormDisplayed = False
    mfrmAddIn.Hide
End Sub
```

The Show method is a little more interesting. You modify this event to change how the form is for your Add-In will get displayed (modally, for example). First off, there is the On Error Resume Next statement to take into account any problems VB might have in doing things like connecting to the Add-In. Next, we actually hook up the mfrmAdddIn local variable to the Add-In form if it is not already set to this object. Finally, we hook the mfrmAddIn local variable up to an instance of the current instance of VBIDE object. Note that this does not hook the Add-In into the current VB project, this is taken care of by the next method.

```
Sub Show()
    On Error Resume Next

    If mfrmAddIn Is Nothing Then
        Set mfrmAddIn = New frmAddIn
    End If

    Set mfrmAddIn.VBInstance = VBInstance
    Set mfrmAddIn.Connect = Me
    FormDisplayed = True
    mfrmAddIn.Show
End Sub
```

The next event is vital. It is the code that actually adds the Add-In to VB. It is called by the Add-In Manager when the user checks off that he or she wants to add that Add-In. It is also called at start up if the line for the Add-In is set to 1 in the VBAdd-Ins32.INI file. Note that you can also call it from an external application such as the Add-In Toolbar. What happens when this event is triggered is that the code inside of it is responsible for connecting our VBInstance local object variables up with the currently running instance of the VB IDE. We also hook things like the mcbMenuCommandBar local variable into the IDE's command bar. (Notice also how the code actually invites you to set a breakpoint, as we did at the beginning of this chapter!)

```
--
Private Sub IDTExtensibility_OnConnection(ByVal VBInst _
As Object, ByVal ConnectMode As vbext_ConnectMode, ByVal _
AddInInst As VBIDE.Add-In, custom() As Variant)

    On Error GoTo error_handler

    'save the vb instance
    Set VBInstance = VBInst

    'this is a good place to set a breakpoint and
    'test various Add-In objects, properties and methods
    Debug.Print VBInst.FullName

    If ConnectMode = vbext_cm_External Then
        'Used by the wizard toolbar to start this wizard
        Me.Show
    Else
        Set mcbMenuCommandBar = _
AddToAddInCommandBar("My Add-In")
        'sink the event
        Set Me.MenuHandler = _
VBInst.Events.CommandBarEvents(mcbMenuCommandBar)
    End If

    If ConnectMode = vbext_cm_AfterStartup Then
        If GetSetting(App.Title, "Settings", _
"DisplayOnConnect", "0") = "1" Then
            'set this to display the form on connect
            Me.Show
        End If
    End If

    Exit Sub

error_handler:
    MsgBox Err.Description
End Sub
```

The next event that is part of the interface is only called after the Add-In is loaded into the IDE.

```
Private Sub IDTExtensibility_OnStartupComplete(custom() As _
Variant)
     If GetSetting(App.Title, "Settings", _
"DisplayOnConnect", "0") = "1" Then
        'set this to display the form on connect
        Me.Show
     End If
End Sub
```

The next event is only given as a stub in the Add-In template. It is called whenever any Add-In is loaded into or removed from the IDE. (Note the comment symbol so that its skeleton will stay in the compiled code.

```
Private Sub IDTExtensibility_OnAddInsUpdate(custom() As Variant)
'
End Sub
```

The final event procedure that is part of the IDTExtensibility interface is triggered when someone tries to remove the Add-In from VB. It is triggered by the Add-In Manager when either the user unchecks the Add-In or if the current instance of the VB IDE is shut down. The code contained in it removes the Add-In from VB; it also unhooks the various local object variables and saves the current settings to the Registry. For example, it unloads and then destroys the mfrmAddIn form object variable used for the Add-In.

```
Private Sub IDTExtensibility_OnDisconnection(ByVal _
RemoveMode As _ vbext_DisconnectMode, _
custom() As Variant)

    On Error Resume Next

    'delete the command bar entry
    mcbMenuCommandBar.Delete

    'shut down the Add-In
    If FormDisplayed Then
        SaveSetting App.Title, "Settings", _
"DisplayOnConnect", "1"
```

```
            FormDisplayed = False
      Else
            SaveSetting App.Title, "Settings", _
"DisplayOnConnect", "0"
      End If

      'destroy the form object
      Unload mfrmAddIn
      Set mfrmAddIn = Nothing
End Sub
```

The Add-In template also contains the following method for hooking up the Add-In to a command bar (menu or toolbar).

```
Function AddToAddInCommandBar(sCaption As String) As _
Office.CommandBarControl
      Dim cbMenuCommandBar As Office.CommandBarControl
      'command bar object
      Dim cbMenu As Object

      On Error GoTo AddToAddInCommandBarErr

      'see if we can find the Add-Ins menu
      Set cbMenu = VBInstance.CommandBars("Add-Ins")
      If cbMenu Is Nothing Then
            'not available so we fail
            Exit Function
      End If

      'add it to the command bar
      Set cbMenuCommandBar = cbMenu.Controls.Add(1)
      'set the caption
      cbMenuCommandBar.Caption = sCaption

      Set AddToAddInCommandBar = cbMenuCommandBar

      Exit Function

AddToAddInCommandBarErr:
Exit Function
```

Connecting Your Add-In

First, the Add-In Manager (shown in Figure 15-19) is a utility found on the AddIns menu in VB's IDE. It is basically a dialog box that lists all of the Add-Ins that have entries in the VBADDIN.INI file located in your \Windows directory. (As you saw earlier, calling the AddToINI function found in the code module of the Add-In template modifies this file.) The point of the Add-In Manager is to check if an Add-In should be loaded into memory when Visual Basic is loaded. If you check an Add-In in this dialog box, the Add-In Manager will load it (via the extensibility interface) into memory as soon as you dismiss the dialog box. The state that you leave the Add-In Manager dialog box when you shut VB down carries over to the next session. Any boxes you have checked determine whether or not VB will automatically load that Add-In the next time you start VB. If you leave an Add-In checked (running) when you close VB, it will automatically load the next time you run VB. Conversely, if you uncheck an Add-In, then exit VB, that Add-In will not be loaded automatically the next time you run VB.

All of the Add-Ins that ship with VB5 automatically appear on the Add-In Manager dialog box. If you check one of the supplied Add-Ins, you probably

Figure 15-19 The Add-In Manager

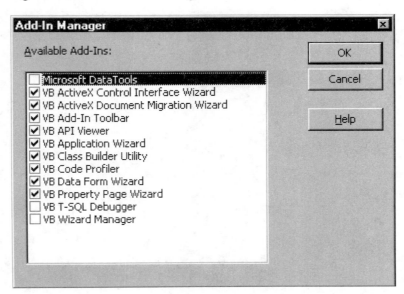

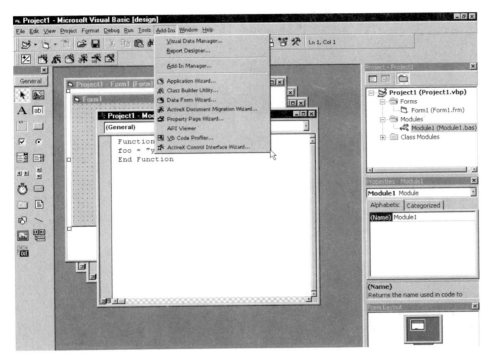

Figure 15-20 The AddIns menu with lots of Add-Ins

won't see anything at that time. This is because checking the box simply loads the Add-In. The Add-In itself will wait for the user to call it by clicking its menu item. What you may notice the next time you select the AddIns menu is that you'll see lots of new items, as shown in Figure 15-20. You now only have to click on the item to activate it.

After you have run the AddToINI function in the Add-In template that changes the VBADDIN.Ini file, you need to start the project. This will also register the Add-In. At this point, as you saw in the previous section, you can start up another VB session and work with the Add-In by:

1. Opening the new sessions Add-Ins menu.
2. Choosing the Add-In from the Add-In Manager. (The default name is MyAddIn.)

Finally, the main advantage of using the Add-In Manager is that you can connect your Add-In via the most appropriate place in the IDE. All of the methods discussed in this section use this approach. The disadvantage of using the Add-In Manager is that the Add-In will be loaded into memory all of the time, even though it sits idle until the user (or some other event) makes it active. The Add-In Toolbar we discuss in the next section makes an Add-In available without loading it into memory until the user chooses to do so.

Using Another Menu to Hook in the Add-In

Another method of connecting your Add-In to the IDE is to add a menu item or items on an existing IDE menu or toolbar where the Add-In seems to be appropriate. The Template Manager discussed in Chapter 17 does this. Although we need to refer you to Chapter 17 for more details, the idea, as you can see in Figure 15-21, is that the Template Manager adds three menu items to the Tools menu. This seemed appropriate because the functionality added by the Template Manager seemed to mesh with the other tools on this menu such as the Menu Editor.

The idea is that a click on each different menu item fires a distinct event in the connection class of the Template Manager. Here is the code that was used to add the three items to the Tools menu:

Figure 15-21 The Tools menu with the Template Manager added

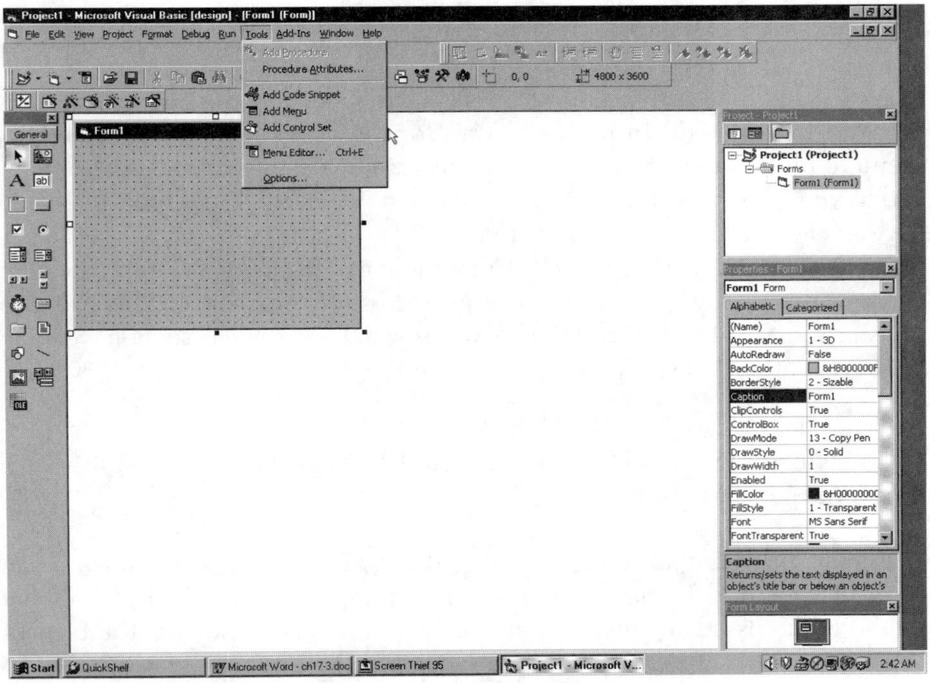

```
'add it to the Tools menu on command bar right above the
'menu editor
  Set mcbMenuCommandBarCode = _
VBInst.CommandBars("Tools").Controls.Add(msoControlButton, , , 3)
  mcbMenuCommandBarCode.BeginGroup = True
  mcbMenuCommandBarCode.Caption = LoadResString(1004)
  mcbMenuCommandBarCode.ToolTipText = LoadResString(1005)
  Clipboard.SetData LoadResPicture(5002, 0)
  mcbMenuCommandBarCode.PasteFace
  Set CodeHandler = _
VBInst.Events.CommandBarEvents(mcbMenuCommandBarCode)
  Set mcbMenuCommandBarMnu = _
VBInst.CommandBars("Tools").Controls.Add(msoControlButton, , , 4)
  mcbMenuCommandBarMnu.Caption = LoadResString(1000)
  mcbMenuCommandBarMnu.ToolTipText = LoadResString(1001)
  Clipboard.SetData LoadResPicture(5000, 0)
  mcbMenuCommandBarMnu.PasteFace
  Set MenuHandler = _
VBInst.Events.CommandBarEvents(mcbMenuCommandBarMnu)
  Set mcbMenuCommandBarCtl = _
VBInst.CommandBars("Tools").Controls.Add(msoControlButton, , , 5)
  mcbMenuCommandBarCtl.Caption = LoadResString(1002)
  mcbMenuCommandBarCtl.ToolTipText = LoadResString(1003)
  Clipboard.SetData LoadResPicture(5001, 0)
  mcbMenuCommandBarCtl.PasteFace
  Set ControlHandler = _
VBInst.Events.CommandBarEvents(mcbMenuCommandBarCtl)

  'add the menu editor's separator
  VBInst.CommandBars("Tools").Controls(6).BeginGroup = True
```

The idea of this code is it first gets a reference to the third item on the Tools menu. This item can obviously have a Caption, ToolTipText and so on. The PasteFace method adds a picture to the left of the menu item. (You can see these in Figure 15-21.) These are all loaded from a resource file. The Add function used here is one that will reappear a lot in your Add-In code. It is used to actually add an item to the Controls collection of a specific component. It's syntax is:

```
Add([Type], [id], [Parameter],[Before], [Temporary]
```

Thus, in the code snippet above, the first line added the new menu item *before* the current third item on the Tools menu; i.e., before the Menu Editor item. (As you can see in Figure 15-21.) By modifying the above code to change the specific menu you can add your Add-In to virtually any menu in the IDE. The trick is to change the string "Tools" that identifies the element in the CommandBars collection to the string that identifies the menu you want to work with and modify the call to add appropriately. Finally, lines like:

```
Set ControlHandler = _
VBInst.Events.CommandBarEvents(mcbMenuCommandBarCtl)
```

give us a way of detecting when the menu item is clicked. Without the click event handler, you would never be notified that the button you added was being clicked by the user.

Toolbar

It may be more appropriate to simply add a button to a toolbar rather than have the Add-In appear on a menu. You can add your Add-In to an existing toolbar such as the Standard toolbar or you can add your own toolbar altogether. The Add-In toolbar provided by VB is explained in detail below. Here is an example of the code needed to add your Add-In to the Standard toolbar as the last item. (It is taken from the TabOrder sample provided with VB. We will discuss this example in detail in a later section.)

```
Set mcbMenuCommandBar = _
gVBInstance.CommandBars("Standard")._
Controls.Add(msoControlButton, , ,    _
gVBInstance.CommandBars("Standard").Controls.Count)
```

The advantage of this is that the Add-In is available with one click of the mouse instead of being hidden on a menu. Be sure to add a meaningful tooltip to your button(s) so that the user will not have to rely on figuring out what your bitmap represents.

Context Menu

The main benefit of placing your Add-In on a context menu is that it is visible at just the right time. The example code below adds a menu item to the Project window's context menu. The trick here is to figure out the distinct name of the context menu you wish to use. To do this, run the utility supplied on the CD called IDEMenus. You will be able to determine the correct menu based upon the items on the menu and its name. The code below is from the VBClone example discussed later in the chapter:

```
'add it to the project window pop-up menu
Set mcbMenuCommandBar = VBInstance.CommandBars ("Project _
Window Project").Controls.Add(msoControlButton, , , 5)
'set the caption
mcbMenuCommandBar.Caption = "&Clone Project"
```

On an Event

The final method for connecting an Add-In that we want to discuss is to activate it in response to an event. This requires silently monitoring for a particular events or events in the IDE. The advantage of doing this is that your Add-In will pop up only when it is needed. An example of this would be an Add-In that checks for Controls events in order to give you a quick and dirty way to change the most common properties of a control after you add it to a form. (By the way, the jargon used around Microsoft for this is to talk about sinking the Controls event.) Suppose, therefore, that you want to have a simple dialog box that automatically pops up when the user adds a control to the form. The user can use this dialog box to enter the name for the control or change the font. This eliminates the need to always have to go to the Properties window just to change the name or font of the new control.

The key to doing this is the ControlHandler_ItemsAdded event, which is triggered when a control is added to the active form. For an Add-In to change the font at this moment the code could be as simple as:

```
Private Sub ControlHandler_ItemAdded(ByVal VBControl _
As VBIDE.VBControl)
   With VBControl
     .ControlObject.Font.Name = "Arial"
     .ControlObject.Font.Size = 12
     .ControlObject.Font.Bold = True
   End With
End Sub
```

(Obviously, a more realistic example might pop up a dialog box for this and then use what the user enters to set these properties.)

Add-In Toolbar

As discussed above, the main advantage of the Add-In toolbar shown in Figure 15-22 is that it makes an Add-In available without having to have it loaded into memory every time Visual Basic is loaded. This not only means less memory use but it also means fewer messages are being monitored by the Add-Ins waiting in the wings. This can make VB seem more responsive. Also, using the Add-In toolbar can reduce the startup time for VB. This is because you can have an arbitrary number of Add-Ins on the Add-In Toolbar but only the Add-In toolbar itself is loaded at startup.

The Add-In toolbar is essentially an Add-In launcher that makes it easy to provide single click access to an Add-In. This means your Add-In does not even need to have entry in the VBADDIN.INI file. (The one exception is any Add-In that uses the CreateToolWindow method discussed in the section on the TabOrder sample below). The Add-In toolbar provides a management dialog box similar to the one used in the Add-In Manager that allows the user to add or remove Add-Ins from the toolbar and the registry.

The Add-In toolbar can become aware of Add-Ins in two ways. The first is the simplest:

- The user clicks on the +/- button on the Add-In toolbar and selects Browse from the dialog box that pops up (see Figure 15-23). This will let he or she find any Add-In that is registered on their system.

Note

This requires the Add-In to be registered. If the Add-In is on your system but not registered, using this method gives an error.

Figure 15-22
The Add-In toolbar

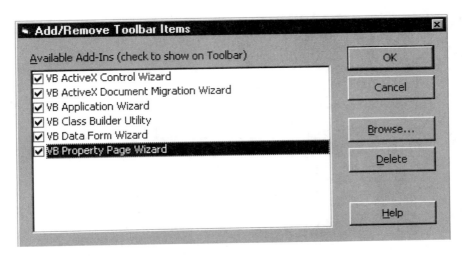

Figure 15-23 The Add/Remove Add-Ins dialog box

(As usual, you use the regsvr32 utility available on the Visual Basic CD in the \Tools\RegUtils directory to execute the following command from a DOS prompt or the Run menu item on the Start Menu:

```
regsvr32 TheAddInName.dll
```

The second way you can make an Add-In available to the Add-In toolbar is by writing the code for a standard EXE with Sub Main as the startup object and the following code in this procedure:

```
Sub Main()
   Dim x As Object
   Set x = CreateObject("AddInToolbar.Manager")
   x.AddToAddInToolbar sFileName:="C:\VB5\MyAdd.DLL", _
      sProgID:="MyAddIn.Connect", _
      sAddInName:="MyAddIn Title" _
      ShowOnToolBar:=True, _
      ForceAddInToolbar:=True
End Sub
```

The final issue that you might be concerned about when using the Add-In toolbar is one of instancing. This only applies to non-modal Add-Ins. If the user loads your non-modal Add-In, then clicks the toolbar button again, the Add-In will be called a second time. The toolbar is smart enough to know not to create another instance of the Add-In.

Removing an Add-In

If you wish to remove an Add-In completely, you have three choices:

- Click on the +/- dialog in the Add-In toolbar and use the dialog box that pops up to delete the Add-In.

- Run a simple EXE with the following code in it:

```
Sub Main()
   Dim x As Object
   Set x = CreateObject("AddInToolbar.Manager")
   x.RemoveAddInFromToolbar sAddInName:="MyAddIn Title"
End Sub
```

- The last method is to edit the registry and remove the key for this Add-In (not recommended unless you know your way around the Registry).

TabOrder Sample

The TabOrder Add-In ships with VB5. You can find it in the \Samples\ CompTool\Addins\TabOrder directory. The TabOrder Add-In demonstrates how to write a non-modal Add-In application that runs in a tool window as an integral part of VB's IDE. The TabOrder window can be docked along with the other the other tool windows such as the Project Explorer, Toolbox, and Property Explorer. This is appropriate for an Add-In that:

- Needs to stay in synch with the IDE.
- Is useful to have open all the time.

As its name suggests, the TabOrder Add-In gives you an easy way to manipulate the TabOrder property for controls on a form. It allows you to set the tab order of controls by dragging and dropping controls in the list, moving them up or down or setting the order based on their position from left to right or top to bottom. If you are like us, then you will rarely add the controls in the same order as they ultimately end up in. This tool helps throughout the form design process to keep the tab order somewhat sensible until you know the design process is complete and you can set the tab order for good. When this Add-In is running, you will see its dialog box filled up with the controls on the form in their tab order. Figure 15-24 shows you how the (slightly enlarged) TabOrder Add-In window looks for the calculator project supplied with VB.

How to Synchronize Add-Ins

There are some problems to be aware of when you write an Add-In like TabOrder that needs to stay in sync with another part of the IDE. The TabOrder Add-In displays all of the controls on the active form that have a TabIndex property and also allows users to change the order in the list and apply the changes to the form. This implies that the list of controls shown must be updated in real time. If a user changes to a different form or changes the current form, the TabOrder window has to update itself. This involves knowing and responding to ("sinking") events.

The events that the TabOrder sample needs to sink are the VBComponentsEvents and VBControlsEvents events. This will allow it to keep everything in synch since:

- Any time the form changes, a VBComponent event will fire.
- Any time controls are added or removed on the active form, a controls event will fire.

Figure 15-24 The TabOrder window for the Calculator project

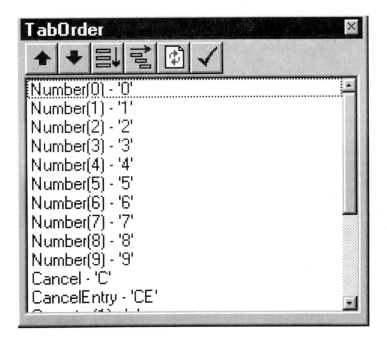

The first potential problem with the TabOrder Add-In is that it does not know when the user changes the control's caption property—because there are no events that are triggered by this action. This can make the list shown in the TabOrder window slightly out of date because it displays the caption property of all the controls that have one to help the user identify controls, such as labels, that will likely be in a control array.

Instancing Problems

Most Add-Ins have a potential problem with instancing. If the user loads the Add-In from an external loader such as the Add-In toolbar described above, the VB IDE does not have the same knowledge of that Add-In as if it had been loaded from the Add-In Manager. The user might load it again and if the Add-In had not been written to handle this, you would get multiple instances of it running at the same time. (Both the Add-In toolbar and the TabOrder app have special code in them to handle this case.)

Here is a code snippet from the Add-In toolbar that shows how it detects that an instance of an Add-In is already running. Each Add-In on the toolbar has its own instance of the ClickHandler class with the following code in it:

```
Dim AppInstance As IDTExtensibility

Private Sub ButtonHandler_Click(ByVal CommandBarControl _
As Object, handled As Boolean, CancelDefault As Boolean)
   On Error Resume Next

   If AppInstance Is Nothing Then
     'not loaded yet so try to create an instance
     Set AppInstance = _
CreateObject(CommandBarControl.OnAction)
```

The TabOrder Add-In has similar code in its Connect class to prevent it from executing its startup code more that one time:

```
If Not winWindow Is Nothing Then
    'already running so just show it
    Show
```

The next way an instancing problem may arise is when you use another Add-In loading tool. (We are not aware of any commercial ones however, and are not sure why you would want to bother rolling your own since the Add-In toolbar and the Add-In Manager seem to do a good enough job.). In the Add-

In toolbar, the code that handles this essentially caches each instance of an Add-In that it loads. Then, when the user tries to load an already running Add-In, the Add-In toolbar detects that an instance is already running and does not create another instance. (The TabOrder Add-In has code to detect that it is already running. If this happens, it simply shows itself instead of executing the code that it uses when it is loaded for the first time.)

Note

This cooperation between Add-Ins is necessary in the current VB environment, whose original architecture was not written to handle Add-Ins being loaded by any mechanism other than the Add-In Manager itself.

A Simple Example: IDEMenus

We want to work through a simple example of an Add-In that we wrote to show you all the menus that the IDE has to offer via a TreeView Control. (It also demonstrates a nifty use of the Tree-View control of course.) Figure 15-25 shows you what the IDEMenus window might display.

This turns out to be a fairly simple Add-In as far as the code that is needed to manipulate the IDTExtensibility model. The Connect class has essen-

Figure 15-25 The IDEMenus Add-In example

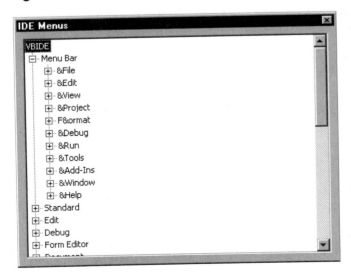

tially boilerplate code modified from the Add-In template. The actual work is done in the Form_Load of the window used for the Add-In. The relevant code looks like this:

```
For Each cmb In VBInstance.CommandBars
    Set nod = tvMenus.Nodes.Add(nodRoot, tvwChild, , cmb.Name)
    LoadChildControls cmb, nod
Next cmb
```

This runs through all the menus and toolbars in the current VB Instance and adds them to a TreeView control. (Remember the CommandBars collection includes both menus and toolbars.) The call to LoadChildControl in the above code uses a similar routine as you can see in the full form code that follows.

Listing 15-1:   The Full Form Code for the IDEMenus Example

```
Public VBInstance As VBIDE.VBE

  Private Sub Form_Load()
  On Error GoTo Form_LoadErr

  Dim cmb As CommandBar
  Dim nod As Node
  Dim nodRoot As Node

  Screen.MousePointer = vbHourglass

  Set nodRoot = tvMenus.Nodes.Add(, , , "VBIDE")
  nodRoot.Expanded = True

  For Each cmb In VBInstance.CommandBars
    Set nod = tvMenus.Nodes.Add(nodRoot, tvwChild, , cmb.Name)
    LoadChildControls cmb, nod
  Next cmb

  Screen.MousePointer = vbDefault

  Exit Sub
Form_LoadErr:
  Screen.MousePointer = vbDefault
  MsgBox Err.Description
End Sub

Sub LoadChildControls(cmb As Object, nodParent As Node)
```

```
On Error GoTo LoadChildControlsErr

Dim ctl As CommandBarControl
Dim nod As Node

For Each ctl In cmb.Controls
   Set nod = tvMenus.Nodes.Add(nodParent, tvwChild, , _
ctl.Caption)
   LoadChildControls ctl, nod
Next ctl

Exit Sub
LoadChildControlsErr:
End Sub

Private Sub Form_Resize()
   tvMenus.Height = ScaleHeight - (tvMenus.Top * 2)
   tvMenus.Width = ScaleWidth - (tvMenus.Left * 2)
End Sub

Private Sub cmdClose_Click()
   Unload Me
End Sub
```

Modal Add-Ins

Modal Add-Ins are utilities that are loaded after some action by the user. This can be done by them selecting a menu item or clicking on a button in the Add-In toolbar. It also may be triggered by a certain event occurring such as a form being added to the current project. The Add-In we chose to build to illustrate this process is a utility that adds what we think is a much needed feature to Visual Basic. It clones the current project to a \BAK directory or to a directory of your own choosing. This way you can always have a backup copy of your project, eliminating the tedious process of using Explorer or doing a series of Save As commands, then reloading the original project. Our Add-In does all the work of saving copies of your project files in one easy step. It is located in the CH15\VBPClone directory. We want to work through its high points.

The VBPClone Add-In Example

First, the Connect class is mostly boilerplate. The main difference is that we want to show the form window that we use to ask about cloning the project, modally. Hence the Show method in the Connect class has to look like this:

```
Sub Show()
    Set mfrmAddIn = New frmAddIn
     'pass the form the vbinstance object
    Set mfrmAddIn.VBInstance = VBInstance
    mfrmAddIn.Show vbModal
    Set mfrmAddIn = Nothing
End Sub
```

where the keyline:

```
mfrmAddIn.Show vbModal
```

is used to show the form for the Add-In modally.

All the work for this Add-In is done in the form that is used to ask the user whether he or she wants to clone the project. At design time, the form we used looks like Figure 15-26. It has an option button group, two command buttons and a Common Dialog box control.

The code shows off how you can use the FileName property of the ActiveVBProject object in order to find out the name of the project in the current instance of VB:

```
sOriginalProject = VBInstance.ActiveVBProject.FileName
```

Then we have the code to save the parts of the project in a new place. For example, if the user wants to save it to a \BAK directory below the current directory, the following code will be processed. (To make the code shorter we use a common trick of trying to create the directory and eating the error that would result if the \BAK directory happened to already exist. We could have written the code to check if that directory existed before trying to create it using the Dir function, of course.). The code also uses helper functions to strip off various unessential parts of the file's full path name. The key point though, is the following code that walks through all the files in the project and saves them all.

```
For Each cmp In VBInstance.ActiveVBProject.VBComponents
    cmp.SaveAs sNewPath & StripPath(cmp.FileNames(1))
Next cmp
'now save the project file
VBInstance.ActiveVBProject.SaveAs sNewPath & "\" & _
StripPath(sOriginalProject)
```

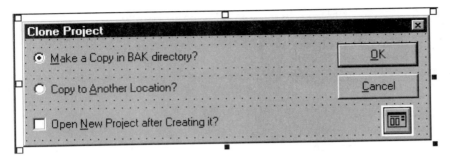

Figure 15-26 The form for the Clone Add-In

Here's the full code attached to the form for the VBPClone Add-In. Notice how we use the common dialog box ShowSave method in case the user clicked the option button that says he or she wants to save it to a different location. (The default is simply a \BAK directory below the current directory.)

Listing 15-2: Full Code for the VBPClone Form File

```
Public VBInstance As VBIDE.VBE

Private Sub cmdCancel_Click()
    Unload Me
End Sub

Private Sub cmdOK_Click()
    On Error GoTo cmdOK_ClickErr

    Dim sOriginalProject As String
    Dim sNewProject As String
    Dim cmp As VBComponent
    Dim sNewPath As String

    sOriginalProject = VBInstance.ActiveVBProject.FileName

    If optChoice(0).Value Then
      'save to BAK dir
      On Error Resume Next
      'try to make the BAK dir
      sNewPath = StripFileName(sOriginalProject) & "BAK\"
      MkDir sNewPath
      If Err Then Err = 0   'eat the error if the dir
                            'already exists
      On Error GoTo cmdOK_ClickErr
```

```
        If Len(Dir(sNewPath & StripPath(sOriginalProject))) _
> 0 Then
            'file exists so prompt for overwrite
            If MsgBox("Project in BAK directory already _
exists, overwrite?", vbYesNo + vbQuestion) = vbNo Then
                Exit Sub
            End If
        End If
        'walk through all files and save them all
        For Each cmp In _
VBInstance.ActiveVBProject.VBComponents
            cmp.SaveAs sNewPath & StripPath(cmp.FileNames(1))
        Next cmp
        'now save the project file
        VBInstance.ActiveVBProject.SaveAs sNewPath & "\" & _
StripPath(sOriginalProject)

    ElseIf optChoice(1).Value Then
        'save to new location
        With CommonDialog1
            .FileName = sOriginalProject
            .Flags = cdlOFNOverwritePrompt
            .ShowSave
            sNewProject = .FileName
        End With
        sNewPath = StripFileName(sNewProject)
        'walk through all files and save them all
        For Each cmp In _
VBInstance.ActiveVBProject.VBComponents
            cmp.SaveAs sNewPath & StripPath(cmp.FileNames(1))
        Next cmp
        'now save the project file
        VBInstance.ActiveVBProject.SaveAs sNewProject
    End If

    If chkOpenNew.Value = vbUnchecked Then
        'reload the original project
        If VBInstance.VBProjects.Count > 1 Then
            '1st remove the new BAK project
            VBInstance.VBProjects.Remove _
VBInstance.ActiveVBProject
            'now reload the original
            VBInstance.VBProjects.Add sOriginalProject, False
        Else
            'reload the original
            VBInstance.VBProjects.AddFromFile sOriginalProject, True
```

```
            End If
        End If

        Unload Me
        Exit Sub
cmdOK_ClickErr:
        If Err = 32755 Then Exit Sub
        MsgBox Err.Description
End Sub

Function StripFileName(rsFileName As String) As String
    On Error Resume Next
    Dim i As Integer

    For i = Len(rsFileName) To 1 Step -1
        If Mid(rsFileName, i, 1) = "\" Then
            Exit For
        End If
    Next
    StripFileName = Mid(rsFileName, 1, i)
End Function

Function StripPath(rsFileName As String) As String
    On Error Resume Next
    Dim i As Integer

    For i = Len(rsFileName) To 1 Step -1
        If Mid(rsFileName, i, 1) = "\" Then
            Exit For
        End If
    Next
    StripPath = Mid(rsFileName, i + 1)
End Function
```

Non-Modal Add-Ins

Some Add-Ins need to be loaded at all times in order to be useful. These are a bit trickier to code as they work much more closely with the IDE and its windows. The preferred method for doing this is to create a tool window much like the one used in the TabOrder sample. We built two samples to show this feature off. The sample we give you is much more sophisticated as far as its actual code goes—and its use of the extensibility model is also deeper than the IDE menus example. What it does is allow you to add and remove line numbers from a procedure with a click of a button. It is very useful where this last ditch debugging technique (using Err.Line is no fun) is needed. (For debugging out-of-process EXEs, for example.)

The Line Number Add-In Example

The form for this Add-In is trivial. As Figure 15-27 shows it simply is a tiny form with two command buttons that are part of a control array. On the other hand this Add-In requires by far the most sophisticated use of the extensibility model. This is because as we said earlier, you have to drill down very deeply to get at the code in your project. (Although because of the power of the model, little code is needed to actually do this.) Also, independently of the extensibility model, the code to add the line numbers once you have the strings that make up the code in hand is somewhat nontrivial. The actual project may be found in the CH15\LineNumb directory. We want to go over the high points of the code in this section.

As usual, the Connect class is mostly boilerplate. The key work is done in the code attached to the form. For example, the cmdLineNumbers_Click event procedure has code like the following to get at the CodeModule object:

```
With VBInstance
    If .ActiveVBProject Is Nothing Then Err.Raise -1
    If .SelectedVBComponent Is Nothing Then Err.Raise -1
    Set modModule = .SelectedVBComponent.CodeModule
End With
```

Next, we have to use the CodePane object associated to the CodeModule object in order to get the lines that are currently selected (if any)

```
    modModule.CodePane.GetSelection lStartLine, lStartCol, _
    lEndLine, lEndCol
```

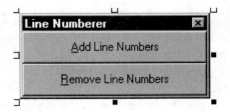

Figure 15-27
The form for the Line Number Add-In

Then we use the ProcOfLine method to find out the name of the function:

```
sProc = modModule.ProcOfLine(lStartLine, vbext_pk_Proc)
If Len(sProc) = 0 Then Err.Raise -1
```

Now we use the ProcBodyLines to get at the line number of the line below the signature of the procedure or function:

```
'adjust for declaration
lLine = modModule.ProcBodyLine(sProc, vbext_pk_Proc) + 1
```

Now we can use the Lines method of the CodeModule to get at the actual text in the lines. The point being that the Lines method requires you to tell it where to start. We used the above code to make sure we are not including the signature of the function or procedure.

```
sLine = modModule.Lines(lLine, 1)
```

That's almost it as far as using the Extensibility model goes. The rest of the code is basically just using lots of string manipulation functions on the sLine string. The one exception are lines like this that uses the ReplaceLine method in order to write the modified string back to the CodeModule object:

```
modModule.ReplaceLine lLine, lLine & sLine
```

Here's the complete code. The string manipulation code is boring but necessary.

Listing 15-3:   Complete Code Attached to LineNumber Form

```
If Len(Trim(sProc)) = 0 Then Err.Raise -1

If Right$(Trim(sLine), 1) = "_" Then

Loop While Left$(Trim(sLine), 4) <> "End "

 Option Explicit

Public VBInstance As VBIDE.VBE
Public Connect As Connect
Private Declare Function SetWindowLong& Lib "user32" Alias _
"SetWindowLongA" (ByVal hwnd As Long, ByVal nIndex _
As Long, ByVal dwNewLong As Long)

Dim mHwnd As Long
```

```
Private Sub cmdLineNumbers_Click(Index As Integer)
   On Error GoTo cmdLineNumbers_ClickErr

   Dim sProc As String
   Dim modModule As CodeModule
   Dim lStartLine As Long, lStartCol As Long, lEndLine _
As Long, lEndCol As Long
   Dim sLine As String
   Dim lLine As Long
   Dim i As Integer
   Dim bLineContinuation As Boolean

   'first we need to check and see if we are inside a function
   With VBInstance
      If .ActiveVBProject Is Nothing Then Err.Raise -1
      If .SelectedVBComponent Is Nothing Then Err.Raise -1
      Set modModule = .SelectedVBComponent.CodeModule
   End With

   modModule.CodePane.GetSelection lStartLine, lStartCol, _
lEndLine, lEndCol
   sProc = modModule.ProcOfLine(lStartLine, vbext_pk_Proc)
   If Len(Trim(sProc)) = 0 Then Err.Raise -1

   'set the start line and end line of the procedure
   lLine = modModule.ProcBodyLine(sProc, vbext_pk_Proc) + 1
   'adjust for declaration
   'get the first line
   sLine = modModule.Lines(lLine, 1)
   sLine = Trim$(sLine)

   'now we need to perform the requested action
   Do
      If Len(sLine) > 0 Then

         If Index = 0 Then    'adding line numbers
            'need to see if the line already starts with a
            'line number
            If Val(sLine) = 0 Then
               'see if this line ends with a "_"
               If Right$(sLine, 1) = "_" Then
                  If Not bLineContinuation Then
                     'set it for the first line
                     bLineContinuation = True
                  End If
               Else
```

```
            If bLineContinuation Then
               'reset after the entire line is done
               bLineContinuation = False
            End If
            'replace the line with the new one
            modModule.ReplaceLine lLine, lLine & sLine
         End If
      End If

      Else                    'removing line numbers
         'need to see if the line doesn't start with a
         'line number
         If Val(sLine) > 0 Then
           'strip off the number
           For i = 1 To Len(sLine)
             If Mid$(sLine, i, 1) = " " Or Mid$(sLine, i, _
1) = vbCr Then
                 Exit For
             End If
           Next
           'replace the line with the new one
           modModule.ReplaceLine lLine, Mid$(sLine, i)
         End If
      End If

    End If

    'get the next line
    lLine = lLine + 1
    sLine = modModule.Lines(lLine, 1)
  Loop While Left$(sLine, 4) <> "End "
  Exit Sub

cmdLineNumbers_ClickErr:
  If Err = -1 Then
    MsgBox "No active procedure." & vbCrLf & _
"Place the cursor inside a procedure, then try again.", _
vbInformation
  End If
  Exit Sub
End Sub

Private Sub Form_Load()
   'parent off the main IDE window so this
   'window will act like a child of the IDE
   mHwnd = SetWindowLong(hwnd, -8,
```

```
VBInstance.MainWindow.hwnd)

    'restore the position of the window
    Move Val(GetSetting(App.Title, "Settings", "Left", "1000")), _
        Val(GetSetting(App.Title, "Settings", "Top", "1000"))
End Sub

Private Sub Form_QueryUnload(Cancel As Integer, _
UnloadMode As Integer)
    If UnloadMode = 0 Then
        'just hide it so it stays running
        Cancel = True
        Hide
        Connect.FormDisplayed = False
    End If
    'save the position
    SaveSetting App.Title, "Settings", "Left", Left
    SaveSetting App.Title, "Settings", "Top", Top
End Sub

Private Sub Form_Unload(Cancel As Integer)
    'reparent the window
    mHwnd = SetWindowLong(hwnd, -8, mHwnd)

End Sub
```

Invisible Add-Ins

Let's say that every time you add a form to a project or a control to a form you want to set the font of the object to a particular value—such as Arial 12 pt. Bold for all text and captions. (For example, so as to achieve a uniform look and feel for your design.) To do this, an Add-In doesn't need a UI, it simply needs to listen for the appropriate events and act accordingly when they occur.

The FontSet Example

This example is in CH15\FontSet directory. It has all its functionality in a single class module whose code follows. Although as you will soon see much of this code is boilerplate added by the Add-In template, there are a few subtle points that you need to be aware of. The first is that in order to trap the events for all of the forms in all of the projects in the IDE, you need to pass Nothing to the event sinking call in the OnConnection event. This is done with a line like the following:

```
Set FormHandler = _
VBInstance.Events.VBComponentsEvents(Nothing)
```

Using Nothing rather than a specific component tells the extensibility model to sink the events for all components, as opposed to a single one that would ordinarily be passed in as you have seen earlier in this chapter. The second problem is that you need to reset the control event handler whenever a new component becomes active because it is not possible to pass Nothing to the control handler. This is done when a component is activated or selected in the project window. You do this in the FormHandler_ItemActivated event using the following code:

```
If VBComponent.Type = vbext_ct_VBForm Then
    Set ControlHandler = _
VBInstance.Events.SelectedVBControlsEvents _
(VBInstance.ActiveVBProject, VBComponent.Designer)
    End If
```

The actual code to set the font is trivial. It is contained in the ControlHandler_ItemAdded event:

```
Private Sub ControlHandler_ItemAdded(ByVal VBControl As _
VBIDE.VBControl)
    With VBControl
        .ControlObject.Font.Name = "Arial"
        .ControlObject.Font.Size = 12
        .ControlObject.Font.Bold = True
    End With
End Sub
```

Listing 15-4: Full Code for the FontSet Example

```
Implements IDTExtensibility
Public VBInstance                As VBIDE.VBE
Public WithEvents FormHandler As VBComponentsEvents
Public WithEvents ControlHandler As SelectedVBControlsEvents
Private Sub IDTExtensibility_OnConnection(ByVal VBInst As _
Object, ByVal ConnectMode As vbext_ConnectMode, ByVal _
AddInInst As VBIDE.Add-In, custom() As Variant)
    'save the vb instance
    Set VBInstance = VBInst
    Set FormHandler = _
```

```
VBInstance.Events.VBComponentsEvents(Nothing)
End Sub
Private Sub IDTExtensibility_OnDisconnection(ByVal
RemoveMode As vbext_DisconnectMode, custom() As Variant)
'
End Sub
Private Sub IDTExtensibility_OnStartupComplete(custom() _
As Variant)
'
End Sub
Private Sub IDTExtensibility_OnAddInsUpdate(custom() _
As Variant)
'
End Sub
'this event fires when a control is added to the active form
Private Sub ControlHandler_ItemAdded(ByVal VBControl _
As VBIDE.VBControl)
   With VBControl
     .ControlObject.Font.Name = "Arial"
     .ControlObject.Font.Size = 12
     .ControlObject.Font.Bold = True
   End With
End Sub
'this event fires when a form becomes activated in the IDE
Private Sub FormHandler_ItemActivated(ByVal VBComponent _
As VBComponent)
   If VBComponent.Type = vbext_ct_VBForm Then
     Set ControlHandler =
VBInstance.Events.SelectedVBControlsEvents _
(VBInstance.ActiveVBProject, VBComponent.Designer)
   End If
End Sub
'this event fires when a form is selected in the project window
Private Sub FormHandler_ItemSelected(ByVal VBComponent _
As VBIDE.VBComponent)
   FormHandler_ItemActivated VBComponent
End Sub
```

Debugging Add-Ins

Add-Ins must be debugged using two instances of the IDE. This is so that they can have access to a VBInstance object just as they would if they were running as an Add-In after they have been built. Notice that this is exactly what we did when we went to watch the VBInst object variable at the beginning of this chapter. Unfortunately, there a few things you cannot do in a debug session like this because you are running out of process. These include things like certain control property access such as adding images to a ListImage control. So if you run into something that won't work while debugging, try it from an ordinary in-process-built DLL and try debugging it that way.

> **Tip**
>
> *Even after you build an EXE or DLL, you can still load your Add-In in this fashion and Visual Basic will figure out that you are using the one running in another instance of the IDE as opposed to the built one. This is certainly useful for building a new version of your Add-In—you won't have to get rid of the previous version!*

It is even possible to have more than two instances of VB running. This is needed to debug an Add-In that communicates with other Add-Ins, such as the Add-In toolbar written in Visual Basic.

Add-In Tips and Tricks

There are a couple of tips and tricks that you may find useful that we want to pass on. Most of these come from situations that Dave needed to work-around when he was building most of the Add-Ins that ship with VB5.

Making a Non-Modal Add-In Act as Part of the IDE

In order to make a non-modal Add-In act as part of the Visual Basic IDE, you need to set its parent to be the main IDE window. This is done with the SetWindowLong API call as shown in the following code:

```
Declare Function SetWindowLong& Lib "user32" Alias _
"SetWindowLongA" (ByVal hwnd As Long, ByVal nIndex _
As Long, ByVal dwNewLong As Long)
Dim mHwnd As Long

Public Sub Form_Load()
   'needed to parent to the IDE window
```

```
    mHwnd = SetWindowLong(hwnd, -8, mVBInstance.MainWindow.hwnd)
End Sub

Sub Form_Unload()
  If mHwnd <> 0 Then
    'restore the window parent
    mHwnd = SetWindowLong(hwnd, -8, GetDesktopWindow())
  End If
End Sub
```

This code gets the window handle in the Form_Load and restores it when the form is unloaded. The main drawback to using this API call is that it will cause problems if the application is loaded from anything other than the normal Add-In Manager discussed above. If it is loaded from another application such as the Add-In toolbar, it may not get shut down before Visual Basic disappears and this can cause a GPF. Therefore, we recommend it only for Add-Ins used in-house that you have control over.

Resolving Instancing Problems with Global Data

This also applies to a non-modal Add-In that you do not want to load more than one time from the IDE. If you place a Global object variable in a BAS module, then each instance of the connection class that gets created can check for the existence of this object and use the already loaded instance if this variable says it is available. Without a mechanism like this in place, multiple copies will be loaded whenever the user clicks the menu that loads the Add-In. This is done in the TabOrder sample. If you look at the TabOrder code you will see that it uses a global variable called gwinWindow. This variable is tested in the OnConnection event to see if an instance of the application is already running.

Determining if the IDE Is in Run Mode or Design Mode

Unlike user controls, the extensibility model has no direct way of telling that the IDE is running, as opposed to developing an application. One way to find this out is to use certain menu items that have a known state at run time. Here is some simple code to check this it from an Add-In.

```
Function InRunMode(VBInst As VBIDE.VBE) As Boolean _
InRunMode = _
(VBInst.CommandBars("Run").Controls("End").Enabled = True)
End Function
```

This function (also used in the TabOrder sample) will return True is the Run|End menu is enabled which only occurs when the IDE is in run mode!

How to Pass Menu Keystrokes to the IDE

Any Add-In written as a tool window like the TabOrder sample needs to include code to pass on the keystrokes it receives to the main IDE menu. (Otherwise, keystrokes such as ALT+F will not be handled when the Add-In has focus.) To fix this, use code like the following in the BAS module of the Add-In:

```
Private Declare Sub PostMessage Lib "user32" Alias _
"PostMessageA" (ByVal hwnd&, ByVal msg&, ByVal wp&, ByVal lp&)
Private Declare Sub SetFocus Lib "user32" (ByVal hwnd&)
Private Declare Function GetParent Lib "user32" (ByVal _
hwnd&) As Long
Const WM_SYSKEYDOWN = &H104
Const WM_SYSKEYUP = &H105
Const WM_SYSCHAR = &H106
Const VK_F = 70    ' VK_A thru VK_Z are the same as their
                   ' ASCII equivalents: 'A' thru 'Z'
Dim hwndMenu As Long 'needed to pass the menu keystrokes
                     'to Visual Basic

Sub HandleKeyDown(ud As Object, KeyCode As Integer, _
Shift As Integer)
If hwndMenu = 0 Then hwndMenu = FindHwndMenu(ud.hwnd)
   PostMessage hwndMenu, WM_SYSKEYDOWN, KeyCode, &H20000000
   KeyCode = 0
   SetFocus hwndMenu
End Sub
```

Next, you must add the following code to the user document that will be loaded as the tool window:

```
Private Sub UserDocument_KeyDown(KeyCode As Integer, _
Shift As Integer)
   If Shift <> vbAltMask Then Exit Sub
   If KeyCode < vbKeyA Or KeyCode > vbKeyZ Then Exit Sub
   If gVBInstance.DisplayModel = vbext_dm_SDI Then Exit Sub
   'pass the keystrokes onto the IDE
   HandleKeyDown Me, KeyCode, Shift
End Sub
```

WIZARDS

Topics in this Chapter

- The Application Wizard
- The Data Form Wizard
- Taking a Wizard Outside the VB5 IDE
- Launching Wizards

Chapter 16

Windows 95 has them, Office has them, Publisher has them, and of course VB5 has them as well. As you know by now, Wizards are an integral part of the VB IDE. VB5 ships with six Wizards: the Application Wizard that was briefly discussed in Chapter 1, the ActiveX Control Interface Wizard (see Chapter 13), the Property Page Wizard (also see Chapter 13), and the ActiveX Document Wizard (see Chapter 18). There's also the Setup Wizard (see Chapter 20) and a Data Form Wizard that we will explain shortly. Wizards are supposed to make features more discoverable, complex operations easy, and tedious tasks not.

Obviously, Wizards differ in how successful they are at accomplishing these rather lofty goals. In particular, only in the most ideal of situations will a Wizard do it all: You almost always have to hand-tweak the code that a Wizard produces. Still, unless you type faster than anyone we know, you will be grateful for how much tedious work Wizards like the Control Interface Wizard can save you.

Note

While VB doesn't ship with a Wizard to make Wizards, it does ship with a Wizard Manager and a Wizard Template to make creating your own Wizard quite easy.

So what's a Wizard? As far as VB is concerned the answer is that a Wizard is merely a special kind of Add-In that puts up a series of step-by-step screens. When you click on the Finish button whenever it is available, the Wizard uses the information you have entered together with the Extensibility model discussed in the last chapter to build what the user asked for.

Note

Microsoft has fairly rigid rules about what a Wizard should look like. If you use the Wizard Template, you will automatically be following them. Even though these seem to be changing all the time, the Wizard Template adheres closely to the Win95 standard.

To illustrate what Wizards can do, we begin this chapter by going over the Application Wizard and Data Form Wizard in detail. Then, it's on to the steps needed to create your own Wizards. We first explain how to hook up Wizards with VB's IDE but, as a bonus, we also explain how easy it is to make Wizards that can be used for the ultimate in user-friendly data-gathering applications. (After all, a series of step-by-step "fill-in-the-blank" screens are about as simple a way to gather information as one can imagine.) For a stand-alone Wizard, of course, you won't be using the extensibility model but rather writing the code to process the information yourself.

The Application Wizard

The Application Wizard is a good example of a multipurpose Wizard. On the one hand, it gives naïve users a gateway to VB's powers and makes reviewers happier since they seem to be able to do things without knowing much. On the other hand, the VB programmer, who realizes that the output of the Application Wizard is usually just the start of his or her job, knows that the Application Wizard is not a cure-all, yet can save them a lot of tedious work. (You saw this, for example, in the section on MDI applications in Chapter 6.) The following is a detailed explanation of the options available in each step and how they affect the application created. Figure 16-1 show you the first screen in the Wizard where you can determine the interface type

As you can see you have three choices. You have already seen the MDI and SDI choices at work. Note that the SDI (Single Document Interface) application format is becoming more popular since applications such as Internet

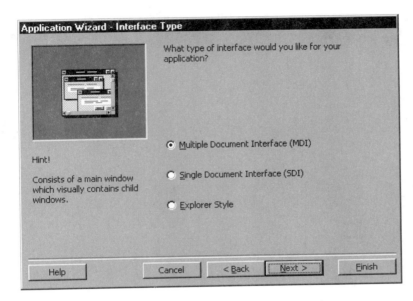

Figure 16-1 Interface Type Step in Application Wizard

Explorer and the Windows 95 Explorer are becoming so familiar to users of Windows 95. SDI applications do not have the ability to have child forms that share their space as MDI applications do. They either spawn other stand-alone windows or they display modal dialogs that the user must close before continuing with the main application. SDI applications rely on the operating system more for managing the forms it uses. The last type of interface available is described as "Explorer" type. The framework you get from this choice looks like Windows Explorer. It is implemented basically as a combination of Treeview and Listview controls. (This type of application choice requires the most additional code from the programmer in order to become functional. The complexity comes from the code needed to create the data structures behind the items displayed.) We suggest using this framework for any type of application that has:

1. A hierarchy of items that are best displayed in a Treeview.
2. Each item in that hierarchy has a dynamic number of members that can be displayed in a Listview.

An example within VB of this type of interface is the Visual Basic Class Builder Add-In. As you know (see Chapter 7), this displays a list of classes in the Treeview with the members of the selected class displayed in the

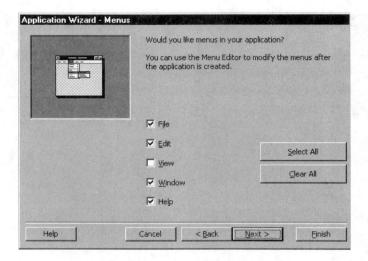

Figure 16-2   The Menu step in the Application Wizard

Listview. The interface enables the user to add code to copy, move, rename, add, and delete items in both the Treeview and Listview.

The next step as shown in Figure 16-2 lets you pick the menus you want. What you end up with is the usual menus such as a File menu with an Exit item as the last entry. The Menus step is fairly self-explanatory but there are some subtleties we think worth mentioning. First, the Window menu only makes sense for MDI applications; therefore, it is unavailable for the SDI and Explorer styles. Secondly, the View menu will be added automatically (even if you uncheck it) if you select any of the following features: Web Browser, Options Dialog, or Database forms. Also worth noting is that you may uncheck any of the menus and add your own at a later time from using the Menu Designer or Template Manager (discussed in Chapter 9). If you use the Template Manager, however, it may be difficult to get the menus to mesh in the desired order without some modifying of the order using the Menu Designer.

The next screen shown in Figure 16-3 is how you can automatically attach a resource file to your application (see Chapter 6). Recall that using a resource file to contain all of your strings and images is useful for many reasons:

- Resource files are easier to maintain since all the information is contained in a single file.

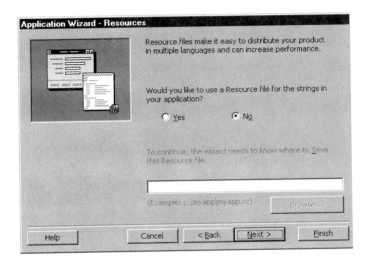

Figure 16-3   The Resource Screen step in the Application Wizard

- Reuse of the information is easier, which leads to less overhead.
- Consistency is more likely because everyone on the team is more likely to conform to the standard set forth in the single file.

And of course, there's the original purpose:

- Resource file makes it possible to localize your application for other languages without changing the application itself.

Note

When you add a resource file using this step, the application will have numbers for all of the menu captions. As you saw in Chapter 6, this subroutine walks through all of the controls and menus on a form at form load and replaces the caption and ToolTipText with strings from the resource file if a number is stored in the Tag or ToolTipText properties of a control. Since menus do not have a Tag property as other controls do, the only property available to store the numeric resource ID is the Caption property. This makes the form look a little strange at design time but the overall efficiency of this routine outweighs the inconvenience of not seeing the menu captions at design time.

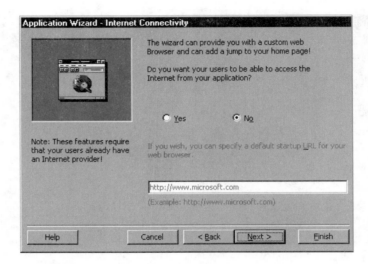

Figure 16-4 The Internet Connectivity step in the Application Wizard

Finally, if you choose to add a resource file using this step, you have to enter a directory to store the resource file. Therefore, you should have a subdirectory ready for the application so that you do not have to subsequently move the RC and RES files once you have saved the application to its final destination.

Figure 16-4 shows you the Internet Connectivity step, which is only available if you have Microsoft Internet Explorer version 3.0 or later installed on your system. This step allows you to add a custom browser to your application using the Web Browser control that is the essence of Internet Explorer 3. The form the Application Wizard builds requires very little code to hook it into the Web (see Chapter 18). We find this special purpose browser form very useful in situations like a corporate intranet where you don't need (or don't want) the user to have full access to the power of a browser like Internet Explorer.

Figure 16-5 shows you the Standard Forms screen. This step allows you to include some typical forms and dialog boxes to your application. As we mentioned in Chapter 10, Splash screens are useful in applications that take some time to start up and show their main form. The Login dialog lets you create an application that requires a user to supply a name and password in order to load. The Options dialog choice is a great way to allow users to set application preferences. It gives you a tabbed dialog box similar to the ones found in most professional applications shipped today, including Visual Basic. Finally the About Box is a dialog box that lets you fill in the information that tells users

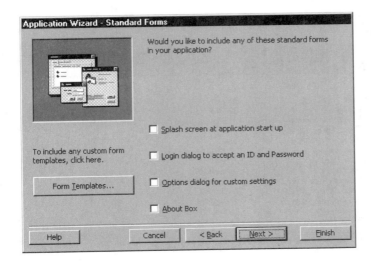

Figure 16-5 The Standard Forms screen in the Application Wizard

about the application such as the author and the current version, It also allows them to click a button to view information about their system by including the code needed to hook up to the Microsoft System Information screen as shown in Figure 16-6! (Which is not fun code to write.)

Note

Choosing the Form Templates button loads a list of all of the templates found in the Template/Forms directory. (See Chapter 17 for more on Templates.) As you will see there, templates makes it possible for you to add your own forms to an application created by the Application Wizard. Keep in mind that template forms will not be hooked up until you add the code to do it.

Figure 16-7 shows you the Data Access step. This is probably the most powerful feature in the Application Wizard and is actually a "two-part" step. The first part as shown in Figure 16-7 allows you to choose whether or not you want to include any forms for working with a database in your application. If you choose yes, then the drop-down list box gives you access to a list of the possible types of databases such as Acesss, FoxPro, Paradox, and so on. (If you need to create forms for data that are not on the list, you can either use an Access database and attach the external tables, or use the Data Form

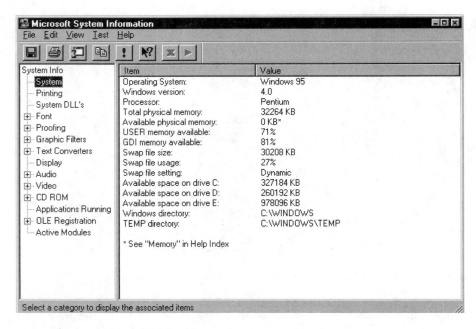

Figure 16-6   The results of adding an About Box when the user clicks on System Info

Figure 16-7   The Data Access step in the Application Wizard

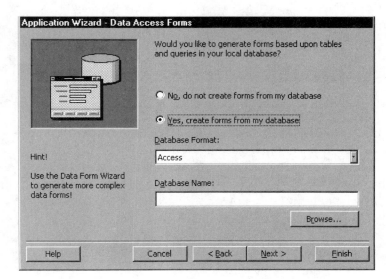

Wizard to add forms for those tables after you have created your application with the Application Wizard. Keep in mind that if you use the Data Form Wizard, you will have to add code to hook up those forms yourself.)

Note that if you choose to have the Application Wizard create forms for database tables, you need to select the database from which to get the data. Once you have done this, you can proceed to the next part of this step by clicking the Next button; you'll see a screen like Figure 16-8. The part allows you to choose which tables and/or queries you want forms generated for. If you chose an Access database as in Figure 16-8, you will also have an item labeled "<Querys List>." This item creates a special form that allows you to create a form dynamically for any query in the database. The data is displayed in a bound grid for viewing and modification. If you wish to, it is easy to modify this form to disallow users from modifying the data. To do this, simply set the AllowAddNew, AllowDelete, and AllowUpdate properties on the grdDataGrid control on the frmDataGrid form to false.

Finally, the finished step shown in Figure 16-9 lets you enter a name for the project other than the default name that the Application Wizard has supplied. This step also has a very important check box that all Wizards (should) have. It allows you to save the settings you have used while running the Wizard so that the next time you run it, you will not have to set all of the preferences again.

Figure 16-8 The Select Tables step in the Application Wizard

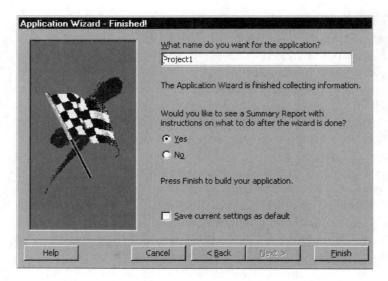

Figure 16-9   The Finished step in the Application Wizard

Tip

It is a good idea to run through the Application Wizard once for each interface type and select all possible features. Then look at the resulting code now that you are completely familiar with Visual Basic's programming language.

The Data Form Wizard

Although we don't have space in this book to cover Visual basic's very powerful database features, we do want to say a few words about the Data Form Wizard. This Wizard lets you bind a database to a form (or more precisely to the controls on the form). First off, the Data Form Wizard is an adaptation of the Data Form Designer that shipped as a sample in Visual Basic 4.0. It has been greatly enhanced so that it now can create three types of database forms: single table, grid view using the data bound grid control, and master/detail providing a view of a one-to-many relationship. It also has the capability to create a form that uses the Remote Data Control (RDC) to access

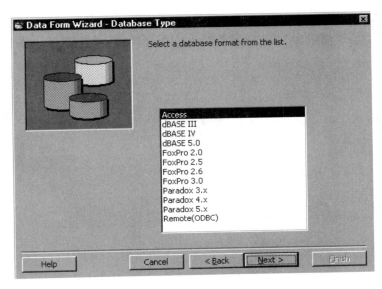

Figure 16-10   First screen in the Data Form Wizard

data from an ODBC data source in the most efficient way possible. And, as you can see in Figure 16-10 you have a lot of possible database types that you can hook up to.

Note

If you have a data type that is not supported, you can create an Access database and attach the tables of that type. Then you can use the Access database as if the data were stored in Access format. If you choose Remote, you will go to a step where you will be prompted to enter all of the connect string information for the ODBC data source you wish to use. If you choose any other type, you will go to a step prompting for the database name.

The next step, shown in Figure 16-11, lets you select the database. As with the similar step in the Application Wizard, if you have chosen an Access type database, you can limit your record source selection to only tables or queries. This is helpful if you want to filter out one or the other in order to minimize the list in the record source step that we discuss next. You cannot continue with the Wizard until you have entered a valid database name.

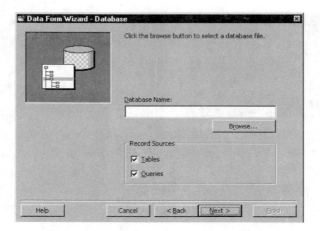

Figure 16-11   Picking the Database step in the Data
Form Wizard

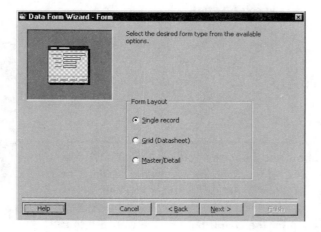

Figure 16-12   The Form step in the Data Form Wizard

Figure 16-12 shows you the Form step. This step lets you decide if you
want to view a single record, a table of the results of a query, or a master/
detail view that links together the master record source in single record format and the data for a record in a grid format.

After that you are taken to the Record Source screen. Once you choose the
Record Source you can choose the Fields you want to display. (Figure 16-13
uses the Biblio.mdb Access style database that ships with VB.)

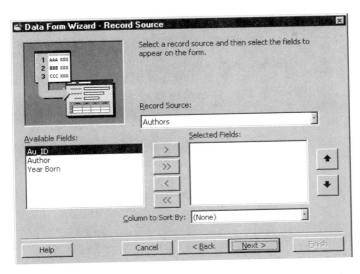

Figure 16-13 Record Source step in the Data Form Wizard

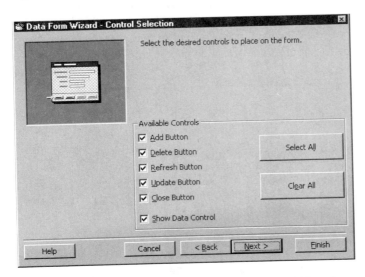

Figure 16-14 The Controls step in the Data Form Wizard

Finally, you are given a choice of what controls you want to place on the form such as an Add or Delete button (see Figure 16-14) and then it's on to the standard Finished step that tells the Wizard to generate the forms and code (and there will usually be a lot of them) needed to do what you asked.

The Wizard Manager

You activate the Wizard Manager (often called *WizMan*) via the Add-Ins menu—it's also on the Add-In Toolbar. WizMan was written completely in Visual Basic (by Dave actually). It is a dockable resizable window that is fully integrated with the IDE. See Figure 16-15, which enlarges the default size of the Wizard Manager's window a little bit.

WizMan is designed to make creating, modifying, and maintaining a Wizard as easy as possible. To understand why a tool like WizMan is such a great help, we want to step back and describe the structure of a Wizard. First off it *does not have a form* for each step. Microsoft tried lots of designs and discovered that using multiple forms exacted too great a performance penalty and created maintenance problems.

So what do they use instead of multiple forms? They use *multiple borderless frames,* only one of which is visible at any step.

Note

At design time, the other frames have a Left property set at −10000 so they are not visible to you. When you use WizMan to manage a step it takes care of moving the appropriate frame to center stage so you can see and work on its UI.

Figure 16-15   The Wizard Manager

Figure 16-16   Wizard Manager opening message box

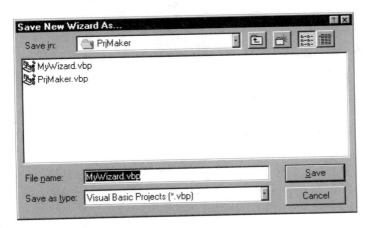

Figure 16-17   Save New Wizard As screen

WizMan only works with Wizards created from the Wizard Template explained below. For this reason, it is best to have WizMan create your new Wizard from the Wizard template instead of trying to create your own Wizard from scratch. To use WizMan:

1. Start up Visual Basic.

2. Load the Wizard Manager from the Add-In manager.

Since it can't find a form named frmWizard, WizMan will prompt you to create this using the message box shown in Figure 16-16.

After you click on Yes in the message box shown in Figure 16-16, WizMan will pop up a modified version of the usual File Save box as shown in Figure 16-17. You need to give the project file for the Wizard a distinctive name. (It

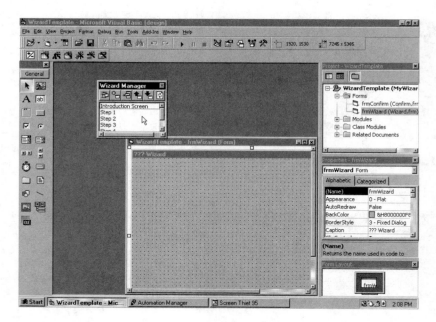

Figure 16-18   The VB IDE when starting to create a Wizard

is best to use a separate directory for each Wizard.) Once you do this and choose the Save option, WizMan will make a copy of the Wizard Template in the location you choose. Your screen will look like Figure 16-18. Note the Project Explorer in Figure 16-18 shows two forms: one for the confirmation step, the other, therefore, will be used via the trick with borderless frames described above to display all the steps.

Let's concentrate on the Wizard Manager's screen. As you can see in Figure 16-18, WizMan has three basic components. The first is the list of the current steps used in the Wizard. A new Wizard starts out with a step for an Introduction Screen, four intermediate steps and a screen for the Finished step. As you will see you can add and remove steps easily using WizMan. To make a step active so you can work on it:

- Simply click on its name in the WizMan's window.

Try this with the Introduction Screen. Your screen should look like Figure 16-19.

Next, double-clicking on a step in WizMan allows you to edit the name used for that step as shown in Figure 16-20. Highlighting a step and pressing

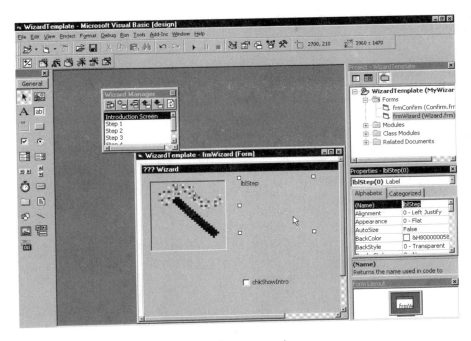

Figure 16-19   The Finished screen for a Wizard

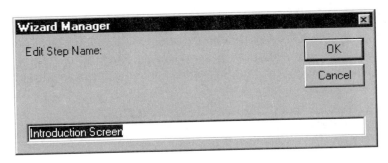

Figure 16-20   Editing a step name in WizMan

the *Delete* key lets you delete a step. Deleting a step removes both the controls and the code attached to that step. (When you ask WizMan to delete a step, it pops up a Yes/No confirmation message box so that you won't delete a step accidentally.)

The following table describes the tools in the Wizard Manager's toolbar reading form left to right:

Table 16-1: The Wizard Manager's Toolbar	
Function	*Explanation*
Move all steps off screen	This moves the frames used for the interface for all the steps off form. This lets you work with a clean form.
Add a new step	This adds a step to the Wizard (i.e., a new borderless frame). New steps always go before the Finished step.
Insert a step	This adds a step in front of the current step.
Move step up	Moves the currently selected step up in the order used for the Wizard. This requires WizMan to change many of the properties such as the borderless frames (control array) index. (This is one of the reasons Dave wrote WizMan since it is a real pain to move steps by hand.)
Move step down	Moves the current step down.
Refresh	This button is useful when you have made some changes to the Wizard and for some reason the display seems out of synch.

The next part of WizMan's UI is its context menu that, as always, you access by right-clicking when the focus is in WizMan. The context menu includes all of the functionality of the toolbar as well as some additional functions that are described in the table below.

Table 16-2: Context Menu Additional Functions	
Function	*Explanation*
Edit name	Same as double-clicking on a step in the list as explained above.
New Wizard	Lets you to create a new Wizard from the Wizard template.
Help	Loads the help file for WizMan.
Show toolbar	Obviously, since all toolbar functions are also on the context menu, you can turn off the toolbar if you want. The value for this setting will be saved when you exit WizMan.

Note

WizMan takes care of all of the work needed to maintain the steps. Without this tool working on a Wizard is very tedious and problem prone. Dave can attest to how much time they saved while he was coding four of the six Wizards that ship with Visual Basic 5.0!

Wizard Template

The forms and other files used in the Wizard Template follow a design that Microsoft arrived at only after trying many others. They had to reject many obvious designs (such as one that used multiple forms) for performance, other designs because maintenance was a nightmare, still others because they relied on outside components. The Wizard Template is written in 100 percent VB, the only outside files that are ever used are those contained in a single (optional) resource file. In the end the design chosen seems to satisfy all these requirements:

1. No outside components needed.
2. Good performance in moving from step to step.
3. Possible to maintain with a simple utility (WizMan explained above).
4. A design that works equally well as an Add-In or stand-alone EXE.

As we said earlier the design is based on a single form. The form has two main components:

- A picture box aligned to the bottom of the form. This contains the navigation buttons and a separator line (navigation bar). By setting the Align property of the picture box to Bottom, we know the form can be resized without needing to move or resize the navigation bar.
- A control array of borderless frames for the information on each step. (Prior to Visual Basic 5.0, the Frame control always had a border and extra space at the top for the caption. Adding a borderless frame gives Visual Basic 5 a container with a caption property where the step names can be stored.)

The key part of the code in the template is in the Click procedure for the command buttons used to navigate through the form. Since these buttons are part of a control array, the Click procedure uses a Select Case to distinguish among them. Let's go through the code framework used in this Click event procedure case by case. First off, the Click procedure's signature looks like this:

```
Private Sub cmdNav_Click(Index As Integer)
```

which is what one would expect when using a control array. Next there are a couple of declarations used to identify the step and the help file index inside the resource file. You would need to add the correct values for your Wizard:

```
Dim nAltStep As Integer
Dim lHelpTopic As Long
Dim rc As Long
```

Finally, we get to the code that does the work; it is a simple Select Case. For example, clicking on the Help button activates:

```
Case BTN_HELP
   mbHelpStarted = True
   lHelpTopic = HELP_BASE + 10 * (1 + mnCurStep)
   rc = WinHelp(Me.hwnd, HELP_FILE, _
   HELP_CONTEXT, lHelpTopic)
```

Clicking on the Cancel button unloads the Wizard form:

```
Case BTN_CANCEL
   Unload Me
```

Clicking on the Back or Forward button changes the value of the nAltStep counter that marks the current step. For example:

```
Case BTN_BACK
   'place special cases here to jump
   'to alternate steps
   nAltStep = mnCurStep - 1
   SetStep nAltStep, DIR_BACK
```

The real work—the place where you have to write the code to hook in the Extensibility model is contained in the BTN_FINISH case. It looks like this:

```
Case BTN_FINISH
   'wizard creation code goes here

   Unload Me
```

```
If GetSetting(APP_CATEGORY, WIZARD_NAME, _
CONFIRM_KEY, vbNullString) = vbNullString Then
    frmConfirm.Show vbModal
End If
```

The comment tells you where to place the code that does the output of the Wizard. The call to GetSetting is there so that the Wizard can have a "Do Not Show" in future check box on its Finish screen. (Remove this code if you always want to show the Confirm screen. Be sure to remove the check box from the Finish screen in that case as well.) Here's all the template code for this key event procedure:

```
Select Case Index
    Case BTN_HELP
        mbHelpStarted = True
        lHelpTopic = HELP_BASE + 10 * (1 + mnCurStep)
        rc = WinHelp(Me.hwnd, HELP_FILE, _
        HELP_CONTEXT, lHelpTopic)

    Case BTN_CANCEL
        Unload Me

    Case BTN_BACK
        'place special cases here to jump
        'to alternate steps
        nAltStep = mnCurStep - 1
        SetStep nAltStep, DIR_BACK

    Case BTN_NEXT
        'place special cases here to jump
        'to alternate steps
        nAltStep = mnCurStep + 1
        SetStep nAltStep, DIR_NEXT

    Case BTN_FINISH
        'wizard creation code goes here

        Unload Me

        If GetSetting(APP_CATEGORY, WIZARD_NAME, _
        CONFIRM_KEY, vbNullString) = vbNullString Then
            frmConfirm.Show vbModal
        End If

End Select
```

A Sample Wizard for the IDE

In this section we want to show you how easy it is to create a Wizard for the VB IDE. We called this Wizard "Project Maker" because it simply asks the user how many Forms, Code Modules, and Class Modules they want in their project. This Wizard took under an hour to create using the Wizard Template and the Wizard Manager. Although it a simple Wizard, it does show you how to interact with the IDE through the VB Extensibility model by adding the necessary code to the Finished case discussed above. Figure 16-21 shows you the Screens that ask for the number of forms.

For the interface of the Wizard all we needed to do was:

1. Add the textbox controls to the frame used for the interface for each step.

2. Place the appropriate captions in the resource (RC) file.

Then we have to write the only code that uses the Extensibility model to add the number of components to the Project of the type requested in the BTN_FINISH case. For example, we first create a New Project:

```
VBInst.VBProjects.Add vbext_pt_StandardExe, True
```

Figure 16-21 Forms screen from Project Maker Wizard

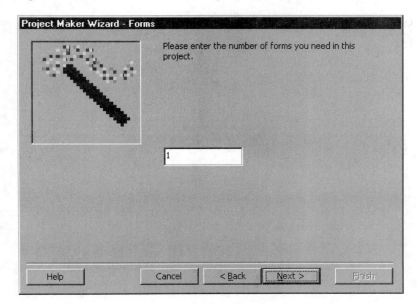

Then we use the input from the textboxes to:

- Add the number of forms requested.
- Add the number of modules requested.
- Add the number of class modules requested.

As you saw so often in the previous chapter, we put everything in a With statement to make the code shorter and clearer:

```
With VBInst.ActiveVBProject
```

Then, for example, since the text Box for the number of forms we want to add is called txtForms, the code looks like this:

```
For i = 1 To txtForms.Text
   .VBComponents.Add vbext_ct_VBForm
Next
```

where all we do is call the Add method using the vbext_ct_VBForm constant that you saw in the last chapter. Finally, we need to set the Start Mode of the project to StandAlone:

```
.StartMode = vbext_psm_StandAlone
```

and the code to set the start-up object to Form1

```
If txtForms.Text > 0 Then
   .VBComponents.StartUpObject = _
   .VBComponents("Form1")
End If
```

Here's the complete code for the BTN_FINISH case. (The CD contains the full source code and the resource file.)

Listing 16-1: Code for BTN_FINISH Case

```
Case BTN_FINISH
    'wizard creation code goes here
    VBInst.VBProjects.Add vbext_pt_StandardExe, True
    With VBInst.ActiveVBProject
      For i = 1 To txtForms.Text
        .VBComponents.Add vbext_ct_VBForm
      Next
      For i = 1 To txtModules.Text
        .VBComponents.Add vbext_ct_StdModule
      Next
```

```
For i = 1 To txtClasses.Text
   .VBComponents.Add vbext_ct_ClassModule
Next
.StartMode = vbext_psm_StandAlone
If txtForms.Text > 0 Then
   .VBComponents.StartUpObject = .VBComponents("Form1")
End If
End With
Unload Me
```

Of course, to make this into a truly useful "Project Wizard" you would need to add error checking to make sure the user enters valid amounts for the number of components of each type. In addition, you could add numerous features such as the ability to create an MDI Form, other project types, other component types, and the like.

Finally like all Add-Ins, you must register it and add the appropriate reference to the Add-Ins32.INI file. The Wizard.bas module contains the necessary code in its AddToIni function that you can call from the Immediate Window to do this.

Taking a Wizard Outside the VB IDE

Although the Wizard Template shipped with Visual Basic is designed to act as an IDE Wizard, with a couple of quick changes, you can create stand-alone Wizards that has nothing to do with the Visual Basic IDE. The example we want to go over may be found in the CH16\BenWiz directory. Figure 16-22 shows you the opening screen.

What we want the remaining screens of this stand-alone Wizard to do is prompt the user for the type of employee benefits they want. Then, when they are all done answering the questions on the various screens, it tallies their responses and *says it* will allow them to send the information they entered off to their human resources department. Obviously, our example does not contain the code to send the information because this would be specific to the company and department the Wizard was built for. Here are the steps needed to convert the Wizard Template to make stand-alone Visual Basic Wizard applications:

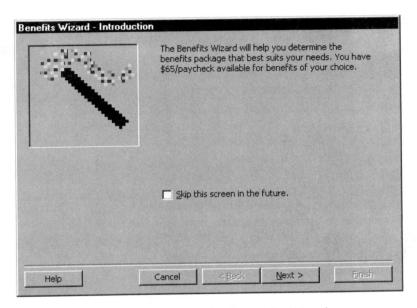

Figure 16-22 The Opening Screen for the Benefits Wizard

1. Load the Wizard Manager utility. (See above for a description of this tool.)

2. Answer "Yes" to the question of creating a new Wizard from the template.

3. After the framework for the new Wizard has been created, remove the "Wizard" class module.

4. Load the Project Properties dialog from the Project|WizardTemplate Properties menu.

5. Select Standard EXE from the Project Type drop-down list.

6. Select frmWizard from the Startup Object drop-down list.

7. Click OK.

You should see a message box saying that the start-up mode has been changed. (Which is, of course, True. We just changed the project type from an ActiveX DLL which cannot be stand-alone to a Standard EXE that must be stand-alone.)

Now:

*   Make the EXE.

That's it. You have just created a stand-alone Wizard with very little coding. Since it is no longer needed, you can remove the Wizard.cls class module from the project.

Tip

We have found this type of Wizardlike application to often be much easier for the beginning user to interact with. This is because the screens are relatively clean and there is plenty of room for explanation of each step. As opposed to a single form that is overly filled with controls that, for lack of space or for some other reason, are not as well described.

Launching Wizards

There are lots of ways to launch Wizards in VB's IDE. Along with the Add-In menu, you can launch Wizards via the:

- Add-In Toolbar

that we discussed in the last chapter. Next, you can have Wizards show up in the:

- Add/New dialog boxes like the New Project Dialog Box.

To get a Wizard to show up in this kind of dialog box requires putting a special file called a VBZ file into a subdirectory of VB's template directory (see Chapter 17 for more details on Templates). A VBZ file contains the information needed to launch a Wizard. For example, the Data Form Wizard can be launched from the Add Form dialog because a VBZ file called "VB Data Form Wizard.vbz" is in the Template\Forms directory. The "VB Data Form Wizard.vbz" file contains the following three lines:

```
VBWIZARD 5.0
Wizard= DataFormWizard.Wizard
Param="other information"
```

The first line identifies the file as an acceptable VBZ file. The second line contains the ProgID of the Wizard and the third line contains optional information (which is not used in this case). So if you want to launch your own Wizard (or any Add-In) this way, simply create a VBZ file with this format and place in the appropriate directory so users see it when they try to add a new component to their project. Next, as with regular Add-Ins, you can load a Wizard:

- In response to Add-In events.

This is similar to the model used for the Add-In toolbar but is less generic. If you have a set of Wizards that you want to pop up at a specific time, such as when user loads a new project or adds a control to a form, you can have a single small Add-In that looks to those events and loads the appropriate Wizard when the event fires. (See the section on Invisible Add-Ins in Chapter 15 for an explanation of how to write an Add-In that synchs events in order to perform certain actions when these events occur.)

Finally, there is the:

- Visual Component Manager.

The new Visual Component Manager has the ability to launch Wizards (or any Add-In) on demand, just like the toolbar. For more information on the Visual Component Manager, see Chapter 20.

TEMPLATES

Topics in this Chapter

- Basics of Templates
- Using Our Templates
- Using One of Our Templates
- Creating Your Own Template
- The Template Manager

Chapter 17

No programmer wants to be constantly reinventing the wheel. Regardless of what language he or she uses, every programmer that we know reuses code snippets and (tries to) reuse user interfaces. The object-oriented approach to programming became the most popular modern programming paradigm precisely because, at its heart, it is one of the most effective ways to reuse your code.

Visual Basic has always been based on reusing work whenever and wherever possible. Much of VB's success comes because controls are the most successful use of objects in the programming universe. On the other hand, to reuse part of a UI that you created in a form in earlier versions of VB meant you had to cut and paste the code from the .frm file. Visual Basic 5 removes this limitation with a new reusable object type called a Template—which is the topic of this chapter.

Note

Templates are also the most effective way for a programming shop to insure that all applications produced there have the same "look and feel."

Basics of Templates

Templates are simply files that the VB5 IDE can understand and reuse. VB ships with a number of templates that are both useful and an ideal way to get ideas for future templates. Microsoft's intent is that you will either create your own templates, obtain templates from vendors, or both. (Make www.microsoft.com\vbasic web site your first stop.) For example, when you choose to add a form and VB pops up the standard Add Form dialog box shown in Figure 17-1, it is actually reporting on all the form templates it knows about.

The default is that templates are stored in the directory called \Template that is off your main VB directory. As you can see in Figure 17-2, there are subdirectories called: Classes, Forms, MDIForms, Modules, Projects, PropPage, UserCtls, and UserDocs. The subdirectory names contain the templates of that type. For example, the Forms subdirectory looks like Figure 17-3 and each one of those files corresponds to a different item in the Add Form dialog box. Notice in Figure 17-3 that the template directories also contain .vbz files. These are pointers to Wizards that can be launched from the same Add dialog box to help create an object of that type. For example, the Data Form Wizard can be launched from the Add Form dialog because a VBZ file called "VB Data Form Wizard.vbz" is in the Template\Forms directory.

When you add a template to your current project, VB simply loads it into memory as if you has created it from scratch and prompts you to save it when you save the rest of the project.

Figure 17-1   The Add Form dialog box

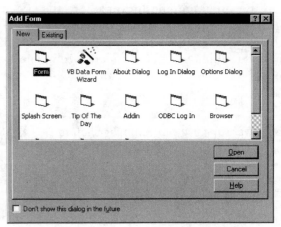

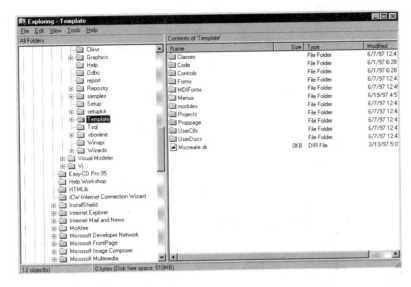

Figure 17-2 The Template directory tree

Figure 17-3   The Template\Forms directory.

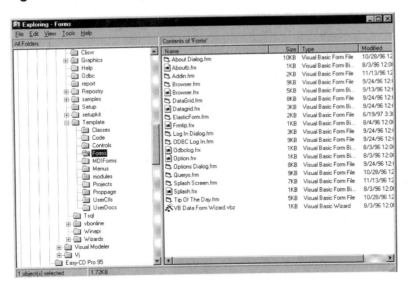

Caution

Make sure you do not use Add File from one of these template directories unless you want to change the base template. Otherwise, every time you save the object, VB will change the existing template.

Tip

You can also store templates on a network server so that many users can access and add to them. To point the VB IDE at a network server (or at any other location other than the default one) for your templates, load the Tools/Options dialog box and select the Environment tab. Enter the location you want for your templates in the Templates Directory text box.

Using Our Templates

The CD supplied with this book contains one "elastic" form template that has our generic resize code built into it. You can use these templates to make your forms start out as elastic. There is also one "elastic" user control form that you can use as a user control form container so that its constituent controls will automatically resize themselves. The CD supplied with this book also contains a set of five User Control templates based on the PictureBox, Label, TextBox, Command Button and ListBox controls. Using our control templates you can easily extend one of these standard five controls. We also added six control group projects that add the necessary EXE project for testing a control you develop from one of the six User Control Templates. Using our control group templates lets you not only extend one of these five controls but test them as well. (These templates let you enhance the most common controls without needing to do any of the kinds of preliminaries outlined in Chapter 13—you won't have to run the Control Interface Wizard because we did it for you.) Also, our templates not only have all the standard properties, methods, and events exposed, they include the extra code needed to allow the use of design time properties such as MultiLine for a TextBox at run time.

To use the templates on the CD, the easiest way is to copy the directories in our Template directory tree over to your Template directory for Visual

Basic. (This is the usually called \Program Files\DevStudio\VB\Template.) Doing this will copy the templates to the correct locations so that they are ready to use. (You can also copy individual files to the appropriate directory by hand.)

Note

Any project or project groups you save to one of the subdirectories of the Template become templates of that type. Form files saved in the Template\Forms directory become form templates, code files saved in the Template\Code directory become code templates, and so on.

We give you seven projects you can use as templates (one for the elastic form and one for each of the six controls). All you need to do to use one of them is load Visual Basic. As you can see in Figure 17-4, the New Project Dialog box automatically includes them. You can also add our elastic form or one of our control templates by choosing Project|Add Form or Project|Add User Control as shown in Figure 17-5 and Figure 17-6.

Figure 17-4 The New Project dialog box
with Templates

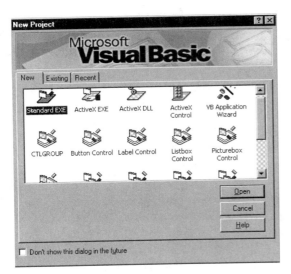

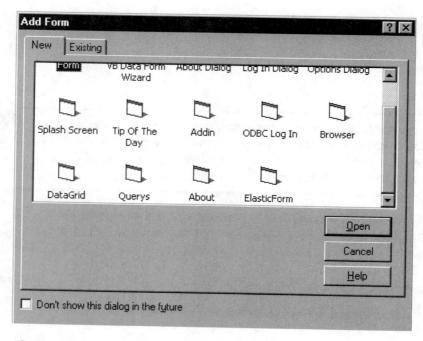

Figure 17-5   The Add Form dialog box with templates

Figure 17-6   The Add User Control dialog box with templates

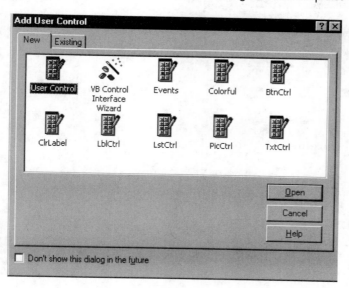

Using One of Our Templates

Let's suppose you want to further customize a label and test it as well. Choose Label Control from the New Project dialog box shown in Figure 17-4. (To further customize our label control, choose LblCtrl from the Add User Control dialog box shown in Figure 17-6.)

Caution

Always use the Add dialog box to work with a template. Never use the Project\Add File option to add a file from a template directory unless you want to change the template. If you choose Project\Add File then once you save the template it will replace the previous version of the template (and may not be as useful anymore).

A Step-by-Step Template Session

In this section we want to run through a step-by-step session with our elastic form template and also one of our user controls (assuming you have added the files to your \Template directory). Let's start with the elastic form. Here's what you have to do:

- Choose Project|Add Form.
- Choose the Elastic form.

That's it—you're done, just start adding controls to the form and they will automatically be resized at run time. (Not much to it, is there? You have to admit this is a whole lot easier than cutting and pasting the necessary resize code like you had to do with earlier versions of VB.)

Let's go through a sample session with one of our user control forms. It is a little bit more time consuming but the idea is still simple.

- Choose Project|New Project.
- Open the LabelControl User Control.

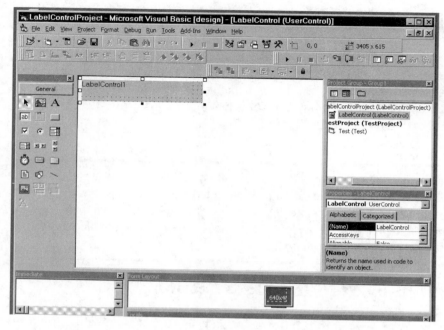

Figure 17-7   Our Label Control template in design mode

You should see a screen like Figure 17-7

We are now going to add some code to the base control so that it will cycle through colors at regular intervals. For this we need a Timer control, so add one from the toolbox by double clicking it. (Recall the Timer control is invisible at run time so you don't need to move it.) Set the Interval property of the Timer to 100 (1/10 of a second).

We now want to run the Control Interface Wizard to:

1. Expose the Timer Interval property.
2. Create a custom property called TimerEnabled.
3. Map the Interval property for the User Control to the Timer1 control's Interval property.
4. Map the custom TimerEnabled property to the Timer1 control's Enabled property.

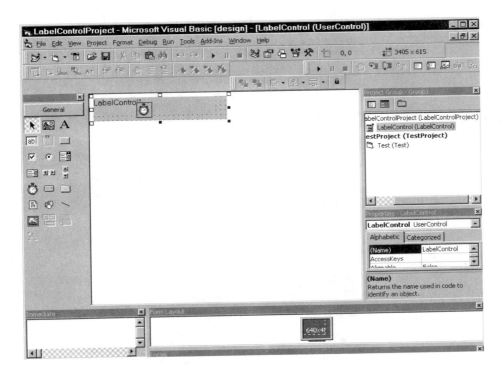

Figure 17-8 Timed Label in design stage

(If you need help with these steps, refer to Chapter 13.)
Add the following code to the User Control:

```
Private Sub Timer1_Timer()
  On Error Resume Next
  Static nColor As Integer
  If Not Ambient.UserMode Then Exit Sub    'don't execute in
                                           'design mode

  If nColor = 15 Then
    nColor = 0                             'start over again
  Else
    nColor = nColor + 1                    'increment it
  End If
  lblLabel.ForeColor = QBColor(nColor)     'set the forecolor
End Sub
```

(One could also use nColor = (nColor + 1) Mod 15 instead of the If-Then-Else.)

Now you are ready to test your new control but first you should save it to a new directory. This prevents you from changing the base template. Save the enhanced label to any directory you wish and name it something like ColorLbl. That way it will have no link to the original template. Notice we built this new control by simply adding a timer, a couple of properties, and some code to our template.

Next, since we used our Label Control project group to build this project we already have the form that we need to test the control. To do this:

1. Close the designer for your User Control.

2. Open up the Test form and add an instance of the user control to the form.

3. The exposed Interval property needs to be set (try 100 or 1/10 second). The TimerEnabled property has a default value of True so all you have to do to test this label is press F5. Visual Basic edition will run the project and you should see a label with the color of the caption changing rapidly.

Next, notice that our label has a Custom property so there is a property page available (as shown in Figure 17-9). This makes it easy to experiment with other settings, such as different font sizes and back ground colors.

Figure 17-9   The Property Page for our Label control

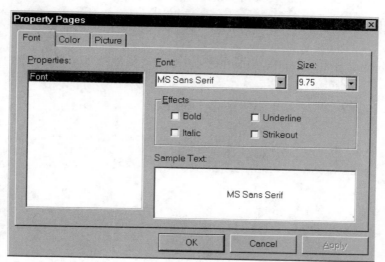

Creating Your Own Templates

It is easy to create your own templates. Simply save an object you wish to make a template out of into the appropriate subdirectory. For example, you might have a copyright splash screen that you like to put in all of your applications. To make a form template out of it:

- Load Visual Basic.
- Load a Standard EXE project.
- Rename Form1 to frmCopyright.
- Add a command button with a caption of OK, and a picture box with the name pctLogo.

Now set the following properties of the form:

Property	Value
BorderStyle	3—Fixed Dialog
Caption	"Welcome"
MaxButton	False
MinButton	False
ControlBox	False
StartUpPosition	2—CenterScreen

Add code in the command button's click event to unload the form:

```
Private Sub cmdOK_Click()
   Unload Me
End Sub
```

Add the Code to the Form_Paint event for the copyright:

```
Sub Form_Paint()
   'code to set the logo
   'code for the copyright notice
End Sub
```

(You can also add code in the Form_Resize event if you want to make the form always be a certain size relative to the actual screen size. Next you should add a comment section to the code, such as:

```
'This is a generic copyright screen. Either make this the
'Startup form or load it first from the Sub Main
```

Now:

1. Give the form a descriptive name so that it will be easily identified next time you start a new project and want to add this screen.

2. Use File|Save As to save the form into the Template\Forms directory with the name you chose.

Tip

Templates work best if they are written as stand-alone objects that do not depend upon other forms, classes or modules in order to function. The code in them should be as generic as possible. If they do require another object in order to do their work, make sure that you make this clear in the comments at the begining of the code. A good example of this is the Querys form template. Using this form template requires adding a couple of global variables and the DataGrid form in order to work. This is stated clearly in the comments at the top of the Querys form code module.

The Template Manager

There are three other types of objects that come in template form but they are not meant to operate on their own. They are Menus, Code Snippets, and Control Sets. These template types are handled by an Add-In called the Template Manager that is included in the Tools\Unsupprt\Tmplmgr directory. It is a little tricky to install it, here's what you have to do:

1. Copy the Template Manager Add-In from the Tools\Unsupprt\Tmplmgr by copying the file named TEMPMGR.DLL from the \Tools\Unsupprt\TmplMgr directory to the directory where VB is located on your drive.

2. Register the TempMGR.DLL Add-In by opening up the Run dialog box in Windows 95 and entering:

    ```
    regsvr32 tempmgr.dll
    ```

(You must have RegSvr32.exe on some other directory in your path. You can find it in the \Tools\RegUtils directory on your VB CD.) When RegSvr finishes you'll see a message box like Figure 17-10.)

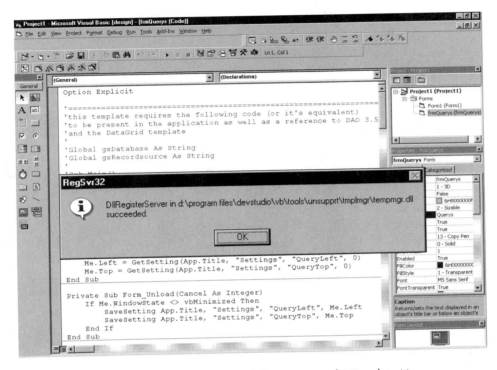

Figure 17-10 Message box after successfully registering the Template Manager

3 Update the VBADDIN.INI file that can be found in your \WINDOWS directory. (As you saw in Chapter 15, this file lists all the VB Add-Ins registered on your computer and it tells Visual Basic which Add-Ins to load on start-up.) You need to add the following line to your VBADDIN.INI file:

```
TempMgr.Connect=0
```

4. Create the new Template directories.

(We suggest copying the Template directory from \Tools\Unsupprt\ TmplMgr to the VB \Template directory.)

Once the Template Manager is installed, you will be able to more easily reuse:

- Code,
- Menus for your forms, and
- Control Sets.

(And, of course, like all other template types, you can create your own menu, control set, and code snippet templates to add to the ones that come with VB. This turns out to not only be a very powerful way to reuse code but also a very convenient way.

Using the Template Manager

You can access the Template Manager from three different menu items on the Tools menu of the IDE as shown in Figure 17-11. They are:

- Add Code Snippet.
- Add Menu.
- Add Control Set.

Figure 17-11   The Tools Menu with the Template Manager active

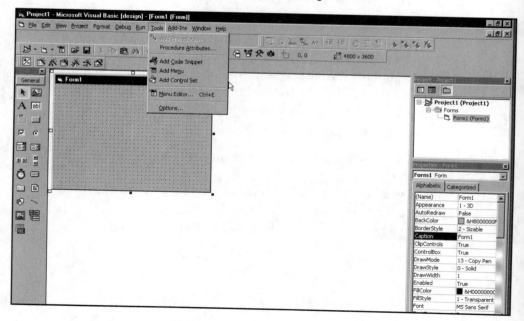

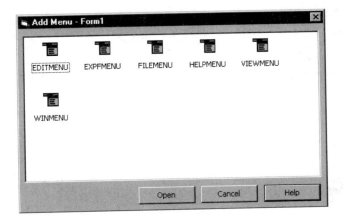

Figure 17-12   The Add Menu dialog box

The idea is that when you choose one of these items, VB displays a dialog box similar to the ones you have seen for things like adding a form. For example, Figure 17-12 shows you the Add Code Snippet box for the menus supplied with the Template Manager.

Now, if you click on the FILEMENU item in Figure 17-12, VB will automatically add the usual File menu to the form you are currently working with as shown in Figure 17-13.

You can actually store multiple menus in a single menu template. This makes it easy to create sets of menus for different types of forms as well as adding a Tools menu or modifying one of the existing menu templates. To create your own menu template:

- Simply create a form with the menu(s) and code that you want to as your template.
- Save it to the Template\Menus directory (with a descriptive name so that it will be easily understood from the template manager dialog box).

Using Code Snippets

Think of these as little code libraries for handling certain tasks such as data conversion, file I/O, or parsing routines. Visual Basic will add the code snippet wherever the cursor is currently located in the code window. This way you can easily add code snippets to form, code, or class modules.

To create a code snippet template:

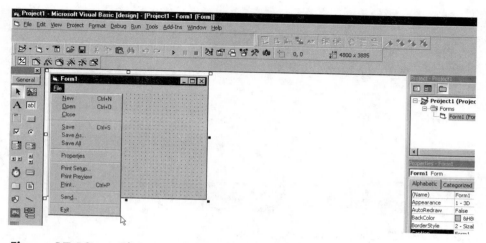

Figure 17-13   A File Menu added by the Template Manager

1. Add a code module to a project.
2. Copy the procedure(s) you want to have in the snippet to this code module.
3. Save it with a descriptive name to the \Template\Code directory.

(VB only ships with one code snippet—for working with resource files, as described in Chapter 6).

Using Control Sets

Control Set templates are a little different then menu or code snippet templates as they are essentially a special kind of ActiveX Control. Instead of creating an OCX file that cannot be changed, a Control Set Template allows you to reuse the code as a starting point for another ActiveX control. You can simply tweak the functionality of controls along with code that may need to be tweaked slightly based on how you want to use them on a given form. Control set templates save you time but still allow you to modify them as needed for new situations. The difference between adding a control set and adding an ActiveX control to your project is that when you add an existing ActiveX Control, you can only do what the writer of the control decided to allow (unless he or she gave you the source).

The Template Manager ships with a list picker control set and a Treeview/Listview with splitter control set. Both of these are good examples of controls and form a great starting point for extensions. The feature set they provide, however, would be tough to encapsulate into a full-featured ActiveX Control. To create your own control set template:

1. Create a user control form with the controls and code that make up the control set.
2. Save it to the Template\Controls directory.

Some possibilities for control set templates might be:

- toolbars,
- button sets, and
- status bars.

Note

Some versions of VB have a bug in the Template Manager that prevents Control Sets from working in the MDI environment. If you get an error message when you use a Control Set that says Invalid file format, you should go to the Microsoft web site to get an update.

VISUAL BASIC AND THE INTERNET

Topics in this Chapter

- ActiveX Documents
- The Visual Basic Internet Controls

Chapter 18

iven the importance of both the Internet and corporate intranets, it should come as no surprise that Visual Basic has a fair amount of power in this arena. Obviously, once the Visual Basic virtual machine is on a user's machine, any ActiveX controls that you create with VB can be used in Internet Explorer (Version 3 or later) running on Windows 95 or NT. (Using the NCompass lab plug-in you can also use ActiveX controls on Netscape Navigator 3 or Communicator.)

This chapter, however, concentrates on using VB5 to interact with Internet in a much more direct fashion. First, we cover ActiveX documents, which are a way of hosting Visual Basic forms in Internet Explorer. ActiveX documents are potentially even more exciting than ActiveX controls since this technology allows Internet Explorer Versions 3 or later to act as a container for a Visual Basic form. The menus in an ActiveX document will even take over IE's menus. Although, as you will see shortly, there are some limitations on the forms that can be embedded in Internet Explorer, most forms will translate with little if any change. ActiveX documents provide a great way to get the functionality you build into your VB projects (such as Wizards) onto an intranet. (Security might prevent many users from working with them over the Internet but for an intranet they are ideal.)

Then, we give a brief introduction to three amazingly powerful controls that are supplied with most versions of Visual Basic. As you will soon see, combining two of these controls allows you to build a special purpose browser with relatively little code. Our special purpose browser lets you restrict the sites you want someone to be able to visit. It even lets you specify certain words or phrases so that our browser will simply not display any page containing them. The third control lets you get at the lowest level of traffic, the ports to which data is posted to or sent from.

ActiveX Documents

ActiveX documents are a return to the roots of ActiveX technologies: object linking and embedding (OLE). One of the cornerstones of OLE was the ability to embed a document in an application. (You can still do this using the OLE container control in VB, for example.) The idea, of course, is that you could embed an Excel spreadsheet in a Word document and then Excel would temporarily take over Word's menus whenever you activated the embedded object. ActiveX documents depend on the same principle although the container is usually Internet Explorer. (The Office 97 Binder can also serve as a host for ActiveX documents.)

ActiveX documents can be built from scratch by choosing ActiveX Document from the New Project dialog box. ActiveX documents can be created either as an ActiveX EXE or ActiveX DLL project. In either case, just as ActiveX controls are based on a User Control form, ActiveX documents are based on a User Document form (see Figure 18-1).

Tip

The ActiveX Document Migration Wizard, available on the Add-Ins menu, gives you a quick and easy way to get an existing form converted to an ActiveX document however, it is limited in what it can convert as some form properties and code is not supported in an ActiveX document as it is in a standard form. The Wizard flags this code with comments so that you know you may have some work to do in order to get the ActiveX document operating the same way it did when it was a VB form.

You work with a User Document form in much the same way as you would work with an ordinary form or a user control form. Of course, since ActiveX documents are hosted in a container application, there are both differences

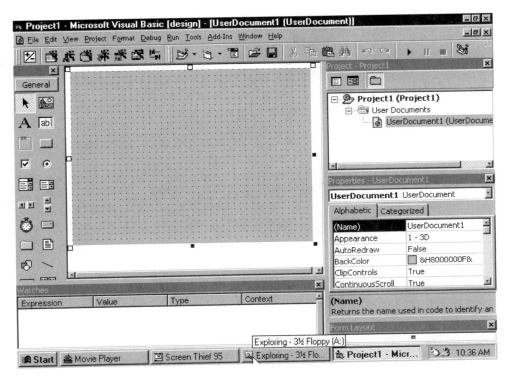

Figure 18-1 Active document is the VB IDE

and limitations. The main limitations on what you can control concern the look of the form. To a great extent, the container application controls this so it should come as no surprise that the following properties are not available at all:

- Left, Top, WindowState, and BorderStyle.

And the Width and Height properties become read-only. Here's the complete list of form properties that are not supported in ActiveX documents:

- BorderStyle, Caption, ControlBox, Enabled, Height, HelpContextID, Hide, Icon, Left, Move, Moveable, LinkMode, LinkTopic, MaxButton, MDIChild, MinButton, NegotiateMenus, NegotiatePosition, OLEDropMode, Show, ShowInTaskbar, StartUpPosition, Top, Visible, WhatsThisButton, WhatsThisHelp, Width, and WindowState.

In addition, the End statement is not allowed in an ActiveX doc. This is because the life of the ActiveX document has to be determined by its container. Finally any occurrence of "Form_" needs to be changed to "UserDocument_". For example:

```
Form_Load
```

becomes:

```
UserDocument_Load
```

ActiveX Document Migration Wizard

Here's a step-by-step example of how to use this tool to convert an existing form-based project to an ActiveX document:

1. Load a project with at least one form in it. (We will use one of the samples supplied with VB: Samples\CompTool\PicClip\Redtop.)
2. Load the ActiveX Document Migration Wizard from the Add-Ins menu or the Add-Ins toolbar.
3. Click Next to go to the Form Selection step (Figure 18-2).

Figure 18-2   Initial screen in the ActiveX Document Migration Wizard

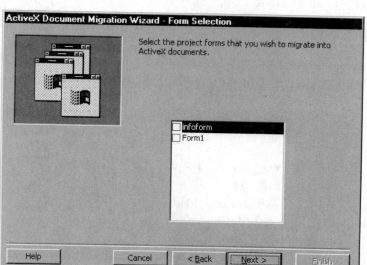

4. Check "Form1" if you used the Redtop sample (or select a form in your application).

5. Click Next.

6. Check the "Comment out invalid code" check box. Note that you have the option of making an EXE or a DLL on this page (Figure 18-3).

7. Click Next.

8. Click Finish.

You'll see a warning box if the Wizard found code that can't be used in an ActiveX document (see Figure 18-4). Now close the Confirmation and Summary dialog boxes.

Figure 18-3   Option screen in the ActiveX Document Migration Wizard

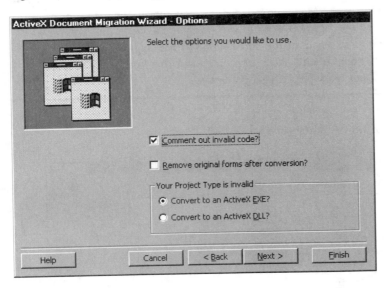

Figure 18-4   Warning message box in the ActiveX Document Migration Wizard

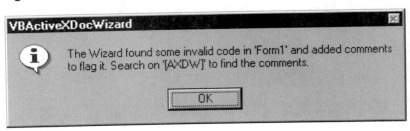

You can now see the ActiveX document hosted in Internet Explorer. To do this:

1. Run the project.
2. Load Internet Explorer 3.0 (or greater).
3. Choose File|Open and load the docForm1.VBD file from the directory you were working with. (You can also load Windows Explorer and drag this file to Internet Explorer.)

You should see the same form in the Internet Explorer as you saw when you ran the application in the Visual Basic IDE: The top spins just as it did before (See Figure 18-5).

Caution

The ActiveX Document Migration Wizard lets you convert as many forms from a specific project as you want to. However, applications that can have more than one form visible at the same time will not migrate well. This is because the mechanism that loads and unloads forms in a Visual Basic application will not work for ActiveX documents.

Figure 18-5   An ActiveX document at work

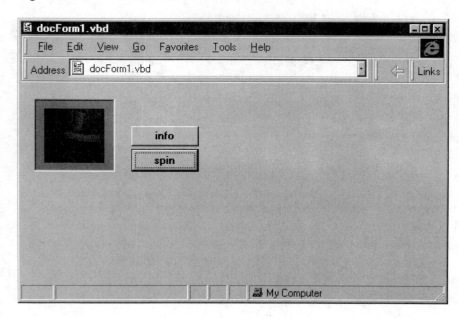

Moving from One Form to Another in an ActiveX Document

Each of the forms in your application becomes a separate document in Internet Explorer. In order to move from one of them to another, you must navigate between them just like you would navigate from one Web page to another. You can do this using your favorite scripting language or VB itself. Here are the steps and code needed to move from one document to another and back again:

1. Get the path of the current document.

    ```
    Dim i As Integer
    Dim sPath As String

    sPath = Trim$(UserDocument.Parent.LocationName)

    'strip off the name of the current document file
    For i = Len(sPath) To 1 Step -1
      If Mid$(sPath, i, 1) = "\" Then
        Exit For
      End If
    Next
    sPath = Left$(sPath, i)
    ```

2. Save any data that is needed by the second document (using global variables—see below).

3. Navigate to the second document via code like:

    ```
    UserDocument.Hyperlink.NavigateTo sPath & "NextDoc.vbd"
    ```

    To navigate back to the one document to the previous one you can use:

    ```
    UserDocument.Hyperlink.GoBack
    ```

Note

This code assumed that all of the VBD files are in the same path.

This seems pretty straightforward, but we should warn you that:

- Depending on the number of forms you are working with, the way they are interrelated, and the various branches and the amount of data that you will need to store in global variables, the needed code gets very complicated very fast.

Tip

Consider using a single form with "virtual" pages on it just as VB Wizards do (See Chapter 16). For example, use a control array of frames or picture boxes and navigate from one to the other by simply moving the current one off the screen and the next one on. The main problem with this design is that it can be tough to maintain. However, the Wizard Manager (also explained in Chapter 16) can help with the maintenance process. Another idea is to design a single form application but use either the Tab Strip or Tabbed Dialog control to yield "virtual" pages. With these controls, navigating from one screen to another is easier, but you are more restricted in the size of the screens you can display. Of course, neither method works well if you have forms that vary a lot in size.

Finally, if you need to communicate information from one form to another in a user document, you *must* place the data in global variables. Since the variables are now global you have to be careful: Any form can read and write to them. When you run or build an application with User Documents in it, Visual Basic creates VBD files in the working directory. As in the example above, this VBD file is the file that gets loaded into Internet Explorer. Visual Basic creates one VBD file for every User Document.

The Visual Basic Internet Controls

Visual Basic comes with three very powerful controls that are Internet enabled, although you may have to install Internet Explorer Version 3 or later to get the Web Browser control:

- The Internet Transfer Control
- The Web Browser Control
- The Winsock Control

We will give short explanations of these controls in the next few sections. Before we can do that we need to remind you that the Internet consists of data sent from one network of computers to another. (It's a network of networks.) Every location on the Internet has a *URL* (uniform resource locator) such as www.microsoft.com, although the actual address consists of four groups of numbers. Domain name servers do the translation between ordinary URLs and things like: 127.0.0.1

Information is sent over the Internet using a protocol called TCP/IP (transmission control protocol/internet protocol). This protocol gives a way to break down a larger amount of data into individual *packets* which can then be reassembled correctly at the target location. (When you use the TCP/IP protocol on a single network you have what people are now calling an *intranet*.) Information is sent or received on what are called *ports*. Certain conventions have sprung up so that certain ports are always used for specific tasks. For example, mail is usually sent through port 25 (SMTP) or 110 (Pop3). The HTML files used for Web documents are sent through port 80. Ports are not physical objects, there is probably only one physical port (such as the communication port or an Ethernet card) on your machine. (A program called socket services lets multiple requests use the same port—this is how Web servers are possible.)

Note

We will assume in what follows that you have a live Internet connection using either a direct connection or Windows "Dial Up Networking."

The Winsock Control

The Microsoft Winsock control (mswinsck.ocx) gives you access to the lowest level of TCP/IP, individual ports, and most VB programmers won't need to be concerned with this level of control, but here is a short introduction for those who may need this information.

First, it is an invisible control. Its properties and methods let you communicate with a specific port on a specific machine. (It can even handle an older, less reliable protocol called UDP.) To use the Winsock control on the client machine you must know:

- The server computer's name or IP address (RemoteHost property).
- The port (RemotePort property) that you want to send or receive information from. (The server must also be "listening.")
- Then, you simply call the Connect method of the WinSock control.

If you are writing code for a server, you must:

- Set the port (LocalPort property) on which the server should listen.
- Call the Listen method. The server will then run in the background waiting for a request received on the port you designated.

When the client computer actually makes a request to connect at the port you designated, the WinSock control will trigger its ConnectionRequest event. The final step is to actually accept the connection. This is done using the Accept method within the ConnectionRequest event procedure.

Once the server has established the connection by calling the Accept method *either* computer can send or receive data. To send data, use the SendData method. Obviously you need to be notified when data arrives at the designated port. When this happens the WinSock control triggers the DataArrival event. You then use the GetData method in DataArrival event procedure to accept whatever data the client sent.

The Internet Transfer Control

This control (MSINET.ocx) works at a higher level than the WinSock control. It is easy to use but can handle only two protocols.

- FTP (file transfer protocol)—used for sending files across the Net

- HTTP (hypertext transfer protocol)—used for sending hypertext files across the Net.

One way of using this control is trivial:

- Use the OpenURL method with a valid URL to get information.

For example:

```
Text1.Text = Inet1.OpenURL("http://www.microsoft.com")
```

stores the raw HTML text of the information available at www.microsoft.com (see Figure 18-6). What we do for our special purpose browser is use the Instr method to check this string before we display it with the Web Browser control.

Figure 18-6   Raw HTML

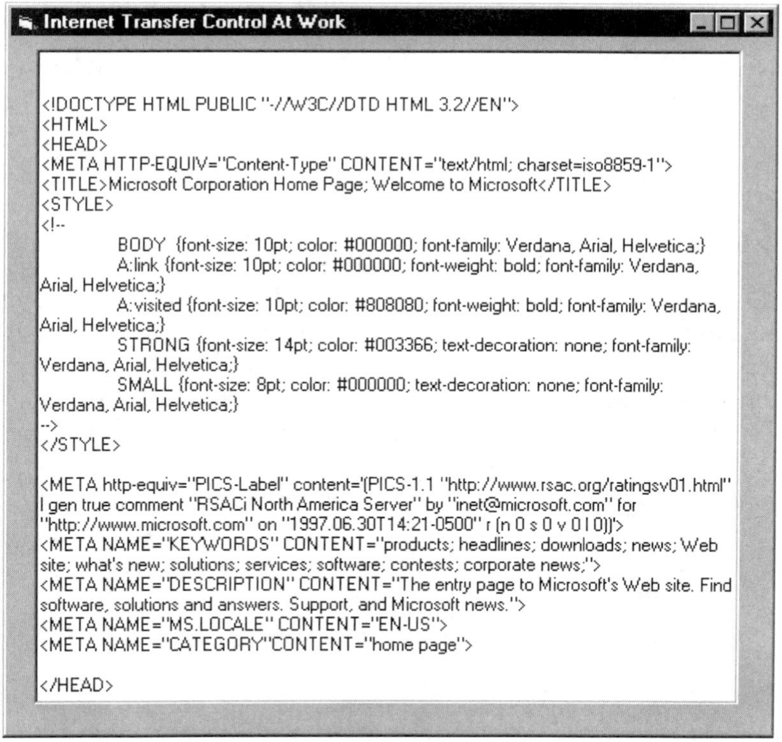

If you give the URL a file name, then the Internet Transfer control will actually grab the file:

```
FileData$ = _
Inet1.OpenURL("ftp://ftp.microsoft.com/disclaimer.txt")
```

Now, of course, you can use the usual file handling techniques (Chapter 6) to save the information.

Tip

The OpenURL method uses a synchronous method to get its data. This means that the data transfer must be completed before any other code can be executed. If you want to allow other activities to go on you need to use the Execute method, which allows asynchronous transmission. If you use the Execute method, you need to monitor what is happening in the StateChanged event procedure. Finally, the Execute method allows you to use the GET, HEAD, POST, and PUT commands which are needed for CGI.

This is obviously only a short introduction to what this very powerful control can do. We need to refer you to the on-line help or Microsoft Knowledge Base for more information. (This is especially true about the Execute method which can be tricky to use depending on the server with which you are working.)

The Web Browser Control

The Web Browser control is actually stored in the form of a DLL. (SHDOCVW.DLL—it is listed as "Microsoft Internet Controls" in Project| Components dialog box.) You can think of Internet Explorer as simply being an automation wrapper around this control! When you place a Web Browser control on a form it is hidden when by default. Visual Basic reveals it either because you have set its Visible property to True or because you called the Navigate (or GoSearch) methods. The simplest way of using this control is to call the Navigate method with a valid URL. For example if:

1. You stick a Web Browser control on a form.
2. Put the following line in the Form_Load:

```
WebBrowser1.Navigate(www.microsoft.com)
```

You'll see Microsoft's Web page properly formatted in the control. You can browse a location on a local disk by giving the full path of the file.

Here's the general syntax for the Navigate method:

```
WebBrowserControlName.Navigate URL [Flags,] _
[TargetFrameName,] [PostData,] [Headers]
```

Following are short description of these options.

URL

A string expression whose value is the URL address of the location you want to display or the full file name for a local file.

Flags

This optional parameter controls whether you want to keep the location cached or stored in the history list (or both). You can also use a special flag to pop up a new browser window for the URL being specified. The possible flags are given in the following table, and you can Or them together to set multiple flags:

Table 18-1: Flags	
Symbolic Constant	**Meaning**
NavOpenInNewWindow	Open the URL or file in a new window.
NavNoHistory	Don't add the location to the history list kept by the control. (The new page replaces the current page in the list.)
NavNoReadFromCache	Don't check if there is a cached copy.
NavNoWriteToCache	Don't write the HTML page to the local cache.

TargetFrameName

This optional parameter allows you display the HTML page in a new frame.

PostData

This optional parameter is used to work with HTML forms and CGI. (For those familiar with HTML forms, if you leave this parameter off, the Navigate method uses the HTML GET method, turn this parameter on and it uses the POST method.) This parameter is ignored when the location you are navigating to is not a Web page.

Headers

This optional parameter allows you to send additional information to the HTML server that contains the page you are trying to download.

Important Properties and Methods of the Web Browser Control

The following table describes the most important methods and properties of the Web Browser control.

Tip

The Help file for the Web Browser control may be found in the Tools\Unsupprt\WebBrwsr directory of your VB CD.

Table 18-2:   Web Browser Control Methods and Properties

Member	*Description*
LocationURL	The current location.
GoBack	Return to the previous page in the cached list.
GoForward	To the next page in the cached list.
Refresh	Reloads the page.

The Most Important Web Browser Events

As you would expect for a VB control, the Web Browser control triggers various events at crucial times. For example, right before the Web Browser moves to a new location it triggers the BeforeNavigate event, whose syntax looks like this:

```
Private Sub WebBrowserName_BeforeNavigate(ByVal URL As _
String, ByVal Flags As Long, ByVal TargetFrameName As _
String, PostData As Variant, ByVal Headers As String, _
Cancel As Boolean)
```

The parameters are described in the following table:

Table 18-3: Web Browser Event Parameters	

Parameter	*Meaning*
URL	The string expression whose value is the URL.
Flags	Not currently used
TargetFrameName	Used if you are going to display the information in a HTML frame.
PostData	Used for posting data to the Web server
Headers	These are various headers you can use in advanced HTML programming to send information to the server about you or what you want done.
Cancel	A True/False option. Use True to stop the operation, False to allow it to proceed.

The ProgressChange event lets you monitor what is happening as the downloading continues. Its syntax is:

```
Private Sub WebBrsowerControl_ProgressChange(ByVal _
Progress As Long, ByVal ProgressMax As Long)
```

Finally, the last event that we want to mention here is the deceptively named DownloadComplete event. This event is triggered when the download is "completed" but this doesn't mean the download was finished nor that it was successful. For example, it is triggered when you halt the download or it *fails*. In fact, this event is always triggered *after* the control starts to go to a URL. (This is different than what happens with the NavigateComplete event, which is triggered only when the browser successfully navigates to a URL.)

Example: A Special Purpose Browser

We built the framework for this browser using the Application Wizard. The idea of this example is that we allow you to:

- set up a list of sites you don't want people to be able to visit or
- (using the Internet Transfer Control) specify words that can't appear on the page.

To make the code simpler we use two rich text boxes: one to store the list of bad sites and one for the bad words. The information is stored in lines that are separated from each other by carriage return line feed combinations. (You can add to the list of the forbidden items simply by clicking on the S or W buttons.) The result, as shown in Figure 18-7 (using the SDI option for VB), is something that pretty much resembles a usual browser. The second form simply holds the rich text boxes.

For example, here's the code to check the text that might be displayed on a Web page. This returns a Boolean that we can use to decide whether to display that site or not in a routine we call GetPage.

```
Private Function SiteHasBadText(sText As String) As Boolean
   Dim sTmp As String
   Dim sWordTmp As String
   Dim nPos As Integer

   sText = UCase(sText)
   sTmp = UCase(rtfBadWords.Text)
```

Figure 18-7   Our Web browser at design time

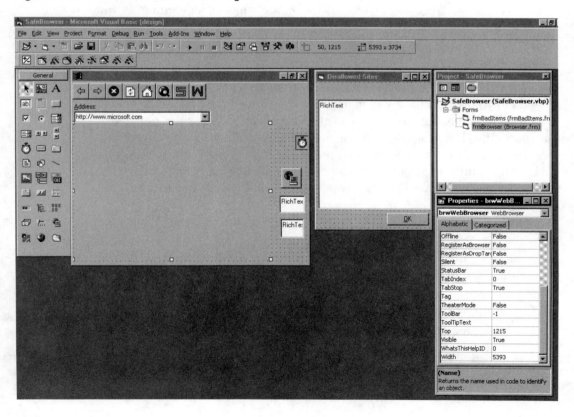

```
    'get the first item
    nPos = InStr(sTmp, vbCrLf)
    Do While nPos > 0
       sWordTmp = Left$(sTmp, nPos - 1)
       If Len(sWordTmp) = 0 Then GoTo SkipIt
       If InStr(sText, sWordTmp) > 0 Then
          MsgBox "'" & sWordTmp & "' is a disallowed word!", _
vbInformation
          SiteHasBadText = True
          Exit Function
       End If
       'knock off the one we just processed
SkipIt:
       sTmp = Mid$(sTmp, nPos + 2)
       nPos = InStr(sTmp, vbCrLf)
    Loop

End Function
```

Here's the GetPage routine. As you can see, it checks if the site is allowed. If the site is not on the forbidden list, we open it using the Internet Transfer control so that we can check the text inside before displaying it.

```
Private Sub GetPage()
    On Error GoTo GetPageErr

    Dim sTmp As String
    Dim sTok As String
    Dim sSite As String

    sSite = cboAddress.Text

    'check for invalid site
    If SiteIsInvalid(sSite) Then
       MsgBox "'" & sSite & "' is a disallowed site!", _
vbInformation
       Exit Sub
    End If

    MousePointer = vbHourglass
    sTmp = CStr(Inet1.OpenURL(cboAddress.Text))
    MousePointer = vbDefault
    'look for bad text
    If SiteHasBadText(sTmp) Then
       Exit Sub
    End If
```

```
'try to navigate to the starting address
timTimer.Enabled = True
brwWebBrowser.Navigate cboAddress.Text

Exit Sub

GetPageErr:
  MousePointer = vbDefault
  MsgBox Err.Description
End Sub
```

Notice that if the site passes all the tests, we display the page in the Web Browser control using the line:

```
brwWebBrowser.Navigate cboAddress.Text
```

The Full Code for the Web Browser Application

Here are the .frm files for the two forms we used in this application:

Listing 18-1:   frmBrowser Code

```
VERSION 5.00
Object = "{6B7E6392-850A-101B-AFC0-4210102A8DA7}#1.1#0"; "COMCTL32.OCX"
Object = "{EAB22AC0-30C1-11CF-A7EB-0000C05BAE0B}#1.0#0"; "SHDOCVW.DLL"
Object = "{48E59290-9880-11CF-9754-00AA00C00908}#1.0#0"; "MSINET.OCX"
Object = "{3B7C8863-D78F-101B-B9B5-04021C009402}#1.1#0"; "RICHTX32.OCX"
Begin VB.Form frmBrowser
    ClientHeight    =    5130
    ClientLeft      =    4065
    ClientTop       =    2310
    ClientWidth     =    6540
    Icon            =     "Browser.frx":0000
    LinkTopic       =     "Form1"
    LockControls    =    -1   'True
    ScaleHeight     =    5130
    ScaleWidth      =    6540
    ShowInTaskbar   =    0    'False
    Begin ComctlLib.Toolbar tbToolBar
        Align           =    1    'Align Top
        Height          =    540
        Left            =    0
```

```
TabIndex            =    3
Top                 =    0
Width               =    6540
_ExtentX            =    11536
_ExtentY            =    953
ButtonWidth         =    820
ButtonHeight        =    794
Appearance          =    1
ImageList           =    "imlIcons"
_Version            =    327680
BeginProperty Buttons {0713E452-850A-101B-AFC0-4210102A8DA7}
   NumButtons       =    8
   BeginProperty Button1 {0713F354-850A-101B-AFC0-4210102A8DA7}
      Key                    =    "Back"
      Object.ToolTipText     =    "Back"
      Object.Tag             =    ""
      ImageIndex             =    1
   EndProperty
   BeginProperty Button2 {0713F354-850A-101B-AFC0-4210102A8DA7}
      Key                    =    "Forward"
      Object.ToolTipText     =    "Forward"
      Object.Tag             =    ""
      ImageIndex             =    2
   EndProperty
   BeginProperty Button3 {0713F354-850A-101B-AFC0-4210102A8DA7}
      Key                    =    "Stop"
      Object.ToolTipText     =    "Stop"
      Object.Tag             =    ""
      ImageIndex             =    3
   EndProperty
   BeginProperty Button4 {0713F354-850A-101B-AFC0-4210102A8DA7}
      Key                    =    "Refresh"
      Object.ToolTipText     =    "Refresh"
      Object.Tag             =    ""
      ImageIndex             =    4
   EndProperty
   BeginProperty Button5 {0713F354-850A-101B-AFC0-4210102A8DA7}
      Key                    =    "Home"
      Object.ToolTipText     =    "Home"
      Object.Tag             =    ""
      ImageIndex             =    5
   EndProperty
   BeginProperty Button6 {0713F354-850A-101B-AFC0-4210102A8DA7}
      Key                    =    "Search"
      Object.ToolTipText     =    "Search"
```

```
         Object.Tag                =      ""
         ImageIndex        =    6
      EndProperty
      BeginProperty Button7 {0713F354-850A-101B-AFC0-4210102A8DA7}
         Key               =     "Sites"
         Object.ToolTipText       =     "List Locked Out Sites"
         Object.Tag                =      ""
         ImageIndex        =    7
      EndProperty
      BeginProperty Button8 {0713F354-850A-101B-AFC0-4210102A8DA7}
         Key               =     "Words"
         Object.ToolTipText       =     "List Disallowed Words"
         Object.Tag                =      ""
         ImageIndex        =    8
      EndProperty
   EndProperty
End
Begin SHDocVwCtl.WebBrowser brwWebBrowser
   Height            =    3734
   Left              =    50
   TabIndex          =    0
   Top               =    1215
   Width             =    5393
   Object.Height            =    249
   Object.Width             =    360
   AutoSize          =    0
   ViewMode          =    1
   AutoSizePercentage=    0
   AutoArrange       =    -1    'True
   NoClientEdge      =    -1    'True
   AlignLeft         =    0     'False
End
Begin RichTextLib.RichTextBox rtfBadWords
   Height            =    555
   Left              =    5760
   TabIndex          =    6
   Top               =    3855
   Visible           =    0     'False
   Width             =    675
   _ExtentX          =    1191
   _ExtentY          =    979
   _Version          =    327680
   Enabled           =    -1    'True
   TextRTF           =    $"Browser.frx":000C
End
```

```
Begin RichTextLib.RichTextBox rtfBadSites
    Height          =       525
    Left            =       5730
    TabIndex        =       5
    Top             =       3195
    Visible         =       0       'False
    Width           =       735
    _ExtentX        =       1296
    _ExtentY        =       926
    _Version        =       327680
    Enabled         =       -1      'True
    TextRTF         =       $"Browser.frx":00DD
End
Begin InetCtlsObjects.Inet Inet1
    Left            =       5790
    Top             =       2430
    _ExtentX        =       1005
    _ExtentY        =       1005
    Protocol        =       4
    RemoteHost      =       "www.microsoft.com"
    URL             =       "http://www.microsoft.com"
End
Begin VB.Timer timTimer
    Enabled         =       0       'False
    Interval        =       5
    Left            =       6180
    Top             =       1500
End
Begin VB.PictureBox picAddress
    Align           =       1       'Align Top
    BorderStyle     =       0       'None
    Height          =       675
    Left            =       0
    ScaleHeight     =       675
    ScaleWidth      =       6540
    TabIndex        =       4
    TabStop         =       0       'False
    Top             =       540
    Width           =       6540
    Begin VB.ComboBox cboAddress
        Height          =       315
        Left            =       45
        TabIndex        =       2
        Text            =       "http://www.microsoft.com"
        Top             =       300
```

```
        Width              =     3795
     End
     Begin VB.Label lblAddress
        Caption            =     "&Address:"
        Height             =     255
        Left               =     45
        TabIndex           =     1
        Tag                =     "&Address:"
        Top                =     60
        Width              =     3075
     End
  End
  Begin ComctlLib.ImageList imlIcons
     Left                =     2670
     Top                 =     2325
     _ExtentX            =     1005
     _ExtentY            =     1005
     BackColor           =     -2147483643
     ImageWidth          =     24
     ImageHeight         =     24
     MaskColor           =     12632256
     _Version            =     327680
     BeginProperty Images {0713E8C2-850A-101B-AFC0-4210102A8DA7}
        NumListImages    =     8
        BeginProperty ListImage1 {0713E8C3-850A-101B-AFC0-4210102A8DA7}
           Picture            =     "Browser.frx":01AE
           Key                =     ""
        EndProperty
        BeginProperty ListImage2 {0713E8C3-850A-101B-AFC0-4210102A8DA7}
           Picture            =     "Browser.frx":0840
           Key                =     ""
        EndProperty
        BeginProperty ListImage3 {0713E8C3-850A-101B-AFC0-4210102A8DA7}
           Picture            =     "Browser.frx":0ED2
           Key                =     ""
        EndProperty
        BeginProperty ListImage4 {0713E8C3-850A-101B-AFC0-4210102A8DA7}
           Picture            =     "Browser.frx":1564
           Key                =     ""
        EndProperty
        BeginProperty ListImage5 {0713E8C3-850A-101B-AFC0-4210102A8DA7}
           Picture            =     "Browser.frx":1BF6
           Key                =     ""
        EndProperty
        BeginProperty ListImage6 {0713E8C3-850A-101B-AFC0-4210102A8DA7}
```

```
              Picture         =      "Browser.frx":2288
              Key             =      " "
          EndProperty
          BeginProperty ListImage7 {0713E8C3-850A-101B-AFC0-4210102A8DA7}
              Picture         =      "Browser.frx":291A
              Key             =      "Sites"
          EndProperty
          BeginProperty ListImage8 {0713E8C3-850A-101B-AFC0-4210102A8DA7}
              Picture         =      "Browser.frx":2FAC
              Key             =      "Words"
          EndProperty
       EndProperty
    End
End
Attribute VB_Name = "frmBrowser"
Attribute VB_GlobalNameSpace = False
Attribute VB_Creatable = False
Attribute VB_PredeclaredId = True
Attribute VB_Exposed = False
Option Explicit

Dim mbDontNavigateNow As Boolean

Private Sub Form_Load()
  On Error Resume Next
  Me.Show
  tbToolBar.Refresh
  Form_Resize

  'load bad sites and bad words
  rtfBadSites.LoadFile App.Path & "\sites.txt"
  rtfBadWords.LoadFile App.Path & "\words.txt"

  cboAddress.Move 50, lblAddress.Top + lblAddress.Height + 15

  If Len(cboAddress.Text) > 0 Then
    GetPage
  End If

End Sub

Private Sub brwWebBrowser_DownloadComplete()
  On Error Resume Next
  Me.Caption = brwWebBrowser.LocationName
End Sub
```

```vb
Private Sub brwWebBrowser_NavigateComplete(ByVal URL As String)
  Dim i As Integer
  Dim bFound As Boolean
  Me.Caption = brwWebBrowser.LocationName
  For i = 0 To cboAddress.ListCount - 1
    If cboAddress.List(i) = brwWebBrowser.LocationURL Then
      bFound = True
      Exit For
    End If
  Next i
  mbDontNavigateNow = True
  If bFound Then
    cboAddress.RemoveItem i
  End If
  cboAddress.AddItem brwWebBrowser.LocationURL, 0
  cboAddress.ListIndex = 0
  mbDontNavigateNow = False
End Sub


Private Sub cboAddress_Click()
    If mbDontNavigateNow Then Exit Sub
    GetPage
End Sub


Private Sub cboAddress_KeyPress(KeyAscii As Integer)
  On Error Resume Next
  If KeyAscii = vbKeyReturn Then
    cboAddress_Click
  End If
End Sub


Private Sub GetPage()
  On Error GoTo GetPageErr

  Dim sTmp As String
  Dim sTok As String
  Dim sSite As String

  sSite = cboAddress.Text

  'check for invalid site
  If SiteIsInvalid(sSite) Then
    MsgBox "'" & sSite & "' is a disallowed site!", vbInformation
    Exit Sub
```

```
    End If

    MousePointer = vbHourglass
    sTmp = CStr(Inet1.OpenURL(cboAddress.Text))
    MousePointer = vbDefault
    'look for bad text
    If SiteHasBadText(sTmp) Then
        Exit Sub
    End If

    'try to navigate to the starting address
    timTimer.Enabled = True
    brwWebBrowser.Navigate cboAddress.Text

    Exit Sub

GetPageErr:
    MousePointer = vbDefault
    MsgBox Err.Description

End Sub

Private Function SiteIsInvalid(sSite As String) As Boolean
    Dim sTmp As String
    Dim sSiteTmp As String
    Dim nPos As Integer

    sSite = UCase(sSite)
    sTmp = UCase(rtfBadSites.Text)
    'get the first item
    nPos = InStr(sTmp, vbCrLf)
    Do While nPos > 0
        sSiteTmp = Left$(sTmp, nPos - 1)
        If InStr(sSite, sSiteTmp) > 0 Then
            SiteIsInvalid = True
            Exit Function
        End If
        'knock off the one we just processed
        sTmp = Mid$(sTmp, nPos + 2)
        nPos = InStr(sTmp, vbCrLf)
    Loop

End Function

Private Function SiteHasBadText(sText As String) As Boolean
```

```
    Dim sTmp As String
    Dim sWordTmp As String
    Dim nPos As Integer

    sText = UCase(sText)
    sTmp = UCase(rtfBadWords.Text)
    'get the first item
    nPos = InStr(sTmp, vbCrLf)
    Do While nPos > 0
      sWordTmp = Left$(sTmp, nPos - 1)
      If Len(sWordTmp) = 0 Then GoTo SkipIt
      If InStr(sText, sWordTmp) > 0 Then
        MsgBox "'" & sWordTmp & "' is a disallowed word!", vbInformation
        SiteHasBadText = True
        Exit Function
      End If
      'knock off the one we just processed
SkipIt:
      sTmp = Mid$(sTmp, nPos + 2)
      nPos = InStr(sTmp, vbCrLf)
    Loop

End Function


Private Sub Form_Resize()
    cboAddress.Width = Me.ScaleWidth - 100
    brwWebBrowser.Width = Me.ScaleWidth - 100
    brwWebBrowser.Height = _
Me.ScaleHeight - (picAddress.Top + picAddress.Height) - 100
End Sub

Private Sub timTimer_Timer()
  On Error Resume Next

  If brwWebBrowser.Busy = False Then
    timTimer.Enabled = False
    Me.Caption = brwWebBrowser.LocationName
  Else
    Me.Caption = "Working..."
  End If
End Sub

Private Sub tbToolBar_ButtonClick(ByVal Button As Button)
  On Error Resume Next
```

```
Dim frm As frmBadItems

timTimer.Enabled = True

Select Case Button.Key
   Case "Back"
      brwWebBrowser.GoBack
   Case "Forward"
      brwWebBrowser.GoForward
   Case "Refresh"
      brwWebBrowser.Refresh
   Case "Home"
      brwWebBrowser.GoHome
   Case "Search"
      brwWebBrowser.GoSearch
   Case "Stop"
      timTimer.Enabled = False
      brwWebBrowser.Stop
      Me.Caption = brwWebBrowser.LocationName
   Case "Sites"
      Set frm = New frmBadItems
      With frm
         .Caption = "Disallowed Sites"
         .Label1.Caption = "Enter disallowed sites below, one per line:"
         .RichTextBox1.Text = rtfBadSites.Text
         .Show vbModal
         If .OK Then
            .RichTextBox1.SaveFile App.Path & "\sites.txt"
            rtfBadSites.Text = .RichTextBox1.Text
         End If
      End With
      Unload frm
      Set frm = Nothing
   Case "Words"
      Set frm = New frmBadItems
      With frm
         .Caption = "Disallowed Words"
         .Label1.Caption = "Enter disallowed words below, one per line:"
         .RichTextBox1.Text = rtfBadWords.Text
         .Show vbModal
         If .OK Then
            .RichTextBox1.SaveFile App.Path & "\words.txt"
            rtfBadWords.Text = .RichTextBox1.Text
         End If
      End With
```

```
     Unload frm
     Set frm = Nothing

  End Select

End Sub
```

Listing 18-2: frmBadItems Code

```
VERSION 5.00
Object = "{3B7C8863-D78F-101B-B9B5-04021C009402}#1.1#0"; "RICHTX32.OCX"
Begin VB.Form frmBadItems
   BorderStyle     =   3    'Fixed Dialog
   Caption         =      "Disallowed Sites"
   ClientHeight    =   4095
   ClientLeft      =   945
   ClientTop       =   3240
   ClientWidth     =   3300
   LinkTopic       =      "Form1"
   MaxButton       =   0    'False
   MinButton       =   0    'False
   ScaleHeight     =   4095
   ScaleWidth      =   3300
   ShowInTaskbar   =   0    'False
   StartUpPosition =   2    'CenterScreen
   Begin RichTextLib.RichTextBox RichTextBox1
      Height       =      3105
      Left         =      30
      TabIndex     =      1
      Top          =      480
      Width        =      3210
      _ExtentX     =      5662
      _ExtentY     =      5477
      _Version     =      327680
      Enabled      =      -1   'True
      TextRTF      =      $"frmBadItems.frx":0000
   End
   Begin VB.CommandButton cmdOK
      Caption      =      "&OK"
      Height       =      345
      Left         =      1950
      TabIndex     =      0
```

```
        Top                 =     3675
        Width               =     1170
     End
     Begin VB.Label Label1
        Height              =     405
        Left                =     45
        TabIndex            =     2
        Top                 =     15
        Width               =     3210
     End
End
Attribute VB_Name = "frmBadItems"
Attribute VB_GlobalNameSpace = False
Attribute VB_Creatable = False
Attribute VB_PredeclaredId = True
Attribute VB_Exposed = False
Option Explicit

Public OK As Boolean

Private Sub cmdOK_Click()
   OK = True
   Hide
End Sub
```

THE VISUAL COMPONENT MANAGER

Topics in this Chapter

- User Interface
- Sharing Components with Other Users
- Creating Templates from the VCM
- The Future of the VCM

Chapter 19

By this point we hope that you are long since convinced that a great deal of the power (and success) of Visual Basic comes from its ability to reuse objects. These objects can be quite varied: controls, servers, templates, code modules, and so on—all the various components that make up an application. One problem with trying to reuse all these various kinds of objects may be obvious but is still worth noting:

- How do you keep track of all of the various objects that you have available to you while building an application?

This is especially true as more and more Visual Basic projects are built by teams of developers. The Visual Component Manager (VCM) (that Dave wrote, actually) was designed to help alleviate this problem. The Visual Component Manager has four major functions:

- Organize (reusable) components in one single place.
- Catalogue those components so that they are easily searchable and sharable both between users and between projects.
- Provide a way to create reusable objects from components in the application currently under development.
- Give another way to create and use components that the

Visual Basic IDE does not inherently support (such as control sets, menus, code snippets, and documents).

Before we begin to describe and explain the interface, structure, and features of the VCM, we need to tell you how to get it! (It did not ship with Visual Basic 5.0.) However, it was made immediately available by Microsoft on the Visual Basic Owners Web site at www.microsoft.com/vstudio/owner. Note that the first time you access this site, you will need to register your copy of Visual Basic. The VCM may be found under the Product Updates and you can download the self-extracting EXE file—it's about (1.2 MB). The only requirement to get (and use) the VCM is that you have a (registered) copy of Visual Basic 5.0 Pro or Enterprise on your system first.

Tip

Besides the VCM, the VB Owner's site has new features added almost every week. It's also where you should go to find the major (roughly quarterly) updates that the VB team plans on releasing. These updates will generally be available on this site long before they make it into the box. For example, there may be updates to the Resource Editor, to the Application Wizard and to the Data Form Wizard. We encourage you to check out this site frequently.

User Interface

The Visual Component manager uses an Explorer-style interface complete with a Find dialog box similar to the one in the Win95 or NT 4.0 Explorer. After a copyright splash screen, Figure 19-1 shows you what the initial screen of the VCM looks like.

If you click on the Local Database item in order to expand it, the tree expands, as you can see in Figure 19-2.

Here are some other features of the VCM that are not immediately obvious from looking at Figure 19-2:

- You will also find every previously opened project (opened while the VCM was running that is) listed in the Projects group. This goes far beyond Visual Basic's limit of 40 in its MRU (most recently used) list.

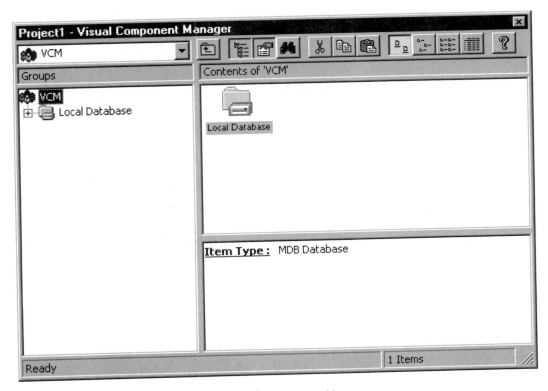

Figure 19-1   The initial screen of the Visual Component Manager

- You will have access to all of the Wizards in a single location.
- The Sample Projects group contains a catalog of all of the samples shipped with Visual Basic for the first time. The samples are automatically loaded with keywords and descriptions making it easy to find an example containing any topic such as "treeview" or "database."

If you are familiar with Explorer, then you will be right at home with the VCM. It also has tool tips and a help file when you need them. (Click on the ? icon to open up the Help System.) As you might expect, looking at Figure 19-2, the idea is that you can open up a folder (the VCM calls them *groups*) in order to see all the objects of that type. The VCM creates a default set of groups the first time you run it. These can also be seen in Figure 19-2. You are also free to create new groups as needed by:

1. Right-clicking.

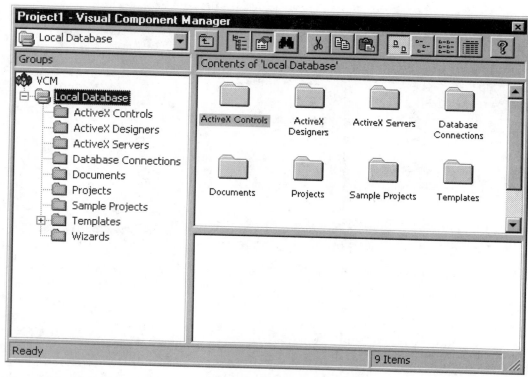

Figure 19-2   The VCM main screen with tree expanded

2. Then choosing New from the context menu that pops up as shown in Figure 19-3.

Next, you can rearrange items in the various groups by dragging and dropping from one group to another. (Obviously you should do this only if it makes sense; the VCM won't stop you from moving an ActiveX control to the Documents group or something equally strange.)

The first time you open a group, the VCM builds a database of all objects of each type that it can find on your system. For example, Figure 19-4 shows you what you might see if you expand the ActiveX control group. (This may take a few moments as the VCM builds its database of the controls on your system.) Notice that you will even see the appropriate icons for the controls. These are the same as what you will see in the toolbox. The status bar of the VCM tells you the number of objects of that type. For example, as Figure 19-4 shows, we have 64 ActiveX controls on the system used for this screen shot. Notice as well that the lower pane of Figure 19-4 gives you a lot of infor-

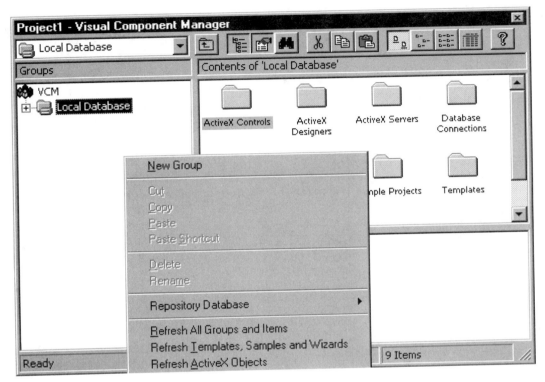

Figure 19-3   The Context menu for the Treeview Group pane

mation about the control such as when it was created, where it is located and
so on. One useful feature of the VCM is that you will find all controls listed
individually so you can see a single control like "Treeview" as opposed to the
OCX library name such as "Windows Common Controls."

Tip

---
*You can also open up multiple databases that can be located anywhere on
a network (either as Access MDB files or SQL Server databases). This
allows components to be shared between everything from small work
groups all the way up to entire corporations. You do this from the context
menu available by right-clicking a node in the treeview control that displays
the groups.*

More generally, the treeview control on the left of the VCM displays the
available databases and groups and the listview control on the right display-

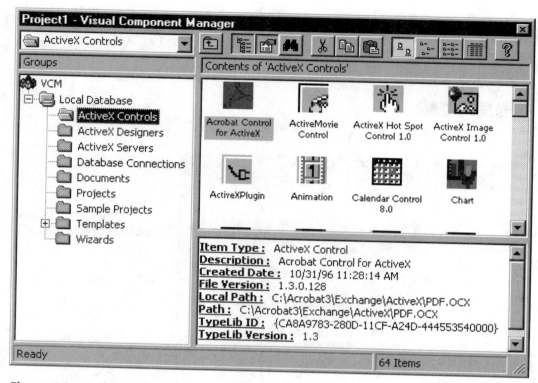

Figure 19-4   The VCM with the ActiveX Controls Group open

ing all of the items in the currently selected group. As shown in Figure 19-4, the VCM will display a third pane under the listview. This pane is called the *property* pane. The property pane lists all of the properties of the currently selected item. Components show the following inherent properties: Item Type, Description (if it is not blank), and the Keyword list (if there are any for this item). Beyond that, the various component types can have any number of different properties such as filename, author, progid, and so on. Next, the context menus (shown in Figure 19-5 for an unopened group and in Figure 19-6 for an item when a group is open) are extremely useful. These context menus are where you go to get at the full power of the VCM. This includes the ability to add keywords, search, move items, perform item specific tasks such as install items on a local system off a server and lots more! (As is usually the case, some but not all of the features available on the context menus are available from the Toolbar.)

Finally, because the VCM was designed to work alongside you when you are working in VB's IDE, it can be made quite small and still provide enough

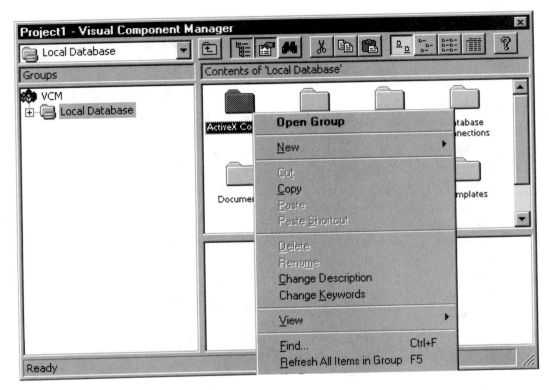

Figure 19-5 Context menu for a group

of its interface to make it easy to navigate between or to find desired items. All you have to do, since the VCM window is resizable, is shrink it down to display relatively few features—you will still be able to navigate to other groups using the "up one level" button on the toolbar. (Double-clicking on white space in the listview will also let you go up one level.)

To make the VCM as small as possible, we suggest:

1. Hiding the treeview by using the toolbar button that has a little treeview control on it. If the button is depressed, the treeview is displayed and vice versa.

2. Eliminating the properties pane in the same way using the properties button on the toolbar.

You can also hide the treeview and the property pane via the context menu by choosing its View item. The context menu also lets you hide the status bar and hide the toolbar as well. (But since the toolbar is pretty useful, we don't

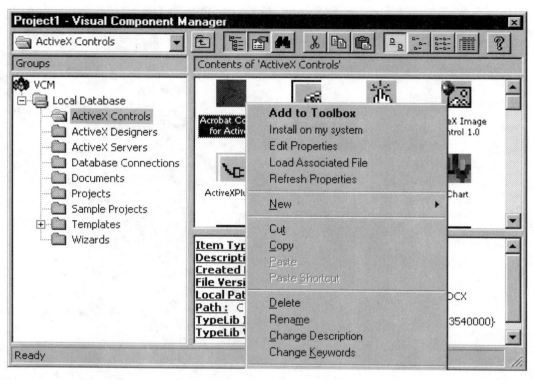

Figure 19-6   Context menu for an item in a group

recommend that you hide it.) Since the listview displays groups as well as items, it is easy to go down a level by simply double-clicking on a group item.

Keywords

Since all components may have keywords, the VCM has a very nice dialog box (shown in Figure 19-7) that lets you add keywords to help describe a selected item. The idea behind adding keywords to an item is simple but useful: It lets the VCM provide a searchable catalogue of items based on commonly used words. You can then search for these keywords using the Find dialog box that we will discuss shortly. Keywords let other users (or even you down the road) find what may sometimes seem like the proverbial needle in a haystack. Obviously, the more keywords you use to describe a component the easier the search will be. For example, if the item is a control, you should add words that describe what it deals with such as "date," "data," "finance," "sales tax," and the like. Since keyword searches must match the complete word (they are *not*

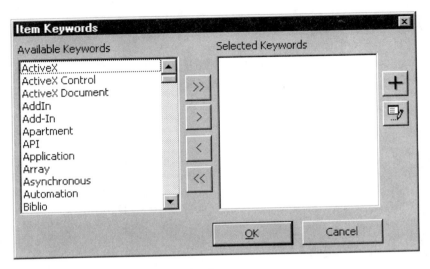

Figure 19-7   The Keyword dialog box

case sensitive however), it is a good idea to add variations on certain words such as "control," "usercontrol," "activex control," and "ocx." The keyword dialog box displays all of the available keywords in the current database and provides a drop-down list of other databases if more than one is currently open. This allows you to avoid creating slightly different variations on the same keyword by reusing the same ones over and over again.

Item Description

Choosing Item Description form the Context menu pops up a dialog box like the one shown in Figure 19-8. The description of an item can be up to 255 characters. Just as with the keyword list, choosing a good description for the component makes it easier to find items. As you will soon see, you can even search through the various descriptions of components using the "like" operator that works exactly as its counterpart does in VB. This will let you find embedded words and phrases (item description is also *not* case sensitive).

Find Dialog Box

Combine a judicious use of keywords and item descriptions with the Find features of the VCM and you won't have any trouble finding what you are looking for in a few short steps—no matter where you start. Figure 19-9

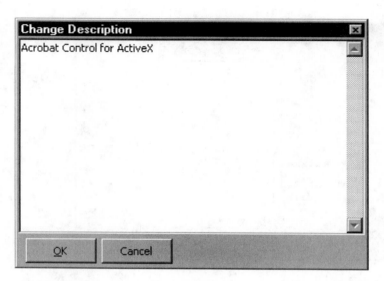

Figure 19-8   The Description dialog box

shows you the Find dialog box that is available either from the toolbar, the context menu, or by the Ctrl+F shortcut. This dialog box was modeled after the Win95 File Find dialog box. As you can see in Figure 19-9, you can search on Name, Description, Keywords, and Property Values. The most efficient searches are single-word searches that do not search through property values. If you can further limit your search to a particular type or types of items, this will help as well. Searching through all properties of all items of the selected type(s) may take a while, depending upon the number of items of the type(s) chosen. You may enter multiple words and they all will be searched for using the operator "OR." If you want to enter a multiple-word phrase, use double quotes, as in "activex document."

You can also load any number of find dialogs at the same time in order to do multiple searches. (When you start a search, the "Stop" button is enabled; a click on it allows you to abort a search at any time.)

Once you have a list of items that match your search criteria, you can right-click any item and use the context menu the same way you can from the main window's list view. You may also open the group containing this item in the main window so that you will be able to see the item's properties and other items in the same group.

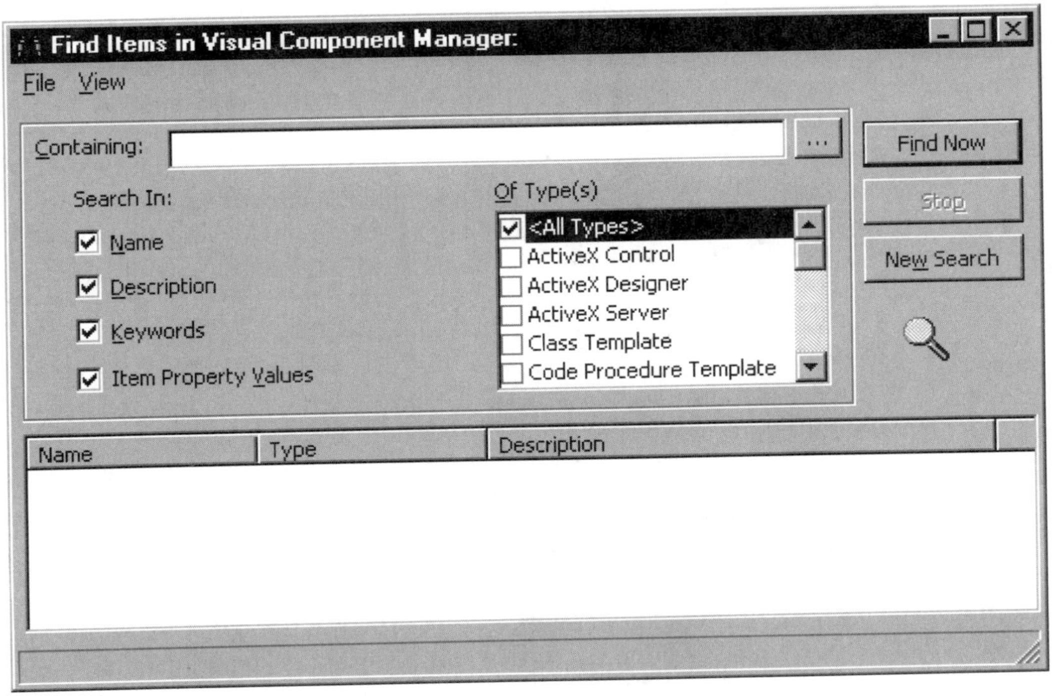

Figure 19-9 The Find dialog box

Sharing Components with Other Users

Workgroups are becoming more important in VB development. One of the niftiest features of the VCM is its ability to let you share components among users in a group working off a central server. This is done by creating shared databases on the server(s) that all members of the team have access to. Once these databases have been created, any member of the team can place copies of the components they have created on the shared database. This way other members of the team may use them easily (and of course, find them easily via the VCM). In the current version of the VCM, this requires a two-step process.

1. Copy the physical files needed by the component to a shared location where other users can access it.

2. Create a new item in the shared VCM database that points to the shared file(s).

In future versions, this will likely be made into a one-step process.

Here is an example of how this might work: Assume that you have created a user control that you want others members of your team to be able to use.

- You need to copy the OCX file to a shared server location.

Assuming you have a shared VCM database currently loaded, you can do one of three things at this point.

1. Drag and drop the control from your local database to the desired group in the shared database. Doing this will make the VCM pop up a dialog box asking you for the UNC location for the .OCX.

2. Using the Windows Explorer, drag and drop the .OCX from the shared location to the desired group in the shared database as shown in the VCM dialog box. Through the magic of OLE drag and drop, this will create a new item with the correct UNC path for you in the VCM.

3. Right-click on the desired group in the shared database as shown in the left pane of the VCM. Then choose "New-ActiveX Control." (If this option is not available, you need to find a group that allows ActiveX Controls to be stored there.) You will be presented with a dialog box like the one in Figure 16-10. This dialog box allows you to browse for the shared file (click on the ellipsis (the three dots) to pop up the File dialog box) as well as enter other cataloging information.

All of these methods work equally as well but the third lets you enter the additional cataloging information that will be most likely to help other users find your component. (If no one can find it, it is not likely that they will use it!)

Once you or a member of your team finds a component on a shared server that they would like to use in their project, they can in most cases just double-click it and the VCM will add it to the current project. There is one "gotcha" for ActiveX Controls and ActiveX Servers. Both of these components must be "Installed" on the local system before they can be used in a

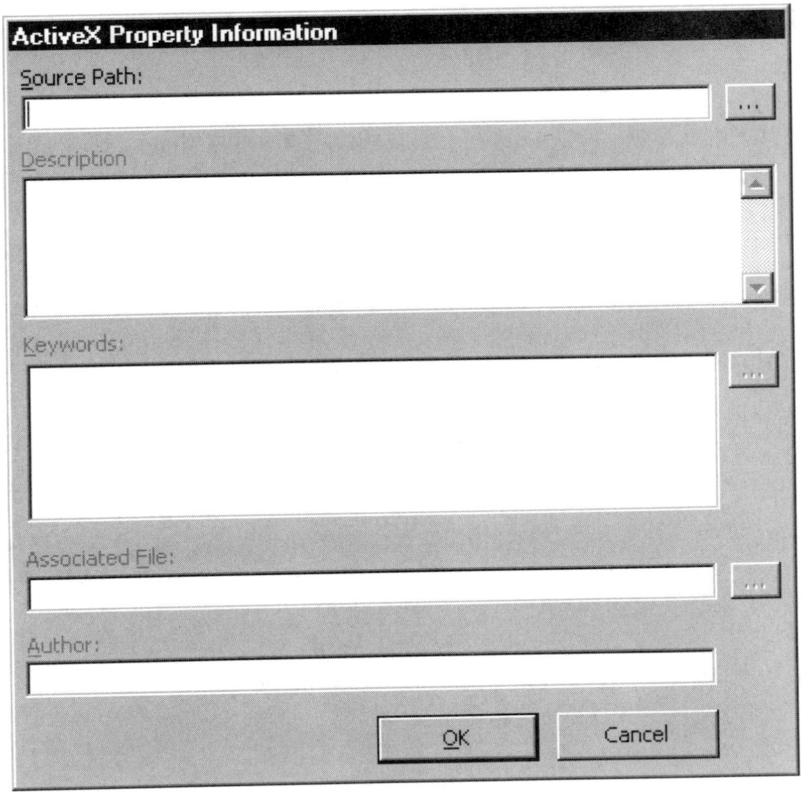

ActiveX Property Information

Source Path:

Description

Keywords:

Associated File:

Author:

OK   Cancel

Figure 19-10   The ActiveX Property Information dialog box

Visual Component Manager

ⓘ 'ActiveMovie Control' has been installed on your system and added to the current project.

OK

Figure 19-11   Successful installation of a control via the VCM.

project. This is done by right-clicking the item and choosing, you guessed it, the item marked "Install on My System" from the Context menu. This will copy the file to a directory of your choice, register it on your system, and copy the item to your local database, making it available to your projects. You'll see a message box like Figure 19-11 when this process is successful.

Creating Templates from the VCM

Although the Visual Basic IDE can and does utilize templates very well (see Chapter 17), it does not make creating them all that easy: You have to manually copy files to the correct directories. We think the VCM does a great job of creating these templates for you from *any* type of project component, control sets, menus, or code snippets. In addition, the VCM does not limit your templates to the VB5\Template tree. You can access templates from anywhere on your hard disk or network. For example, to create a template from a form in your current project, follow these steps:

1. Right-click in a group that allows Form Templates. The default one is called "Templates\Forms."

2. Select "New-Form Template" from the context menu.

3. A dialog box will appear like the one shown in Figure 19-12. This dialog box lists all of the forms in the current project with the active one already selected for you.

4. If this is the form you wish to make a template from, simply click the OK button. (If the form has never been saved, you will be prompted to save it first.)

5. You will also be prompted for the location where you wish to create this template file. The default is the VB5\Template\Forms directory.

6. Now you can add keywords and a description to the item if you want to.

The Future of the VCM

We hope that we have convinced you that the Visual Component Manager *today* will be quite helpful for your work with VB. We expect, however, that the VCM will be greatly improved in the near future. One reason for this hope is that the database that the VCM uses is the Microsoft *Repository* database. The number of types of objects the Repository can handle will only increase as more and more types of data are stored in the Repository. Also, as vendors of third-party tools begin to use the Repository, a lot of information

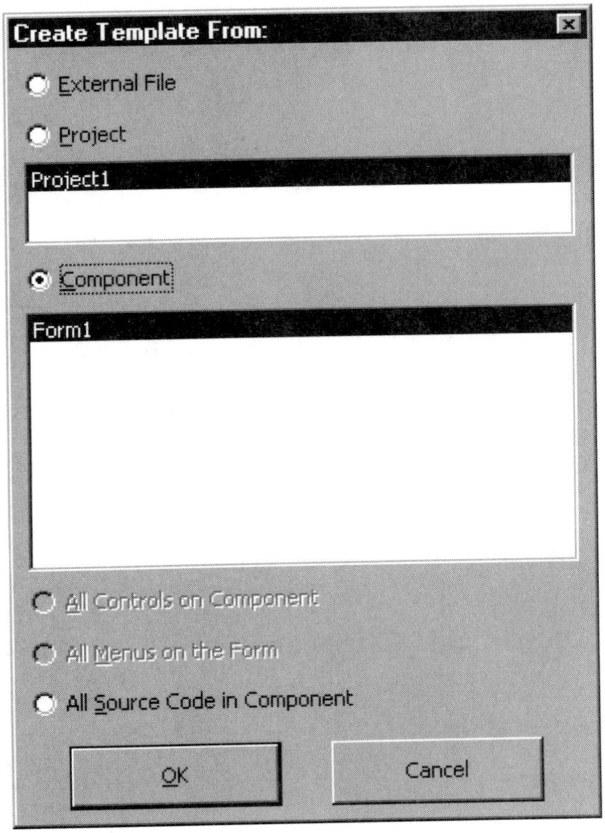

Figure 19-12　The Create Template From dialog box

about the objects they add will be accessible from the VCM. (The VCM is currently the only front-end application that we know of that exploits the repository.) We also expect other features to be added to the VCM. This may include: versioning, using related objects, associated files, and item browsing. Dave's goal is to make the VCM the most powerful labor-saving Add-In in Visual Basic's IDE. (E-mail him with your suggestions for improvements to it: daveje@microsoft.com.)

DEPLOYMENT

Topics in this Chapter

- Setting Up an Application
- Control Deployment

Chapter 20

Once you have written and tested your application, Add-In, Wizard or control, you may want to make it available to others. To do this, you need to install not only the applications files themselves but also any supporting files such as the Visual Basic run time that are not already on the users system. Depending on the controls and the libraries you used, you may also need to distribute various additional OCXs and DLLs along with the VB run time. (Make sure that you have the proper license to do this before distributing a custom control or a library purchased from someone else. If you are not sure, contact the company for this information.) This chapter shows you how to use the Setup Wizard that comes with all versions of VB to make most installations a snap.

Note

The Setup Wizard does virtually all of the work needed to create a fully functional setup for your application but it may not do everything. For example, as you saw in the chapter on add-ins, you need to write a string to the VB add-in INI file before the add-in will be available. If you find that the Setup Wizard is proving inadequate for your needs you might want to consider getting a full-featured Installation program. The InstallShield line is the most popular—for very good reason—we recommend it highly (http://www.installshield.com).

Setting Up an Application

To see the Setup Wizard at work, we want to walk through a session using the Wizard to prepare one the applications that we have created in this book for distribution. For this, we will use the GetFiles application created in Chapter 5. (If you did not build it by hand, you can always copy it from the CD in the CH5 directory to your system now.) Here's what you need to do to use the Setup Wizard:

1. Launch the Application Setup Wizard from the VB submenu on the Start menu. (It is not available from within VB's IDE.) You'll see an introductory screen like Figure 20-1 (or possibly the screen in Figure 20-2, which is what you would get if you hit the Next button in Figure 20-1.)

2. Click the Browse button, shown in Figure 20-2, and find the GetFiles.vbp file from wherever you placed it (or from the CD).

3. In the Options frame shown in Figure 20-2, select "Create a Setup Program" because we want to set up the application for use on other systems. (If you also select the "Rebuild the Project" checkbox you will be sure that you get an up-to-date EXE.)

4. Click Next to continue and you will be at the "Distribution Method" step shown in Figure 20-3.

Figure 20-1 The Information Startup screen for the Setup Wizard

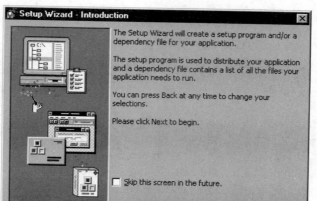

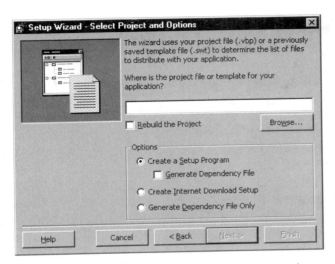

Figure 20-2   The initial screen for the Setup Wizard

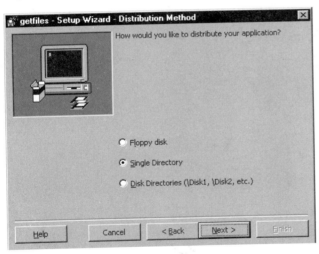

Figure 20-3   The Distribution screen

5. Choose "Disk Directories" and click Next. This will keep an image of the setup disks on your hard drive. This allows you the option of copying the image to a CD or a bunch of floppies down the road.

You should now be on the "Multiple Directories" step shown in Figure 20-4. If the defaults are not acceptable, choose the appropriate settings from the drop-down list's boxes.

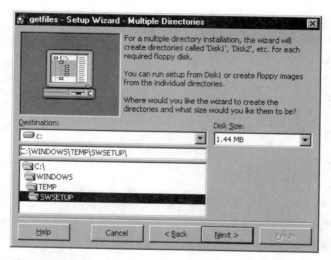

Figure 20-4   The Multiple Directories step in the
Setup Wizard

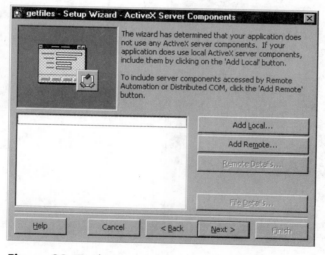

Figure 20-5   The ActiveX Server Components step

Click Next to go to the ActiveX Server Components step as shown in
Figure 20-5. This step is where you would tell the Wizard to add in any other
necessary components such as specialized libraries and other OCXs if you
used them in your application. Since we do not have any such dependencies
for our GetFiles application, we will just move on.

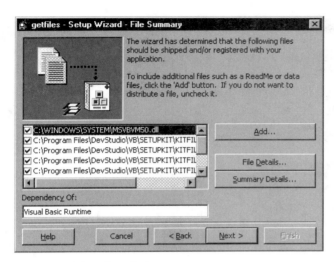

Figure 20-6 The File Summary step

Click Next one last time and the Wizard will perform its magic. After a short delay, where you will see a "Working" screen, you should be looking at the File Summary step shown in Figure 20-6. This screen displays a list of all of the files needed to distribute this application.

Tip

Notice the first file listed in Figure 20-6 is the MSVBVM50.dll—the VB Run time. This file alone requires roughly one 1.4 meg floppy. If you have complete control over where you are distributing your application, and know that all those systems have the VB run time, you can safely remove this file.

Click Next to go to the Finished step as shown in Figure 20-7. (If you think you will be creating this setup again, you may want to save the template to save you the trouble of going through the steps every time. Finally, click Finish button as shown in Figure 20-7. The Wizard will start compressing all of the files it needs and place them in the directories you chose in step 5. These directories can easily be copied to floppy disks or just run over a local area network.

That's all there is to it. The \Disk1 directory will contain the Setup program that the user needs to run.

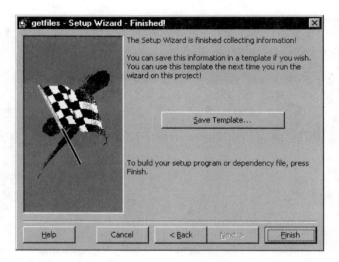

Figure 20-7   The Finished step in the Setup Wizard

Control Deployment

The Setup Wizard makes it really easy to create professional setups for your applications. Since Visual Basic 5.0 lets you create other types of projects such as ActiveX Controls, we want to discuss the creation of a setup routine for these projects in these sections. Obviously, once you have created a control, you may wish to give it to others or maybe even try to sell it. In order to use the control on another system, you must first install it (usually in \Windows\System unfortunately). As with an application, if you used any other controls or libraries on your user control, you will need to distribute the needed OCXs and DLLs along with the OCX for your control.

If you only used the VBA language and the standard controls as we have in this book, then all you need to distribute is the .ocx itself and the MSVB-VM50.DLL library. If you used any of the other OCX controls that come with Visual Basic you are free to distribute them as well.

Note

For a commercial distribution of a control, you will probably want to sign your controls using a digital certificate available (for a small fee) from Verisign (www.verisign.com). Their Web site has full details on the process of obtaining a certificate for your controls.

The simplest installation for a control involves copying the files to the target system and registering the user control and any controls and libraries that it uses. You can register an OCX or DLL using the Regsvr32.EXE utility that you saw in the Add-In chapter. As we mentioned there, Regsvr32.EXE may be found in the Tools\Regutils directory on your VB CD if you have the Professional or Enterprise edition of VB. (Microsoft makes this utility freely available from their Web site if you are using a different version of VB.) To use the registration utility, first copy `Regsvr32.EXE` to your system in a directory in your path such as your `\Windows` directory. Then open up a DOS window and from the command line type:

```
Regsvr32 mycontrol.ocx
```

This will register the control and make it available to any host application that uses this OCX.

As with applications the Setup Wizard does virtually all of the work needed to create a fully functional setup for your control. To see this at work, we will walk through a session with the Wizard to set up one of the controls that we have created in this book. For this, we will use the Banner created in Chapter 13. (If you did not build it by hand, you can always copy it from the CD in the CH13 directory to your system now.)

Most of the steps are the same as with an application. This time however we will choose the Floppy Disk setup so you can see what you get for this option. Here's what you need to do to use the Setup Wizard. As before, launch the Application Setup Wizard from the VB submenu on the start menu. Click the Browse button, shown in Figure 19-18, and find the Banner.VBP file from wherever you placed it (or look at the CH13\Banner directory on the CD). When you get to the "Confirm Dependencies" step shown in Figure 20-8, you should see the stdole2.tlb file. This is the library needed for OLE; most controls will need it.

Click Next, and the Wizard will again start performing its magic. You should see a message box as shown in Figure 20-9. This message box asks you whether you want to add the PropertyPage.DLL with the message "if you wish to use this control in a design environment other than Visual Basic." Answer Yes to this prompt so that any font, color, or picture properties your control has will be able to be set with the property pages and will be available to the user of the control.

After a short delay, you should be looking at a version of the File Summary step you saw in Figure 20-6. Click Next to go to the Finished step. Finally, click Finish. The Wizard will start compressing all of the files it needs and prompt you to put disk 1 of 2 in drive A:. Now it will copy the files to the

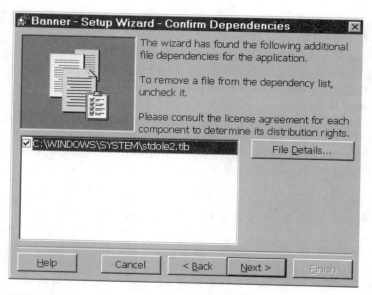

Figure 20-8   Confirm Dependencies box

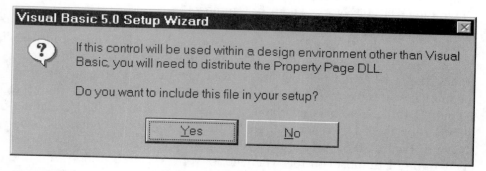

Figure 20-9   Property Page message box

floppy disks. That's it, you're finished. You now have 2 disks that make it possible to set up this control on another system. If the system you work on is available to others across a network, you could have chosen "Single Directory" on Step 5 and the files would have been copied to a directory on your hard drive instead of the floppy disks.

Note

Two disks with 1.5 MB may seem like a lot considering the OCX file is only about 20k. Most of the needed files are probably already on the user's system. If you are in a controlled environment like a corporation, you can be sure that say the STDOLE.TLB library and the VBVM is already on the user system. This cuts the installation files down to a few hundred k.

Finally, if you need to deploy the control across the Internet, run the Wizard again and choose "Create Internet Download Setup" on the first step. This will create a CAB file and an HTM file that can be loaded into Internet Explorer. The Internet Explorer will handle the setup for you since it knows exactly what to do with CAB files.

Note

A CAB file (which stands for Cabinet) is Microsoft's archive format. It usually gives about a 2:1 compression ratio in most nongraphical situations. (For graphics, the possible compression ratios are much higher.)

Appendix

Overview of the \Tools Directory on the VB CD

The \Tools directory contains lots of useful programs, samples and information. Unfortunately, although individual items within its subdirectories may have readmes or help files, there's no overview in the \Tools directory itself. This short appendix is designed to give you that missing overview. (We will leave it to you to look in the subdirectory that has the tool you need for more information about it.)

Aperedis

This is available on the Enterprise edition of VB. It contains subdirectories for the Client, Manager, Server, and Worker components of the Application Performance Explorer suite that lets you do performance tuning.

Cabinets

This contains CAB files (see Chapter 20) for the controls supplied with VB and various support libraries such the Jet (database) engine. Since CAB files are compressed, this reduces the amount of information you need to send over the Internet.

Catalog

This is an on-line version of a catalog of Component Objects and Companion Products for Visual Basic that is published by Fawcette Technical Publications (http://www.windx.com), the publisher of the *Visual Basic Programmers Journal*.

Controls

This directory contains all of the ActiveX controls that shipped with Visual Basic 4.0 Professional and Enterprise Editions. These are technically no longer part of VB5, although they work perfectly well in VB5 after you register them (see the readme file). The following controls are included: AniBtn32.ocx (animated button), Gauge32.ocx (a gauge control), Graph32.ocx (Gsw32.EXE, Gswdll32.DLL) (a great graphing control), Grid32.ocx (a grid control, the FlexGrid control is usually a better choice), KeySta32.ocx (a control for checking the status of the CAP, SCROLL, and NUM LOCK keys—see Chapter 12 for a way to do this using API calls.), MSOutl32.ocx (an outline control), Spin32.ocx (a spin button), and Threed32.ocx (a 3-D container control).

Datatool

This directory comes only with the Enterprise edition of VB. It includes some powerful tools for helping you with your database development, including a Database Designer and an SQL Query Designer.

Dcom95

The files necessary to run Distributed COM (DCOM) for Windows 95.

Docs

This has Word documents for the VB 5.0 documentation that is available in, for example, Books Online.

Hcw

This contains the Help Compiler Workshop. The Help Workshop is a program that you use to create Help (.hlp) files, edit project and contents files, and test and report on help files. Help Workshop takes the information in the project

(.hpj) file to combine the topic (.rtf) files, bitmaps, and other sources into one Help file that can be viewed using the Microsoft Windows Help program.

Idgen

Both GUIDGEN and UUIDGEN are tools for generating globally unique identifiers GUIDs (see Chapter 8 and Chapter 12). VB generates GUIDs automatically when you compile a class or control so these tools are useful only for developers who want to generate IDL (Interface Description Language) or ODL (Object Description Language.) IDL and ODL are used with the MIDL.EXE and MKTYPLIB.EXE tools to generate type libraries that can be used with VB and viewed with the Object Browser.

Imagedit

This contains a reasonably good image editor. This kind of application lets you create and edit icons, bitmaps, and cursors. (You might want to check out some of the better shareware ones, like those at www.hotfiles.com.)

LPK_tool

This directory contains the License Package Authoring Tool (LPK) which is needed to build an LPK file. The idea is that an HTML page that uses licensed ActiveX controls needs an associated license package. This package stores the run-time licenses for all the controls used on the page. The HTML page should point to the correct license package via a relative URL.

Mfc42

This directory contains some files that you may need if you do not have MFC (Microsoft Foundation Classes) Version 4.2.

Msd

A sampler of what Microsoft's "Mastering Series" CDs have to offer.

Msie

This directory probably contains Microsoft Internet Explorer version 3.01. You will want to upgrade at least to IE 3.02 if not to IE 4.0. (There are at least three other copies of IE 3.01 in the Tools directory of the CD we worked from!) This version of the Internet Explorer runs on Windows 95 and Windows NT 4.0 only, it does not run on Windows NT 3.51.

Nt351SP5.a

This is the Windows NT 3.51 U.S. Service Pack 5.

Nt40.sp2

This is the Windows NT Service Pack 2. Since Service Pack releases are cumulative, you should therefore get Service Pack 3 or later!

Odbcspy

ODBC stands for open database connectivity, which is Microsoft's database architecture that allows one to work with many different types of relational databases. ODBC Spy allows you to log the ODBC API calls produced by your VB application. This tool is useful for tracking down problems in VB applications that use ODBC drivers to access data since the error messages can be obscure. For example, the log produced by ODBC Spy is usually easier to read than the log produced by the ODBC driver manager. ODBC Spy can also log to the screen as well as to a file.

Olemsg

OLEMSG.HLP is a Windows Help file that documents the entire OLE Messaging library that lets you work with MAPI. This help file has complete reference information, a programmer's guide, and brief code examples, many of which are written using VB.

Oletools

The OLETools directory contains five tools for working with OLE (i.e., COM) applications. Particularly useful are the two OLEViewer tools that let you see the classes and interfaces in a project. For example, you can see what interfaces are in any DLL with them. For more information on all these tools, consult the OLETOOLS.HLP file and the readme.

Pspy

This is used when you are trying to see how much memory is allocated for the DLLs in memory. For those who can remember that far back, Pspy is much like WPS.EXE in Windows 3.1.

Pview

This directory contains process viewers (see Chapter 14 for more on processes). You can use these tools to view or terminate processes that are currently running on your system. PVIEW.EXE runs under Windows NT and PView95 runs under Windows 95. Under Windows NT 4.0, the task manager has most of the same capabilities as PVIEW.EXE.

Regutils

This directory contains three tools for registering in-process ActiveX (OLE) servers, including the all-important regsvr32.exe program that is used to register DLLs or EXEs (see the Add-Ins chapter for samples of this tool). You will definitely want to copy these tools to a directory in your path.

Repostry

The repository is used by the Visual Component manager (Chapter 20) to store information. This directory gives you some samples that let you use the repository to store objects of your own choosing.

Resource

This directory contains the Resource Compiler RC.EXE (see Chapter 6). For more information on how to use the Resource Compiler, see the RESOURCE.TXT and RC.HLP files in this directory.

Spy

Spy++ (SPYXX.EXE) is a Win32-based utility that will run on both Windows 95 and Windows NT. It gives you a graphical view of the system's processes, threads, windows, and window messages. Using it you can, for example, see what messages are going to which windows. (Remember, controls are usually windows in this sense.) This uses the files in the \MFC42 directory.

Stoolkit

This directory contains the localized versions of Setup.EXE for the Setup Toolkit. These let you build localized setup routines for different languages.

Tsql

This directory is available only in the Enterprise edition of VB and contains SQL6.5 Service Pack 2 and the T-SQL Debugging Server Setup that lets you setup the Transact-SQL Debugging feature on a Microsoft SQL Server.

Unsupprt

Our favorite. We showed you how to use the Code Profiler in Chapter 10. These subdirectories contain unsupported tools and samples. Here are descriptions of the subdirectories:

Subdirectory	Contains
Calendar	Calendar control.
DlgObj	The Microsoft Dialog Automation Objects component, which provides Common Dialog functionality without requiring that you place a control on a form.
HTTPExpl	A sample HTTP application (see Chapter 18).
Ihandler	The Icon Handler application.
MCIWinDx	Documentation for the MCIWndX OLE control.
MigrWiz	Upscale Wizard to convert MDB files to SQL server.
ShellLnk	A shell extension sample.
Ssaver	A screen saver sample.
SysTray	System tray sample.
TmplMgr	Template Manager explained in Chapter 17.
Typlib	Make Typelib utility.
VBCP	The Visual Basic Code Profiler explained in Chapter 10.
Voice	Sample voice application.

WebBrwsr	The Help file for the Web Browser control (see Chapter 18).
WSView	Working Set Viewer utility (used with OLE messaging).
Xtnsblty	Extensibility header file needed to write VB Add-Ins in C++.

Tip

Many more of these interesting (unsupported) tools may be found on the VB Owner Web Site: http://www.microsoft.com/vstudio/owner.

Index

A

Abs function, 188
Absolute coordinates, 304
Accelerator keys, 36, 108
Access keys, 36
access parameter, Open statement, 245
Active Platform, 5
ActiveX, 5
    calendar control, 6
    COM (common object model), 5, 436, 458-63
    Control Interface Wizard, 357, 634-58, 773, 808
    controls, 5-7
    definition of, 5
    Document Wizard, 773
    libraries for, 561
    See also ActiveX Component; ActiveX Control Pad;
ActiveX controls; ActiveX DLLs; ActiveX Document
Migration Wizard; ActiveX documents; ActiveX EXEs
ActiveX Component, 691
ActiveX Control Pad, 6, 682-83
    with HTML Object tag, 685
    inserting a control with, 684-86
    Script Wizard, 687-89

ActiveX controls, 606-89
    address control, building, 650-58
    Control Interface Wizard, 634-58
    Extender object, 630-32
        events, 632
        methods, 632
        properties, 631-32
    guaranteed-to-drive-your-user-crazy command
        button, 633-34
    properties, mapping, 613-16
    Property Pages, creating, 658-79
    scripting, 686-89
    simple control, building, 18-25
    testing, 23-25, 679-89
        in Internet Explorer, 682-83
        platform testing, 680-82
    user control:
        anatomy of, 607-9
        appearance of, 621-25
        integer text box, 625-29
        life cycle of, 619-21
        managing state of, 618-19
        writing the code, 609-16
    user interaction, 629-34
    See also Control Interface Wizard

G

LICENSE AGREEMENT AND LIMITED WARRANTY

READ THE FOLLOWING TERMS AND CONDITIONS CAREFULLY BEFORE OPENING THIS DISK PACKAGE. THIS LEGAL DOCUMENT IS AN AGREEMENT BETWEEN YOU AND PRENTICE-HALL, INC. (THE "COMPANY"). BY OPENING THIS SEALED DISK PACKAGE, YOU ARE AGREEING TO BE BOUND BY THESE TERMS AND CONDITIONS. IF YOU DO NOT AGREE WITH THESE TERMS AND CONDITIONS, DO NOT OPEN THE DISK PACKAGE. PROMPTLY RETURN THE UNOPENED DISK PACKAGE AND ALL ACCOMPANYING ITEMS TO THE PLACE YOU OBTAINED THEM FOR A FULL REFUND OF ANY SUMS YOU HAVE PAID.

1. **GRANT OF LICENSE:** In consideration of your payment of the license fee, which is part of the price you paid for this product, and your agreement to abide by the terms and conditions of this Agreement, the Company grants to you a nonexclusive right to use and display the copy of the enclosed software program (hereinafter the "SOFTWARE") on a single computer (i.e., with a single CPU) at a single location so long as you comply with the terms of this Agreement. The Company reserves all rights not expressly granted to you under this Agreement.

2. **OWNERSHIP OF SOFTWARE:** You own only the magnetic or physical media (the enclosed disks) on which the SOFTWARE is recorded or fixed, but the Company retains all the rights, title, and ownership to the SOFTWARE recorded on the original disk copy(ies) and all subsequent copies of the SOFTWARE, regardless of the form or media on which the original or other copies may exist. This license is not a sale of the original SOFTWARE or any copy to you.

3. **COPY RESTRICTIONS:** This SOFTWARE and the accompanying printed materials and user manual (the "Documentation") are the subject of copyright. You may <u>not</u> copy the Documentation or the SOFTWARE, except that you may make a single copy of the SOFTWARE for backup or archival purposes only. You may be held legally responsible for any copying or copyright infringement which is caused or encouraged by your failure to abide by the terms of this restriction.

4. **USE RESTRICTIONS:** You may <u>not</u> network the SOFTWARE or otherwise use it on more than one computer or computer terminal at the same time. You may physically transfer the SOFTWARE from one computer to another provided that the SOFTWARE is used on only one computer at a time. You may <u>not</u> distribute copies of the SOFTWARE or Documentation to others. You may <u>not</u> reverse engineer, disassemble, decompile, modify, adapt, translate, or create derivative works based on the SOFTWARE or the Documentation without the prior written consent of the Company.

5. **TRANSFER RESTRICTIONS:** The enclosed SOFTWARE is licensed only to you and may <u>not</u> be transferred to any one else without the prior written consent of the Company. Any unauthorized transfer of the SOFTWARE shall result in the immediate termination of this Agreement.

6. **TERMINATION:** This license is effective until terminated. This license will terminate automatically without notice from the Company and become null and void if you fail to comply with any provisions or limitations of this license. Upon termination, you shall destroy the Documentation and all copies of the SOFTWARE. All provisions of this Agreement as to warranties, limitation of liability, remedies or damages, and our ownership rights shall survive termination.

7. **MISCELLANEOUS:** This Agreement shall be construed in accordance with the laws of the United States of America and the State of New York and shall benefit the Company, its affiliates, and assignees.

8. **LIMITED WARRANTY AND DISCLAIMER OF WARRANTY:** The Company warrants that the SOFTWARE, when properly used in accordance with the Documentation, will operate in substantial conformity with the description of the SOFTWARE set forth in the Documentation. The Company does not warrant that the SOFTWARE will meet your requirements or that the operation of the SOFTWARE will be uninterrupted or error-free. The Company warrants that the media on which the SOFTWARE is delivered shall be

free from defects in materials and workmanship under normal use for a period of thirty (30) days from the date of your purchase. Your only remedy and the Company's only obligation under these limited warranties is, at the Company's option, return of the warranted item for a refund of any amounts paid by you or replacement of the item. Any replacement of SOFTWARE or media under the warranties shall not extend the original warranty period. The limited warranty set forth above shall not apply to any SOFTWARE which the Company determines in good faith has been subject to misuse, neglect, improper installation, repair, alteration, or damage by you. EXCEPT FOR THE EXPRESSED WARRANTIES SET FORTH ABOVE, THE COMPANY DISCLAIMS ALL WARRANTIES, EXPRESS OR IMPLIED, INCLUDING WITHOUT LIMITATION, THE IMPLIED WARRANTIES OF MERCHANTABILITY AND FITNESS FOR A PARTICULAR PURPOSE. EXCEPT FOR THE EXPRESS WARRANTY SET FORTH ABOVE, THE COMPANY DOES NOT WARRANT, GUARANTEE, OR MAKE ANY REPRESENTATION REGARDING THE USE OR THE RESULTS OF THE USE OF THE SOFTWARE IN TERMS OF ITS CORRECTNESS, ACCURACY, RELIABILITY, CURRENTNESS, OR OTHERWISE.

IN NO EVENT, SHALL THE COMPANY OR ITS EMPLOYEES, AGENTS, SUPPLIERS, OR CONTRACTORS BE LIABLE FOR ANY INCIDENTAL, INDIRECT, SPECIAL, OR CONSEQUENTIAL DAMAGES ARISING OUT OF OR IN CONNECTION WITH THE LICENSE GRANTED UNDER THIS AGREEMENT, OR FOR LOSS OF USE, LOSS OF DATA, LOSS OF INCOME OR PROFIT, OR OTHER LOSSES, SUSTAINED AS A RESULT OF INJURY TO ANY PERSON, OR LOSS OF OR DAMAGE TO PROPERTY, OR CLAIMS OF THIRD PARTIES, EVEN IF THE COMPANY OR AN AUTHORIZED REPRESENTATIVE OF THE COMPANY HAS BEEN ADVISED OF THE POSSIBILITY OF SUCH DAMAGES. IN NO EVENT SHALL LIABILITY OF THE COMPANY FOR DAMAGES WITH RESPECT TO THE SOFTWARE EXCEED THE AMOUNTS ACTUALLY PAID BY YOU, IF ANY, FOR THE SOFTWARE.

SOME JURISDICTIONS DO NOT ALLOW THE LIMITATION OF IMPLIED WARRANTIES OR LIABILITY FOR INCIDENTAL, INDIRECT, SPECIAL, OR CONSEQUENTIAL DAMAGES, SO THE ABOVE LIMITATIONS MAY NOT ALWAYS APPLY. THE WARRANTIES IN THIS AGREEMENT GIVE YOU SPECIFIC LEGAL RIGHTS AND YOU MAY ALSO HAVE OTHER RIGHTS WHICH VARY IN ACCORDANCE WITH LOCAL LAW.

ACKNOWLEDGMENT

YOU ACKNOWLEDGE THAT YOU HAVE READ THIS AGREEMENT, UNDERSTAND IT, AND AGREE TO BE BOUND BY ITS TERMS AND CONDITIONS. YOU ALSO AGREE THAT THIS AGREEMENT IS THE COMPLETE AND EXCLUSIVE STATEMENT OF THE AGREEMENT BETWEEN YOU AND THE COMPANY AND SUPERSEDES ALL PROPOSALS OR PRIOR AGREEMENTS, ORAL, OR WRITTEN, AND ANY OTHER COMMUNICATIONS BETWEEN YOU AND THE COMPANY OR ANY REPRESENTATIVE OF THE COMPANY RELATING TO THE SUBJECT MATTER OF THIS AGREEMENT.

Should you have any questions concerning this Agreement or if you wish to contact the Company for any reason, please contact the publisher, in writing at the address below.

Robin Short
Prentice Hall PTR
One Lake Street
Upper Saddle River, New Jersey 07458

MICROSOFT CORPORATION NON-DISCLOSURE AGREEMENT

ACTIVEX CONTROL PAD

IMPORTANT: PLEASE READ CAREFULLY

This Microsoft End-user License Agreement (EULA) is alegal agreement between you (either an individual or a single entity) and Microsoft Corporation for the Microsoft software product(s) listed above, which includes computer software and associated media and printed materials (if any), and may include online or electronic documentation and software product (collectively, the "SOFTWARE PRODUCT(s)"). By installing, copying, or otherwise using the SOFTWARE PRODUCT, you agree to be bound by the terms of this EULA. If you do not agree to the terms of this EULA, you are not authorized to use the SOFTWARE PRODUCT. The SOFT-WARE PRODUCT is protected by copyright laws and international copyright treaties, as well as other intellectual property laws and treaties. The SOFTWARE PRODUCT is licensed, not sold.

1,   GRANT OF LICENSE.

(a) MS grants to Recipient a limited, non-exclusive, nontransferable, royalty-free license to use one copy of the executable code of the Product software on a single CPU residing on Recipient's premises, solely to test the compatibility of Recipient's application or other product(s) which operate in conjunction with the Product and to evaluate the Product for the purpose of providing feedback thereon to MS. Recipient shall not rent, lease, sell, sublicense, asign, or otherwise transfer the Product, including any accompanying printed materials. Recipient may not reverse engineer, decompile or disassemble the Product except to the extent that this restriction is expressly prohibited by applicable law. MS and its suppliers shall retain title and all ownership rights to the Product.

(b) Recipient agrees to provide reasonable feedback to MS, including but not limited to usability, bug reports and test results, with respect to the Product testing. Recipient will use reasonable efforts to review and comment on all documentation supplied. All bug reports, test results and other feedback made by Recipient shall be the property of MS and may be used by MS for any purpose. Due ot the nature of the development work, MS is not certain as to when errors or discrepancies in the Products may be corrected.

2.   TERM OF AGREEMENT. The term of this Agreement shall commence on the Effective Date and shall continue until terminated by MS in writing at any time, with or without cause. The Agreement will terminate without notice upon the commercial release of the Product. Upon the termination of this Agreement, Recipient shall promptly return to MS, or certify destruction of, all full or partial copies of the Product and related materials provided by MS.

3.   PRODUCT MAINTENANCE. MS is not obligated to provide maintenance or updates to Recipient for the Product. However, any maintenance or updates provided by MS shall be covered by this agreement.

4.   DISCLAIMER OF WARRANTY. Product is deemed acceptable by Recipient. The Product constitutes pre-release code and may be changed substantially before commercial release. The PRODUCT is provided "AS IS" WITHOUT WARRANTY OF ANY KIND. TO THE MAXIMUM EXTENT PERMITTED BY APPLICABLE LAW, MICROSOFT FURTHER DISCLAIMS ALL WARRANTIES, INCLUDING WITHOUT LIMITATION ANY IMPLIED WARRANTIES OF MERCHANTABILITY, FITNESS FOR A PARTICULAR PURPOSE, AND NONINFRINGEMENT. THE ENTIRE RISK ARISING OUT OF THE USE OR PERFORMANCE OF THE PRDUCT AND DOCUMENTATION REMAINS WITH RECIPIENT. TO THE MAXIMUM EXTENT PERMITTED BY APPLICABLE LAW, IN NO EVENT SHALL MICROSOFT OR ITS SUPPLIERS BE LIABLE FOR ANY CONSEQUENTIAL, INCIDENTAL, DIRECT, INDIRECT, SPECIAL, PUNITIVE, OR OTHER DAMAGES WHATSOEVER (INCLUDING, WITHOUT LIMITATION, DAMAGES FOR LOSS OF BUSINESS PROFITS, BUSINESS INTERRUPTION, LOSS OF BUSI-

NESS INFORMATION, OR OTHER PECUNIARY LOSS) ARISING OUT OF THIS AGREEMENT OR THE USE OF OR INABILITY TO USE THE PRODUCT, EVEN IF MICROSOFT HAS BEEN ADVISED OF THE POSSIBILITY OF SUCH DAMAGES. BECAUSE SOME STATES/JURISDICTIONS DO NOT ALLOW THE EXCLUSION OR LIMITATION OF LIABILITY FOR CONSEQUENTIAL OR INCIDENTAL DAMAGES, THE ABOVE LIMITATION MAY NOT APPLY TO RECIPIENT.

5.　　GOVERNING LAW; ATTORNEYS' FEES. This Agreement shalll be governed by the laws of the State of Washington and Recipient further consents to jurisdiction by the state and federal courts sitting in the State of Washington. If either MS or Recipient employs attorneys to enforce any rights arising out of or relating to this Agreement, the prevailing party shall be entitled to recover reasonable attorneys' fees.

6.　　U.S. GOVERNMENT RESTRICTED RIGHTS. The Product is provided with RESTRICTED RIGHTS. Use, duplication, or disclosure by the Government is subject to restrictions as set forth in subparagraph (c)(1)(ii) of The Rights in Technical Data and Computer Software clause of DFARS 252.227-7013 or subparagraphs (c)(1) and (2) of the Commercial Computer Software—Restricted Rights at 48 CFR 52.227-19, as applicable. Manufacturer is Microsoft Corporation, One Microsoft Way, Redmond, WA 98052-6399.

7.　　EXPORT RESTRICTIONS. Recipient acknowledges that the Product licensed hereunder is subject to the export control laws and regulations of the U.S.A., and any amendments thereof. Recipient confirms that with respect to the Product, it will not export or re-export it, directly or indirectly, either to (i) any countries that are subject to U.S.A. export restrictions (currently including, but not necessarily limited to, Cuba, the Federal Republic of Yugoslavia (Serbia and Montenegro), Haiti, Iran, Iraq, Libya, North Korea, South Africa (military and police entities), and Syria); (ii) any end user who Recipient knows or who has reason to know will utilize them in the design, development or production of nuclear, chemical or biological weapons; or (iii) any end user who has been prohibited from participating in the U.S.A. export transactions by any federal agency of the U.S.A. government. Recipient further acknowledges that the Product may include technical data subject to export and re-export restrictions imposed by U.S.A. law.

8.　　ENTIRE AGREEMENT. This Agreement constitutes the complete and exclusive agreement between MS and Recipient with respect to the subject matter hereof, and supersedes all prior oral or written understandings, communications or agreements not specifically incorporated herein. This Agreement may not be modified except in a writing duly signed by an authorized representative of MS and Recipient.

ABOUT THE CD

All the significant code from the book may be found in the various subdirectories of the CodeFromBook directory—usually with an accompanying .vbp (project) or .vbg (project group) file.

To use the templates given in the \Template directory please consult the Template chapter for directions on how to merge our templates with VB's own Template directory.

To use our Add-Ins please follow the directions given to register them in the Add-Ins chapter. Note that you will need to have access to regsvr32 which can be found on the VB CD in the Professional or Enterprise editions. (You can also get it off the Microsoft web site at www.microsoft.com.)

Next, the \Microsoft directory contains the following programs all are executables so that they can be installed by simply double clicking on the file name in Windows Explorer.

Internet Explorer 3.02 (in the IE 3.02 directory WIndows 95 version.)
The VBScript DLL
The VBScript documentation
The ActiveX Control Pad (The last three all may be found in the VBScript directory.)

Please note the following:

The programs in the \Microsoft directory were reproduced by Prentice Hall under a special arrangement with Microsoft Corporation. For this reason, Prentice Hall is responsible for the product warranty and for support. If your CD-ROM is defective, please return it to Prentice Hall, which will arrange for its replacement. PLEASE DO NOT RETURN IT TO MICROSOFT CORPORATION. Any product support will be provided, if at all, by Prentice Hall. PLEASE DO NOT CONTACT MICROSOFT CORPORATION FOR PRODUCT SUPPORT. End users of these Microsoft programs shall not be considered "registered owners" of a Microsoft product and therefore shall not be eligible for upgrades, promotions or other benefits available to "registered owners" of Microsoft products.